DATE DUE

DEMCO 38-296

Anderson's Travel Companion

Anderson's Travel Companion

A Guide to the Best Non-fiction and Fiction for Travelling

Sarah Anderson

$\mathbb{S}$COLAR
PRESS

Croft Road
Aldershot
Hants GU11 3HR
England

Ashgate Publishing Company
Old Post Road
Brookfield
Vermont 05036
USA

British Library Cataloguing in Publication Data

Anderson's Travel Companion: Guide to the
best non-fiction and fiction for travelling
  I. Anderson, Sarah
  016.910202

Library of Congress Cataloging-in-Publication Data

Anderson, Sarah
    [Travel Companion]
    Anderson's Travel companion : a guide to the best non-fiction and
fiction for travelling/Sarah Anderson
        p. cm.
    Includes index.
    ISBN 1-85928-013-7 (hard)
    1. Travel–Bibliography.   I. Title
  Z6004.T6A53 1995
  [G151]
  016.91'02'02–dc20   94-24094 CIP
ISBN 1-85928-013-7

Typeset by Cappella, Ipswich and printed in Great Britain by Biddles
Ltd, Guildford

Contents

Acknowledgements

Thanks to Michael Barker, T.J. Binyon, Dea Birkett, Stephen Brook, David Campbell, Robert Erskine, Alexander Fyjis-Walker, the Knight of Glin, John Hatt, Peter and Kath Hopkirk, Michael Jacobs, Natania Jansz, John Keay, Laurence Kelly, Norman Lewis, Carola Lott, Tom Lloyd, Patrick Marnham, Philip Marsden, Jonathan Mirsky, Geoffrey Moorhouse, Jan Morris, Dervla Murphy, Eric Newby, Michael Palin, Jeremy Paxman, Jonathan Raban, Anthony Sattin, Lucretia Stewart, Patricia Sullivan, Paul Theroux, Andrew Threipland, Colin Thubron, Sara Wheeler, William and Lynn Wilkins and Sebastian Wormell, many of whom gave me special quotes for the book and all of whom helped me in various ways; special thanks to Mark Ellingham and Rough Guides for allowing me to make use of their excellent bibliographies and to Sue McNaughton, my editor, and others at Scolar Press, and to the staff at the British Library, the London Library, the Royal Geographical Society Library and Books for Cooks – and of course to everyone, both staff and customers, at the Travel Bookshop where I learnt what I know about travel books.

All mistakes are, of course, mine alone.

Introduction

The idea behind this book is very much the same as the idea behind the Travel Bookshop which I started in 1979. It seemed to me then, and still does now, that when you travel you often want to know more about a country than can be found in a guide book; reading about a country makes any trip, however short, more worthwhile and reading widely about a country and finding out about its art, history and natural history makes travelling far more interesting. I have often found that a place comes most alive through reading fiction set there and for this reason I have included many novels and short stories by both local and foreign authors.

But it is not always easy to discover what literature exists on a country without having a great deal of time and access to a good library. This book should help you, I hope, to find out which are the most important and/or interesting books to a particular place. The book is inevitably unbalanced, as somewhere like France has a huge literature whereas Gabon, in Africa, virtually none. For places like Britain, I had to make tough choices and be ruthless with what I left out.

I am not claiming to have produced a definitive and comprehensive guide to books about countries, but rather I have made a personal choice, which the reader can sift through and I hope find the kind of book which will make his or her trip more enjoyable. Some people might disagree with my choices and think that I have left out essential reading; I would welcome ideas for the next edition. I have included old and out of print books if I felt they were relevant and that nothing in print had superseded them; old books can still be the seminal books to places and are often out of print.

The book is divided by continent, subdivided into countries and each country's books are then further subdivided into subject sections.

Rather than describe each guide book, there is a section at the front which examines each series of guide. Obviously each series is not uniformly consistent, but I hope that the reader will be able to discover the kind of guide which will suit his or her needs.

Regrettably this book will be out of date by the time it comes out, as new books are being published all the time and some of the books that were in print at the time of going to press will be out of print by then, but the core of the book will remain solid and I hope it will provide many happy hours of browsing. Maybe some people will immediately want to go and find the books I have written about, while others may decide that they can get enough of the feel of the place by just reading about the books.

I hope that the book will appeal to all kinds of different people, especially since it covers such a wide range of books. I would like to feel that not only travellers and armchair travellers, but also journalists, diplomats and business people will benefit from finding out about the literature to the country of their choice.

SA

Guidebook Series

The motive behind guides has almost completely changed since Karl Baedeker brought out his first guide to Koblenz in 1829. Then the emphasis was on seeing and learning rather than on the consuming which is so prevalent in most of today's guides. Those guides published in the nineteenth century are much collected today: Baedekers, Cooks, Murray and Augustus Hare are all names which evoke a past era of travel. Many travellers today still find them useful as there is often a better description of a building in an old guide. They can also be invaluable for novelists and researchers who need to check facts. Guides in those days assumed a fair amount of knowledge from their readers. To quote a Thorough guide at the turn of the century: 'It may be taken for granted that those who go out of their way to visit Bury will be familiar with Carlyle's *Past and Present* and the early history of the Abbey of St. Edmund.' Unfortunately an inconceivable statement today. The following short résumés are an attempt to conduct travellers through the maze of guide book series which are published today.

AA BAEDEKER

The AA Baedeker series used to be published in a very awkward format, but are now much more manageable. They have fold out maps in a pocket at the back and put all their practical information towards the end, leaving the front as a gazetteer. There are colour pictures throughout. Worthy but dull.

AA ESSENTIAL

Essential Guides are a small pocket-sized series on towns. Very basic but quite useful for a whistle-stop tour.

ACCESS

A series imported from America to major cities: Boston, Chicago, Florence, Los Angeles, New York City, Paris, Rome, San Francisco and Washington. An original and easy-to-use layout; the text is in four different colours according to category, making these guides, which are full of useful line drawings, plans and maps, a joy to use.

AMERICAN EXPRESS

The great advantage of the original American Express guides was their format and size. They really did fit in a pocket. Now they look like any other guide book. Most are city guides; there are good descriptions of hotels and shops, plenty of clear maps and ample accounts of sites for a relatively short stay.

ARCHITECTURAL GUIDES FOR TRAVELLERS

Guides to specific themes or areas have an advantage on general guides which try to cram everything in. This worthwhile series which focuses on architecture is full of plans, maps and photographs.

THE BERKELEY GUIDES

A new series for budget travellers from the west coast of America. The books are written by Berkeley students (as opposed to the Harvard students and their 'Let's Go' series). The annual guides claim to be extremely up-to-date as well as brutally honest. They say that their writers are 'a motley collection' which I'm not sure is a recommendation.

BERLITZ

Apart from the small basic pocket guides which are of very limited use, Berlitz have a newer series called 'Discover . . .'. These are certainly bigger and have more detail, but are not in any sense unique.

BLACK'S ITALIAN REGIONAL GUIDES

Since the guides deal with one region of Italy at a time, they are able to cover unusual and out-of-the-way places which other guides omit. Illustrated with colour photographs and maps.

BLUE GUIDES

The Blue Guides have recently improved their image, but have not been able to shake off entirely their somewhat worthy appearance. They began in 1915 and until 1933 collaborated with the French 'Guide Bleu' series. Now there are over forty titles in print covering cities, countries and areas. They have good maps and plans and there are some good introductory essays but they are weak on practical information. On the whole the guides are arranged in the form of itineraries which can be useful, but can also be maddening when you are trying to follow a route backwards.

BRADT

Hilary Bradt, the publisher and author of some of the books, was a pioneer in publishing off-the-beaten-track guides, mostly about South America. They are very practical, aimed at budget travellers and hikers, and carry a good selection of maps and plans throughout.

CADOGAN

The Cadogan guides seem to be going from strength to strength: they are now adding city guides and island guides to their country series. Aimed at 'independent travellers on all budgets', they proudly use a quote from the *Independent* on most of their back covers: 'It is difficult to praise the Cadogan Guide series too highly.' The guides to Morocco and Tunisia are extremely well researched and full of precisely the kind of things you want to know, with ample historical descriptions as well as what kind of hotel to expect. They make a point of finding places off the tourist route and of explaining how to get there. Useful tips are scattered throughout the text, e.g. the guide to Morocco advises you to inspect hinges and locks, as 'skill with wood is seldom matched with much love for metalwork'. However they are not without their flaws; no series can be consistently good when so many different authors are involved and the descriptions of paintings in the Italian series does not match up to the generally high standard.

CHARMING SMALL HOTELS

An excellent series, attractively produced and recommending rather special hotels. Each entry is described in detail and most are illustrated.

COMPANION GUIDES

This superb series, originally published by Collins, and recently rescued from oblivion by Everyman, is a must for any serious traveller. The guides become friends which you can dip into or read at leisure. My favourite is Georgina Masson's *Companion Guide to Rome*, a real friend in need when I was abandoned there one summer.

DARWEN COUNTY HISTORY SERIES

A fascinating series which covers the history of England, county by county, from prehistoric times until 1974 when there was the local government reorganization of counties. Each book is illustrated with photographs and line drawings and would prove invaluable to anyone who wants to get to know England better either from an armchair or from actual travel.

DISCOVERY

Michael Haag, the publisher and author of the North African books in this series, is a historian and very knowledgeable about his subject. It is reassuring to know that what you are reading is almost bound to be correct. The guides have in-depth background coverage, but scanty practical information.

EVERYMAN

A welcome and completely new concept in guidebooks. Each book in the series, originated by Gallimard in France, is crammed with fascinating nuggets of information and in-depth essays on various subjects. The original layout is full of diagrams and pictures, for example, illustrating the different architectural styles of buildings in a city. The kind of book that you learn something from every time you pick it up.

EYEWITNESS TRAVEL GUIDES

The initial impression is that this series is similar to the Everyman guides; they certainly *look* much the same, but in fact there is far less information. However, certainly useful for the less committed traveller.

FODOR

Fodor guides, which come from the US, are updated annually. They have been around for fifty-eight years and publish over 130 titles. They now have uniformly gold covers; some of the volumes have interesting essays and there is much practical information – hotels and restaurants have informative and useful descriptions. Useful, but not overly exciting.

FOOTPATHS OF EUROPE

A regional footpath series, created in agreement with the French Ramblers' Association from their 'Topo' guides to the Grande Randonnée routes. Each has clear colour maps.

FROMMER'S

A well-known American series which has its loyal followers, judging by the extracts from satisfied readers on the back, but which is geared to the American market and has a dated feel about it.

GATWICK ENTREÉ GUIDES

Recently renamed, these guides, most of which are by Patricia Fenn, were originally called 'French Entreé'. It is an excellent series, not least because each guide guarantees that every place mentioned has been personally visited by the author. You know you can trust places that Patricia Fenn recommends.

GROC'S CANDID GUIDES TO THE GREEK ISLANDS

Very good on local information, these slightly wacky guides *do* 'get down to the nitty gritty' and uphold their proud claim: 'One of the important corner stones of the guide's philosophy has been unflinchingly maintained, that is candour and readers may rest assured that no punches are pulled in the text.'

HELM FRENCH REGIONAL GUIDES

France has been split up into ten areas, including Paris. The Paris guide has been compiled as a series of ten walks and includes bars and restaurants along the way. It is packed with history and interesting information and you can feel that the author has a true love of Paris. The regional guides are not as comprehensive, but are nonetheless useful as they include hotels and restaurants.

HIDDEN PLACES

Descriptions of the well known tourist sites as well as those lesser known places. Hotels and restaurants are included; there are line drawings throughout and eventually they hope to cover the whole of the UK. Very reasonably priced, but not dated.

HISTORIC HOTELS

These select guides describe each hotel in detail: the history, practical details, special features and menus. The large-format paperback books are published by Thames and Hudson and are full of colour photographs.

INSIGHT

Everytime you blink there seems to be a new batch of Insight guides. They cover countries, areas and themes, e.g. *Native America* and *East African Wildlife*. Filled with colour pictures they also have interesting anecdotal material but are short on practical information. They can be good for deciding where to go and also would make good souvenirs after returning from a trip.

KAREN BROWN

An American series of books which recommends either bed and breakfasts or country inns. Each entry has a page of description and a line drawing of the establishment.

LET'S GO

The original budget guide series, compiled by Harvard/Radcliffe students during their holidays for other students to use on *their* holidays. The series is updated every year and is written with enthusiasm by alumnae travelling on tight budgets. Useful.

LONELY PLANET

The immensely successful Australian series was started by Tony and Maureen Wheeler who travelled across Asia on a tight budget in the early 1970s and realized that there was not a suitable guide. They wrote and published *Across Asia on the Cheap* from one room in Sydney. Today there are over eighty titles in print: the travel survival kits cover a single country and a range of budgets; the shoestring guides cover a region and are more for budget travellers. There are also walking guides and phrasebooks. They have been criticized recently for being irresponsible in encouraging people to travel to out-of-the-way places, but since people are going to travel anyway surely it is better that they go well informed about their destinations. Lonely Planet donates a percentage of its income from the guides to the country concerned and tries to make its readers take a responsible attitude. As most of the world is now covered by Lonely Planet Guides, this is an important role. There is a problem in that because the guides are so popular 'a quiet hotel' cannot remain so. They are packed with interesting information and facts and are easy and fun to read.

MICHELIN

Still probably the one series that everyone has heard of, the Michelin green guides are wholly for sightseeing. There are twenty-four to the regions of France, the twelve most popular have been translated into English. Other countries and towns worldwide also come under the Michelin umbrella. They are arranged alphabetically by place with the famous star rating system. You can generally be sure that when they say something is worth the detour, it will be.

The Michelin red guides concentrate on hotels and restaurants: the one to France has over 1,300 pages, crammed with places to eat and stay, arranged alphabetically by town. The famous Michelin symbols are easy to decipher and the town plans are excellent.

MOON PUBLICATIONS

The flagship of this series was the excellent *Indonesia Handbook*, which is still the best guide to Indonesia. Mostly to South East Asia and North America, the guides are full of practical information as well as having much about the culture and background of the areas.

MOORLAND

The Moorland Visitor's guides have a nice chunky format, arranged in routes with symbols in the margins for churches, parks, museums etc., which are meant to be helpful but can become maddening and disruptive when reading the text. Very little practical information, e.g. hotels are not mentioned by name. There are over 50 titles in print. New from Moorland is their 'Independent Traveller' guide series, which are slightly larger format and have more information than their Visitor's guides.

MURRAY

The Literary Companions is a new series from John Murray, the doyen of travel publishers. The thoughts and writings of known and not so well known travellers and writers are quoted – essential for those who want to know what somewhere was like and who have an interest in reading more about it. So far guides to Paris, Florence, Rome, Venice, London, Ireland, Greece, China, Spain and India have been published.

NATIONAL TRAIL GUIDES

Walking guides to national trails throughout Britain. The routes are split into convenient sections with relevant ordnance survey maps for each.

NELLES

A German series full of photographs, with some interesting essays on aspects of the countries by different authors (there are about thirty titles in print), but which are of limited use as practical guides.

ODYSSEY

One of the newer names in the ever growing guide book market, this quickly expanding series is published in Hong Kong; the guides are entitled 'Introduction to . . . '. There are over fifty titles in print with ample text and a mass of colour pictures. The few hotels mentioned are listed without descriptions which makes the series slightly less useful than it might otherwise be. The series includes guides to many of the American states, something quite hard to find in the UK.

ORDNANCE SURVEY

Ordnance Survey publish two sets of walking books to accompany their maps: The Landranger series and the Pathfinder series. Each contains coloured ordnance survey mapping with local information and points of interest on each walk.

PALLAS GUIDES

One wishes that there were more titles in this excellent and in-depth series. These are the kind of books which become invaluable companions and are as useful for residents as for casual visitors. Recommended.

PERIPLUS INDONESIA TRAVEL GUIDES

Invaluable guides to the lesser known parts of Indonesia; full of maps and colour photographs and fairly strong on regional culture as well as practical information.

PEVSNER – BUILDINGS OF ENGLAND

A must for anyone interested in learning about the architecture of where they are living or visiting. Extremely detailed descriptions of buildings with masses of architectural terms. However each volume has a glossary at the end. Invaluable if somewhat arcane.

PHAIDON

The Phaidon cultural guides are devoted to the art and culture of countries and towns. They are arranged alphabetically by town or region and have detailed information about the churches, museums and other interesting buildings; the descriptions are accompanied by colour reproductions, maps and plans.

PHILIP'S TRAVEL GUIDES

A large format series of illustrated books. The word 'guide' is somewhat of a misnomer, as they are certainly not the kind of books that you would want to travel with – more the kind to buy before a trip to give you ideas, or afterwards as a souvenir.

ROUGH GUIDES

Rough Guides are a real success story. Started on a shoestring by young graduates, they have gone through a variety of publishers and distributors before landing firmly on their feet at Penguin.

There are currently over fifty in print with many new titles planned for next year. They began with a student market in mind, but soon found that they were selling to a much wider audience, now to both up-market and down-market travellers. As the *Independent* recently said they are also 'helpful, at a different level, when they tell you where to find cheap tickets or a tranquil hotel, though their search for gay helplines in remote Catholic hill villages seems doomed to disappointment'. They are independent and irreverent and have marvellous sections on history, art and architecture and wildlife. Each book has an authoritative bibliography at the end.

SHELL GUIDES

One of the best, and only, series of guides to the counties of England. Now unfortunately out of print.

SMITHSONIAN GUIDES

A series which concentrates on historic America. Each volume is well researched and is filled with colour photographs and maps. The guides include many out-of-the-way and not so famous historical sites as well as the more obvious ones.

SPECTRUM GUIDES

The series is packed with colour photographs and background essays by the Camerapix team.

SUNFLOWER COUNTRYSIDE GUIDES – LANDSCAPES OF . . .

Small practical guides which are useful for touring whether by public transport, car or on foot. Most are arranged in a series of tours.

THOMAS COOK TRAVELLERS GUIDES

A newish series which uses writers who really know their subject. Published in a handy, small format and interspersed with colour photographs throughout.

TIME OUT GUIDES

Pocket-sized books which stick to the *Time Out* look and which have a wealth of information; this series would be extremely useful for residents as well as for the casual visitor.

TIMES BARTHOLOMEW GUIDES

A series of international guidebooks to only the most obvious places and which have nothing particular to recommend them.

TRADE & TRAVEL

Trade & Travel publish the vastly successful South American Handbook now in its sixty-eighth edition. A few years ago they decided to expand the series by dividing the South American Handbook into three: *Mexico & Central America* and the *Caribbean*. They have since added new titles: the *South Asian Handbook, Thailand, Indochina & Burma Handbook, Indonesia, Malaysia & Singapore Handbook*. These guides are extremely informative, printed on India paper they are packed with interesting facts with new editions coming out annually.

TRAVEL RESOURCE GUIDES

A new series of multi-resource travel guides which aims to cover the travel literature of various countries. They will have critical reviews of mainstream and special interest guidebooks, maps and videos as well as information about bookshops, libraries and clubs. Very expensive.

TRAVELLER'S LITERARY COMPANIONS

An original series of literary guides which contains extracts from books by both native and foreign writers about particular countries. There are short biographies of the writers; there is no question that the countries are brought to life by this kind of book.

TRAVELSCAPES

A narrative guide series in which each chapter is devoted to a particular area. Strong on history; would be a good accompaniment to a more practical guide.

VACATION WORK

Targeted primarily at students and full of ideas on what to do either on short vacations or for longer periods abroad. Their guides are called *Travellers' Survival Kit*, confusingly similar to the Lonely Planet name, but much more budget oriented.

VERSATILE GUIDES

A new series of guides which are refreshingly opinionated and clearly laid out. Each region is divided alphabetically; there are clear road references and restaurants and hotels are described and recommended.

VIRAGO WOMAN'S TRAVEL GUIDES

At last a series of practical guides aimed at women, on their own, with other women or with their families, which are good guides in their own right. Includes sections which describe women's contributions to the history, art and culture of the cities and countries. Clearly set out and easy to read with maps and plans.

WHICH? GUIDES

The fairly dense text with few maps makes this series seem somewhat old-fashioned. However, the contents are quite discerning and useful.

WINDRUSH ISLAND GUIDES

Portable and easy to use; concentrating on one island at a time, and containing a good deal of information. Illustrated.

OLD SERIES OF GUIDES

The original *Baedeker* guides which were first published in 1829 are not only collectors' items today, but can be very useful for travellers with their detailed descriptions of buildings. They are eye-openers about what travel was like in the nineteenth century which makes them suitable for research. This also applies to *Murray's* guides, the most famous of which is the *Handbook to Spain* written by Richard Ford. Other series of interest are *Cook's* and Augustus *Hare's Walk's in* . . .

I have occasionally included some of these in the main text, and they are always worth looking for in second-hand bookshops as they can add substantial enjoyment and interest to travelling.

About the book

I have arranged the book to make it as easy as possible to use. By looking up the country of your choice you will be able to find a selection of books in various categories; it would also always be worth looking under the general section at the start of each continent for additional books about the country in which you are interested, e.g. books which include belgium might be found in the general Europe section. There is an extensive index; it can be frustrating to know, for example, that Evelyn Waugh wrote a book about Africa, but not to be able to remember its name or where it was about. Alternatively, you might want to know where *Scoop* was about. The comprehensive indexes should help solve all these problems.

Key

✔ = in print at time of going to press
[ ] = a book recommended by ... especially for this book

AFRICA

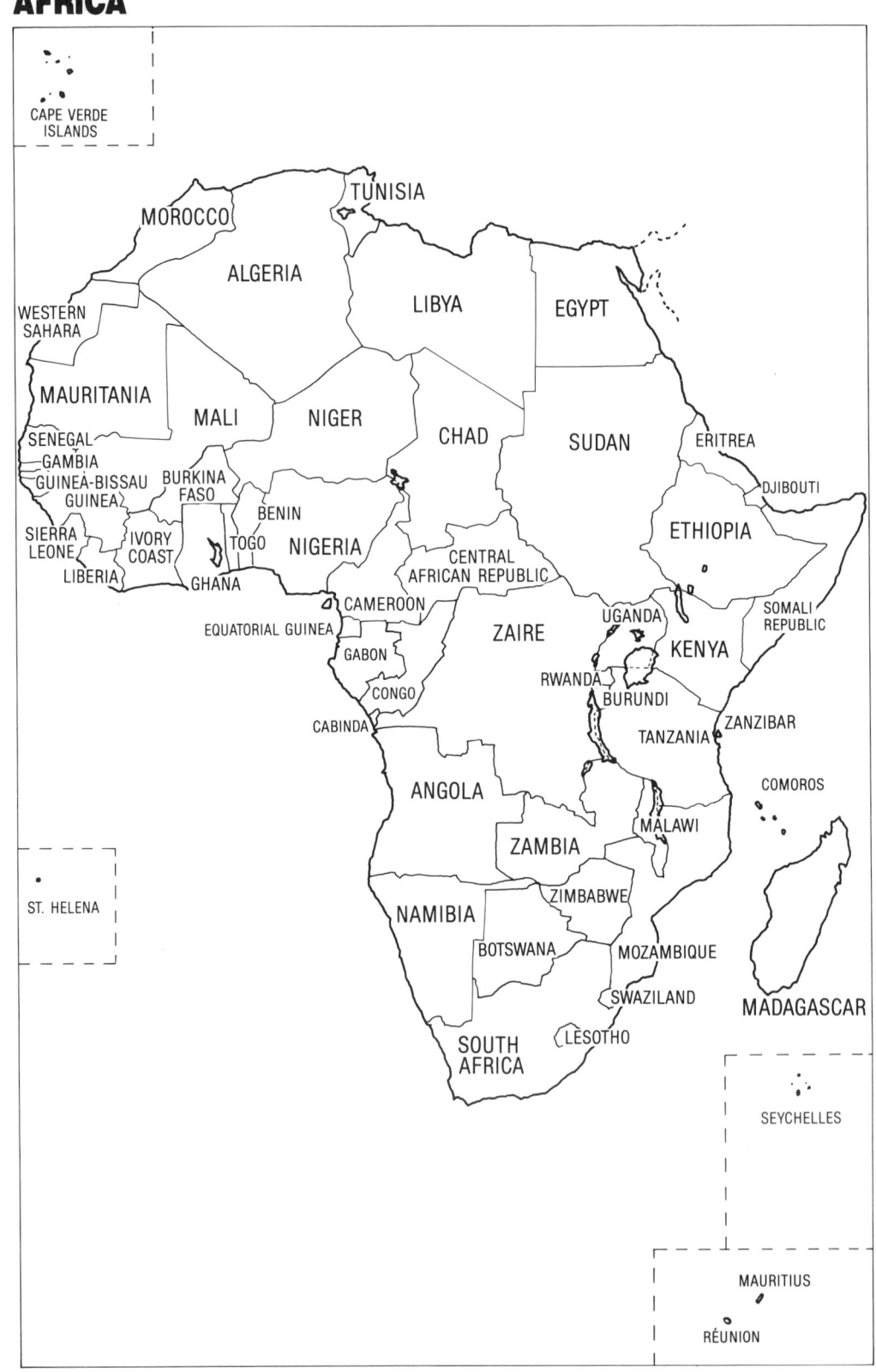

CAPE VERDE ISLANDS

MOROCCO
TUNISIA
ALGERIA
LIBYA
EGYPT
WESTERN SAHARA
MAURITANIA
MALI
NIGER
CHAD
SUDAN
ERITREA
DJIBOUTI
SENEGAL
GAMBIA
GUINEA-BISSAU
GUINEA
BURKINA FASO
BENIN
ETHIOPIA
SIERRA LEONE
IVORY COAST
TOGO
NIGERIA
CENTRAL AFRICAN REPUBLIC
SOMALI REPUBLIC
LIBERIA
GHANA
CAMEROON
UGANDA
KENYA
EQUATORIAL GUINEA
ZAIRE
GABON
RWANDA
CONGO
BURUNDI
CABINDA
TANZANIA
ZANZIBAR
COMOROS
ANGOLA
ZAMBIA
MALAWI
ST. HELENA
ZIMBABWE
NAMIBIA
MOZAMBIQUE
BOTSWANA
SWAZILAND
MADAGASCAR
SOUTH AFRICA
LESOTHO
SEYCHELLES
MAURITIUS
RÉUNION

NORTH and CENTRAL AMERICA

ARCTIC

GREENLAND

ALASKA (U.S.A.)

CANADA

UNITED STATES OF AMERICA

MEXICO

HAWAII

BELIZE
HONDURAS
GUATEMALA
EL SALVADOR
NICARAGUA
COSTA RICA
PANAMA

SOUTH AMERICA

GALAPAGOS

TRINIDAD AND TOBAGO

VENEZUELA

GUYANA

COLOMBIA

SURINAM

FRENCH GUIANA

ECUADOR

PERU

BRAZIL

BOLIVIA

CHILE

PARAGUAY

EASTER
ISLAND

URUGUAY

ARGENTINA

FALKLAND Is.

TIERRA DEL
FUEGO

CARIBBEAN

TROPIC OF CANCER

BERMUDA

BAHAMAS

CAYMAN
Is.

CUBA

GREATER ANTILLES

JAMAICA

CAICOS Is.

TURK Is.

HAITI

DOMINICAN
REPUBLIC

PUERTO RICO (U.S.A.)

VIRGIN Is. (U.S.A.)

LEEWARD Is.

ANGUILLA

ST. MARTIN

ST. KITTS

NEVIS

MONSERRAT

ANTIGUA & BARBUDA

GUADELOUPE

DOMINICA

LESSER ANTILLES

MARTINIQUE

ST. LUCIA

ST. VINCENT & GRENADINES

WINDWARD Is.

BARBADOS

GRENADA

TOBAGO

TRINIDAD

CENTRAL ASIA and the INDIAN SUB-CONTINENT

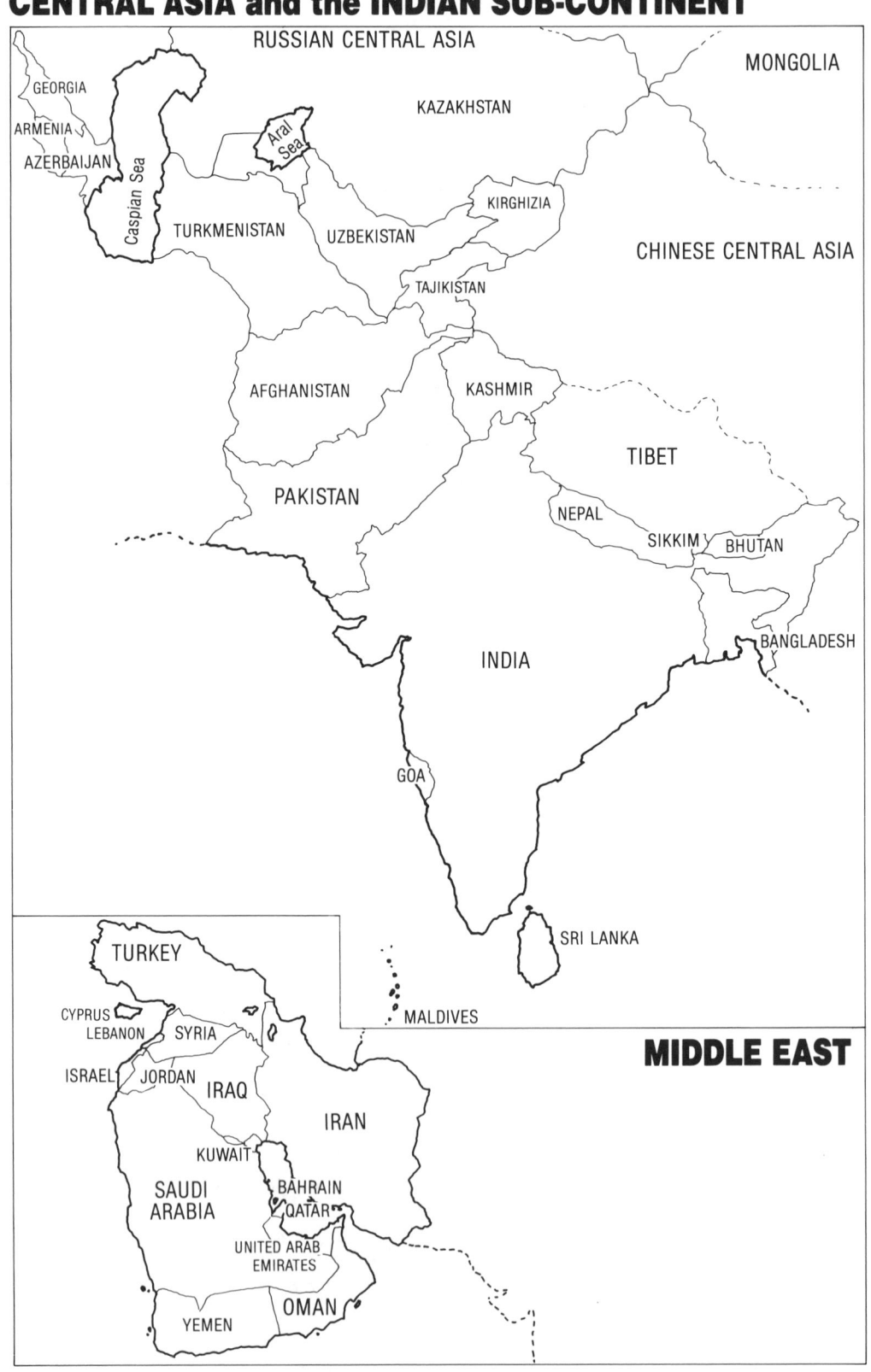

RUSSIAN CENTRAL ASIA

MONGOLIA

GEORGIA

ARMENIA

AZERBAIJAN

Caspian Sea

KAZAKHSTAN

Aral Sea

TURKMENISTAN

UZBEKISTAN

KIRGHIZIA

CHINESE CENTRAL ASIA

TAJIKISTAN

AFGHANISTAN

KASHMIR

TIBET

PAKISTAN

NEPAL

SIKKIM

BHUTAN

INDIA

BANGLADESH

GOA

SRI LANKA

TURKEY

CYPRUS

LEBANON

SYRIA

ISRAEL

JORDAN

IRAQ

IRAN

KUWAIT

SAUDI
ARABIA

BAHRAIN

QATAR

UNITED ARAB
EMIRATES

OMAN

YEMEN

MALDIVES

MIDDLE EAST

FAR EAST and SOUTH EAST ASIA

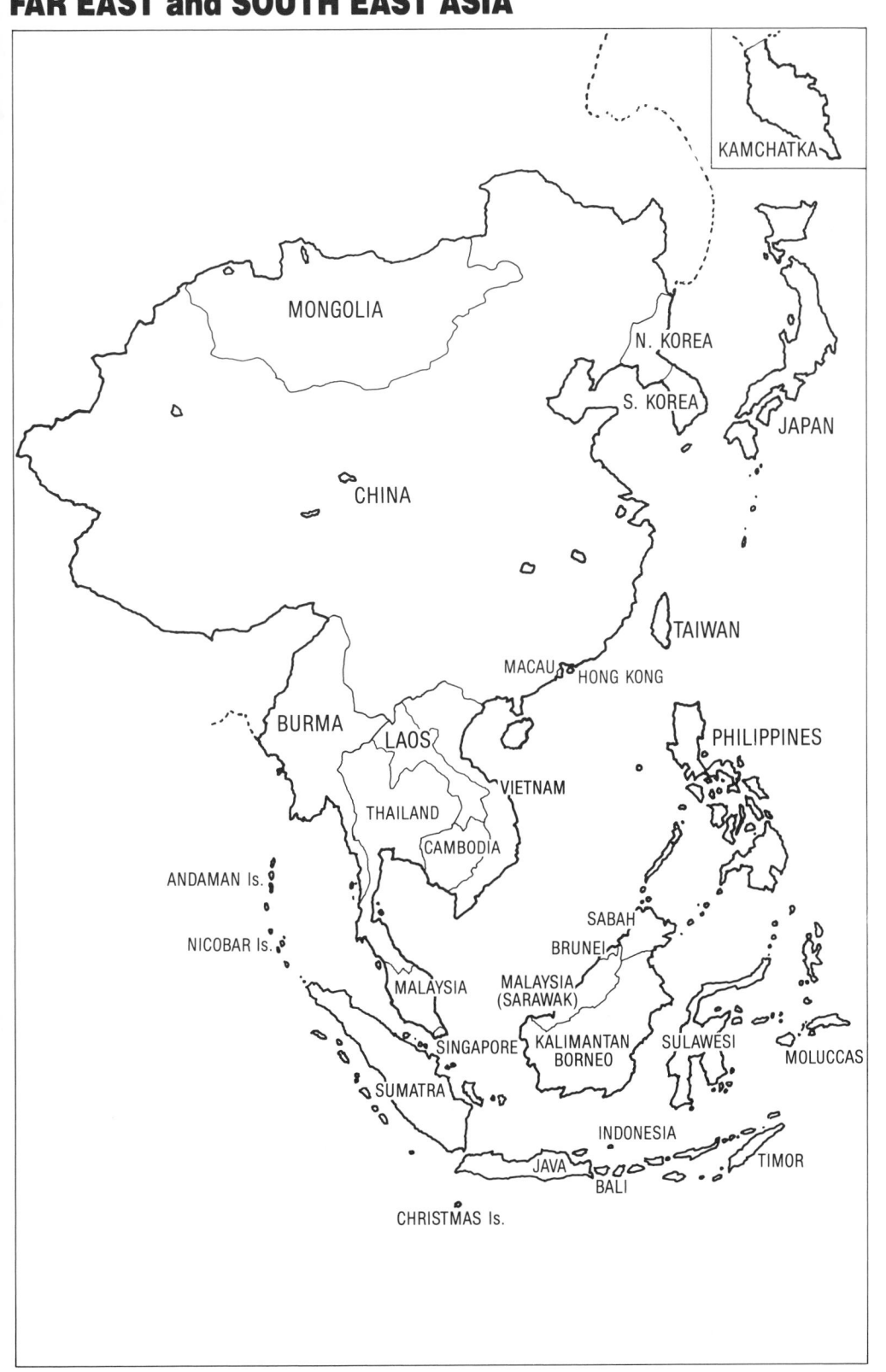

KAMCHATKA

MONGOLIA

N. KOREA

S. KOREA

JAPAN

CHINA

TAIWAN

MACAU

HONG KONG

BURMA

LAOS

PHILIPPINES

VIETNAM

THAILAND

CAMBODIA

ANDAMAN Is.

NICOBAR Is.

SABAH

BRUNEI

MALAYSIA
(SARAWAK)

MALAYSIA

SINGAPORE

KALIMANTAN
BORNEO

SULAWESI

MOLUCCAS

SUMATRA

INDONESIA

TIMOR

JAVA

BALI

CHRISTMAS Is.

PACIFIC   AUSTRALASIA

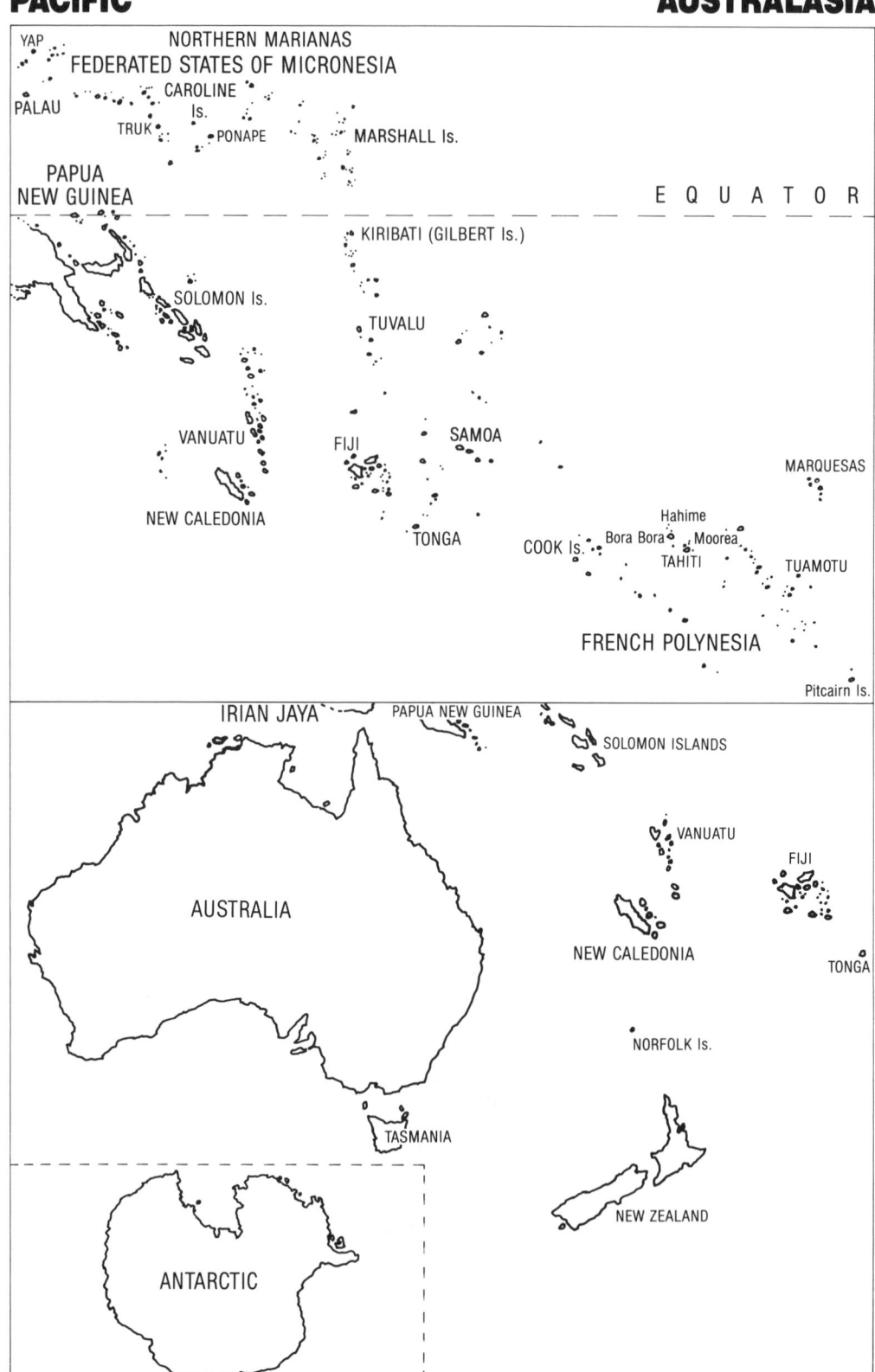

YAP
NORTHERN MARIANAS
FEDERATED STATES OF MICRONESIA
CAROLINE
PALAU
Is.
TRUK
PONAPE   MARSHALL Is.
PAPUA
NEW GUINEA   E Q U A T O R

KIRIBATI (GILBERT Is.)

SOLOMON Is.

TUVALU

VANUATU   FIJI   SAMOA   MARQUESAS

NEW CALEDONIA   Hahime
COOK Is. Bora Bora Moorea
TONGA   TAHITI   TUAMOTU

FRENCH POLYNESIA

Pitcairn Is.

IRIAN JAYA   PAPUA NEW GUINEA
SOLOMON ISLANDS

VANUATU

FIJI

AUSTRALIA

NEW CALEDONIA
TONGA

NORFOLK Is.

TASMANIA

NEW ZEALAND

ANTARCTIC

WESTERN EUROPE

ICELAND

LAPLAND

FINLAND

SWEDEN

NORWAY

FAROE Is.

SHETLAND
Is.

HEBRIDES

ORKNEY
Is.

SCOTLAND

N. IRELAND

Glasgow Edinburgh

DENMARK

RUSSIA

EIRE Dublin

BRITISH ISLES

ENGLAND

WALES

NETHERLANDS

SCILLY
Is.

London

Berlin

CHANNEL Is.

BELGIUM

GERMANY

LUXEMBOURG

Paris

FRANCE

LIECHTENSTEIN

SWITZERLAND

AUSTRIA

SLOVENIA

CROATIA

PORTUGAL

Venice

BOSNIA

YUGOSLAVIA

Florence

Madrid

ANDORRA

MONACO

SAN MARINO

MACEDONIA

Lisbon

SPAIN

Barcelona

CORSICA

ITALY

Rome

MAJORCA

ALBANIA

BALEARICS

Ischia

CAPRI

GREECE

GIBRALTAR

SARDINIA

SICILY

CORFU

IONIAN Is.

Athens

GREEK Is.

RHODES

GOZO

MADEIRA

MALTA

CRETE

CANARIES

CYPRUS

CENTRAL and EASTERN EUROPE

SIBERIA

ESTONIA

LATVIA

LITHUANIA

RUSSIA

POLAND

BELORUSSIA

CZECH
REPUBLIC

SLOVAK
REP.

UKRAINE

HUNGARY

MOLDAVIA

SLOVENIA

ROMANIA

CROATIA

BOSNIA

YUGOSLAVIA

Black Sea

BULGARIA

ALBANIA

MACEDONIA

AFRICA

Africa

GENERAL

Anthropology

Black Skin, White Masks   *Frantz Fanon*
1967 (1952)
This book was not published in England until after Fanon's death in 1961. He uses psychoanalysis and psychology to explain his theory about the feelings of dependency and inadequacy that black people experience in a white world. *The New York Times* wrote 'One feels a brilliant, vivid and hurt mind walking the thin line that separates effective outrage from despair', and *Newsweek* described the book as 'A strange, haunting mélange of existential analysis, revolutionary manifesto, metaphysics, prose, poetry and literary criticism'.

The Africans   *David Lamb   1990*
The author tries to cram too much into this book making it a somewhat muddled overview.

Art and Architecture

✔ **African Traditional Architecture**
Susan Denyer   1982
A survey of architecture in sub-Saharan Africa; the text is broken down into Rural Settlements; States and Towns; Sacred, Ceremonial and Community Buildings; Defence; The Building Process; Decoration; a Taxonomy of House Forms; Distribution of Styles; The Impact of Modernization. Thorough, but accessible to the general reader; detailed line drawings and photographs make this a useful book.

✔ **A Short History of African Art**
Werner Gillon   1988 (1984)
A concise and comprehensive history of African art illustrated with many black and white photographs. Gillon examines the worldwide influences on African culture through the ages and includes an invaluable bibliography at the end. Very useful for reference and for a general appreciation of the many different art forms in Africa.

The Dance, Art and Ritual of Africa
Jean-Louis Paudrat   Photographs by Michel Huet.
1978
More than 260 photographs of dances recorded during thirty years in sub-Saharan Africa. The significance of the ritual and dances is explained in the text.

✔ **African Textiles**   *John Picton and John Mack   1991 (1979)*
A book showing how textiles are produced in the different countries of Africa. The mostly black and white photographs show the processes of preparing the raw materials, dyeing, appliqué and embroidery etc. Sixty colour illustrations show the finished result.

✔ **Africa Explores**   *Susan Vogel   1991*
An exploration of the major themes in twentieth century African art. Susan Vogel divides the sub-Saharan African art of today into five main themes: traditional art, New Functional art, Urban art, International art and Extinct art. Many people have contributed a variety of essays to the book and it is well illustrated with colour photographs throughout.

✔ **African Art**   *Frank Willett   1991 (1971)*
A very good introduction and survey of African art which shows the variety and power of the different forms of art. The book is easy to use and has many colour illustrations.

Biography

✔ **The Devil Drives**   *Fawn Brodie   1990 (1967)*
A riveting biography of Richard Burton, the explorer, botanist, swordsman, zoologist, geologist, pornographer, author of forty-three books and speaker of forty languages.

✔ **The Arabs**   *Peter Mansfield   1992 (1976)*
(see 'Middle East')

Food

✔ **The Africa News Cookbook: African Cooking for Western Kitchens**
Tami Hultman (ed.)   1986 (1985)
The book includes the best of regional African dishes adapted for Western kitchens: coriander chicken from Algeria, pigeon pie from Morocco, Tunisian couscous, hot spiced prawns from Mozambique, mango snow from Tanzania and vegetable mafé from Senegal.

✔ **Les Merveilles de la Cuisine Africaine**   *Rose-Marie Mendy   n.d.*
Recipes from all over Africa, in French.

General Background

✔ **The Soccer War**   Ryszard Kapuscinski
1991 (1990) (see 'Central America')
Among the revolutions and coups that Kapuscinski covered were incidents in Algeria, the Congo and Ghana.

✔ **Traveller's Literary Companion to Africa**   Oona Strathern   1994

Guides

✔ **Africa Overland. A Route & Planning Guide**   David Brydon   1991 (1987)
Practical information about planning a trip across the Sahara and onwards as well as an account of the author's overland journey from England to South Africa.

✔ **Africa on a Shoestring**   Geoff Crowther etc.   1992 (1977)

✔ **Through Africa. The Overlander's Guide**   Bob Swain and Paula Snyder   1991
Information about travelling through Africa by four-wheel drive, motorbike, bicycle or organized truck tour.

History

The History and Description of Africa   Leo Africanus   1896 (translated into English in 1600 by John Pory, Hakluyt Society)
Born in Grenada in 1491, Leo Africanus went to Africa as a child when the Moors surrendered to Ferdinand and Isabella. Morocco was in a period of disintegration and decay, with the exception of Fez, a great centre of Arab learning, where Leo studied. He went on various pilgrimages and undertook diplomatic missions, travelling to Tunis, Timbuktoo, Central Africa, Constantinople, Egypt, Algiers, along much of the Niger and to much of Arabia. He was captured by Christians and taken as a present to Pope Leo X (a Medici), who converted and renamed him. He spent many years in Rome, but when the pope died he returned to Tunis where he died in 1552, as a Moslem. He was very adaptable and 'at home' everywhere – explaining his easy transitions to different religions. He wrote in Arabic and Italian, but interestingly does not mention his contemporaries Columbus, Vasco da Gama and Cortes. There was nothing known about Africa at the time, which makes his detailed descriptions of the shops and artisans of sixteenth century Fez and other places especially fascinating. He writes about the different religions in Africa at the time. An important and neglected work.

✔ **Tales from the Dark Continent**   Charles Allen (ed.)   1979
(Images of British Colonial Africa in the twentieth century)
A distillation of the experiences of fifty British men and women who lived and worked in Africa in the days of colonial rule. They originally went to Africa as traders, missionaries, soldiers and policemen and here tell their candid and often funny reminiscences.

Africa in History   Basil Davidson   1968
A very clear introduction to Africa's past. Davidson uses interviews in the text as well as a wide variety of other sources making this a far ranging and useful book.

✔ **Africa Explored**   Christopher Hibbert   1984 (1982)
Subtitled 'Europeans in the Dark Continent 1769–1889'; this is a very readable account of the exploits of the white explorers in Africa before colonial times. The book is arranged chronologically and Hibbert writes about lesser known people as well as the more famous names of Park, Stanley and Livingstone. Most of his research is based on the diaries, letters and books of the explorers themselves.

In Quest of Spices   Sonia E. Howe   c. 1946
A history of the explorers and discoverers who in pursuit of spices ended up by discovering new countries. Alexandria, West Africa, Zanzibar and Madagascar were all important in the development of the spice trade; Sonia Howe charts the journeys of the explorers who visited these places and shows how, for example, seeds and seedlings from cloves and nutmeg were sent from the Moluccas and ended up in Zanzibar and Madagascar which today supply the world with cloves.

✔ **The Exploration of Africa. From Cairo to the Cape**   Anne Hugon   1993 (1991)
A small profusely illustrated book about some of the great explorers of Africa: Burton, Speke, Grant, Baker and Kingsley.

✔ **Europe's Myths of Orient**   Rana Kabbani   1986
An intriguing reassessment of why Europeans travelled and travel to the east. The majority of travellers come from societies which exercise a high degree of political power; inevitably they take their preconceptions with them and their observations and writings are geared to their fellow countrymen. Through the writings of Naipaul, Blunt, Canetti, Thesiger, Burton, Galland, Doughty and Lawrence among others,

Rana Kabbani makes a fascinating case as to why there was and is the great pull to the east.

✔ **The Scramble for Africa**
Thomas Pakenham 1992 (1991)
The last twenty years of the nineteenth century saw a mad 'scramble' for Africa. Between 1880 to 1902 five European powers had grabbed most of Africa and divided it up between them; the rush started after Livingstone had exposed the horrors of the slave trade and said that what Africa needed was Commerce, Christianity and Civilization. Thomas Pakenham has written a fascinating book on this huge subject.

The History of the World *Pliny (translated by Philemon Holland) 1962*
Pliny was writing in the first century AD and this translation first published in 1601 was probably the one read by Shakespeare. Pliny was insatiably curious; he lived in a permanent state of astonishment, accumulating sensational 'facts' to emphasize the extraordinary world in which he lived. Book Five deals briefly with Africa: the inhabitants of Aethyopia, the Source of the Nile and Alexandria which he compares to a 'Macedonian cloak, full in the skirts'.

Natural History

✔ **A Field Guide to the Larger Mammals of Africa** *Jean Dorst and Pierre Dandelot 1990 (1970)*
Full of colour photographs, line drawings and detailed descriptions of the animals, including their measurements, colour, markings, habitat, behaviour and habits. The book also has distribution maps making it an invaluable reference work.

✔ **Field Guide to the Mammals of Africa including Madagascar**
T. Haltenorth and H. Diller 1992 (1977)
The guide covers every species of mammal found in continental Africa. Each family of species has its own introduction and this is followed by detailed descriptions and illustrations.

✔ **Field Guide to the Butterflies of Africa** *John Williams 1969*
A general guide which covers all of Africa except Madagascar. Colour illustrations and line drawings and descriptions of over 400 of the most common butterflies.

Photography

✔ **Visions of a Nomad** *Wilfred Thesiger 1993 (1987)*
A selection of Thesiger's black and white photographs from Africa, the Arab World and Asia.

Travel Literature

From the Niger to the Nile *Boyd Alexander 1907*
The expedition which took place between 1904–7 ended in the death of two of Alexander's companions including his brother. He succeeded in reaching the Nile carrying out much mapping and wild-life investigation en route.

Behind God's Back *Negley Farson 1983 (1941)*
Just before the Second World War, Negley Farson, an American journalist, spent four months crossing Africa overland. He gives a very good account of colonial Africa.

From the Cape to Cairo *Ewart S. Grogan 1900*
(The First Traverse of Africa from South to North)
Grogan was a Cambridge undergraduate at the time of his expedition which he undertook on foot; in the introduction Cecil Rhodes writes how 'humorous' it is that a 'youth from Cambridge during his vacation should have succeeded in doing that which the ponderous explorers of the world have failed to accomplish'.

✔ **Native Stranger** *Eddy L. Harris 1993 (1992)*
Eddy Harris is a black American who travelled throughout Africa in order to understand just how little and yet how much it had to do with himself. He went to Tunisia, Algeria, Morocco, Western Sahara, Mauritania, Senegal, The Gambia, Guinea-Bissau, Mali, Ivory Coast, Liberia, Burkina Faso, Togo, Benin, Nigeria, Cameroon, Central African Republic, Zaire, Rwanda, Burundi, Zambia, Zimbabwe and South Africa.

No Man's Land *John Heminway 1983*
A personal memoir in which Heminway travels through Africa focusing on the expatriates who cannot call Africa home and yet cannot leave it. 'A literary gem that belongs on your shelf beside the best of Isak Dinesen and Elspeth Huxley, Ernest Hemingway and Laurens van der Post, or currently Edward Hoagland and Peter Matthiessen.' (*Los Angeles Herald Examiner*). Heminway has also written *African Journeys* (1990), a per-

sonal guidebook and *The Imminent Rains*, the account of a car journey from South Africa to Kenya with Mary Ann Fitzgerald.

Fantastic Invasion   Patrick Marnham
1988 (1979)
Patrick Marnham went on many trips to Africa in the 1970s including one in which he wrote a report on the Nomads of the Sahel after a drought. This book, for which he had much trouble finding a publisher, was widely acclaimed when it was published; Paul Theroux said of it: 'An absolutely horrifying chronicle which, better than any book I know, explains Africa and finds a pattern in what

has baffled every other observer up to now. It is a courageous and brilliant effort.'

✔ **When the Going Was Good**
Evelyn Waugh   1992 (1946)
A collection of abridged travel writing which includes a train trip from Djibouti to Abyssinia en route for Haile Selassie's coronation; an expedition to Aden, Zanzibar, Kenya and the Congo; and a return trip to Addis Ababa to report on the war between Abyssinia and Italy. He was a perceptive traveller: 'That merciless eye illuminated all it saw with a brilliant and lurid light' *(TLS)*. Originally published in full as *Remote People* (1931).

North Africa

ALGERIA AND THE SAHARA

'Man eats you; the desert does not.' Arab proverb quoted by Richard Burton

Art and Archaeology

✔ **A Guide to the Archaeological Sites of Israel, Egypt & North Africa**
Courtland Canby and Arcadia Kocybala   (1990)
Over 300 sites are covered, but the black and white photographs are disappointing. The book is divided into three sections: each begins with a history of the area and is followed by a fairly detailed gazetteer of each site.

✔ **The Art and Architecture of Islam 650–1250**   *Richard Ettinghausen and Oleg Grabar   1991 (1987) (see 'Middle East')*

✔ **Africa Adorned**   Angela Fisher   1987 *(1984)*
Jewellery and body adornment are collected here in over 400 stunning photographs. Angela Fisher travelled through North Africa looking out for different kinds of decoration; the ingenuity and diversity of what she found is interesting, as much for what it means, as for its beauty.

Islamic Architecture of North Africa
Derek Hill and Lucien Golvin   n.d.
A photographic survey with notes on the monuments.

North Africa: Islamic Architecture
Anthony Hutt   (1977)
A brief introduction, illustrated with copious well annotated plates, to Islamic architecture in Morocco, Algeria, Tunisia and Libya.

The Search for the Tassili Frescoes. The Story of the pre-historic rock-paintings of the Sahara   *Henri Lhote   1959*
The rock-paintings of the Sahara were not discovered until 1933, but due to the Second World War, no real expedition to explore the Tassili frescoes was mounted until 1956. Lhote faithfully copied the hundreds of paintings of people and animals that he discovered, providing a new understanding of eight millennia of life in the Sahara.

✔ **Rome in Africa**   Susan Raven   1993
An interesting book which has recently been updated and reprinted.

✔ **Islamic Art**   David Talbot Rice   1991 *(1965) (see 'Middle East')*
Only a few chapters refer to North Africa and Morocco in particular, but this is definitely a book worth perusing, since it is interesting to be able to place Islamic art in North Africa into context.

Autobiography/Biography

The Life of Isabelle Eberhardt
Annette Kobak   1991
A biography of Isabelle Eberhardt who became part of the Saharan legend.

The Private Life of Islam   *Ian Young*
1992
An Algerian diary of 1970 of a medical student in a provincial maternity unit.

Fiction

✔ **The Golden Ass**   *Apuleius (translated by Robert Graves)   1976*
Apuleius was born in Madaurus (Soul Ahras in Algeria) and trained as a lawyer in Carthage. This novel is set in Greece where the hero became involved with witchcraft.

L'escargot entêté   *(1982)*
Le Désordre des Choses   *(1991)*
La Pluie   *(1987)*
Le Vainqueur de Coupe   *Rachid Boudjedra   (1981)*
In French only.

✔ **Everything is Nice**   *Jane Bowles   1989*
The collected stories of Jane Bowles were put together by her husband Paul Bowles after her death. The indications are that she would have been reluctant to publish them, but the stories, some of which are set in North Africa, although strange, are full of precision and wit. Unlikely things happen – a true reflection of life.

✔ **The Sheltering Sky**   *Paul Bowles (see Paul Bowles, fiction, Morocco)*
Probably Bowles' most famous book is *The Sheltering Sky* 1990 (1949) – now a major feature film. He describes it as 'a novel just like any other novel: a triangle laid in the Sahara', but of course it is much more than 'just a novel' and it *is* the Sahara, which helps make it so different. The power of the desert is tangible in his work and raw emotion is powerfully near the surface.

✔ **The Plague**   *Albert Camus   1960 (1947)*
Albert Camus (1913–1960) was born in Algeria. *The Plague* is ostensibly set in a French port in Algeria, but the destruction of the town could as easily be an analogy for the sufferings of France under German occupation in the Second World War. *The Immoralist* 1986 (1902) is about a young man, newly married, who goes to live in Algeria; he discovers he has tuberculosis and while recovering goes through a voyage of self-discovery. He realizes in Gide's words 'To know how to free oneself is nothing; the arduous thing is to know what to do with one's freedom'.

✔ **Tea in the Harem**   *Mehdi Charef   1989 (1983)*
The author was born in Algeria; this novel is set in the Paris suburbs and is about a young boy growing up split between two cultures: at home the Arab culture and at school the French culture.

L'Espèce Errante   *Afsaneh Eghbal   1983*
In French only.

✔ **The Mysteries of Algiers**   *Robert Irwin   1993 (1988)*
Set in 1959 in Algiers when the French were making a last stand against the FLN liberation army. It was described in the *Listener* as 'Entertaining and very nasty, this calculatedly intellectual comedy succeeds well as an unheroic quest starring Philippe, an interesting monster of disarming honesty'.

La Ceinture de l'Ogresse   *(1990)*
Le Fleuve détourné   *(1982)*
The Honour of the Tribe   *(1993)*
Une Paix à vivre   *Rachid Mimouni   (1983)*
Most of Rachid Mimouni's books have not yet been translated into English.

Desert Love   *Henry de Montherlant   1960 (1955)*
Extracts from the novel called *La Rose de Sable* which de Montherlant wrote in Algiers between 1930 and 1932 and which has as its subject the colonial question seen through the problem of the natives of North Africa. The translation leaves out the politics and concentrates on the love story in which a stupid, but sensitive young French lieutenant who is stationed at a remote oasis in French North Africa, becomes obsessed by a young Arab girl Ramie, who has to remain a virgin. Graham Greene described it as 'Fascinating, brilliant and aseptic in its analysis of lust'.

✔ **The Little Prince**   *Antoine de Saint-Exupéry   1982 (1945)*
A parable which tells of an air pilot who after making a forced landing in the Sahara Desert meets the little prince who tells him wonderful stories about the planet where he lives. The book was written a year before Saint Exupéry died.

General Background

A Dying Colonialism   *Frantz Fanon   1980 (1959)*
Fanon had worked as a psychiatrist in an Algerian hospital during the Algerian revolution. Here he identifies the justice of the Algerian cause and analyses the relations between colonial and subject peoples. He also shows how this nationalist struggle altered traditional attitudes to family, women, technology and medicine.

The Wretched of the Earth   *Frantz Fanon   1967 (1961)*
A study of the Algerian revolution which has served as a model for other liberation struggles. Fanon exposes the economic and psychological degradation of imperialism and points the way forward (through violence if necessary) to socialism.

✔ **The Sahara**   *Jeremy Swift   (1975)*
A survey of the Sahara through contemporary photographs, history and fascinating text. As an overall view of this vast area of North Africa, there is no better introduction.

Guides

✔ **Sahara Handbook**   *Simon Glen 1990(1987)*
Invaluable as a practical guide for anyone intending to travel across the Sahara. There is information on the climate, how to choose and maintain a vehicle as well as detailed routes. Since the last edition, crossing the Sahara has become very dangerous; few tour operators risk the journey because of outbreaks of violence among the Tuareg and banditry 'liberation' actions. Be warned!

✔ **Morocco, Algeria & Tunisia. Travel Survival Kit**   *1992 (1989)*
Biased in favour of Morocco, there is, however, enough information on Algeria, both practical and historical, to make it a worthwhile buy.

✔ **North African Handbook 1995**
Published by Trade & Travel
Includes sections on Andalucia, Morocco, Mauritania, Algeria, Tunisia, Libya, Egypt and Sudan.

History

✔ **Modern Algeria. A History from 1830 to the Present**   *Charles-Robert Ageron 1991 (1964)*
A balanced political, social and economic account of the colonial period in Algeria from the beginning of the French conquest in 1830 until 1962.

The Golden Trade of the Moors   *E.W. Bovill   1968 (1958)*
This book shows what an important part the Sahara played in linking the sophisticated cities of North Africa with the great markets to the South. Bovill argues that Berbers, Arabs, Jews and Christians all drew on the wealth and industry of the Sudanese and that it was the routes through the Sahara that made this possible. Both areas gained

from this interchange of merchandise, salt and above all differing cultures.

Alamein to Zem Zem   *Keith Douglas   1979 (1966)*
Keith Douglas was one of the few poets who wrote about the North African campaign during the Second World War. He had been a pacifist as a student, but against orders drove a truck to El Alamein and reported for duty in the Sherwood Rangers. He portrays his experiences in vivid prose; he was both curious and detached.

A Savage War of Peace. Algeria 1954-1962   *Alistair Horne   1987 (1977)*
Around a million Muslim Algerians were killed in the savage colonial war and as many Europeans were made homeless. Alistair Horne's book documents the course of the war and includes an excellent bibliography.

The Conquest of the Sahara   *Douglas Porch   1986 (1984)*
A history which describes the French attempt to colonize the Sahara in the late nineteenth century. The men who attempted it were often driven mad by the adverse conditions of heat, thirst, insects and sandstorms which they encountered, but they were driven on by dreams of grandeur and imperialist policy.

Natural History

✔ **Birds of Britain & Europe with North Africa and the Middle East**
H. Heinzel, R.F. Fitter and J. Parslow   1992 (1972)
The birds are arranged by family; all the illustrations are in colour and the text indicates the points most useful for identification.

✔ **The Flowers of the Mediterranean**
O. Polunin and A. Huxley   1990 (1965)
The whole of the Mediterranean, including Morocco, is covered with over 300 colour illustrations and 200 line drawings. The descriptive text makes the plants easily identifiable.

Photography

Sahara. Magic Desert   *Jean-Marc Durou 1986*
A series of evocative images of land, life and ecology in the Sahara, with a short introduction and text by Theodore Monod.

Travel Literature

✔ **Impossible Journey**   Michael Asher
1989 (1988)
Michael Asher embarked on the crossing of
the Sahara from west to east, by camel, with
his wife of five days. This is one of the most
punishing journeys left for man to make and
Asher tells of his and and his wife Marianto-
nietta's 4,500 mile trek, with an honesty from
which he emerges both as a traveller and as
a writer with credit.

✔ **Ibn Battuta. Travels in Asia and
Africa 1325–1354**   *1984 (1929)*
Ibn Battuta was born in Tangier and as a
good Muslim made a pilgrimage to Mecca. As
both pilgrim and theologian he was warmly
welcomed along the route and discovered the
joys of travel for its own sake. He spent seven
years in India amassing both wealth and
fascinating memories about life in a medieval Muslim court, which he wrote about. He
was eventually sent as an envoy to China but
to get there he took a circuitous route via the
Maldives and Sumatra, finally arriving in
Peking. He was known as 'The Traveller of
Islam' and is the only known person to have
visited the lands of every Muhamadan ruler,
as well as many others, covering about
75,000 miles.

✔ **Their Heads Are Green**   Paul Bowles
(see 'Morocco')

Tangier to Tunis   Alexandre Dumas   *1959*
A tour of the North African coast undertaken
by Dumas while he was waiting for the return of the governor of Algiers. The English
translation is an abridged version of the original, but concentrates on all the exciting
parts including a visit to the bey's palace in
Tunis.

✔ **The Passionate Nomad**
Isabelle Eberhardt   1987 (1944)
Isabelle Eberhardt was born in 1877 near
Geneva, the illegitimate daughter of an ex-
pope of the Russian Orthodox Church and a
Prussian/Russian mother. She and her
mother went to North Africa, where they
both converted to Islam. When her mother
died she started her desert wanderings,
dressed as a man and known as Si Mahmoud.
The Passionate Nomad is the collection of her
journals found in notebooks after she was
killed by a flash flood in 1904. She suffered
from constant illness and poverty, but
through her writing shines a real love of the
desert and Arab culture. She also wrote an
unfinished novel *Vagabond* 1988 (1922) and
a collection of short stories, The *Oblivion
Seekers*, set in North Africa. Isabelle Ebe-

rhardt is one of the four women referred to in
Lesley Blanch's *Wilder Shores of Love*. (q.v.)

The Lands of Barbary   Geoffrey Furlonge
1966
Furlonge travelled through North Africa in
1960 and 1964. He writes convincingly about
all the different landscapes, people and scenery that he encounters.

Amyntas   André Gide   *1988 (1906)*
These North African journals were written
over a seven-year period at the turn of the
century. Gide's descriptions of Tunis and Algiers are an 'articulation of consciousness'
and mark an interesting evolution in his
writing, as he said 'Few realise I have never
written anything more perfect than *Amyntas*'.

North African Notebook   Robin
Maugham   1948
Robin Maugham travelled through the countries of North Africa to discover the politics
in each. He also gathers much information
about the social climate.

The Fearful Void   Geoffrey Moorhouse
1974
A personal odyssey of a journey across the
Sahara west to east. [Stephen Brook, Colin
Thubron]

Wind Sand and Stars   Antoine de
Saint-Exupéry   1990 (1939) (see 'Argentina')
Much of Saint-Exupéry's flying takes place
in the Sahara. [Colin Thubron]

In Search of Sheba   Barbara Toy   *1961*
Barbara Toy started her journey in northern
Libya, crossed the Central African Republic,
the Sudan, Tanganyika, Uganda and into
Ethiopia where she was reminded of the
glassy look that came into people's eyes who
had been there. She was eager to discover for
herself the people and the country about
whom so much myth had been written.

Forbidden Sands   Richard Trench   *1978*
Trench sets out across the Sahara by camel
caravan ostensibly to try to find out what was
happening at the notorious salt mines in
Mali. The reality was an attraction to the
desert and a desire to pit himself against its
difficulties. He endured great hardship, but
recounts his journey with humour.

EGYPT

'Egypt is an acquired country, the gift of the river.' Herodotus *History*

Anthology

The Nile. A Traveller's Anthology
Deborah Manley 1991
Deborah Manley opens her book with a quote by G.W. Steevens 'Egypt is the Nile' and proceeds to trace travellers' age old fascination with the river. She begins with a section of short biographies of the travellers and continues geographically through the country introducing each section with a short description. The diverse quantity of people who travelled in Egypt is staggering and reading what they wrote would certainly enhance a present day trip to Egypt.

✔ **Egypt – An Anthology** *C. Pick 1991*
Extracts ranging from the nineteenth to the twentieth centuries.

Art and Archaeology

'He who wants to see his time rightly, must look upon it from a
distance. How great a distance? Quite simply, just far enough away
so that he cannot discern Cleopatra's nose.' (Ortega Y. Gasset)

Egyptian Antiquities in the Nile
Valley *James Baikie 1932*
This book 'confines' itself to descriptions of objects of Egyptian architecture and art, leaves out Roman, Coptic and Arab culture and only describes objects *in situ* in Egypt. It is therefore wonderfully detailed and although somewhat dated is well worth trying to find in a library. Surprisingly Baikie never went to Egypt.

Gods, Graves and Scholars *C.W.*
Ceram 1984 (1949)
An entirely fresh approach to archaeology which was quite revolutionary when it was first published; the stories of Schliemann, Evans, Champollion, Belzoni, Petries, Howard Carter, Grotefend, Rawlinson, Layard, George Smith, Stephens and Thompson. [Anthony Sattin]

Early Muslim Architecture *(1969 2nd edn.)*
Muslim Architecture of Egypt *K.A.C.*
Cresswell (1951/9)
Massive and well-illustrated volumes: *Early Muslim Architecture* covers the first three centuries of Islam in all countries and the volumes *The Muslim Architecture of Egypt* deal solely with Egypt from the point where the previous volumes left off. [Anthony Sattin]

✔ **The Pyramids of Egypt**
I.E.S. Edwards 1991 (1947) (revised edn.)
One of the classic books on Egyptian archaeology, the revised edition includes recent discoveries and scholarship. Dr Edwards uses a combination of his own and other people's research, ensuring a comprehensive whole.

✔ **Archaic Egypt** *W. Emery 1991*
Aimed at the general reader; not much detail about the archaeological sites.

✔ **Architectural Guides for Travellers: Ancient Egypt**
Delia Pemberton 1993 (1992)

✔ **Art & Archaeology of Ancient Egypt** *W. Stevenson Smith 1984 (1958)*
Over 400 illustrations accompany a detailed text to the monuments of Ancient Egypt. Copious notes at the end provide those who want to pursue a particular area with many further sources.

✔ **The Search for Ancient Egypt**
Jean Vercoutter 1992 (1986)
One of a series translated from the French, this little book is crammed full of photographs, pictures and snippets of fascinating information. The kind of appetite whetter which could lead you into all kinds of other avenues.

Biography

Leisure of an Egyptian Official
Lord Edward Cecil 1931 (1921)
Edward Cecil well known at the time for his wit, wrote these sketches for his family. They give a rather irreverent but highly amusing account of his eighteen years spent serving in Egypt. Many of his observations are hilarious; he is especially acute at analysing people's characters.

Fiction

A Woman of Cairo *Noel Barber 1985 (1984)*
Set in Farouk's Cairo; westernized Egyptians mingle with ex-patriots.

Collected Poems *C.P. Cavafy Translated by Edmund Keeley and Philip Sherrard 1984 (1975)*
The Greek poet Cavafy (1863–1933) was born in Alexandria and lived most of his life there; during his lifetime he only circulated his poems to a select few people. It was not

until after his death that he won international acclaim; today he is considered as 'one of the greatest writers of our times' (*TLS*). His rich use of history, myth and eroticism and his commitment to Hellenism and cynicism about politics all combine to make his poetry relevant today, while giving us an understanding of history and of the times in which he lived. [Anthony Sattin]

✔ **Death on the Nile** *Agatha Christie* 1937
Agatha Christie stayed in Aswan while she wrote this book about a murder on the Nile which was solved by Hercule Poirot.

✔ **The Alexandria Quartet** 1991 (1962)
✔ **Justine** (1957)
✔ **Balthazar(1958)**
✔ **Mountolive(1958)**
✔ **Cleo(1960)** *Lawrence Durrell*
The quartet intended to be read as a continuous novel has the rich background of Alexandria in the 30s and 40s. It is easy to get completely enmeshed in the exotic world created by Durrell. [Anthony Sattin]

✔ **Woman at Point Zero** *Nawal El Saadawi* 1983 (1975)
Nawal El Saadawi is an Egyptian novelist and militant writer on women's issues. Her novel is based on the true case of a woman sentenced to death for murder in Cairo. The story of her life as a prostitute is simply and directly told and very powerful. She also wrote *God Dies by the Nile* (1974), *The Hidden Face of Eve* (1980) and *The Circling Song* (1989).

✔ **Beer in the Snooker Club**
Waguih Ghali 1987 (1964)
Ram and Font both lived in England and drank pints of Bass from two mugs which now hang in a bar in Cairo where there is no Bass. The Bass is a symbol for their longing to leave a country where there is a revolution and where they feel stranded between two cultures. [Anthony Sattin]

The Cheapest Nights *Yusuf Idris* 1978
A collection of short stories by a fine writer of short stories; also *Rings of Burnished Brass* (1984) and *A Leader of Men* (1988).

✔ **The Search** *Naguib Mahfouz* 1991 (1964)
Naguib Mahfouz (1911–) is one of the most widely read authors in the Arab world and was the winner of the Nobel Prize in 1988. He has written more than thirty novels which are now beginning to be translated into English. *The Search* is a compelling and lyrical account of a man's search for his father which moves from Alexandria to

Cairo. The Cairo Trilogy composed of *Palace Walk* 1991 (1956), *Palace of Desire* 1991 (1957), and *Sugar Street* 1993 (1957) is a rich family saga set at the beginning of the century. Other books by Mahfouz include *Midaq Alley* [Anthony Sattin], *Wedding Song* 1984 (1981) and *Autumn Quail* 1985 (1962).

✔ **The Levant Trilogy** *Olivia Manning* 1982
Wartime Cairo is the setting for Olivia Manning's trilogy, *The Danger Tree*, *The Battle Lost and Won* and *The Sum of Things*. Guy and Harriet Pringle have their own problems as well as those of rumours of a bloody desert campaign. A compelling read which was made into a television serial.

Journey to the Orient *Gérard de Nerval* 1973 (1851)
De Nerval, poet, visionary and dreamer, made his first voyage to the East in 1843 visiting Cairo, Alexandria, Lebanon, Syria, Cyprus, Rhodes, Constantinople and Malta. He was encouraged to write this collection of exotic tales by his doctor as therapy: 'I feel the need to liken myself unto the entire universe of nature . . . foreign women . . . memories of having lived there.'

Guides

Baedeker Egypt
The 1929 Baedeker to Egypt is the most sought after, as it includes the discovery of Tutankhamun's tomb. These old Baedekers are full of maps, plans and diagrams and advice to travellers; although of course well out of date, they are always worth reading. [Anthony Sattin]

The Nile. Notes for Travellers in Egypt and in the Egyptian Sudan *E.A. Wallis Budge* 1910
The book was written for people who had only a few weeks to spend in Egypt and concentrates almost entirely on the Ancient Egyptians excluding almost everything about the Persians, Ptolemies, Romans, Arabs and Turks. It is, however, very much more detailed than almost any guide available today and well worth trying to find.

✔ **Everyman Guide: Egypt** 1995

✔ **Egypt: the Rough Guide**
Dan Richardson and Karen O'Brien 1993 (1991)

✔ **Cadogan Guide Egypt** *Michael Haag* 1993

✔ **Penguin Guide to Ancient Egypt**
William J. Murnane (1983)
The first half gives an interesting back-

ground survey of Ancient Egypt and is followed by itineraries taking in nearly all the important Pharaonic remains and some Christian ones too. The Cairo Museum is described in detail, room by room, and the whole book is full of useful plans and diagrams.

✔ **Egypt and The Sudan. Travel Survival Kit**   *Damien Simonis   1994 (1987)*

History

The Dwellers on the Nile   *E.A. Wallis Budge   1977 (1926)*
(The Life, History, Religion and Literature of the Ancient Egyptians)
The book begins with a history of Ancient Egypt and follows this with descriptions of the Ancient Egyptians' everyday life from birth to death. Budge writes about their work, manners, schools, food and drink, literature and writing methods and finishes with what they did with their dead and their beliefs about the after life. Very informative and interesting.

The Vanished Library   *Luciano Canfora 1990 (1987)*
The library at Alexandria was one of the wonders of the Ancient World; the ambition of the Ptolemaic kings of Egypt was to house all of the books ever written under one roof. In 196 BC the library in Pergamum was established and became its great rival but by the fourth century AD all of the great libraries, Rome, Pergamum, Alexandria, Antioch and Athens had been destroyed. The history of what happened is unravelled here.

✔ **Cairo in the War 1939–45**
Artemis Cooper   1989
A look at Cairo society during the war especially through the eyes of writers who were there at the time.

The Mountains of Pharaoh
Leonard Cottrell   1955
In this book the pyramids are described from the viewpoint of explorers and adventurers to Egypt starting with Herodotus in the fifth century BC. Cottrell concentrates on little known anecdotes such as Colonel Howard-Vyse in 1837 who was so desperate to find hidden chambers within the pyramids that he used gunpowder.

Letters from Egypt 1863–1865   *Lady Duff-Gordon   1865 (2nd edn.)*
Informal letters like the ones written by Lady Duff-Gordon are an extremely good way of learning about a country. She combines domestic details, 'A number of camels sleep in the yard under my verandah; they are pretty and smell nice, but they growl and swear at night abominably', with observations about the country, 'One must come to the East to understand absolute social equality'. The unfortunate lady seems to have suffered from a variety of ailments, but in one instance perked up considerably when she was finger fed pigeons and rice by her loyal servant Omar. [Anthony Sattin]

Egypt. Land of the Valley.
Robin Fedden   1977
Robin Fedden gives an interpretation of contemporary Egypt through its history and emphasises the importance of both the Nile and the Nile Valley to its development. Despite the many attempted conquests Fedden concludes, as did Herodotus, that Egypt is averse to being anything but Egypt.

Alexandria. A History and Guide.
E.M. Forster   1986 (1922)
Forster had thought Alexandria worthy but dull until he encountered Cavafy who supplied him with the link 'The "sights" of Alexandria are in themselves not interesting, but they fascinate when we approach them through the past'. The book was written during a hiatus in the writing of *A Passage to India* and is described by Lawrence Durrell: 'The whole historical perspective of the city in all its variety, has been captured and fixed in a series of short essays brightly starred with all the virtues of this fine artist . . . It is a work of deep affection and a noble monument raised to this most haunting of cities.' [Anthony Sattin]

Lovers on the Nile   *Richard Hall   1981 (1980)*
Samuel and Florence Baker were lionized in Victorian England as national heroes and explorers. Florence was the first white woman to have sailed to the source of the Nile, but her dubious origins, she was bought by Samuel from a slave market in Bulgaria, reached Queen Victoria's ears and she refused to meet her, despite Samuel's friendship with the Prince of Wales. They remained a devoted couple for the whole of their lives.

The Histories   *Herodotus   c. 460 BC (see 'Turkey')*

✔ **Cleopatra**   *Lucy Hughes-Hallett   1991 (1990)*
The myth and fantasy that have been woven around Cleopatra over the years are here brilliantly described and analysed. A fascinating look at the historical Cleopatra and the many different portrayals of her throughout the ages.

✔ **Egypt the Living Past** *T.G.H. James Photographs by Graham Harrison) 1992*
T.G.H. James was Keeper of Egyptian Antiquities at the British Museum and his book is an authorative look at the continuity which exists between Ancient Egypt and the Egypt of today and the importance that the Nile plays in this continuity. The text is accompanied by 115 colour illustrations.

Cavafy's Alexandria *Edmund Keeley 1977*
An analysis of everything that Alexandria meant to Cavafy (q.v.). The book is divided into 'metaphoric', 'sensual' and 'mythical' Alexandria, the World of Hellenism and the Universal Perspective.

An Account of the Manners and Customs of the Modern Egyptians 1833–5 *Edward William Lane 1836*
Lane was well placed to study the 'modern' Egyptians since he spoke Arabic and lived as an Egyptian Muslim while he was compiling notes for this book. Lane got to know the Egyptians better than any other European of his time and has detailed chapters on charms, magic, the bath and marriage as well as every other aspect of life. [Anthony Sattin]

The British in Egypt *Peter Mansfield 1971*
The British remained in Egypt for a period of seventy-four years from 1882. The relationship between the two countries was unique. Britain really saw Egypt as a stepping stone to India and did not view it as an imperial mission. A readable account of the period. [Anthony Sattin]

The Blue Nile *1984 (1962)*
The White Nile *Alan Moorehead 1973 (1962)*
The Blue Nile is a compelling historical narrative of the events on the Nile from 1798–1869. Alan Moorehead traces the course of the Blue Nile through its history from the Ethiopian Highlands, through the Sudan and Egypt to the sea. Four ambitious and powerful people dominated the period: James Bruce, Napoleon, Mohammed Ali and Emperor Theodore of Ethiopia. They are all vividly described here. *The White Nile* continues the history and takes the period from 1856–1900, with descriptions of all its early explorers, including those brave pioneers who were searching for the source. [Anthony Sattin]

Egypt's Belle Epoque: Cairo 1869–1952 *Trevor Mostyn 1989*
An account of the ex-patriot community in Cairo from the time of Ismail to the overthrow of King Farouk.

Lifting the Veil: British Society in Egypt 1768–1956 *Anthony Sattin 1988*
Anthony Sattin realized on a trip up the Nile that very little had been written about the foreigners who had been visiting the Ancient Egyptian sites for hundreds of years; he decided to tell the story of why and how those visitors came. Many had left graffiti as evidence of their presence and he quotes at length from these voices from the past.

Natural History

The Butterflies of Egypt *T.B. Larsen 1990*
The author, although trained as an economist, has spent most of his life investigating and writing about butterflies. The book contains ample descriptions of the butterflies and their habitat, followed by several pages of colour plates.

Photography

✔ **Egypt from the Air** *Max Rodenbeck 1991*
Glossy aerial photographs of Egyptian sites.

✔ **Philip's Egypt** *Peter Stocks (photography David Couling) 1992*
The book includes Egypt both ancient and modern.

Travel Literature

Libyan Sands. Travel in a Dead World (Jordan, Egypt, Sudan, Libya) *R.A. Bagnold 1987 (1935)*
In the 1920s, Brigadier Ralph Bagnold and a group of young officers used all their free time from the army to explore the Libyan Desert in a Ford Model T. They drove the car along camel tracks and were able to cover huge distances in a short amount of time finding places which had probably not been explored since the Stone Age. An energetically written and interesting book.

✔ **A Thousand Miles Up the Nile** *Amelia Edwards 1993 (1877)*
Amelia Edwards arrived in Egypt unexpectedly in 1873 and stayed on to become an eminent Egyptologist.

✔ **The Travels of Sir John Mandeville**   *Translated by C.W.R.D. Moseley* *1983 (see 'Middle East')*
During his travels Mandeville reputedly served with the Sultan of Egypt.

Letters from Egypt: a Journey on the Nile 1849–50   *Florence Nightingale   1987*
Florence Nightingale wrote a prodigious amount of letters during her five-month journey in Egypt. This edition is well illustrated with paintings and sketches contemporary with her travels. [Anthony Sattin]

Flaubert in Egypt   *Francis Steegmuller (ed.)   1983 (1972)*
An amalgamation of Flaubert's diaries and letters written in Egypt during the years 1849–50. Flaubert arrived in Egypt as a Romantic and he and his friend, Maxime Du Camp, spent much time photographing Egyptian antiquities. However, much of Flaubert's time was devoted to sensual pursuits and pleasure and within a year of returning to France, as a Realist, he wrote *Madame Bovary* the novel which was to have such a profound effect on literature. [Anthony Sattin]

The Other Nile   *Charlie Pye-Smith   1986*
Several journies made along the length of the Nile in Sudan, Ethiopia and Egypt from 1975–1985. Much changed in Africa during those years – famine and civil war prompted him to quote Evelyn Waugh: 'There is no room for tourists in a world of displaced persons.'

The Innocents Abroad   *Mark Twain 1988 (1869)*
A record of a pleasure-trip, which as Jonathan Raban points out in the introduction is ironic, since the fashionable thing to do nowadays is to mock package tours and those who take them. What we need suggests Raban is a 'Twain – or a Waugh – to chronicle them'. Twain visits Egypt towards the end of his cruise and writes 'We were very glad to have seen the land which was the mother of civilisation.' [Stephen Brook]

LIBYA

'The land of Libya . . . because of over mickle heat is barren and bears no manner of fruit.' John Mandeville *The Book of John Mandeville*, c. 1360

General Background

✔ **The Book of Mordechai. A Study of the Jews of Libya**   *Mordechai Hakohen 1993 (1980)*
A fascinating record of Jewish life written in the early years of this century by a Talmudic scholar who was also a teacher, itinerant pedlar and amateur anthropologist.

Guide

Green Mountain   *Gwynn Williams   1963 (An informal guide to Cyrenaica and its Jebel Akhdar)*
The author lived in Libya for six years and wrote this book as a series of itineraries. Although it is out of date and tourism in Libya is not exactly popular, it has worthwhile descriptions of the sites, the history and peoples who were subjected to so many administrations: Greek, Roman, Byzantine, Arab, Turkish, Italian and British. Gwynn Williams even discovered that the Celts had been there.

Travel Literature

✔ **A Cure for Serpents**   *Duke of Pirajno 1985 (1955) (Libya, Eritrea, Ethiopia & Somaliland)*
The Duke of Pirajno arrived in North Africa as a doctor in 1924 and stayed for eighteen years. A doctor sees facets of life hidden to most other people and as Cyril Connolly says: 'Doctors who are good raconteurs make wonderful reading'. This collection of reminiscences and stories does make wonderful reading.

A Fool in the Desert   *Barbara Toy   1956*
Barbara Toy was driven back to Libya by the desert which she had glimpsed from Egypt: 'for the desert means different things to different people. Men have cursed it, come to love it and died in it.' She realized that there was no escape once you had come under its spell and that the magic would always draw you back. She had fallen party to this spell and embarked on a journey through the Libyan desert.

MAURITANIA

'But Mauretania's giant-shadows frown From mountain-cliff to coast descending sombre down.'
Lord Byron *Childe Harold's Pilgrimage* 1812

Travel Literature

Travels in Mauritania   Peter Hudson
1991 (1990)
Very little has been written about Mauritania, so Peter Hudson was able to approach it with few preconceptions. The result is an engaging and descriptive account of his journey.

Barefoot in Mauritania
Odette du Puigaudeau   1937
A journey by camel through an unknown Mauritania.

MOROCCO

'If you like your romance dark, Fez is probably the most romantic
city on earth. It might have been dreamed up by Edgar Allan Poe –
almost sinister in its secretiveness, a twisted city, warped and closed.'
John Gunther *Inside Africa* 1955

Anthology

✔ **Morocco: the Traveller's Companion**   Margaret and Robin Bidwell
1992
A collection of excerpts from writers over the last five centuries.

Anthropology

Beyond the Veil   Fatima Mernissi   1975
(Male-Female Dynamics in a Modern Muslim Society)
Fatima Mernissi asks whether there is a nascent female liberation movement in the Morocco of today similar to those in the west. She describes the politics of Islam, the traditional Muslim view of women and the effect that the modern world has had on traditional views.

Ritual and Belief in Morocco
Edward Westermarck   2 vols 1926
Westermarck made twenty-one journeys to Morocco between 1898 and 1926, spending a total of seven years. His work is still recognized as one of the most authoritative on the country. He travelled throughout Morocco with a Moorish friend Shereef 'Abdsslam I-Baqqâli, enabling him access and assistance in places which otherwise would have been difficult to visit. Westermarck wrote many articles on Morocco and *Marriage Ceremonies in Morocco* (1914).

Art and Architecture

The Moors. Islam in the West
Michael Brett   1980
A well illustrated book which relates the rise of the Moors, their achievements, the society they lived in, a general picture of the world at that time and their eventual decline.

✔ **Fez; City of Islam**   Titus Burckhardt
1992 (1960)
The author went to Morocco in 1933–4 and 'Seeking a spiritual master, I settled in Fez, where I divided my time between this search and the study of Arabic'. He returned twenty-five years later and the book, an illustrated history, personal interpretation and description of Fez, was published in Germany in 1960, but not in England until very recently.

✔ **Matisse in Morocco**   Jack Cowart et al
1990
The paintings and drawings of Matisse in Morocco between 1912–1913. Matisse visited Tangier twice and made full use of the exotic environment. This large book was published to coincide with the travelling exhibition, in 1993.

Biography

✔ **The Track**   Arturo Barea   1984 (1943)
(see 'Spain')
The Track is the second volume in Barea's autobiographical trilogy in which he records his life in the army during the Spanish war in Morocco in the 1920s. It is, at times, a very shocking account dealing with the sordid life of conscript soldiers in North Africa and vividly describing the vermin, disease, brothels and foul food which were part of that life.

Look and Move On   Mohammed Mrabet
Translated by Paul Bowles

✔ **An Invisible Spectator**   Christopher Sawyer-Lancanno   1990
A biography of Paul Bowles.

Fiction

✔ **The Spider's House**   Paul Bowles   1985
(1955)
Paul Bowles was a great traveller and composer who lived in many different countries, until coming to Morocco, which he now rarely leaves. He made Tangier his home in the late 40s and since then has written and translated and become an expert on Moroccan folklore and magic. His best Moroccan novel is probably *The Spider's House* set in Fez. He has written several collections of short

stories: *Collected Stories 1939–76, Call at Corazon* 1989 (1939), *Points in Time* 1990 (1982), *100 Camels in the Courtyard* 1991 (1962). Travel books include *Their Heads are Green* 1990 (1963) (which includes a superb piece on the Sahara) *Two Years Beside the Strait – TangierJournal 1987–9.* 1990 (1989). He has translated much of Mohammed Mrabet's work.

✔ **Earthly Powers**   Anthony Burgess   1980
Includes descriptions of life in 1950's Tangiers.

Jean Genet in Tangier
Mohamed Choukri   1990
Paul Bowles translated this and *Tennessee Williams in Tangier* also by Mohamed Choukri.

The Process   Brion Gysin   1985 (1969)
A novel which was written in Tangier between 1965–8. The American character, on a Fulbright fellowship, smokes his way through various encounters in the Sahara in prose reminiscent of Burroughs.

In the Lap of Atlas   Richard Hughes   1979
An article about Hughes' own experiences in Morocco, and his retelling of some traditional Moroccan stories.

The Sand Child   Tahar Ben Jelloun   1988 (1985)
The shame felt by a father of eight daughters made him bring up his youngest daughter as a boy. The fear of being found out and the pain suffered by the child makes this a haunting book. The solitary life at home contrasts with the bustle of the Marrakesh bazaar. Other books by Jelloun include *Silent Day in Tangier* 1991 (1989), *The Sacred Night* 1989 (1985) and *With Downcast Eyes* (1991).

Yesterday and Today   Larbi Layachi   1985
Layachi, who now lives in America, was born in 1937 in a small town in Morocco. He moved to Tangier when he was three years old and in 1961 he met Paul Bowles and told him many Moghrebi stories which Bowles then translated. Other titles include *A Life Full of Holes* and *The Jealous Lover*.

✔ **Leo the African**   Amin Maalouf   1994 (1988)   Translated by Peter Sluglett
A novel closely based on the life of Leo Africanus (q.v.). It is narrated in the first person, starts in Granada and moves on to Fez, Cairo and Rome.

The Beach Café and The Voice
Mohammed Mrabet   1980
Paul Bowles taped and translated this and other works by Mrabet including *Marriage*

with Papers (1986) and *Love With a Few Hairs* (1986).

✔ **The High Flyer**   Nicholas Shakespeare   1993
Thomas Wavery arrives in Gibraltar en route to take up his post as HM Consul General in Abyla in North Africa. The variety of people he comes into contact with are brilliantly observed.

Food

✔ **Good Food from Morocco**
Paula Wolfert   1989 (1973)
The author lived in Morocco for two years and indulged her love of the adventurous and exotic life. The recipes include couscous, Moroccan bread, fish tagine, chicken stuffed with almond paste and briouats (pastry stuffed with almond paste and dipped in honey).

General Background

✔ **The Dream at the End of the World**   Michelle Green   1992
The literary life and people of Tangier.

Guides

✔ **Morocco, Algeria and Tunisia. A Travel Survival Kit**   Geoff Crowther and Hugh Finlay   1992 (1989)

✔ **Everyman Guide: Morocco**   1994

✔ **Morocco: the Rough Guide**
Mark Ellingham, Shaun McVeigh and Don Grisbrook   1993 (1985)

✔ **Cadogan Guide to Morocco**   Barnaby Rogerson   1994 (1989)

History

Morocco   Nevill Barbour   1965
Morocco has a long and interesting history and unlike the rest of the Arab world was never subject to the Turks. Barbour writes about it from the earliest times right up to the twentieth century in an accessible and easy to read manner.

✔ **Tangier. City of the Dream**
Iain Finlayson   1992
Tangier has a long and exotic history and in recent years has attracted many writers: William Burroughs, Jack Kerouac, Allen Ginsberg, Tennessee Williams, Joe Orton, Paul Bowles and Truman Capote are among

those who have lived there. Finlayson's book tells how all these and many more came to be here in a city which was full of the kind of drugs and sex banned in Europe.

✔ **The Muqaddimah. An Introduction to History.** *Ibn Khaldun 1987 (1967) (see 'Middle East')*
The Muqaddimah was written in 1377 by the Arab scholar Ibn Khaldun as an introduction to a history of the world. It is the summing up of the achievements of Islam and is remarkable for its insights; the abridged version contains the essence of all he wrote. He was the first person who attempted to find a pattern in the changes that occur in man's political and social organization.

✔ **Lords of the Atlas** *Gavin Maxwell 1991 (1966)*
The history of the Glaoua family who rose and fell from power in Morocco from 1893–1956. Gavin Maxwell draws on Walter Harris (q.v.), but writes an exciting and bloodthirsty account of this once obscure tribe who within a few years had become frighteningly powerful and controlled Morocco until Independence in 1956.

The Conquest of Morocco
Douglas Porch 1986 (1982)
The French conquest of Morocco took from 1844–1934. The meeting of Islam and Christianity make it a compelling story. Douglas Porch concentrates here on what happened at the beginning of the century when Hubert Lyautey, an eccentric and colonial soldier who played such an important part in events, but who has, nonetheless, been ignored by biographers in France. An illuminating historical account.

Leisure

Atlas Mountains. Morocco *Robin G. Collomb 1987 (1980)*
A basic and practical guide: divided into walks, giving distances and describing the terrain and various routes.

Natural History (See North Africa)

✔ **Mediterranean Wildlife. The Rough Guide** *Pete Raine 1990*
Includes Morocco and Tunisia.

Photography

The Berbers *Alan Keohane 1991*
A well-illustrated book about the Berbers.

Travel Literature

✔ **Morocco Its People and Places**
Edmondo de Amicis 1982 (1885)
A fresh, original and lively account of Morocco in 1882, which was popular when it was published and is now considered a classic.

✔ **The Voices of Marrakesh**
Elias Canetti 1982 (1967)
Canetti, who won the Nobel Prize for Literature in 1981, uses a series of sketches to convey his impressions of Marrakesh. Each scene that he selects is so vivid and so full of imagery that the rich diversity of life in a bazaar-town shines through.

Saints and Sorcerers *Nina Epton 1958*
Good on background history and interesting anecdotes. Nina Epton's journey covered much of Morocco from Tetouan to the High Atlas including a meeting with the magicians of Sous. An easy and enjoyable read.

✔ **Hideous Kinky** *Esther Freud 1992*
Esther Freud was taken, aged five, during the sixties by her hippy mother to Morocco. The book brilliantly conveys how a five-year-old thinks and feels about travelling. The shock of having her hair hennaed and turn orange is balanced by 'magic' sugared almonds appearing out of nowhere. The relationship between her and her sister Bea who was two years older is sensitively drawn. The book which is an extraordinary feat of memory rings true and is by turn both funny and sad.

Mogreb-el-Acksa *R.B. Cunninghame Grahame 1988 (1898)*
Cunninghame Grahame, much opposed to imperialism, disguised himself as a Turkish doctor in order to travel and find out about Moorish life. He was arrested on the way to Taroudant; this is the account of that episode. His book was praised by Joseph Conrad for its 'skill, pathos, wit, indignation'.

✔ **Morocco That Was** *Walter Harris 1983 (1921)*
Walter Harris arrived in Tangier in 1886 and became *The Times* correspondent there until his death in 1933. He approached his work seriously but always with a certain amount of humour. Morocco was virtually unknown to Westerners when Harris arrived, a closed country; his descriptions may seem excessive, but they were representative of life in the then wild and primitive country.

✔ **See Ouarzazate and Die**
Sylvia Kennedy 1992
The author spent twelve months and three different trips travelling round Morocco on

buses, trains and coaches with a variety of travelling companions in order to write this gutsy and amusing book. She describes many local customs in detail conveying the feeling that she really threw herself into whatever she was seeing or doing.

Morocco and the Moors   Arthur Leared
1876 (Being an Account of Travels With a General Description of its People)
The author kept prolific notes while travelling and talked at length to people who were resident there. The country was relatively unknown to outsiders then and he decided that with its excellent climate it was a very desirable place for invalids.

Journey into Barbary   Wyndham Lewis
(edited by C.J. Fox)   1983
Wyndham Lewis went to Morocco in 1931 for a few months, writing two books from his experiences, *Filibusters in Barbary* (1932) and *Kasbahs and Souks* which had not been published prior to inclusion in this edition. He was fascinated by the Berbers and their energy and did many drawings of them; it is interesting to note the different ways he translated what he observed as a writer and as a painter. He read about Morocco in depth before he went: 'I always desire the fullest information regarding any habitation or work of man, strange to me, which I propose to approach and interrogate . . . before I set foot in the Maghreb I knew more about the inhabitants of, say, the hinterland of Tetouan than they know themselves.'

Into Morocco   Pierre Loti   1889
Loti makes no pretence of trying to write about the politics of Morocco, indeed he makes a point of trying not to offend anybody. He does however immerse himself in the culture of the Maghreb having always felt himself half Arab at heart, thrilling 'to the sound of the little Africa flutes, of the tam-tams and the iron castanets'.

✔ **A Year in Marrakesh**   Peter Mayne
1990 (1953)
Peter Mayne lived much of his life in India and Pakistan and had a fundamental understanding of Muslim life by the time he moved to Morocco. He lived in a small house in Marrakesh and wrote this book (originally published as *The Alleys of Marrakesh*) from his observations. The style is simple and easy to read and shows what everyday life was like in Marrakesh.

Life in Morocco and Glimpses Beyond   Budgett Meakin   1905
Sketches and observations gathered from many visits by an enthusiast. 'Nothing . . .

elsewhere excels Morocco in point of life and colour save Bokhara'. Meakin's style is somewhat over the top, but he is good on detail and gives fascinating insights into Moorish domestic life. His most interesting book is *The Moors: A Comprehensive Description*. [Mark Ellingham]

In Morocco   Edith Wharton   1920
Rather patchy but with some good insights into harem life.

Blue Nile
White Nile   A. Moorehead   (see 'Egypt – History')

TUNISIA

'Carthage had not desired to create, but only to enjoy: therefore she left us nothing.' Hilaire Belloc *Esto Perpetua* 1906

Anthropology

Cave-Dwellers of Southern Tunisia
D. Bruun   1898
Bruun was one of the first Europeans to live with the cave-dwelling people of Matmata and Haddej.

Biography

Confessions   Augustine   1970
Saint Augustine's spiritual autobiography from which you can learn about the times in which he lived.

Augustine of Hippo   Peter Brown   1969
Brown writes very interestingly about the Africa of Augustine's time.

Fiction

✔ **The Golden Ass**   Apuleius (see 'Algeria')

✔ **Salammbo**   Gustave Flaubert   1977 (1862)
A visually rich and exotic novel set in North Africa after the first Punic War with Rome. Flaubert was criticized for making the history surrounding the passionate story too accurate, but it is through this kind of book that you can really imagine life in the time of the Carthaginian army under Hamilcar, secure in the knowledge that it *is* accurate.

Strangers   Albert Memmi   1958
Memmi, a Tunisian Jew, tells the story of a Tunisian Jew who marries a French Catholic girl while he is studying in Paris. She returns to Tunisia with her husband but finds it

impossible to settle down and to adapt to the new society. Her husband is torn between her needs and those of his family and when she decides to return to France, the suggestion is that such a mixed marriage cannot work. Other books by Memmi include *The Pillar of Salt* (1992), *Colonizer and the Colonized* (1990) and *The Scorpion* (1975).

Guides

Tunisia   *Nina Nelson   1974*
More of a travel narrative than a guide and now somewhat out of date; there are however some good descriptions of the country.

✔ **Cadogan Guide Tunisia**   *Barnaby Rogerson and Rose Baring   1992*

✔ **Tunisia: the Rough Guide**   *Peter Morris et al   1993 (1985)*

History

✔ **The Muqaddimah. An Introduction to History**   *Ibn Khaldun (See 'Morocco')*

✔ **The Jugurthine War**   *Sallust   1969*
An amusing account of war and morality.

✔ **The Aeneid**   *Virgil   1991*
Includes the tragic love story of Queen Dido, founder of Carthage and Aeneas, founder of Rome.

Natural History (see North Africa)

✔ **Mediterranean Wildlife. The Rough Guide**   *Pete Raine   1990*
Includes Morocco and Tunisia.

Travel Literature

About Tunisia   *John Anthony   1961*
Anthony lived in Sidi Bou Said for five years and during that time travelled widely throughout Tunisia; the book is an account of his experiences and the people he met.

Fountains in the Sand   *Norman Douglas 1986 (1912)*
Norman Douglas bravely set out into the deserts of Tunisia, but sadly for such a widely travelled person, never shook off his prejudices about the aridity of Arab culture. However, worth reading for the descriptive passages.

Tangier to Tunis   *Alexandre Dumas (see 'North Africa – General')*

Amyntas   *André Gide (see 'Algeria')*

The Olive Tree   *Aldous Huxley   1973 (1936)*
A travel piece in this collection called *In a Tunisia Oasis* is about a trip Huxley took to Tunisia.

A Journey through the Tunisian Sahara   *Sir Harry Johnston   1898*
Johnston was one of the first European travellers to attempt to understand the people among whom he travelled in the Sahara.

Tunis, Kairouan and Carthage   *Graham Petrie   1908*
The author visited these three towns at the beginning of the century and writes interesting descriptions of the life that he encountered there.

West Africa

GENERAL

Biography

✔ **Mary Kingsley. Imperial Adventuress**   *Dea Birkett   1992*
There is no one better qualified to write about Mary Kingsley than Dea Birkett. She first wrote about her in an undergraduate essay and since then has written many articles and followed her routes all over West Africa. Dea Birkett 'creates' Mary Kingsley in this biography, showing her to have been a complex character who took on many roles.

Fiction

✔ **The Crystal World** *J.G. Ballard   1993 (1966)*
A forest area in West Africa is gradually becoming crystallized – everything has to keep moving to ensure that they too do not get trapped.

✔ **A Good Man in Africa** *William Boyd 1982 (1981)*
William Boyd was born in Ghana and lived there and in Nigeria and set this very funny novel in tropical 'Kinjanja'. Morgan Leafy, the not very successful and overweight British Government representative, finds himself involved in all kinds of local bribery, which he has to use guile to deal with.

General Background

✔ **East and West Africa. Travel Resource Guide** *Louis Taussig   1994*

Guides

✔ **Backpacker's Africa. A guide to West and Central Africa for walkers and overland travellers** *David Else 1990 (1989)*
You are told what to expect in no uncertain language: 'The boat trip is very long and you will be very hot and hungry'. A very basic guide, but information such as the above can prove invaluable.

✔ **West Africa. The Rough Guide**
Jim Hudgens and Richard Trillo   1990

✔ **Discovery Guide to West Africa, the Niger and Gambia river route**
Kim Naylor   1989
About the Sahel region of West Africa.

✔ **West Africa a Travel Survival Kit**
Alex Newton   1992 (1988)

Traveller's Guide to West Africa *IC Publication   1988*
Straight facts, no opinions and out of date – as are most things on West Africa.

History

✔ **A History of West Africa 1000–1800** *Basil Davidson, F.K. Bush and J.F.A. Ajayi   1990 (1965)*
A new edition of a clear and all-encompassing history.

✔ **An Economic History of West Africa** *A.G. Hopkins   1993 (1973)*
The standard text on the economic history of the whole of West Africa which ranges from prehistoric times up to independence.

✔ **The Revolutionary Years. West Africa Since 1800** *J.B. Webster et al   1992 (1967)*
A new edition of a classic text on West African history from 1800.

Natural History

Birds of West Central and Western Africa (2 vols.) *C.W. Mackworth-Praed and C.H.B. Grant   1973*
This large and comprehensive work is of use as a reference book, but can also be used 'in the field'. It took twenty years to compile and is full of maps, sketches and detailed descriptions, as well as many colour photographs.

✔ **Collins Field Guide Birds of West Africa** *W. Serle, G.J. Morel and W. Hartwig 1992 (1977)*
Over 500 species of bird are illustrated and described with their identifying characteristics, distribution, habitat and eggs etc.

Photography

✔ **African Canvas**
Margaret Courtney-Clarke   1990
Every year, after the harvest, the women of West Africa get together to restore and paint their houses. This is a beautifully coloured photographic book which records the event in Nigeria, Ghana, Burkina Faso, Ivory Coast, Senegal, Mauritania and Mali.

Religion

A History of Islam in West Africa
J. Spencer Trimingham   1962
An historical background into the penetration of Islam into West Africa; by understanding how a religion enters a country it is easier to understand its implications in contemporary society.

Travel Literature

✔ **One Dry Season. In the Footsteps of Mary Kingsley** *Caroline Alexander   1989*
Caroline Alexander was intrigued by Mary Kingsley's travels and decided to follow her journey to the Gaboon (Gabon) as closely as possible.

✔ **Jella**   *Dea Birkett   1994 (1992)*
Dea Birkett was the only woman on a cargo ship going from Lagos to Liverpool. She was nicknamed 'Jella', meaning small boy, and dressed in blue overalls, as this somehow made her more acceptable to the male crew. An interesting look at life in a confined community, with reflections about West Africa.

✔ **Wanderings in West Africa**   *Richard F. Burton   1991 (1863)*
In 1861 Richard Burton joined the Foreign Office as consul in Fernando Po, an island off the coast of West Africa. Using that as his base he made many expeditions on to the mainland amassing a huge quantity of information which he later used in his books of travel and exploration. He wrote very good descriptions of the people he encountered, which anthropologists have found invaluable.

Zanzibar to Timbuctoo   *Anthony Daniels 1989 (1988)*
Anthony Daniels worked for years as a doctor in Africa in Zimbabwe, South Africa and Tanzania. He decided to travel back to Europe overland, disillusioned about Africa after two years in Tanzania. His journey takes him through Burundi, Rwanda, Zaire, Gabon, Equatorial Guinea, Cameroon, Nigeria, Niger and Mali. Inevitably he encounters much corruption, poverty and ignorance en route, but overall he reckons that most Africans have an ability to enjoy life which we have largely lost.

✔ **Africa Dances**   *Geoffrey Gorer   1990 (1935)*
Gorer went to West Africa with Feral Benga, a dancer from Paris, in order to study music and dance. This book ends up as much more than that: he describes everything with which he comes into contact so that we learn about fetish, magic, wrestling, dancing, marriage and the military. [John Keay]

Four Guineas. A Journey Through West Africa   *Elspeth Huxley   1954*
Elspeth Huxley was aware of the disadvantages of travelling by car to the Gambia, Sierra Leone, the Gold Coast and Nigeria, however she manages to capture the atmosphere and is good on background.

✔ **Travels in West Africa**   *1982 (1897)*
✔ **West African Studies (1863–1900)**
Mary Kingsley
Mary Kingsley first went to Africa in 1893. Ostensibly she chose Africa to continue her father's natural history research (West Africa was one of the few places he had not visited) but desolate with grief after her par-

ents' death she probably wanted a complete change of life. She was very sympathetic to and about the Africans she lived among: 'As it is with the forest, so it is with the minds of the natives. Unless you live among the natives, you never get to know them. If you do this you gradually get a light into the true state of their mind-forest.' This was an extraordinarily enlightened view in an age when Africa was known as the 'dark continent'. She considers her *Travels in West Africa* an 'interim report' and was amused by being called 'an intrepid explorer'. In *West African Studies* she uses some of the material collected on her first trip, but most of it is as a result of further reflection and research. She died of heart failure after a fever in South Africa in 1900 and was buried, at her request, at sea.

Captain Clapperton's Last Expedition to Africa   *Richard Lander   1967 (1830)*
Lander agreed to join a British government party under Clapperton to go in search of the Niger. Many people urged him not to go because of the danger and because of what had happened to Mungo Park (q.v.). Here he describes the trip via the Madeiras, Canaries and Cape Verde Islands, the arrival in Sierra Leone and the departure into the interior. Clapperton died of fever during the trip but Lander continued to Badagry which was a market for the sale of slaves to European merchants. He was picked up here by an English vessel and returned to England.

✔ **Travels into the Interior of Africa**   *Mungo Park   1983 (1799)*
Mungo Park, a young Scottish doctor, made his first journey in 1795, in search of the Niger, into what was the almost uncharted territory of inland West Africa. Although he found the river he accomplished little else and a year later returned to Scotland exhausted. In 1805 he went on a second expedition which ended in death for all forty-six Europeans, including himself. He documented what he saw diligently, but brought back little new information. The account of his travels appeared in 1799 and shows him to have been a tough and resolute explorer who according to Joseph Banks had 'opened a gate into the interior of Africa'. [John Keay]

Lake Chad   *Sylvia K. Sikes   1972*
Lake Chad is situated in the southern part of the Sahara where Tchad, Niger, Nigeria and Cameroon meet. It is now very shallow, but still vast and has a mass of fascinating lagoons and islands with tribes called the 'Yedina' (formerly 'the pirates of the papyrus'), living on the floating islands.

✔ **Malaria Dreams**   *Stuart Stevens   1992*
(1989) (Cameroon, Chad, Niger and Mali)
Stevens was almost completely unprepared
for this trip and would probably make the
most infuriating travelling companion; he
has however written a very funny account of
his journey from *Bangui to Algeria, driving through*
Cameroon, Chad, Niger and Mali.

BENIN

Fiction

✔ **Snares Without End**
Olympe Bhely-Quénum   1981 (1978)
The only novel from Benin translated into
English. Anatou awakens a monster in
Ahouna which leads him to a motiveless mur-
der.

✔ **The Viceroy of Ouidah**
Bruce Chatwin   1982 (1980) (see 'Brazil')
A poor Brazilian sailed to Dahomey, now
Benin, in the early 1800s determined to
make a fortune and to return triumphantly
to Brazil. He never returned but managed to
establish an outpost of Brazil in Africa by
siring an enormous amount of children. Ma-
cabre and funny.

History

✔ **A Short History of Benin**
Jacob Egharevba   1991 (1968)
A very slight history of the country from the
founding of the Benin empire in about 900
AD

BURKINA FASO

Most of the little written about Burkina Faso
is in French.

General Background

Benin, Congo and Burkina Faso
Joan Baxter and Keith Somerville   1989
In the Marxist régime series.

CAMEROON

'Farewell, Camaroons! Farewell, beautiful
heights! where so many
calm and quiet days have sped without
sandflies or mosquitoes, or

prickly heat. Adieu! happy rustic wilds.'
Richard Burton
Abeokuta and the Camaroons Mountains 1863

Anthropology

✔ **The Innocent Anthropologist**
Nigel Barley   1986 (1983)
The hilarious account of Barley's first field
trip to the Dowayo in the Cameroons. All the
theory he had learnt was seemingly completely useless in the field, but he managed
to turn his experiences into a very revealing
book.

Leaf of Honey   *Joseph Sheppherd   1988*
An American anthropologist's delightful
book about the Ntuumu people of Cameroon.

Fiction

The Poor Christ of Bomba   *Mongo Beti*
1971
A cynical novel which deals with political
satire; a French priest tries to convert a
whole village. Other books by Beti include
Mission to Kala (1957) and *King Lazurus*
(1960).

The White Man of God   *Kenjo Jumbam*
1980
Childhood in a strict Christian family in the
early days of colonialism; a time mixed with
both sorrow and happiness.

History

The Cameroons   *Mark DeLancey   1989*
A survey of politics, economics and history.

Natural History

✔ **The Overloaded Ark**   *Gerald Durrell*
1987 (1953)
Durrell's first book is about an expedition to
the Cameroons to collect animals for his zoo.
'A delightful book . . . you can feel his bush-
shirt sticking to his back . . . Bagging a monitor, smoking out a Pangolin (scaly anteater),
celebrating the capture of the rare Angwan-
tibo (small lemur), bird liming for Giant
King-fishers on the warm milky waters of
Lake Soden: he communicates every detail of
his experiences with just the right degree of
zest.' (*New Statesman*) His other books about
the Cameroon are *The Bafut Beagles* (1954)
and *A Zoo in My Luggage* (1960).

Travel Literature

Cameroon With Egbert *Dervla Murphy*
1990 (1989)
Dervla Murphy trekked through Western Cameroon with her daughter and a horse named Egbert. She and her daughter are intrepid travellers and get themselves into all kinds of scrapes from which they always seem to emerge unscathed.

CAPE VERDE ISLANDS
'These llands are held to bee scituate in one of the most unhealthiest Climates of the world, and therefore it is wisedome to shunne the sight of them, how much more to make abode in them?' Sir Richard Hawkins 1593 in *Purchas his Pilgrimes* 1625

General Background

The Fortunate Isles – a Study in African Transformation *Basil Davidson*
1989
History as well as present-day impressions of these generally unwritten-about islands.

Leisure

✔ **Atlantic Islands** *Anne Hammick and Nicholas Heath* *1989*
A sailors' pilot with navigational charts, including much on the Cape Verde Islands.

Travel Literature

Black and White Make Brown: An Account of a Journey to the Cape Verde Islands in Portuguese Guinea
Archibald Lyall *1938*
Lyall went to the Cape Verde Islands because they 'are easily the least known of all the Atlantic islands'. He discovered a wealth of bird life, but most of the natural vegetation and animal life had disappeared due to endless droughts, much changed since they were discovered by a captain of Prince Henry the Navigator in 1460 when they had been covered with trees.

CHAD
'Who holds Chad holds Africa.' French maxim, quoted by John Gunther *Inside Africa* 1955

Fiction

Descent from the Hills *Stanhope White*
1963
The Wakara tribe live above Lake Chad: leadership is passed down by secret rites and there has been an unbroken succession from Wakara, the founder, through the Gidigils (guardians). This story is set in 1890 and documents the disintegration of the tribe through three generations.

Travel Literature

Travels in the Congo *André Gide* *1986 (1927)*
In 1925–6, Gide travelled as a special envoy of the Colonial Ministry to the Congo and Chad. He was appalled by the injustices of French colonialism and wrote a book which is part travel, but filled with reforming zeal. He dedicated it to Conrad.

EQUATORIAL GUINEA
'Seen from the sea, or from the continent it looks like an immense single mountain that has floated out to sea.' Mary Kingsley *Travels in West Africa* 1897 (about Fernando Po)

GABON
'The majesty and beauty of the scene fascinated me, and I stood leaning with my back against a rock pinnacle, watching it.' Mary Kingsley *Travels in West Africa* 1897 (about Sierra del Cristal from the Ogowe River)

GAMBIA
'Gambia is more English than England, more English even than India.' Richard West *The White Tribes of Africa* 1965

Fiction

Chaff in the Wind *Ebou Dibba* *1986*
The author now lives in Britain, but here describes life in Gambia in the 1930s.

Roots *Alex Haley* *1990 (1976)*
The first part of this epic saga is set in the Gambia.

The Second Round *Lenrie Peters* *1965*
A young doctor returns home to the Gambia

after several years of medical school in England and encounters family hate and disloyalty.

Guides

✔ **The Gambia & Senegal. Insight Guide** *1991*

History

History of the Gambia *J.M. Gray 1966*
A rather turgid history which finishes before the Second World War.

Photography

Gambia *Michael Tomkinson 1991 (1987)*
A rather slight, illustrated book which does give an idea of the place and which is accompanied by a fair amount of text.

Travel Literature

✔ **Our Grandmothers' Drums**
Mark Hudson 1992 (1989)
Mark Hudson spent a year in Dulaba in the Gambia. For some, largely unexplained, reason he was allowed to be with the women of the village at times and in places where men were not allowed, so he spent much of his time with them gaining interesting insights into their lifestyle. The book is written with feeling and conviction. [Colin Thubron]

GHANA

'Accra . . . is one of the five West Coast towns that look well from the sea . . .
What there is of beauty in Accra is oriental in type.' Mary Kingsley *Travels in West Africa* 1897

Biography

✔ **All God's Children Need Travelling Shoes.** *Maya Angelou 1991 (1986)*
The fifth volume of Maya Angelou's autobiography, emigrating to Ghana from the US via Cairo. She discovers that 'you can't go home again' but finds untold riches in love and friendship, describing in her inimitable way her feelings about Africa.

Fiction

✔ **The Dilemma of a Ghost**
✔ **Anowa** *Ama Ata Aidoo 1991 (1965)*
Two plays which show very plainly the differences between Western culture and the traditions of Africa. In *The Dilemma of a Ghost* Ato returns to Ghana, having lived in North America bringing with him a sophisticated black American wife. Their idealism is soon shattered.

The Beautiful Ones Are Not Yet Born
Ayiu Kwei Armah 1968
A novel about politics, greed and corruption as told by a railway clerk. Armah also wrote *Fragments* (1970) and *The Healers* (1978).

General Background

✔ **A View of the World** *Norman Lewis 1987 (1986)*
A collection of selected journalism which includes an essay called *A Few High-Lifes in Ghana*.

History

✔ **African Eldorado. Ghana from Gold Coast to Independence** *John Carmichael 1993*
The book looks at the legend of ancient Ghana, the arrival of the Europeans and their quest for gold, the slave trade and the Ashanti wars, as well as examining the Ghana of today, the first Black African state to gain independence.

GUINEA

Fiction

The African Child *1969 (1953)*
A Dream of Africa *Camara Laye 1968 (1954)*
When his first book was published Camara Laye soon became established as the leader of new African literature. His novels are full of the feeling of the spirit world enclosing the everyday world.

I Was a Savage *Prince Modupe 1969 (1958)*
Modupe wrote this autobiographical novel after living for many years in the United States. He was born in French-speaking Guinea and here recounts his early life as a Sousou boy.

GUINEA-BISSAU

General Background

Guinea-Bissau: Politics, Economics and Society *Rosemary E. Galli and Jocelyn Jones 1987*
A rather heavy background survey.

History

No Fist is Big Enough to Hide the Sky: the Liberation of Guiné and Cape Verde *Basil Davidson 1981*
An account of the war and its aftermath by a sympathetic observer.

IVORY COAST

'Grand Bassam . . . is for connoisseurs of decay.' Richard West
The White Tribes of Africa 1965

Autobiography/Biography

✔ **Finding the Centre** *V.S. Naipaul 1985 (1984)*
The first part of the book recounts Naipaul's return to his native Trinidad; the second part describes his exploration of African magic on the Ivory Coast and shows how far his writing grows out of his contact with other people.

Fiction

Climbié *Bernard B. Dadié 1971 (1953)*
Largely autobiographical and reminiscent of Camara Laye (q.v.). A pre-independence Ivory Coast childhood.

LIBERIA

'There is a distinctly Stuart air about the civilization of the Liberian Coast.' Graham Greene *Journey Without Maps* 1936

Fiction

Love in Ebony: a West African Romance *Varfelli Karlee (pseudonym Charles Edward Cooper) 1932*
There are very few works about the hinterland of Liberia, which is inhabited by Africans native to the area, rather than those who were sent from America to occupy coastal areas.

General Background

✔ **A View of the World** *Norman Lewis 1987 (1986)*
Selected journalism which includes an essay on Liberia called 'Tubman Bids Us Toil'.

Travel Literature

Monrovia Mon Amour *Anthony Daniels 1992*
Anthony Daniels arrived in Liberia in the aftermath of its civil war to find a country shattered by what it had gone through. Its leaders Samuel Doe, Charles Taylor and Prince Y. Johnson had all in their turn resorted to brutal killings and laid trails of destruction. Daniels who has lived in Africa paints an accurate portrayal of what he found.

✔ **Too Late To Turn Back** *Barbara Greene 1990 (1938)*
The twenty-three-year-old Barbara Greene accompanied her cousin Graham to the unmapped Liberia. She was used to a rather luxurious London life, missing the Savoy Grill and smoked salmon on her travels, but although she never meant this book to be published it is riveting to read it in conjunction with *Journey Without Maps* (q.v.). This was the first time that either of them had been to Africa and the portrait of Graham Greene through Barbara's book is fascinating. We learn an immense amount about him through her observations, while he only mentions her by name once in his book.

✔ **Journey Without Maps** *Graham Greene 1980 (1936)*
The journey across Liberia with his cousin Barbara was Greene's first book about Africa. It is interesting to read both of their books: it is hard to imagine that they were on the same journey. Greene's acute observations of the differences in other cultures make him one of the best writers with whom to travel.

MALI (see also 'North Africa – Sahara')

'To that impracticable place Timbuctoo, where Geography finds no one to oblige her
With such a chart as may be safely stuck to.'
Lord Byron *Don Juan* 1819-24

Most of what is written about Mali is in French.

Autobiography/Biography

The White Monk of Timbuctoo
William Seabrook 1934
The biography of Pere Yakouba a white priest who married a woman from Timbuctoo.

Fiction

L'Assemblée des Djinns Massa Makan Diabaté 1985
In Mali the 'griots' (wandering musicians) have kept power and influence; this novel tells of the struggle for that power. In French only. Also *Lieutenant, Coiffeur, Boucher de Houta* and *Comme une Pîque de Guêpe*.

✔ **Sundiata: an Epic of Old Mali**
D. Niane 1993 (1960)
Sundiata grew up to fulfil the prophecies that he would unite the twelve kingdoms of Mali into a powerful empire. The tale has been told by generations of griots.

Bound to Violence Yambo Ouologuem 1971 (1968)
An epic of a fictitious empire in which the author writes that three historical forces are responsible for the fate and character of the black African: African emperors, Arabs and Europeans.

Gone to Timbuctoo John Pearson 1967 (1962)
A non-violent thriller about a collection of odd characters who are involved in a journey from Dakar to the River Niger and through remote parts of West Africa to Timbuctoo, where the climax of the book takes place. Vivid descriptions of the country as well as an exciting plot.

Photography

✔ **Masked Dancers of West Africa: the Dogon** Stephen Pern and Bryan Alexander 1982
A well illustrated book with ample text in the Time Life series.

Travel Literature

The Quest for Timbuktoo Brian Gardner 1968
A collection of biographies of explorers to Timbuktoo.

NIGER
Most books about Niger are in French.

Anthropology

In Sorcery's Shadow: a Memoir of Apprenticeship among the Songhay
Paul Stoller 1987
Paul Stoller writes about mystery and magic in Niger. Another book is *Fusion of the Worlds: an Ethnography of Possession among the Songhay of Niger* (1987).

Photography

✔ **Nomads of the Niger** Carol Beckwith 1983
A glorious photographic account of eighteen months spent with the Wodaabe of Niger, following a herdsman, his wife and kinsmen on a year's migration. The text is ample and readable.

NIGERIA
'Nigeria is a place where the best is impossible but where the worst never happens.' Old saying, quoted *The Economist* 18th April 1953

Anthropology

Return to Laughter Elenore Smith Bowen 1954
'Smith Bowen is a pseudonym for an American woman academic, an anthropologist, who conducted fieldwork amongst the Tiv people of central Nigeria in the 1950s. Fearing that writing an account which included her own personal reactions and problems would dent her academic reputation, Smith Bowen wrote fiction under a pseudonym. *Return to Laughter* is an agonising account of a woman's struggle to be accepted in a society which is governed by principles other than her own. It is the story of her attempt to hold on to who and what she is when surrounded by strangeness. She does this through small things, such as dressing for dinner and reading Jane Austen in the bush. Without these simple gestures, she soon realises, she does not become 'one of the Tiv', but simply a nobody, a person without any principles at all, neither governed by their rules nor hers. It's a warning to all of us.' (Dea Birkett)

Autobiography/Biography

Aké *Wole Soyinka* *1982*
An autobiographical account of Soyinka's childhood in Abeokuta.

Fiction

Anthills of the Savannah
Chinua Achebe *1988 (1987)*
Achebe was born in Eastern Nigeria. He writes movingly and powerfully about the troubled recent history in West Africa by making 'His Excellency', a defeated officer, into a dictator. Fact is woven with fiction creating an exciting novel. Other novels by Achebe include: *Things Fall Apart* (1958), *No Longer at Ease* (1960), *The Arrow of God* (1964) and *A Man of the People* (1966).

Orimili *Amechi Akwanya* *1991*
The author was born in Nigeria in 1952, became a priest and lived in Ireland before returning to Nigeria. His novel is set in pre-colonial Nigeria in a small but complex community which he uses as a structure for exploring human relationships.

Mister Johnson *Joyce Cary* *1985 (1939)*
Joyce Cary fought in the Nigerian Regiment during the First World War and subsequently rejoined the Nigerian Political Service. However he suffered from ill health and was advised to retire. He left Africa and began to write. Mr Johnson is a minor government clerk at an outpost in Nigeria who has ideas of grandeur. Cary captures colonial life well and manages to combine it with a real understanding of Africa and the Africans.

Slave Girl *Buchi Emecheta* *1979*
The theme of Buchi Emecheta's novels, which include *Second Class Citizen* (1977), *Double Yoke* (1984) and *Bride Price* (1978), is the struggle of being both a Nigerian woman and an independent person.

✔ The Famished Road *Ben Okri* *1992 (1991)*
A lyrical and compelling book, full of flights of fancy, but also very instructive as to life in a West African village. After finishing it you begin to see the world around you in a different way. Okri's first novel was *Flowers and Shadows* (1980) and he has written collections of short stories including *Incidents at the Shrine* (1986) and *Stars of the New Curfew* (1988).

Loyalties *Adewale Maja Pearce* *1987*
Short stories about a society in disarray.

The Interpreters *Wole Soyinka* *1965*
About a group of young intellectuals living in Lagos.

General Background

The Trouble with Nigeria
Chinua Achebe *1983*
The complexities of Nigeria are examined in a brief but informative book.

Guides

✔ Survive Lagos *Elizabeth Cox and Erica Anderssen* *1984*
A useful little book which advises about the 'do's and don'ts' when visiting Lagos.

✔ Enjoy Nigeria *Ian Nason* *1991*
A very basic guide to the country, published there.

Travel Literature

Equiano's Travels *Paul Edwards (ed.)* *(abridged)* *1969 (1789)*
Olaudah Equiano was born in 1745 in what is now Nigeria. He was taken as a slave to the West Indies, managed to buy his freedom when he was twenty-one and in 1773 took part in Phipps' expedition to the Arctic. He was an ardent member of the Anti-Slavery movement. This account of his life was extremely popular, going into seventeen editions in Britain between 1789 and 1827.

In My Father's Country
Adewale Maja-Pearce *1987*
The author was revisiting his country for the first time in many years.

SENEGAL

'Dakar has been fittingly called 'the boomingest boom town on the continent.''
John Gunther *Inside Africa* 1955

Fiction

So Long a Letter *Mariama Bâ* *1982 (1979)*
The novel deals with the problems of polygamy and social inequality faced by women in present-day Africa. Portrayed through the eyes of two women, both deserted by their husbands, whose lives take different courses.

A Dakar Childhood   *Nafissatou Diallo*
1982
The account of a middle-class girl growing up
in Dakar in the postwar years.

General Background

**Senegal – An African Nation Between
Islam and the West**   *Sheldon Gellar   1982*
A very readable general survey of Senegal.

SIERRA LEONE

'Sierra Leone, charming as it is, has a sort
of Christy Minstrel air about it.' Mary
Kingsley *West African Studies* 1899

Fiction

The African   *William Conton   1960*
Kisimi Kamara is awarded a scholarship to
study in England where he meets a white
South African girl; colour prejudice ends
their affair, so he returns to Sierra Leone
disillusioned and bitter, but turns his energies to politics.

✔ **The Heart of the Matter**
Graham Greene   1992 (1948)
Graham Greene sets this novel in an imaginary West African country; he was stationed
in Sierra Leone from 1941–43 and inevitably
draws much from his experiences there.
Scobie, a police officer, is passed over for
promotion so has to borrow money in order to
send his wife on holiday. While she is away
he falls in love; the moral dilemma which
follows shows Graham Greene at his best.

History

✔ **A New History of Sierra Leone**
Joe A.D. Alie   1990
An illustrated overall history of Sierra Leone
from early times up until the present.

TOGO

General Background

The Village of Waiting   *George Packer*
1990
The experiences of a Peace Corps volunteer
in Togo.

East Africa

General

Anthropology

✔ **The Tree Where Man Was Born**
Peter Matthiessen   1994 (1972)
Difficult to classify as this is really a book
that feels and understands *Africa* in all its
many facets. Although Matthiessen went to
Africa primarily to see animals he also writes
in a compelling way about the environment,
history, politics, people and the landscape.
He feels that 'Something has happened here,
is happening, will happen – whole landscapes seem alert'.

Fiction

✔ **Henderson the Rain King**
Saul Bellow   1990 (1979)
Bellow has created Henderson as a hero in

the great tradition yet set in contemporary
America and Africa. Very funny, punchy
prose which has a thread of pathos running
through it.

✔ **An Ice-Cream War**   *William Boyd   1983*
Set in East Africa during the times of the
campaigns in the First World War. The book
is about the Europeans who took part, Africans seeming only to appear incidentally and
in bizarre roles; the two cultures are seen
here as stereotypes.

✔ **The Weather in Africa**
Martha Gellhorn   1991 (1978)
Three novellas set in East Africa: *On the
Mountain, By the Sea* and *In the Highlands*.
All three are about Europeans who for one
reason or another do not quite fit in Europe
and so have either come or come back to East
Africa. Their preconceptions of Africa are
very different from the reality; all three are
compelling stories.

The Year of the Lion   Gerald Hanley   1966 (1953)

An inexperienced but eager young man arrives from England to work on a farm in East Africa. He has to learn to cope with the heat and uncertainties of Africa as well as dealing with people and animals; by doing so he grows up. An exciting story which has wonderful descriptions of the hunt for a man-eating lion. Also Hanley's first novel *The Consul at Sunset* (1951).

✔ **Fong and the Indians**   Paul Theroux 1992 (1968)

Paul Theroux's perceptive and funny novel is set in East Africa where a Chinese immigrant, Sam Fong, had been transplanted and where he had lived for thirty-five years.

✔ **Antonia Saw the Oryx First**   Maria Thomas   1988 (1987)

Maria Thomas has lived in Africa for the last twenty years and with her first novel has managed to get under the skin of it, understanding the corruption and writing satirically about its transition from colonial times. The novel is about two women: one black, one white.

General Background

✔ **East and West Africa. Travel Resource Guide**   Louis Taussig   1994

Guides

✔ **Backpacker's Africa. East and Southern Africa for Walkers and Overland Travellers**   Hilary Bradt   1994 (1977)

✔ **East Africa. Travel Survival Kit** Geoff Crowther and Hugh Finlay   1991 (1987)

✔ **East African Handbook 1995** Published Trade and Travel

Traveller's Guide East Africa and the Indian Ocean   Published by IC Publications 1990

Contains countries not included in other guides e.g. Djibouti, Ethiopia, Somalia and Sudan, although there is very little about each.

History

The Lunatic Express   Charles Miller   1987 (1972)

George Whitehouse arrived in Mombasa in 1895 to build a railway. The danger and folly of the enterprise soon became apparent as the railway would have to cross deserts and the Great Rift Valley as well as contend with malarial swamps and wild animals. The saga of the controversial but extraordinary Victorian engineering feat is written here as an exciting history. Miller is also good on general early East African history.

In the Grip of the Nyika   J.H. Patterson 1909

An account of the adventures that befell Colonel Patterson on two trips through the nyika (wilderness) in British East Africa. It seemed almost standard that some members of the party would die en route, nevertheless there are interesting descriptions of what a safari was like at the turn of the century.

The Man-Eaters of Tsavo; and Other East African Adventures   J.H. Patterson 1979 (1907)

The author's terrifying adventures (which impressed President Roosevelt) with man-eating lions when he was an engineer during the building of the Uganda Railway. The chapters on construction of the railway and bridges are also interesting; well illustrated with his photographs.

East African Explorers   Charles Richards (ed.)   1968 (1960)

One of the World's Classics series, this is an anthology devoted to the writings of the first travellers and explorers to East Africa, such as Livingstone, Stanley, Teleki, Burton, Speke, Baker, Lugard and Emin Pasha. Rather limited in its coverage.

Leisure

✔ **Trekking in East Africa. A Lonely Planet Walking Guide**   David Else   1993

Natural History

✔ **A Field Guide to the Wild Flowers of East Africa**   Michael Blundell   1992 (1987)

Over 1200 detailed descriptions of species and 864 colour photographs of wild flowers in Kenya, Tanzania, Uganda, Mozambique and Zimbabwe. Invaluable.

Collins Pocket Guide to the Coral Reef Fishes: Indo-Pacific and Caribbean Edward Lieske and Robert Myers   1994

Over 2000 species illustrated in colour.

✔ **Insight Guide East African Wildlife**   1989

The first half of the book describes specific animals and is illustrated by 'artistic' photographs, this is followed by descriptions of the game parks and reserves. A rundown of various safaris follows.

On Safari in East Africa   Ernest Neal
1991
A useful background book which explains how the animals have evolved, their behaviour and their habitat. Each chapter is arranged under type of animal or type of habitat.

✔ **A Field Guide to the Birds of East Africa**   J.G. Williams and N. Arlott   1993 (1980)
An easy-to-carry pocket guide with many colour illustrations and ample descriptions of nearly 1300 birds of East Africa.

✔ **A Field Guide to the National Parks of East Africa**   J.G. Williams   1991 (1967)
A guide to the parks, game reserves and other game areas in Kenya, Tanzania and Uganda. The pocket-sized guide includes identification of nearly 400 birds and mammals.

Photography

The End of the Game   Peter Beard   1988 (1963)
A documentary history of East African wildlife. Over 300 black and white photographs show the widespread destruction of the African elephant. The text tells of the explorers, missionaries and game hunters and quotes many of them at length. A powerful and disturbing book.

East Africa   Tim Beddow   1988
A lengthy and interesting introduction by Dominic Sasse is followed by 78 colour photographs which show the diversity of landscape and people in East Africa.

Valley of Life   Chris Johns   1991
National Geographic photographer Chris Johns spent eighteen months following the 3,500 miles of the African Rift Valley which stretches from Ethiopia to Mozambique via Djibouti, Kenya, Uganda, Tanzania, Zaire and Malawi. The diverse country, people and animals along the rift are shown here by stunning and original photographs, many of them taken from the air.

Religion

Islam in East Africa   J.S. Trimingham   1964
Islamic history in East Africa and the extent to which it has merged with African culture and produced the mix that exists today.

Travel Literature

✔ **Travels with Myself and Another**
Martha Gellhorn   1991 (1978) (see 'China', 'Caribbean' and 'Israel')
Part of this entertaining and observant book about Martha Gellhorn's 'horror journeys', takes place in East Africa.

✔ **Green Hills of Africa**
Ernest Hemingway   1991 (1935)
Most of Hemingway's love for Africa seems to come from big-game hunting; however there is more to it than that, because his descriptions of the landscape and of smells mean that Africa really did get into his blood. His encounter with a European in the bush and discussion of Rilke is on a par with Kinglake's encounter in *Eothen* (q.v.).

✔ **West With the Night**   Beryl Markham
1992 (1942)
Beryl Markham was taken to Kenya by her father in 1906, when she was four. She learned to train racehorses and in 1931 started flying, regularly piloting mail for East African Airways as well as game hunting from the air. In 1936 she became the first person to fly solo across the Atlantic from east to west. This was her only book and although there is some dispute as to whether she actually wrote it, it is a riveting read.

Straight on till Morning   Mary S. Lovell
1988 (1987)
The acclaimed story of Beryl Markham's life.

✔ **North of South**   Shiva Naipaul   1980
(1979)
A brilliant travel narrative about journeying through Kenya, Tanzania and Zambia. Naipaul was extremely observant and with a novelist's eye for detail could be devastatingly accurate and cynical about what he saw.

Discovery of Lakes Rudolf and Stefanie   Lt. Ludwig von Höhnel   1894
A narrative of Count Samuel Teleki's exploring and hunting expedition in Eastern Equatorial Africa in 1887 and 1888. This account was written for the general reading public and deals with the big game hunting aspect of the trip rather than with the scientific observations which were made; the wealth of animals that they both saw and pursued do not exist today.

A Tourist in Africa   Evelyn Waugh   1960
A slight book, but a funny one, about a short trip to Kenya, Tanganyika and Rhodesia.

DJIBOUTI

'Jibuti, white and neat and empty, looked as if it had just been washed and dumped out in the sun to dry.' Rosita Forbes *From Red Sea to Blue Nile* 1925

Photography

African Ark *Carol Beckwith and Angela Fisher 1991 (1990)*
The photographers spent five years in the Horn of Africa collecting material for this book which contains 320 pages of colour photographs as well as explanatory line drawings in the text. Racked by famine and war today, the region covers sophisticated Christian and Muslim cultures as well as nomads and primitive tribes.

Travel Literature

✔ **Hashish. A Smuggler's Tale**
Henry de Monfreid 1994 (1935)
De Monfreid sailed from Marseilles to Djibouti and on to Suez with a dream of being completely independent. He saw smuggling hashish as a way of achieving his ambition: 'I didn't know exactly what hashish was . . . I knew only two things – that it was grown in Greece and sold very dear in Egypt.'

ERITREA

Fiction

✔ **Towards Asmara** *Thomas Keneally 1990 (1989)*
A powerful novel which uses war-torn Eritrea as its focus for four people travelling under rebel escort to Asmara. Keneally travelled with the Eritrean Relief Association, so much of the book reads as fact, making it especially moving.

General Background

✔ **The Challenge Road** *Amrit Wilson 1989*
Women's experiences during the revolution in Eritrea. The author shows how the revolution addressed women's issues.

ETHIOPIA

'I saw parch'd Abyssinia rouse and sing.'
John Keats *Endymion* 1818

Art

The Abyssinians. Ancient Peoples and Places *David Buxton 1970*
The book documents the country, its people, their history, religion and way of life. The architecture, literature, painting and other arts including music and metalwork are illustrated throughout by line drawings and 128 photographs.

✔ **African Zion. The Sacred Art of Ethiopia** *Roderick Grierson (ed.) 1993*
A magnificent illustrated catalogue with lengthy descriptions of Ethiopia's sacred art.

Fiction

✔ **The History of Rasselas, Prince of Abyssinia** *Samuel Johnson 1986 (1759)*
The story of how Rasselas and his companions escape from their valley in Abyssinia and flee to Egypt to find out how people live. Dr Johnson's moral tale which is really asking 'what is happiness, and how can we find it?' includes discussions on a wide range of subjects including greatness, marriage, solitude and astronomy. A wise and thought-provoking book.

✔ **The Emperor** *Ryszard Kapuscinski 1994 (1983)*
'The only book I've read about Ethiopia, but I can't imagine that had I read a library it would have been any less memorable.' (Jeremy Paxman) [Stephen Brook]

Firebrands *Sahle Sellassie 1979*
A political novel culminating in 1974 and showing the massive corruption that existed in pre-revolutionary Ethiopia, portrayed through the eyes of one family.

✔ **Black Mischief** *Evelyn Waugh 1992 (1932)*
The Emperor Seth and his Minister of Modernization, Basil Seal, are pitted against the cruelty, treachery and cannibalism in the mythical country of Azania (loosely based on Abyssinia) which is racked by civil war; but they find it a losing battle. Cynical and funny.

✔ **Scoop** *Evelyn Waugh 1992 (1938)*
William Boot, Countryman, is mistakenly sent to Ishmaelia by Lord Copper to cover the war. As Boot blunders through, the novel

becomes an hilariously funny satire on Fleet Street and war reporting.

History

The Nile Tributaries of Abyssinia and the Sword Hunters of the Hamran Arabs   *Sir Samuel Baker   1867*
Baker spent twelve months exploring every river that is a tributary to the Nile from Abyssinia. During the journey he found time to learn Arabic and to study the character of the peoples he encountered; his wife, Florence, accompanied him throughout this tough trip which was beset by every kind of problem, but which ultimately led to his success in reaching the 'Albert N'yanza'. Although written after *The Albert N'yanza* (q.v.), the part of the expedition it describes actually took place before.

The Sacred City of the Ethiopians
J. Theodore Bent   1893
A record of four months of travel and research in Abyssinia in 1893 to Aksum, the sacred city of the Ethiopians. The author was the first to find Sabœan inscriptions in a temple proving a connection between the peoples of South Arabia and of Abyssinia mentioned in the tenth chapter of Genesis and alluded to by Greek authors.

Travels to Discover the Source of the Nile   *James Bruce   1964 (1790)*
Bruce wanted to discover the Ethiopian source of the Nile. He set off in 1768 and in 1769 arrived at Massawah in Ethiopia. His second attempt to reach the source was successful. On returning to England he was initially acclaimed, but his travels were subsequently disbelieved. His account of his own travels is lively and accessible to the general reader, whereas his volume on the history of Ethiopia is somewhat confused. [Anthony Sattin]

Photography

African Ark   *Carol Beckwith and Angela Fisher*
(see 'Djibouti')

Religion

Islam in Ethiopia   *J. Spencer Trimingham   1952*
The account of the impact of Islam upon the nomadic and settled peoples of Ethiopia, the reaction of indigenous cultures and the way the converts to Islam moulded it into their lives.

Travel Literature

The Fountain of the Sun   *Douglas Busk   1957*
The author was posted to the embassy in Addis Ababa and from there made many trips into Ethiopia and the Ruwenzori. His main love was for the mountains, but he found so much else in Ethiopia to interest him that mountains are given less coverage than he had anticipated.

Travels in Ethiopia   *David Buxton   1949*
The author, a biologist, worked for mosquito control and travelled throughout Ethiopia in the 40s.

✔ The Sign and the Seal. A Quest for the Lost Ark of the Covenant
Graham Hancock   1992
In 1983 Graham Hancock had visited a building in the Ethiopian Highlands which was alleged to contain the Ark of the Covenant. He was unable to see it, but was fired with enthusiasm and curiosity to find out all he could about it and the Queen of Sheba.

✔ Journey to the Jade Sea
John Hillaby   1993 (1964)
Formerly known as Lake Rudolf, now Lake Turkana, the Jade Sea is on the borders of Kenya and Ethiopia. The lava beds which surround the lake are often too hot to touch, but the colour is a stunning green and unusually large crocodiles live in the lake. John Hillaby walked over a thousand miles to the lake and along its shores and recounts his adventures in this book.

✔ A Far Country   *Philip Marsden-Smedley   1991 (1990)*
A combination of travelogue and a book tracing Ethiopia's past. The author remains detached but describes the many people he meets, letting them talk. The result is a book which makes you feel you have travelled through the country.

✔ In Ethiopia With a Mule
Dervla Murphy   1968
Dervla Murphy is an intrepid traveller and went from Massawah in the north of Ethiopia to Addis Ababa in the south. Much of her journey was on foot, or rather with a mule named Jock, about whom we hear everything. Written in diary form so we learn much about the habits and lifestyles of the people she meets and what the landscape looks like; as she says 'every local detail interests me'.

Desert and Forest   *L.M. Nesbitt   1934*
(The exploration of Abyssinian Danakil)
Already in the 1920s people seemed to be

aware of the impossibility for the would-be explorer to find a 'virgin field for his enterprise on the earth'. Nesbitt appreciated his good fortune in being one of the last to be able to experience virgin territory; his three-and-a-half-month expedition traversed the Danakil territory south to north in 1927 and he presented the scientific results to the Royal Geographical Society in 1928.

The Mountains of Rasselas
Thomas Pakenham 1959
Thomas Pakenham found himself involved in going to Ethiopia to climb Mount Wachni, near Lake Tana, where the King's sons had been confined (see Johnson's *Rasselas*). He would be the first to give an eye-witness account of all three summits. (Bruce had only visited two of the three mountains.) The unknown shape of the mountain became a fixation and when he eventually saw one of the peaks, shaped like a thumb, his stomach contracted with fear. Pakenham writes clearly, blending history with the myth surrounding the area.

In Search of Sheba   *Barbara Toy (see 'Algeria and the Sahara')*

✔ Waugh in Abyssinia   *Evelyn Waugh 1984 (1936)*
Waugh went to Abyssinia in 1935 to cover the Italian–Abyssinian war for the *Daily Mail* and with his witty prose takes a look at the crisis and its build up. His descriptions of the lives of war correspondents and their encounters with the local people are very amusing and perceptive.

KENYA
'In Kenya any eccentricity gets blamed on the altitude.' Richard West *The White Tribes of Africa* 1965

Anthropology

✔ Being Maasai   *Thomas Spear and Richard Waller (eds.) 1993*
A collection by historians, archaeologists, anthropologists and linguists which examines how the Maasai identity has been created.

Biography

My Pride and Joy   *George Adamson 1988 (1986)*
George Adamson first went to Kenya in 1924 and retired from being a game warden in 1963. His autobiography tells of his life with lions (including the famous Elsa) and of the murder of his wife Joy in 1980. Especially interesting because of the long span of time he spent in Kenya.

✔ Out of Africa   *Karen Blixen (Isak Dinesen) 1991(1937)*
In 1914 Karen Blixen went to Kenya to run a coffee farm which failed. She subsequently returned to Denmark where she wrote this unsentimental but moving and introspective account of her experiences there. The friends and animals that she came across in Kenya are vividly portrayed and we share her sense of loss both for the farm and in a wider sense for an era.

✔ The Flame Trees of Thika   *1991 (1959)*
✔ The Mottled Lizard   *1981 (1962)*
✔ Out in the Midday Sun   *Elspeth Huxley 1987 (1985)*
These three volumes of autobiography begin when Elspeth Huxley goes with her parents to Thika to become pioneering settlers among the Kikuyu. The memoirs of her African childhood are captivatingly written; they vividly conjure up landscapes, episodes and people from another era but make valid reading for today.

Nellie: Letters from Africa   *Nellie Grant 1980*
Nellie Grant, born in 1885, was Elspeth Huxley's mother; she married a settler farmer and lived in Kenya for most of her life. Her letters describe the domestic details of life during the pioneer period and are very illuminating.

Kenya Diary   *Richard Meinertzhagen 1906*
The diary of a young British officer takes a cold-blooded approach to his 'punitive expeditions' as well as the endless slaughter of wild animals.

A Nice Place to Live   *Pamela Scott 1991*
Pam Scott was left a farm to run in Kenya when she was eighteen; the farm was sold forty-five years later, but she stayed on and was in Kenya during the Mau Mau emergency. Her straightforward account of life during and after that time is refreshing in its honesty.

✔ My Kenya Days   *Wilfred Thesiger 1994*
Thesiger's autobiography of the thirty years he spent in Kenya. During the 1960s he made many long expeditions on foot with camels to Lakes Turkana and Marsabit and other remote areas; he writes about these as well as giving insights into his reasons for travelling and his love of Kenya.

✔ **The Life of Isak Dinesen**
Judith Thurman   1984 (1982)
A biography of Isak Dinesen (Karen Blixen).

Fiction

The Slums   Thomas Akare   1981
Rather rambling book set in the Nairobi
slums, but which nonetheless does nothing to
sentimentalize the reality of slum life.

Maasai Dreaming   Justin Cartwright   1993

Murder on Safari   Elspeth Huxley   1938
A detective story about a big game safari
which gives an accurate portrayal of the reality of such an event.

Master and Servant   David Mulwa   1987
(1979)
A novel which explores Kenyan society at the
end of the colonial period through the eyes of
an adolescent sent to a Dickensian-type
school by a cruel father. A good balance to the
normal colonial literature from Kenya.

Going Down River Road   Meja Mwangi
1976
Other books by Mwangi who writes easy-to-
read, rather hip novels, include *Bread of Sorrow* (1987), *Cockroach Dance* (1979), *Weapon
of Hunger* (1989) and *Striving for the Wind*
(1992 (1990)).

Petals of Blood   1977
Secret Lives
Weep Not Child   Ngugi Wa Thiong'o   (1964)
Weep not Child was the first novel to be
published in English by an East African
writer. It begins with the period just before
the Emergency and rise of the Mau-Mau and
continues through into the Emergency. *Petals of Blood* is a long and complex and much
praised novel which is political, didactic and
full of passion.

Food

✔ **More Specialties of the House from
Kenya's Finest Restaurants**   collected by
Kathy Eldon   1989
Recipes from various hotels, restaurants and
chefs in Kenya.

✔ **Kenya Traditional Dishes**
A.B.N. Wandera   1983
A pamphlet of traditional Kenyan recipes.

Guides

✔ **Kenya and Northern Tanzania. The
Thornton Cox Guide**   Richard Cox   1992

✔ **Kenya. Travel Survival Kit**
Geoff Crowther and Hugh Finlay   1993 (1991)

✔ **Insight Guide Kenya**   1991

✔ **Introduction to Kenya. An Odyssey
Guide**   Dennis Lakin   1992

✔ **Kenya. The Rough Guide**
Richard Trillo   1993 (1991)

History

✔ **White Mischief**   James Fox   1988 (1982)
The 'Happy Valley' set in Kenya was thrown
into confusion when Lord Erroll, founder of
the set, was murdered in 1941. Much upper-
class decadence was revealed in the scandal
that ensued, but the culprit was never found.
James Fox has written a social history/detec-
tive story which makes very exciting reading.

The Hunt for Kimathi   Ian Henderson
1958
The author spoke Kikuyu fluently and writes
very interestingly about the Mau Mau emergency. He was a Superintendent in the Special Branch.

A History of Kenya   William R. Ochieng
1985
A very accessible book aimed at students
which is based on lectures the author gave at
Kenyatta University and UCLA. It goes from
pre-history to the present and is well illustrated with maps and photographs. It was
the first book to deal with the period.

Themes in Kenyan History   William R.
Ochieng (ed.)   1990
Each chapter is about a theme in Kenyan
history: migrations, population growth, food
production, agriculture, pastoralism, urban-
ization, industrialization, religion, government and trade. The contributors all teach at
Kenyan universities and create a good mix,
as some are historians and others academics.

✔ **The Kenya Pioneers**   Errol Trzebinski
1991 (1985)
Using letters, diaries and interviews, Trzebinski amasses an interesting record of what
it was like to be an early pioneer in Kenya.
The life was exceptionally tough but as one
settler said 'Why should I retire to England?
In this country I am somebody; in England I
would only be a number on a door'.

Leisure

✔ **Guide to Mount Kenya and Kilimanjaro** *Ian Allan (ed.) 1991 (1959)*
A guide for walkers and climbers published by the Mountain Club of Kenya. A convenient size with a large foldout map at the back.

✔ **Camping Guide Kenya**
David Else 1990 (1989)
Everything you could possibly want to know about camping in Kenya including lists of campsites.

✔ **Mountain Walking Kenya** *David Else 1991 (1990)*
Designed for the recreational walker rather than the serious climber, there is much practical information on the different walks and hikes as well as health and supplies. Maps and routes of the various treks are scattered throughout the book.

Natural History

Birds of Kenya and Uganda
Frederick Jackson 1938 (3 vols.)
Frederick Jackson was Governor of Uganda from 1911–17 and while he was there became an expert on the birds of the area.

✔ **The Beautiful Plants of Kenya**
John Karmali 1988
A small book with many colour illustrations of plants and trees but with rather scanty text.

✔ **Elephant Memories** *Cynthia Moss 1989 (1988)*
The author is director of the Amboseli Elephant Research Project and has written of her experiences spanning the twenty years she has spent in Africa. The majesty of elephants and her love for them shine through this book with its combination of personal experience and scientific material.

Photography

On God's Mountain *Mohamed Amin, Duncan Willetts and Brian Tetley 1991*
A photographic history of the story of Mount Kenya which was once one of the world's highest mountains but which has shrunk as a result of wind, sun and rain. It is now much climbed and this makes an interesting record for climbers and non-climbers alike.

✔ **Maasai Mara** *Karl Ammann 1990*
A large format paperback with pictures of one of Kenya's most famous game reserves. There are some wonderful closeups of animals in over 200 pages of full colour; there is no text and minimal captions.

✔ **Maasai** *Photographs by Carol Beckwith Text by Tepilit Ole Saitoti 1991 (1980)*
The author is a Maasai and the text describes the ancient legends, songs, prayers and daily lives of his people. Accompanied by line drawings and beautifully descriptive photographs.

Vanishing Africa *Mirella Ricciardi 1984 (1971)*
A stunning black and white photographic book showing the traditional customs of some of the Kenyan peoples which are fast disappearing. An important historical document as well as a book which is visually pleasing.

Travel Literature

The Desert's Dusty Face *Charles Chenevix Trench 1964*
A district commissioner's account of life with the Turkana just before independence; he writes about the problems on the borders with Ethiopia and Somalia as well as the politics of Kenya at the time.

Letters from Africa 1914–1931
Isak Dinesen 1981
These letters which were written to various members of her family during the time that she spent in Kenya portray the often very lonely life that Isak Dinesen led among the other European settlers.

Shadows on the Grass *Isak Dinesen 1961 (1960)*
Episodes of her life in Africa, written twenty-five years later, under the chapter headings of Farah, Barua and Soldani, the Great Gesture and Echoes from the Hills. These everyday incidents are an evocative portrayal of the life she led.

✔ **I Dreamed of Africa** *Kuki Gallmann 1992 (1991)*
A book of tremendous courage and spirit which conveys a true love of Africa. The author has many tragedies in her life, but nevertheless manages to come through them and write about them upliftingly, with her father's words helping her: 'The most important thing you can ever learn in life, Kuki, is to be able to be alone'. She has set up a conservation project and does much work in helping to conserve the black rhinoceros.

Journey to the Jade Sea   *John Hillaby (see 'Ethiopia')*

The Frozen Leopard   *Aaron Latham   1991*
As much a search for himself as a straight travel book, Latham suffering from 'the rainy season in the soul' travels through Kenya to Rwanda observing the wildlife and trying to pull himself out of his depression. A fascinating odyssey which follows paths set by ancient man.

Another Land, Another Sea: Walking Round Lake Rudolph   *Stephen Pern   1979*
Pern walked round the lake, now called Lake Turkana, with two companions and three donkeys. Lake Rudolph was the last of the great lakes of East Africa to be discovered in 1888 and Pern's journey contains elements of real adventure as well as good descriptions of the country he was passing through.

✔ **A Small Town in Africa. Kenyan Journal**   *Daisy Waugh   1994*
Daisy Waugh spends six months in a remote and poor Kenyan town, Isiolo, describing well the feelings of loneliness and frustration as well as the happiness of being there.

SOMALIA

'British Somaliland is the only country I know where you see camels walking in the sky and goats climbing trees. This of course, is the effect of the mirage, and not the result of exposing your head to the sun.' Geoffrey Harmsworth *Abyssinian Adventure* 1935

Autobiography/Biography

✔ **Warriors. Life and Death among the Somalis**   *Gerald Hanley   1993 (1971)*
Gerald Hanley spent several years in Somalia where he got to know the local people well: 'Of all the races of Africa, there cannot be one better to live among than the most difficult, the proudest, the bravest, the vainest, the most merciless, the friendliest: the Somalis'. The book was originally published under the title *Warriors and Strangers*.

Fiction

From a Crooked Rib   *Nuruddin Farah   1970*
The first work of fiction to be published by a Somali writer in English, the title is from a Somali proverb 'God created woman from a crooked rib; and any one who trieth to

straighten it, breaketh'. The novel, set in pre-independence Italian Somaliland is about a girl from the country who survives the transition to city life by learning to cheat when she is cheated.

History

✔ **First Footsteps in East Africa**
Richard F. Burton   1987 (1856)
The account of Burton's epic and brave journey into the forbidden East African Muslim city of Harar (in present day Ethiopia) is an extraordinary story. Burton spoke fluent Arabic and so was able to enter the city disguised as an Arab, becoming the first European to do so without being executed. His observations about Muslim beliefs and customs make this an invaluable historical document, but it is also a very readable book. .

Two Dianas in Somaliland
Agnes Herbert   1908
(The record of a shooting trip)
The author was aware of the glut of 'hunting' books being published, but she had decided to write this one because 'simply – I want to write'. She embarked on the four month trip with a female cousin and had many alarming adventures which she recounts with a great sense of humour.

Natural History

Lone Dhow   *Adrian Conan Doyle   1963*
Conan Doyle was sent by the Natural History Museum of Geneva to find an adult tiger shark off the Somali coast. He used a Somali crew and gives good descriptions of the Somali coastal area.

Photography

✔ **African Ark**   *Carol Beckwith and Angela Fisher (see 'Djibouti')*

Travel Literature

The Prophet's Camel Bell
Margaret Laurence   1963
The author's husband went to the then Somaliland Protectorate as an engineer to construct thirty earth dams over an area of 6500 miles. Margaret Laurence wrote a perceptive account of their travels and life.

SUDAN

'It has the intense virility of something newly born and its vibrant will to live derives from sound old roots.' John Gunther *Inside Africa* 1955

Autobiography/Biography

An Arab Tells His Story   *Edward Atiyah 1946*
Several chapters are devoted to the author's life and work in the Sudan; he has many interesting observations about Khartoum between the wars and his feelings towards the British are vividly portrayed.

The Camel's Back   *Reginald Davies   1957*
The author was in service for twelve years in rural Sudan at the beginning of the century. He writes about the people he encountered in his day-to-day life, as he reckoned that there had been very little written about the Sudanese as individuals.

Traveller Extraordinary. The Life of James Bruce of Kinnaird   *J.M. Reid 1968*
A biography of the Scottish explorer James Bruce (1730–94) who travelled in the Sudan at the end of the eighteenth century.

Fiction

Their Finest Days   *Sir Hassan Fadl   1969*
Two long short stories: the first is based on the Sudanese revolution of 1964 when the military régime was overthrown; the second portrays the revolution through the eyes of a young partisan.

**Season of Migration to the North
The Wedding of Zein**   *Tayeb Salih   1980 (1969)*
Salih, a Sudanese, is one of the leading Arab writers of today who knows Europe well. In the first story a student returns to his village after having experienced 'the mysterious west', where he met women who were obsessed by 'the mysterious east'. In the second, a village buffoon marries a sought-after girl from a Sudanese village.

Guide

✔ **Egypt and the Sudan. Travel Survival Kit**   *Damien Simonis   1994 (1987)*

History

The Wind of Morning   *Hugh Bousted   1974*
Bousted was a soldier and administrator in the Sudan during the Condominium period at the turn of the century.

The River War. An Account of the Reconquest of the Soudan
Winston Churchill   1899
The Anglo-Egyptian conquest of the Sudan described here by Winston Churchill in his readable style.

✔ **The Blue Nile**
✔ **The White Nile**   *Alan Moorehead (see 'Egypt – History)'*

Fire and Sword in the Sudan. A Personal Narrative of Fighting and Serving the Dervishes 1879–1895
Colonel Sir R. Slatin Pasha   1907 (1895)
Slatin Pasha, an Austrian, having held high posts in the Sudan, was then held in captivity for many years. He was unable to take any notes during his imprisonment so he relied entirely on his memory to write this book which describes the events leading up to his captivity as well as his time as a prisoner.

Natural History

The Cry of the Fish Eagle   *Peter Molloy 1957*
Most of the travelling that Peter Molloy did with his wife, in his capacity as Game Warden of the Southern Sudan, was on foot. His love of nature, skill as an observer and ability to communicate make this an unusually sympathetic book.

Photography

People of Kau   *Leni Riefenstahl   1978 (1976)*
The Nuba of Kau live in South East Nuba. Riefenstahl focuses on what makes them different from other peoples in the area; they are a wild and passionate people and show this by the way they paint their faces and bodies and by the kind of dances they do. Riefenstahl spent about four months living with them gathering material for this book.

Sudan   *Nick Worrall   1980*
A selection of colour photographs taken all over the Sudan.

Religion

Turabi's Revolution. Islam and Power in Sudan *El-Affendi 1991*
An historical and political look at Islam in the Sudan.

Islam in the Sudan *J. Spencer Trimingham 1949*
The classic book on Islam in the Sudan which aims to help those interested in the Sudanese to understand the significance of Islam in their lives. A broad background on which to base a deeper knowledge of the country through its religion.

Travel Literature

In Search of the Forty Days Road
Michael Asher 1986 (1984)
Michael Asher determined to follow an ancient trade route through the Sudan by camel. He encountered much danger and hardship, but it is the variety of people he met, who became his friends and whom he felt it was a privilege to know, that make this an interesting book.

Travels in Nubia *J.L Burckhardt 1822*
Burckhardt, who was Swiss, visited the Sudan in 1812–14 and wrote this account of his travels; it is still relevant today as his powers of observation were acute.

African Calliope *Edward Hoagland 1981 (1979)*
The Sudan covers such a diverse range of territory and peoples: an Arab north, a black south, rain forests and desert. There are over 115 languages spoken across the country and it is this diversity which appealed to Edward Hoagland who specifically wrote this as a 'travel book, not a book of history'. However Hoagland weaves the richness of Sudanese history and culture into his narrative making this an ideal travel book.

TANZANIA/ZANZIBAR

'How can one convey the power of Serengeti? It is an immense, limitless lawn, under a marquee of sky . . . The light is dazzling, the air delectable.' Cyril Connolly
The Evening Colonnade 1973

Anthropology

✔ **Being Maasai** *Thomas Spear and Richard Waller (eds.) 1993 (see 'Kenya')*

Autobiography/Biography

Memoirs of an Arabian Princess: an Autobiography *Emily Ruete 1907*
The author was daughter of one of the rulers of Zanzibar; she married a German and left for Europe. The book gives an interesting insight into the lives of women in Zanzibar at the time.

Fiction

✔ **Paradise** *Abdulrazek Gurnah 1994*
Set around Zanzibar in the early years of European involvement. Yusuf, a young Muslim boy, is taken into the service of his merchant uncle and we see Europeans, as colonizers, through his eyes.

The Wicked Walk *W.E. Mkufya 1977*
Set in contemporary Dar-es-Salaam, the novel deals with the themes of prostitution and corrupt management and the attempts to deal with them.

Three Solid Stones *Martha Mvungi 1975*
Twelve oral tales from the traditions of the Wahehe and the Wabena which are recounted here in a simple and direct style.

Dying in the Sun *Peter K. Palangyo 1968*
A son alienated from his father tries to piece together a new life after his father's death. Set in post-independence Tanzania, the novel is more about the universal suffering of man.

Guides

✔ **Guide to Tanzania. A Bradt Guide** *Philip Briggs 1993*

✔ **Guide to Zanzibar and Pemba. A Bradt Guide** *David Else 1993*

✔ **Spectrum Guide to Tanzania** *edited by Camerapix 1992*

✔ **Kenya and Northern Tanzania. The Thornton Cox Guide** *Richard Cox 1992 (1986)*

History

Princes of Zinji: the Rulers of Zanzibar *Genesta Hamilton 1957*
The reign of Seyyid bin Sultan and back-

ground information on life under Omani in-fluence.

Zanzibar: its History and its People
W.H. Ingrams   1967
A detailed history of Zanzibar.

Photography

✔ **Journey Through Tanzania**
Mohamed Amin, Duncan Willetts and Peter Marshall   1988 (1984)
Tanzania is the largest country in East Africa; it has the Indian Ocean on one side and the natural beauty of Mount Kilimanjaro, Lake Tanganyika, Lake Victoria, the Serengeti and Ngorongoro. This book shows a cross section of all of these as well as the people and the way they live.

Maasai   Photographs by Carol Beckwith   Text by Tepilit Ole Saitoti (see 'Kenya')

✔ **Ngorongoro**   Reinhard K kel   1992
A magnificently lavish photographic book.

Travel Literature

The Lake Regions of Central Africa: a picture of exploration   Richard Burton
1961 (1860)
A description of Burton's journey with Speke in 1857–8 to Lake Tanganyika. He was an acute observer and writes in detail about the areas they crossed; since he was such an extraordinary linguist, he was able to record many of the conversations that he had with Arab traders.

Zanzibar: city, island and coast   Richard Burton   1967 (1872)
Burton gives an account of the main coastal towns as well as the islands and describes his visit to Usambara.

Heaven Has Claws   Adrian Conan Doyle
1953
Conan Doyle and his wife went sailing in the Indian Ocean in search of freedom. They started in the Red Sea and sailed to Mombasa before moving on to Zanzibar and getting a boat in which they sailed through the Mafia Channel and visited the east coast of Tanzania, Kilwa Kisiwani and the ruins of Songa Manra.

✔ **Dancing with the Dead**
Helena Drysdale (see 'Madagascar')

✔ **Filosofa's Republic**   Thursday Msigwa
(pseud. Anthony Daniels)   1992
Banned in Lambeth, Anthony Daniels has only recently revealed that he is the author of this controversial book about Tanzania. The book is written as if by a white visitor to Ngombia, a mythical republic, which has adopted Human Mutualism as its philosophy.

Isle of Cloves   F.D. Ommanney   1955
Ommanney was sent to Zanzibar by the Colonial Office to improve local methods of fishing, but here he mixes what he saw on the land with history and observations of Islam. He visited the leper colony on the island of Pemba and describes the rich sea life on the coral reefs.

Journal of the Discovery of the Source of the Nile   John Hanning Speke   1864
Speke played an important role in the British exploration of Tanganyika; he thought he had found the source of the Nile when he made his journey with Burton to Lake Victoria, but the two men never agreed on the issue. Speke returned in 1860–2 to pursue the matter, following the Nile right up to the Mediterranean, but still failing to convince Burton. On the morning that Speke and Burton were going to debate the matter, Speke shot himself; it is not known whether this was suicide or an accident.

How I Found Livingstone   Henry Morton Stanley   1872
Stanley was given lavish support by his newspaper to find Livingstone in Central Africa in 1871–2. He set out from Zanzibar and crossed Tanganyika before encountering him and uttering the famous phrase 'Dr Livingstone, I presume?'

✔ **Through the Dark Continent**   Henry Morton Stanley   1878
The account of Stanley's second journey which began in 1874. He started in Zanzibar and crossed to Victoria Nyanza and into Uganda and to Lake Tanganyika before going into Zaire. Stanley encountered Tippu Tip, an important Arab trader, who eventually wrote his autobiography in Swahili; as a result of this meeting much new information came out of the expedition.

UGANDA
'But the forests of Uganda, for magnificence, for variety of form and colour, for profusion of brilliant life –plant, bird, insect, reptile, beast –for the vast scale and awful fecundity of the natural processes that are beheld at work, eclipsed, and indeed effaced, all previous

impressions.' Sir Winston Churchill *My African Journey* 1908

Fiction

Return to the Shadows
Robert Serumaga 1969
The idealistic Joe Musizi encounters many difficulties in the tough new world of independent Africa.

General Background

✔ **Changing Uganda** *Holger Bernt Hansen and Michael Twaddle (eds.) 1991*
A series of articles by a team of Ugandan and international scholars which analyse the situation in Uganda today from many different angles.

Guides

✔ **Guide to Uganda. A Bradt Guide**
Philip Briggs 1994

History

The Albert N'yanza. Great Basin of the Nile and Explorations of the Nile Sources *Samuel White Baker 1866*
An account of the equatorial lake system from which the Egyptian Nile derives its source. Baker discovered that the lake-sources of Central Africa support the *life* of

Egypt by supplying a stream throughout the year, but that this source unaided could never overflow the banks of the Nile creating the fertile delta that it does.

Uganda *Harold Ingrams 1960*
In a series called the 'Corona Library' the book contains descriptions of how the people live and the way they are governed and has many maps and photographs illustrating the text.

Natural History

Birds of Kenya and Uganda *Frederick Jackson 1938 (see 'Kenya')*

Travel Literature

✔ **Touching the Moon** *John Preston 1991 (1990)*
Inspired by a childhood dream, John Preston went to Uganda to see the fabled Mountains of the Moon. Inevitably, in post-Idi Amin Uganda, what he found was incredible poverty and corruption not the romance he was looking for. However he manages to turn his experiences into an extremely funny and informative book.

Journal of the Discovery of the Source of the Nile *John Hanning Speke 1864 (see Tanzania)*

✔ **Through the Dark Continent** *Henry Morton Stanley 1878 (see 'Tanzania')*

Central and Southern Africa

Art

Southern Africa During the Iron Age. Ancient Peoples and Places *Brian M. Fagan 1965*
The last two thousand years of the prehistoric period in South Africa, when farmers and metalworkers first settled there. Descriptions of the Iron Age peoples of Rhodesia, South Africa and Zambia. When the book was written much of Southern Africa had not been explored by archaeologists or ethno-historians making this a somewhat patchy appraisal. Illustrated throughout by line drawings.

Fiction

✔ **Collected African Stories**
Doris Lessing. Vol.1 This Was the Old Chief's Country 1992 (1951) and vol.2 The Sun Between Their Feet
Doris Lessing was brought up in Southern Rhodesia and her stories are from childhood experience; many of them are set in Zimbabwe and South Africa. She states in the preface that she really enjoyed writing the stories and that enjoyment shines through her prose.

✔ **A Bend in the River** *V.S. Naipaul*
1979
Salim, whose forebears had come to the east coast of Africa, is offered a business in central Africa, which he accepts realizing that it is up to him to make what he can of his life. He travels to the town on a bend in the river and this is the story of his life as a trader in the town which comes vividly alive in Naipaul's prose.

✔ **Penguin Book of Southern African Stories** *1985*
This diverse and varied anthology compares the different literatures of Southern Africa and includes stories from Botswana, Lesotho, Malawi, Namibia, South Africa, Swaziland and Zimbabwe.

General Background

✔ **Central and Southern Africa. Travel Resource Guide** *Louis Taussig*
1995

Guides

✔ **Backpacker's Africa. East and Southern Africa for Walkers and Overland Travellers** *Hilary Bradt 1994 (1977)*

✔ **A Traveller's Companion to Southern Africa** *Mike Crewe-Brown 1990*
Arranged in routes, the guide picks out the worthwhile hotels, restaurants and tourist attractions.

✔ **Guide to Southern African Safari Lodges** *Peter Joyce 1993*
A guide to private lodges, rest camps, bush camps and private hotels in South Africa, Namibia, Botswana, Zimbabwe and Zambia.

✔ **Discovery Guide to Southern Africa** *Pamela McKinstry 1994*
A guide to Botswana, Namibia, South Africa and Swaziland.

✔ **Central Africa. A Travel Survival Kit** *Alex Newton 1993 (1989)*

Traveller's Guide: Central and Southern Africa *1990*

History

The Remarkable Expedition
Olivia Manning 1947
When Emin Pasha arrived in Khartoum in 1875, he said he was a Turk, but he was soon found out to be a Prussian doctor named

Schnitzer who spoke Arabic, Turkish, Albanian, French, Italian, Latin and Greek, who played good chess and excellent piano. He was disillusioned by his early life and eventually found his way to Central Africa. Olivia Manning tells the story and his eventual rescue from Equatorial Africa by Stanley.

Leisure

✔ **The Guide to Backpacking and Wilderness Trails** *Willie and Sandra Olivier*
1989
Information on guided wilderness trails, backpacking areas, safaris and pony trekking.

Natural History

Field Guide to the Snakes and other Reptiles of Southern Africa *Bill Branch*
1988
There are almost 400 species of reptile in Southern Africa and this guide describes each, with a physical description, habitat and range and information about the biology and breeding habits. There are distribution maps and numerous colour plates. Comprehensive and useful.

Guide to the Sharks and Rays of Southern Africa *L.J.V. Compagno, D.A. Ebert and M.J. Smale 1989*
The authors write reassuringly about the low instance of shark attacks, but when you see the immense variety of sharks and rays illustrated in this guide you would inevitably feel wary about venturing into the sea. An informative and useful book.

Robert's Birds of Southern Africa
Gordon Lindsay Maclean 1988
The standard and definitive work on the birds of Southern Africa, but too heavy to take on a trip.

A Field Guide to the Trees of Southern Africa *Eve Palmer 1977*

✔ **Field Guide to the Birds of Southern Africa** *Ian Sinclair 1985*
A handy and reliable pocket guide.

✔ **Field Guide to the Mammals of Southern Africa** *Chris and Tilde Stuart*
1988
Colour photographs, identification pointers and detailed descriptions of each animal make this an extremely useful and easy to use handbook.

Travel Literature

Zanzibar to Timbuktoo   *Anthony Daniels*
(see 'West Africa')

✔ **The Ukimwi Road**   *Dervla Murphy*
1993
Dervla Murphy made a 3000 mile bicycle journey from Kenya through Uganda, Tanzania, Malawi and Zambia to Zimbabwe. 'Ukimwi' of the title is AIDS and Dervla Murphy discussed the implications of this devastating disease. She discovered that some communities in Africa are reverting to traditional ways of organizing village life.

✔ **Journey to the Vanished City**   *Tudor Parfitt   1992*
A fascinating journey in which Tudor Parfitt attempts to track down the origins of the Lemba tribe, who claim to be Jewish, and their lost city of Sena. His journey takes him through South Africa, Zimbabwe, Malawi and Tanzania. No one knows who were the architects and builders of Great Zimbabwe; interesting theories as to its origins abound and Parfitt adds others.

Travel and Adventure in South East Africa   *Frederick Courtenay Selous   1984 (1893)*
Selous was in Zimbabwe before, during and after colonization.

✔ **Through the Dark Continent**   *Henry Morton Stanley   1988 (1878)*
This was the expedition in which Stanley explored the great lakes of Central Africa, searched for the sources of the Nile and traced the unknown Congo River to the sea. His followers were decimated by disease but he persevered, being nicknamed Bula Matari 'the rock breaker'. The book is packed with exciting accounts of his exploits but also detailed descriptions of the people, flora and fauna that he encountered.

Following the Equator   *Mark Twain   1897*
Twain started a lecture trip which took him round the world from Paris via America. He sails from Ceylon to Mauritius via Mozambique to South Africa. His funny and acute observations and anecdotes make you wish that he had written more about South Africa. He tells one story of a famous doctor in Cape Town who was wild but well respected and for some odd reason never got into trouble despite endlessly misbehaving. It was only on the doctor's death that it was discovered he was a woman in exile from a scandal in England.

ANGOLA
'The Countrie is Champain plaine, and drie blacke earth, and yeeldeth verie little Corne.' Anthony Knivet, 1601, in *Purchas his Pilgrimes* 1625

Fiction

South of Nowhere   *Antonio Lobo Antunes*
1983 (1979)
The narrator leaves Portugal for Angola on a ship full of troops and in the process 'becomes a man'. Good descriptions of the torpor, lassitude and heat felt in Africa.

Sacred Hope   *Agostinho Neto   1974*
Neto was a medical doctor and writer who became the first president of Angola; his collection of poems which are very politically committed speak of love, harmony and freedom and the humiliations caused by colonialism.

Travel Literature

Another Day of Life   *Ryszard Kapuscinski*
1988 (1976)
Kapuscinski went to Angola during the last months of Portuguese rule, when many internal factions were fighting for power and both South Africa and Cuba were involved in propping up their protégés. His observations of what he terms 'the incommunicable image of war' are as enlightening as it is possible to be about the evil of war.

BOTSWANA
'The miraculous thing about the Kalahari is that it is a desert only in the sense that it contains no permanent surface water. Otherwise its deep fertile sands are covered with grass glistening in the wind like fields of gallant corn.' Laurens van der Post *The Lost World of the Kalahari* 1958

Fiction

When Rain Clouds Gather   *1969*
Maru   *Bessie Head   1972*
Novels which examine the relationship between the Bushmen and the African villagers.

Whites   *Norman Rush   1987*
Short stories by a US Peace Corps worker about the lives of whites in Botswana.

Love on the Rocks *Andrew Sesinyi 1981*
Pule Nkgogan is driven from home by family conflicts and tries to start a new life in the city, only to discover the difficulties of breaking with the past.

✔ **A Story Like the Wind** *Laurens Van der Post 1987 (1972)*
A bushman is rescued from a horrible death and life for Francois immediately changes dramatically as he meets and becomes friends with many new people; all this within the context of the African bush. A novel which highlights the conflicts between African and European cultures.

Food

✔ **Cooking in Botswana** *Pauline Cuzen 1983*
Recipes compiled by different people and brought up to date so that they can be made with current ingredients.

Guides

✔ **Zimbabwe, Botswana and Namibia. A Travel Survival Kit** *Deanna Swaney and Myra Shackley 1992*

✔ **Zimbabwe and Botswana. The Rough Guide** *Barbara McCrea and Tony Pinchuck 1993 (1990)*

Visitor's Guide to Botswana *Mike Main and John and Sandra Fowkes 1987*
The Visitor's Guides to the various countries in Southern Africa are practical and basic and when they were written were often the only ones available. They are all by people who know and love the countries and have useful and detailed directions.

History

History of Botswana *T. Tlou and A. Campbell 1984*
A school textbook, but about the only history available.

Photography

✔ **Kalahari** *Jacques Gilliéron 1989*
Photographs of the animals and landscape of the Kalahari. Very little text.

The Bushmen *Photographs by Peter Johnson and Anthony Bannister Text by Alf Wannenburgh 1979*
A record of a fast disappearing group of hunter-gatherers who are inexorably being drawn into the big cities. The book begins with sixty pages of text and is followed by photographs.

✔ **Okavango. Africa's Last Eden** *F. Lanting 1993*
A large and colourful photographic book.

✔ **Okavango. Jewel of the Kalahari** *Karen Ross 1992 (1987)*
A book based on the three part television series which shows the mass of wildlife in the Okavango Delta; the fragile environment is fast disappearing and this book explains why.

Travel Literature

✔ **Cry of the Kalahari** *Mark and Delia Owens 1988 (1984)*
In 1974 the authors sold everything they possessed in America in order to go and study wildlife in the Kalahari. They spent seven years living and researching there before returning to the States where they published scientific papers. This is the account of their everyday existence, which was often very hard, in the desert and among the animals.

✔ **The Lost World of the Kalahari** *Laurens Van der Post 1992 (1958)*
The Bushmen had been driven by successive invaders of South Africa into the waterless Kalahari desert. Van der Post rediscovers the Bushmen with their cave art, music-making and hunting skills and records what he found of a fast disappearing culture. *The Heart of the Hunter* is a sequel and goes into much more detail about the life and lore of the Bushmen as well as much soul searching about how badly the Bushmen were treated. [Colin Thubron]

BURUNDI

The Last Elephant. An African Quest *Jeremy Gavron 1993*
There has been one solitary elephant left to wander round Burundi for the last several years. No one knows where it came from, but it is left alive since killing it would be taboo; by killing the last of a species, an African would lose a fragment of his belief system. Only the first part of this book is about Burundi.

CENTRAL AFRICAN REPUBLIC

'It was the only place in the world where I have seen almost the entire French community drunk at 10 o'clock in the morning.' (Bangui) Negley Farson *Behind God's Back* 1940

CONGO

'In the management of a bargain I should back the Congoese native against Jew or Christian, Parsee or Banyan, in all the round world.'
Henry Morton Stanley *The Congo* 1885

Fiction

✔ **Heart of Darkness** *Joseph Conrad* 1967 (1902)
Conrad went to the Belgian Congo in 1890 to command a river steamer, an event which physically weakened, but psychologically strengthened him. In Conrad's words *'Heart of Darkness* is experience, too; but it is experience pushed a little (and only very little) beyond the actual facts of the case for the perfectly legitimate, I believe, purpose of bringing it home to the minds and bosoms of the readers. There it was no longer a matter of sincere colouring. It was like another art altogether. That sombre theme had to be given a sinister resonance, a tonality of its own, a continued vibration that, I hoped, would hang in the air and dwell on the ear after the last note had been struck.'

Travel Literature

Travels in the Congo *André Gide* 1986 (1927) (see 'Chad')

✔ **East Along the Equator**
Helen Winternitz 1987
The author travelled east along the Congo river by boat to Kisangani in Zaire, before striking out over land through the Ituri rain forest, visiting the Pygmies and travelling past the Mountains of the Moon and into the Great Rift Valley. She contrasts well the abundance of nature with the greed of mankind and her book contains politics, history and ecology.

LESOTHO

'Basutholand is the Switzerland of South Africa, and very appropriately, is the part of South Africa where the old inhabitants, defended by their hills, have retained the largest meaasure of freedom.' James Bryce *Impressions of South Africa* 1897

Fiction

Wrath of the Ancestors and other plays *Bob Leshoai* 1972
The writer is believed to be his people's first writer in English. He has also published a collection of freely adapted traditional tales *Masilio's Adventures and Other Stories* (1968)

MALAWI

Autobiography

I Will Try *Legson Kayira* 1967
The author walked 2500 miles across Africa in search of an American education, eventually ending up at the University of Washington.

Fiction

The Looming Shadow *(1968)*
The Detainee *Legson Kayira* *(1974)*
A novel of village life and feuding and a novel about dictatorship.

Jungle Lovers *Paul Theroux* 1982 (1971)
A comedy about love and guerilla war set in Malawi. Calvin Mullet of Homemakers International is taken prisoner by the ruthless Marais and inevitably his life gets intertwined with theirs.

Guides

✔ **Malawi** *A. Hülsbömer and P. Belker* 1991
Translated from the German.

✔ **Visitor's Guide to Malawi** *Martine Maurel* 1990

Travel Literature

✔ **Venture to the Interior** *Laurens Van der Post* 1992 (1952)
After the war Van Der Post was sent by the British to what was then Nyasaland to explore the region around Mount Mlanje and

the Nyika plateau area to obtain information about these remote areas. As in his later books he is introspective and questions his own motives for wanting to go; this inner journeying is accompanied by interesting descriptions of what he sees. The book starts with a quote by Sir Thomas Browne 'We carry with us the wonders we seek without us: there is all Africa and her prodigies in us.'

MOZAMBIQUE

'Mozambique is a curious mixture – Shangri La with a bullwhip behind the door.' John Gunther *Inside Africa* 1955

Fiction

The Returning Hunter   *Mario J. Azevedo   1978*
The author was born in Mozambique and set his novella there. Bento, a Portuguese African, has his confidence in his colonial government shattered.

Guides

✔ **Guide to Mozambique. A No Frills Bradt Guide**   *Bernhard Skrodzki   1994*

Politics

Mozambique: São Tomé and Príncipe
Jens Erik Torp and L.M. Denny and Donald I. Ray 1989
There is so little on Mozambique that this has been included; a book which is in the Marxist Régimes series of politics, economics and society. A serious introduction to the country by people who know the areas well.

NAMIBIA

'This hilly capital [Windhoek] is God's gift to the picture postcard industry. Its sky is

just that incredible blue.' Negley Farson *Behind God's Back* 1940

Guides

✔ **Guide to Namibia and Botswana**
(Pub. Bradt) Chris McIntyre and Simon Atkins   1991

✔ **Insight Guide Namibia**   *1993*

✔ **Visitor's Guide to Namibia**   *Willie and Sandra Olivier   1989*

✔ **Zimbabwe, Botswana and Namibia. A Travel Survival Kit**   *Deanna Swaney and Myra Shackley   1992*

History

The Devils are Among Us   *Denis Herbstein and John Evenson   1989*
The story behind the eventual South African withdrawal from Namibia. The book exposes the brutality of the occupation and the extraordinary resistance of the Namibian people to the occupying army.

RWANDA

Anthropology

✔ **The Dark Romance of Dian Fossey**   *Harold Hayes   1992 (1990)*
Hayes discovers what Dian Fossey was really like. He describes her early life in Kentucky and her turbulent love life as well as her work with the gorillas. The film *Gorillas in the Mist* was largely based on Hayes' article published in *Life* magazine, but in this book he has uncovered much more material.

Travel Literature

The Frozen Leopard   *Aaron Latham (see 'Kenya')*

South Africa

'The light in South AfricaAfrica . . . replaces architecture.' Cyril Connolly *The Evening Colonnade* 1973

Autobiography

✔ **White Boy Running**   Christopher Hope
1991 (1988)
Christopher Hope returned to his native South Africa in 1987 to cover the May election. He tried to make sense of what he saw but the more he saw the more nonsensical it all seemed; he traces his childhood and describes the South Africa of the 1950s and using straight reporting writes about the madness of the modern South Africa which he found in the 1980s.

✔ **My Traitor's Heart**   Rian Malan   *1990*
An extraordinarily powerful book about the reality of being brought up in South Africa. Malan left South Africa for America, but returned after eight years to face up to what he had left. He is extremely tough on his conscience and on himself with the result that he has produced an honest, moving and instructive book. 'I'm bored with the torrent of travel books about gimmicky journeys, and much prefer to read a book that attempts to get into the heart of a place. Such a book is *My Traitor's Heart* – brilliantly paced, beautifully written, and a revelation about both black and white South Africa.' (John Hatt)

✔ **Journey Continued**   Alan Paton   *1989 (1988)*
This volume of autobiography begins in 1948, the year that *Cry the Beloved Country* (q.v.) was published. Paton died before it was published but he writes about literature and politics, both of which played such an important part in his life, in a direct and simple style which shows a deep understanding of South Africa.

Fiction

✔ **A Dry White Season**   *1989 (1979)*
✔ **Rumours of Rain**   André Brink   *1984 (1978)*
André Brink was born in South Africa and now teaches modern literature and drama at Rhodes University. His novels are all set in South Africa and he uses real events making his fiction seem very true to life.

The Trap and a Dance in the Sun
Dan Jacobson   1988 (1955)
Although these novels were written in the 1950s, they are as relevant today as they were then; Jacobson was inspired by the bleak and forlorn landscapes around his home town of Kimberley in the Northern Cape and uses this setting to describe the issues between blacks and whites living uneasily together.

✔ **Cry, The Beloved Country**
Alan Paton   1988 (1948)
Even today this book remains one of the classics about racial tension in South Africa. In Johannesburg a father looking for his delinquent son encounters the worlds of murder, prostitution, racial hatred and eventually reconciliation. The simplicity and compassion of the prose make it an extremely moving book.

✔ **Mittee**   Daphne Rooke   *1991 (1951)*
A best seller when it was published, this novel set in late nineteenth-century Transvaal describes the intense love–hate relationship between Selina, a young servant girl, and Mittee her mistress who both vie for the love of the same man.

✔ **Flamingo Feather**   Laurens Van der Post   *1992 (1955)*
A story of international intrigue about how a rich white South African foils a Soviet plot to flame a co-ordinated tribal revolution.

Guides

✔ **Bradt Guide to South Africa**   Philip Briggs   *1991*

✔ **Cadogan Guide Africa: South Africa**   *1994*

✔ **South Africa, Lesotho and Swaziland. Travel Survival Kit**   Richard Everist and Jon Murray   *1993*

✔ **Traveller's Guide to South Africa**
Peter Joyce   1992
The same kind of format as an Insight guide with colour pictures scattered throughout the text, however, this guide bills itself as 'first and foremost a functional guide'. It includes brief profiles of South Africa's land neighbours: Namibia, Botswana, Lesotho, Swaziland, Mozambique and Zimbabwe.

History

Hidden Lives, Hidden Deaths
Victoria Brittain   1990 (1988)
The author has travelled as a journalist over much of Africa; in this book she exposes the reality of how the South African government really behaves and how so much of what it does is covered up by the United States and Britain.

The Washing of the Spears
Donald Morris   1978 (1966)
Described by Colin Legum in *New Society* as 'enormously readable and tremendously exciting', *The Washing of the Spears* describes how Zulu power rose and fell in a period of just fifty years. 'But my own favourite book about the place is Donald Morris' *The Washing of the Spears*, about the Zulu Wars.' (Jeremy Paxman)

✔ Shaka Zulu   *E.A. Ritter   1992 (1955)*
Shaka Zulu who founded the Zulu nation was a contemporary of Napoleon; within the space of twelve years he organized an army and conquered an area larger than Europe. His exploits had been handed down by word of mouth, but are recorded here by an author who grew up with the Zulus and gained their trust and respect.

✔ The Mind of South Africa
Alister Sparks   1991 (1990)
The author was formerly editor of the *Rand Daily Mail* and in this book surveys the rise and fall of apartheid. He analyses the history, culture and warped mythology of apartheid and the reasons why it still has such a powerful hold. 'The best shortish and easily comprehensible history of that country.' (Jeremy Paxman)

A History of South Africa
Leonard Thompson   1990
A new and fresh look at South African history written by an eminent professor at Yale; it is objective and focuses primarily on the black majority rather than the white minorities. Authoritative and full of insight.

✔ White Tribe Dreaming
Marq de Villiers   1990 (1987)
The history of South Africa traced through the author's Afrikaner ancestors and family who arrived in South Africa in 1688. It is a compassionate and illuminating attempt by a white liberal to understand the roots of apartheid; the book won the Alan Paton prize.

Natural History

Jock of the Bushveld   *Sir Percy Fitzpatrick*
1925 (1907)
Life could be very lonely in the South African Bush at the turn of the century; one way of dealing with this was to have a dog. In this case 'Jock' became the narrator's best friend and his exploits are recounted here in a lively way. The original illustrations were by E. Caldwell.

✔ South African Eden. The Kruger National Park   *James Stevenson-Hamilton*
1993 (1937)
The story of the founding of the Kruger National Park told by the man who was its first warden.

✔ Field Guide to the Wild Flowers of the Witwatersrand and Pretoria Region   *Braam van Wyk and Sasa Malan   1988*
The 763 species in the guide are divided into colour groups and within the colour groups into families. Each species is illustrated by a colour photograph and line drawings of the leaves accompany the concise text. A glossary to the terms used and indexes to both the scientific names and Afrikaans names complete this useful guide.

Photography

✔ This Is South Africa   *Peter Borchert*
1993
An illustrated book covering some of the scenery and natural history of South Africa.

✔ South Africa in Focus   *Willem Drechsel (ed.)   1992*
A well illustrated book full of text, accompanied by small photographs, showing the many faces of South Africa.

Travel Literature

Impressions of South Africa   *James Bryce   1897*
Bryce travelled from Cape Town to Fort Salisbury in Mashonaland in 1895. The book is not a narration of his journey but is divided into various sections: the physical character of the country, the characteristics of the people, the history of the natives and of the European settlers, the present conditions and the economic resources.

✔ Innocents in Africa   *Drury Pifer   1994*
The author's father, a young, idealistic newly-married mining engineer, went to South Africa in the 1930s. He was soon caught between the hostility of the Afri-

kaners and the arrogance of the British, and the new 'apartheid'; however, he persisted and brought up his family there.

SWAZILAND

'In all Africa there is no more vividly African place than Swaziland.'
James Morris *Swaziland, Places* 1972.

Fiction

Tell Me No More *Senzenjani Lukhele* *1980*
The story of a court case and the family problems that ensue because of Gugu interfering in a village affair and subsequently being banished by her adoptive father.

ZAIRE

Anthropology

The Forest People *Colin Turnbull* *1988 (1961)*
The Bambuti, the pygmies, who live in the forest in north-east Zaire are an ancient people who were mentioned by both Homer and Aristotle. Turnbull spent a long time living in the forest with them writing this book for the lay reader, as well as his more serious anthropological studies. Turnbull conveys the pygmies love of the forest as well as his intense love and friendship for them.

Fiction

✔ **A Burnt Out Case** *Graham Greene 1992 (1960)*
Greene went to what was then the Belgian Congo with an idea for a novel in mind but on his return to England found the writing of *A Burnt Out Case* very depressing. Querry, a famous but disillusioned architect arrives at a leper colony and is diagnosed as the mental equivalent of a 'burnt out case'. However as he throws himself into work with the lepers he begins to get better, but then his identity is discovered by the white community. Full of thought-provoking ideas.

General Background

✔ **The Return of Eva Peron**
V.S. Naipaul 1988 (1980)
The last two essays in this book are called *A New King for the Congo: Mobutu and the*

Nihilism of Africa and *Conrad's Darkness*. Having examined Mobutu's society and the legacy left by colonialism, Naipaul reflects on Conrad's reactions to a similar society.

Guide

✔ **Zaire** *Christa Mang 1991*
A small practical guide translated from the German.

Travel Literature

Back to the Congo *Lieve Joris 1992 (1987)*
The Amsterdam based author's uncle had been a missionary in the Belgian Congo. She was intrigued by his experiences and travels to Zaire: she visits his old missionary haunts and embarks on journeys of her own. Much has changed, but much, including the attitudes of many of the white colonials she encounters, has stayed the same.

A Congo Diary *V.S. Naipaul 1980*
A well-observed short essay on the Congo, published in a limited edition.

✔ **In Southern Light** *Alex Shoumatoff 1988 (1986) (see 'Amazonia' – 'South America – Amazonia')*
The second half of Shoumatoff's book tells of his trek into the heart of the Ituri Forest where the BaMbuti and Efe pygmies live.

Through the Dark Continent *Henry Morton Stanley 1878 (see 'Tanzania')*

East Along the Equator *Helen Winternitz (see 'Congo')*

ZAMBIA

'The capital, Lusaka, looks like a Wild West set in early, shabby movies.' John Gunther *Inside Africa* 1955

Fiction

The Tongue of the Dumb *Dominic Mulaisho 1971*
A symbolic novel about the struggles by the new élite against the traditional powers of the chiefs, written from a very westernized viewpoint. In his second novel *The Smoke That Thunders* (1979), the author had become economic advisor to President Kaunda and he sets the book in a mythical country between Rhodesia and Zambia.

Natural History

✔ **Survivor's Song**   *Delia and Mark Owens   1993 (1992)*
The authors were expelled from Botswana after writing *Cry of the Kalahari*. They went to the North Luangwa Valley in Zambia where they discovered that the locals lived by poaching elephants. This is their account of how they tried to change the villagers' attitude to poaching.

Photography

Zambia   *Photographs by Ian Murphy, Richard Vaughan (ed.)   n.d.*
A cross section of the whole country showing as many urban scenes as rural ones; the photographs were taken over a four-year period by Ian Murphy who travelled the length and breadth of the country. So little has been written about Zambia that the text in this book is important as reference.

ZIMBABWE

Art & Archaeology

The Painted Caves   *Peter Garlake   1987*
An illustrated look at San rock art in Zimbabwe.

Fiction

Nervous Conditions   *Tsitsi Dangarembga   1988*
About growing up in colonial Rhodesia.

The Grass is Singing   *Doris Lessing   1973*
A depiction of white Rhodesia with powerful descriptions of the physical landscape.

The House of Hunger   *Dambudzo Marechera   1978*
This collection of short stories won the 1979 Guardian Fiction Prize. Angela Carter wrote: 'But it is rare to find a writer for whom imaginative fiction is such a passionate and intimate process of engagement with the world.'

Bones   *Chenjerai Hove   1991*
Experiences of the war; also by Hove is *Shadows* a story of lovers who choose death.

The Mourned One   *(1975)*
Year of the Uprising   *Stanlake Samkange (1978)*
History and fiction are melded together. *Year of the Uprising* is set in 1896, the time of the uprising between the Matabele and the Mashona. *The Mourned One* is the narrative written by 'Ocky' (Muchemwa) looking back over his life while awaiting execution in a Salisbury jail in the 1930s.

Food

✔ **A Zimbabwean Cookery Book**
Yvonne Hayward (ed.)   1984 (1967)
A collection of 87 recipes.

General Background

✔ **African Laughter**   *Doris Lessing   1993 (1992)*
Doris Lessing visited Zimbabwe four times between 1982 and 1992 and interviewed many people, some of whom had recently returned disillusioned from South Africa. An excellent introduction to the country.

Guides

✔ **Guide to Zimbabwe and Botswana. A Bradt No Frills Guide**   *David Else   1994*

✔ **Zimbabwe and Botswana. The Rough Guide**   *Barbara McCrea and Tony Pinchuck   1993 (1990)*

✔ **Discovery Guide to Zimbabwe**
Melissa Shales   1993

✔ **Spectrum Guide to Zimbabwe**
compiled and edited by Camerapix   1991

✔ **Zimbabwe, Botswana and Namibia. Travel Survival Kit**   *Deanna Swaney and Myra Shackley   1992*

History

Zimbabwe: A New History for Primary Schools   *David Beach   1986 (1982)*
A readable history spanning 15,000 years.

None But Ourselves. Masses vs Media in the Making of Zimbabwe   *Julie Frederikse   1982*
Interviews, quotes and photographs from the media.

Photography

✔ **Journey Through Zimbabwe**
Mohamed Amin, Duncan Willetts and Brian Tetley 1990
Over 150 colour photographs of the wilderness and the animals that inhabit it, Lake Kariba (at 280 kilometres long the largest

manmade lake), flora, botanical parks and the cities. Ample text accompanies the glossy pictures.

✔ **Zimbabwe**   *Photographs by Ian Murphy Text by Richard Vaughan   1991*
The book covers every aspect of life in Zim-babwe. Scenes of wildlife and scenery are of course included but there is a great emphasis on showing how the country works, by including many photographs of people and their work. This makes it much more interesting than most other 'coffee table' books.

African Islands

General

Pirates of the Eastern Seas 1618–1723
Charles Gray   1971 (1933)
Piracy in the Indian Ocean was rife at this period; crews of pirates from Réunion, the Comoro Islands, Mauritius and Madagascar preyed on ships which were engaged in trade with India and the spice-producing islands of South Asia.

Guides

✔ **The Complete Guide to the Southwest Indian Ocean**   *Iain Walker 1993*
A guide to the following island groups: Comores, Madagascar, Mauritius, Réunion and the Seychelles.

MADAGASCAR

'Magastar, one of the greatest and richest Isles of the World, three thousand miles in circuit, inhabited by Saracens, governed by foure old men.' Marco Polo *Purchas his Pilgrimes* 1625

Guides

✔ **Guide to Madagascar. A Bradt Guide**   *Hilary Bradt   1992 (1988)*

✔ **Madagascar and Comoros. Travel Survival Kit**   *Deanna Swaney   1993 (1989)*

History

Madagascar Rediscovered
Mervyn Brown   1978
Mervyn Brown traces the history of Madagascar from its origins to the recovery of independence in 1960 in a clear and objective manner. After the French conquest in 1895 most contacts with non-French speaking countries were severed and the opening of the Suez Canal meant that Madagascar was no longer on major shipping routes so that there was very little written in English; Mervyn Brown here rediscovers the past and varied history of the island.

History of Madagascar   *Rev. William Ellis 1838*
(subtitled: Comprising also The Progress of the Christian Mission Established in 1818; and an Authentic Account of the Persecution and Recent Martyrdom of the Native Christians.)
Originally conceived as a history of the missions in Madagascar, it was then decided to include a history of the island from the earliest times. It became a much more comprehensive book containing chapters on the climate, natural history and native customs.

The Drama of Madagascar   *Sonia E. Howe   1938*
The author approached this book from a different viewpoint to most other histories of the island in that she writes about the role that Madagascar has played in history – the interrelation between it and Britain, France and Portugal. Madagascar owes its economic and historical interest solely to its geographical situation; it lay on the route to India and was therefore of vital importance to mariners of all nations.

Natural History

Zoo Quest to Madagascar
David Attenborough   1961
One of Attenborough's trips which was sponsored by the BBC to collect animals for the London Zoo. Many of the creatures that he returned with had never been seen alive in

England before; he also did a great deal of filming and recording of animal sounds.

A World Like Our Own Alison Jolly 1980
(Man and Nature in Madagascar) Alison Jolly is a biologist and she travelled the thousand mile length of Madagascar recording what she saw. Madagascar broke away from Africa one hundred million years ago and managed to preserve many of the species which eventually became extinct on the mainland.

Madagascar. A Natural History.
Ken Preston-Mafham 1991
Madagascar has many species of flora and fauna which do not exist anywhere else; this large format book with ample text and over 300 colour photographs shows many of them in their natural habitats.

A Naturalist in Madagascar
James Sibree 1915
(A Record of Observation Experiences and Impressions made during a period of over Fifty Years' Intimate Association with the Natives and Study of the Animal and Vegetable Life of the Island.)
Sibree was a missionary in Madagascar, but this book is an account of the natural history of the island rather than of his missionary work, which he considered had had enough written about it; the author was rare for his time in that he admits that he takes 'more delight in silently watching the birds . . . than in shooting them to add a specimen to a museum'.

Photography

✔ **Madagascar** Hilary Bradt (ed.) 1988
A collection of colour photographs and text by a number of experts on Madagascar, the world's fourth largest island.

Travel Literature

✔ **Dancing with the Dead**
Helena Drysdale 1991
Helena Drysdale's journey to Madagascar was made more interesting because she discovered that her family had had trading connections with the island in the nineteenth century. She and her husband travel from Zanzibar to the Comoro Islands and all over Madagascar by a variety of different kinds of transport which often seems very uncomfortable. They attend the fascinating death ritual *famadihana*, whereby ancestors are exhumed, in the middle of Madagascar.

✔ **Muddling Through in Madagascar**
Dervla Murphy 1990 (1985)
Dervla Murphy travelled through Madagascar with her fourteen-year-daughter Rachel; they encountered many disasters and mishaps on their journey, but maintained a curiosity about what they saw and who they met, so that you do get some idea of what the country is like.

The Great Red Island Arthur Stratton
1965 (1964)
A mixture of personal anecdote and history which jumps backwards and forwards in time in an opinionated way. A badly edited book which nonetheless contains some interesting information.

Lemurs of the Lost World Jane Wilson
1990
The 'Lost World' is the Ankàrana Massif in northern Madagascar which is hidden behind vertical cliffs and dense, thorny shrubs. Jane Wilson penetrated this area through sixty miles of caves and canyons and discovered a wealth of wildlife including lemurs, chamaeleons, blind fish, twenty-foot long crocodiles and six-inch hairy spiders. Good descriptions of the animals, the people, the trip and the realities of ecological fieldwork.

MAURITIUS

'This is, by heavens, a Paradise, and not without angels.' Theodore Hook, Letter to Charles Mathews. 24th March 1814

Art and Architecture

✔ **Living in Mauritius. Traditional Architecture of Mauritius** Photographs by Christian Vaisse 1990
A lavishly illustrated book showing the traditional architecture of Mauritius in colour photographs.

Fiction

The Hell-Hot Bungalow Azize Asgarally
1967
A play about a family quarrel; it was originally banned but when it was eventually performed was a great success.

Food

✔ **Genuine Cuisine of Mauritius**
Guy Félix 1988
African, European and Asian recipes are

combined to make up the Creole and Indian Ocean dishes.

Guides

✔ **Bradt Guide to Mauritius**
Royston Ellis   1990 (1988)

✔ **Moorland Visitor's Guide to Mauritius, Rodrigues and Réunion**
Katerina and Eric Roberts   1992

✔ **Mauritius, Réunion and Seychelles. Travel Survival Kit**   *Deanna Swaney and Robert Strauss   1993 (1989)*

Travel Literature

Island of the Swan   *Michael Malim   1952*
The Portuguese were the first to call Mauritius the 'Island of the Swan', although the origin of the name is unknown and it is thought unlikely that they ever went there. Following the Dutch withdrawal, the French rechristened it 'L'Isle de France', and held it until 1810 when it became British; the British returned La Réunion to France in 1816 but held on to Mauritius. The book is an account of a trip through the island and contains some fairly detailed historical background.

✔ **Darwin and the Beagle**   *Alan Moorehead   1969*
Darwin landed and collected specimens at Mauritius and the Bourbon Islands (Réunion) and kept detailed diaries of what he saw and found.

Mauritius   *Carol Wright   1974*
An account of the island's geology, early history, wildlife, people and landscape written in a straightforward way.

SEYCHELLES

Guides

✔ **Baedeker Seychelles**   *1992*

✔ **Mauritius, Réunion and Seychelles. A Travel Survival Kit**   *Deanna Swaney and Robert Shaw   1993*

✔ **Spectrum Guide to Seychelles**
edited by Camerapix   1991

Travel Literature

Beyond the Reefs   *William Travis   1990*
Beyond the Reefs (1959) and *Shark for Sale* (1961) are accounts of diving and sailing in the Indian Ocean. Travis left the RAF and flew small planes round the world before deciding to make his living by diving and shark fishing. He now lives in Samoa where he runs a fishing business.

THE
AMERICAS

USA

GENERAL

'We are a people who do not want to keep much of the past in our heads. It is considered unhealthy in America to remember mistakes, neurotic to think about them, psychotic to dwell on them.'
Lillian Hellman *Scoundrel Time* 1976

Anthropology

✔ **Native American Stories**
Joseph Bruchac 1991
A collection of myths drawn from the native cultures of North America.

✔ **Native American Mythology**
Page Bryant 1991
Myths, historical people and places are arranged alphabetically with a short entry about each.

✔ **North American Indians**
George Catlin 1989 (1841)
George Catlin's classic 'complete' account of the Plains Indians, at the height of their culture, was made by canoe and by horse during the 1830s.

Art, Architecture and Archaeology

✔ **Lost Cities of North and Central America** *David Hatcher Childress 1992 (see 'Central America')*
The author searches for lost cities in Texas, Arizona, New Mexico, the Mississippi Valley, Florida, New England, the Rockies and California.

✔ **Kingdoms of Gold, Kingdoms of Jade. The Americas Before Columbus**
Brian M. Fagan 1991
A well illustrated book which has chapters on Clovis and the Bison Hunters, the Coastal Peoples of the Far West and North, the Farmers and the Pueblos and Moundbuilders of the Southwest and East.

The New Moderns. From Late to Neo-Modernism *Charles Jencks 1990*
A large illustrated study of neo-modernist architecture with interviews with Philip Johnson, Peter Eisenman and Richard Meier.

Biography

Daughter of Earth *Agnes Smedley 1977 (1929)*
Agnes Smedley was born into a very poor family in Missouri in 1892. She educated herself and moved to New York where she worked for a birth-control magazine and was imprisoned for her involvement in the Indian nationalist cause. She lived in Berlin from 1921–8, in a disruptive relationship with an Indian revolutionary, which led to her interest in psychoanalysis. She wrote *Daughter of Earth* as a kind of therapy. In 1928 she went to China as a correspondent where she participated in most of the major events of the 1930s, becoming a friend of Mao's.

Fiction/Poetry

✔ **Stories** *Raymond Carver 1985*
'Read it. Read everything he wrote.' (Salman Rushdie).

✔ **The Penguin Book of American Short Stories** *James Cochrane (ed.) 1969*
The collection includes stories by Poe, Hawthorne, Melville, Twain, Henry James, Willa Cather, William Faulkner and John Updike.

✔ **Martin Chuzzlewit** *Charles Dickens 1991 (1843–4)*
Mark Tapley accompanied Martin on a voyage of self-discovery to America.

✔ **America** *Franz Kafka 1992 (1928)*
The story of Karl Rossman who is banished to America by his father, having been seduced by a servant girl, is a bewildering novel and a vehicle for Kafka's obsessions and beliefs.

✔ **On the Road** *Jack Kerouac 1991 (1957)*
The classic book about fifties underground America which has become the epitome of the Beat generation.

Food

✔ **The Joy of Cooking** *Irma Rombaugh*

✔ **The Silver Palate Cookbook**
Julee Rosso and Sheila Lukins 1982 (1979)
Recipes, menus and tips from the celebrated gourmet food shop in Manhattan.

General Background

The Moronic Inferno Martin Amis 1986
A collection of disparate pieces which Amis had written about America over the years for various newspapers and journals.

✔ **Talk About America 1951–1968**
Alistair Cooke 1981 (1968)
A selection of 'letters' on a wide-ranging number of subjects.

✔ **Slouching Towards Bethlehem**
Joan Didion 1993 (1961)
Passionate essays about the state of America in the 1960s.

✔ **Cities on a Hill** Frances Fitzgerald
1986 (1981)
An exploration of four contemporary, but very different, visionary communities, all of whom want to shake off the past and build anew: The Castro, Liberty Baptist, Sun City and Rajneeshpuram.

✔ **America. A User's Guide**
Simon Hoggart 1991 (1990)
Hoggart was fascinated by the 'ordinariness' of most Americans, despite the huge extremes and contrasts found there.

USA John Dos Passos 1976 (1938)
A trilogy written between 1930 and 1938 which aims to unravel the complicated first thirty years of the century.

Guides

✔ **Family USA** Frank Barrett 1993
Aimed at independent travellers who want to plan their own holiday, under whatever guise: how to get there, where to stay (self-catering and otherwise), how to get about; it also includes specialist and activity holidays.

✔ **USA and Canada. Travellers Survival Kit** Simon Calder 1993 (1985)

✔ **USA. The Rough Guide**
Samantha Cook, Jamie Jensen, Tim Perry and Greg Ward 1994

✔ **The National Trust Guide to Historic Bed and Breakfasts, Inns and Small Hotels** Suzanne G. Dane 1992
Five hundred historic establishments ranging from one-room guest houses to 100 room resorts, all with an individual feeling. Arranged by state.

✔ **Frommers USA '93–'94**

✔ **Frommer Where to Stay USA** 1993
(1974)

✔ **Insight Guide Crossing America**
1992

✔ **Elegant Small Hotels. A Connoisseur's Guide** Pamela Lanier 1993
(1986)
A guide to unique hotels – many of which have delicious food. Arranged by state.

✔ **Let's Go USA 1995**

✔ **Country Inns and Back Roads North America 1993–1994** Jerry Levitin
1993
A selection of 200 small inns and bed-and-breakfast establishments throughout North America.

✔ **USA By Rail. Plus Canada** John Pitt
1992
Each of the 28 long-distance routes is examined in detail and there is information about stations and hotels.

History

✔ **Hard Travellin'** Kenneth Allsop 1993
(1967)
Kenneth Allsop travelled 9,000 miles through America reconstructing the history of the migrant worker by following the old hobo routes.

✔ **America as Seen By Its First Explorers. The Eyes of Discovery**
John Bakeless 1989 (1950)
The book describes America region by region as it would have appeared to the first explorers and settlers.

✔ **The Penguin History of the United States of America** Hugh Brogan 1990
(1985)
A complete general history of the States, starting from early British colonization and going up to the fall of Richard Nixon. Brogan looks at the pre-Independence period from both the British and American points of view and shows how America developed so rapidly from such small beginnings to global dominance: 'A superb piece of work ... written with grace and style.' (J.K. Galbraith *The Sunday Times*)

✔ **Bury My Heart at Wounded Knee. An Indian History of the American West** Dee Brown 1990 (1970)
The epic bestseller which tells the Indian side of the story through the voices of chief-

tains such as Sitting Bull, Cochise, Crazy Horse and Geronimo.

✔ **Passage to America** *Terry Coleman*
1992 (1972)
Coleman uses original diaries and letters in his history of the two million people who were herded across the Atlantic during the last century.

Battle Cry of Freedom
James M. McPherson 1990 (1988)
A very readable history of the Civil War which explains the complex social, economic, political and military factors: 'Mr McPherson wears with equal ease the hats of biographer, economist, sociologist and military historian . . . Probably the best single-volume history of America's Civil War yet written.' (*Economist*)

✔ **The Great Explorers**
Samuel Eliot Morison 1986 (1978)
The great European voyages of discovery to the New World: Cabots, Verrazzano, Cartier, Gilbert, Frobisher, Davis, Columbus, Magellan and Drake.

Leisure

✔ **Rivers Running Free** *Judith Niemi and Barbara Wieser (eds.) 1992 (1987)*
A collection of writings spanning a century of women's canoeing adventures including trips on the Yukon River, the George River in Labrador, the Hudson and the Mississippi.

Natural History

✔ **Fodor's Guide to America's National Parks** *1994–5 1994*

Pilgrim at Tinker Creek *Annie Dillard 1990 (1974)*
The winner of the Pulitzer Prize in 1974 was described as 'one of the truly beautiful books of this or any other season' (*Publishers Weekly*). Dillard went on to write *An American Childhood, The Writing Life, Tickets for a Prayer Wheel, Holy the Firm, Living by Fiction* and *Teaching a stone to Talk*.

Field Guide to the Birds of North America *Jon L. Dunn and Eirik A.T. Blom*

A Sand County Almanac and Sketches Here and There *Aldo Leopold 1968 (1949)*
A classic book with natural history essays.

✔ **Crossing Open Ground** *Barry Lopez 1989 (1988)*
Essays which reflect the importance of nature, of landscape touching the soul and of friendship and community in present-day America.

Photography

✔ **America in Passing**
Henri Cartier-Bresson 1991
Cartier-Bresson's black and white photographs from all over America which were taken between the 1940s and the 1970s.

✔ **America** *1989*
Photographs and text, arranged by category. Published by Flint River.

Travel Literature

✔ **The Lost Continent. Travels in Small Town America** *Bill Bryson 1993 (1989)*
Born in Des Moines, Bryson left as soon as he could, but after ten years in England he was lured back and drove around small town America producing an hilarious acount of his travels: 'A savagely funny portrait of modern America as seen by expat Bill Bryson as he travels across the continent of his birth.' (*GQ*)

✔ **Coast to Coast. A Rock Fan's US Tour** *Andy Bull 1993*
Andy Bull determined to get to the roots of American popular music of the last forty years, went to Nashville, Memphis and California, met the real Peggy Sue and discovered where Roy Orbison's 'Only the Lonely' was composed.

✔ **American Notes** *Charles Dickens 1985 (1842)*
Dickens went to America in 1842, curious to find out what was happening with the 'new experiment'.

The American Scene *Henry James 1987 (1907)*
A collection of articles which were published in various magazines about New England, New York, Philadelphia, Baltimore, Washington, Richmond and Charleston. Includes portraits of many of the socialites who wintered in Florida at the turn of the century, especially in St Augustine and Palm Beach.

✔ **Peter Kalm's Travels in North America** *Peter Kalm 1987 (1770)*
The botanist Peter Kalm was sent to North America in 1747 to search for hardy plants to take back to Sweden. He spent three years travelling through New York, New Jersey, New England, Pennsylvania and southern Canada, observing not just natural history

but also food, language, architecture, climate, religion and fashion.

✔ **The Great American Bus Ride**
Irma Kurtz 1994 (1993)
The expatriate Irma Kurtz, armed only with the bare essentials, decided to explore America by Greyhound: 'The truth is, I am a hussy of low appetites who yearns shamelessly for rough travel . . . Greyhound and I were made for each other.' The minutiae of the habits of the people she meets are very well observed.

✔ **Blue Highways. A Journey into America** *William Least Heat-Moon 1993 (1983)*
After losing his job in a college in Missouri, the author drives through America in a half-ton Ford van tracking various ancestors and sensitively getting the best out of the people he meets: 'Least Heat-Moon is a witty, generous, sophisticated, and democratic observer. His modesty, his subtle, kindly humor, and his uncanny gift for catching good people at good moments make *Blue Highways* a joy to read.' (Annie Dillard)

✔ **The Great Divide** *Stephen Pern 1990 (1987)*
The Continental Divide runs for nearly 3,000 miles from Mexico to Canada; Pern spent six months following it on foot.

✔ **Hunting Mr Heartbreak**
Jonathan Raban 1991 (1990)
Setting out from Liverpool Docks, Jonathan Raban followed in the steps of Hector St John de Crèvecoeur and many other immigrants, in order to have a new look at what the immigrants experienced: 'He is most certainly the finest writer afloat since Conrad, and few landlubbers have equalled either his acuteness or his sense of style.' (Geoffrey Moorhouse *The Guardian*)

✔ **The Divine Supermarket. Travels in Search of the Soul of America**
Malise Ruthven 1991 (1989)
Malise Ruthven travelled in a camping van throughout America looking for its religious spirit since so many of the attitudes and beliefs of Americans are shaped by religions of every type and hue.

Travels with Charley *John Steinbeck 1990 (1962)*
Steinbeck travelled with his dog Charley for company, in a pick-up truck coast to coast, in order to reacquaint himself with his country; acute observations about America.

✔ **Roughing It** *Mark Twain 1985 (1872)*
A record of several years 'variegated vaga-

bonding' in the States. Twain writes about the growth and culmination of silver-mining fever in Nevada, which he reckons he is the first to do; inevitably he includes many interesting facts although does not want to write 'a pretentious history or a philosophical dissertation'.

✔ **The Plains Across. Emigrants, Wagon Trains and the American West**
John D. Unruh 1992 (1979)
The author uses contemporary newspapers, diaries, journals and letters to tell the story of the wagon train migrations across America in the middle of the last century.

✔ **States of Desire** *Edmund White 1986 (1980)*
White's purpose in travelling through America was to examine the lives and changes that had happened to homosexuals after the first decade of the gay liberation movements. He concentrates on New York and San Francisco.

No Particular Place to Go
Hugo Williams 1981
Hugo Williams crossed America from coast to coast, mostly by Greyhound, appearing at the odd poetry meeting and having a series of lurid adventures. Scintillating and funny prose.

NEW YORK CITY AND MID-ATLANTIC STATES: NEW YORK STATE, NEW JERSEY, PENNSYLVANIA

'The semi-colon of the Eastern seaboard– that's modern New Jersey.' Irvin S. Cobb
Some United States 1926

Fiction

✔ **Bullet Park** *John Cheever 1992 (1969)*
Life in suburban upstate New York; two disparate neighbours become inextricably linked because of their names – Eliot Nailles and Paul Hamme: 'In a class by itself, not only among Cheever's work but among all the novels I know'. (Joseph Heller) *Short Stories* [Jan Morris]

Ragtime *E.L. Doctorow 1975*
A mingling of fact and fiction about three families with totally different backgrounds who find their lives entwined in the era of ragtime in New York State.

An American Tragedy *Theodore Dreiser*
1978 (1925)
Set in upstate New York a young man murders a woman who gets in his way on his path to wealth.

Drums Along the Mohawk
Walter Dumaux Edmonds 1963 (1936)
A novel about upstate colonial New York.

✔ **The Great Gatsby** *F. Scott Fitzgerald*
1967 (1926)
Mostly set among the estates of Long Island; the mysterious Gatsby entertained lavishly in his fabulous Long Island house in order to impress a woman he had loved but who had subsequently married a rich good-for-nothing.

Legs *1983 (1975)*
Billy Phelan's Greatest Game *1983 (1978)*
Ironweed *1983 (1979) William Kennedy*
A cycle of novels set in the depression in Albany, New York.

Only Children *Alison Lurie 1979*
A Fourth of July weekend in the Catskills is beset with problems.

The Groves of Academe *Mary McCarthy 1952*
A detailed dissection of life at a small college in Pennsylvania.

Rich Man, Poor Man *Irwin Shaw 1970*
The fortunes of the Jordache family in New York State from the 1940s to 1970s.

The Hack *Wilfrid Sheed 1968*
A satirical novel about Catholicism set in New Jersey.

The Poorhouse Fair *John Updike 1977 (1959)*
An eccentric cast of characters in a New Jersey poorhouse. Updike's books set in Pennsylvania are: *Rabbit, Run* (1960), *Rabbit Redux* (1971) and *Rabbit is Rich* (1981).

Guides

✔ **Bed and Breakfast in the Mid-Atlantic States** *Bernice Chesler 1993*
Delaware, Maryland, New Jersey, New York, North Carolina, Pennsylvania, Virginia, Washington DC, West Virginia.

✔ **Fodor's Bed and Breakfasts and Country Inns: Mid-Atlantic Region**
1993
New York, Pennsylvania, New Jersey, Delaware, Maryland, Virginia, West Virginia.

✔ **Fodor's Vacations on the Jersey Shore** *(undated) 1991*

✔ **Frommer's Atlantic City and Cape May** *1993*

✔ **Frommer's New York State** *1994 (1988)*

✔ **Frommer's Philadelphia '93–'94** *1993 (1981)*

✔ **Insight Guide Philadelphia** *1993*

NEW YORK CITY

'It is altogether an extraordinary growing, swarming, glittering, pushing, chattering, good-natured, cosmopolitan place, and perhaps in some ways the best imitation of Paris that can be found (yet with a great originality of its own.)' Henry James, Letter to George du Maurier, 17 April 1883

Art and Architecture

New York Art Guide
Deborah Jane Gardner 1982
Very useful for listings of all the private galleries.

New York. A Guide to the Architecture of Manhattan *Paul Goldberger 1982*
An up-to-date guide to the most important buildings in Manhattan. Well worth having.

New York. A Physical History
Norval White 1987
An architectural history which describes and explains how New York developed through its buildings.

AIA Guide to New York City
Norval White and Elliot Willensky 1989
A gazetteer to almost every building with suitably pithy comments.

Fiction

✔ **The New York Trilogy** *Paul Auster*
1988 (1987)
The trilogy consists of: *City of Glass*, *Ghosts* and *The Locked Room* and has been described as 'A shatteringly clever piece of work . . . utterly gripping, written with an acid sharpness that combines Tom Wolfe with Raymond Chandler, and it leaves an indelible dent in the back of the mind'. (*The Sunday Telegraph*)

✔ **Go Tell it On the Mountain**
James Baldwin 1991 (1954)
Set in Harlem in the 1930s, Baldwin deals with his relationship with his father. Also by Baldwin *Another Country* about the search for meaningful relationships among a group of 1960s Bohemians, *No Name on the Street*, *Fire Next Time* and *Evidence of Things Not Seen*.

✔ **Stars and Bars** William Boyd 1985 (1984) (see 'The South')
Set partly in New York and partly in the Deep South. Henderson Dores starts off in New York but is sent south by his art-dealer firm to try and persuade a millionaire to part with his collection of Impressionists: 'Speed, skill and fun . . . the intricacies of the slithering plot leave you weak with suspense and laughter'. (*Listener*)

✔ **The Beautiful and the Damned**
F. Scott Fitzgerald 1950 (1922)
Set in Manhattan among the 'fast set'.

✔ **Walter Winchell. A Novel**
Michael Herr 1991 (1990)
Walter Winchell was a ruthless broadcaster and newspaper columnist who made and broke reputations; the novel is scattered with people like Ernest Hemingway, Damon Runyon, Hedy Lamarr, William Randolph Hearst and Josephine Baker: 'Some of the best dialogue you're ever going to read'. (*Harpers and Queen*)

✔ **Washington Square** Henry James 1986 (1880)
An early James novel set in New York about divided loyalties and innocence betrayed. James catches the naive vigour and parochialism of mid-century New York.

I'll Take Manhattan Judith Krantz 1986
The heroine's career is in the New York publishing world.

The Group Mary McCarthy 1989 (1954)
A group of eight Vassar graduates arrive in New York in the thirties for the wedding of one of them and set about discovering the city and themselves; each is a 'distinct individual' and within their sheltered limits they surge forward into the technological era.

✔ **Bright Lights, Big City**
Jay McInerney 1986 (1984)
A witty, fast-moving novel, which captures the bright lights and fast pace of New York and questions whether it is better to live an illusion or to lose it.

The Assistant Bernard Malamud 1957
About a Jewish grocer and his family, set in Brooklyn.

✔ **The Bell Jar** Sylvia Plath 1963
Esther Greenwood visits New York in the summer of 1953, the year they electrocuted the Rosenbergs.

✔ **The Godfather** Mario Puzo 1991 (1969)
A fast-moving saga about the Mafia in New York, with the unforgettable character of Don Corleone whose attitude to death is: 'Why should I be afraid now? Strange men have come to kill me ever since I was twelve years old.'

Runyon On Broadway Damon Runyon 1975 (1950)
Rip-roaring stories about low-life New York.

✔ **The Catcher in the Rye** J.D. Salinger 1951
The young Holden Caulfield runs away from school in Pennsylvania to New York and embarks on a journey of self-discovery.

Duplicate Keys Jane Smiley 1984
Two rock musicians are found dead in the apartment of a librarian's friend.

The Hothouse by the East River
Muriel Spark 1973
A family live in a suffocating apartment on the East River.

✔ **The Age of Innocence** Edith Wharton 1992 (1920)
Edith Wharton's satire on New York society, with the pressures brought to bear by that society on two of its members who are having an illicit affair. She had been urged by her friend Henry James in 1902 to 'DO NEW YORK', but waited until 1920 and a time in which she was in urgent need of money before she wrote what many consider her finest novel.

✔ **The Bonfire of the Vanities**
Tom Wolfe 1990 (1987)
An assorted cast of characters have their lives welded together after an accident involving a Mercedes in the Bronx. Wolfe's aim was to 'cram as much of New York City between covers' as possible, a challenge in which he most certainly succeeds.

General Background

✔ **New York** Djuna Barnes 1990 (1989)
The first collected edition of Djuna Barnes' lively pieces about New York which were written at the beginning of the century: 'The greater part of New York is as soulless as a department store; but Greenwich Village has recollections like ears filled with muted music and hopes like sightless eyes straining to catch a glimpse of the beatific vision'.

Imperial City   *Geoffrey Moorhouse*   *1992*
(1988)
'I can find no higher praise for *Imperial City*
than to say that its a worthy successor to his
Calcutta. Mr Moorhouse is superb.' (Mervyn
Jones *Sunday Telegraph*)

**The Great Port. A Passage Through
New York**   *James Morris*   *1970*
A romantic look at New York Harbour and
Port Authority.

Domestic Manners of the Americans
Frances Trollope   *1984 (1839)*
Very funny and perceptive account of nineteenth-century America. Frances Trollope,
mother of the novelist, had married Thomas
Trollope, a lawyer, in 1809; he brought the
family almost to a state of collapse, so the
energetic Fanny crossed the Atlantic with
some of her children, with the aim of selling
exotic goods in Cincinnati. The enterprise
was a disaster and through desperation Mrs
Trollope turned her hand to writing, producing the then scandalous and controversial
Domestic Manners of the Americans which
caused a sensation on both sides of the Atlantic.

Guides

✔ **The Food Lover's Guide to the Real
New York**   *Myra Alperson and Mark Clifford*
1987
Ethnic restaurants, markets and shops
divided into boroughs.

✔ **The Woman's Travel Guide New
York**   *Josie Barnard*   *1993*

✔ **New York. The Rough Guide**
Martin Dunford and Jack Holland   *1994*

✔ **Eyewitness Travel Guide New
York**   *1993*

✔ **Fodor's Flashmaps: New York**   *1991*

✔ **The Companion Guide New York**
Michael Leapman   *1991 (1983)*

✔ **Cadogan City Guide New York**
Vanessa Letts   *1991*

✔ **American Express New York**
Herbert Bailey Livesey   *1993 (1983)*

✔ **Michelin New York City**   *1991*

✔ **Blue Guide New York**
Carol von Pressentin   *1983*

✔ **Thomas Cook Travellers New
York**   *1993*

✔ **Time Out Guide New York**   *1994*

✔ **Access Guide New York City**
Richard Saul Wurman   *1991*

History

The Great Crash   *John Kenneth Galbraith*
1975
An investigation into the causes of the Wall
Street Crash.

Manhattan '45   *Jan Morris*   *1989 (1987)*
New York as it was, when it greeted returning GIs in 1945.

Photography

✔ **Inside New York: Discovering New
York's Classic Interiors**
Richard Berenholz   *1992*
Foreword by Paul Goldberger.

Travel Literature

✔ **New York Days, New York Nights**
Stephen Brook   *1985 (1984)*
Stephen Brook's observations of the many
faceted New York are wry, energetic and
amusing.

✔ **The Heart of the World**   *Nik Cohn*
1993 (1992)
Cohn's book about a walk up Broadway
proves that 'travel writing' can be just as
effective and mind opening when its about a
small area and that it is not necessary to go
to the ends of the earth. '*The Heart of the
World* is a walk up Broadway, an imaginative leap into its past and its present. Runyon
wrote fiction based loosely on fact. Cohn
writes fact with the vividly colourful brush-
stroke of fiction.' *(The Sunday Telegraph)*

✔ **A Walk Up Fifth Avenue**
Bernard Levin   *1992 (1989)*
Bernard Levin brilliantly captures the variety and contrasts of Fifth Avenue, a microcosm of New York with Trump Towers and
excessive riches side by side with bag ladies,
drunks and poverty.

✔ **Maximum City**   *Michael Pye*   *1993*
(1991)
A biography of New York City which through
its use of history establishes why it is like it
is today.

NEW ENGLAND: CONNECTICUT, MAINE, MASSACHUSETTS, NEW HAMPSHIRE, RHODE ISLAND, VERMONT

'I saw but one drunken man through all New England, and he was very respectable. He was, however, so uncommonly drunk that he might be allowed to count for two or three.' Anthony Trollope *North America* 1862

Art and Architecture

The AIA Guide to Boston   *Michael and Susan Southworth   1984*
An architectural guide which is arranged by neighbourhood.

Fiction/ Poetry

The Lovely Ambition   *Mary Ellen Chase 1960*
A Methodist minister and his family emigrate to Maine in the early 1900s. Other novels set in Maine include *Mary Peters* (1934), *Silas Crockett* (1935) and *Windswept* (1941).

✔ **The Scarlet Letter**
Nathaniel Hawthorne   1990 (1850)
An elderly English scholar sends his young wife to set up house in puritanical Boston; he follows two years later to find her ostracized with an illegitimate child, whose father she refuses to name. She is sentenced to wear a scarlet 'A' for adulteress and her husband embarks on a manic search for her lover. Henry James described it as 'beautiful, extraordinary, admirable', but then went on to criticize it, saying that Hawthorne had created unintentional physical comedy rather than moral tragedy.

✔ **The Rise of Silas Lapham**
William Dean Howells   1982 (1885)
A humourous characterization of a self-made millionaire in Boston society. Silas Lapham had moved from Vermont to Boston as a rich man; eventually his company went almost bankrupt and he returned to Vermont with his family. *Hazard of New Fortunes* 1965 (1890) takes as its subject the future of America; Howells saw something rotten in society after eight anarchists were arbitrarily arrested when eight policemen were killed in a bomb attack in Chicago in May 1886.

Class Reunion   *Rona Jaffe   1979*
Four Radcliffe classmates meet for their twentieth reunion.

✔ **The Bostonians**   *Henry James   1973 (1886)*
'I wished to write a very American tale, a tale very characteristic of our social conditions, and I asked myself what was the most salient and peculiar point in our social life. The answer was: the situation of women, the decline of the sentiment of sex, the agitation in their behalf' wrote Henry James on his reasons for writing *The Bostonians*.

The Country of the Pointed Firs
Sarah Orne Jewett   1896
Set in a Maine town by the sea.

✔ **Favorite Poems**
Henry Wadsworth Longfellow   1992
Paul Revere's Ride, part of the selection Tales of a Wayside Inn, was published in 1863, and tells of the famous night ride by Paul Revere through Mystic, Lexington and Concord on 4th April 1775.

Tough Guys Don't Dance
Norman Mailer   1984
Set in Provincetown, Mass. a writer wakes after a night's drinking to find two decapitated heads hidden with his marijuana.

✔ **Moby Dick**   *Herman Melville   1992 (1851)*
As well as being a compelling account of whaling and having many layers of meaning, Melville gives detailed descriptions of nineteenth- century life in New England (and the Pacific). Melville himself described the book as follows: 'Here, then, was this grey-headed, ungodly old man, chasing with curses a Job's whale round the world, at the head of a crew, too, chiefly made up of mongrel renegades, and castaways, and cannibals . . . '

A Day No Pigs Would Die
Robert N. Peck   1973
Written by a Shaker, this autobiographical novel evokes life on a Shaker farm in Vermont in the 1920s.

The Professor's Daughter
Piers Paul Read   1971
A father and daughter get caught up with radicals on a Massachusetts campus.

Arundel   *Kenneth Roberts   1938*
Colonial period novels; Arundel is a chronicle of the Province of Maine and the secret expedition against Quebec. *Rabble in Arms* (1939) is a chronicle of Arundel and the Burgoyne invasion. Also *The Lively Lady* (1944) and *Lydia Bailey* (1947) which moves on to the Haiti of the Slave Rebellion.

✔ **Picture Palace** *Paul Theroux* *1978*
Set in Cape Cod, a photographer reflects on
her life.

Marry Me *John Updike* *1976*
Adulterous affairs in Connecticut in the
1960s. *Witches of Eastwick* (1984) is about
three very different women in Rhode Island,
who all get involved with a devil in the guise
of a newcomer to the area.

Theophilus North *Thornton Wilder* *1973*
A dissection of the different classes of Newport, Rhode Island society in the 1920s.

General Background

**A Week on the Concord and
Merrimack Rivers** *(1849)*
Walden; or Life in the Woods *(1854)*
The Maine Woods *(1864)*
Cape Cod *(1865)* *Henry David Thoreau*
1985 edn
Thoreau made a lifelong exploration of the
countryside around him; he studied natural
history at the Concord Lyceum, before going
to Harvard. *A Week on the Concord and Merrimack Rivers* is a day-to-day description of
a trip he made with his brother in 1839.
Walden was written when Thoreau lived
alone in the woods in a house he had built
himself on the shores of Walden Pond, in
Concord, Massachusetts. In 1846 he left Concord for Bangor and the backwoods of Maine
by railroad and steamboat, and visited Cape
Cod in October 1849, June 1850 and July
1855, walking around the Cape.

✔ **A Year in Thoreau's Journal: 1851**
(1993)
Observations of life and natural history in
Concord which also shows Thoreau's intellectual development.

Guides

✔ **Guide to Martha's Vineyard**
Polly Burroughs *1990 (1979)*
The author is a long-term resident of the
Vineyard and includes notes on architecture
and history as well as practical information.

✔ **Fodor's Bed and Breakfasts and
Country Inns: New England** *1993*

✔ **Fodor's Guide Boston 1994**

✔ **Fodor's Guide Cape Cod, Martha's
Vineyard, Nantucket 1994**

✔ **Fodor's Guide Maine. Vermont,
New Hampshire** *(undated)* *1993*

✔ **Fodor's Guide New England 1994**

✔ **Insight Guide Boston** *1993*

✔ **Country Inns and Back Roads New
England 1993–1994** *Jerry Levitin* *1993*
A selection of 100 of the best small inns and
bed-and-breakfasts.

✔ **Michelin Green Guide New England**

✔ **The Smithsonian Guide to Historic
America. Northern New England**
Vance Muse *1989*
Vermont, New Hampshire, Maine.

✔ **Thomas Cook Travelers Boston and
New England** *1994*

✔ **The Smithsonian Guide to Historic
America. Southern New England**
Henry Wiencek *1989*
Massachusetts, Connecticut and Rhode Is-
land.

✔ **Access Guide Boston**
Richard Saul Wurman *1993*

History

Who Killed Society *Cleveland Amory* *1960*
A social history of Massachusetts which in-
cludes descriptions of now dead resorts like
Jekyl Island as well as Newport. *The Proper
Bostonians* (1955) is a history of Boston.

Leisure

✔ **Halliday's New England Food
Explorer** *Fred Halliday* *1993*
The book concentrates on unusual places
which are off the beaten track and includes a
selection of recipes.

Natural History

✔ **The Outer Lands. A Natural
History Guide to Cape Cod, Martha's
Vineyard, Nantucket, Block Island and
Long Island** *Dorothy Sterling* *1978 (1967)*
Interesting facts about the creatures and
plants found along the coast of New England.

Photography

✔ **A New England Autumn** *Gerd Kittel*
1987
Emphasis on the colours of the New England
autumn.

✔ **Maine** *Eliot Porter* *1986*
Superb colour photographs.

Travel Literature

The Boat and the Town
Geoffrey Moorhouse 1979
A coastal New England town and its fishermen seen through the seasons.

GREAT LAKES STATES: ILLINOIS, INDIANA, MICHIGAN, MINNESOTA, OHIO, WISCONSIN
'It rained and fogged in Chicago and muddy-flowing people oozed thick in the canyon-beds of the streets. Yet it seemed to me more alive and more real than New York.' D.H. Lawrence, letter to Mrs Bessie Freeman, August 1923

Fiction

✔ **Winesburg, Ohio** *Sherwood Anderson*
1987 (1919)
A collection of short stories which get to the heart of small town Midwest America at the turn of the twentieth century.

✔ **Adventures of Augie March**
Saul Bellow 1984 (1983)
Augie March was born and bred in Chicago and his escapades take him all over the city, as well as on a jaunt to Mexico: 'A rich, various, fascinating, and important book, and from now on any discussion of fiction in America in our time will have to take acount of it'. *(The New Republic)*

The Hills Stand Watch
August W. Derleth 1960
A woman from the east marries a Wisconsin tradesman in the 1840s. Also *Wind Over Wisconsin* (1938) and *Still Is the Summer* (1937).

✔ **Sister Carrie** *Theodore Dreiser 1991*
(1900)
A novel about lower-middle class life in Chicago; a young woman is seduced by city life, while a middle-aged man is seduced by desire for her. Publication was delayed for twelve years because the realism and immorality depicted were deemed likely to cause offence.

The Torrents of Spring
Ernest Hemingway 1972 (1926)
A working-class satire set in Michigan; it was Hemingway's first full-length novel written while he was living in Paris and it parodies and rejects the literary heroes of the day.

✔ **Lake Wobegon Days** *Garrison Keillor*
1993 (1985)
Keillor started telling his Lake Wobegon, Minnesota stories on his radio show, eventually turning his humorous monologue into a book.

Freaky Deaky *Elmore Leonard 1988*
A tough, brutal, funny thriller set in Detroit.

Main Street *Sinclair Lewis 1950*
Minnesota in the 1920s.

Sula *Toni Morrison 1974*
The story of the friendship of two black women in Medallion, Ohio.

Do With Me What You Will
Joyce Carol Oates 1973
An adulterous affair, in Michigan, prompts two people to look back at their lives.

Letting Go *Philip Roth 1962*
Jewish academic life at the University of Chicago in the 1950s.

✔ **Chicago Loop** *Paul Theroux 1991 (1990)*
A gripping and sexy thriller set in Chicago: '*Chicago Loop* is a first-rate thriller . . . cunningly structured and full of insights into erotic psychosis'. *(Daily Mail)*

The Eighth Day *Thornton Wilder 1967*
At the turn of the century the lives of two families from Coaltown, a small mining centre in Southern Illinois, intermingle over the years, after a miscarriage of justice.

Guides

✔ **Fodor's Bed and Breakfasts, Country Inns and Other Weekend Pleasures: The Upper Great Lakes Region** *1993*
Michigan, Minnesota, Wisconsin.

✔ **Fodor's The Upper Great Lakes Region: The Best of Michigan, Wisconsin and Minnesota** *(undated) 1991*

✔ **Frommer's Chicago '93–'94**

✔ **Frommer's Minneapolis and St. Paul** *1993 (1988)*

✔ **The Smithsonian Guide to Historic America. The Great Lakes States**
Louise Winckler 1989
Ohio, Indiana, Illinois, Michigan, Wisconsin, Minnesota.

Photography

✔ **Indiana** *Photography by Darryl Jones* Text *by Jared Carter* *1984*
A cross-section of the landscape in colour photographs with ample text.

Travel Literature

✔ **Places** *Jan Morris* *1973*
This collection includes an essay on Chicago.

VIRGINIA AND THE CAPITAL REGION: WASHINGTON DC, VIRGINIA, WEST VIRGINIA, DELAWARE, MARYLAND

'The dead calm which is so often felt in Washington and leaves a man more tired in the morning than he was the night before.'
Charles Francis Adams *Diary* 8 July 1834

Fiction

Democracy *Henry Adams* *1980 (1879)*
The political society of Washington during President Ulysses S. Grant's second administration. The book was published anonymously.

The Sot-Weed Factor *John Barth* *1967*
A seventeenth-century historical novel set in Maryland. Also by John Barth *The End of the Road* (1967), set in a small college town and *Sabbatical: A Romance* (1982) about a boat trip from Chesapeake Bay to the Caribbean.

The Spike *Arnaud de Borchgrave and Robert Moss* *1982 (1980)*
A spy novel which ranges from Vietnam to Moscow to Washington, Rome, Geneva and New York, about Soviet infiltration of the government and the media.

Angel of Light *Joyce Carol Oates* *1981*
A novel about revenge and justice which takes place between New York, Ontario, Maine, but mostly in Washington DC

Machine Dreams *Jayne Anne Phillips* *1984*
How people's lives were transformed from the time of the depression up until the Vietnam war. Set in West Virginia.

The Confessions of Nat Turner
William Styron *1967*
A novel set in Virginia about the 1831 slave rebellion.

Guides

✔ **Bed and Breakfast in the Mid-Atlantic States** *Bernice Chesler* *1993*
Delaware, Maryland, New Jersey, New York, North Carolina, Pennsylvania, Virginia, Washington DC, West Virginia.

✔ **Fodor's Bed and Breakfasts and Country Inns: Mid-Atlantic Region** *1993*
New York, Pennsylvania, New Jersey, Delaware, Maryland, Virginia, West Virginia.

✔ **Fodor's Guide Virginia and Maryland** *(undated) 1993*

✔ **Fodor's Guide Washington DC '94**

✔ **Frommer's Delaware and Maryland '94–'95**

✔ **Frommer's Washington DC '94**

✔ **The Smithsonian Guide to Historic America: The Carolinas and the Appalachian States** *Patricia L. Hudson and Sandra L. Ballard* *1989*
North Carolina, South Carolina, Tennessee, Kentucky and West Virginia.

✔ **Insight Guide Washington DC** *1992*

✔ **Let's Go Washington DC 1995**

✔ **American Express Washington DC**
Christopher McIntosh and Elisavietta Ritchie *1992 (1987)*

✔ **Michelin Washington DC** *1991*

✔ **Smithsonian Guide to Historic America: Virginia and the Capital Region** *Henry Wiencek* *1989*

✔ **Access Guide Washington DC**
Richard Saul Wurman *1989*

Travel Literature

✔ **Voyages to the Virginia Colonies**
Richard Hakluyt (modernized by A.L. Rowse) *1986 (c.1590)*
Hakluyt was geographical advisor to the East India Company and one of the original members of the Virginia Company; this modern English version shows his significant contribution to history and exploration.

✔ **Destinations** *Jan Morris* *1980*
Both this and *Travels* have essays on Washington DC

THE SOUTH: NORTH CAROLINA, SOUTH CAROLINA, GEORGIA, KENTUCKY, TENNESSEE, ALABAMA, MISSISSIPPI, LOUISIANA, ARKANSAS

'See Naples and die," says the proverb. My view of things is that you should see Canal-street, New Orleans, and then try to live as much longer as ever you can.' G.A. Sala *America Revisited* 1882

Autobiography/Biography

✔ **I Know Why the Caged Bird Sings**
Maya Angelou 1988 (1984)
The first volume in this autobiography tells of how a black girl comes to terms with her childhood in Arkansas in the 1930s.

✔ **Sound Shadows of the New World**
Ved Mehta 1987 (1986)
At the age of 15, Ved Mehta was sent from India to the Arkansas School for the Blind in Little Rock; although the book ends with his graduation from there and was written thirty-five years later, it is extraordinarily vivid.

Georgia O'Keefe *Georgia O'Keefe* 1976
The artist's thoughts about her work.

Fiction

Kinflicks *Lisa Alther* 1981
A woman experiences every kind of political 'movement' and tells of her life in Tennessee in a series of flashbacks.

King of the Roses *V.S. Anderson* 1984 (1983)
A thriller set around the Kentucky Derby. Someone with millions to spend determines that the favourite, a thoroughbred called Knidos, is not going to win.

✔ **Stars and Bars**
William Boyd (see 'New York')

Tobacco Road *Erskine Caldwell* 1978 (1934)
The demise of a poor white family in Georgia, who persisted in having faith in nature, the earth and in plants, despite the frequent failure of the harvests. *God's Little Acre*, full of passion, violence and humour is the story of down-trodden whites in the Southern States.

Other Voices, Other Rooms
Truman Capote 1978 (1948)
Joel Knox's mother dies and he is sent to Louisiana in the Deep South to live with his father whom he has never met and who remains elusive. All set against a shimmering landscape of heat and decadence.

The Awakening *Kate Chopin* 1972
Set at the turn of the century in Louisiana, a bourgeois married woman's fight for independence ends in tragedy.

The Prince of Tides *Pat Conroy* 1988 (1986)
Set in Beaufort, South Carolina, the story of Tom Wingo and his troubled twin sister Savannah and their turbulent family, spans forty years.

✔ **Absalom, Absalom!** *William Faulkner* 1975 (1936)
Sutpen, a poor white boy, was turned away from a plantation owner's mansion and as a result determined to become a Virginia plantation owner himself; he realizes his ambition but after returning from the Civil War finds his estate in ruins. 'The novel in which Faulkner most profoundly and completely says what he has to say about the South and the human condition' (Walter Allen). The *Reivers* 1970 (1962) is about the eleven-year old Lucius Priest who in 1905 took his grandfather's new car and went to Memphis: 'A wildly comic and brilliantly invented tale' (V.S. Pritchett). Other novels by Faulkner include *Sanctuary* (1931), *The Sound and the Fury* (1929) and *Go Down Moses* (1942).

Black Sunday *Thomas Harris* 1977 (1975)
A plot by Arab extremists to blow up the Super Bowl and 80,000 people, making it the bloodiest Sunday America would ever have experienced, all depends on one man: 'A frightening, suspenseful, cleverly plotted cat-and-mouse battle played out against the clock.' *(Publishers Weekly)*

Porgy *DuBose Heyward* 1970 (1925)
The story, which takes place in South Carolina, about the love of Porgy for his Bess, on which the opera was based.

Savannah Purchase *Jane A. Hodge* 1971 (1970)
An historical novel set in Savannah at the time of Napoleon; two cousins who look like each other as children are thrown together again as adults.

Dinner at Antoine's
Frances Parkinson Keyes 1977 (1948)
Dinner in the famous 1850 room at Antoine's restaurant in New Orleans is the start of a

murder mystery. Orson Foxworth is giving a dinner party to mark the re-opening of an old romance with a Creole widow; the following day her daughter, Odile, is found dead. Also *Steamboat Gothic* (1952), a romance set in the south; the prologue begins in 1869 and is followed by books one and two which are set in 1894 and 1895.

To Kill a Mocking Bird   Harper Lee   1960
A tale of racial conflict in Alabama and how society reacts to an outsider; a father defends a black man accused of rape, bringing violence into the lives of two children.

✔ Gone With the Wind
Margaret Mitchell   1936
Good descriptions of life during the Civil War – a romantic blockbuster.

The Moviegoer   Walker Percy   1961
Set in New Orleans with a carnival background.

Three O'Clock Dinner   Josephine Pinckney
1946
Set in Charleston, the story is told through the eyes of a young widow who learns to deal with her dead husband's relations and an adoption.

On Leaving Charleston   Alexandra Ripley
1993 (1984)
The fortunes of Ashley Barony, a plantation in Charleston, which started disintegrating on the day of Margaret Tradd's scandalous wedding. The first book was *Charleston* (1992 (1981), which is the story of Lucy Tradd as a child after the Civil War in which her father had died and her brother was crippled.

A Confederacy of Dunces
John Kennedy Toole   1981 (1980)
The antihero Ignatius O Reilly wreaks havoc in a surreal New Orleans. John Kennedy Toole wrote his novel in the 1960s and having tried, unsuccessfully, to get it published became so depressed by his failure that he committed suicide: 'I succumbed, stunned and seduced, page after page . . . It is a masterwork of comedy' *(The New York Times)*

In Love and Trouble   Alice Walker   1984
(1973)
A powerful collection of moving, loving and angry stories of black women in the South.

The Ponder Heart   Eudora Welty   1954
Life in a small Mississippi town. She also wrote *Delta Wedding* (1946) the story of a large southern family, and *Losing Battles* (1970), *The Optimist's Daughter* (1972) and *The Golden Apples* (1949).

A Streetcar Named Desire
Tennessee Williams   1947
An unhappy couple have to deal with her wacky sister.

Look Homeward, Angel   Thomas Wolfe
1984 (1929)
An autobiographical novel about a boy growing up in Asheville, North Carolina (called Altamont in the book), who raids literature and the world for fresh ideas and wonders.

Folklore

✔ The Sanctified Church
Zora Neale Hurston   1981
A collection of essays on Afro-American folklore, legend, popular mythology and the Southern Black Christian church, by Zora Neale Hurston, described as somebody who despite the Depression 'Went right on collecting, maintaining, celebrating the genius of Blacksouth folks'.

Food

✔ Chef Paul Prudhomme's Louisiana Kitchen   1984
Cajun and Creole recipes from South Louisiana.

General Background

New Orleans Sketches   William Faulkner
1968
Stories and articles written when Faulkner was living and working in New Orleans.

✔ Praying for Sheetrock
Melissa Fay Greene   1992
The political awakening of a small black community in McIntosh County, Georgia, told through the voices of the people themselves: 'This is a truly extraordinary book – a marvellous evocation of a changing rural southern world as seen by a conscientious, thoughtful, morally alert observer who also happens to be a wonderfully talented writer.' (Robert Coles)

✔ The Land Where the Blues Began
Alan Lomax   1994 (1993)
A new insight and fresh look at the music which was born in the Mississippi Delta around 1900 and which gradually became known and loved worldwide.

Guides

✔ **Bed and Breakfast in the Mid-Atlantic States** *Bernice Chesler 1993*
Delaware, Maryland, New Jersey, New York, North Carolina, Pennsylvania, Virginia, Washington DC, West Virginia.

✔ **Fodor's Guide The Carolinas and the Georgia Coast 1994**

✔ **Fodor's Guide The South '94**

✔ **Frommer's Atlanta '93–'94**

✔ **Frommer's The Carolinas and Georgia** *1994*

✔ **Frommer's New Orleans '93–'94**

✔ **The Smithsonian Guide to Historic America: Texas and the Arkansas River Valley** *Alice Gordon, Jerry Camarillo Dunn and Mel White 1990*
Texas, Oklahoma, Arkansas.

✔ **Hippocrene Guide to Exploring Mid-America. A Guide to Museum Villages** *Gerald and Patricia Gutek 1990 (see 'Plains States')*

✔ **The Smithsonian Guide to Historic America: The Carolinas and the Appalachian States** *Patricia L. Hudson and Sandra L. Ballard 1989*
North Carolina, South Carolina, Tennessee, Kentucky and West Virginia.

✔ **Insight Guide New Orleans** *1992*

✔ **The Smithsonian Guide to Historic America: The Deep South**
William Bryant Logan and Vance Muse 1989
Louisiana, Mississippi, Alabama, Georgia, Florida.

Photography

The Bayous *Peter S. Feibleman 1973*
Part of the Time-Life American Wilderness series.

Ozarks *Richard Rhodes 1974*
The Ozark Mountains of Arkansas in the Time-Life Wilderness series.

✔ **New Orleans. Elegance and Decadence** *Richard Sexton and Randolph Delehanty 1993*
An impressionistic photographic essay featuring both interiors and exteriors.

Travel Literature

✔ **Mississippi Madness. Canoeing the Mississippi–Missouri** *Nicholas Francis and William Butcher 1990*
Starting in the Rocky Mountains, Nicholas Butcher made the first canoe trip down Mark Twain's 'crookedest river in the world', ending up in the Gulf of Mexico.

✔ **A Turn in the South** *V.S. Naipaul 1989*
Naipaul aims to come to terms with the complexities of the South with all its many contradictions and paradoxes: 'A supremely interesting, even poetic glimpse of a part of America foreigners either neglect or patronize'. [Clancy Sigal *The Guardian*]

✔ **Old Glory** *Jonathan Raban 1986 (1981)*
Inspired by memories of reading *Huckleberry Finn* as a child, Jonathan Raban takes a boat up the Mississippi; the physical journey, often full of danger, is mingled with childhood dreams and his sharp observations of the America he passes through result in a marvellous book. [Colin Thubron]

✔ **Life on the Mississippi** *Mark Twain 1990 (1883)*
A nostalgic and humorous mixture of journalism and autobiography written in the heyday of steamboating on the Mississippi; Twain's love of the river shines through his prose.

FLORIDA

'Florida . . . does beguile and gratify me – giving me my first and last (evidently) sense of the tropics, or à peu pres, the subtropics, and revealing to me a blandness in nature of which I had no idea.' Henry James, letter to Edmond Gosse, 16 February 1905

Fiction

✔ **Miami** *Pat Booth 1992*
A novel of seduction and desire set against the backdrop of Miami's South Beach.

Nine Florida Stories
Margaret Stoneman Douglas 1990
Margaret Stoneman Douglas concerned herself with Florida's environment throughout her long life. She fought for over sixty years to save the Everglades. These stories are all set in Florida and were originally published in the *Saturday Evening Post*.

✔ **To Have and Have Not**
Ernest Hemingway 1972 (1937) (see 'Cuba')

✔ **Double Whammy** *Carl Hiaason 1990 (1988)*
An extraordinarily funny fishing thriller that brings together a diverse collection of Florida characters. Also *Skin Tight* about plastic surgery in Miami; *Native Tongue* about a Florida theme park, and *Tourist Season* which has as its theme destruction of the Florida environment.

✔ **Their Eyes Were Watching God**
Zora Neale Hurston 1986 (1937)
Descriptions of the founding of Eatonville, the author's home town and the state's first all-black town. Also by Hurston: *Jonah's Gourd Vine* and her autobiography *Dust Tracks on a Road.*

Stick *Elmore Leonard 1983*
Like *La Brava* and *Gold Coast* this is a Florida-set thriller; *Stick* is about the rise of a black opportunist through money, sex and drugs.

✔ **Ninety-Two in the Shade**
Thomas McGuane 1989 (1976)
An unstable young man aspires to become a fishing guide in Key West; *Panama* (1978) is also set in Key West.

✔ **Killing Mister Watson**
Peter Matthiessen 1991 (1990)
Edgar Watson arrived in the unspoilt Florida Everglades 100 years ago and began to plunder the mangrove swamps for unusual feathers, investing his profits in a sugar plantation. His success bred envy and the killings began culminating in the Great Hurricane of October 1910: 'A profound and convincing account of our battle with both inner and external nature, and of the violence we have done to the world and to ourselves'. (Brian Morton *The Times*)

Cross Creek *Marjorie Kinnin Rawlings 1984 (1970)*
About the people the author knew while she lived in Cross Creek. Also *The Yearling* 1972 (1938) about life in the brush country.

✔ **Los Gusanos** *John Sayles 1992 (1991)*
A novel set around the lives of Cuban exiles in Miami at the beginning of the 1980s. 'Los Gusanos' are Castro's 'worms', the landowners, liberals, criminals and counter-revolutionaries who live in America but dream of Cuba.

✔ **The Way We Die Now**
Charles Willeford 1992 (1988)
One of a series starring Hoke Moseley, a Miami cop. The *Way We Die Now* involves Moseley growing a beard and going on an ultra-secret mission. Others in the series include *Miami Blues* 1985 (1984) about a psychopathic criminal released from jail who arrives in Miami carrying the stolen credit cards of three men, *Kiss Your Ass Goodbye* 1989 (1987) and *Sideswipe* 1988 (1987). 'No one writes a better crime novel.' (Elmore Leonard)

Guides

✔ **Access Guide Miami and South Florida** *1992,*

✔ **Access Guide Orlando and Central Florida** *1992*

✔ **Fodor's Guide Florida '94**

✔ **Frommer's Florida '94**

✔ **Frommer's Miami '93–'94**

✔ **Frommer's Orlando '94**

✔ **Frommer's Tampa and St. Petersburg '93–'94**

✔ **Insight Guide Florida** *1993*

✔ **Hidden Florida Keys and Everglades** *Candace Leslie 1994 (1990)*
Concentrates on the lesser known parts of the two areas, as well as the places that Hemingway wrote about.

✔ **The Smithsonian Guide to Historic America: The Deep South**
William Bryant Logan and Vance Muse 1989
Louisiana, Mississippi, Alabama, Georgia, Florida.

✔ **Visitor's Guide: Florida. A Moorland Guide** *Brian Merritt 1991*

✔ **Explore the Everglades**
Miriam Lee Ownby 1992
The book guides you through the Everglades, explaining the significance of what you see.

✔ **The Florida Where-to-Stay Book**
Phil Philcox 1993
Over 4500 different places to stay across the price range.

✔ **The 1994 Unofficial Guide to Walt Disney World** *Bob Sehlinger 1994*
Includes information on Epcot, Disney–MGM Studios and Universal Studios.

✔ **Florida. The Rough Guide**
Mick Sinclair 1994 (1991)

✔ **Thomas Cook Travellers Florida**
1993

History

Florida. The Long Frontier
Marjory Stoneman Douglas 1967
The story of Florida from its geological formation to the present. She also wrote *The Everglades. River of Grass.*

Leisure

✔ **The Florida Bicycle Book**
Jackalene Crow Hiendlmayr 1990
The best cycling areas in each county and where to stay and what to see.

Photography

The Everglades *Archie Carr 1973*
Part of the Time-Life American Wilderness series.

Travel Literature

✔ **Miami** *Joan Didion 1988 (1987)*
Concentrates on the Cuban exiles in Miami: 'To understand America, which is in many ways the British future . . . I recommend *Miami* . . . No one depicts place or passion or dislocation with more accuracy; no one can move us more deeply with the staccato repetition of the crazy facts of personal–political life than Joan Didion.' *(New Statesman)*

✔ **Journeys** *Jan Morris 1984*
The collection includes an essay on Miami.

Going to Miami: Exiles, Tourists and Refugees in the New America
David Rieff 1987
Miami as seen through the eyes of its many differing residents; more than half the population is Spanish speaking and includes refugees from Cuba, Nicaraguan Contras, Hondurans, Haitians as well as Vietnamese boat people, black Americans and rich Jewish retirees.

TEXAS

'The province of Techas will be the richest state of our Union without any exception.'
Thomas Jefferson, letter to James Monroe, 15 May 1820

Fiction

The Edge of Time *Loula Grace Erdman 1950*
Frontier life in 1885 with emphasis on the role of women and of one particular woman.

Giant *Edna Ferber 1952*
Good descriptions of ranch life (meant to be the King Ranch) and the scenery and unremitting heat of Texas. Jet Rinh is a portrait of the great wildcatter Sid Richardson.

Stand Proud: A Texas Saga
Elmer Kelton 1988 (1984)
A mystery novel and western set in West Central Texas. Frank Claymore had been praised as a hero of the frontier during the Civil War, but was subsequently on trial for murder.

Terms of Endearment *Larry McMurty 1975*
A Texas widow tries to wield power over those around her, but changes her way of living when her daughter dies of cancer.

Guides

✔ **The Smithsonian Guide to Historic America: Texas and the Arkansas River Valley** *Alice Gordon, Jerry Camarillo Dunn and Mel White 1990*
Texas, Oklahoma, Arkansas.

✔ **Insight Guide Texas** *1992*

✔ **Best Places to Stay in the Southwest** *Anne E. Wright 1993*
230 of the best places to stay in Arizona, New Mexico, Oklahoma and Texas.

Travel Literature

✔ **Journeys** *Jan Morris 1984*
The collection includes a piece on Houston.

THE PLAINS STATES: NORTH DAKOTA, SOUTH DAKOTA, IOWA, KANSAS, MISSOURI, NEBRASKA, OKLAHOMA

'Oh, they chew tobacco thin in Kansas, Oh, they say that drink's a sin in Kansas.'
Kansas folksong, quoted by John Gunther *Inside USA 1947*

Biography

✔ **Geronimo. The Man, His Time, His Place** *Angie Debo 1993 (1976)*
In 1886 it took 5,000 army troops to capture Geronimo, the Apache war leader, 'tiger of the human race' and sixteen other warriors. This sympathetic biography shows Geronimo as a man of interest, energy and drive and not the bloodthirsty savage as he has so often been portrayed.

Fiction

The Emigrants *Johan Bojer 1974 (1924)*
A group of poverty stricken Norwegian immigrants settle in the Red River Valley area of North Dakota.

The Kincaids *Matthew Braun 1976*
A family saga spanning several generations of the Kincaids in Oklahoma.

✔ **My Ántonia** *Willa Cather 1954 (1918)*
The famous and well-loved portrait of a pioneer woman which captures the strengths and passions of the early settlers and their strong feeling for the land they settled. Also *O Pioneers!* (1913).

✔ **The Prairie** *James Fenimore Cooper 1992 (1827)*
Cooper realized the consequences that America's inexorable advance westward would have on the Indians and the countryside. He tells this through the voice of the aged trapper, Natty Bumppo, who preaches the conservation of nature. Also by Fenimore Cooper *The Last of the Mohicans* (1826), *The Deerslayer* (1841) and *The Pioneers* (1823).

✔ **Americana** *Don Delillo 1990 (1971)*
David Bell flees New York for a small Kansas town with his 16mm film camera; the townsfolk are drawn into the bizarre movie that he starts to make in his motel room.

✔ **Tracks** *Louise Erdrich 1989 (1988)*
'One of the most exciting and surprising novelists writing in English tells of America's dispossessed, her Indian forefathers, in a compassion untainted by sentimentality. And she has given the Chippewas of North Dakota a lasting place in fiction.' Paul Bailey *(The Sunday Times)*

Yonnondio: From the Thirties
Tillie Olsen 1974 (1937)
South Dakota in the 1920s and a family tries to make their living as tenant farmers.

Even Cowgirls Get the Blues
Tom Robbins 1981 (1976)
Sissy Hankshaw a small-town girl with big dreams from Virginia, ends up after a series of adventures in Manhattan, in the Dakota Badlands where FBI agents, cowgirls and whooping cranes all congregate.

✔ **A Thousand Acres** *Jane Smiley 1992 (1991)*
Three sisters are given a farm by their father; the two eldest accept, but the youngest has misgivings and as a result is cut out by her father. The *King Lear* story transposed to Zebulon County, Iowa.

The Grapes of Wrath *John Steinbeck 1939 (see 'California')*

The Adventures of Tom Sawyer *1982 (1876)*
The Adventures of Huckleberry Finn *Mark Twain (1883)*

General Background

✔ **PrairyErth** *William Least Heat-Moon 1992 (1991)*
Chase County, in the Flint Hills of Kansas, 'the last remaining grand expanse of tall-grass prairie in America', is the subject of William Least Heat-Moon's evocation of the American land, its people, its past, its hopes.

✔ **In the Spirit of Crazy Horse** *Peter Matthiessen 1992 (1983)*
In 1975 there was a shoot-out between FBI agents and American Indians near Wounded Knee in South Dakota. Four Indians were indicted on murder charges after two FBI agents died; Matthiessen investigates what really happened and is convinced of the innocence of Peltier, who was given two consecutive life sentences.

Guides

✔ **Frommer's St Louis and Kansas City** *(undated) 1993 (1991)*

✔ **The Smithsonian Guide to Historic America: Texas and the Arkansas River Valley** *Alice Gordon, Jerry Camarillo Dunn and Mel White 1990*
Texas, Oklahoma, Arkansas.

✔ **Hippocrene Guide to Exploring Mid-America. A Guide to Museum Villages** *Gerald and Patricia Gutek 1990*
A guide and descriptions to the near west as it was.

✔ **The Smithsonian Guide to Historic America: The Plains States: Missouri, Kansas, Nebraska, Iowa, South Dakota, North Dakota** *Suzanne Winckler 1990*

✔ **Best Places to Stay in the Southwest** *Anne E. Wright 1993*
230 of the best places to stay in Arizona, New Mexico, Oklahoma and Texas.

History

✔ **A Place Called Bird** *Tony Parker 1990 (1989)*
Tony Parker spent three months in a small Kansas town talking to the residents about their hopes and fears for the future and collecting a series of oral interviews.

Travel Literature

✔ **The Big Muddy. Adventures up the Missouri** *Peter Holt 1991*
The American explorers Meriwether Lewis and William Clark travelled 3,000 miles up the Missouri River between 1804 and 1806; Peter Holt followed in their footsteps from St Louis to the headwaters near the Rockies.

SOUTH WEST – DESERT STATES: ARIZONA, NEVADA, NEW MEXICO, UTAH

'The country looks something like a singed cat, owing to the scarcity of shrubbery, and also resembles that animal in the respect that it has more merits than its personal appearance would seem to indicate.'
[Nevada] Mark Twain, *Washoe– Information Wanted –San Francisco Golden Era*, 22 May 1864

Biography

Crossing the 100th Meridian *Wallace E. Stegner*
The biography of John Wesley Powell, the first man to descend the Colorado.

✔ **Refuge** *Terry Tempest Williams 1991*
As the author's mother dies of cancer, she writes in parallel about the death of the country around Salt Lake City. Beautifully written.

Fiction

Death Comes for the Archbishop
Willa Cather 1971 (1927)
In the mid-nineteenth century Father Latour, who was to become Archbishop of Santa

Fé, arrived in the Southwest in order to try and convert the area to Catholicism; after forty years he died 'of having lived'.

A Study in Scarlet *Arthur Conan Doyle 1977 (1887)*
Although much of this mystery takes place in London, there is a sub-plot about two Mormons in Utah who take revenge on a girl and her lover.

Children of God *Vardis Fisher 1977 (1939)*
The history of the Mormons, their trek West and establishment in Salt Lake City, in novel form.

The Arizona Clan *Zane Grey 1958*
Family feuds in the Tonto Basin. Dodge Mercer drifts into Tonto Basin country looking for a quiet life, but ends up defending the Lilly clan against the moonshiner Buck Hathaway. *Riders of the Purple Sage* (1974) is set in southwestern Utah in 1871. Also *The Rainbow Trail* (1985).

✔ **The Blessing Way** *Tony Hillerman 1990 (1970)*
The first of many murder mysteries starring Lt Joe Leaphorn of the Navajo Tribal Police. Brilliant evocation of life in the Southwest and compulsive reading. Others include: *Talking God, A Thief of Time, Sacred Clowns, Coyote Waits, Skinwalkers, The Ghostway* and *The Dark Wind*.

✔ **Animal Dreams** *Barbara Kingsolver 1992 (1990)*
Codi Noline returns to her home town of Grace, Arizona after fifteen years absence, to confront her family and her past. She finds a threatened town, but is able to learn much about herself and to unravel her past.

Laughing Boy *Oliver La Farge 1930*
A novel which tries to be accurate about Navajo customs, character, ceremonies and rites.

St Mawr and Other Stories
D.H. Lawrence 1983 (1925)
A psychological novella which starts in England and moves to New Mexico.

The Desert Rose *Larry McMurty 1983*
Written in three weeks; about Las Vegas.

✔ **Fools Die** *Mario Puzo 1992 (1978)*
Set between New York and Las Vegas in the 1950s and 1960s in the interconnecting worlds of bigtime gambling, publishing and the film industry.

✔ **Fear and Loathing in Las Vegas**
Hunter S. Thompson 1993 (1971)
A savage dissection of the American Dream; Thompson enters Las Vegas armed with

massive quantities of different drugs and while 'under the influence' encounters casino operators, bartenders and the police whom he approaches with a cutting black humour.

General Background

The Biggest Game in Town   A. Alvarez
1991 (1983)
Sketches of the big poker players at the annual World Series of Poker: 'The ruthless, mind-boggling world of the poker professionals is vividly described by poker-playing poet Al Alvarez in his engrossing, shimmeringly well written account of the world poker knockout championship.' *(The Sunday Times)*

Guides

✔ **Introduction to Las Vegas. An Odyssey Guide**   Deke Castleman   1991

✔ **Las Vegas**   Deke Castleman   1991

✔ **Nevada Handbook. A Moon Publication**   Deke Castleman   1993 (1989)

✔ **The Smithsonian Guide to Historic America: the Desert States**
Michael S. Durham   1990

✔ **Bet on It! The Ultimate Guide to Nevada**   Mary Jane and Greg Edwards   1992
A complete guide to gambling in Nevada – where to go and how to do it.

✔ **Fodor's Guide Arizona '94**

✔ **Fodor's Las Vegas, Reno, Tahoe '94**

✔ **Frommer's Arizona '93–'94.**

✔ **Frommer's Las Vegas '93–'94**

✔ **Frommer's New Mexico '93–'94.**

✔ **Introduction to New Mexico. An Odyssey Guide**   Nancy Harbert   1992

✔ **Las Vegas and Beyond. The Ultimate Guidebook**   David Stratton   1993
A guide to the casinos, but also to the unknown parts of Las Vegas.

✔ **Hidden Southwest**   Ulysses Press   1992
Arizona, New Mexico, Southern Utah and Southern Colorado.

✔ **Ultimate Santa Fé and Beyond**
Ulysses Press   1993

✔ **Utah Handbook. A Moon Publication**   Bill Weir   1993 (1988)

✔ **Introduction to Utah. An Odyssey Guide**   Tom and Gayen Wharton   1991

✔ **Best Places to Stay in the Southwest**   Anne E. Wright   1993
230 of the best places to stay in Arizona, New Mexico, Oklahoma and Texas.

History

Great River: the Rio Grande in North American History   Paul Horgan   1968
A deep and moving insight into the story of New Mexico by *the* historian of the Southwest.

The Gathering of Zion: The Story of the Mormon Trail   Wallace E. Stegner
1982 (1964)
The story of the Mormon's migration, mixing contemporary accounts with the history of their trek.

Natural History

✔ **Cortez Crossroads**
Frederick W. Lange   1989
A guide to the natural history and Anasazi Heritage of the Four Corners region (where Colorado, New Mexico, Arizona and Utah meet).

Photography

✔ **The Grand Canyon**   Eliot Porter   1992
Sixty-four pages of full-colour illustrations; these were taken from the 2,000 photographs that Porter took on three trips to the Grand Canyon between 1967 and 1969.

Travel Literature

✔ **Desert Solitaire. A Season in the Wilderness**   Edward Abbey   1992 (1968)
Funny, scathing and moving account of life in a desert in Utah where Abbey spent several seasons and where, to his anguish, tourism and the modern world rapidly encroached.

✔ **Scenes in America Deserts**
P. Reyner Banham   1989 (1982)
The visual delight that Banham, an architectural historian, discovers as he travels through the American desert is infectious.

He is as much intrigued by the manmade buildings as by the beauty of the desert landscape.

✔ **The Place Where Souls Are Born**
Thomas Keneally 1993 (1992)
Inspired by the Westerns of his childhood, Keneally sets out on a journey of exploration from the Colorado Rockies to the Mexican border, a land he found more beautiful and richer than he had imagined.

✔ **Journeys** *Jan Morris 1984*
This collection of essays includes Las Vegas and Santa Fé.

ROCKY MOUNTAIN STATES: COLORADO, IDAHO, MONTANA, WYOMING
'I am in love with Montana . . . Montana seems to me to be what a small boy would think Texas is like from hearing Texans.'
John Steinbeck *Travels with Charley* 1962

Anthropology

✔ **Black Elk Speaks** *as told through John G. Neihardt 1993 (1932)*
The classic account of the vision and life of a Sioux holy man who fought against Custer at the battle of Little Bighorn. John Neihardt described his meeting with Black Elk as the most memorable experience of his life and Joseph Campbell describes the book as 'a key statement to the understanding of myth and symbols'.

Autobiography/Biography

✔ **A River Runs Through It and Other Stories** *Norman Maclean 1990 (1976)*
Humour and tragedy mingle in these stories about living and fishing in the Blackfoot River country of Montana. Wonderful.

Fiction

Strangers in the River *Carol Brink 1960*
The story of a group of foresters who were trying to conserve the forests in Idaho at the turn of the century.

The Song of the Lark *Willa Cather 1915*
The novel charts the fortunes of a young girl from Moonstone, Colorado who becomes a great singer.

The Wrong Case *James Crumley 1991 (1975)*
Detective story with not much plot, but with vivid descriptions of Montana. *Dancing Bear* 1991 (1983) is also set in Montana.

English Creek *Ivan Doig 1984*
One of a trilogy about a family called McCaskill, who were homesteaders and who emigrated from Scotland after the clearances. The second in the trilogy was *Dancing at the Rascal Fair* (1987) and the third *Ride with Me, Mariah Montana* (1991) 1990.

✔ **Wildlife** *Richard Ford 1991 (1990)*
The summer of 1960 was a time of great change: the town of Great Falls, Montana was surrounded by fire and a family's life was thrown into disarray.

The Big Sky *A.B. Guthrie 1965 (1947)*
An historical novel about Boone Caudill who runs away from his Kentucky home aged sixteen to both fight and trade with the Blackfoot Indians and who ends up by falling in love with Teal Eye. One of many by the Pulitzer Prize Winner. Others include *Arfive* (1971) and *The Last Valley* (1975).

The Lady in Kicking Horse Reservoir *Richard Hugo (1973)*
Poetry, much of it to do with Montana, also *Death and the Good Life* a detective story by the poet.

The Shining *Stephen King 1977*
A horror story set in the Overlook Hotel in Colorado which involves dead spirits.

Rest and Be Thankful *Helen MacInnes 1949*
A rich widow gets stranded in Wyoming as the result of a storm; she falls in love with the country and stays.

✔ **Lonesome Dove** *Larry McMurty 1986 (1985)*
An epic novel and classic western set in the 1880s, Lonesome Dove is the story of a cattle drive from the Rio Grande to the highlands of Montana.

Fools Crow *James Welch 1986*
The impact of white civilization on Blackfoot Indians. Also *The Death of Jim Loney* 1987 (1979) about Jim Loney a half white and half native American who goes mad while living in a small Montana town.

The Virginian *Owen Wister 1928 (1902)*
Subtitled 'A Horseman of the Plains', this colonial romance is set in Wyoming between the years 1874 and 1892 when the state was still very wild. In 1892 there was a clash between the Wyoming Stock Growers Asso-

ciation who wanted an open range and roaming cattle and the Northern Wyoming Farmers and Stockgrowers Association who wanted to divide and fence the range. Wister had already visited the West and took this as the basis for his novel.

General Background

✔ **Miles from Nowhere**   Dayton Duncan 1993
Duncan goes to places in the Rocky Mountain States where very few people live and interviews them. Very interesting about the new versus the old West.

Montana Spaces   William Kittredge   1988
Original essays about the land and people of Montana. Also ✔ *The Last Best Place* (1988) an anthology of history, poetry and literature about Montana.

✔ **Places**   Jan Morris   1973
There is an essay on Wyoming in this collection.

Guides

✔ **The Smithsonian Guide to Historic America: Rocky Mountain States: Colorado, Wyoming, Idaho, Montana**
Jerry Camarillo Dunn   1989

✔ **Frommer's Colorado**   (undated) 1992

✔ **Frommer's Denver, Boulder and Colorado Springs**   1993 (1990)

✔ **Idaho Handbook. A Moon Publication**   Bill Loftus   1992

✔ **Montana Handbook. A Moon Publication**   W.C. McRae and Judy Jewell 1992

✔ **Wyoming Handbook. A Moon Publication**   Don Pitcher   1993 (1991)

✔ **Introduction to Montana. An Odyssey Guide**   Norma Tirrell   1992 (1991)

✔ **Hidden Southwest**   Ulysses Press   1992
Arizona, New Mexico, Southern Utah and Southern Colorado.

✔ **Hippocrene USA Guide to Rocky Mountain States**   Henry Weisser   1992

History

This House of Sky   Ivan Doig
A non-fiction account of Doig's family who came to Montana from Scotland.

✔ **Roadside History of Colorado**
James McTighe   1989 (1984)
A history of Colorado as seen and passed through from the highway.

Across the Wide Missouri
Bernard de Voto   1975 (1947)
De Voto is the classic historian of the west. Among his many books is *The Year of Decision 1846* (1989) (1942).

✔ **The Journals of Lewis and Clark**
Bernard de Voto (ed.)   1981 (1953)
The classic edition of the Lewis and Clark journals.

Natural History

Wild Life on the Rockies   Enos A. Mills 1988 (1909)
Enos Mills spent three successive winters on the slopes of the Rockies with a camera and notebook, recording the weather and topography for the government and animals and plants for himself.

✔ **The Rites of Autumn**   Dan O'Brien 1989 (1988)
In 1986 Dan O'Brien went to the Rocky Mountains of Montana to work as an endangered-species biologist; from there he travelled 2,000 miles from the Canadian border to the Gulf of Mexico. His purpose was to imitate the natural movement of wild falcons by following the autumnal migration of waterfowl in order to teach a young peregrine he had rescued to survive on her own.

Photography

✔ **Rocky Mountains**   David Muench   1975
A range of colour photographs spanning the seasons.

✔ **The Rocky Mountains**
Bryce S. Walker   1989
In the Time–Life World's Wild Places series.

Travel Literature

✔ **A Lady's Life in the Rocky Mountains**   Isabella Bird   1992 (1879)
In 1873 Isabella Bird rode her horse, Birdie, through the 'Wild West', meeting her 'dear (one-eyed) desperado', Rocky Mountain Jim, whom she described as 'a man any woman might love, but no sane woman would marry'.

✔ **A Mountain Boyhood**   Joe Mills   1988 (1926)
Joe Mills, the brother of Enos Mills (q.v.), climbed, watched wild animals, hunted and

trapped in Estes Park which became Rocky Mountain National Park in 1915, meeting many of the early settlers.

WEST COAST - CALIFORNIA

'California is a queer place —in a way, it has turned its back on the world, and looks into the void Pacific. It is absolutely selfish, very empty, but not false, and at least, not full of false effort . . . It's sort of crazy-sensible. Just the moment: hardly as far ahead as *carpe diem.*' D.H. Lawrence, letter to J.M. Murry (sic), 24 September 1923

Fiction/Poetry

Complete Short Stories   Ambrose Bierce
In the Midst of Life (Tales of Soldiers and Civilians) (1892), *The Monk and the Hang-mans Daughter, Fantastic Fables, The Eyes of the Panther*

The Abortion: an Historical Romance, 1966   Richard Brautigan   1974 (1971)
Brautigan writes convincingly about contemporary hedonistic Californian life. A public library in California becomes a place where authors can bring their unpublished manuscripts and where nothing is rejected.

✔ **The Happy Man**   Robert Easton   1993 (1942)
A vivid portrayal of the American west in the 1940s: 'Haunting as the tule-fogs of the Delta – a picture of one of those romantic, raunchy, – a picture of one of those romantic, raunchy, womanless worlds of work that men invent and inhabit – as strange as science fiction and as common as cattle ranching. These are the real cowboys. This is the real West, vintage 1940'. (Ursula Le Guin)

The Maltese Falcon   Dashiell Hammett
1982 (1929)
The Sam Spade mystery. Also set in San Francisco *The Dain Curse* 1975 (1928), *The Big Knockover, 106,000 Dollars Blood Money* and others: 'Hammett gave murder back to the kind of people that commit it for reasons, not just to provide a corpse; and with the means at hand, not with hand-wrought duelling pistols, curare and tropical fish. He took murder out of the Venetian vase and dropped it into the alley. He was spare, frugal, hard-boiled, but he did over and over again what only the best writers can ever do at all. He wrote scenes that seemed never to have been written before'. (Raymond Chandler)

Ramona   Helen Jackson   1884
A romantic love story in which Ramona falls in love with Alessandro, an Indian in southern California. Good descriptions of sheep-shearing and farming.

Tales of the City   Armistead Maupin   1989 *(1978)*
More Tales of the City 1989 (1980) and *Further Tales of the City* 1989 (1982) are all tales, many about the gay life in San Francisco. The novels began as a serial for the *San Francisco Chronicle*, in the tradition of Dickens and Thackeray and were very controversial in their original form.

✔ **Moby Dick**
Herman Melville (see 'New England')

The Golden Gate   Vikram Seth   1986
A novel in verse which brillianty captures Californian life in the early 1980s.

Cannery Row   John Steinbeck   1945
A novel set in Monterey which includes a range of differing characters. Also set in Monterey is *Sweet Thursday* (1954). *East of Eden* (1952) and *Of Mice and Men* (1937) are both set in Salinas. *The Grapes of Wrath* (1939) is about Okies who fled the Oklahoma dust-bowl during the depression.

The Wrecker   Robert Louis Stevenson   1982 *(1892) (see 'Oceania')*
Some of Dodd's piratical adventures take place in pre-earthquake San Francisco.

The Electric Kool-Aid Acid Test
Tom Wolfe   1968
A factual novel about the hippie generation in Haight-Ashbury.

General Background

Beyond the Wall   Edward Abbey   1984
A collection of well-written essays which explore the wilderness by the environmentalist and conservationist.

Guides

✔ **Access Guide Northern California Wine Country**   Richard Saul Wurman   1992

✔ **Access Guide San Francisco**
Richard Saul Wurman   1993

✔ **California and West Coast USA. The Rough Guide** *Deborah Besley, Wendy Ferguson, Jamie Jensen and Mick Sinclair 1994*

✔ **San Francisco. The Rough Guide** *Deborah Bosley and Jamie Jensen 1994*

✔ **Karen Brown's California Country Inns and Itineraries** *Clare Brown, June Brown and Karen Brown 1992 (1989)*

✔ **The Definitive California Bed and Breakfast Touring Guide** *1994–95* Over 300 inns, many of them illustrated with colour photographs.

✔ **American Express San Francisco and the Wine Regions** *Brian Eads 1992*

✔ **Everyman Guide San Francisco 1994**

✔ **Fodor's Bed and Breakfasts, Country Inns and Other Weekend Pleasures: The West Coast** *1992* California, Oregon, Washington.

✔ **Fodor's San Francisco '94.**

✔ **Frommer's California '94**

✔ **Frommer's San Francisco '94**

✔ **Insight Guide Northern California** *1992*

✔ **Insight Guide Southern California** *1992*

✔ **Let's Go California and Hawaii 1995**

The Smithsonian Guide to Historic America: The Pacific States, California, Oregon, Washington, Alaska, Hawaii *William Bryant Logan and Susan Ochshorn 1989*

Frommer's San Diego '93–'94

✔ **Catalina Island Handbook. A Moon Publication** *Chicki Mallan 1992*

✔ **Visitor's Guide California. A Moorland Guide** *Jackie and Brian Merritt 1993*

✔ **Undiscovered Islands of the US and Canadian West Coast** *Linda Lancione Moyer and Burl Willes 1992 (1991)* Many of the islands off the coast between British Columbia and northern California are uninhabited. Details of how to get there and what to see and do.

✔ **Where to Stay in Northern California** *Phil Philcox 1993* Descriptions of over 3,000 places to stay.

✔ **Where to Stay in Southern California** *Phil Philcox 1993* Descriptions of over 3,500 places to stay in Southern California.

✔ **Hidden Coast of California** *Ray Riegert 1993 (1988)* Everything to do and see on the thousand miles of Californian coast.

✔ **Ultimate California** *Ray Riegert 1993 (1990)* Seaside hotels, gourmet restaurants, campgrounds, desert hideaways, walking tours and ski resorts.

✔ **California. The Versatile Guide. A Duncan Petersen Guide** *Mick Sinclair 1994*

✔ **Thomas Cook Travellers California** *1993*

✔ **Northern California Handbook. A Moon Publication** *Kim Weir 1994*

✔ **Bed and Breakfast Guide. West Coast: California, Oregon, and Washington** *Courtia Worth, Terry Berger and Naomi Black 1989 (1984)* The 126 bed-and-breakfasts covered range from private houses and estates to country inns.

Leisure

✔ **California. Public Gardens. A Visitor's Guide** *Eric Sigg 1991* Major and minor gardens of California.

✔ **Webster's Wine Tours: California, Oregon and Washington** *Bob Thompson 1987* Detailed wine routes and profiles of over 400 wineries and vineyards with places to stay.

Natural History

✔ **The Mountains of California** *John Muir 1991 (1894)* Descriptions of what the naturalist John Muir found on his first trips into the then completely unspoilt Sierras. A facsimile edition with fifty-three engravings.

Photography

✔ **Yosemite and the Range of Light** *Ansel Adams 1979* Yosemite in black and white photographs during every season.

✔ **San Francisco**   *Morton Beebe*
233 photographs.

Fog and Sun, Sea and Stone
Steve Crouch   1980
Colour photographs of the Monterey coast.

Travel Literature

✔ **Nordhoff's West Coast. California,
Oregon and Hawaii**   *Charles Nordhoff*
1987 (1874)
Charles Nordhoff was a respected American
journalist, political commentator and descriptive writer who arrived in America from
Germany aged four. His descriptions of life
on the Pacific coast in the latter part of the
nineteenth century give us a fine historical
account: 'The California of those days was a
most unproductive or rather nothing-produc-
ing country – a great fertile waste in which
everything would grow but nothing was
made to grow except, indeed, beef . . . there
was nothing eatable but beef, beef, beef – a
never ending round of boiled beef.'

✔ **The Southwest Expedition of
Jedediah S. Smith. His Personal
Account of the Journey to California,
1826–1827**   *George R. Brooks (ed.)   1989*
(1977)
The journals of the travels of the 'mountain
man' who did so much to open the American
West had been lost and were rediscovered in
1967.

✔ **Two Years Before the Mast**
R.H. Dana   1841
Dana left his law studies at Harvard in 1834
and got a job as a sailor on a trading ship
bound for California; the voyage lasted two
years and he has fine descriptions of the
Californian coast.

LOS ANGELES

'Thought is barred in this city of Dreadful
Joy, and conversation is unknown.' Aldous
Huxley *Jesting Pilate* 1926

Art and Architecture

✔ **Los Angeles. The Architecture of
Four Ecologies**   *P. Reyner Banham   1990*
(1971)
'A fascinating and loving account of this most
exciting of cities.' (Angus Wilson *Observer*)

Fiction

✔ **The Big Sleep**   *Raymond Chandler   1948*
(1939)
Chandler's first novel, introducing the legendary Philip Marlowe, was an instant success when it was published – 'a new type of
crime novel in which ingenuity of plot and
detection combine with a distinctive and distinguished literary style'. Other titles include *Farewell, My Lovely* (1940), *The High
Window* (1942), *The Lady in the Lake* (1944)
and *The Long Good-Bye*.

The Last Tycoon   *F. Scott Fitzgerald   1969*
(1941)
An unfinished novel about a Hollywood pro-
ducer.

Blood Test   *Jonathan Kellerman   1987 (1986)*
Alex Delaware, a young but burned out child
psychologist, is called to the scene of a blood-
stained motel room with his LA cop friend,
Milo. This and *When the Bough Breaks*, *Private Eyes* and *Over the Edge* are psychological thrillers set in Los Angeles and written
by a psychologist.

The Nowhere City   *Alison Lurie   1986*
(1965)
A Harvard historian and his wife end up in
Los Angeles; he, enthusiastically, to write
the history of a corporation, she reluctantly.
However living in this 'foreign country'
changes both them and their marriage.

The Underground Man   *Ross Macdonald*
1971
Detective novel set in Southern California.

Guides

✔ **American Express Los Angeles and
San Diego**   *Brian Eads   1993 (1990)*

✔ **Fodor's Guide Los Angeles '94**

Travel Literature

✔ **L.A. Lore**   *Stephen Brook   1994 (1992)*
An in-depth exploration of Los Angeles which
examines the familiar, but also ferrets out
the unusual.

✔ **Destinations**   *Jan Morris   1980*
This collection includes an essay on Los
Angeles.

Los Angeles Without a Map
Richard Rayner   1988
Richard Rayner flew from London to Los
Angeles in search of adventure and Barbara,
a bunny girl whom he relentlessly pursues

and finally marries: 'I was living a movie and it turned into something which might have been invented by the Marx Brothers'.

✔ **Los Angeles. Capital of the Third World** David Rieff 1993 (1991)
Los Angeles, the epitome of the American Dream, has been radically transformed in recent years by the new immigrants from Asia and Latin America: 'A disturbing and brilliant examination of the America we have not yet faced'. (Joan Didion)

PACIFIC NORTH WEST: WASHINGTON, OREGON

'There is a great deal in the remark of the discontented traveller: 'When you have seen a pine forest, a bluff, a river, and a lake, you have seen all the scenery of western America. Sometimes the pine is three hundred feet high, and sometimes the rock is, and sometimes the lake is a hundred miles long. But it's all the same don't you know. I'm getting sick of it.'''
Rudyard Kipling From Sea to Sea 1889

Autobiography/Biography

Hole in the Sky, A Memoir
William Kittredge 1992
Memoirs of a boyhood spent in Southeast Oregon.

Fiction

Trask Don Berry 1960
Semi-factual novel based on the life of Eldridge Trask who was a pioneer in Oregon in the 1840s.

The Hawkline Monster
Richard Brautigan 1974
In this weird spoof set in Oregon in 1902, much revolves round a strange pair of sisters.

Honey in the Horn H.L Davis 1975 (1935)
A novel about pioneers and homesteading in Oregon at the turn of the century.

The Sniper Willo Davis Roberts 1984
The heroine inherits a Victorian house and a series of murders ensue.

Wild Geese Calling Stewart E. White 1940
A young couple meet in Oregon, live in Seattle and are lured north to Alaska by the call of the wild geese.

✔ **This Boy's Life** Tobias Wolff 1992 (1989)
A semi-autobiographical novel about growing up in Oregon. Also The *Barracks Thief* and *Hunters in the Snow*.

Guides

✔ **On the Loose in the Pacific Northwest and Alaska. A Berkeley Guide** 1992

✔ **Fodor's Bed and Breakfasts, Country Inns and Other Weekend Pleasures: The Pacific Northwest** 1993
Oregon, Washington, Western British Columbia.

✔ **Fodor's Bed and Breakfasts, Country Inns and Other Weekend Pleasures: The West Coast** 1992
California, Oregon, Washington.

✔ **Fodor's Guide Pacific North Coast** 1994
Oregon, Washington, British Colombia and Southeast Alaska.

✔ **Fodor's Guide Seattle and Vancouver** 1992

✔ **Frommer's Seattle and Portland '94–'95**

✔ **Insight Guide Seattle** 1993

✔ **Pacific Northwest. The Rough Guide** Phil Lee and Tim Jepson 1994

✔ **The Smithsonian Guide to Historic America: The Pacific States, California, Oregon, Washington, Alaska, Hawaii** William Bryant Logan and Susan Ochshorn 1989

✔ **Washington Handbook. A Moon Publication** Dianne J. Boulerice Lyons and Archie Satterfield 1992

✔ **Oregon Handbook. A Moon Publication** Stuart Warren and Ted Long Ishikawa 1991

✔ **Bed and Breakfast Guide. West Coast: California, Oregon, and Washington** Courtia Worth, Terry Berger and Naomi Black 1989 (1984) (see 'California')

History

Skid Road Murray Morgan 1988
'On this city where I now live (Seattle), I'd nominate Murray Morgan's brilliant urban history . . . ' (Jonathan Raban)

Leisure

✔ **Webster's Wine Tours: California, Oregon and Washington** Bob Thompson
1987
Detailed wine routes and profiles of over 400 wineries and vineyards with places to stay.

Travel Literature

✔ **Astoria. Adventure in the Pacific Northwest** Washington Irving 1987 (1839)
The story of John Jacob Astor's dream to establish a trading empire on the northwest coast of America that via the Pacific would reach China. The book is based on Astor's private papers and is a saga of daring, intrigue, heroism and betrayal.

✔ **Nordhoff's West Coast. California, Oregon and Hawaii** Charles Nordhoff
1987 (1874) (see 'California')

HAWAII

'The loveliest fleet of islands that lies anchored in any ocean.' Mark Twain

Fiction/Poetry

From Here to Eternity James Jones
1952 (1980)
Considered shocking when it was first published because of its brutally realistic portrayal of army life, *From Here to Eternity* is set in pre-Pearl Harbour Hawaii and tells the story of love and admiration between the Top Sergeant and the GI.

Murder Between Dark and Dark
Max Long 1939
An Hawaiian policeman, Komako Koa, is asked to solve a series of murders in the haole community. He also appears in *The Lava Flow Murders* (1940) and *Death Goes Native* (1941).

Hawaii James Michener 1959
A controversial historical novel, written in the year that Hawaii became the fiftieth American state, which shows the cultural kaleidoscope of Hawaii after waves of people came from Asia, the Pacific and the United States. The period covers from millions of years ago, before the geological formation of the islands, up until 1954.

✔ **The Whiteness of Bones**
Susanna Moore 1991 (1989)
After a childhood spent in Hawaii, Mamie

Clarke arrives in New York. Also *My Old Sweetheart* 1984 (1982).

✔ **Lucky Come Hawaii** Jon Hiroshi Shirota
1965
The author is a Japanese–American and writes about a Maui family during the year of the Pearl Harbour attack.

✔ **Island Nights' Entertainments**
Robert Louis Stevenson 1987 (1893)
Two stories from this collection are set in Hawaii: *The Bottle Imp* and *The Isle of Voices*.

Guides

✔ **Hawaii. Travel Survival Kit**
Glenda Bendure and Ned Friary 1993 (1990)

✔ **Big Island of Hawaii Handbook**
J.D. Bisignani 1990

✔ **Kauai Handbook. A Moon Publication** J.D. Bisignani 1989

✔ **Maui Handbook (Including Molokai and Lanai)** J.D. Bisignani 1991 (1986)

✔ **Insight Guide Hawaii** 1992

✔ **Let's Go California and Hawaii 1995**

The Smithsonian Guide to Historic America: The Pacific States, California, Oregon, Washington, Alaska, Hawaii William Bryant Logan and Susan Ochshorn 1989

✔ **Odyssey Illustrated Guide Hawaii**
Moana Tregaskis 1993 (1992)

✔ **Access Guide Hawaii**
Richard Saul Wurman 1992

Leisure

✔ **Hawaii. A Walker's Guide**
Rodney N. Smith nd
A practical guide to walking on all the main islands of Hawaii.

Natural History

The Indigenous Trees of the Hawaiian Islands Joseph F. Rock 1974 (1913)
The definitive book on Hawaii's indigenous trees which was a pioneering work in its day. Each species is annotated with descriptions of the habitat.

Travel Literature

A Residence of Twenty-One Years in the Sandwich Islands Hiram Bingham
1969 (1847)
Bingham was a missionary from Vermont who according to Michener ' . . . is one of the most difficult great men of history to love . . . and I consider his awkward and unlovely book . . . the most significant volume yet published on the islands.'

Six Months Among the Palm Groves, Coral Reefs, and Volcanoes of the Sandwich Islands Isabella Bird 1876 (1875)
Isabella Bird remained in the Hawaiian Islands for nearly seven months after stopping there on a trip she was making for health reasons. She travelled on a horse through many of the islands, exploring the interior, climbing mountains and visiting active volcanoes and remote places. She was urged to write about Hawaii since she had got to know it so well and was considered a kamaina (old resident) rather than a stranger. Written as letters to her sister in Scotland.

Fire Fountains: The Kingdom of Hawaii, Its Volcanoes and the History of the Missions C.F. Gordon-Cumming 1883
Constance Gordon-Cumming made an extensive tour of the Hawaiian Islands, writing about Honolulu and the rest of Oahu, Hilo, Kilauea Volcano and Lahaina. She includes a history of the Hawaiian peoples.

The Cruise of the Snark Jack London
1911 (see 'Pacific Islands')
A chapter describes a trip through the 'House of the Sun', the dormant crater of Haleakala and a stay at the famous Parker Ranch on the big island of Hawaii. He also visited the isolated leper colony on Molokai.

✔ Nordhoff's West Coast: California, Oregon and Hawaii Charles Nordhoff
1987 (1874) (see 'USA West')
Nordhoff ran away from home with $25 and departed from Philadelphia on a journey which after two years took him to Hawaii. He writes that 'Honolulu at that time (just before the discovery of gold in California) was a straggling, rather poorly constructed town . . . The whole place had a listless, impassive look, as though the inhabitants were only taking a rest, preparatory to starting on a journey.'

Travels in Hawaii Robert Louis Stevenson
1973
Stevenson first arrived in Hawaii on the yacht *Casco* in 1889 and spent five months exploring the islands. *Travels in Hawaii* includes ten sketches of life at the Kona Coast, the City of Refuge and on Molokai.

Summer Cruising in the South Seas
Charles Warren Stoddard (1874)
'There are but two writers who have touched the South Seas with genius, both Americans: Melville and Charles Warren Stoddard.' (Stevenson) Stoddard loved Hawaii and in this collection writes about a servant lad 'Joe of Lahaina' on Maui, about dancers of the forbidden hula in 'The Night-Dancers of Waipio' and about a description of a ride by mule into the dormant crater of Haleakala (named because the demigod Maui is supposed to have captured the sun in his net there).

Letters from Hawaii Mark Twain 1975
Twain arrived in Honolulu in 1866 to spend four months as a roving reporter for the Sacramento *Union*. This was the first time that Twain left the United States and he wrote twenty-five sketches of his impressions during his travels to Maui and Mount Haleakala, Hawaii's Kona Coast and Honolulu. These letters were published in the *Union* and cover the sugar and whaling industries as well as descriptions of ther scenery, climate and people.

Canada

GENERAL

'If Canada did not exist it would be to the interest of the United States to invent her.'
James Bryce, quoted by H.A.L. Fisher *An Unfinished Autobiography* 1940

Anthropology

Maps and Dreams   Hugh Brody   1986 (1981)
An extremely interesting book about the Beaver people of northwest Canada: 'A wonderful book, full of travel and people. Most of all, it is superb anthropology, challenging many of the accepted notions about the lives of hunters.' (Paul Theroux)

✔ **Arctic Dreams. Imagination and Desire in a Northern Landscape**
Barry Lopez   1986 (see 'Arctic')

Art and Archaeology

Canadian Folk Art   Michael Bird   1983
A catalogue of a cross-section of Canadian folk art. Well illustrated.

✔ **A Concise History of Canadian Painting**   Dennis Reid   1988
A comprehensive and well illustrated book about Canada's leading artists from 1665 up until 1980.

Fiction/Poetry

✔ **Wilderness Tips**   Margaret Atwood 1992 (1991)
A collection of short stories: 'Vintage, gleaming, catch-your-breath Atwood.' (*Scotsman*). Other books by Margaret Atwood include *Surfacing*, (1973) about two couples on holiday together in Quebec, *Cat's Eye*, *Life Before Man* (1980) set in Toronto and *Lady Oracle*.

Mountain Meadow   John Buchan   1941
A man is given a year to live and decides to spend his time searching for a man who has disappeared in northern Canada.

Shadows on the Rock   Willa Cather   1984 (1931)
Set in the late seventeenth and early eighteenth centuries in French Quebec when a French family, the Auclairs, begin a new and completely different life from the one they had left in Paris.

I Heard the Owl Call My Name
Margaret Craven   1974 (1973)
The story of one man's discovery of the ultimate truths of life and love and courage and dignity in a small village among the Indians of the Northwest: 'Rare and beautiful . . . you will never be the same again.' (*Seattle Times*)

✔ **The Cornish Trilogy**   Robertson Davies
The Cornish trilogy is made up of *The Rebel Angels* (1982), *What's Bred in the Bone* (1985) and *The Lyre of Orpheus* (1988). 'A master storyteller . . . The murkier areas of the soul are the author's forte . . . energy, historical sweep, humorous understanding of moral inconveniences, sympathy for the unfulfilled.' (*Listener*)

✔ **The Deptford Trilogy**
Robertson Davies   1983 (1975)
The Deptford Trilogy is made up of *Fifth Business*, *The Manticore* (see 'Switzerland') and *World of Wonders* and is a complex and labyrinthian novel woven around a mysterious death; includes myth, history and magic.

The Land God Gave to Cain
Hammond Innes   1958
A thriller set in Labrador about the hardships suffered by the grandson of a murdered prospector.

✔ **A Jest of God**   Margaret Laurence   1966
Most of Margaret Laurence's books are set in the fictional prairie backwater of Manawaka and are about the frustrations of women in small town life. *The Fire Dwellers* (1969) is set in Vancouver and *Diviners* (1974) is about a middle-aged writer living in the backwoods of Ontario.

Call of the Wild   Jack London   1903
London lived in the Yukon goldfields during the Klondike gold rush. He also wrote *White Fang and Other Stories* (1906).

✔ **Hear Us O Lord from Heaven thy Dwelling Place**   Malcolm Lowry   1991 (1962)
Lowry spent much of his adult life on the wild west Pacific coast in log cabins and shacks he built for himself.

✔ **The Lost Salt Gift of Blood**
Alistair MacLeod   1991 (1976)
A collection of stories set in Cape Breton, Nova Scotia, a region where Gaelic is still spoken: 'MacLeod writes with the sort of intensity that gives his beautifully shaped sen-

tences the haunting power of the Gaelic songs which are within him'.

✔ **Anne of Green Gables**
L.M. Montgomery 1993 (1905)
Anne is sent from the local orphanage to help out an old man and his sister on their farm. Initially she is very outspoken and upsets the local community, but eventually her kind heart is discovered. Set in Avonlea, a peninsula which juts out into the Gulf of St Lawrence.

Black Robe Brian Moore 1985
A missionary's journey in the seventeenth century, into native territory in Canada, allows Moore to write about Catholicism, repression and redemption. *The Luck of Ginger Coffey* (1960) is about an Irish family in Montreal.

Lives of Girls and Women Alice Munro 1982 (1978)
Most of Alice Munro's short stories deal primarily with the lives of women in rural, protestant southwest Ontario. Her other books include *The Progress of Love, Dance of the Happy Shades* (1973), *The Beggar Maid* (1979), *The Moons of Jupiter* (1983) and *Friend of My Youth*.

✔ **In the Skin of a Lion**
Michael Ondaatje 1988 (1987)
The threads of different people's lives weave in and out of this beautifully written novel which concentrates on work and workers.

✔ **The Shipping News** E. Annie Proulx 1994
A compelling book about fishing and newspaper life in Newfoundland. Winner of the Pulitzer prize.

✔ **The Apprenticeship of Duddy Kravitz** Mordecai Richler 1980 (1959)
Richler grew up in Montreal's Jewish working-class ghetto and sets most of his book against this background.

✔ **The Republic of Love** Carol Shields 1993 (1992)
Set in Winnipeg, Fay, a folklorist who studies mermaids, falls in love with Tom, who hosts a late night radio show: 'Perfectly rendered, a touching, elegantly funny, luscious work of fiction . . . I read it with awe and delight' (*The New York Times*). Also by Carol Shields *Mary Swann* and *Happenstance*.

The Engineer of Human Souls
Josef Skvorecky 1984
An emigré from Czechoslovakia observes and writes about his fellow emigrés in Toronto. Subtitled 'An entertainment on the old

themes of life, women, fate, dreams, the working class, secret agents, love and death'.

By Grand Central Station I Sat Down and Wept Elizabeth Smart 1991 (1945)
Elizabeth Smart was born in Ottawa. This semi-autobiogaphical novel describes her intense and tragic love affair with the poet George Barker: 'A passion between a man and two women, one of them his wife – a love both despairing and triumphant upon which the reader may gaze, awed, appalled, or even, perhaps, envious.' (*The Times*)

The Chrysalids John Wyndham 1983 (1955)
Science-fiction about a group of telepathic children in post-holocaust Labrador. The groups of 'normal' people who have survived become obsessed that everything different is evil and must be eliminated. A small boy, a chrysalid, dreams of the past, but is discovered by the authorities and driven out.

Guides

✔ **USA and Canada. Travellers Survival Kit** Simon Calder 1993 (1985)

✔ **Ontario. Ulysses Travel Guide**
Pascale Couture 1992
A guide to the whole of Ontario including the Niagara Falls, Ottawa and Toronto.

✔ **Fodor's Bed and Breakfasts, Country Inns, and Other Weekend Pleasures: The Pacific Northwest** 1993
Oregon, Washington, Western British Columbia.

✔ **Fodor's Canada '95**

✔ **Fodor's Montréal and Québec City 1995**

✔ **Fodor's Guide Pacific North Coast '95**
Oregon, Washington, British Columbia, Southeast Alaska.

✔ **Fodor's Guide Seattle and Vancouver** (undated) 1992

✔ **Insight Guide Canada** 1993

✔ **Canada. The Rough Guide**
Tim Jepson, Phil Lee and Tania Smith 1993

✔ **British Columbia Handbook. A Moon Guide** Jane King 1992

✔ **Elegant Small Hotels. A Connoisseur's Guide** Pamela Lanier 1993 (see 'USA')

✔ **Let's Go USA and Canada 1995**

✔ **Country Inns and Back Roads.
North America 1993–1994** *Jerry Levitin
1993*

✔ **Canada. Travel Survival Kit**
Mark Lightbody and Tom Smallman 1992 (1983)

✔ **Introduction to Canada. An
Odyssey Guide** *Garry Marchant 1991*

✔ **Michelin Green Guide Canada** *1993*

✔ **Michelin Green Guide Quebec** *1992*

✔ **Undiscovered Islands of the US and
Canadian West Coast**
Linda Lancione Moyer and Burl Willes 1992 (1991)

✔ **USA By Rail. Plus Canada** *John Pitt
1992 (See 'USA')*

✔ **Thomas Cook Traveller's
Vancouver and British Columbia** *1993*

History

✔ **Come From Away** *David Macfarlane
1991*
The Newfoundland colonial experience seen
through the eyes of one family.

✔ **The Penguin History of Canada**
Kenneth McNaught 1988 (1969)
A good general history from the earliest ex-
peditions up until the 1980s.

**History of the Conspiracy of Pontiac,
and the War of the North American
Tribes against the English Colonies
after the Conquest of Canada**
Francis Parkman 1851
Also by Parkman: *France and England in
North America* (1865), a seminal history in
seven volumes.

A Social History of Canada
George Woodcock 1989 (1988)
A book about the dramatic changes in lifestyle that people had to adapt to when life in
the wilderness became life in the city.

Leisure

✔ **Rivers Running Free** *Judith Niemi and
Barbara Wieser (eds.) 1992 (1987) (see 'USA –
General')*

✔ **High Summer. Backpacking The
Canadian Rockies** *Chris Townsend 1989*

Natural History (see 'USA')

✔ **Pocket Guide to Mammals of North
America** *John Burton*

✔ **The Pocket Guide to Birds of Prey
of North America** *Philip Burton*

✔ **The Macmillan Field Guide to
North Atlantic Shorebirds**
Richard Chandler
A well-illustrated and comprehensive hand-
book.

✔ **The Pocket Guide to Wild Flowers
of North America** *Pamela Forey*

✔ **The Pocket Guide to Trees of North
America** *Alan Mitchell*

✔ **The Pocket Guide to Birds of
Western North America** *Frank Shaw*

Photography

✔ **Panoramic Canada** *nd*
Lavish colour photographs.

✔ **Labrador** *Robert Stewart 1989*
In the Time-Life World's Wild Places series.

Travel Literature

**Maple Leaf Rag. Travels Across
Canada** *Stephen Brook 1987*
An amusing journey across the 'vast and
daunting country' of Canada; Brook admits
that he was full of prejudices before he went,
gaining some new ones while he was there,
but during his travels he saw and discovered
much that one does not normally hear or read
about.

✔ **Down the Wild River North**
Constance Helmericks 1993 (1969) (see 'Arctic')

**Roughing it in the Bush: Or Forest
Life in Canada** *Susanna Moodie 1987
(1852)*
The experiences and decline of a pioneering
English couple in southeastern Ontario.

O Canada: Travels in an Unknown
Country *Jan Morris 1992*
Ten essays about Canadian cities by one of
Britain's best travel writers.

✔ The Thousand Miles with a Dog
Sled *Hudson Stuck 1988 (1914) (see 'Arctic')*

Central America

GENERAL

Anthropology

✔ **Aztec and Maya Myths** *Karl Taube
1993*
Descriptions of Aztec, Maya and Mesoamerican mythology. The author explains the
major areas and sources of research and
shows how the Maya and flood myths have
survived in various forms in pre-Hispanic
writing and art.

Art and Archaeology

✔ **The Ancient Americas** *W.M. Bray,
F.H. Swanson and I.S. Farrrington 1989 (1975)*
A well illustrated book which deals with the
archaeology and pre-Columbian cultures of
North and South America and Mesoamerica.

✔ **Lost Cities of North and Central
America** *David Hatcher Childress 1992*
A search for the lost cities of Honduras, Guatemala, Belize, the Yucatan and northern
and southern Mexico. The author calls himself a maverick archaeologist and has been
all over the world seeking ancient cities, pyramids, ruins, tunnels and treasure.

✔ **The Maya** *Michael Coe 1993 (1987)*
A new enlarged good, clear introduction to
the archaeology, life and culture of the Maya
which has now become a classic. Full of black
and white photographs, line drawings and
plans.

✔ **Kingdoms of Gold, Kingdoms of
Jade. The Americas Before Columbus**
Brian M. Fagan 1991 (see 'South America')
The book includes the civilizations of ancient
Mesoamerica: the Olmecs, the Maya, the Az-
tecs, Teotihuacan and the Toltecs.

✔ **Maya. The Riddle and Rediscovery
of a Lost Civilization** *Charles Gallenkamp
1987 (1959)*
A slightly sensationalist account of Maya

archaeology which attempts to unravel the
mystery of why the Maya at the height of
their Classic Period in 800 AD suddenly
ceased all activity, abandoned their cities,
left temples unfinished and vanished.

✔ **The Art and Architecture of
Ancient America** *George Kubler 1990
(1962) (see 'South America')*
The first two sections are about Mexico and
Central America; the book is chiefly about
the architecture, sculpture and painting of
the areas and explains the art rather than
the archaeology in detail.

✔ **Latin American Art of the
Twentieth Century** *Edward Lucie-Smith
1993 (see 'South America')*

✔ **The Art of Mesoamerica from
Olmec to Aztec** *Mary Ellen Miller 1991
(1986)*
A well-illustrated survey of the art and architecture of Mesoamerica which includes the
Olmec, Maya, Teotihuacan, Toltec and Aztec
civilizations as well as some lesser known
ones.

✔ **Incidents of Travel in Central
America, Chiapas and Yucatan**
John L. Stephens 1969 (1841)
Stephens writes with excitement and wonder
at discovering the city of Copan: 'It is impossible to describe the interest with which I
explored these ruins. The ground was entirely new . . . The beauty of the sculpture,
the solemn stillness of the woods, disturbed
only by the scrambling of monkeys and the
chattering of parrots, the desolation of the
city, and the mystery that hung over it, all
created an interest higher, if possible, than I
had ever felt among the ruins of the Old
World.' He also explores Palenque, Quirigua,
Patinamit, Utatlan, Gueguetenango, Ocos-
ingo and Uxmal. His pioneering work is accompanied by 111 detailed illustrations by
Frederick Catherwood.

Fiction/Poetry

✔ **The Penguin Book of Latin American Short Stories**
Thomas Colchie (ed.)   1993 (1991) (see 'South America')

General Background

✔ **Memory of Fire**   *Eduardo Galeano*
The trilogy comprised *Genesis* 1987 (1982), *Faces and Masks* 1989 (1984) and *Century of the Wind* 1989 (1988). They are a series of vignettes which tell the story by weaving fact and fiction, of the conquest of Latin America through the voices of such people as Simon Bolivar, Benito Juarez and Abraham Lincoln.

Open Veins of Latin America. Five Centuries of the Pillage of a Continent
Eduardo Galeano   1973 (1971)
Galeano sees Latin America's underdevelopment and 'losing' as a product of the capitalist world's 'winning'. 'Our defeat was always implicit in the victory of others; our wealth has always generated our poverty by nourishing the prosperity of others – the empires and their native overseers.' His book is divided into two parts: 'Mankind's Poverty as a Consequence of the Wealth of the Land' and 'Development Is a Voyage with More Shipwrecks than Navigators'.

✔ **The Soccer War**   *Ryszard Kapuscinski*
1991 (1990) (see 'Africa')
Kapuscinski spent ten years as the Polish Press Agency's only foreign correspondent, five of them in Latin America; he witnessed twenty-seven revolutions and coups and gives an 'astonishing account of how he covered the bloody, scarcely believable conflict that Honduras and El Salvador waged in 1969 over a pair of soccer games'. (*Vanity Fair*)

The Missionaries   *Norman Lewis   1988*
The third in Norman Lewis' trio of autobiographical books which is also a travel book; he had found that missionaries played an increasingly prominent part in his travels: 'I encountered so many abuses and saw so much damage to the human environment inflicted behind a pseudo-religious front, I found it impossible to remain silent.' He looks at areas in the world where he encountered these abuses.

✔ **You Can't Drown the Fire**
Alicia Partnoy (ed.)   1989 (1988) (see 'South America')

✔ **Latin America. The Writer's Journey**   *Greg Price (see 'South America – General')*

✔ **Traveller's Literary Companion South and Central America**
Jason Wilson   1993

Guides

✔ **Guatemala, Belize and Yucatan. La Ruta Maya. A Travel Survival Kit**
Tom Brosnahan   1994

✔ **The Maya Road. Eastern Mexico, Belize, Lowland Guatemala: Natural History and Mayan Sites. A Bradt Guide**   *Jim Conrad   1992*

✔ **Everyman Guide: Route of the Mayas**   *1995*

✔ **The Maya Route. The Ultimate Guidebook**   *Richard Harris and Stacy Ritz   1993*
Clearly laid out practical guide.

✔ **Travellers Survival Kit Central America**   *Emily Hatchwell and Simon Calder   1991*

✔ **Central America on a Shoestring**
Nancy Keller, Tom Brosnahan and Rob Rachowiecki   1992

✔ **Cadogan Guide Central America**
Natascha Norton and Mark Whatmore   1993

✔ **Mexico and Central American Handbook 1995**   *Published by Trade and Travel*

History

A History of Latin America
George Pendle   1967 (1963)
An authoritative and concise introduction to Latin America: economics, politics and history.

✔ **The Penguin History of Latin America**   *Edwin Williamson   1992 (see 'South America')*

Leisure

✔ **Adventure Travel in Latin America**   *Scott Graham   1990 (see 'South America' and 'Caribbean')*

Natural History

South America and Central America: a Natural History *Jean Dorst 1967 (see 'South America')*

Photography

✔ **The Jungles of Central America**
An illustrated Time-Life book about the jungles and their wildlife.

✔ **Other Americas** *Sebastiao Salgado 1986*
A powerful collection of black and white photographs, taken over seven years, of Indians in Brazil, Mexico, Ecuador, Peru, Bolivia and Guatemala.

✔ **Lost Kingdoms of the Maya**
Gene S. Stuart and George E. Stuart 1993
An illustrated book with plenty of text by a team of archaeologists, includes up-to-date information on the latest discoveries.

Travel Literature

✔ **The Fever Coast Log** *Gordon Chaplin 1992*
The account of a journey by a couple in a 36-foot boat down the Caribbean coasts of Belize, Honduras, Guatemala and Nicaragua. Their onshore adventures are combined with their life at sea.

✔ **Reality is the Bug that Bit Me in the Galapagos** *Charlotte Du Cann and Mark Watson 1994*
In 1991 the authors sold everything in London and embarked on life out of a suitcase in the Americas. They started in Mexico and travelled through Guatemala, Honduras, Ecuador, Bolivia and Chile. Highly original and well written.

✔ **Tekkin a Waalk Along the Miskito Coast** *Peter Ford 1993 (1991)*
Ford travels from Belize through Guatemala, Honduras, Costa Rica and Panama and through the wild territories of the Garifuna and Miskito indians; in Creole he was 'tekkin a waalk'.

Fire Down Below. A Journey of Exploration from Mexico to Chile
Robert Harvey 1988
Robert Harvey who had been Latin American correspondent for *The Economist* travels through Central and South America trying to discover the character of each nation. He looks at current news reports as well as describing the landscapes and peoples of each country.

Beyond the Mexique Bay *Aldous Huxley 1991 (1934)*
Huxley travelled through Belize, Guatemala and Mexico in 1934. He writes something refreshingly original, albeit sometimes eccentric, about everyone he meets and everything he sees.

So Far From God *Patrick Marnham 1985*
After travelling through California, Marnham goes to Mexico, Guatemala, El Salvador and Nicaragua. He went to investigate the old Spanish colonial empire from which the United States had evolved and records everything he encounters with a razor sharp eye. His vivid interpretations and impressions make this an excellent book. [Colin Thubron]

✔ **Nothing to Declare** *Mary Morris 1988 (1987)*
Mary Morris travelled on her own from Mexico down through Central America. The book is a reflective account of her journey which she made so that 'life would begin to make sense to me again'.

Through the Volcanoes *Jeremy Paxman 1989*
A semi-political travel book which investigates the turmoil in every country in Central America.

A Butterfly Sings to Pacaya *Nigel Pride 1978*
A journey by jeep through Mexico, Guatemala and Belize which has a good description of the climb of the Pacaya volcano.

Travels in Central America particularly in Nicaragua *E.G. Squier 1853 (see 'Nicaragua')*

✔ **Time Among the Maya. Travels in Belize, Guatemala and Mexico**
Ronald Wright 1993 (1989)
'A brilliant, highly engaging travelogue, sparkling with wit, incisive observation and sheer good writing . . . Wright is the ideal travelling companion.' (*Toronto Star*) Wright attempted to find the roots of the Maya and to see how they had survived after all the invasions they had had to contend with. His own journey is combined with their history and civilization.

MEXICO

Anthropology

The Children of Sanchez *Oscar Lewis 1964 (1961)*
Subtitled 'The Autobiography of a Mexican

Family', this book was described by Stuart Hampshire as 'The most vivid, complete, and internal description of modern poverty, and of the survival of poverty, that I have ever read'. Oscar Lewis was an anthropologist who wove what he recorded and saw into a work of art. *A Death in the Sanchez Family* (1970) continues the saga. [Colin Thubron]

✔ **Unknown Mexico. Explorations in the Sierra Madre and Other Regions 1890–1898**   *Carl Lumholtz   1987 (1902)*
The mountainous northwestern area of Mexico in which the Norwegian Lumholtz mounted three expeditions was almost completely unknown at the turn of the century. Lumholtz went in search of cliff-dwelling tribes and although he did not find any he did find primitive tribes living in caves. He also amassed a huge collection of plants, animals and birds and his second expedition to the region was under the auspices of the American Museum of Natural History. On his third expedition he lived with the cave-dwelling Tarahumare Indians (descendants of the Aztecs), quickly winning their trust through his compassionate attitude and by learning their language.

✔ **Sons of the Earth. The People of Mexico and Guatemala – Their Land, History, and Culture**   *Eric Wolf   1959*
Eric Wolf, a professor of anthropology, attempts to trace the lifeline of Middle American culture by synthesis rather than in great detail, making an accessible and readable book.

Art and Archaeology

✔ **Mexico**   *Michael D. Coe   1988 (1962)*
A well-illustrated book describing the ancient civilizations.

✔ **The Ancient Kingdoms of Mexico**
Nigel Davies   1990 (1982)
An archaeological study of ancient Mexico which spans four civilizations: the Olmecs, the culture of Teotihuacan, the Toltec dynasty and the Aztecs.

✔ **The Cities of Ancient Mexico. Reconstructing a Lost World**
Jeremy A. Sabloff   1992 (1990)
Descriptions of life during the Olmec, Zapotec, Maya, Toltec and Aztec cultures. Sabloff emphasizes the unity of these cultures and his text is accompanied by photographs, plans and line drawings.

✔ **Incidents of Travel in Yucatan**
John L Stephens   1963 (1843)
Before Stephens went to the Yucatan in 1841

very little was known about the country. He discovered forty-four Maya sites which he wrote about and which are illustrated with realistic drawings and engravings by Catherwood.

✔ **Mysteries of the Mexican Pyramids**
Peter Tompkins   1976
The author concentrates on trying to unravel the secrets of the ancient pyramids, many of which lie probably still undiscovered in the Mexican jungle. He pays particular attention to the Pyramid of the Sun and the Pyramid of the Moon at Teotihuacan.

Autobiography/Biography

Life in Mexico   *Frances Calderon de la Barca 1987 (1843)*
The author was the Scottish wife of the Spanish ambassador to Mexico; they were in Mexico for nearly two years until 1841 and the book is a mixture of letters and her personal journals. It gives riveting insights into the minutiae of daily life in Mexico at the time as well as looking at the overall political and social scene. After Mexico they lived in the United States, Paris and Madrid where she eventually became governess to the daughter of Queen Isabela II of Spain.

Reminiscences of the Mexican Revolution   *Patrick O'Hea   1981 (1966)*
Patrick O'Hea was an Anglo-Mexican farm manager who found himself in the midst of the Mexican Revolution in 1910. He managed to protect his lands from the shellfire of both sides and saved many lives by courageous negotiation.

My Art, My Life   *Diego Rivera   1960*
The book began as a newspaper interview which Rivera gave Gladys March in 1944. She was immediately impressed by his quick mind and staggering imagination and realized that much he had said orally could stand up as writing. The book is written as if by him.

Fiction/Poetry

✔ **The Adventures of Augie March**
Saul Bellow   1966 (1953)
Augie Marsh grows up in Chicago, and on his first trip abroad goes to Mexico with a rich lover to hunt iguanas in the south. The Mexico which drives Augie to a crisis is one where there are many expatriate Americans who are trying to escape the materialism of the States.

Queer William Burroughs 1986 (1984)
An autobiographical novel written when Burroughs had had to flee to Mexico City on account of drugs charges. Lee (the rich junkie in the novel) eventually ends up in Ecuador. Burroughs also wrote *Junkie* (1953) about his experiences as an addict in Mexico.

Mexico Set Len Deighton 1989 (1984)
A spy thriller with scenes set in Mexico City and along the Pacific coast.

✔ **Like Water for Chocolate**
Laura Esquivel 1994 (1989)
An original novel which is the bizarre history of the all-female De La Garza family; it is written in monthly instalments with recipes, romances and home remedies.

The Ultimate Good Luck Richard Ford
1981
Set in a violent Oaxaca, where a Vietnam vet is trying to get his brother out of jail; it envokes the druggy low life of the city.

✔ **Terra Nostra** Carlos Fuentes 1987 (1975)
A huge and complex novel about the life and times of Philip II of Spain as he builds El Escorial, marries Elizabeth Tudor and witnesses the discovery of the New World. The *Sunday Times* described it as 'a whacking great affirmation of fiction as the only proper vehicle for poetry, speculation, prophecy, surmise, heroic optimism . . . ' Other novels by Fuentes include *Christopher Unborn* 1990 (1987), *Where the Air is Clear*, *The Death of Artemio Cruz*, *The Old Gringo*, *A Change of Skin* and *Myself and Others*.

✔ **The Power and the Glory**
Graham Greene 1971 (1940)
The 'whisky' priest of Graham Greene's novel had done everything wrong in the eyes of the Church: had a 'wife', fathered a daughter, had an addiction to brandy and yet obstinately remained a priest. The descriptions of Mexico and the struggles with a catholic conscience are vintage Greene.

✔ **Eyeless in Gaza** Aldous Huxley 1989
(1936)
The lives of a group of schoolfriends are followed up to the Second World War; Anthony Beavis goes to Mexico to help a friend support a Mexican revolutionary.

The Dead Girls Jorge Ibarguengoitia 1983
(1981)
This and *Two Crimes* (1984 (1979)) are black comic thrillers; *The Dead Girls* is based on the true story of the murders of six prostitutes in a Mexican brothel.

✔ **The Plumed Serpent** D.H. Lawrence
1983 (1926)
Through the eyes of Kate, the heroine of the novel, we learn much about both post-revolutionary Mexico and the landscape, people and religion. Lawrence is fascinated by reincarnation and the possibility of rebirth; this is explored through Kate's lover, Cipriano who is involved with the Quetzalcoatl cult. Lawrence described the book as 'nearer to my heart than any other work of mine'.

✔ **Under the Volcano** Malcolm Lowry
1990 (1947)
Set in Cuernavaca where the alcoholic British consul Firmin has a breakdown and finally dies, *Under the Volcano* has now become a cult book, although when it was published it sold only two copies in two years in Canada. Although written as a stream-of-consciousness, there are very accurate descriptions of the surroundings. [Stephen Brook]

✔ **Collected Poems** Octavio Paz
1957–87 Edited and translated by Eliot Weinberger
1988

✔ **Calling All Heroes**
Paco Ignacio Taibo II 1990 (1982)
The prize-winning novel, which has been attacked as irreverent and improbable, about the incident prior to the Olympic Games when the Mexican army fired on student protesters killing 49 and wounding 500. 1500 were jailed.

✔ **Air and Fire** Rupert Thomson 1994
(1993)
A couple arrive in the Mexican copper-mining town of Santa Sofia at the turn of the century. Théo has come to build a metal church designed by his mentor Eiffel and his wife, a clairvoyant, has insisted on accompanying him.

The Rebellion of the Hanged B. Traven
1970 (1936)
A novel about Indian exploitation under the dictatorship of Porfirio Diaz; the workers finally rebel. Other books by the mysterious Traven (no one has ever discovered his origins), include *The Carreta*, *The Treasure of the Sierra Madre*, *The Cotton Pickers* and *The General from the Jungle*.

Food

✔ **The Taste of Mexico**
Patricia Quintana 1986
More than 225 regional recipes – lavishly illustrated.

General Background

✔ **The Labyrinth of Solitude**
Octavio Paz   1990 (1961)
The latest edition includes *The Other Mexico, Return to the Labyrinth of Solitude, Mexico and the United States* and *The Philanthropic Ogre*. The collection of essays analyses Mexico's history and psyche and looks at United States–Mexican relations. Paz won the Nobel Prize for Literature in 1990 and in its citation the committee praised him for 'his impassioned writing with wide horizons, characterized by sensuous intelligence and humanistic energy'. [Paul Theroux]

✔ **Distant Neighbours: A Portrait of the Mexicans**   Alan Riding   (1984)
The author was once based in Mexico as a reporter for *The New York Times*.

Guides

✔ **Mexico. Access Guide. The Best Coastal Resorts with Mexico City and the Yucatan**

✔ **Mexico. Travel Survival Kit**
Tom Brosnahan, John Noble, Nancy Keller, Mark Balla and Scott Wayne   1992 (1982)

✔ **Baja Handbook**   Joe Cummings   1992

✔ **Mexico. The Rough Guide**
John Fisher   1994

✔ **Fodor's Acapulco, Ixtapa and Zihuatanejo**   1992

✔ **Fodor Mexico 1995**

✔ **Michelin Mexico**   1989

✔ **Mexico By Rail**   Gary A. Poole   1993

Terry's Guide to Mexico
(Published between 1922 and 1947)
The Baedeker equivalent to Mexico – out of date but full of fascinating information.

✔ **Cadogan Guide Mexico**   Katharine and Charlotte Thompson   1991

✔ **Mexico. American Express Guide**
James and Oliver Tickell   1993 (1984)

✔ **Mexico and Central American Handbook 1995**   Published by Trade and Travel

✔ **Hippocrene Language and Travel Guide to Mexico**   Ila Warner   1992

✔ **Baja California. Travel Survival Kit**   Scott Wayne   1991 (1988)

History

✔ **A Short Account of the Destruction of the Indies**   Bartolomé de las Casas
Translated by Nigel Griffin   1992 (1542)
'The conquest of Latin America as told by a humane priest horrified by the massacre of the Indians. It should be read as balance to Bernal Diaz' (q.v.) account from the Conquistadores' point of view.' [Jeremy Paxman]

✔ **The Conquest of New Spain**
Bernal Diaz del Castillo   Translated by J.M. Cohen
1963 (1568)
An eyewitness account, by one of Cortés' companions, of the Spanish arrival. 'I once read everything I could get my hands on about Mexico with the intention of writing a book (which never happened) on Central American history and culture. From these Bernal Diaz del Castillo stands out for the excellent descriptions of the country as well as the Conquest as seen through the eyes of a soldier in the ranks.' (Norman Lewis)

✔ **Aztec: The World of Montezuma**
Jane S. Day   1992
A clearly laid out and well illustrated book to the Aztec capital of Tenochtitlan and Aztec culture just before the Spanish arrival in 1519.

✔ **Mexico. A Traveller's Cultural History**   Peter McGregor Eadie   1991
A clearly laid out, well-illustrated concise history of Mexico.

✔ **The Aztecs. Rise and Fall of an Empire**   Serge Gruzinski   1992 (1987)
An excellent little book stuffed with colour photographs and interesting facts as well as a brief history; in the Thames and Hudson New Horizons series.

✔ **Yucatan Before and After the Conquest**   Friar Diego de Landa   1978 (1566)
Landa did all he could to destroy Maya civilization: 'We found a great number of books in these letters, and since they contained nothing but superstitions and falsehoods of the devil we burned them all'. In July 1562 he destroyed 5000 'idols' and 27 hieroglyphic rolls. Ironically, Landa's book which he wrote to defend himself, gives us according to William Gates, the Mayan scholar, 99 per cent of what we know today about the Mayas. However one can only surmise at the huge quantity of knowledge that was irretrievably lost at the auto-da-fé at Mani in July 1562.

The Conquest of Mexico   W.H. Prescott
1933 (1843)
Before Prescott began writing his history he heard that Washington Irving was conside-

ring the same topic; after a civilized exchange of letters, Irving stood aside with magnanimity and Prescott spent the next five years researching and writing his book, although he never actually went to Mexico.

Insurgent Mexico   John Reed   1983 (1914)
Reed lived with Pancho Villa's troops throughout the 1910 Mexican revolution.

✔ **The Conquest of Mexico**
Hugh Thomas   1993
Hugh Thomas uses much new material in this vast book about the collapse of Montezuma's Mexican empire under the onslaught of Cortés' troops.

✔ **The Aztecs**   Richard F. Townsend   1992
An integrated portrait of the Aztecs which reconciles their bloodthirstiness with their creativity. War and human sacrifice were certainly used as instruments of terror but the Aztecs believed that human blood ensured fertility for the land.

Leisure

✔ **No Frills Guide to Hiking in Mexico**   Jim Conrad   1992
Thirty-three different hikes over six regions of Mexico are described; the maps are basic, but seem easy to follow.

✔ **The People's Guide to RV Camping in Mexico**   Carl Franz with Steve Rogers   1989
How to find a campsite, repel mosquitoes, avoid bandits and find spare parts.

Natural History

A Field Guide to the Birds of Mexico
R.T. Peterson and E.L. Chalif   1973

Photography

✔ **Return to Mexico. Journeys Beyond the Mask**   Abbas   1992
Black and white photographs by Abbas, a *Magnum* photojournalist who now lives in Paris. He made nine trips to Mexico during three years, taking these revealing and passionate photographs and also keeping a journal of his experiences, published at the end of the book.

✔ **Mexico. Feast and Ferment**
Tom Owen Edmunds   1992
A collection of colour photographs of all aspects of Mexican life and landscape.

Religion

The Teachings of Don Juan
Carlos Castaneda
Castaneda first met Don Juan, a Yacqui Indian in Sonora; the local people were afraid of him because of his unnatural powers, but Castaneda spent five years with him as his pupil learning about magic, sorcery and supernatural powers. He wrote several other books about his experiences including *A Separate Reality*, *Journey to Ixtlan* (1975) and *The Power of Silence* 1990 (1987).

✔ **The Gods and Symbols of Ancient Mexico and the Maya. An Illustrated Dictionary of Mesoamerican Religion**
Mary Miller and Karl Taube   1993
This useful book, in dictionary form, explains and illustrates some of the myths and beliefs of the Precolumbian civilizations of Mesoamerica.

Travel Literature

✔ **Mexico**   Alice Adams   1992 (1990)
Alice Adams has spent thirty years visiting Mexico; her understanding of the country and her love affair with it are evident from this rather off-beat travel book which goes to many out-of-the-way places.

✔ **A Visit to Don Otavio**   Sybille Bedford   1982 (1953)
Sybille Bedford describes the horrors of her train journey to Mexico in graphic detail; when she arrives in Mexico 'a country with a long nasty history in the past, and as little present history as possible', she stays with Don Otavio, a bankrupt who still has seventeen servants to wait on him. Bruce Chatwin wrote that it is 'A work which evokes that disturbing and paradoxical country as vividly as anything by D.H. Lawrence, and, to my mind, far more vividly than Malcolm Lowry's *Under the Volcano* . . . A wonderful book.' [Colin Thubron]

Mexico South   Miguel Covarrubias   1946
Detailed descriptions of the life and customs of the Zapotecs on the Isthmus of Tehuantepec in the southwest of Mexico.

✔ **Viva Mexico! A Traveller's Account of Life in Mexico**   Charles Flandrau   1990 (1908)
Flandrau, a rich American, spent almost five years based in Mexico; for much of the time he was on his brother's coffee plantation where he became well acquainted with the Mexican people about whom he writes so well. *He* thought of himself as a lousy writer but *Viva Mexico* has been variously described

as 'probably the best travel book I have ever read' (Miles Kington), 'the best travel book written by an American' (Alexander Woollcott) and he is 'a marvellous writer with something of Mark Twain's high spirits and Henry James's suavity' (Geoffrey Smith).

Mexican Mosaic   Rodney Gallop   1939
Most of Rodney Gallop's journeys were day and weekend trips from Mexico City; as he shows, a great deal can be accomplished even given such limited time. He compares Monte Alban to Mycenae: 'the loneliness and natural beauty of the spot. The very light is Greek in quality, and so are the contours and texture of the mountains.'

✔ **The Volcanoes from Puebla**
Kenneth Gangemi   1979
The author travelled through Mexico on a motorcycle and has written his experiences as an expanded guidebook. The sections which are arranged alphabetically include chocolate, drinking, films, Guanajuato, tacos, volcanoes and Zapata.

✔ **The Lawless Roads**   Graham Greene
1982 (1939)
Graham Greene was commissioned to go to Mexico in 1938 to find out how the people had reacted to the religious persecution and the anti-clerical purges of the then President Calles. The journey which inspired his novel *The Power and the Glory* was through a small part of Mexico, the Chiapas and Tabasco. Shortly after Greene left the area the Bishop of Tabasco was allowed to return and became the first resident Bishop for fourteen years.

✔ **A Trip to the Light Fantastic. Travels with a Mexican Circus**
Katie Hickman   1994 (1993)
Katie Hickman became absorbed into the nomadic life of a Mexican circus and became a performer in her own right, known as 'La Gringa Estrella'. By being with the circus she discovered the magic she was searching for and was able to unravel some of the complicated psyche of modern Mexico.

✔ **Mornings in Mexico**   D.H. Lawrence
1986 (1927)
Lawrence maintained that it was the few years that he spent in Mexico in the 1920s that changed him forever. He is fascinated by the animistic spirit of the Mexican Indians, who can become completely immersed in their own drama and religion since it has no beginning, no end and is all-inclusive and cannot be judged because there is nothing to judge it. He shows how this contrasts with the West and with Greek drama where there

is always an onlooker, often in the shape of a god or goddess.

One Man's Mexico   John Lincoln   1983 (1967)
Lincoln travelled in Mexico between 1958 and 1964, a time which under the presidency of Adolfo Lopez Mateos, was politically fairly stable and economically progressive. By visiting many out-of-the-way places he discovered much about the Mexicans including the fact that they make the best and most generous friends in the world. [Stephen Brook]

Barbarous Mexico   John Kenneth Turner
1969
An American journalist's account at the turn of the century of the Porfirio Diaz régime.

GUATEMALA

Anthropology

✔ **I, Rigoberta Menchu. An Indian Woman in Guatemala**
Elisabeth Burgos-Debray (ed.)   1993 (1983)
Rigoberta Menchu, who won the Nobel Peace Prize, was born a Quiché Indian, one of the largest ethnic groups in Guatemala. Aged twenty she decided to teach herself Spanish and this book was narrated to the editor three years later, before she had become world famous. Her experiences are typical of the lives of many women in Latin America: she tells of everyday life in an Indian community but sees it in the broader context of what is happening in Central America today.

✔ **Sons of the Shaking Earth. The People of Mexico and Guatemala – Their Land, History and Culture**
Eric Wolf (see 'Mexico')

Autobiography/Biography

✔ **Rites. A Guatemalan Boyhood**
Victor Perera   1991 (1972)
An autobiography of life in Guatemala City's Jewish community; Perera's father was a first-generation immigrant who worked his way up from being an itinerant pedlar to a leading merchant. 'One closes this short book with a sharpened perception not only of life in mid-twentieth century Guatemala, but of life in Latin America as a whole . . . Perera demonstrates a lively wit on almost every page.' (*TLS*)

Fiction/Poetry

Men of Maize Miguel Angel Asturias 1949
Asturias, who won the Nobel Prize for Literature, leans heavily on Guatemalan history and culture in his work which is typical of the Latin American magic realist style. Maize is taken as the yardstick for how much men have changed; in Mayan times it was considered sacred whereas today it is sold for money.

✔ **Everything is Nice: Collected Stories of Jane Bowles** Jane Bowles 1993
The trip that Jane Bowles made with her husband Paul Bowles in the 1930s is used for the setting of *A Guatemalan Idyll.*

✔ **Up Above the World** Paul Bowles 1991 (1982)
A novel set in Guatemala in the late 1930s.

✔ **The Long Night of White Chickens** Francisco Goldman 1993 (1992)
Set between Boston and Guatemala City the novel is about a boy who grows up between the two cultures; at the same time it is a love story and a mystery about an unsolved murder. 'It is a meditation, investigation and chronicle written in a lyrical, evocative English'. (*Boston Sunday Globe*)

The Volcanoes Above Us Norman Lewis 1969 (1957)
An adventure story which shows the effects of revolution on a young man and includes much of recent Guatemalan history; depressingly the conclusions Lewis drew turned out to be prophetic.

Staying with Relations Rose Macaulay 1930
Rose Macaulay never got to Guatemala, but must have read about it extensively since her descriptions are exact. She satirizes the Bloomsbury set by showing over-educated Britons having to survive in the Guatemalan jungle.

Popol Vuh: the definitive edition of the Mayan book of the dawn of life and the glories of gods and kings Translated by Dennis Tedlock 1985
The great mythological poem of the Quiché which was written just after the conquest in order to try and preserve the tribe's knowledge of history. The Rough Guide recommends this translation.

Dust on Her Tongue Rodrigo Rey Rosa 1989
A collection of brutal stories by a Guatemalan writer, translated by Paul Bowles who wrote that they were involved with 'a present-day Central America troubled by atavistic memories of its sanguinary past'. Another collection is entitled *The Beggar's Knife.*

Food

False Tongues and Sunday Bread: A Guatemalan and Maya Cookbook Copeland Marks
The American food writer spent years ferreting out the best Guatemalan recipes which vary from hen in chocolate sauce to the regular black beans.

General Background

✔ **Inside Guatemala** Tom Barry 1992
An analysis of the political, social and economic sectors of Guatemala. The broad spectrum of information is both accurate and useful.

✔ **A View of the World** Norman Lewis 1987 (1986)
A Quiet Evening in Huehuetenago about Guatemala is included in this collection.

✔ **Guatemala. Eternal Spring. Eternal Tyranny** Jean-Marie Simon 1987
The author spent much time in Guatemala following events which had been largely ignored by the news. She records the testimonies of people, who have to remain unnamed, whose situation was daily changing for the worse. The book is also a powerful photographic record of people, places and events.

Guides (see 'Central America – General')

✔ **Guatemala Guide** Paul Glassman 1991 (1975)

Four Keys Guide to Guatemala Lily de Jongh Osborne 1939
Reputedly the best guidebook to Guatemala ever written.

✔ **Guatemala and Belize. The Rough Guide** Mark Whatmore and Peter Eltringham 1993 (1990)

✔ **Mexico and Central American Handbook 1995** Published by Trade and Travel

History

Garrison Guatemala George Black 1984
A history of Guatemala from 1945 up until the present day.

✔ **Conquest and Survival in Colonial Guatemala. A Historical Geography of the Cuchumatan Highlands 1500–1821**   *W. George Lovell   1992 (1985)*
The book examines the impact of Spanish rule in the isolated north-west of the country. Although Spanish imperialism made its mark there, the Maya culture, which exists there to this day, was not obliterated.

Bitter Fruit   *Stephen Schlesinger and Stephen Kinzer   1982*
The CIA boast that they carried out a successful clandestine military operation in Guatemala when they removed the elected President Jacobo Arbenz from power and replaced him with a little known military man, Castillo Armas. This book asks whether 'Operation Success' was necessary and whether it really advanced US interests. 'The best telling of the story of the United Fruit Company's coup in Guatemala in 1954 – the big event in that country's history.' (Jeremy Paxman)

Photography

✔ **Guatemala Rainbow**
Gianni Vecchiato   1989
A photographic book which concentrates on the brightly coloured textiles of Guatemala.

Travel Literature

✔ **Sweet Waist of America**
Anthony Daniels   1991 (1990)
Anthony Daniels, then an itinerant doctor, went to Central America to write a book about the whole isthmus, but decided, wisely, to concentrate on the most fascinating and beautiful country of the region, Guatemala. His revisionist view of the country's perennial troubles is a clear and decisive rejection of the usual liberal views.

Bird of Life, Bird of Death. A Central American Journey
Jonathan Evans Maslow   1987 (1986)
An impressionistic account of a trip to Guatemala in search of the rare and endangered resplendent quetzal, the killing of which was to the Maya a capital crime. Maslow was motivated by an obsessional curiosity about nature and he combines this with a love of travel and observations about politics.

BELIZE

Biography

Beka Lamb   *Zee Edgell   1986 (1982)*
An account of growing up in Belize in the 1950s: the problems of adolescence and the Belizean independence movement and the power of the Catholic Church.

On Heroes, Lizards and Passion
Zoila Ellis
A collection of seven short stories written by a Belizean woman.

Fiction/Poetry

Shots from the Heart
An anthology of three poets from Belize: Yasser Musa, Kiren Shoman and Simone Waight.

General Background

✔ **Inside Belize**   *Tom Barry   1992*
Chapters on government, politics, economy, society and ethnicity, social forces and institutions, the environment and foreign influence.

✔ **A View of the World**   *Norman Lewis   1987 (1986)*
A collection of journalism which includes *A Letter from Belize*.

✔ **The Overcrowded Barracoon**
V.S. Naipaul   1984 (1972)
The Ultimate Colony in this collection is about Belize.

Guides (see 'Central America–General')

✔ **Belize. Ecotourism in Action**
Meb Cutlack   1993
The author moved to Belize from Australia in 1981 and here writes about the Mayan ruins, the rainforest and barrier reefs – all of which are as yet unspoilt by tourism.

✔ **Mexico and Central American Handbook 1995** *Published by Trade and Travel*

✔ **Guatemala and Belize. The Rough Guide** *Mark Whatmore and Peter Eltringham 1993 (1990)*

History

A History of Belize *Narda Dobson 1973*
Belizean history from Maya times up to independence, including the early settlers and details of some of the many treaties between Britain and Spain over territorial disputes.

Natural History

✔ **Belize. A Natural Destination**
Richard Mahler and Steele Wotkyns 1992 (1991)
A guide which concentrates on the natural history of the country.

HONDURAS

Fiction/Poetry

Cabbages and Kings *O'Henry 1904*
William Sydney Porter (alias O'Henry) fled America following accusations of embezzling; he lived in Mexico on his ill-earned money and then went to Honduras where his dying wife eventually made him give himself up. He spent three years in jail where he wrote this collection of short stories, about the Central American republic of Anchuria (Honduras).

✔ **The Mosquito Coast** *Paul Theroux 1982 (1981)*
Allie Fox takes his family to live in the Honduran jungle and struggles to keep them alive with his mad inventions. It turns into an adventure story which is 'As oppressive and powerful as its central character. It bursts with inventiveness.' *(The Times)*

Guides (see 'Central America – General')

✔ **Mexico and Central American Handbook 1995** *Published by Trade and Travel*

Travel Literature

Jungle in the Clouds
Victor W. von Hagen 1945
An expedition into Honduras in search of the rare quetzal, the sacred bird of the Aztecs which had never been photographed or captured alive.

Explorations and Adventures in Honduras *William W. Wells 1857*
The author was keen to explore the gold regions of Central America and had heard that there were large deposits in Olancho in Honduras. He had problems finding any books or maps about the country, but assumed that had he been able to track down information, it would have been, with the exception of Squier (q.v.) useless 'owing to the author's ignorance'. He spent a year travelling, mostly by mule and visited thirty-eight Central American towns and settlements: 'It is the New World at its best – its summit of beauty and utility. The aphorism of Lord Bacon, that knowledge is power, and by converse, that ignorance is weakness, exemplifies itself in the ignorance of the American people regarding the real character of the interior of tropical America.'

EL SALVADOR

Fiction/Poetry

✔ **Ashes of Izalco** *Claribel Alegría and Darwin J. Flakoll 1989*
A classic Salvadorean novel with historical significance.

Cuzcatlan *Manlio Argueta 1987*
The illiterate peasants of El Salvador and how they were driven to support the guerrillas in the 1980s.

A Book of Common Prayer *Joan Didion 1986 (1977)*
Set in the imaginary state of Boca Grande. Through Charlotte, a hapless American tourist, we see America's unwillingness to take notice of what is happening in Latin America.

General Background

✔ **El Salvador** *Tom Barry 1991 (1990)*
A very useful book on war, economy, politics and social issues published by the Inter-Hemispheric Education Resource Center in New Mexico.

Salvador *Joan Didion 1983*
A study of 'the exact mechanisms of terror.'

✔ **Promised Land. Peasant Rebellion in Chalatenango El Salvador**
Jenny Pearce 1986
The author crossed the front line in El Salvador in order to talk to the people who were living in an area controlled by the FMLN guerillas and to collect together their testimonies. After fifty years of repression the peasants had begun to organize themselves into a union in the 1970s; this had finally led to a civil war and the formation of a guerilla army.

Guide (see 'Central America – General')

✔ **Mexico and Central American Handbook 1995** *Published by Trade and Travel*

NICARAGUA

Fiction/Poetry

✔ **Perfect English** *Paul Pickering 1987 (1986)*
Johnny Morgan comes down from Cambridge and joins his American girlfriend in Nicaragua in order to be with Perfect English, a group dedicated to the peaceful support of the Sandanistas.

General Background

✔ **The Tiger's Milk. Women of Nicaragua** *Adriana Angel and Fiona Macintosh 1987*
'This book deserves to be read. It is a tribute to people of courage and spirit whose voices are rarely heard' (Julie Christie). This well illustrated book records the lives of Nicaraguan women, both young and old, whose narrow domestic lives and traditional values suddenly had to change.

✔ **Life Stories of the Nicaraguan Revolution** *Denis Lynn Daly Heyck 1990*
The biographies of twenty Nicaraguans from a cross-section of society are divided into three categories: political lives, religious lives and survivors' lives.

✔ **Nicaragua** *Kent Norsworthy 1990 (1989)*
An attempt to find out what is really going on in Nicaragua by looking at the revolution and counterrevolution. Published by the Resource Center in New Mexico.

Guide (see 'Central America – General')

✔ **Mexico and Central American Handbook 1995** *Published by Trade and Travel*

History

Triumph of the People *George Black 1981*
The standard work on the Nicaraguan Revolution which has been described as 'an invaluable account of the Revolution and the subsequent attempt by the Sandanista government to reconstruct this devastated country'.

Natural History

The Naturalist in Nicaragua
Thomas Belt (1874)
Belt was an engineer by profession so his natural history observations were made in his leisure time. His descriptions of new, strange and beautiful things in nature all contain a sense of wonder and Charles Darwin described this book as 'the best of all natural history journals which have ever been published'. [Norman Lewis]

Photography

✔ **Nicaragua** *William Frank Gentile 1989*
A combination of photographs which show the landscape and people in ordinary daily life as well as images of how the army has pervaded every area of life. Also contains an interview with Sergio Ramirez, author and vice-president of Nicaragua.

Travel Literature

✔ **The Jaguar Smile. A Nicaraguan Journey** *Salman Rushdie 1987*
Salman Rushdie first went to Nicaragua in 1986 and was overwhelmed by what he saw. He met a huge variety of different people whom he weaves in and out of fantasy: '*The Jaguar Smile* is about power, powerlessness, beauty, blood, death'.

Travels in Central America particularly in Nicaragua: with a Description of its Aboriginal Monuments, Scenery and People, their Languages, Institutions, Religion etc.
E.G. Squier 1853
The author visited Nicaragua as an accredited Representative of the United States which he reckons enabled him to see the

country under a very favourable aspect; he hoped by writing about his experiences, to 'awaken a true sympathy in the hearts of the American people, for their simple, but unfortunate friends and allies in Central America'. His style is very readable and the book is full of ethnological facts which had not previously been known.

✔ **Hurricane in Nicaragua. A Journey in Search of Revolution**   Richard West   1989

West mixes anecdote, history, travelogue and analysis as he travels through Nicaragua, a country racked by revolution and natural disasters. 'I like the way (Richard West) writes, I like what he has to say. He is a humanist who does not accept facile solutions, a judge of character, and unraveller of contradictory authorities . . . ' (Cyril Connolly)

COSTA RICA

Fiction/Poetry

✔ **The Children of Mariplata. Stories from Costa Rica**   Miguel Benavides   1992
Eleven fables, each with a twist in its tail.

General Background

Costa Rica and Her Future   Paul Biolley   1889
Biolley who had lived in Costa Rica for several years thought that it deserved to be better known, since probably all that Americans or Europeans would know about it, is that it produced 'coffee which is quoted rather high on the market'. The book is a good introduction to the country, its culture and people.

✔ **Lost Illusions. Latin America's Struggle for Democracy, as Recounted by its Leaders**   Paul H. Boeker   1990 (see 'South America – General')

Guides

✔ **Costa Rica Handbook. A Moon Publication**   Christopher P. Baker   1994

✔ **Berlitz Travellers Guide Costa Rica**   1994

✔ **The New Key to Costa Rica**   Beatrice Blake and Anne Becher   1993

✔ **Costa Rica**   Paul Glassman   1989 (1984)

✔ **Choose Costa Rica. A Guide to Wintering or Retirement**   John Howells   1992
The guide includes Guatemala.

✔ **Insight Guide Costa Rica**   1992

✔ **Costa Rica. A Travel Survival Kit**   Rob Rachowiecki   1994 (1991)

✔ **Mexico and Central American Handbook 1995**   Published by Trade and Travel

Leisure

The Rivers of Costa Rica: A Canoeing, Kayaking and Rafting Guide   Michael W. Mayfield and Rafael E. Gallo   1988

Natural History

A Year of Costa Rican Natural History   Amelia Smith Calvert and Philip Powell Calvert   1917
The completion of the Panama Canal made a huge difference to the neighbouring countries, but since Costa Rica was still relatively unknown, the aim of this book was to introduce visitors to some of the features of tropical life. Although the authors' prime research was into dragonflies, there is much interesting general material.

✔ **In the Rainforest**   Catherine Caulfield   1986
The problems of the disappearing rainforest.

✔ **A Guide to the Birds of Costa Rica**   F. Gary Stiles and Alexander F. Skutch   1989
A very thorough guide.

PANAMA

Fiction/Poetry

✔ **Canal Dreams**   Iain Banks   1989
A Japanese musician is trapped in Panama during a war, on her way to give concerts in Europe. She is raped, escapes and manages to kill off many of the fake revolutionaries.

✔ **The Captain and the Enemy**   Graham Greene   1989 (1988)
The narrator goes to Panama where he meets an adventurer and gets caught up in the fighting; much is based on fact including the murders of the narrator and Captain by the CIA.

General Background

✔ **Panama**   *Tom Barry   1990*

✔ **Getting to Know the General**
Graham Greene   1986 (1984)
Graham Greene was about to go to Panama
for the fifth time when he heard that his host,
General Omar Torrijos Herrera, had died.
The idea then came to him to write a memoir
of the man he had 'grown to love', but he
realized that he also wanted to write about
Chuchu the only member of the National
Guard whom the General completely
trusted.

**In the Time of the Tyrants. Panama
1968–1989**   *R.M. Koster and
Guillermo Sanchez Borbon   1990*
An eyewitness account of how Panama fell
victim to a line of military dictators who used
the misery of the country for their own ends.

✔ **A View of the World**   *Norman Lewis
1987 (1986)*
A Collection of journalism which includes
High Adventures with the Chocos of Panama.

Guides (see 'Central America – General')

✔ **Getting to Know Panama**
Michèle Labrut   1994
A paperback guide with illustrations in pen
and wash and a full colour pull-out map.

✔ **Mexico and Central American
Handbook 1995**   *Published by Trade and Travel*

History

**The Impossible Dream. The Building
of the Panama Canal**   *Ian Cameron   1971*
In 1513, the Spaniard Alvaro de Saavedra
first suggested that a strait connecting the
Atlantic and the Pacific oceans 'might not be
impossible to make'. But it was not until 1916
after many thwarted schemes that the canal
was finally completed. 'Never before have so
much labour, so much scientific knowledge

and so much administrative skill been concentrated on a work designed to serve the
interests of mankind.' (Sir James Bryce, British Ambassador to Washington)

The Golden Isthmus   *David Howarth   1966*
A very readable history of the Isthmus of
Panama which starts with the Spanish ex-
plorers of 1502 and continues up until 1966.
Based mostly on first-hand accounts.

**The Path Between the Seas. The
Creation of the Panama Canal
1870–1914**   *David McCullough   1977*
'A wonderful account of the building of the
Panama Canal. There are all sorts of inade-
quate guidebooks and companions to Central
America, but this book really tells you everything you need to know about Panama. The
country only came into existence to create the
canal, and the story of its construction is the
story of the country. It's brilliantly told.'
(Jeremy Paxman).

The Darien Disaster   *John Prebble   1968*
In 1695 the Parliament of Scotland defied the
King to establish a trading company, The
Company of Scotland Trading to Africa and
the Indies. The dream of William Paterson,
the erratically brilliant Scot who had helped
found the Bank of England, was to found a
colony – Darien on the Isthmus of Panama;
he called it 'this door of the seas, and the key
of the universe'. The Scots put half of the
nation's capital into the enterprise and sailed
into Caledonia Bay in 1698. After only three
years it went disastrously wrong: the leaders
quarelled, it was deliberately obstructed by
the English Government and over 2000 of the
men, women and children who had gone
there died.

Travel Literature

Through the Panama   *Malcolm Lowry
1991 (1961)*
In the posthumous autobiographical collection *Hear Us O Lord from Heaven Thy Dwelling Place.* Lowry went through the Panama
Canal in 1947.

South America

GENERAL

Art and Archaeology

✔ **Lost Cities and Ancient Mysteries of South America** David Hatcher Childress 1989 (1986)
Childress combines adventure and archaeology in his search for the lost cities of South America which include Nazca, Cuzco, Machu Picchu and the Matto Grosso, Bahia and the Jungles of Bolivia. 'Whether we get through, and emerge again, or leave our bones to rot in there, one thing's for certain. The answer to the enigma of Ancient South America – and perhaps of the prehistoric world – may be found when those old cities are located and opened up to scientific research. That the cities exist, I know . . . ' (Colonel Fawcett)

✔ **Kingdoms of Gold, Kingdoms of Jade. The Americas Before Columbus** Brian M. Fagan 1991 (see 'Central America')
A well illustrated book which describes the Inca and pre-Inca periods of Peru as well as the civilizations of Mesoamerica and North America; he describes what life would have been like and how the European conquerors reacted to what they found.

✔ **Art in Latin America** Published by the Hayward Gallery, South Bank Centre.
A well illustrated catalogue of the 1989 exhibition.

✔ **The Art and Architecture of Ancient America** George Kubler 1990 (1962) (see 'Central America')
The third part of the book which is in the Pelican History of Art series, concentrates on the Andean civilizations. The text is accompanied by line drawings, maps, plans and photographs.

✔ **Latin American Art of the Twentieth Century** Edward Lucie-Smith 1993. (see 'Central America')
Magic Realism and Expressionism are just two of the concepts which Latin American art shares with its literature. This Thames and Hudson guide has 171 illustrations, 38 of which are in colour.

Biography

✔ **Charles Waterton 1782–1865. Traveller and Conservationist** Julia Blackburn 1989
An up-to-date biography of the eccentric Waterton who turned his park in Yorkshire into a sanctuary for animals and birds. Julia Blackburn emphasizes the importance of Waterton's pioneering conservation ideas.

The Squire of Walton Hall Philip Gosse 1940
The life of Charles Waterton (q.v.) who came from an old Catholic family in Yorkshire, and who became a great natural historian in South America, bringing many birds and animals to Yorkshire for the first time.

Bolivar and the Independence of Spanish America J.B. Trend 1946
A short, sharp and exciting life of Bolivar which was published in the 'teach yourself library', but which remains concise and readable today.

Don Roberto A.F. Tschiffely 1937
A biography of Robert Boutine Cunninghame Graham (1852–1936), the distinguished South American traveller and poet, horseman, scholar, romantic and Scottish Nationalist.

Fiction/Poetry

✔ **The War of Don Emmanuel's Nether Parts** Louis de Bernières 1992 (1990)
Set in an imaginary South American country, but uses many real but jumbled facts. This exotic mixture of myth, poetry and fact combines to produce a 'fat, juicy, tropical fruit of a narrative' (*Independent on Sunday*).

✔ **The Penguin Book of Latin American Short Stories** Thomas Colchie (ed.) 1993 (1991) (see 'Central America')
A collection of twenty-six short stories from all over Latin America; the anthology includes well known writers and some who had never before been published in English.

Food

✔ **The Book of Latin American Cooking**   Elisabeth Lambert Ortiz   1984
The recipes, from both South and Central America, are arranged in sections.

✔ **The Art of South American Cooking**   Felipe Rojas-Lombardi   1991
Shows how South American cooking combines the agricultural greatness of pre-Colombian peoples with Spanish cuisine.

General Background

✔ **Lost Illusions. Latin America's Struggle for Democracy, as Recounted by its Leaders**   Paul H. Boeker   1990
An analysis of the prospects of democracy in Latin America and of the challenges to American foreign policy, by a career diplomat who since 1988 has been president of the Institute of the Americas.

Memory of Fire
Eduardo Galeano (see 'Central America')

✔ **After the Despots**
Andrew Graham-Yooll   1991
Conversations with writers on politics and literature. There are interviews with Borges, Jorge Amado, Mario Vargas Llosa and Ariel Dorfman among others.

✔ **You Can't Drown the Fire**
Alicia Partnoy (ed.)   1989 (1988) (see 'Central America')
A collection of essays, stories, poetry, letters and song from Latin American women in exile.

✔ **Latin America. The Writer's Journey**   Greg Price   1990
Interviews with writers from Uruguay, Peru, Chile, Argentina, Paraguay, Brazil, El Salvador, Guatemala, Mexico and Cuba. Many, like Isabel Allende and Mario Vargas Llosa, are well known in the West but Price also visits and talks to lesser known writers, some of whom have not been translated into English.

The Conquest of Paradise
Kirkpatrick Sale   1991 (1990)
A reassessment of Columbus' arrival in the 'New World' in 1492. Kirkpatrick Sale, anticipating the inevitable backlash that would occur over Columbus, examines the original documents and presents him as a rootless, lonely man who never understood the nature of the world he had discovered.

✔ **South American Travel Resource Guide**   Betty Wagenhauser   1994

✔ **Traveller's Literary Companion to South and Central America**
Jason Wilson   1993

Guides

✔ **Insight Guide South America**   1990

✔ **South American Handbook 1995**
Published by Trade and Travel

✔ **South America on a Shoestring**
Wayne Bernhardson, Rob Rachowiecki, Krzysztof Dydynski et al.   1993

History

A Vanished Arcadia
R.B. Cunninghame Graham   1901
The rise and fall of the Jesuit missions in South America from 1607 to 1767. The book begins with their early history and growth and then states the reasons for their unpopularity which, strangely, was most prevalent among Catholics – Protestants having often written as apologists for them.

Open Veins of Latin America
Eduardo Galeano   1973 (see 'Central America')
The social, cultural and political struggles of Latin America.

A History of Latin America
George Pendle   1968 (see 'Central America')
A good general history of the area.

✔ **The Penguin History of Latin America**   Edwin Williamson   1992 (see Central America)
Five hundred years of history from the time of Columbus up until the present day. 'An excellent general history . . . clear in its narrative, interesting in its analysis and consistently intelligent in its judgements.' (The Times Higher Education Supplement)

Leisure

✔ **Adventure Travel in Latin America**   Scott Graham   1990 (see 'Central America' and the 'Caribbean')
A guide to backpacking, camping and 'finding adventure' in South America, Mexico, the Caribbean and Central America.

✔ **South America Ski Guide**
Chris Lizza   1992
Descriptions of thirty-five ski areas, the history of skiing in South America and twenty-five original trail maps.

Natural History

South America and Central America: a Natural History *Jean Dorst* 1967
A well-illustrated survey of Latin America fauna and flora.

South American Birds: A Photographic Aid to Identification *John S. Dunning* 1987.

Birds of South America . Illustrations from the lithographs of John Gould 1972
A selection of colour plates and descriptions.

South America Called Them
Victor W. Von Hagen 1949
Biographies of four of the great naturalists who went to South America: Charles-Marie de la Condamine (1701–74), Alexander von Humboldt (1769–1859), Charles Darwin (1809–82) and Richard Spruce (1817–93). They represent four different time periods, four geographical regions and four distinct sciences.

✔ **Personal Narrative of Travels to the Eqinoctial Regions of America during the years 1799–1804**
Alexandre von Humboldt 1993 (extracts) (pub. 1814–29)
From his youth Von Humboldt had been devoted to the study of nature and 'experienced in my travels, enjoyments which have amply compensated for the privations inseparable from a laborious and often agitated life'.

A Guide to the Birds of South America *Rodolphe Meyer de Schauensee* 1970
The nearly 3000 species of birds found in South America are identified in a single volume aimed at both the professional and amateur ornithologist. The layout seems to require some prior knowledge of the subject, as not all the species are illustrated.

Wanderings in South America, the North-West of the United States and the Antilles in the Years 1812, 1816, 1820 and 1824 *Charles Waterton* (1878)
Waterton gives wonderful descriptions of the flora and fauna, both benign and dangerous, which he discovered during his wanderings: 'At the close of day, the Vampires leave the hollow trees, whither they had fled at the morning's dawn, and scour along the river's banks in quest of prey. On waking from sleep, the astonished traveller finds his hammock all stained with blood. It is the vampire that hath sucked him. Not man alone, but every unprotected animal, is exposed to his depre-

dations: and so gently does this nocturnal surgeon draw the blood, that instead of being roused, the patient is lulled into a still profounder sleep.'

Photography

✔ **The Forbidden Rainbow. Images and Voices from Latin America**
Photographs by Julio Etchart   Edited by Amanda Hopkinson 1992
Military oppression, urban displacement and poverty throughout the countries of Latin America.

✔ **Other Americas** *Sebastiao Salgado* 1986 (see 'Central America')

Travel Literature

Across South America. An Account of a Journey from Buenos Aires to Lima by Way of Potosi *Hiram Bingham* 1911
Parts of the old trade route between Lima, Potosi and Buenos Aires had been used over the years by the Incas, their conqueror Pizarro, Spanish viceroys and mine owners, the liberating armies of Argentina and by Bolivar and Sucre. This historic highway therefore made an interesting route for Hiram Bingham who went to Santiago as a delegate of the United States Government and of Yale University, to the First Pan-American Scientific Congress in December 1908.

✔ **Beyond the Silver River. South American Encounters** *Jimmy Burns* 1989
'Each South American country is idiosyncratic – it brings out our individual fantasies and forces us to interpret anew' writes Jimmy Burns who was based in Buenos Aires for five years as a journalist. During that time he travelled to other parts of Argentina and to Brazil, Peru, Ecuador, Bolivia and Chile.

✔ **In the Realms of Gold. Travels Through South America** *Quentin Crewe* 1989
Quentin Crewe travelled 24,000 miles through ten countries in South America. His book is a mixture of anecdote, history, travelogue and description and shows the enormous contrasts between the different countries and the people he meets.

Coups and Cocaine. Two Journeys in South America *Anthony Daniels* 1986
Anthony Daniels's aim is to find the spirit of the people and places he visits. His journeys take him from smart hotels to doss-houses; quite rightly he realizes that to understand

a country you need to cover a broad spectrum. He goes to Peru, Bolivia, Ecuador, Brazil, Paraguay and Chile.

✔ **Reality is the Bug that Bit Me in the Galapagos**   *Charlotte Du Cann and Mark Watson   1994 (see 'Central America – General')*

✔ **Land Without Evil. Utopian Journeys Across the South American Watershed**   *Richard Gott   1993*
Richard Gott became intrigued about the different countries he visited in South America. The result of his curiosity is an unique kind of travel book in which he charts a journey that he and his wife made across the central belt of South America from the town of Campo Grande in western Brazil, via the swamps of the upper Paraguay river in the Matto Grosso do Sul and the flat plains of Chiquitos in eastern Bolivia, to the Beni in northern Bolivia. The book also aims to illuminate the past as much as the present. The development of each area is discussed along with the people who had previously travelled there.

✔ **The Ra Expeditions**   *Thor Heyerdahl 1990 (1971)*
Heyerdahl's crossing of the Atlantic from North Africa to South America in a forty-five foot papyrus boat, which followed a possible migratory route made by early man.

The Condor and the Cows
Christopher Isherwood   1949
Based on a diary which Isherwood kept during a trip to Colombia, Ecuador, Peru, Bolivia and Argentina; full of detail and idiosyncrasy due to his unique way of observing people and situations.

✔ **Out of Chingford. Round the North Circular and Up the Orinoco**   *Tanis and Martin Jordan   1989 (1988)*
Tanis was a hairdresser and Martin a house painter when they first saved enough money to make a jungle expedition to Surinam. They travelled with little money and no back-up, often by paddling a canoe; they had some extraordinary adventures and after the success of their first trip they went on to Venezuela, Peru and Brazil. A good reminder that anything is possible if you want to do it enough.

The Cruise of the 'Falcon'. A Voyage to South America in a 30-ton Yacht
E.F. Knight   1884
The author spent twenty months with two other barristers and a cabin-boy, sailing about 22,000 miles in South American and Caribbean waters, including a five-month journey up the Rivers Parana and Paraguay.

✔ **The Cloud Forest: A Chronicle of the South American Wilderness**
Peter Matthiessen   1988 (1961)
Peter Matthiessen wandered around South America in 1960 experimenting with the drug ayahuasca and looking at birds.

Across Unknown South America
A. Henry Savage-Landor   1913
Savage-Landor expected South America to be a *terra incognita*, but found to his disappointment that (a) 'it is possible for any experienced traveller to cross Brazil in any direction' and (b) that the 'millions of savage Indians' supposed to be swarming all over the interior of Brazil do not exist at all'. Since he could not find any suitable officers in Brazil to accompany him he had to do all the 'tedious scientific work of the expedition' and complains that he filled the posts of 'surveyor, hydrographer, cartographer, geologist, meteorologist, anthropologist, botanist, doctor, veterinary surgeon, painter, photographer, boat-builder, guide, navigator, etc.'

Half a Dozen of the Other
Sebastian Snow   1972
Snow answered an advertisement in the personal column of *The Times* to join an expedition to Peru to try and establish the 'true' source of the Amazon from a hydrological survey of its headwater areas. This expedition is recounted in the first part of the book and other equally adventurous journeys make up the rest.

✔ **The Old Patagonian Express. By Train Through the Americas**
Paul Theroux   (1979)
Paul Theroux quotes Robert Louis Stevenson's Amateur Emigrant at the start of his book: 'That train was the one piece of life in all the deadly land; it was the one actor, the one spectacle fit to be observed in this paralysis of man and nature.' Theroux's journey from Boston to Patagonia was full of contrasting trains – some ramshackle and old and others superb and new; he started in freezing temperatures and went through a variety of climate zones, scenery, attitudes and altitudes on his journey.

Southern Cross to Pole Star. Tschiffely's Ride   *A.F. Tschiffely   1982 (1932)*
In 1925–28 Tschiffely made an epic 10,000 mile journey from Buenos Aires to Washington on two Argentine Criollo ponies, aged fifteen and sixteen. The book was published to great acclaim. [Stephen Brook]

ANDES

History

Kingdom of the Sun God. A History of the Andes and Their People
Ian Cameron 1990
How the mountains were formed and how, when the hunter-gatherers arrived from North America, *ayllus*, village communes, developed. Pre-Inca civilizations who built temples emerged from these settlements until they were conquered by the Incas, who in turn were conquered by a paltry collection of 160 Spaniards. The bloody Spanish conquest was succeeded by a degree of concern shown by the Catholic church, but it was the great naturalists La Condamine, Humboldt and Darwin who first undermined Spanish rule in the Andes. An interesting and well illustrated book.

Photography

✔ **The Andes** *Tony Morrison 1976*
A superbly illustrated book in the Time/Life 'World's Wild Places' series.

Travel Literature

✔ **Eight Feet in the Andes**
Dervla Murphy 1983
Dervla Murphy and her nine-year-old daughter Rachel travelled 1300 miles by mule through the Andes. They only vaguely followed the conquistadores' route, often through necessity as there are so few routes through the Andes. Murphy's trip was at roughly the same time of year as Pizarro – the conquistadores took around three months to get from Cajamarca to Cuzco; Dervla Murphy, her daughter and the mule took about three and a half months.

✔ **High Cities of the Andes**
Celia Wakefield 1988
Personal impressions of why the author liked travelling in the Andean regions of Peru, Bolivia and Ecuador.

Travels Amongst the Great Andes of the Equator *Edward Whymper 1987 (1892)*
Whymper is interested by altitude sickness, the concept of which was very much in its infancy: 'While the greatest heights in Europe are annually ascended by throngs of persons without perceptible inconvenience, multitudes of others in Asia and America suffer acutely at lower elevations; and it would therefore seem that there are in-fluences at work on the latter continents which do not operate in Europe.' He climbs many peaks in the Andes, describing in detail what he observed and the problems he encountered.

ARGENTINA

Biography

Uttermost Part of the Earth
E. Lucas Bridges 1948
Written by the son of the first white missionaries to the Yahgan Indians in southern Tierra del Fuego. The Bridges founded a cattle farm in 1887 and got to know the local inhabitants so well that their record of Indian customs and language is unique.

✔ **A State of Fear** *Andrew Graham-Yooll 1986*
The author was News Editor of the *Buenos Aires Herald* for ten years while all round him people were 'disappearimg'. He was held in deep suspicion and eventually fled to Britain, making several return journeys to Argentina. His experience and understanding of what was happening under the brutal military dictatorship make his account of events all the more chilling.

✔ **Far Away and Long Ago. A Childhood in Argentina** *W.H. Hudson 1991 (1918)*
Hudson's seemingly unremarkable childhood on the Argentinian pampas is full of delightful detail and observations of people and wildlife. 'One cannot tell how this fellow gets his effects; he writes as the grass grows. It is as if some very fine and gentle spirit were whispering to him the sentences he puts down on the paper. A privileged being.' (Joseph Conrad)

Juan Peron and the Reshaping of Argentina *Frederick Turner and José Enrique Miguen 1983*
An important biography of Peron.

Fiction/Poetry

✔ **The Book of Sand** *Jorge Luis Borges 1979 (1971)*
A collection of stories and poems which although Borges wrote them in his seventies and called them 'blind man's exercises', show him at his sharpest and most imaginative. Other books by Borges include *Labyrinths, The Book of Imaginary Beings, Doctor Bro-*

die's Report and *A Universal History of Infamy.*

✔ **The Campaign**   Carlos Fuentes   1992
(1990)
The first in a trilogy about independence, this volume concentrates on the decade between 1810 and 1820 when an Argentinian, Balthasar Bustos, performs a revolutionary deed by secretly changing babies . . .

✔ **Hand in Hand Alongside the Tracks. Contemporary Argentine Stories**   Norman Thomas di Giovanni (ed.)
1992
A collection of eighteen short stories, all by different writers, many of which combine the realistic and the fantastic. Contributors include Rodrigo Fresan, Elvira Orphée, Sylvia Iparaguirre, Mario Paoletti, Juan José Hernandez, Ana Maria Shua, Alicia Steimberg, Daniel Moyano and Rodolfo Rabanal.

✔ **The Honorary Consul**
Graham Greene   1983 (1973)
An insignificant British diplomat is kidnapped in the slums of Corrientes instead of the American ambassador. He has married a young whore, Clara, who becomes the mistress of Dr Eduardo Plarr. Jealousy, alcoholism and religion all play a part in this typical Greene novel. *Travels With My Aunt* (see 'Paraguay') is also partly set in Argentina.

The Peron Novel   Tomas Eloy Martinez
1988
A fictionalized account of Peron's life and his return to Argentina in 1973. The author mixes historical people into his fiction, imagining what they might have said to Peron.

✔ **The Duke**   Enrique Medina   1984 (1976)
One of the few critical novels to appear during the repression. It was inevitably banned by the military junta. A boxing idol becomes brutalized by the system and a paid assassin for the armed squads. Medina's first book was *Las Tumbas* (The Tombs), an autobiographical novel published in 1972.

✔ **The Devil's Trill**   Daniel Moyano   1988
(1974)
A violinist goes to Buenos Aires in search of work, only to become involved in the silence that occurs after the toppling of the President. Musical metaphor is used throughout this political novel which shows Argentina's turmoil and violence.

Heartbreak Tango: A Serial
Manuel Puig   1987 (1969)
Four women who were at school together lead very different lives when they leave. Other books by Puig include: The *Buenos Aires Affair: A Detective Novel* (1976), *The Kiss of the Spider Woman* (1979) – filmed by the Brazilian director Hector Babenco – and *Tropical Night Falls* (1992).

✔ **Triste's History**   Horacio Vazquez Rial
1990 (1987)
Triste had learnt his way of living from the streets and the pool hall; a chance meeting with a disillusioned priest changes him into a member of the Argentinian death squad.

✔ **The Witness**   Juan José Saer   1990 (1983)
A sixteenth century cabin boy recalls, when he is an old man, sailing to the New World on an expedition which was attacked by Indians.

✔ **A Funny Dirty Little War**
Osvaldo Soriano   1989 (1982)
The story of a political confrontation in a village in Argentina; the differences eventually lead to a massacre. *Winter Quarters* (1989), which became a best seller in Argentina after the fall of the military dictatorship in 1983, is a sequel set in the same village.

A Summer in Buenos Aires
Isobel Strachey   1947
An English governess runs off with an Argentinian aristocrat who seduces her on a train; she becomes temporarily liberated riding alone across the pampas and doing what she wants without the burden of chaperones.

✔ **Imagining Argentina**
Lawrence Thornton   1989 (1987)
A first novel which uses the tradition of magic realism to relate the awful times when people 'disappeared'. In this case Carlos Rueda's wife disappears, but he acquires the gift of being able to envisage the fate of the 'disappeared'.

✔ **The Snake Tree**   Uwe Timm   1988
(1986)
A German engineer goes to South America to work, but on his way from the airport his car crushes a snake. The superstition is that whoever kills such a snake will die by drowning . . .

General Background

✔ **The Return of Eva Peron**
V.S. Naipaul   1988 (1980)
The essay which forms the title of this book was written between 1972 and 1975 and describes Peronism and what happened to a country which is full of corruption and which had been deprived due to colonialism.

Life in the Argentine Republic in the Days of the Tyrants
Domingo Faustino Sarmiento   1960 (1868)
A popular contemporary account of post-independent Argentina.

Guides

✔ **Argentina, Uruguay and Paraguay. Travel Survival Kit**   *Wayne Bernhardson and Maria Massolo   1992*

✔ **Travel Companion: Argentina**
Gerry Leitner   1990
A very detailed guide of the country arranged by province; 417 cities and towns are described and hotels and restaurants are listed and graded.

History

The Conquest of the River Plate
R.B. Cunninghame Graham   1924
The remarkable Cunninghame Graham, friend of Conrad, and who was for a while a cattle rancher, has been somewhat neglected since his death. This history starts with the discovery of the River Plate and ends with the founding of Buenos Aires in 1580.

Argentina. A City and a Nation
James R. Scobie   1971 (1964)
A comprehensive short history of Argentina; life on the pampas is contrasted with life in the cities and the development of both is explored.

Leisure

✔ **Backpacking in Chile and Argentina**   *Hilary Bradt   1989*

The Springs of Enchantment. Climbing and Exploration in Patagonia   *John Earle   1981*
John Earle accompanied Eric Shipton on an expedition to Patagonia in 1963; this forms the first part of the book. A second expedition in 1979 was undertaken in order to make a film about the Bridges family (*Uttermost Part of the Earth* q.v.).

✔ **Trekking in the Patagonian Andes. Lonely Planet Walking Guide**
Clem Lindenmayer   1992

Natural History

✔ **The Whispering Land**   *Gerald Durrell   1964 (1961)*
One of Durrell's expeditions to find animals for his private zoo in Jersey. He spent eight months in Argentina and describes the animals and the setbacks and successes of his trip with great humour. 'In conclusion, it appears to me that nothing can be more improving to a young naturalist than a journey in distant countries' (Charles Darwin *The Voyage of HMS Beagle*). Durrell also wrote *The Drunken Forest* about Argentina and Paraguay.

Idle Days in Patagonia   *W.H. Hudson 1984 (1893)*
Hudson returned to Patagonia for a year on a scientific mission to study birds; 'the passion of the ornithologist took me'. He had to remain 'idle' after he accidentally shot himself in the knee.

The Naturalist in La Plata
W.H. Hudson   1988 (1892)
A collection of pieces on natural history which originally appeared in magazines; among others, he writes about spiders, dragonflies, humming-birds, wasps, pumas and skunks with his keen naturalist's eye.

Travel Literature

✔ **In Patagonia**   *Bruce Chatwin   1979 (1977)*
Bruce Chatwin never forgot the piece of leathery skin with strands of coarse red hair belonging to a Patagonian brontosaurus, that he found in his grandmother's cabinet; it was this that eventually inspired him to go to Patagonia. [Jeremy Paxman]

✔ **Patagonia Revisited**   *Bruce Chatwin and Paul Theroux   1993 (1985)*
The first books of both authors on Patagonia are credited with starting the travel writing boom, but as Chatwin says 'if we are travellers at all, we are literary travellers'; here they explain, in lecture form, their reasons for going to Patagonia.

An Englishman in Patagonia
John Pilkington   1991
Pilkington spent eight months travelling round Patagonia, discovering that being a Patagonian is more how you feel than where you live; mostly immigrants, they have worked out a set of values which include a hatred of towns and their petty rivalries.

Wind, Sand and Stars
Antoine de Saint-Exupéry   1990 (1939) (see 'North Africa', 'Sahara')
Saint-Exupéry's description of the weather he encountered on his flight to the Patagonian Argentine, as if he had 'exposed himself to the enemy', is remarkably vivid.

Land of Tempest: Travels in Patagonia
1958–62   *Eric Shipton   1963* .
A series of glaciological and botanical expeditions to the volcanoes and glaciers in the Patagonian Andes.

Mischief in Patagonia   *H.W. Tilman   1957*
The boat, Mischief, sailed from England to southern Chile and the crew then crossed the ice-cap to Lago Argentino; most descriptions are of sailing and climbing.

This Way Southward: a Journey through Patagonia and Tierra del Fuego   *A.F. Tschiffely   1940*
A 7,000 mile car journey which started down the Patagonian Atlantic coast, through Chile, up the Andean side of Patagonia and finished in Buenos Aires.

Fat Man in Argentina   *Tom Vernon   1990*
Vernon travelled round the central pampas and northern Patagonia on a bicycle; the journey was a two-part television programme.

FALKLAND ISLANDS

General Background

Antarctica and the South Atlantic: Discovery, Development and Dispute
Robert Fox   1985

Battle for the Falklands   *Max Hastings and Simon Jenkins   1983*
One of the most readable and best books on the Falklands War.

From the Falklands to Patagonia
Michael Mainwaring   1983
The history of pioneer sheep farming in the Falklands.

The Falkland Islands   *Ian J. Strange   1983*
A fairly dry book on the geography, history and natural history of the islands.

✔ Falkland People   *Angela Wigglesworth   1992*
Interviews with a cross-section of people who live in the Falkland Islands.

Natural History

The Falkland Islands and their Natural History   *Ian J. Strange   1987*
A large book illustrated with colour and black and white photographs which shows the connection between the people and their environment. The author is a resident of the

Falklands where he has established a conservation trust on New Island (South).

Falkland Islands Birds   *Robin Woods 1982*
Excellent photographs and fairly practical to use.

BOLIVIA
(For many of the books see 'Argentina')

Fiction/Poetry

Mask of the Andes   *Jon Cleary   1971*
A group of foreigners, including an American priest, his sister and a Briton, get involved in Bolivian politics during the 1950s and 1960s.

A Cloak of Monkey Fur   *Julian Duguid 1936*
Both this and *Father Coldstream* (1938) are set in the Bolivian jungle.

✔ Rising   *R.C. Hutchinson   1982 (1976)*
Through the lives of two brothers who are trying to save their mine from saboteurs we see the tensions that exist between the various strata of Bolivian society.

✔ At Play in the Fields of the Lord
Peter Matthiessen (see 'Amazonia')

General Background

Beyond Lake Titicaca   *Angela Caccia 1969*
The author's husband was a diplomat who was posted to La Paz. She determined to find out as much as possible about Bolivia's history and people during the time she spent there.

✔ A View of the World   *Norman Lewis 1987 (1986)*
The essay called *The White Promised Land* is about Bolivia.

My Quest for El Dorado   *Ross Salmon 1979*
Salmon was intrigued by what had happened to the Incas who had fled from the Spaniards and whose descendants live on the Altiplano; he made four expeditions into Bolivia gathering both archaeological and anthropological information.

Guides

✔ **Bolivia. Travel Survival Kit**
Deanna Swaney and Robert Strauss   1992 (1988)

Leisure

✔ **Backpacking and Trekking in Peru and Bolivia**   *Hilary Bradt   1994*

Natural History

(see 'Amazonia')

Travel Literature

Gate of the Sun   *Margaret Joan Anstee   1970*
The author spent nearly six years in Bolivia as head of the United Nations programme; she travelled widely within the country and describes the people, their history and towns and the landscape she travelled through.

Green Hell: A Chronicle of Travel in the Forests of Eastern Bolivia
Julian Duguid   1931
An expedition to the then unexplored Bolivian Chaco, made by the author, a BBC reporter, with the Bolivian Consul General to London and an Argentinian photographer.

✔ **In Quest of the Unicorn Bird**
Oliver Greenfield   1992
Oliver Greenfield seized the opportunity to leave his job in a building society to go and work for the director of a national park in Bolivia. He had collected natural history books since childhood but is often quite bemused by the reality of the creatures he comes across.

The Incredible Voyage   *Tristan Jones*
1984 (1978)
The book includes several months of sailing on Lake Titicaca.

Summer at High Altitude
Gordon Meyer   1968
A train and bus trip to Bolivia in 1967 during which Meyer investigates what happened to the Jesuits.

✔ **Sons of the Moon**   *Henry Shukman*
1991 (1990)
The Aymara 'the sons of the moon' live on a high plateau, the Altiplano, in the Bolivian Andes. The few who remain are descendants of the moon worshipping pre-Columbian empire which was conquered by the sun-loving Incas. Shukman travelled among the Indians in their desolate and inhospitable terrain recording what he saw and learnt.

AMAZONIA

Anthropology

✔ **Rio Tigre and Beyond. The Amazon Jungle Medicine of Manuel Cordova**
F. Bruce Lamb   1985
Manuel Cordova was abducted at the beginning of the century by tribes people, to be trained as their new shaman. Lamb was a forester in the upper Amazon in the 1960s and was entrusted with Cordova's story of the seven years he had spent in a pre-Columbian world at the turn of the century; he subsequently wrote the book *Wizard of the Upper Amazon* about those experiences. *Rio Tigre and Beyond* summarizes the previous book and continues with what happened to Cordova next. 'Since man is a product of nature, I believe that a cure for all of his ills will be found in nature and these cures are natural, in my opinion, and not miraculous at all.' (Manuel Cordova in *Wizard of the Upper Amazon*)

Biography

Henry Walter Bates, Naturalist of the Amazons   *George Woodcock   1969*
Bates met Alfred Russel Wallace. Both were self-taught naturalists, and in 1848 they decided to go to the Amazon Rivers to do fieldwork. Bates stayed for eleven years, paying his way by selling specimens to British museums and discovering over 8000 hitherto unknown species of insects, birds and mammals.

Fiction

✔ **At Play in the Fields of the Lord**
Peter Matthiessen   1989 (1965)
Two American missionaries and their wives find themselves on a remote strip in the middle of the Amazon jungle; their idealism is tested when they see the struggle between the Indian tribe and 'civilization'. Although this is one of Peter Matthiessen's earlier books his observations as a naturalist and traveller, for which he became so well known, are evident.

Dead Man Leading   *V.S. Pritchett   1984*
(1937)
A son travels along one of the tributaries of the Amazon to try and find out why his father died.

General Background

✔ **Amazon Watershed**   George Monbiot
1992 (1991)
Monbiot investigates the underlying reasons
for the deforestation of the Amazon. He saw
peasants being forcibly moved from their
homes into the Amazon and watched a vast
military project being opened in the north;
much to the chagrin of the military police
who tried to kill him, he followed timber from
the Amazon all the way back to retailers in
Britain.

✔ **The Burning Season**   Andrew Revkin
1990
Chico Mendes, a Brazilian rubber tapper,
was killed in December 1988 by prospectors
who were intent on plundering the forest for
short term gain.

History

The Amazon   Robin Furneaux   *1969*
If the north bank of the Amazon was in London, the south bank would be in Paris; this is
just one of the staggering facts that Robin
Furneaux mentions in his book. The Amazon's history had been little written about,
because as it flows through six countries
authors have tended to concentrate on their
own country or their own travels. Robin Furneaux writes about the explorers, colonists,
Jesuits and naturalists who visited the area.

✔ **The Amazon Past, Present and
Future**   Alain Gheerbrant   *1992 (1988)*
A concise and well illustrated history in the
Thames and Hudson New Horizons series.

✔ **Explorers of the Amazon**
Anthony Smith   *1990*
Short biographies of some of the most import-
ant explorers of the Amazon: Pedro Cabral,
Francisco de Orellana, Lope de Aguirre,
Pedro de Teixeira, Charles Marie de la Con-
damine, Monsieur and Madame Godin,
Baron von Humboldt, Richard Spruce, Henry
Wickham and Julio Arana.

Natural History

The Naturalist on the River Amazons
(sic)   Henry Walter Bates   *1975 (1863)*
Bates spent eleven years travelling in the
Amazon region recording his adventures, the
habits of animals, sketches of Brazilian and
Indian life and other aspects of nature.

The Fate of the Forest   Susanna Hecht and
Alexander Cockburn   *1990*
A natural history of the Amazon with much
emphasis on the politics.

✔ **Insight Guide Amazon Wildlife**
1992

✔ **In Search of Flowers of the Amazon
Forests**   Margaret Mee   *1988*
Margaret Mee did not start travelling in the
Amazon until she was forty-seven, after
which she made fifteen journeys. Her paintings and sketches of flowers and plants have
been compared to Ehret and Redouté; tragically she was killed in a car accident when
she came to England to celebrate the publication of this book.

**A Narrative of Travels on the Amazon
and Rio Negro**   Alfred Russel Wallace   *1889
(1853)*
When Wallace first suggested going to the
Amazon with Bates in addition to collecting
natural history specimens he also hoped to
acquire knowledge 'towards solving the problem of the origin of species'. He travelled on
the Rio Negro and to the upper waters of the
Orinoco and up the rapid Uaupés recording
what he saw of the natural history and the
people. Much of what he collected was destroyed when the boat on which he was returning to England caught fire, but he
salvaged enough to write this book before
leaving for the Malay archipelago.

Travel Literature

✔ **Mad White Giant. A Journey to the
Heart of the Amazon Jungle**
Benedict Allen   *1985*
The author travelled from the mouth of the
Orinoco to the mouth of the Amazon, living
in the jungle with the Indians who taught
him how to survive; an ability he had great
need of when finally he had to leave the area
in fear of his life.

✔ **The Decade of Destruction**
Adrian Cowell   *1990*
The author, a film director who has been
going to the area since the 1950s, describes
the events of the last thirty years in the
Amazon rainforest, through the eyes of the
people who live there and from the perspective of the variety of different people who
both exploit and try and protect it.

✔ **Into the Heart**   Kenneth Good   *1992
(1991)*
Kenneth Good went to study the Yanomama
Indians as an anthropologist but fell in love
with Yarima, a Yanomama woman. Their

struggle to stay together forms the basis of this book.

✔ **Running the Amazon** Joe Kane 1991 (1989)
Evidently the first attempt at travelling the entire length of the Amazon by a combination of kayak, raft and on foot. The expedition started 17,000 feet up in the Andes and of the original eleven participants only four completed the hazardous journey.

✔ **Tristes Tropiques** Claude Lévi-Strauss 1978

✔ **True Hallucinations**
Terence McKenna 1994
In 1971 the author went in search of the hallucinogenic drug oo-koo-hé in the Amazon basin; from this extraordinary journey he developed his theory that the psychoactive ingredient in the *Stropharia cubensis* mushroom is the missing link in the development of human consciousness and language.

✔ **Amazon Beaming** Petru Popescu 1993 (1991)
Nearly twenty years ago Loren McIntyre attempted to look for the source of the Amazon with the help of the Mayoruna tribe, who were said to be the only people who knew the true source. He was kidnapped by them but developed telepathic communication – 'beaming' – with the head shaman. This is his story told by Popescu.

✔ **In Trouble Again. A Journey Between the Orinoco and the Amazon** Redmond O'Hanlon 1989 (1988)
Parallel to descriptions of jungle torments, dangerous natives, frightening diseases, stressed-out photographers and hilarious incidents, O'Hanlon writes with knowledge and learning, in the tradition of the great nineteenth-century masters, about the natural history of the region.

✔ **An Amazon and a Donkey**
Natascha Scott-Stokes 1991
The author claims to be the first woman on her own to follow the Amazon from one of its headwaters to the sea. Her journey was dangerous not only because of the difficult terrain but also because of the *Senderos* who were threatening to kill the next foreigner they encountered.

✔ **In Southern Light** Alex Shoumatoff 1988 (1986) (see 'Zaire')
In the first half of the book the author explores the Nhamunda River, a little known and unspoilt tributary of the Amazon where the fabled Amazon women are said to have lived.

BRAZIL

Anthropology

✔ **Savages. The Life and Killing of the Yanomami** Dennison Berwick 1993 (1992)
Since the mid-eighties nearly a quarter of the Yanomami have died from either western diseases or bullets; Berwick lived with them in the Amazon jungle and describes their fight for survival against the greed of the invaders.

Xingu. The Indians, Their Myths
Orlando and Claudio Villas Boas 1973 (1970)
The Villas Boas brothers led an expedition 'Brazil's March to the West', which was intended to open up the interior for colonization. At that time little was known about the Xingu and when the expedition disbanded the brothers stayed behind to protect them from future exploitation. Their book is about the history, ritual, myth, symbolism, material culture and social structure of the tribes of the Alto-Xingu.

Shabono Florinda Donner 1982
Florinda Donner, an anthropologist, spent time deep in the jungle between Brazil and Venezuela studying the witchcraft practices of various Indian tribes. She becomes completely caught up in their lives and customs and is accepted by the Iticoteri as one of themselves. She eventually has to leave, albeit reluctantly.

The Valley of the Latin Bear
Alexander Lenard 1965
An account of village life in the interior of southern Brazil, by the same author who wrote *Winnie ille Pu*.

Biography

✔ **The Diary of Helena Morley**
Alice Dayrell Caldeira Brant (Helena Morley) 1977
The diary of a thirteen-year-old-girl written between 1893 and 1895. She describes family life and social customs in a mining town.

The Bandit King: Lampiao of Brazil
Billy Jaynes Chandler 1978
A fast-moving reconstruction of the life of the famous social bandit Lampiao.

Fiction/Poetry

✔ **Shepherds of the Night** Jorge Amado 1989 (1964)
Much of the action of the novel takes place on the waterfront in Bahia, a place packed with

prostitutes, pimps, drunks and homeless. 'Amado is by turns, realist, fantastical, episodic, direct, angry, humorous and, above all, characterful.' (*Scotsman*). He has written twenty-one novels mostly concerned with social justice, including *The Violent Land*, *Tent of Miracles*, *Dona Flor and Her Two Husbands* and *Gabriela, Clove and Cinnamon*.

Macunaima   Mario de Andrade   1984 (1928)
A comic tale of the adventures of the popular hero Macunaima; considered one of the greatest works of Brazilian literature.

Epitaph of a Small Winner
Machado de Assis   1977
Assis was the son of a freed slave and worked as a journalist in Rio in the late nineteenth century. His other novels include *Posthumous Memoirs of Bras Cubas*, *Philosopher or Dog* (1982) and *Dom Casmurro* (1980) and short story collections: *The Devil's Church and Other Stories* and *Helenas*.

Complete Poems 1927–1979
Elizabeth Bishop   1983
The poet Elizabeth Bishop fell ill while visiting Rio in 1951 and decided to stay on there until her death in 1979. She travelled widely in Brazil and wrote many poems about Brazil.

✔ The Viceroy of Ouidah
Bruce Chatwin (see 'Benin')
Francisco Manoel goes from Brazil to Africa where he is made the Viceroy of Ouidah and where all his aspirations turn to dust. The Werner Herzog film *Cobra Verde* is based on the novel.

Rebellion in the Backlands
Euclides da Cunha   1957 (1902)
The odd rebellions by the followers of the mystic Antonio Conselheiro are fictionalized with a mixture of history, geography and philosophy by da Cunha who describes the wild parts of Brazil which were often omitted from many more European looking novels. Both Cunninghame Graham and Mario Vargas Llosa used his accurate descriptions for their writings.

The Lost World
Arthur Conan Doyle. (see 'Guyana')

✔ Gerontius   James Hamilton-Paterson
1991 (1990)
A novel based on Elgar's trip to Brazil. Much of it takes place on the ship but there are many descriptions of the plants and animals seen on the way to Manaus.

✔ The War of the End of the World
Mario Vargas Llosa   1985
The story of the rebellion by Conselheiro

which was written about by da Cunha (q.v.) and was described by *The Times* as 'A vast, fantastic . . . thunderous novel.'

Childhood   Graciliano Ramos   1979 (1946)
A collection of short stories by Ramos who was the eldest of fifteen children of a shopkeeper. He was a member of the Brazilian communist party and visited Russia in 1952. Other works by Ramos include *Barren Lives* and *Memories of Jail*.

Emperor of the Amazon   Marcio Souza
1980
Souza, a satirist who lives in Manaus, parodies Brazilian history in his novels include *Mad Maria* (1985) and *The Order of the Day* (1986).

✔ Blues for a Lost Childhood
Antonio Torres   1989 (1986)
An amalgam of Brazilian life is shown through a period of thirty years: Calunga breaks out of his background and becomes a journalist in the city; the city finally defeats him and his land reclaims him, leaving him only his irony. Torres also wrote *The Land* (1976).

The Animal Game   Frank Tuohy   1957
Most of the novel takes place on the coast of Brazil; the characters feel alienated and live in a world dominated by passion. *The Warm Nights of January* (1960) continues his theme of exiles in Brazil.

Food

✔ The Art of Brazilian Cookery
Dolores Botafogo   1993 (1960)
Over 300 varied recipes.

✔ Tasting Brazil. Regional Recipes and Reminiscences   Jessica B. Harris   1992
The wide-ranging and varied recipes are taken from Brasilia to the Atlantic.

General Background

✔ A View of the World   Norman Lewis
1987 (1986)
A long essay in this collection of journalism is entitled *Genocide*.

✔ It's All True   Paul Rambali   1993
In the 1940's Orson Welles attempted to make a film about Brazil called *It's All True*; it was never made since the footage was lost. Rambali looks at all the facets of Brazil: the tensions, the carnival, Catholicism, poverty and wealth which all go to make up this complex nation which is 'gazing up at dizz-

ying perspectives of rapid development across an abyss of debt'.

An Introduction to Brazil *Charles Wagley*
A very good introduction to Brazil and the Brazilians, though somewhat out of date.

Guides

✔ **Brazil: the Rough Guide** *David Cleary, Dilwyn Jenkins and Oliver Marshall 1994*

✔ **Brazil. Travel Survival Kit**
Andrew Draffen, Robert Strauss and Deanna Swaney 1992 (1989)

✔ **Fodor's Brazil** *1991*

✔ **Insight Guide Brazil** *1992*

History

The Masters and the Slaves: A Study in the Development of Brazilian Civilization *Gilberto Freyre 1986*
A good book on Brazil's colonial period. Although many of his ideas are flawed there is much interesting detail on the folklore, myths, superstitions and religion.

✔ **Amazon Frontier. The Defeat of the Brazilian Indians** *John Hemming 1987*
Covers the period from the mid-eighteenth to the early twentieth century during which time the Portuguese government issued legislation freeing the tribes who had been appallingly treated during the previous two hundred years, only to find that they were subjected to even greater oppression at the hands of lay directors. A definitive account full of original research.

Red Gold. The Conquest of the Brazilian Indians *John Hemming 1978*
The history of the conquest and colonization of Brazil up to the mid-eighteenth century as experienced by the native Indian populations. John Hemming shows how the coastal areas were conquered and settled and how the strength of the Portuguese and Spanish colonists soon overcame the weaker French and Dutch colonies. Thoroughly researched from many original documents.

Natural History

Mato Grosso *Anthony Smith 1971*
A joint Royal Society/Royal Geographical Society expedition went in 1967–69 to the Mato Grosso to investigate the flora, fauna, climate, soils, rocks and peoples of the 'green

hell' of Colonel Fawcett (q.v.). Illustrated with many photographs.

Notes of a Botanist on the Amazon and Andes *Richard Spruce 1908 (see 'Peru')*

Travel Literature

Explorations of the Highlands of Brazil, with a Full Account of the Gold and Diamond Mines, Including Canoeing Down Fifteen Hundred Miles of the Great River Sao Francisco, from Sabara to the Sea
Richard F. Burton 1968 (1869)
One of Burton's reasons for going to Brazil was so that he could explore a country that had had relatively little written about it: 'Central Africa is fast becoming better known to Europe than the Central Brazil'. His wife Isabel accompanied him for much of the time and although she acknowledges that it had been 'her privilege, during those three years, to have been his almost constant companion' she goes on to write 'I protest vehemently against his religious and moral sentiments . . . I point the finger of indignation particularly at what misrepresents our Holy Roman Catholic Church, and at what upholds that unnatural and repulsive law, Polygamy, which the Author is careful not to practice himself, but from a high moral pedestal he preaches to the ignorant as a means of population in young countries'. The project of the journey was to visit the head-waters of the Rio de Sao Francisco and to 'float down its whole length' ending with the rapids, Paulo Affonso.

Exploration Fawcett *Lt. Col. P.H. Fawcett 1953*
The disappearance of Colonel Fawcett in the Matto Grosso remains one of the great unsolved mysteries of today. In 1925 Fawcett was convinced that he had discovered the location of a lost city; he set out with two companions, one of whom was his eldest son, to destination 'Z', never to be heard of again. Brian Fawcett has compiled this book from letters and records left by his father whose last written words to his wife were: 'You need have no fear of any failure . . . .' Fawcett had tried to find lost cities for ten years: 'That the cities exist I know'. The story is both thrilling and astonishing.

Brazilian Adventure *Peter Fleming 1968 (1933)*
Peter Fleming answered an advertisement in the Agony Column of *The Times*: 'Exploring and sporting expedition, under experienced guidance, leaving England June, to explore

rivers Central Brazil, if possible ascertain fate Colonel Fawcett; abundance game, big and small; exceptional fishing; ROOM TWO MORE GUNS; highest references expected and given. – Write Box X, The Times, E.C.4.' He deliberated for a while before replying with just his age (24) and school (Eton); he was accepted on to the expedition for which as he says, Rider Haggard might have written the plot and Conrad designed the scenery.

Samba   *Alma Guillermoprieto*   *1990*
An account of a year spent in Rio *favela* by one of Mexico's leading journalists. A compelling read, revelling in the drama of everyday life in the run-up to Carnival.

Journeys in Time   *Rudyard Kipling*   *1946*
Rudyard Kipling was advised to take a sea voyage by his doctor in 1927; he went to Brazil and wrote *Brazilian Sketches*, included in the above book.

Matto Grosso   *Waclaw Korabiewicz*   *1954*
The author was a refugee, job-hunting in Rio de Janeiro, when he was offered the opportunity to go on a bird-hunting expedition in the Matto Grosso. Many descriptions of the animals and fishes of the jungle.

The Sea and the Jungle   *H.M. Tomlinson*
1989 (1912)
In 1911 Tomlinson decided to leave the English winter and travel up the Amazon on a ship which was delivering coal to Porto Velho.

CHILE

Biography

Uttermost Part of the Earth
E. Lucas Bridges   *1948 (see 'Argentina')*

✔ **Death in Chile**   *Tony Gould*   *1992*
Cristian Huneeus, whom Tony Gould had known at Cambridge, dies of a brain tumour; Gould uses this as an opportunity to go to Chile to find out what happened to this friend whose early success as a novelist had seemed so rich with promise.

Child in Chile   *Bea Howe*   *1957*
The reminiscences of a childhod spent in Valparaiso at the end of the last century.

Sweet Waters: a Chilean Farm
C.J. Lambert   *1975 (1952)*
Life on a large estate in Chile during the 1920s; an ancestor of the author had made his fortune in copper.

Fiction/Poetry

The Chilean Spring   *Fernando Alegria*
1980 (1975)
The fictional account of a photographer called Cristian and what happened to him during the Pinochet coup. He has also written *Allende: A Novel* (1992) and *The Funhouse* (1984).

✔ **The House of the Spirits**
Isabel Allende   *1993 (1985)*
A family saga spanning four generations and full of unforgettable characters, spirits, history and forces of nature. 'This is a novel like the novels no one writes any more: thick with plot and bristling with characters who play out their lives over four generations of conflict and reconciliation.' (*El Pais*, Madrid) Other books by Isabel Allende include *Of Love and Shadows* and *Eva Luna* (see 'Venezuela').

Hell Has No Limits   *José Donoso*   *1973*
(1966)
A novel which explores the emotions, set in a brothel in central Chile. *Curfew* (1988 (1986)) takes place in Santiago under Pinochet; a returning folk singer gets involved in local politics. *Coronation* (1965 (1957)) is an attack on the Chilean aristocracy and *The Obscene Bird of Night* (1974 (1970)) is a powerful novel set in a retreat house in Santiago.

The Last Song of Manuel Sendero
Ariel Dorfman

Selected Poems of Gabriela Mistral
Gabriela Mistral   Translated and edited by Doris Dana   1971
A Nobel prize-winning Chilean author.

✔ **Selected Poems**   *Pablo Neruda*   *1975*
(1970)
Neruda chronicles nature and history through his poetry: 'I have never thought of my life as divided between poetry and politics'.

✔ **Watch Where the Wolf Is Going**
Antonio Skarmeta   *1991 (1969)*
A collection of stories, both old and new, published to celebrate the return of Skarmeta to Chile. Two novels by Skarmeta in English are *I Dreamt the Snow was Burning* (1985) and *Burning Patience* (1985)

General Background

✔ **Clandestine in Chile**
Gabriel Garcia Marquez   *1990 (1986)*
Miguel Littin returned to Chile twelve years after the military coup, using a false identity,

in order to let the world know of the horrors of Pinochet's régime. Marquez retells his story which he adapted from eighteen hours of taped interviews.

Guides

✔ **Chile and Easter Island. Travel Survival Kit** *Wayne Bernhardson* 1993 (1987)

✔ **Insight Guide Chile** 1991

History

The Last Two Years of Salvador Allende *Nathaniel Davis* 1985
The author was US ambassador to Chile during the last two years of Allende's régime. He is fairly critical of Allende's methods but, on the whole, sympathetic to his beliefs.

Small Earthquake in Chile
Alistair Horne 1972
Horne visited Chile at a time when the Popular Unity government seemed to be quite successful; here he combines an assessment of the political scenario with a look at the country and its people.

Chile: The Legacy of Hispanic Capitalism *Brian Loveman* 1979
A history of Chile from the Spanish conquest to the late 1970s.

The Conquest of Chile *H.R.S. Pocock* 1967,
An account of the conquest of Chile by Pedro de Valdivia up until his death in 1554.

Leisure

✔ **Backpacking in Chile and Argentina** *Hilary Bradt* 1989

✔ **Trekking in the Patagonian Andes. A Lonely Planet Walking Guide**
Clem Lindenmayer 1992

Natural History

(see 'Argentina': Earle and Hudson)

Travel Literature

(For travel in Chile see 'Argentina' books on Patagonia by: Chatwin, Pilkington, Shipton, Tilman, Tschiffely and Vernon)

✔ **What Am I Doing Here?**
Bruce Chatwin 1989
Includes an essay on Chiloé Island.

Back to Cape Horn *Rosie Swale* 1986
The account of a 400-day trip by horse from the Atacama Desert to Cape Horn; there are many 'off the beaten track' descriptions of Chile.

Cucumber Sandwiches in the Andes
John Ure 1973
John Ure was a diplomat in Santiago; while he was there he decided to follow by horse, General San Martin's route across the Andes, though in the opposite direction.

✔ **Travels in a Thin Country**
Sara Wheeler 1994
Sara Wheeler spent six months on her own travelling through Chile, at 2,600 miles, the longest country in the world. She covered extraordinarily diverse landscapes and met a variety of people all of whom she writes about with a freshness and originality.

EASTER ISLAND

Art and Archaeology

Aku-Aku: the Secret of Easter Island
Thor Heyerdahl 1958
An account of an archaeological expedition to Easter Island; the mysteries of Easter Island's history and pre-history are examined and there is a fascinating description of a visit to the secret Raakau cave where surprising ethnographic artefacts were found.

The Art of Easter Island *Thor Heyerdahl* 1976
One of the fundamental archaeological books of the island.

General Background

✔ **Easter Island Earth Island** *Paul Bahn and John Flenley* 1992
Much new research has gone into this book and many previous theories have been overthrown. The book speculates on where the Easter Islanders came from, how they got there and how the statues were moved; some interesting conclusions are reached.

The Secrets of Easter Island
Jean-Michel Schwartz 1975
Schwartz tries to analyse the cryptic rongo-rongo writing of Easter Island and finds striking similarities between it and symbols found in the Indus Valley (a script which has never been deciphered). Schwartz thinks that the statues on Easter Island acquired

their character through the interaction of Asian influences from the West.

Guides

✔ **Chile and Easter Island. Travel Survival Kit**   Wayne Bernhardson   1993 (1987)

History

Easter Island: A Stone-Age Civilization of the Pacific   Alfred Métraux   1957
A readable overview of the culture and what is known of the history, based on an expedition made in 1934/5. The author admits that certain mysteries concerning Easter Island are 'only half-solved and will perhaps never be fully elucidated'.

Photography

Easter Island. The Mystery Solved
Thor Heyerdahl   1989
Thor Heyerdahl was asked to return to Easter Island many years after writing *Aku Aku* (q.v.); still haunted by the mystery of the statues – who made them and how were they moved – he compiled a book with many photographs.

Travel Literature

Easter Island: Island of Enigmas
John dos Passos   1971
An account by dos Passos of a trip he made to Easter Island.

The Mystery of Easter Island. The Story of an Expedition
Mrs Scoresby Routledge   1919
Katherine Routledge was the only female member of the expedition that went to Easter Island in 1913 to try to discover the origin of the statues, how they got there and who brought them. They had asked the anthropological department of the British Museum what work needed to be done in the Pacific and the authorities had replied 'Easter Island'. She was persuaded to write a book partly because after giving a lecture a woman came up to her and said 'I was disappointed in what you told us. You never said what you had to eat.'

JUAN FERNANDEZ ISLANDS

Fiction

✔ **Robinson Crusoe**   Daniel Defoe   1991 (1719) (see 'Caribbean')

COLOMBIA

Biography

Bolivar and the Independence of Spanish America   J.B. Trend   1946 (see 'South America –General')

Fiction/Poetry

✔ **Call at Corazon**   Paul Bowles   1989
The collection of short stories has two by Bowles set in Colombia which he visited in 1934: *Call at Corazon* and *The Echo*.

The Lost Steps   Alejo Carpentier   1956
An American musicologist searches for mysticism and spirituality in the jungles of Colombia.

✔ **Nostromo**   Joseph Conrad   1990 (1904)
In the imaginary republic of Costaguana, (a thinly veiled Colombia), Conrad creates a surprisingly modern novel but one which nonetheless shows his typical pessimism; his lifelike picture captures the essence of South American politics and he draws acute character sketches of people whose potential for good turns bad.

Maria   Jorge Isaacs   1890 (1867)
The author studied medicine in Bogota and London, eventually becoming Consul in Chile. He was drawn to the countryside and to the Indians and his romantic novel *Maria* is set in the surroundings he knew so well.

✔ **One Hundred Years of Solitude**
Gabriel Garcia Marquez   1978 (1967) (see also 'Chile' and 'Venezuela')
A wonderfully imaginative and rich novel about a group of people who establish a town in the middle of the South American jungle. What happens to them during the next century is the basis for this book which was described by the *Sunday Times* as 'An immensely rich piece of writing, dense as the jungle foliage and packed with learned allusion, action and humour – full of incidents to enjoy and philosophies to wonder at'. Other books by Marquez include: *Innocent Eréndira, No One Writes to the Colonel* and *Leaf*

Storm (all short stories) [Jan Morris] and *Chronicle of a Death Foretold, In Evil Hour* and *The General in His Labyrinth* (a novel which is also a portrait of Simon Bolivar).

General Background

In Bogota   *Joan Didion   1979*
An essay from the book *The White Album* which describes the people, politics and attitudes of the Colombians and of the Americans to the Colombians.

Guides

✔ **Colombia. A Travel Survival Kit**
Krzysztof Dydynski   1988

✔ **Cadogan Guide Ecuador, the Galapagos and Colombia**
John Paul Rathbone   1991

History

The Golden Man: the Quest for El Dorado   *Victor W. von Hagen   1974*
An illustrated account of the people who searched for the 'golden man': Nicolaus Federmann, Ambrosius Dalfinger, George Hohermuth, the Quesadas, Gonzalo Pizarro, Francisco Orellana and Sir Walter Raleigh.

The Search for El Dorado
John Hemming   1978
'Every explorer needs a vision, some goal to keep him and his men struggling forward.' With these words Hemming begins his clearly laid out and well-illustrated book on the early explorations of Venezuela and its neighbouring countries.

Natural History

The Hills of the Boasting Woman
Stephen Earl   1962
The observations of the zoologist Stephen Earl in the Maraena mountains.

Photography

Colombia   *Patrick Rouillard   1985*
A large photographic book published in Colombia.

Travel Literature

✔ **The Heart of the World**   *Alan Ereira*
1992 (1990)
The Kogi, who call themselves the Elder Brothers, had lived for years in the lost dense mountain jungle city of the Taironas. When pre-Columbian gold objects appeared on the market in the 1970s, their city was 'discovered' and the Elder Brothers decided to speak to the rest of the world, warning that greed and ignorance would destroy life on earth if the balance between man and nature and the spiritual world were ignored. A forceful and moving book.

Travels Through the Interior Provinces of Colombia   *John P. Hamilton 1828*
Hamilton was a British diplomat who travelled from Santa Marta up the Magdalena to Bogota, taking in many side trips en route.

✔ **The Fruit Palace**   *Charles Nicholl   1985*
Charles Nicholl first came into contact with the Colombian drug trade in the early seventies and twelve years later went back to find out as much about this dangerous world as he could: '. . . ruefully witty, shrewdly observant, eminently sensible, far too intelligent to get mixed up in a story like this one, and lucky enough to have survived it.' (Jay McInerney)

ECUADOR

Fiction/Poetry

Seven Serpents and Seven Moons
Demetrio Aguilera-Malta   1979
A novel set in a tropical village of Santoronton; the theme is the perennial struggle between good and evil.

Huasipungo   *Jorge Icaza   1962 (1934)*
The exploitation of the Indians who were forced to build a road through the jungle of Ecuador after oil had been discovered. The Indians saw the road as a bridge to civilization, whereas Don Alfonso, the landowner, saw it as a means of increasing his wealth.

General Background

A Saint Among Savages
Rosemary Kingsland   1980
Rachael Saint, a missionary, lived for twenty years with the violent and hostile Waorani (Auca) Indians who had killed her brother and four companions in 1956; she befriended an Auca woman, Dayuma, and her son Sam.

Guides

✔ **Insight Guide Ecuador**   *1991*

✔ **Ecuador and the Galapagos Islands. A Travel Survival Kit**
Rob Rachowiecki   1992 (1986)

✔ **Cadogan Guide Ecuador, The Galapagos and Colombia**
John Paul Rathbone   1991

History

Ecuador   *Victor W. Von Hagen   1978*
A history of the country, region by region.

Leisure

Climbing and Hiking in Ecuador
Rob Rachowiecki and Betty Wagenhauser   1991

Natural History

Notes of a Botanist on the Amazon and Andes   *Richard Spruce   1908 (see 'Peru')*

Photography

Ecuador. Island of the Andes
Kevin Kling   1988 (1987)
Photographic books about Ecuador too often concentrate on the Galapagos to the detriment of the rest of the country; this is an exception and shows 100 colour photographs of the Indians and the landscape.

Jungle Nomads of Ecuador: the Waorani   *John Man   1982*
The Waorani (Auca) live in the western fringes of the Amazon Basin; many colour photographs – in the Time-Life series of the World's Wild Places.

Travel Literature

✔ **The Donkey Inside**
Ludwig Bemelmans   1990 (1968)
The author and illustrator of the children's classic *Madeleine* books, made three trips to South America and kept six large notebooks and a portfolio of drawings. His approach and descriptions of people, animals and the landscape is refreshingly original and humorous: 'Bemelmans is not like anyone who has ever written about South America'. (*New York Times* Book Review).

Interlude in Ecuador   *Janet Mackay   1934*
A refreshing book by a Canadian woman barrister who took time off from her very male working world, to visit her sister in Santa Elena, Ecuador.

Ecuador – A Travel Journal
Henri Michaux   1970 (1929)
In 1927/8 Michaux journeyed from Amsterdam through the Panama Canal to Quito, down the Amazon to Para, Brazil and back to France. He wrote it as a journal but as Robin Magowan, the translator, writes 'Much of the originality of *Ecuador* lies in Michaux's awareness of the fact of incompleteness, his and everything else's . . . The traveler is 'He Who Seeks to Attach Himself' and throughout the book Michaux is trying to attach himself to anything and everything he comes across – mountains, natives, the sea, a horse, a boat . . .

The Panama Hat Trail   *Tom Miller   1988 (1986)*
A very amusingly written travelogue which takes as its theme the search for the source of the Panama hat. How is the hat made? What from? How is it sold? Miller seeks the answer to all these questions and puts them in the broader context of the workings of world trade.

✔ **Living Poor**   *Moritz Thomsen   1989 (1971)*
Thomsen joined the American Peace Corps late in life and farmed near Esmeraldas in Ecuador, where he dispensed with American values.

✔ **The Saddest Pleasure: A Journey on Two Rivers**   *Moritz Thomsen   1990*
A trip up the Amazon which Thomsen made after twelve years of 'living poor' in Ecuador. He started writing late in life and sadly died in poverty before receiving the acclaim he deserved. 'The book so affected me that reading it I suddenly wondered where is that smell of charcoal cooking and over ripe fruit coming from? It was the smell of South America.' (Norman Lewis) [Colin Thubron]

Travels Amongst the Great Andes of the Equator   *Edward Whymper   1987 (1891) (see 'Andes')*

GALAPAGOS ISLANDS

'Take five and twenty heaps of cinders dumped here and there in an outside lot; imagine some of them magnified into mountains and the vacant lot the sea; and you will have a fit idea of the general aspect of the Encantadas.' (Herman Melville)

Biography

Floreana   *Margret Wittmer   1989 (1961)*
The Wittmers arrived in the Galapagos in 1932 in search of a cure for their twelve-year-old invalid son. On arrival Margret was confined to the practical problems of living on a day-to-day basis and had no time for the 'philosophy' that some of the other inhabitants were preaching. However, their lives became entangled and tragedies struck their island paradise.

Fiction/Poetry

✔ **The Encantadas or Enchanted Isles**   *Herman Melville   1967*
This story which is included in *Billy Budd and Other Stories* is about the life that Melville had seen in the Galapagos.

Galapagos   *Kurt Vonnegut   1987*
A group of people get stuck in Guayaquil on their way to the Galapagos. This satirical novel looks at the possible extinction of the human race and its survival as sea creatures.

General Background

The Galapagos Affair   *John Treherne   1983*
An investigation into the mystery surrounding the disappearance of a group of German settlers on Floreana in the 1920s.

Guides *(See 'Ecuador –General')*

History

The Enchanted Islands. The Galapagos Discovered   *John Hickman 1985*
The fragmented history of the Galapagos from Inca times up until this century. The Galapagos have attracted a collection of strange people, many of whom Hickman chronicles here.

Natural History

Galapagos. World's End   *William Beebe 1924*
The author was Director of the Department of Tropical Research of the New York Zoological Society but describes the flora and fauna of the Galapagos in a very comprehensible manner. Well illustrated with 24 colour illustrations and 83 photographs.

✔ **A Field Guide to the Birds of Galapagos**   *Michael Harris   1978*
Each bird in the guide is described with its identifying features such as voice, breeding, habitat and food etc.

✔ **Galapagos. A Natural History Guide**   *Michael H. Jackson   1985*
The book combines a travel guide with an introduction to and descriptions of the natural history of the islands. Colour photographs.

Field Guide to the Fishes of Galapagos   *Godfrey Merlen   1988*
One hundred and seven fish that are found in the Galapagos are illustrated.

✔ **Darwin and the Beagle**
Alan Moorehead   1971 (1969)
An illustrated and readable account of Darwin's round-the-world voyage in the *Beagle* via South America and the Galapagos, where he observed the finches which helped him form his theory of evolution.

Plants of the Galapagos   *Eileen Schofield 1984*
Brief descriptions of the plants, illustrated with line drawings.

GUYANA, FRENCH GUIANA AND SURINAME

Anthropology

The Gentle People. A Journey Among the Indian Tribes of Guiana
Colin Henfrey   1964
Guiana has always had many myths and fables written about it: Raleigh saw it as El Dorado, sending his men up the Orinoco in search of gold and Laurence Keymis wrote in 1596 of 'men who had eminent heads like dogs and live all day in the sea and speak the Carib language'. Henfrey sees Guiana as having been neglected and by travelling among the Indian tribes he aimed to put the record straight.

Fiction/Poetry

✔ **A Plan for Escape**   *Adolfo Bioy-Casares 1988 (1969)*
A Frenchman, Nevers, is sent for a year to work in a penal colony off the islands of French Guiana. This dreamlike, metaphysical novel, full of black humour proves Borges' point, as he has described the author as 're-

ally and secretly the master' of Latin American literature.

The Lost World   Arthur Conan Doyle   1980 (1932)

Conan Doyle's 'Lost World' is a real place – a twenty-five mile square plateau more than 9,000 feet high, at the top of Mount Roraima where the border of Guyana meets Venezuela and Brazil. In the adventure story four men travel up the Amazon accompanied by the incessant drumming of unseen tribes; on the plateau they discover dinosaurs and pterodactyls and to the very end the plot retains suspense and has some unexpected twists.

Guinea-Pig   Paul Marlee   1990

Set in the Suriname of the author's childhood; the narrator has a dream which proves that he is a writer.

✔ **My Bones and My Flute**
Edgar Mittelholzer   1989 (1955)

A ghost story set in pre-Independence Guyana: in the jungle the bones of a Dutch plantation owner are found unburied next to his deserted mill; a haunting flute plays insistently.

✔ **A Hot Country**   Shiva Naipaul   1984 (1983)

'Cuyama' is a thinly disguised Guyana; the novel mocks post-colonial 'intellectual' life.

✔ **A Handful of Dust**   Evelyn Waugh
1951 (1934)

Tony Last sails through the Caribbean on his way to search for a city: 'to Brazil. At least it may be Brazil or Dutch Guiana. One cannot tell. The frontier has never been demarcated', but 'it did not come easily to him to realize that he was an explorer'.

The Eye of the Scarecrow
Wilson Harris   1970

A series of somewhat disjointed reminiscences by the narrator who meets a childhood friend. *Tumatumari* (1968), in which a woman comes to terms with the death of her child, takes place near some waterfalls in the interior.

Orealla   Roy Heath   1984

Set at the turn of the century in a mythical Indian location where oppression and slavery do not exist. Heath has also written a Georgetown trilogy *From the Heat of the Day* (1979), *One Generation* (1981) and *Genetta* (1981)).

General Background

✔ **Beyond the Dragon's Mouth**
Shiva Naipaul   1985 (1984)

A collection of pieces including one on Surinam.

✔ **Black and White**   Shiva Naipaul   1981 (1980)

Shiva Naipaul went to Jonestown two weeks after Jim Jones and his followers had committed mass suicide. He interviewed many people and pieced together the events which led up to the horrifying massacre.

British Guiana   Raymond T. Smith   1962

A general background book which includes chapters on natural resources, history, the economy, social structure, social services, government and politics.

History

Papillon   Henri Charrière   1986 (1970)

Charrière was named 'Papillon' (Butterfly) when he was a criminal in France. He was sent to Devil's Island having been wrongly convicted of murder and tried to escape nine times between 1931 and 1943. He ended up in Venezuela.

✔ **The Making of Guyana**   Vere T. Daly
1990 (1974)

A straightforward history of the country.

✔ **Devil's Island. Colony of the Damned**   Alexander Miles   1988

Seventy thousand of France's toughest criminals were sent to either St Laurent or Devil's Island to serve their sentences. Conditions were so dire that only one in ten survived the ordeal. Miles interviewed some of the survivors and their guards.

Natural History

Zoo Quest to Guiana   David Attenborough
1956

David Attenborough spent three months in British Guiana filming for the BBC and collecting animals for London Zoo.

Wai Wai   Nicholas Guppy   1958

The author worked for the Forest Department in Georgetown, the capital of British Guiana, and managed to persuade his superiors that his brief should take him into the interior; he decided to go to the very south of the country, along the mountainous Brazilian border, to meet the Wai-Wai Indians in the Serra Acarai. He not only wanted to collect new plant species, but also to examine the nature of the almost certainly virgin forests before they were disturbed.

Birds of Surinam   F. Haverschmidt   1968
An illustrated handbook with information on the habitat, identification, nesting and food of about 600 species found in Suriname.

Travel Literature

✔ **Journey to Guyana**   Margaret Bacon
1993 (1970)
The author spent two years in Guyana and describes her everyday life there, married to a civil engineer in the 1960s. Since British Guyana was the only British territory in South America, much in the past had been written about it, but little that was up to date.

A Young Man's Journey   Nicholas Guppy
1973
The book is the account of Guppy's time, as a young 'over-educated' graduate, in Guyana in the early 50s. However it was written over twenty years afterwards and he reflects 'Could I ever have been so innocent as he?' By observing plants and seeing their parallels with people, he 'learned much of what I believe I know about people' and makes plants the heroes and heroines of his book.

Out of Chingford   Tanis and
Martin Jordan (see 'South America – General')

Dutch Guiana   W.G. Palgrave   1876
The author spent two weeks as a guest of the British consul in Suriname and wrote very positively about it, calling it a 'Creole paradise' and urged 'The gates are open: enter'.

Expedition to Surinam being the narrative of a five years expedition against the revolted negroes of Surinam in Guiana on the wild coast of South America from the year 1772 to 1777 elucidating that country and describing its productions with an account of Indians of Guiana and negroes of Guinea   Captain John Stedman
1963 (1796)
Stedman was an officer in the expedition which was sent by the Dutch in 1772 to crush the slave revolts. His account of the expedition and the prevailing conditions in the colony were remarkably humane for the time. The original version contains much on the flora and fauna of Guiana, but most of this has been omitted from the 1963 Folio Society edition. 'Gives an unique picture of the Caribbean of his day. It is also very exciting.' (Norman Lewis)

✔ **Ninety-Two Days**   Evelyn Waugh   1991
(1934)
'One does not travel, any more than one falls in love, to collect material. It is simply part of one's life . . . there is a fascination in distant and barbarous places,' writes Evelyn Waugh explaining why he went to British Guiana and Brazil in 1933. Often throughout the book he philosophizes about travel: ' . . . the delight of travel . . . is a delight just as incommunicable as the love of home'. And two pleasures he had missed in Europe which he rediscovered while travelling were washing and reading.

PARAGUAY

Anthropology

An Unknown People in an Unknown Land   W. Barbrooke Grubb   1911
An account of the life and customs of the Lengua Indians of the Paraguayan Chaco, written by a pioneer missionary and explorer who spent twenty years in the country. Inevitably he is biased in his attempt at trying to convert the Indians to Christianity but he did become a great authority on the Indians and writes about their mythology, superstitions and witchcraft.

Biography

Life in Paraguay   Constance Kent   1958
Constance Kent arrived in Paraguay with her family in 1905 intending to grow rubber. The book is disorganized but gives a good idea of the pioneering life.

✔ **Forgotten Fatherland. The Search for Elisabeth Nietzsche**   Ben Macintyre
1992
In 1886 Elisabeth Nietzsche, sister of the philosopher, went to Paraguay with a group of selected blond, blue-eyed Germans to found a colony in Paraguay called New Germany. Ben Macintyre follows her journey and discovers the colony, Nueva Germania, still existing, with the people there, breeding among themselves and maintaining their original manners, customs and language.

Fiction/Poetry

Son of Man   Augusto Roa Bastos   1988 (1961)
A novel which ties together several episodes in Paraguayan history. Also by Bastos, who has spent most of his life in exile, *I the*

Supreme, a novel about the paranoid dictator Francia.

✔ Travels with My Aunt
Graham Greene   1977 (1969)
Aunt Augusta's nephew Henry Pulling decides to stay on in Paraguay after travelling up the River Parana from Argentina. Pulling discovers the joys of travel and the contrast to his suburban existence where he was a bank manager.

✔ The Green Child   *Herbert Read   1989 (1935)*
Much of *The Green Child* is set in 'Roncador' which is a thinly disguised Paraguay. This was Read's only novel and is about a South American President who returns to his native Yorkshire and disappears with the Green Child into a mythical world.

✔ Candide   *Voltaire   1966 (1947)*
Candide is subtitled 'Optimism', but as Robert M. Adams points out in his translation it could just as easily be called 'Civilization and Its Discontents'. When Candide arrived in the New World he discovered that the Jesuits had just been expelled; he first travelled to Paraguay before going on to Surinam and French Guiana. By the end of this satire Candide comes to the conclusion that the New World has nothing new to offer and that which he had been taught by Dr Pangloss is meaningless.

The Paraguayan Experiment
Michael Wilding   1985
A novel, based on fact, about a group of Australian socialists who emigrated to Paraguay in 1893 to set up a 'utopian' colony.

General Background

South American Sketches
R.B. Cunninghame Graham   1978.
One of the essays in this collection is entitled *The Jesuit* (1896). The Jesuits had been expelled from Paraguay in 1767; here he writes about one who returned.

Paraguay   *W.H. Koebel   1917*
A good, if somewhat dated, general background to Paraguay with chapters on the original inhabitants, the Jesuits, the colonial period, the war, the geography, immigration, agriculture and trade.

Guides

✔ Argentina, Uruguay and Paraguay. Travel Survival Kit   *Wayne Bernhardson and Maria Massolo   1992*

History

Letters from the Battlefields of Paraguay   *Richard F. Burton   1870*
Burton twice visited the battlefields of the War of the Triple Alliance as a reporter for *The Times.*

Paraguay. A Riverside Nation
George Pendle   1967 (1954)
Since the problems the Paraguayans faced in the 1960s were very similar to those they had been confronted with for four centuries, much space is given to the history of Paraguay in this small book.

Natural History

Zoo Quest in Paraguay
David Attenborough   1959
The expedition to Paraguay was primarily to look for armadillos: 'The armadillos are the only surviving relations of the Glyptodons. To look at them is to see a link with the strange, primitive beasts of prehistory . . . '

The Drunken Forest   *Gerald Durrell   1980*
(see 'Argentina')

Travel Literature

The River and the People
Gordon Meyer   1966
Gordon Meyer travelled up the River Parana from Argentina to Paraguay researching a book on the dictator Solano Lopez which in fact he never wrote. There are good descriptions of the history and countryside.

PERU

Art and Archaeology

Lines to the Mountain Gods: Nazca and the Mysteries of Peru
Evan Hadingham   1987
The Nazca lines are the geometric designs found in the desert in southern Peru; Hadingham links them with lines found in California and the Midwest and suggests that shamanism could be the link between them.

Monuments of the Incas *John Hemming*
1982
A clear book with over 200 black and white photographs about the building techniques of the Incas; it concentrates primarily on the sites at Sacsahuaman, Machu Picchu and Ollantaytambo.

✔ **The Ancient Civilizations of Peru**
J. Alden Mason 1991 (1957)
A very readable book about the archaeological, historical, artistic, geographical and ethnological discoveries from the sites of Machu Picchu, Cuzco and Titicaca.

✔ **The Incas and Their Ancestors**
Michael E. Moseley 1993 (1992)
The archaeology and history of Peru from over 10,000 years ago up until the Spanish conquest. He examines the pre-Inca civilizations: Chavin, Moche, Nazca, Tiwanaku, Huari and Chimú. Maps, line drawings and photographs.

Fiction/Poetry

Broad and Alien is the World
Ciro Alegria 1941
A political novel which describes the sufferings in an Indian community.

✔ **The Time of the Hero**
Mario Vargas Llosa 1986 (1967)
This novel so outraged the Peruvian authorities that copies were publicly burned; it is set in the Military Academy in Lima and by making the academy a microcosm of Peruvian life becomes a powerful social satire. Other novels by Llosa include *The Real Life of Alejandro Mayta* ('a brilliant novel of a hopeless Peruvian revolutionary' [*The Times*]), *Aunt Julia and the Scriptwriter* ('This is a novel as full of fizz as a giant pack of sherbet, witty, wise and wonderful in equal proportions . . . as tense as a thriller and as racy as a romance.' [*The Sunday Times*], *Conversation in the Cathedral*, *The Green House* and *The Storyteller*.

✔ **Selected Poems** *Pablo Neruda 1975 (1970)*
Neruda wrote an epic poem called *The Heights of Machu Picchu*.

✔ **The Vision of Elena Silves**
Nicholas Shakespeare 1990 (1989)
A young Catholic girl, Elena falls in love with the Marxist Gabriel: 'They represent the two different strains which promise hope in the bereaved and wasted land' (Alan Massie). Shakespeare's combination of magic realism with European traditions of fiction makes an extremely effective and successful mixture.

On the Other Side of Life and Death
César Vallejo 1987 (1922)
From the collection entitled *The Eye of the Heart* which Vallejo published just before leaving Peru for Paris in 1923; he went on to become a founder member of the Spanish Communist Party. This story is autobiographical and tells of his return to his home town after the death of his mother.

The Bridge of San Luis Rey
Thornton Wilder 1941 (1927)
A fictional recreation of life in colonial Peru which begins with the 'finest bridge in all Peru' breaking on 20th July 1714, killing five travellers. A witness to the event, Brother Juniper, decided to find out all he could about the people who had died to establish whether there is a plan to the universe.

General Background

✔ **In the Forests of the Night**
John Simpson 1993
John Simpson went to investigate what was happening in contemporary Peru. He writes at a cracking pace about the terrorism, drug running and military oppression he encountered and relates how he was close on the trail of Abimael Guzman when he was arrested.

✔ **Shining Path** *Simon Strong 1993 (1992)*
The ruthless and dedicated members of the Sendero Luminosa (Shining Path) exploit the divisions and weaknesses in Peru. This 'excellent study' is 'diligently researched and written with brio'. (*The Guardian*).

Guides

✔ **Insight Guide Peru** *1991*

✔ **Peru. The Rough Guide**
Dilwyn Jenkins 1991 (1985)

A Traveller's Guide to El Dorado and the Incan Empire *Lynn Meisch*
Full of detail about the antiquities.

✔ **Peru. Travel Survival Kit**
Rob Rachowiecki 1991 (1987)

Reparaz's Guide to Peru *1991*
A very detailed guide packed with information published in Lima and sponsored by the National Tourism Chamber of Peru.

History

The Conquest of the Incas
John Hemming 1970
A scholarly, yet clear and readable account of the conquest of Peru from the arrival of Pizarro to the execution of the last Inca Emperor, Tupac Amaru, in 1572.

Everyday Life of the Incas   *Ann Kendall 1973*
One in a very useful series of books which explains what life was like under the Incas. It shows how economic and ideological values formed the basis of a very organized structure, which was enforced by strict laws and punishments and which existed parallel to a mystical religion.

The Kingdom of the Sun: A Short History of Peru   *Luis Martin 1974*
A general, easy-to-read and straightforward overall history.

History of the Conquest of Peru
William H. Prescott 1961 (1847)
When Prescott first published his history of Peru, it was considered a pioneering and revolutionary work. The modern edition has been abridged.

Coricancha (garden of gold): Being an Account of the Conquest of the Inca Empire   *A.F. Tschiffely 1943*
A popular account of the conquest which relies on well-known sources.

Leisure

Trails of the Cordilleras Blanca and Huayhuash of Peru   *Jim Bartle 1990*
A new edition has supposedly been published in Lima.

✔ The Peruvian Andes   *Ph Beaud 1988*
Written in French, English and Spanish; useful for climbing routes.

✔ Backpacking and Trekking in Peru and Bolivia   *Hilary Bradt 1994*

✔ Yuraq Janka. Cordilleras Blanca and Rosko   *John F. Ricker 1977*
Aimed at mountaineers and mountain travellers, the book begins with general information about the Andean region of Peru before going onto more specific information for climbers.

Natural History

The Flight of the Condor: a Wildlife Exploration of the Andes
Michael Alford Andrews 1982
A book that accompanied a television series about the flora and fauna of the Andes. Well illustrated.

Notes of a Botanist on the Amazon and Andes   *Richard Spruce 1908*
Spruce collected more than 7,000 specimens of flowering plants during the time he spent in Brazil, Ecuador and Peru from 1849–64. He returned to England to die in poverty in 1893 and his notes were eventually made into book form by his friend Alfred Russel Wallace.

Photography

Martin Chambi: Photographs of Peru
Martin Chambi 1920–1950
A collection of photographs by Peru's most famous photographer, published by the Banco de la Republica.

Travel Literature

Lost City of the Incas   *Hiram Bingham 1951*
A vivid first-hand account of the explorations at Machu Picchu. He also writes about the ancient Peruvians' daily life and shows how many things we take for granted today come from them: the white potato, many varieties of Indian corn, quinine and cocaine.

✔ Three Letters from the Andes
Patrick Leigh Fermor 1992 (1991)
A slim collection of letters which the author wrote to his wife during a trip he made to the Peruvian Andes with five friends in 1971. Starting in Lima they travel into increasingly remote parts of the country where they camp under blankets of snow and need ice axes and ropes to traverse glaciers; his descriptions of these exploits, the landscape and the people, both his travelling companions and the ones he meets, are all keenly observed.

✔ Inca-Kola   *Matthew Parris 1993 (1990)*
An account of Matthew Parris' fourth trip to Peru in which he encountered bandits, prostitutes, peasants and riots.

✔ Touching the Void   *Joe Simpson 1989 (1988)*
A compulsivly readable book about a climbing accident in the Peruvian Andes. Joe Simpson breaks his leg and the rope on which he is

being lowered gets stuck; the decisions which have to be made as a result are agonizing and courageous.

Golden Wall and Mirador: Travels and Observations in Peru   Sacheverell Sitwell   1961
One learns much about Sitwell and somewhat less about the country, since he finds coping with the altitude somewhat taxing.

Keep the River on Your Right
Tobias Schneebaum   1970
The author was a Fulbright fellow who achieved notoriety during his travels in Peru as it was thought that he had been killed by Indians. He gives an interesting summary of what life was like in a jungle mission station.

Peru. Incidents of Travel and Exploration in the Land of the Incas
E. George Squier   1877
Squier was inspired to travel to Peru by having read Prescott as a youth: 'The hand of the conquerors fell heavily on the venerable monuments of Peru; and, in their blind and superstitious search for hidden treasure, they caused infinitely more ruin than time or the earthquake.' Squier spent a year and a half covering the area more closely than anyone had before and wrote a detailed book about his investigations.

✔ Peregrinations of a Pariah
1833–1834   Flora Tristan
Flora Tristan, an ardent feminist and socialist, went to Peru in order to claim a share of her father's fortune (which she failed to do). However, she left us an account of her voyage, of the manners and customs in Peru at the time and of how she acted as an intermediary in Peru's revolution.

Incas and Other Men: Travels in the Andes   George Woodcock   1959
The author travelled through much of Peru in the 1950s and describes life in the Andes as he saw it.

Cut Stones and Crossroads
Ronald Wright   1986 (1984)
Travels through Peru in search of its history and archaeology: 'The book is a marvelous mixture of science and color reporting, antiquities and contemporary politics'. (*Christian Science Monitor*)

URUGUAY

Fiction/Poetry

The Form of the Sword   Jorge Luis Borges
1965 (1962)
In the collection of pieces called *Fictions*; the story is set in northern Uruguay and has an Irishman as a narrator who tells a story about betrayal which turns out to be about himself.

The Purple Land   W.H. Hudson   1979
(1885)
A story set in the 1860/70s which recounts the narrator's wanderings in the interior, mostly on a horse, against a background of civil wars.

✔ The Shipyard   Juan Carlos Onetti   1992
(1961)
Set in the fictional but very real country of Yoknapatawpha, Larsen is offered the job as General Manager of the bankrupt Jeremias Petrus shipyard. Many other vivid characters live in the present reality of the struggling shipyard, but often have glimpses of the past and its glory. Other books by Onetti are *No Man's Land* and *A Brief Life* 1993 (1950).

Ariel   José Enrique Rodo   1976
An essay written at the turn of the century by the famous Uruguayan writer, Rodo, which contrasts North American and Latin American civilizations.

General Background

Uruguay   W.H. Koebel   1911
Chapters on a general survey of the country, history, manners and customs, aboriginal tribes, Montevideo, the campo, estancia life, the geography, industries, communications, commerce and politics and revolutions. Somewhat worthy.

Guide

✔ Argentina, Uruguay and Paraguay. Travel Survival Kit   Wayne Bernhardson and Maria Massolo   1992

History

The Conquest of the River Plate
R.B. Cunninghame Graham   1924 (see 'Argentina')

Uruguay   George Pendle   1957 (1952)
A small book written for the Royal Institute of International Affairs, with chapters on Uruguay under Spanish and British rule and

the struggle for independence as well as on the people, the land, industry and finance.

Natural History

The Naturalist in La Plata
W.H. Hudson (see 'Argentina')

Travel Literature

Travels in Uruguay, South America; together with an account of the Present State of Sheep-farming and emigration to that country
Rev. John H. Murray 1871
The author arrived in Montevideo in February 1868 during a cholera epidemic and was there at the time of the assassinations of General Flores and Bernardo Berro. After his eighteen days in Montevideo he spent nine months travelling in the interior.

VENEZUELA

Anthropology

Shabono *Florinda Donner (see 'Brazil')*

Fiction/Poetry

✔ **Eva Luna** *Isabel Allende 1989 (1987)*
When Isabel Allende was exiled to Venezuela she wrote this novel about the development of a natural story teller. Her collection of short stories The Stories of Eva Luna (1990) are also set in a remote Venezuelan backwater, Agua Santa.

The Lost World
Arthur Conan Doyle (see 'Guyana')

Dona Barbara *Romulo Gallegos 1948*
Based on a real person, an evil-hearted plainswoman, who cultivated the myth that she was a witch. Gallegos, who was later to become President of Venezuela, also wrote *Canaima* (1934), about the harsh life in the hinterland of the Orinoco.

Green Mansions: A Romance of the Tropical Forest *W.H. Hudson 1990 (1904)*
Abel Guevez de Argensola flees from Caracas and travels down the Orinoco where he decides to hide. He gets caught up in the jungle and its lore and meets Rima who, soon after they meet, is burnt for being a sorceress; he goes mad, wanders the jungle, eventually recovering his composure when he reaches Georgetown, by transferring her to a 'Rima of the mind'. There is an Epstein statue of Hudson (who never went to Venezuela) and Rima in Hyde Park.

✔ **Autumn of the Patriarch**
Gabriel Garcia Marquez 1991 (1977)
The composite dictator in the novel is based largely on the Venezuelan dictator Juan Vicente Gomez. *The General in His Labyrinth* is an historical novel about Simon Bolivar (see 'Colombia').

✔ **Keepers of the House**
Lisa St. Aubin de Teran 1982
A family saga about the demise of a dynasty into which a young English girl has married (paralleling her own life). *The Tiger* (1985) is also set in Venezuela.

Guides

✔ **Venezuela. A Bradt Guide**
Hilary Dunsterville Branch 1993

✔ **Hayit's Budget Travel Venezuela**
1994
A chunky little guide translated from German.

✔ **Insight Guide Venezuela** *1993*

✔ **Venezuela. Travel Survival Kit**
1994

History

The Search for El Dorado (see 'Colombia')

Natural History

Narrative of travels on the Amazon and Rio Negro, with an account of the native tribes and observations on the climate, geology, and natural history of the Amazon valley
Alfred Russel Wallace (see 'Amazonia')

Travel Literature

We Dared the Andes. Three Journeys into the Unknown *Gustaf Bolinder 1958*
The journeys, made in 1915, 1920 and 1936, were into the Sierra de Perija on the Colombian–Venezuelan border.

The Sons of El Dorado: Venezuelan Adventure *Donald Cameron 1968*
The author was a Scottish seaman who visited Caracas and Ciudad Bolivar.

Desolate Marches. Travels in the Orinoco Llanos of Venezuela
L.M. Nesbitt 1935
The Llanos, the plains of the Orinoco basin, are huge level grasslands with occasional forests; they were populated by Spanish–Indian half-castes, the Llaneros, who bred horses and cattle and who went over to Bolivar in 1817. When Spain recognized the independence of Venezuela in 1845, they no longer existed as a race, but a few remained and worked with the author who remembers them for their 'warm-hearted courtesy and hospitality'.

Caribbean

GENERAL

'The Caribbean has been described as Europe's other sea, the Mediterranean of the New World.' V.S. Naipaul *The Middle Passage* 1962

Art and Architecture

Historic Architecture of the Caribbean *David Buisseret 1980*
A well illustrated book in which the buildings are grouped in the text by function.

Fiction

A Wreath for Udomo *Peter Abrahams 1956*
The central character is a political leader who is driven by an impersonal vision of his country's status. *This Island, Now* is also set in the Caribbean.

Caribbee *Thomas Hoover 1986 (1985)*
By the middle of the seventeenth century, the largest colony in the New World was in the eastern islands of the Caribbean. This historical novel tells of the strange assortment of people who landed up there in this 'cockpit of violence, greed, drunkenness, piracy and voodoo'.

A Sea-Grape Tree *Rosamond Lehmann 1980 (1976)*
'Anonyma' arrives alone at a guest house in the Caribbean; across the bay beside a seagrape tree lies Johnny, handsome and crippled.

Caribbean *James A. Michener 1989*
Michener dedicates the book to Alec Waugh who once said to him 'Someday you must write about my Caribbean.' Written as a novel based on fact, it spans the history of many of the islands.

West Indian Stories *Andrew Salkey (ed.)*
1960
A collection of twenty-five short stories.

✔ **A Handful of Dust** *Evelyn Waugh*
1976 (1934)
Tony Last, who had 'no very ambitious ideas about travel' embarks on a ship bound for Demerara in search of a city.

Food

✔ **Caribbean Cooking**
Elisabeth Lambert Ortiz 1977 (1973)
Recipes collected from islands all over the Caribbean.

✔ **Caribbean Cooking** *Devinia Sookia*
1994
A large format book with tempting looking photographs of food from all parts of the Caribbean.

General Background

✔ **Caribbean Pirates** *Warren Alleyne*
1992 (1986)
A demythologization of the pirates of the Caribbean which shows what they were really like.

✔ **Caribbean Companion. The A to Z Reference. A Handbook to the People, Places, Plants, Animals, Culture and Major Historical Events of the West Indies** *Brian Dyde 1992*
A very useful companion, arranged alphabetically.

Black Skin, White Masks *Frantz Fanon*
1986 (1952)
Fanon was born in Martinique in 1925 and studied medicine in France, later specializing in psychiatry. He was sent to a hospital in Algeria during the war against the French

and joined the national liberation movement; he never saw Algeria liberated as he died from leukaemia in 1961. In this book Fanon uses psychoanalysis and psychological theory to explain the feelings of dependency and inadequacy that black people experience in a white world.

The West Indian Islands George Hunte
1972
The first section is a general background to the area, this is followed by sections on the various groups of islands.

✔ **Caribbean Travel Resource Guide**
Jeremy Poynting 1994

The Sugar Islands Alec Waugh 1958
A mixed collection of pieces about the West Indies which Waugh had written for magazines and books between 1928 and 1953. He did not update his material for this book, saying that 'the whole point of a travel book is that it should be dated'. Waugh had travelled much in the West Indies and his essays on the various islands are well worth reading.

Guides

The Pocket Guide to the West Indies
Sir Algernon Aspinall 1911 (1907)
An early guide which went into many editions and which is still useful today for its background and history.

✔ **Cadogan Guide to the Caribbean and the Bahamas** James Henderson 1994 (1990)

✔ **Romantic Island Getaways: the Caribbean, Bermuda and the Bahamas** Larry Fox and Barbara Radin-Fox
1991
A selection of romantic beaches, resorts, hotels, villas and restaurants.

✔ **Nelles Guide to The Caribbean** 1992

✔ **Caribbean Islands Handbook 1995**
Published by Trade and Travel

History

✔ **The Overthrow of Colonial Slavery 1776–1848** Robin Blackburn 1990 (1988)
The most recent and comprehensive analysis of the process that led to the end of slavery.

The English in the West Indies or the Bow of Ulysses James Anthony Froude 1888
The author visited the islands in order to find out about the condition of the British Col-

onies; he travelled extensively and wrote about what he heard and saw.

✔ **A Short History of the West Indies**
J.H. Parry, Philip Sherlock and Anthony Maingot
1991 (1956)
An authoritative introduction to West Indian history, beginning with the arrival of Columbus and continuing through to independence in most of the British Caribbean.

West Indian Summer. A Retrospect
James Pope-Hennessy 1943
A book about many of the travellers who had visited the West Indies including Raleigh, Trollope, Froude, Kingsley and Hans Sloane. The essays are meant to be historically accurate although they are held together by mainly fictional episodes.

The Golden Antilles Timothy Severin 1970
Britain early on fell under the spell of the myth of untold riches in the Caribbean. This book is the story of the travellers, adventurers and soldiers of fortune who searched for a promised land in the Caribbean.

A Family of Islands Alec Waugh 1964
A history of the West Indies from 1492 to 1898 with an epilogue oulining the events from the Spanish American War to the 1960s.

From Columbus to Castro. The History of the Caribbean 1492–1969
Eric Williams 1984 (1970)
A classic history of the region by Trinidad and Tobago's most famous prime minister who oversaw independence. He wrote it as a foundation for the economic integration of the region.

Leisure

✔ **A Walking Guide to the Caribbean. From the Virgin Islands to Martinique**
Leonard M. Adkins 1988
A combination of where to walk in the Caribbean and practical information about how to do it.

✔ **Adventure Travel in Latin America**
Scott Graham 1990 (see 'South America' and 'Central America')

✔ **Caribbean Divers' Guide** Peter Vine
1990 (1988)
An illustrated guide to the fishes and diving sites of the Caribbean.

✔ **Deck with a View. Vacation Sailing in the Caribbean** Dale Ward and Dustine Davidson 1992
This book gives advice on every kind of boat

and sailing: crewed charters, tall ships, flotilla charters, resorts with sails, shore and sail charters, bareboat charters, head boat charters, day charters, expedition sails and sailing schools.

Natural History

✔ **Birds of the West Indies** *James Bond 1979*
A comprehensive field guide to the birds of the Caribbean.

✔ **Fruits and Vegetables of the Caribbean** *M.J. Bourne, G.W. Lennox and S.A. Seddon 1988*
A guide to forty-eight of the most commonly found fruits and vegetables with a description of each species origin, its botanical characteristics and its uses.

✔ **Birds of the Eastern Caribbean**
Peter Evans 1990
Descriptions of 180 species of bird in the area from the Virgin Islands to Grenada in the Eastern Caribbean. Colour photographs.

✔ **Caribbean Wild Plants and their Uses** *Penelope N. Honychurch 1986*
About 100 plants which have medicinal or folkloric uses are described and illustrated. There is a glossary of botanical terms and indexes of French and patois names, English names and scientific names.

Sea Shells of the West Indies: A Guide to the Marine Molluscs of the Caribbean *Michael Humfrey 1975*
Around 497 shells are described and illustrated and the author describes where they can be found.

✔ **Flowers of the Caribbean**
G.W. Lennox and S.A. Seddon 1978
The book is divided into three sections: herbs and shrubs, trees and orchids. Each entry has a colour photograph and common, local and scientific names.

✔ **A Field Guide to the Butterflies of the West Indies** *Norman D. Riley 1975*
Descriptions of 293 species with their scientific and common names. There is also a general section on butterfly morphology and classification and collecting methodologies.

✔ **Trees of the Caribbean** *S.A. Seddon and G.W. Lennox 1980*
A basic guide to the trees of the area. The book is divided into four sections: ornamental trees, fruit trees, coast trees and palm trees.

✔ **Butterflies and other Insects of the Eastern Caribbean** *Peter D. Stiling 1986*
An illustrated handbook.

✔ **Fishes of the Caribbean Reefs**
Ian F. Took 1992 1979
Eighty-five species are covered with descriptions which include length, habitats, habits and common and scientific names.

Photography

✔ **Caribbean Camera. A Journey Through the Islands** *Oliver Benn Text by Lennox Honychurch 1992*
A photographic book which captures the moods of the different islands.

Caribbean Isles *Peter Wood and the editors of Time-Life Books 1975*
A cross-section of the many different kinds of landscape and scenery, both above and under, water, found in the Caribbean.

Travel Literature

Touch the Happy Isles: a Journey through the Caribbean *Quentin Crewe 1988 (1987)*
Quentin Crewe travels from Trinidad to Jamaica visiting many different islands. He recognizes that on most islands there are two completely separate strands of life. 'I had a fantasy that tourism is a vast nation with huge armies that march across continents, destroying just as effectively as conquering, armed hordes like the Mongols, Huns, Vandals, Visigoths or whatever. The Tourist Empire will grow to be the biggest ever known.'

✔ **Travels with Myself and Another**
Martha Gellhorn 1991 (1978) (see 'East Africa', 'China' and 'Israel')
Although Martha Gellhorn was living in the Caribbean during the war, she had no conception of what was happening, since most naval activity was highly classified information. Later she went and investigated.

✔ **Sequins for a Ragged Hem** *Amryl Johnson 1988*
Amryl Johnson had arrived in England aged eleven and in 1983 embarks on a six-month journey in the Caribbean. She is searching for lost memories at the same time as wanting to escape; she finally succeeds in uniting her two selves.

At Last. A Christmas in the West Indies *Charles Kingsley 1910 (1871)*
A journey through the Lesser Antilles and to Trinidad. Kingsley had wanted to visit the

West Indies all his life and during his childhood had spent time studying their natural history and charts. He travels in many islands and gives vivid descriptions of the flora and fauna that he sees.

✔ The Traveller's Tree. A Journey through the Caribbean Islands *Patrick Leigh Fermor 1984 (1950)*
It is impossible to generalize about the Caribbean, since each island is distinct and idiosyncratic. Short of writing a thesis in many volumes, Leigh Fermor decides to approach the topic in a haphazard manner. He and two companions made their Odyssey through the islands writing about Voodoo, superstitions, sorceries, songs, religions, politics and race. The book does not attempt to be a comprehensive guide to the islands; those which were formerly Spanish are left out because of their enormity, radically different history and social structure. However his personal and random account of the journey succesfully transmits the interest and enjoyment he experienced. [Jan Morris, Colin Thubron]

✔ Tap Taps to Trinidad. A Caribbean Journey *Zenga Longmore 1990 (1989)*
Zenga Longmore, a black woman living in Brixton, had long been intrigued by what she had heard about 'back home'. Her journey to the Caribbean includes Jamaica, the Dominican Republic, Haiti, Dominica, Guadeloupe, Martinique, St Lucia and Trinidad.

✔ Beyond the Dragon's Mouth *Shiva Naipaul 1985 (1984)*
A collection of pieces which includes *The Rise of the Rastaman* and *Grenada – a Postcript.*

✔ The Middle Passage. Impressions of Five Societies – British, French and Dutch – in the West Indies and South America *V.S. Naipaul 1988 (1962)*
Naipaul's impressions of British Guiana, Surinam, Martinique, Trinidad and Jamaica. He looks at the five different societies and how their British, French and Dutch colonialist past influenced them.

Around the Spanish Main: Travels Around the Caribbean and Guianas *Hugh O'Shaughnessy 1991*
The author who wrote for *The Observer* describes the history and politics of the Caribbean and his travels in Cuba, Grenada, the Leeward Islands and Guadeloupe.

✔ Travels With My Trombone. A Caribbean Journey *Henry Shukman 1993 (1992)*
Playing his trombone as he travels through the Caribbean enables Shukman to meet all kinds of different people. He joined a calypso band and was therefore able to meet musicians and get to know the islands through them and their music.

A Voyage to the Islands Madeira, Barbados, Nieves, St Christophers and Jamaica, with the Natural History of the . . . last of those islands *Sir Hans Sloane 1707–25*

Cruising Among the Caribbees: Summer Days in Winter Months *Charles Augustus Stoddard 1895*
Sympathetic descriptions of the islands.

The Cradle of the Deep *Sir Frederick Treves 1908*
Treves sailed round much of the Caribbean and describes the history and legends of the islands he visited.

The West Indies and the Spanish Main *Anthony Trollope 1985 (1859)*
In 1858 Trollope was asked to reorganise the ailing postal system in the West Indies. He visited many of the islands in the Caribbean: Jamaica, Cuba, the Windward Islands, Barbados, Trinidad, Bermuda and St Thomas as well as making extensive trips in Central America and British Guiana. This was his first travel book and it was immediately successful.

✔ Hot Countries *Alec Waugh 1989 (1930)*
A journey around the tropics including stays in Martinique and Haiti.

Where the Clocks Chime Twice *Alec Waugh 1952*
The first section of Waugh's book is about his travels around islands in the Caribbean that he had not been to before. The purpose of this journey was to 'go off the map'. Because people are often asleep or not listening when the clocks chime the first time, three minutes later they chime again. (Other sections are about the Lebanon, the Seychelles, Ceylon, Iraq, Egypt, Syria and France).

BERMUDA

'The infamous Iland of Bermuda, notorious with unmercifull and incredible stormes of fearefull thunder and lightning.' George, Earl of Cumberland, 1596, *Purchas his Pilgrimes* 1625

'The far Bermoothes' in Shakespeare's *The Tempest* refer to the then newly discovered Bermuda. He did not use Bermuda as the setting, but rather used facts about it to create his enchanted island.

'You go to heaven if you want –I'll just stay here', said Mark Twain about Bermuda.

'For the islands of the Barmudas, as every man knoweth that hath heard or read of them, were never inhabited by a Christian or heathen people but were ever esteemed and reputed a most prodigious and enchanteed place, affording nothing but gusts, storms and foul weather, which made every navigator and mariner to avoid them as Schylla and Charybdis or as they would shun the Devil himself.' *A Plaine Description of the Barmudas* 1612

Fiction/Poetry

Song of the Emigrants in Bermuda
Andrew Marvel
Marvel, who certainly never went to Bermuda, exaggerated its richness which had been much talked about after the famous shipwreck of 1609:
'Where the remote Bermudas ride
In ocean's bosom unespied.'

Verses written to the Marchioness of Donegall by Tom Moore in 1804:

'The moon was lovely, every wave was still,
When the first perfume of a cedar-hill
Sweetly awaked us, and with smiling charms
The fairy harbour woo'd us to its arms.'

✔ **The Tempest** *William Shakespeare*
The Tempest was used as a guide book to Bermuda by Christopher Morley who declared that 'none better had ever been written'. In 1898 Rudyard Kipling discovered the perfect setting for the beach referred to in Act II Scene 2; Shakespeare had probably heard from sailors (who were addicted to playgoing) the accounts of the shipwreck of Admiral Somers in 1609.

✔ **Indigo** *Marina Warner* 1993 (1992)
Indigo, which explores the intertwined histories of the Everard family, was inspired by *The Tempest*. 'The use of *The Tempest* in *Indigo* is a tribute to the play's contemporary power of focusing and symbolising the issues of exploitation, usurpation, racism and slavery – those issues which emerge so inescapably from the identification of Caliban with the Caribbean.' (*London Review of Books*)

General Background

Bermuda *John J. Jackson* 1988
A good straightforward background book in the David and Charles island series containing chapters on geography, history, geology, people, customs, government, politics and economy.

✔ **The Islands of Bermuda. Another World** *David F. Raine* 1990
Bermuda was formed from a volcanic eruption and was uninhabited until the seventeenth century; today it is Britain's oldest self-governing colony.

A Man Called Intrepid. The Secret War 1939–1945 *William Stevenson* 1977 (1976)
'Intrepid' was the code name of Sir William Stevenson who lived in Bermuda (but modestly, rather than like James Bond whose chief Stephenson was at one time supposed to be). However Bermuda was known as 'Bletchley-in-the-Tropics' and at one time had ·1200 British experts (unknown to the Americans) working underground intercepting postal, telegraph and radio traffic between the Western hemisphere and enemy-occupied Europe.

Guides

✔ **Fodor Guide Bermuda 1995**

✔ **Insight Guide Bermuda** *1991*

History

Isle of Devils. Bermuda under the Somers Island Company 1609–1685
Jean Kennedy 1971
Sir George Somers was the Admiral of the Fleet and commander of the *Sea Venture* the ship that was spectacularly shipwrecked off Bermuda in 1609. He ensured a supply of fresh fish for the survivors of the wreck and then proceeded to map the islands which were called Summers Isles for many years. The Somers Island Company was formed in 1612 with Sir Thomas Smith as Governor.

The Story of Bermuda *Hudson Strode* 1935
Chapters on history, Bermuda in the 1930's, architecture, gardens and, especially interesting, on the many writers who used Bermuda for 'loafing' and writing.

Bermuda – Today and Yesterday 1503–1980s *Terry Tucker* 1983 (1975)
A history and introduction of the known and not so known islands of the Caribbean.

Natural History

Nonsuch. Land of Water *William Beebe*
1932
The author was Director of the Department
of Tropical Research of the New York Zoological Society and wrote a series of books about
life in the water around Nonsuch, Bermuda.
Illustrated with black and white photographs.

Photography

✔ **A Scape to Bermuda**
Ian Macdonald-Smith 1991
A photographic journey, east to west,
through the islands of Bermuda.

LESSER ANTILLES
Grenada, St Vincent and Grenadines,
Barbados, St Lucia, Dominica, Antigua and
Barbuda, Monserrat, St Kitts and Nevis,
Anguilla, British Virgin Islands, US Virgin
Islands, French Antilles: Martinique,
Guadeloupe, St Martin, Dutch Antilles.
'The head-quarters of the world for fruit'
[Grenada]. Anthony Trollope *The West
Indies and the Spanish Main* 1859

Biography

**Smile Please: An Unfinished
Autobiography** *Jean Rhys* 1979
Jean Rhys died while she was working on
this book; the first half contains vignettes
and scenes from the author's childhood in
Dominica.

**To Shoot Hard Labour. The Life and
Times of Samuel Smith, an Antiguan
Workingman 1877–1982** *Keithlyn B. Smith
and Fernando C. Smith 1988 (1986)*
Samuel Smith's words are quoted on the back
of the book which is written by two of his
grandchildren: 'I want you to write down
exactly what I am telling you. If you do, the
people will see how far down in the mud we
came from. This generation will take care of
what is happening to them. I hope that the
day will never come again when our people
have to suffer indignity like my generation
and others have to. I am here to watch and
see until the lord take me home.'

Fiction/Poetry

✔ **The Orchid House** *Phyllis Shand Allfrey*
1991 (1953)
Three white Creole girls grow up on Dominica; eventually they leave their enclosed
and decaying world for Europe and America,
but feel the pull back to the island, which
they all return to. *Wide Sargasso Sea* by Jean
Rhys (q.v.) was influenced by *The Orchid
House*, the only novel by Allfrey who founded
the Dominica Labour Party in 1955.

Cahier d'un Retour au Pays Natal
Aimé Césaire 1983
Césaire was born in Martinique in 1913 and
since he is an important poet who does not
seem to have been translated into English, I
have included this collection in French.

✔ **Rotten Pomerack** *Merle Collins 1992*
This collection of poems, many with the
theme of a longing for 'home', has a Grenadian author.

The Spoils of Eden *Robert H. Fowler 1987
(1985)*
A seventeenth century novel set in Barbados;
certain liberties have been used when describing historical figures and their dialogue,
but it is accurate enough to give a very good
idea of what life was like.

Duet in Discord *Elizabeth Garner 1937*
Elizabeth Garner was the nom de plume of
Elma Napier. The narrator falls in love with
a visiting writer and embarks on a stormy
relationship which finally leads to the writer
withdrawing emotionally and leaving the island due to his impotence.

✔ **Annie John** *Jamaica Kincaid 1985 (1983)*
A girl grows up and becomes a woman on the
island of Antigua. We see the island's lush
vegetation and mysteries through her adolescent eyes, knowing that she must leave it
and her childhood behind her.

✔ **In the Castle of My Skin**
George Lamming 1992 (1953)
An autobiographical novel, considered a classic, about cultural differences in the Caribbean. It is about a poor village boy growing
up in colonial Barbados and is at the same
time playful, thoughtful and poignant. Other
books by Lamming include *The Emigrants*
(1980) and *The Pleasure of Exile* (1984).

✔ **The Violins of Saint-Jacques**
Patrick Leigh Fermor 1990 (1953)
Patrick Leigh Fermor's only novel has a lush
Caribbean island as its background. The
mysterious sound of violins rises from the
water and conceals drama and mystery.
(Martinique)

The Hurricane John Levo 1930
The struggle of growing coconut palms on Tortola in the early twentieth century is followed by their devastation in a hurricane. John Levo also wrote *Virgin Islanders* (1933).

✔ **A State of Independence**
Caryl Phillips 1989 (1986)
A British West Indian who has spent twenty years away from the Caribbean goes back just before Independence to see the end of colonial rule; however he has to come to terms with finding himself an outsider. Set in St Kitts.

The Taking of Agnès Jennifer Potter 1985
Agnès went to Martinique to visit her Aunt Alicia who lived on the edge of a plantation; she enchanted people with her seductive beauty, but was then kidnapped; many different people were implicated in her disappearance.

Sleep it Off Lady Jean Rhys 1979 (1976)
A collection of sixteen short stories, seven with the West Indies for background: *Pioneers, oh Pioneers*, *Goodbye Marcus*, *Goodbye Rose*, *The Bishop's Feast*, *Heat*, *Fishy Waters* and *The Insect World*.
The collection *Tigers Are Better Looking* (1973) also includes three short stories set in the West Indies.

✔ **Wide Sargasso Sea** Jean Rhys 1968 (1966)
The novel, set in Dominica and Jamaica, covers the lives of Edward Rochester and his mad wife before their introduction into Charlotte Brontë's Jane Eyre. It explores the alienation of white creole West Indians from the newly emerging post-emancipation West Indian societies.

Ruler in Hiroona. A West Indian Novel
G.C.H. Thomas 1989 (1972)
A very funny political novel in which Jerry Mole has a meteoric rise and becomes Chief Minister in Hiroona (based on St Vincent), followed by an equally meteoric fall.

✔ **Selected Poetry** Derek Walcott 1993 (1981)
The poet was born and brought up on St Lucia; this collection of verse spans nearly twenty years. Another collection by Derek Walcott is *The Star-apple Kingdom* (1980).

The Fatal Gift Alec Waugh 1973
Fact and fiction are blended together in this novel narrated in the first person by Raymond Peronne, the second son of an English peer.

Don't Stop the Carnival Herman Wouk 1967 (1965)
Set in St Thomas in the 1950s, a disillusioned New York publicity agent buys a hotel on a Caribbean island and gets involved with local life and characters. His efforts to finance his whim and to cope with the strange characters he encounters lead to many explosive situations, but whatever sadnesses occur, 'Carnival is Sweet'.

General Background

Lettres Créoles. Tracées Antillaises et Continentales de la Littérature 1635–1975 Patrick Chamoiseau and Raphaël Confiant 1991
The Martinique authors are passionate about preserving Créole; the book begins with a collection of photographs of paintings, maps and sculpture relevant to Haïti, Guadeloupe, Martinique and Guyane and continues with essays about the area and its literature. In French.

Dominica Basil E. Cracknell 1973
Chapters on scenery, natural history, the Carib people, war, communications, agriculture, tourism and society.

Le Discours Antillais Édouard Glissant 1981
Not translated into English, but an important book by an important writer.

Mount Joy Stephen Hawys 1968
The author moved to Dominica in 1929 after getting his fingers burnt on the London Stock Exchange. He lived on Mount Joy Estate and here gives a personal view of his friends, the estate, the island's flora and fauna and historical personages.

Our Island Culture Lennox Honychurch 1982
A general introduction and survey of the cultural aspects of Dominica: fishing, herbs, religious festivals, literature, music, art, theatre and dance.

Barbados George Hunte 1974
A straightforward practical introduction by a resident of Barbados, with chapters on Tobacco and Cotton, Sugar, Empire, Bridgetown, The Gold and Platinum West Coast, the North and the Scotland District, People, Language, Flora and Fauna, Food and Drink and Pirates, Treasures and Legends.

✔ **The Overcrowded Barracoon**
V.S. Naipaul 1984 (1972)
Pieces on St Kitts, Trinidad and Anguilla are included in this collection.

Guides

✔ **Cadogan Guide Caribbean: The Leeward Islands** *1994*

✔ **Cadogan Guide Caribbean: The Windward Islands** *1994*

✔ **Antigua and Barbuda. The Heart of the Caribbean** *Brian Dyde 1986*
A small illustrated guide.

✔ **Islands to the Windward. Five Gems of the Caribbean** *Brian Dyde 1987*
A small guide to Sint Maarten and Saint-Martin, Saint-Barthélemy, Anguilla, Saba and Sint Eustatius.

✔ **St Kitts. Cradle of the Caribbean**
Brian Dyde 1993 (1989)
A small illustrated guidebook.

✔ **Saint Lucia. Helen of the West Indies** *Guy Ellis 1993 (1986)*
A brief introduction and guide to St. Lucia.

✔ **Montserrat. Emerald Isle of the Caribbean** *Howard A. Fergus 1992 (1983)*
Montserrat, which is about eleven miles long and seven miles wide, lies between Antigua and Guadeloupe.

✔ **Fodor's Barbados** *1992*
An undated Fodor guide.

✔ **Fodor Guide The US and British Virgin Islands 1993**

✔ **Nevis. Queen of the Caribees**
Joyce Gordon 1991 (1985)
Nevis is only thirty-five square miles, but has a rich and varied history: Horatio Nelson met and married Fanny Nisbet in 1787; it was the birthplace of Alexander Hamilton, the first person to advocate the federation of the American states which was eventually adopted.

✔ **Barbados. The Visitor's Guide**
F.A. Hoyos 1988 (1982)
An introduction to the history, geography and cultural heritage of Barbados.

✔ **Insight Guide Barbados** *1991*

✔ **Discover ... St Kitts. Columbus' Favourite Island** *Frank Sharman and Amalia Stone 1987*
A very basic little guide.

✔ **The British Virgin Islands. Treasure Islands of the Caribbean**
Larry and Reba Shepard 1991 (1989)
A brief introduction and guide.

History

St Lucia: Historical, Statistical, and Descriptive *Henry H. Breen 1970 (1844)*
St Lucia was one of the least known of the British possessions, hardly noticed until Henry Breen, who lived there for thirteen years, decided to write about it.

The Dominica Story: a History of the Island *Lennox Honychurch 1984*
A survey of the history of Dominica from the time of settlement by the Amerindians to Associated Statehood in 1967 and the first years of independence from 1978 to 1983. The author is a native of the island.

Leisure

Sailors' Guide to the Windward Islands *Chris Doyle 1988*
Invaluable for anyone wanting a detailed guide to sailing in the Windward Islands: there are useful aerial photographs of the entrances into harbours and there is a practical listing section which includes accommodation and restaurants.

Natural History

Up Hill and Down Dale in Grenada
Raymund Devas 1926
Descriptions of the flora, fauna and scenery of Grenada which would be of much use today.

✔ **Reptiles and Amphibians of the Virgin Islands** *William P. Maclean 1982*
A short guide illustrated with photographs and line drawings.

Photography

Grenada: Isle of Spice *Norma Sinclair 1987*
All aspects of Grenadian life, including cooking, are described in this well illustrated book.

Travel Literature

Virgin Islands *George T. Eggleston 1959*
The author sailed round the Virgin Islands for a month on a fifty-foot ketch. He visited St Thomas, St John, Norman Island, Peter Island, Dead Man's Chest, Tortola, Beef Island, Guana Island, Marina Cay, Virgin Gorda, Anegada, Little Thatch, Jost Van Dyke and St Croix.

The Memoirs of Père Labat *John Eaden
1931*
An abridged version of the memoirs of Père Labat who spent ten years in the Caribbean until 1705, mostly in Martinique. His book is full of accounts of how he defended people with cannons, distilled sugar into rum and ate stupendous meals. He was interested in everything and very funny; strangely he is wrongly accused of introducing slavery into Martinique.

Antigua and the Antiguans
Mrs Lanaghan 1844
The author was the wife of a planter; she describes the island and the customs of the people.

Outposts: Journeys to the Surviving Relics of the British Empire
Simon Winchester 1985
Includes a visit to Montserrat.

The Weather Prophet *Lucretia Stewart
1995*
A personal account of a single woman's foray into the the wider reaches of the Antilles.

PUERTO RICO
'It is a kind of lost love-child, born to the Spanish Empire and fostered by the United States.' Nicholas Wollaston *Red Rumba*
1962

Art and Archaeology

**The Art Heritage of Puerto Rico:
pre-Columbian to present** *Published by
the Metropolitan Museum of Art 1974*
A bilingual exhibition catalogue showing 500 years of Puerto Rican art. Well illustrated with biographies of the artists represented.

Fiction/Poetry

If Beale Street Could Talk
James Baldwin 1974
A novel set between New York City and Puerto Rico.

Family Installments *Edward Rivera 1982*

Macho Camacho's Beat
Luiz Rafael Sanchez 1981
The title of the book is a song which plays constantly on the radio.

Cuentos: an anthology of short stories from Puerto Rico *Kal Wagenheim (ed.)
1978*
A collection of twelve short stories which have as a theme the conflict between Hispanic and American cultural values.

General Background

Puerto Rico *Robert A. Crampsey 1973*
A general introduction in the David & Charles Island series.

The Puerto Rican's Spirit
Theresa Maria Babin 1971
An introduction to the history, literature, people and fine arts of Puerto Rico.

Puerto Rico. An Introduction
Raoul Gordon 1982

La Vida *Oscar Lewis 1982 (1966)*
A study of Puerto Rican families and their relatives in New York.

Guides

✔ **Fodor's Pocket Puerto Rico** *1992*

✔ **Puerto Rico Insight Guide** *1992*

✔ **The Adventure Guide to Puerto Rico** *Harry S. Pariser 1989*

History

Puerto Rico: A Political and Cultural History *Arturo Morales Carrion (ed.) 1983*
At the end of the last century Robert T. Hill, an American geologist, wrote that Puerto Rico was less known to the United States 'than even Japan or Madagascar . . . The sum total of the scientific literature of the island since the days of Humboldt would hardly fill a page of this book'. Things have changed dramatically since then and this history, aimed at the general reader, has a large section on suggested further reading.

TRINIDAD AND TOBAGO

'A small country like ours only has principles.' Dr Eric Wiliams *Observer* 27 June 1965

Autobiography/Biography

✔ **Finding the Centre** *V.S. Naipaul* 1985 (1984)

The first piece in this book describes Naipaul's return to his native Trinidad where he goes in search of his roots as a writer and his literary beginnings. It took him time to find 'the centre' for the book, but began his narrative with the writing of his first story. The second part of the book is set on the Ivory Coast.

Fiction

Green Days by the River
Michael Anthony 1973 (1967)

The story of a boy growing up in Trinidad. Other novels by Anthony include *The Year in San Fernando* (1965) and *The Games Were Coming* (1963).

✔ **Crown Jewel** *Ralph de Boissiere* 1981

A powerful political novel about a charismatic black activist who attempts to unify blacks in Trinidad.

✔ **Robinson Crusoe** *Daniel Defoe* 1991 (1719)

The story of a ship-wrecked sailor who lives on an island (meant to be Tobago) for thirty years.

Minty Alley *C.L.R. James* 1971
The only novel by James, the Trinidadian Marxist.

✔ **The Jumbie Bird** *Ismith Khan* 1992 (1961)

An East Indian family is stranded in Trinidad having been betrayed by the authorities. The story of three generations seen through the eyes of Rahim deals with the issues of indenture and repatriation.

✔ **Caribbean Folk Legends**
Theresa Lewis 1989

The legends are all set in Trinidad and Tobago and are about the world of the supernatural.

✔ **The Dragon Can't Dance**
Earl Lovelace 1992 (1979)

Shanty-town life in Trinidad includes stories about Aldrick Prospect who lives for his once a year chance to play the dragon during Carnival, Miss Cleothilda, the aging Carnival queen and Philo the Calypsonian. The carnival and its ramifications permeate the whole book.

✔ **The Chip-Chip Gatherers**
Shiva Naipaul 1973

The story of two Trinidadian East Indian families: the Ramsarans and the Bholais.

✔ **Fireflies** *Shiva Naipaul* 1971

The fortunes of three generations of the Khojas, a Hindu family in Trinidad. His observations about the idiosyncrasies and ironies of family life are acute.

Guerrillas *V.S. Naipaul* 1990 (1975)

Set on a troubled Caribbean island where Asians, Africans, Americans and former British colonials coexist uneasily – a novel about colonialism and revolution.

✔ **House for Mr Biswas** *V.S. Naipaul* 1984 (1961)

Naipaul considers this book to be the one 'that is closest to me', since it is the most personal and he thinks contains some of his funniest writing. Mr Biswas was the son of a labourer who had died when he was a child; he scraped a living from sign-writing and was press-ganged into marrying Shama, a daughter of the Tulsi family. He became part of the furniture in the Tulsi household, but he longed for independence and the house of his own, which he eventually got, became a symbol of everything he had ever wanted.

✔ **In a Free State** *V.S. Naipaul* 1971

A collection of travel essays and short stories about people trapped in alien cultures.

✔ **The Suffrage of Elvira** *V.S. Naipaul* 1987 (1958)

The candidate in the district election in Trinidad has to have both the Hindu and Muslim votes as well as wooing people away from his rival candidate. As a result his expenses soar and his path to the Legislative Council is further complicated by two Jehovah's Witnesses. Other novels by Naipaul set in Trinidad include *The Mystic Masseur* and *Miguel Street* and a collection of short stories set in London and Trinidad *A Flag on the Island* (1967).

✔ **Ways of Sunlight** *Sam Selvon* 1987 (1957)

The first half of this collection of short stories contains vignettes of rural village life in Trinidad including gossip, labour and superstitions; the second half is set in London. Other books by Sam Selvon include the novels *A Brighter Sun* 1991 (1952), *Turn Again Tiger* (1979), *Those Who Eat the Cascadura* (1972), *The Plains of Caroni* (1970) and a collection of stories and articles *Foreday Morning* 1989.

General Background

✔ **Trinidad Sweet. The People, Their Culture, Their Island** *Adrian Curtis Bird* *1992*
A comprehensive portrait of Trinidadian life today from its cooking to its Carnival, its natural history to its scandals. Published in Trinidad.

Trinidad and Tobago. Isles of the Immortelles *Robin Bryans* *1967*
'Any intentions I had of being objective vanished the moment I arrived. The magic was too powerful. Bewitched from that moment on I succumbed, and this book attempts to reveal the secret of its spell . . . And if there is a way of breaking the spell they cast over me, I don't wish to know about it.' wrote Robin Bryans in his introduction to this part history, part travel, part general background book.

✔ **Beyond a Boundary** *C.L.R. James* *1990 (1963)*
A seminal book about the Caribbean which uses cricket as the theme to hold it together. James also includes much about his family.

✔ **The Middle Passage**
V.S. Naipaul (see 'Caribbean –General')

✔ **The Return of Eva Peron** *V.S. Naipaul* *1988 (1980)*
One of the essays in this collection is about Michael X and the Black Power killings in Trinidad.

Calypso and Society In Pre-Independence Trinidad
Gordon Rohlehr *1960*
The book describes the development of the Trinidad Calypso from pre-emancipation times to the late 1950s. It explores the issues of immigration, social conflict, race, humour, World War II and the development of the recording industry and the change in Calypso. Published in Trinidad.

Guides

✔ **Trinidad and Tobago. A Lascelles Caribbean Guide** *Mike East* *1992*

✔ **Insight Guide Trinidad and Tobago** *1992*

✔ **Trinidad and Tobago. An Introduction and Guide** *Jeremy Taylor* *1993 (1991)*
A new edition of a book that was originally published as *Masquerade*.

History

✔ **The Loss of El Dorado; a History**
V.S. Naipaul *1973*
Naipaul picks out two important incidents in Trinidad's history: Sir Walter Raleigh's search for 'El Dorado' and the trial of Thomas Picton, a Governor of Trinidad, for the torture of Luisa Calderon.

Natural History

The Birds of Trinidad and Tobago
G.A.C. Herklots *1961*
Illustrated with sixteen colour plates, four black and white plates and fourteen line drawings.

HAITI AND DOMINICAN REPUBLIC

'Smart life in Haiti – the dazzling white tropical suits, the dark heads and hands – resembles a photographic negative.' Patrick Leigh Fermor *The Traveller's Tree* 1951

Biography

Black Majesty; the Life of Christophe, King of Haiti *John W. Vandercook* *1928*
A fictionalized biography.

Fiction/Poetry

✔ **The Kingdom of this World** *Alejo Carpentier* *1990 (1957)*
A magical representation of the time under Christophe when life was horrific and cruel; through the eyes of the slave Ti Noël. The novel records the destruction of this black régime: 'A tour de force of voluptuous savagery and dark splendour' (*Punch*).

The Tragedy of King Christophe
Aimé Césaire 1969
A drama based on the life of Henri Christophe, Emperor of Haiti.

✔ **Cathedral of the August Heat**
Pierre Clitandre 1987 (1982)
In 1791 there was an uprising under Toussaint L'Ouverture which made Haiti the world's first independent black republic and the first society to abolish slavery after the French Revolution. This novel of contemporary Haiti draws much on historical events.

El Derrumbe (The Collapse)
Federico Garcia Goday 1975
The novel criticizes American imperialism and was declared illegal by the United States occupation authorities in 1916.

✔ **The Comedians** *Graham Greene 1980 (1966)*
Greene makes it clear at the beginning of the book that the narrator, Brown, although a Catholic, is not himself. However life in Haiti under the oppressive régime of Papa Doc Duvalier is not invented; in fact the Tontons Macoute are full of men more evil than Concasseur and Greene writes that things in Santo Domingo had changed 'for the worse' by the time the book was published.

Murder on the Way! *Theodore Roscoe 1935*
A mystery set in Haiti among Voodoo drums and zombies.

General Background

✔ **Bitter Sugar** *Maurice Lemoine 1985 (1981)*
A graphic account of a migrant labourer who enrols to cut cane in the Dominican Republic and finds he has been sold into virtual slavery. The names of the people and labour camp have been changed, but the story is horrifyingly true.

✔ **The Magic Island** *W.B. Seabrook 1989 (1929)*
The author managed to attend many ceremonies with Voodoo rites and black sorcery and writes in detail about the various functions at which he was present. He was guided into the Voodoo Holy of Holies across hideous ravines and gorges, over the mountains and beyond the clouds, by his 'yard-boy', Louis, from whom he began to learn about the invisible world of marvels, miracles and wonders.

Naboth's Vineyard *Sumner Wells 1972*
An excellent view of life in the Dominican Republic in the 1920s.

✔ **The Rainy Season. Haiti Since Duvalier** *Amy Wilentz 1994 (1989)*
Amy Wilentz arrived in Haiti in 1986 just before the ousting of 'Baby Doc' Duvalier. She reports in detail what she observed and heard while she was there.

Guide

✔ **Adventure Guide to The Dominican Republic** *Harry S. Pariser 1993*

History

Enriquillo *Manuel de J. Galvan 1981 (1944)*
The story of a Taino nobleman who took to the hills and waged a guerrilla war against the Spaniards in the 1520s, becoming a national hero.

✔ **The Black Jacobins. Toussaint L'Ouverture and the San Domingo Revolution** *C.L.R. James 1989 (1963)*
The definitive account of the Haitian Revolution of 1791–1803, which began in the wake of the Bastille and became the model for Third World liberation movements. Toussaint L'Ouverture, an almost illiterate slave, led the black people of San Domingo in a successful struggle against successive invasions.

From Dessalines to Duvalier
David Nicholls 1988 (1980)
A detailed history of Haiti since rebellion and Independence.

Religion

Voodoo Gods. An Inquiry into Native Myths and Magic in Jamaica and Haiti *Zora Hurston 1939 (1938)*
Voodoo is a religion of creation and life, the old, old mysticism of the world in African terms; the worship of the sun, the water and other natural forces. But because the symbolism is not properly understood it is often taken too literally. Zora Thurston writes clearly about the cult and its misconceptions. This book was also called *Tell Me Horse*.

Travel Literature

✔ **Best Nightmare on Earth. A Life in Haiti** *Herbert Gold 1991*
Herbert Gold first travelled to Haiti forty

years ago and it still remains his second home. He finds Haiti a land of 'unlimited possibility', full of paradox and extremes and writes about the history, politics, culture and folklore.

Island Possessed Katherine Dunham 1969
The author was a black American dancer and anthropologist and an initiate in the Voodoo cult.

Voodoo Fire in Haiti Richard A. Loederer 1935
The Viennese artist Loederer spent several months in Haiti; the book was criticized for being inaccurate when it was published.

✔ **Bonjour Blanc. A Journey Through Haiti** Ian Thomson 1992
'This adventurous book by Ian Thomson is outstandingly the best account in recent years of life in the weirdest of all tropical islands' (Norman Lewis). Thomson's book is part history and part travelogue; he was greeted by the words 'Bonjour blanc' wherever he went through the island during his gruelling but amusing journey.

JAMAICA

'We had, close over our port bow, the most beautiful island in the world.' H.M. Tomlinson *The Sea and the Jungle* 1912

Autobiography/Biography

Catch a Fire, The Life of Bob Marley
Timothy White 1989 (1983)
A biography of the singer's life: how he rose from poverty to become an international star.

Fiction/Poetry

✔ **The View from Coyaba**
Peter Abrahams 1985
The book spans 150 years of history. It is set in the rugged Red Hills area behind Kingston, Jamaica, and the main family is descended from runaway slaves whose ancestors had been brought from the Guinea coast of Africa.

✔ **Gwendolen** Buchi Emecheta 1990 (1989)
Gwendolen grows up in the harsh environment of rural Jamaica, before arriving in England where she feels alienated.

Doctor No Ian Fleming 1958
Set partly in Jamaica.

The Fair Green Weed
Elisabeth Hargreaves 1972
A well-observed thriller about the ganja racket.

The Faces of Love John Hearne 1957
Set on the imaginary island of Cayuna (which is Jamaica thinly disguised), with good descriptions of the countryside as well as social interest. Other novels by John Hearne include *Land of the Living* (1961) and *Voices Under the Window* (1973).

✔ **A High Wind in Jamaica**
Richard Hughes 1994 (1929)
Childhood fantasy gets caught up with pirates and a tropical landscape, which the children have to leave to cross the ocean.

✔ **Two Roads to Mount Joyful and other stories** Earl McKenzie 1992
A collection of short stories set in rural Jamaica.

The Hills Were Joyful Together
Roger Mais (1953)
Full of social realism based on slum-life in pre-independenc Jamaica. Other novels by Roger Mais include *Brother Man* (1954) and *Black Lightning* (1955).

✔ **The Children of Sisyphus**
Orlando Patterson 1965
A prostitute attempts to rise in Jamaican society.

✔ **Wide Sargasso Sea** Jean Rhys 1968 (1966) (see 'Dominica')

Food

✔ **Traditional Jamaican Cookery**
Norma Benghiat 1985
The recipes are placed in their social and historical context and include bammy, jerked pork, escovetch fish, stew peas and curry goat. Many of the recipes had never been written down before.

General Background

Ian Fleming Introduces Jamaica
Morris Cargill (ed.) 1965
Written by a team of writers, including Ian Fleming who spent part of the year in Jamaica from 1946 to 1964. There are chapters on the country, its people, politics, religion, archives, historic houses, natural history, literature, art, recreation and cooking.

Guides

✔ **Jamaica and the Greater Antilles. A Crowood Travel Guide** *Elizabeth Booth 1991*
Includes the Cayman Islands, the Dominican Republic, Haiti and Puerto Rico.

✔ **Fodor's Pocket Jamaica** *1992*

✔ **Frommer's Jamaica and Barbados '93–'94**

✔ **Insight Guide Jamaica** *1992*

✔ **Jamaica Handbook. A Moon Publication** *Karl Luntta 1992 (1991)*

✔ **Jamaica. A Visitor's Guide**
Harry S. Pariser 1993

History

History of Jamaica *Clinton V. Black 1983 (1958)*
A thousand years of Jamaican history from the arrival of the Arawaks to the present day, covering the arrival of the Spaniards, the extermination of the Amerindians, the coming of the British and the fight for independence. Clearly written and laid out.

Natural History

✔ **Birds of Jamaica. A Photographic Field Guide** *Audrey Downer and Robert Sutton 1990*
A pocket record of all the species and sub-species of birds endemic in Jamaica. Notes for identification as well as information on voice, habits, habitats and range.

Religion

Voodoo Gods. An Inquiry into Native Myths and Magic in Jamaica and Haiti *Zora Hurston 1939 (1938) (see 'Haiti')*

The Ras Tafari Movement
Anita M. Waters 1985
Rastafarian thought in an historical and religious context.

Travel Literature

A Descriptive Account of the Island of Jamaica: with remarks upon the cultivation of sugar-cane, throughout the different seasons of the year, and chiefly considered in a picturesque point of view; also observations and reflections upon what would probably be the consequences of an abolition of the slave-trade, and of the emancipation of the slaves
William Beckford 1790
Beckford lived in Jamaica for thirteen years; he describes the natural beauties and writes sympathetically about the condition of slaves.

Journal of a Residence in Jamaica 1801–1803 *Lady Nugent*
One of the earliest books about Jamaica.

CUBA
'A thousand tongues would not suffice to describe the things of novelty and beauty I saw, for it was all like a scene of enchantment.' Christopher Columbus writing from Baracoa, on his first voyage to Cuba in 1492

Fiction/Poetry

✔ **The Harp and the Shadow**
Alejo Carpentier 1992 (1979)
Carpentier was born in Havana and inspired many writers of Latin American literature; this novel is an imaginative exploration of Christopher Columbus – his myth, morality and historical legacy.

✔ **Dreaming in Cuban** *Cristina Garcia 1992*
Four strong women of the del Pino family, two in Cuba and two in New York, are at the centre of this visionary novel.

✔ **Our Man in Havana** *Graham Greene 1971 (1958)*
Wormwold, a vacuum-cleaner salesman who is short of money, becomes an agent for MI6 in Havana.

✔ **Islands in the Stream**
Ernest Hemingway (see 'Bahamas')

✔ **The Old Man and the Sea**
Ernest Hemingway 1976 (1952)
Lavishly praised when it came out, Hemingway won the Nobel Prize for this long short story about an old man who fished alone in a skiff in the Gulf Stream. 'Not only the finest long short story that Hemingway has ever

written, but one of the finest written by any-one anywhere.' (*The Listener*)

✔ **To Have and Have Not**
Ernest Hemingway 1972 (1937)
An exciting novel about Harry Morgan (a typical hard-living Hemingway hero) who ran rum and revolutionaries from Cuba to the Florida Keys.

✔ **View of Dawn in The Tropics**
G. Cabrera Infante 1990 (1974)
A lyrical and fictional history of Cuba up to the early seventies. 'A collection of images, moments, anecdotes, and chilling moral tales that together form a history of Cuban strug-gle' (*The Times*). Other novels by Infante set in Havana include *Infante's Inferno* and *Three Trapped Tigers*.

Cuban Passage *Norman Lewis 1982*
A man leaves his teenage son alone with his mother and her Cuban lover when he goes off on business trips. The boy rebels, turns to violence and gets swept along by corruption and confusion; parallel to his rebellion is Castro's insurrection which also gathers force and speed.

✔ **Los Gusanos** *John Sayles 1991*
'Los Gusanos' (Castro's 'worms'), people of all ages, professions and colours, live in Miami but dream of Cuba . . . 'Savvy and savage . . . a broad and impressive portrait of the last 50 years of Cuban life.' (*Washington Post*)

✔ **Far Tortuga** *Peter Matthiessen 1975*
Men look for the last turtles of the season on a remote islet, south of Cuba.

Cup of Gold *John Steinbeck 1980 (1929)*
A fictionalized life of Sir Henry Morgan.

✔ **Cuban Bluff** *Nigel West 1991 (1990)*
A thriller about what happened behind the scenes in 1962 when the world trembled on the brink of nuclear war.

Food

✔ **A Taste of Cuba** *Linette Creen 1991*
Over 190 recipes for appetizers, soups, sa-lads, breads, entrées, vegetables, desserts and drinks.

General Background

✔ **A View of the World** *Norman Lewis 1987 (1986)*
Several essays in this collection of journalism are about Cuba.

✔ **Cuba: the Test of Time** *Jean Stubbs 1989*
The author has lived in Cuba for twenty years and describes the mixture of achieve-ment and obstacle which exists in Cuba today and how this affects the ordinary Cuban.

Guides

✔ **Cuba. Travellers Survival Kit**
Simon Calder and Emily Hatchwell 1993

✔ **Cuba Official Guide**
A. Gerald Gravette 1988
Since this is approved by INTUR (the Cuban Tourist Board), it is inevitably very biased.

History

Cuba Libre – Breaking the Chains?
Peter Marshall 1987
A readable and wide-ranging history of the Cuban Revolution.

✔ **Cuba. Between Reform and Revolution** *Louis A. Pérez 1988*
A history from pre-Columbian times to the present which examines Cuba's political and economic development within the context of international relations.

The Pageant of Cuba *Hudson Strode 1935*
A readable history of Cuba from Christopher Columbus until 1934. Strode writes that, in Cuba, even when you are relaxed, you are vibrantly alive; his method of making the history come alive is to place much emphasis on the people.

Photography

✔ **Havana. Portrait of a City**
Juliet Barclay 1993
A collection of colour and black and white photographs and paintings which show all aspects of Havana.

✔ **Havana – 1933** *Walker Evans 1989*
A collection of photographs of Cuba's past.

✔ **Old Havana, Cuba** *Nicholas Sapieha 1990*
Concentrates on photographs of the architec-ture of old Havana but has ample text.

Travel Literature

✔ **Driving Through Cuba** *Carlo Gébler 1991 (1988)*
Well-observed experiences of a trip through

Cuba in 1987 in a Russian Lada. At a time when it was relatively unusual to visit Cuba, Gébler goes off the beaten track and records the conversations of the people he meets.

✔ **Cuba. A Journey** *Jacobo Timerman 1994 (1990)*
A serious look at Cuba which Timerman visited in 1987: 'A devastating portrait of a ruined country.' (*Wall Street Journal*)

BAHAMAS

Fiction

Bahama Crisis *Desmond Bagley 1982 (1980)*
A rich white Bahamian hotel owner, Tom Mangan, who entices people to his hotels, stumbles on murder, kidnapping and arson in his attempt to save the Bahamian tourist industry from criminals.

✔ **Thunderball** *Ian Fleming 1961*
James Bond deals with SPECTRE in this thriller set in the Bahamas.

✔ **Islands in the Stream**
Ernest Hemingway 1970
Hemingway's semi-autobiographical last novel, set in the 1930s, is divided into three parts – the first is about the life of an artist in Bimini, an island in the Gulf Stream; there is a wonderful description of a deep sea fishing episode. The second part is set in Cuba and the third part is about the war at sea. 'This book contains some of the best of Hemingway's descriptions of nature: the waves breaking white and green on the reef off the coast of Cuba; the beauty of the morning on the deep water . . . a big barracuda stalking mullet . . . the mosquitoes in clouds from the marshes.' (Edmund Wilson, *New Yorker*)

An Affair of Honour *Robert Wilder 1969*
The parallel lives of a white Bahamian, Max Hertog, and a black Bahamian, Royal Keating. Another novel by Wilder is *Wind from the Carolinas* (1964), a saga set over generations of the Cameron family.

General Background

✔ **Grand Bahama** *Peter Barratt 1990 (1982)*
Peter Barratt, as a town planner, was in charge of developing Freeport and writes with first hand knowledge about the extraordinary experiment which changed Grand Ba-

hama from a barren island to the second most populated island in the Bahamas.

The Bahamas *George Hunte 1975*
A good general background, history and description.

Who Killed Sir Harry Oakes
James Leasor 1989 (1983)
Sir Harry Oakes, a self-made millionaire, was brutally murdered at his home in Nassau in July 1943. On the surface he had no enemies; many questions needed to be asked, for example why did the Duke of Windsor insist on taking over the investigation and prevent the news of Oakes' death leaving the Bahamas? Leasor assembles all the facts of this unsolved crime.

Guides

✔ **Bahamas. A Traveller's Guide**
Mike East and Adrian Jones. (A Lascelles Caribbean Guide) 1991

✔ **Fodor Guide Bahamas 1995**

✔ **Fodor Pocket Guide Bahamas** *1991*

✔ **Insight Guide Bahamas** *1992*

✔ **Greater Antilles: Bermuda, Bahamas. A Nelles Guide** *1991*

✔ **The Bahamas. A Family of Islands**
Gail Saunders 1990 (1980)
A brief guide to most of the well known places among the 700 islands of the Bahamas.

History

✔ **Paradise Island Story** *Paul Albury 1987 (1984)*
Paradise Island is now linked by bridge to Nassau and plays an important role in the tourist industry of the Bahamas.

The Story of the Bahamas *Paul Albury 1975*
An easy-to-read description of people and events in Bahamian history.

✔ **The Lucayans** *Sandra Riley 1991*
Within fifteen years of Columbus landing in the Bahamas, the entire population of the Lucayan Indians had been eliminated by the Spaniards.

Leisure

✔ **Diving and Snorkeling Guide to the Bahamas: Family Islands and Grand Bahama** *Bob and Charlotte Keller 1988*
Detailed descriptions of the best dive sites in the Bahamas.

Natural History

✔ **The Birds of New Providence and the Bahama Islands** *P.G.C. Brudenell-Bruce 1988 (1975)*
An illustrated guide to the ninety-three species of Bahamian birds.

The Ephemeral Islands: a Natural History of the Bahamas
David G. Campbell 1986 (1978)
Descriptions of the geological, climatic, biological and social conditions which made the Bahamas the way they are today. Also about birds, coral, fishes, flora, reptiles and spiders.

The Bahama Islands *George Burbank Shattuck 1905*
An expedition was sent out by the Geographical Society of Baltimore in 1903. Although out of date, Shattuck's account remains the most comprehensive natural history written. The expedition visited: Abaco, New Providence, Andros, Green Cay, Eleuthera, Cat Island, Long Island, Rum Cay and Watlings Island.

Travel Literature

Islands in the Sun *Rosita Forbes 1949*
Rosita Forbes visited Nassau and Eleuthera during her travels.

A Unicorn in the Bahamas *Rosita Forbes 1940*
An account of the Bahamas in the 1930s. In Eleuthera a little girl gives the author a sea horse with a horn and since a 'unicorn' is a metaphor for her dreams, she decides to build a house on Eleuthera.

A Winter in Paradise *Alan Parsons 1926*
Parsons spent much time in Nassau when other visitors tended only to go there during 'the season', from December to March. Parsons writes about 'the season' but also gives a broader view.

TURKS AND CAICOS ISLANDS

Fiction/Poetry

The Island *Peter Benchley 1979*
An American writer and his son are kidnapped while researching a story about the disappearance of hundreds of boats. Their captors take them to a remote island in the Turks and Caicos.

Dildo Cay *Nelson Taylor Hayes 1940*
Adrian Ainsworth takes over the family's salt business on his father's death; he is torn between continuing to run the business and his love for a beautiful woman.

Guide

✔ **The Turks and Caicos Islands. Lands of Discovery** *Amelia Smithers 1991 (1990)*
A brief introduction and guide.

Travel Literature

✔ **Outposts** *Simon Winchester 1985*
Winchester writes about all the remaining outposts of the British Empire and describes the islands' history and present conditions.

ASIA

Middle East

GENERAL

Art, Architecture and Archaeology

✔ **Islamic Ceramics** James Allan 1991
A clear, straightforward, well-illustrated introduction to Islamic ceramics.

✔ **Islamic Art** Barbara Brend 1991
This easy-to-read book really takes over from where the Ettinghausen/Grabar book finishes, as it gives the history of Islamic art from the seventh to nineteenth centuries.

✔ **Persian Painting** Sheila Canby 1993
A good, well-illustrated introduction to Persian painting from 1300 to 1900.

Gods, Graves and Scholars
C.W. Ceram 1984 (1949) (see 'Egypt')

✔ **The Art and Architecture of Islam**
650–1250 Richard Ettinghausen and
Oleg Grabar 1991 (1987)
History, culture and arts of the period are shown in relationship to each other throughout the Islamic world: the Arab countries, Turkey, Iran and Central Asia. The book has over 400 illustrations and maps and line drawings.

Middle Eastern Mythology S.H. Hooke
1991 (1963)
Professor Hooke explains how mythology plays a role in ritual and customs throughout the Middle East; he demonstrates this with myths from the Assyrians to the Hebrews and shows how they throw new light on the Hebrew scriptures and the Gospels.

✔ **Kilims: the art of tapestry weaving in Anatolia, the Caucasus and Persia**
Yanni Petsopoulos 1979
A beautifully illustrated and comprehensive book which deals separately with the history of kilim weaving in each of the localities.

✔ **Islamic Art** David Talbot Rice 1993
(1965)
A concise, well illustrated chronological survey of Islamic art with ample descriptions of objects and buildings.

✔ **Islamic Metalwork** Rachel Ward 1993
A good general, well-illustrated introduction to the many forms of Islamic metalwork.

Biography

✔ **The Wilder Shores of Love**
Lesley Blanch 1993 (1954)
Biographies of four women: Isabel Burton, Jane Digby, Aimee Dubucq de Rivery and Isabelle Eberhardt: 'Four variations on the theme of the nineteenth century woman who turns to the East for her adventurous life and love . . . an odd quartet, well selected, and fully deserving Miss Blanch's lively and expressive portraiture.' (*The Times*)

A Pilgrimage of Passion. The Life of Wilfred Scawen Blunt 1982 (1979)
Blunt who lived between 1840 and 1922 was the embodiment of a past era; he combined being a poet, diarist, politician and explorer with a strong romantic streak which made him very attractive to women. He was full of energy and travelled, with his wife Lady Anne Blunt (q.v.), to remote and unmapped parts of Central Arabia.

✔ **The Jewish People. Their History and Their Religion** David Goldberg and
John Rayner 1989 (1987)
The book is divided into two parts: the first is a survey of Jewish history and literature, and the second is an analysis of the teachings and practices of Judaism.

Glubb Pasha. A Biography James Lunt
1984
Lunt traces the life and fascinating career of Sir John Bagot Glubb – a Special Services Officer in Iraq, Officer Commanding the Desert Areas in Transjordan and commander of the Arab Legion, which he transformed into a modern army before he was dismissed by King Hussein of Jordan in 1956.

✔ **The Arabs** Peter Mansfield 1992 (1976)
An introduction to the modern Arab world from both political and historical aspects; the second half of the book looks at each Arab state separately.

Philby of Arabia Elizabeth Monroe 1980
(1973)
Elizabeth Monroe embarked on her biography of Philby anticipating that she would get enormous pleasure from the 'hunt'. She found her task both geographically and intellectually rewarding as he had left mountains of papers. But since he found difficulty in seeing a point of view which was not his own, most of the papers were entirely subjective. Ironically for him, he was thought to be over-

whelmingly English by the Arabs and considered out of touch with England by the English. 'My ambition is fame, whatever that may mean and for what it is worth. I have fought for it hard . . . If my ambition had been to make money, it would have been easier to understand.'

✔ **Mohammed**   *Maxime Rodinson   1991 (1971)*
As well as being a fascinating biography of Mohammed, this book shows the tremendous impact that the ideology which grew around him, had on a society which was evolving from a nomadic to a settled economy.

✔ **Desert Traveller: the Life of Jean Louis Burckhardt**   *Katherine Sim   1969*
A biography of the Swiss traveller who spent so much time in Arabia. He learnt Arabic in Aleppo in preparation for travelling, in disguise, to Mecca.

✔ **Traveller's Prelude 1893–1927**

✔ **Beyond Euphrates 1928–1933**

✔ **The Coast of Incense 1933–1939**

✔ **Dust in the Lions Paw 1939–1946**
Freya Stark
The four volumes of Freya Stark's autobiography span a fascinating and changing time in the Middle East. The text is interspersed with letters and extracts from her diaries. *Traveller's Prelude* begins with her childhood which was spent between France, Italy and England; she began to learn Arabic in 1921. *Beyond Euphrates* is mainly about her life in Baghdad, Damascus and Persia; *The Coast of Incense* includes her first journey to Southern Arabia and travels in Iraq and Syria; *Dust in the Lion's Paw* begins in Syria and continues with Aden, the Yemen and includes the siege of the embassy in Baghdad.

✔ **The Life of My Choice**
Wilfred Thesiger   1992 (1987)
Thesiger's autobiography explains his yen for travel and who it was that influenced him: 'He is, unquestionably, one of the greatest travellers the British have ever produced, the last of our recognizable primitives. He also writes with much distinction and honesty.' (Geoffrey Moorhouse *The Daily Telegraph*)

✔ **Lawrence of Arabia. The authorised biography.**   *Jeremy Wilson 1990 (1989)*
Extremely detailed account of Lawrence's life (although there is an abridged version). Jeremy Wilson, the acknowledged expert on Lawrence, spent ten years researching this book and uncovered much new material. He

gets to grips with the odd, eccentric, obsessive and intensely private Lawrence, ironically now a household name.

Fiction

Opening the Gates: a Century of Arab Feminist Writing   *Margot Badran and Miriam Cooke (eds.)   1990*
An anthology in three sections: 'Awareness', 'Rejection' and 'Activism'; it includes both fact and fiction and has a long explanatory introduction.

✔ **Coming up Roses**   *Michael Carson 1991 (1990)*
King Fadl wants to acquire an imaginary Arab kingdom, Zibda; GCHQ is listening to his conversation and sends Charlie Hammond to gather information.

✔ **The Arabian Nights**   *Translated by Husain Haddawy   1992 (1907)*
The Everyman edition of the translation by Haddawy of the Mahdi edition of the Arabian Nights, the definitive Arabic edition which is in the Bibliothèque Nationale in Paris. The stories told by the Princess Scheherazade and collected from Arabia, Persia and India were first published in the West in 1700.

Arabic Short Stories   *Translated by Denys Johnson-Davies   1983*
A collection of twenty-four stories from Saudi Arabia, the Yemen, Iraq, the Lebanon, Syria and other countries of the Arab world.

Journey to the Orient   *Gérard de Nerval 1973 (1851) (see 'Egypt')*

ʿAntar and ʿAbla. A Bedouin Romance
Diana Richmond (ed.)   1978
A short selection from the original work which was transcribed into thirty-two volumes by a courtier of Haroun ar Rashid. The stories were from the 'time of ignorance' (before the birth of the prophet); this collection concentrates on ʿAntar's love for ʿAbla and his success in gaining his rightful place in the tribe, something which was of extreme importance to the Bedouin.

Food

✔ **Traditional Arabic Cooking**
Miriam Al Hashimi   1993

✔ **A New Book of Middle Eastern Food**   *Claudia Roden   1986 (1965)*
A classic book on Middle Eastern food which revolutionized the West's attitude. Paul Levy wrote in the Literary Review: 'This is one of those rare cookery books that is a work of

cultural anthropology and Mrs Roden's standards of scholarship are so high as to ensure that it has permanent value.'

General Background

✔ **A Rock and a Hard Place**
Gerald Butt 1994
A hard and thought-provoking look at the origins of Arab–Western conflict in the Middle East.

✔ **New Jerusalems** Daniel Easterman
1992
A collection of essays, articles and lectures about Islamic fundamentalism, the Iranian revolution, the Rushdie affair and other topics pertaining to the Islamic world which show how pervasive is the Western myth of the Orient and the Islamic myth of the decadent west.

✔ **From Beirut to Jerusalem**
Thomas Friedman 1990 (1989)
The author delved deep into the complex history of the recent conflicts in the Middle East and has produced an analysis and understanding of the situation which is well worth reading.

✔ **The Modern Middle East**
Albert Hourani, Philip S. Khoury and Mary C. Wilson (eds.) 1993
Key writings of the modern history of the Middle East from 1789 up until the present day. There is an introductory essay by Hourani followed by twenty-seven articles arranged in four sections: Reforming elites and changing relations with Europe 1789–1918; Transformations in society and economy 1789–1918; The construction of nationalist ideologies and politics up to the 1950s; The Middle East since the Second World War.

Guides

✔ **Middle East on a Shoestring**
Tom Brosnahan etc 1994

✔ **The Times Guide to the Middle East. The Arab World and its Neighbours** Peter Sluglett and Marion Farouk-Sluglett (eds.) 1991
This is a political guide to the region; inevitably the politics change so quickly that it is impossible to have an up-to-date book, but this guide attempts to put what happens and has happened into an accessible historical framework.

Traveller's Guide to The Middle East
Pat Lancaster (ed.) 1988
A good general overview of the region; with such a general guide there is not much detail about any one country, but since many of those mentioned do not have specific guides written about them, this one often proves to be essential.

History

The Arab Awakening George Antonius
1938
The classic study of the Arab national movement with its origins, development and problems taken from European and American sources as well as from first hand Arab evidence.

The Arabs Edward Atiyah 1955
An analysis of the Arabs as a people, their World and how it came into being and what is happening to it and what are its future prospects. Useful for understanding the politics and events in the Middle East today.

✔ **A Peace to End all Peace. Creating the Modern Middle East 1914–1922**
David Fromkin 1991 (1989)
A history of what happened from the time of the Allies' destruction of the Ottoman Empire in 1914, up until the emergence of eight separate states in 1922.

✔ **Arab Historians of the Crusades**
Francesco Gabrieli 1984 (1957)
Extracts from seventeen Arab authors who wrote about the crusades.

Britain and the Arabs John Bagot Glubb
1959
A study of the fifty years between 1908 and 1958.

A Soldier with the Arabs
John Bagot Glubb 1957
'The self-portrait of an honest man, as true as steel, marvellously unembittered, and sustained through all these anxieties and disappointments by an unyielding spiritual faith.' (James Morris *Manchester Guardian*)

The Story of the Arab Legion John Bagot Glubb 1948
'Glubb Pasha tells his exhilarating story of adventure and achievement – a story made more vivid by a real gift for the portrayal of the desert scene, by excellent illustrations and by many revealing little anecdotes and excursions into history. I find it entrancing.' (General Sir John Burnett-Stewart *Sunday Times*)

✔ **The Hittites**   *O.R. Gurney   1990 (1952)*
The Hittites, often mentioned in the Old Tes-
tament, were an advanced civilization; politically well organized and with their literature
inscribed on clay tablets in cuneiform writing. Their stone monuments were figurative
and powerful and can still be seen on rock
faces.

Inside the Middle East   *Dilip Hiro   1982*
In the late 1970s Hiro spent much time
travelling in the Middle East, a term he
defines as the Arab East which includes the
countries of Lebanon, Jordan, Syria, Iraq,
Saudi Arabia, the Yemen, Oman, the UAE,
Qatar, Bahrain, Kuwait and Egypt (and geographically Israel). Born in Pakistan, he felt
at home in an Islamic environment and was
able to get under the skin of the countries he
visited.

✔ **History of the Arabs**   *Philip K. Hitti*
1970
A very readable book.

✔ **A History of the Arab Peoples**
Albert Hourani   1992 (1991)
A large and readable, yet scholarly, book
which sums up the whole history of the Arab
peoples from the seventh century and the rise
of Islam until the present day.

The Bedouin   *Shirley Kay   1978*
A comprehensive well illustrated overview of
the bedouin, their roles, and the changes that
wealth and education have brought to them.
She questions whether they will be able to
survive in contemporary society.

✔ **Politics in the Middle East**
Elie Kedourie   1992
An historical analysis which attempts to explain why ideological politics, such as nationalism and fundamentalism, have triumphed
in the Middle East and why constitutional
governments have not worked in Islamic
countries.

✔ **The Muqaddimah. An Introduction
to History**   *Ibn Khaldun   1987 (see 'Morocco')*

✔ **The Essential T.E. Lawrence. A
Selection of his Finest Writings**
David Garnett (ed.)   1992 (1951)
Extracts both by and about Lawrence which
include many of his letters.

✔ **The Letters of T.E. Lawrence**
*Selected and edited by Malcolm Brown   1991
(1988)*
A collection of letters written by Lawrence
between 1905 and 1935 which give interesting insights into Lawrence the man, as well
as the political and historical situation of the
time.

✔ **Seven Pillars of Wisdom**
T.E. Lawrence   1962 (1935)
Seven Pillars of Wisdom has been criticised
for its historical inaccuracy as it is a very
personal account of the Arab Revolt, but
Lawrence's lively prose ensures that this
book will remain a classic; it is essential
reading for anyone interested in the Middle
East. It's a great, great book – a heady mixture of war, politics and history.' (Peter Hopkirk)

✔ **A History of the Middle East**
Peter Mansfield   1992 (1991)
Peter Mansfield's book is the history of the
turbulent last 200 years in the Middle East.
It starts with Napoleon in Egypt and follows
the collapse of the Ottoman Empire which
brought with it the emergence of new nations.
He explains how the discovery of oil affected
the whole region and ends with what he
considers the propects for the twenty-first
century. *The Arabs* (q.v.), an earlier book by
Mansfield, is an introduction to the politics,
economy and history of the modern Arab
world.

✔ **The Cambridge Encyclopedia of
the Middle East and North Africa**
Trevor Mostyn and Albert Hourani (eds.)   1988
An invaluable reference work to the culture,
history and geography of the Middle East;
the background economy, peoples, history,
culture and religion of each country are described as well as contemporary history and
politics.

The Background of Islam
H. StJ. B. Philby   1947
A sketch of pre-Islamic Arabian history
which attempts to cover most of the area
affected by Islam rather than just the northern countries which at the time of Philby's
book were the only ones written about.

✔ **The British in the Middle East**
Sarah Searight   1979 (1969)
The author concentrates on the social and
cultural aspects of British interest in the
Middle East with vivid descriptions of 400
years of visitors and travellers.

**The Arabs: the Life-story of a People
who have left their deep impression
on the world**   *Bertram Thomas   1937*
Thomas travelled into unknown places and
got to know the Middle East so well that his
account of the culture and history of the
Arabs became a classic. He begins by describing the Arabs of antiquity and continues with
the birth of Muhammad, Arab civilization,
its arts and sciences, the disintegration of

Arabia and the effect of the West on Arab culture.

Heart Beguiling Araby   Kathryn Tidrick
1989 (1981)
Kathryn Tidrick explores two themes in her book; firstly the idea that the Bedouin were a pure race and as such were independent, noble, honourable and led simple lives until spoilt by contact with the outside world: an idea which came to fruition in the work of Niebuhr and Burckhardt. Her second theme is the idea that there is a natural affinity between the English and the Arabs; many of the early explorers to Arabia were misfits in their own culture and she traces the origin of this illusory idea to the inequality of power: 'those who lie under the power of another are always conscious of it, while those who possess power may be unaware of it'.

Leisure

Falconry in Arabia   Mark Allen   1980
Beautifully illustrated book which describes falconry in Arabia.

Natural History

In Unknown Arabia   R.E. Cheesman   1926
Descriptions of the flora and fauna of Arabia.

✔ **The Birds of Britain and Europe with North Africa and the Middle East**   Hermann Heinzel, Richard Fitter and John Parslow   1992 (1972)
A field guide which aims to describe and illustrate every bird in the regions covered.

Birds of Arabia   Richard Meinertzhagen
1954
This was the first serious book about birds in Arabia and, as a result, has become extremely sought after on the second-hand market by anyone taking an interest in the subject.

✔ **Flowers of the Mediterranean**
Oleg Polunin and Anthony Huxley   1965
A well illustrated guide to the flowers of the Mediterranean, including those parts of the Middle East which border the Mediterranean. Over 700 species are described and 300 are illustrated with colour photographs.

Photography

✔ **Bedouin. Nomads of the Desert**
Alan Keohane   1994
Colour photographs taken all over the deserts of the Middle East, with ample text.

✔ **Desert, Marsh and Mountain**
Wilfred Thesiger   1979
A selection of some of the sixty volumes of photographs that Thesiger took during his many years of travelling. He quotes extensively from *Arabian Sands* and *The Marsh Arabs*, but the prologue includes an account of his childhood in Abyssinia: 'The urge to travel and explore probably originated in my childhood. Certainly it was an unusual childhood.'

✔ **Visions of a Nomad**   Wilfred Thesiger
1993 (1987)
A collection of Thesiger's black and white photographs from Africa, the Arab World and Asia: 'These photographs capture the total confidence and naturalness of the subject created by long and trusting relationships.' (Stephen Haggard *Literary Review*)

Arabia and the Gulf: in Original Photographs 1880–1950
Andrew Wheatcroft
Divided into six parts through which it is possible to get a fairly comprehensive historical overview of what life was like in Arabia and the Gulf.

Religion

✔ **The Koran**   Translated by A.J. Arberry
1991 (1964)
The Koran is a fusion of prose and poetry and in its 114 Suras (chapters) comprises the revelations believed to have been communicated to Muhammed by God, between 610–632 AD.

✔ **Islam**   Alfred Guillaume   1990 (1956)
Professor Guillaume deals with the massive influence that Islam has had on the culture of the Arab peoples; he begins with its historical background and writes about Muhammad and the Quran before describing the evolution of Islam and its different schools as systems of faith, law, religion and philosophy.

✔ **Judaism**   Nicholas de Lange   1991 (1986)
A short book which explains what Judaism is and defines its history, ethics and code.

✔ **Islam in the World**   Malise Ruthven
1991 (1984)
The author tries to get behind the reason why Islam has become such a powerful political force in the modern world.

Travel Literature

Travellers in Arabia
Robin Leonard Bidwell   1976
A collection of some of the travels and explorations that were undertaken by Europeans in the Middle East. The book includes chapters on Niebuhr, Burckhardt, Burton, Palgrave, Doughty, and Philby. Bidwell reckons that there is probably more written on Arabia than on any other part of the world, so he chose what he thought was interesting, amusing or important; inevitably he had to miss out much of value, but the end result is a good brief introduction.

Far Arabia: Explorers of the Myth.
Peter Brent   1977
The myth of Arabia was often promulgated by what the explorers and travellers wrote; this book discusses these unrealities and the effect they had, while also describing various journeys.

✔ Tribes With Flags   *Charles Glass   1992 (1990)*
Charles Glass lived in Lebanon from 1972–1976 and from 1983–1984 and has travelled throughout much of the Middle East. Here he recounts some of his many journeys leading up to his capture and subsequent escape from Hizballah.

✔ Baghdad Without a Map
Tony Horwitz   1992 (1991)
A very entertaining book written with a journalist's desire for 'hot stories' about the author's travels through Yemen, the Persian Gulf, Egypt, Iraq, Iran, Libya, Sudan and the Lebanon with an additional epilogue on Iraq, written after the Gulf War, where Horowitz was sent as a reporter.

✔ Eothen   *Alexander Kinglake   1991 (1844)*
One of *the* classic travel books; written by the young Kinglake in 1844. After the book's publication, Kinglake became known as 'Eothen' Kinglake, which means 'from the East'. He travelled at a time when the European wars had ended and 'gentlemen' were able to resume the Grand Tour, but Kinglake wanted travel that would take him to the heart of the country and that might involve danger. He travelled over fifteen months to Turkey, Beirut, Jordan, Palestine and Egypt, visiting Lady Hester Stanhope in a convent near Sidon. The account of his travels is interesting as much for the effect of what he saw had on him as for descriptions of what he was seeing. [Jonathan Raban]

✔ Crusader Castles   *T.E. Lawrence   1992 (1936)*
Lawrence walked 1,100 miles through Palestine and Syria visiting every Crusader Castle of importance; this was his first introduction to the Middle East. He described the great Krak des Chevaliers as 'the most wholly admirable castle in the world', but noted that in terms of scientific defence it could not begin to compare with Coucy in France or Caerphilly.

✔ The Travels of Sir John Mandeville   *Translated by C.W.R.D. Moseley   1983*
Little is known about Sir John Mandeville and where he actually travelled between 1322 and 1356 – some critics maintain that he never got further than the nearest library. Nevertheless it is known that Leonardo and Columbus both possessed his book, which is written with wit and skill.

The Market of Seleukia   *James Morris   1957*
This is an impression of the Muslim Middle East written at a crucial and changing time in its history, 'frozen for a moment in all its varied attitudes, before the hot breath of history melted the tableau.' Morris writes about Egypt, the Sudan, Syria, Jordan, the Arabian Peninsula, Iraq and Persia in a down to earth yet evocative manner.

✔ The Afghan Amulet   *Sheila Paine   1994*
Sheila Paine spent over two years searching for a particular amulet pattern which was relevant to her work as a textile expert. She was constantly told that it was 'in the next valley', so her trip took her to Makran, Iran, Baluchistan, Afghanistan, Iraqi and Turkish Kurdistan, ending up in eastern Bulgaria.

✔ Arabia   *Jonathan Raban   1987 (1979)*
Jonathan Raban was living in Earls Court in the 1970s when it began to fill up with Arabs; he decided to go and see for himself their countries of origin and produced 'one of the most delightful travel books in thirty years'. (*New York Times*). He travelled through much of the Middle East and the book 'in its ingenious understanding . . . should do a great deal to dispel the easiest and therefore the most prolific paranoid deception which the Western imagination has now fabricated in its desperate attempt to avoid facing reality'. (Angus Wilson)

✔ Beyond Ararat   *Bettina Selby   1994 (1993)*
Bettina Selby cycled from the Black Sea coast of Turkey through the mountains to Ani and to Mount Ararat and through Kurdistan, near the borders of Iran, Iraq and Syria at the end of the Gulf War.

✔ **Riding to Jerusalem** *Bettina Selby*
1994 (1989)
Bettina Selby bicycled across Europe and through Turkey and Syria to Israel.

✔ **East is West** *Freya Stark 1991 (1945)*
At the outbreak of war in 1939, Freya Stark travelled to the Middle East to start work as an official in the Diplomatic Corps. She travelled through Arabia, Egypt, Palestine, Syria, Iraq and Persia. The book is a combination of personal anecdote and observations.

Alarms and Excursions in Arabia
Bertram Thomas 1931
Thomas was a political officer in Mesopotamia and Trans-Jordan before becoming Financial Adviser in Muscat and Oman. Due to his good relationship with several Arab leaders, he was able to make several important journeys into previously unknown territory.

ARAB GULF STATES

General Background

✔ **The Turbulent Gulf. People, Politics and Power** *Liesl Graz 1992*
A country by country account of the Gulf in the post-Cold War era, including the Gulf War and its consequences: 'Liesl Graz is a sharp-eyed observer and probably the best European correspondent working in the area . . . Excellent.' (Malise Ruthven *Sunday Telegraph*)

Guides

The Economist Business Traveller's Guide: Arabian Peninsula *1987*
Covers Saudi Arabia, Kuwait, Bahrain, Qatar, UAE, Oman and Yemen Arab Republic. It subdivides each country into the political scene, resources, industry, finances, the business scene, banks, planning and reference. Primarily of importance for business people, it also provides important background information for the general traveller.

✔ **Arab Gulf States. Travel Survival Kit** *Gordon R. Robison 1993*
Information on Bahrain, Kuwait, Qatar, Oman, Saudi Arabia and the United Arab Emirates.

History

The Gulf: Arabia's Western Approaches *Molly Izzard 1979*
Molly Izzard describes the history and culture of the Gulf including the arrival of the British, as well as writing about her own life in the area. An excellent introduction and survey to the area when 'Arabia proper was still a poor country'.

Arabia, the Gulf and the West
J.B. Kelly 1980
An overview of the economy of oil in the Gulf; the author is very critical of the British political and military withdrawal from the area and remarks that when the British relinquished their responsibilities, the rest of the world paid little attention. Kelly attempts to offer a new interpretation of the recent history of Arabia which tries to dispel any complacency about what happened.

Natural History

The Wild Flowers of Kuwait and Bahrain *Violet Dickson 1955*
An illustrated guide to the flora of Kuwait, North-east Arabia, Dubai and Bahrain. Violet Dickson was the wife of Col. H.R.P. Dickson who had been Political Agent in Bahrain and Kuwait. She was still living in Kuwait when it was invaded by Iraq.

Mammals of the Arabian Gulf
David L. Harrison 1981
Fifty different kinds of animals found in the Gulf and neighbouring areas are described.

BAHRAIN
'And here are the best Pearles, which are round and Orient.' Joseph Salbancke, letter to Sir Thomas Smith, 1609 in *Purchas his Pilgrimes.* 1625.

Art and Archaeology

Looking for Dilmun *Geoffrey Bibby 1972 (1970)*
An account of the Danish excavations in Arabia between 1953 and 1965, in search of the ancient civilization of Dilmun. Much was discovered about the pre-history of Bahrain.

Arabian Fantasy *Herbert Chappell 1976*
The author went to Bahrain to film a musical score which had been combined with traditional music by David Fanshawe. The book of the project is a good introduction to the

country with particular emphasis on its music and famous pearl fishing.

Guides

✔ **Immel's New Guide to Bahrain**
Peter Vine 1988
A brief guide illustrated with colour photographs.

Bahrain. A MEED Practical Guide
John Whelan (ed.) 1983
A good introduction to Bahrain for both short- and long-term visitors. The book deals with background information, practical advice, the economy, doing business and also contains a section on what to do and see. The *Middle East Economic Digest* also publishes special reports on Bahrain.

✔ **Bahrain. A Travel Guide**
Philip Ward 1993
Bahrain deserves more than the short airplane stop-overs which people usually give it as it has over 5,000 years of history. Philip Ward's guide describes some of that history and also lists hotels and useful information. The map of the State of Bahrain is supplied by the Ministry of Information and is extremely hard to fathom.

Travel Literature

✔ **Ibn Battuta. Travels in Asia and Africa 1325–1354** *1984 (1929) (see 'North Africa– Travel Literature')*
Ibn Battuta describes Bahrain in his book of travels: 'a fine large city with gardens, trees and streams . . . The city has groves of date-palms, pomegranates, and citrons, and cotton is grown there.'

The Pirate Coast *Charles Belgrave 1966*
Based on the diaries of Francis Erskine Loch, written between 1818 and 1820. Bahrain is mentioned many times, especially in connection with Portuguese activity in the area and the relocation to Bahrain of the British Residency in the Gulf in 1946.

Arabia Phoenix *Gerald de Gaury 1946*
Included in this book of his travels, De Gaury discusses the fall of Bahrain to the Wahabbis at the beginning of the nineteenth century.

Ben Kendim. A Record of Eastern Travel *Aubrey Herbert 1924*
Herbert provides a summary of Bahrain's history and an account of the kind of life he found there on his visit.

KUWAIT

Biography

Forty Years in Kuwait *Violet Dickson*
1971
Violet Dickson was the wife of the British Political Agent in Kuwait. Although this is her personal account of the years between 1922 and 1962 she also includes profiles of the various Arab leaders.

General Background

✔ **Kuwait. A Nation's Story** *Peter Vine*
1992
A large format illustrated book with good general background information.

History

Kuwait and Her Neighbours
H.R.P. Dickson 1956
Dickson was the British Political Agent in Kuwait and therefore had first hand knowledge of all that was going on in the Saudi–Kuwait frontier problems.

OMAN

'In the months of August and September, it is here so incredible hot and scorching that I am not able to express the condition strangers are in, being as if they were in boiling Cauldrons or in sweating-tubs, so that I have known many who were not able to endure the heat would jump into the sea and remain there till the Heat of the day be over.' John Struys The Voyages of John Struys, translated from the Dutch by John Morison 1684 – of 1673

History

The Wind of Morning *Hugh Boustead*
1971
Development in Oman under Sultan Said bin Taimur looked at from the British point of view.

Oman. The Reborn Land *F.A. Clements*
1980
It was not until 1967 and the discovery of oil, that Oman started to become modernized; prior to the late sixties, as a deliberate policy, Oman had been completely cut off from the outside world. A coup in 1970 changed this

and Clements examines the background to the coup and the emergence of the 'new' Oman.

Where Soldiers Fear to Tread
Ranulph Fiennes 1975
Ranulph Fiennes fought in Dhofar, and writes from first hand experience about this and the changes that were taking place in Oman.

Oman: A History   *Wendell Phillips 1967*
A readable general history of Oman. The author was at one time economic adviser and director of general antiquities to Sultan Said bin Taimur.

Arabian Assignment   *David Smiley 1975*
David Smiley commanded the forces of the Sultan of Muscat and had to expel the Saudi-backed rebels from the mountainous Jebel Akhdar; he writes convincingly about what it must have felt like to have been a European in Arabia.

Travel Literature

✔ Atlantis of the Sands
Ranulph Fiennes 1993 (1992)
Ranulph Fiennes determined to find the lost city of Ubar which legend had it was buried under the sand dunes of southern Oman. In 1991 armed with aerial photographs from the space shuttle 'Challenger', he began his search. The book recounts his search and eventual discovery of the city.

Sultan in Oman   *James Morris 1990 (1957)*
Morris accompanied Sultan Said Bin Taimur on a rushed journey through Oman in the hope of quashing a rebellion and wrote about the incident with insight and humour. *The Times Literary Supplement* wrote that the book should have 'a place on the shelf not so far from those of the great Arabian travellers, Doughty, Gertrude Bell, Lawrence and others'.

Unknown Oman   *Wendell Phillips 1966*
Phillips wrote his two books on Oman in conjunction with each other; this is the account of his travels, excavations and explorations throughout the country. J.R. Wellsted had remarked in his book *Travels in Arabia* published in 1838 'Is this Arabia, this the country we have looked on heretofore as a desert? Verdant fields of grain and sugar cane stretching along for miles, are before us; streams of water, flowing in all directions, intersect our path.' Phillips also describes the landscape and has chapters on women, disease, religion and archaeology.

✔ The Southern Gates of Arabia
Freya Stark   1990 (1936) (see 'Yemen')

✔ Arabian Sands   *Wilfred Thesiger   1991 (1959) (see 'Saudi Arabia')*

Alarms and Excursions in Arabia
Bertram Thomas   1931 (see 'Middle East – General')

✔ Travels in Oman. On the Track of the Early Explorers   *Philip Ward 1987*
A compendium of all the significant travellers, explorers and adventurers who went to Oman. The book includes Bent, Cole, Cox, Eccles, Geary, Haines, Hamdani, Hamerton, ibn Battuta, Kaempfer, Loyd, Miles, Pengelley, Stiffe, Bertram Thomas, C. Ward, Wellsted and Whitelock. Their writings are quoted and Philip Ward adds his own narrative of Oman today.

QATAR

General Background

In Defiance of the Elements: a Personal View of Qatar   *John Moorehead 1977*
A general introduction to the history and contemporary culture of Qatar.

✔ If the Sun Doesn't Kill You, the Washing Machine Will   *Peter Wood 1993*
In 1991 Peter Wood was sent to work in Qatar and, finding the way that everything was done was so completely different, wrote an amusing book about his experiences.

SAUDI ARABIA

Art and Archaeology

The Art of Arabian Costume. A Saudi Arabian Profile   *Heather Colyer Ross 1981*
The author compares collecting costumes in modern Arabia to an exciting treasure hunt. Spurred on by her enthusiasm in hunting down rare and exotic dress she decided to write about her discoveries; the resulting book has much interesting text and is full of photographs, artist's impressions and line drawings illustrating Arabian costume throughout the region.

Bedouin Jewellry in Saudi Arabia
Heather Colyer Ross 1978
Much of the book is based on the author's collection of Bedouin silver jewellery which she and her husband had bought in the

Women's Suq in Riyadh. The different techniques, materials, types of jewellery and historical influences are illustrated with drawings and photographs and ample text.

Biography

Captain Shakespear: a Portrait.
H.V.F. Winstone   1978 (1976)
Captain Shakespear, a Kiplingesque figure who combined being an explorer, diplomat, soldier, botanist and photographer, was killed in battle whilst fighting with Ibn Saud against Ibn Rashid of Hail in 1915. Winstone pieced together the fragments of information he found to write this entertaining 'portrait'.

Fiction

Crash of '79   *Paul Erdman   1980*
A retired banker working for the Saudis observes the events of 1979 that lead to a war in the Middle East and the crash of 1979.

The Doomed Oasis   *Hammond Innes   1896*
An adventure story about saving an oasis from extinction.

✔ **Eight Months on Ghazzah Street**
Hilary Mantel   1989 (1988)
A horror story full of twists and suspense; a woman joins her husband in Jeddah and due to boredom starts speculating about the empty flat upstairs. Gripping to the end.

Endings   *'Abd al-Rahman Munif   Translated by Roger Allen   1988 (1977)*
This was probably the first translation ever made of a Saudi novel set in the desert; drought is a recurring theme, for it is the environment and climate which play such an important part in the daily lives of the people who live there. The author's descriptions of nature and hunting are superb.

Food

✔ **Recipe Memories of Desert Storm**
Mona Gabbori
The only book in English on Saudi cooking. Recipes include: jareesh, fattush, ghraybi (butter cookies), and shredded nut pastries.

Guide

How to Live and Work in Saudi Arabia. A Handbook for Short and Longstay Visitors   *J. McGregor and M. Nydell   1991*
Covers essential practical topics for anyone

intending to visit Saudi Arabia, a country the size of Western Europe, with advice on visas, transport, housing, schools, money matters and etiquette; it also gives a pointer to useful contacts throughout the country.

History

The House of Saud   *David Holden and Richard Johns   1982 (1981)*
The book was started by David Holden before his murder in 1977 and completed by Richard Johns. It tells the extraordinary story of the emergence of an unknown Saudi prince, Ibn Saud, who rose from obscurity to fame and power with the discovery of oil, and of British intrigue and involvement in the kingdom.

The Kingdom   *Robert Lacey   1981*
A history of Saudi Arabia which inevitably includes much about all the surrounding countries. The book was written after four years of living in the country.

The Queen of Sheba   *H. StJ. B. Philby   1981*
Philby's last journey in Central Arabia was with the aim of finding out all he could about the Queen of Sheba, believed to have been loved by King Solomon. Published posthumously.

Flowered Men and Green Slopes of Arabia   *Thierry Mauger   1988*
An illustrated travel journal of a journey through the South-west of Arabia, Arabia Felix, which emphasizes the abundant richness of the traditional environment.

Travel Literature

A Pilgrimage to Nejd   *Lady Anne Blunt   1985 (1881)*
In 1878 Anne Blunt and her husband, Wilfred Scawen Blunt, embarked on a 2,000 mile trek to find the Bedouins in remotest Central Arabia; she was only the second woman to travel into the inhospitable interior of Arabia. Unlike most other Victorians Wilfred and Anne Blunt travelled rough, with the minimum of fuss, and again, unusually for the time, they were interested in the details of ordinary life and insatiably curious about the places they visited.

✔ **Personal Narrative of a Pilgrimage to Al-Madinah and Meccah**
Richard Burton   1964 (1893)
Burton went to Mecca and Medina in 1853; disguised as a wandering dervish, he managed to get to the Kaabah and to the Tomb of the Prophet at Medina, joining in the Hadj.

He was a very sharp observer of all that he saw and his book is of great interest to the traveller today.

✔ **Travels in Arabia Deserta**
Charles Doughty 1979 (1888)
'The place book I find most unforgettable is Doughty's *Travels in Arabia Deserta*: partly because of its sonorous prose, partly because of Doughty's own stately character, self-presented so majestically between its lines, but chiefly because it evokes so magically the strangeness, the beauty, the danger and the excitement of travel in the Arabian desert a century ago.' (Jan Morris) [Colin Thubron]

Arabia of the Wahhabis   *H. StJ. B. Philby 1977 (1928)*
The third volume in Philby's *The Heart of Arabia* which was published in 1922. It completes the account of his experiences in Arabia in 1917 and 1918 when he was sent on missions by Ibn Sa'ud; his primary task was to prepare a campaign against Ibn Rashid, Ibn Sa'ud's northern neighbour. The mission was not a great success, something Philby found it hard to concede, but his belief in Ibn Sa'ud was vindicated, since he now ruled Arabia from sea to sea.

The Empty Quarter   *H. StJ. B. Philby 1933*
The description of Philby's travels in the *Rub' al Khali* or Empty Quarter, the Great South Desert of Saudi Arabia. He had planned the journey for fifteen years, having been inspired by Dr D.G. Hogarth; Bertram Thomas was the pioneer, nevertheless Philby's book is important. He wrote much of the draft as he wandered around the desert, but actually completed the book in North Wales.

A Pilgrim in Arabia   *H. StJ. B. Philby 1946*
A collection of essays from Philby's time in Arabia, including the pilgrimage he made to Mecca.

Sheba's Daughters   *H. StJ. B. Philby 1939*
A record of three months' travel in 'unknown' Southern Arabia. Philby was constantly looking for new areas to explore and Sir Percy Cox reckoned 'that his journey from Mukalla right along the hinterland, through the Western confines of the great Arabian desert to Täif would be a very fine piece of travel, about the only piece of the Arabian peninsula that is entirely unexplored'.

✔ **Arabian Sands**   *Wilfred Thesiger 1991 (1959)*
Most of Thesiger's journeys described in this book, are about crossing the Empty Quarter; much had not been seen by a European before and although he had no intention at the time of writing a book, his combination of intimate detail and anecdote brings wherever he is very much alive, making this one of the classic works of travel. Thesiger says of the book: 'For me this book remains a memorial to a vanished past, a tribute to a once magnificent people.'

Arabia Felix: Across the Empty Quarter of Arabia   *Bertram Thomas 1932*
In his foreword to the book, T.E. Lawrence explains that he had been doubtful of Bertram Thomas' achievements, but having read the draft he was assured that Thomas 'has snatched, at the twenty-third hour, feet's last victory and set us free..'. Lawrence was reluctant to say how much he liked the book in case Jonathan Cape used what he said for the blurb, but he thinks Thomas 'a master of every desert art'.

UNITED ARAB EMIRATES

Autobiography

The Wind of Morning   *Hugh Boustead 1971 (see 'Oman')*
The author was Political Agent in Dubai and writes interestingly about his time there.

General Background

✔ **Dubai. Gateway to the Gulf**
Ian Fairservice (ed.) 1992 (1986)
An illustrated general introduction.

Guide

UAE. A MEED Practical Guide   *1990*
The United Arab Emirates are a group of seven: Abu Dhabi, Dubai, Sharjah, Ras al-Khaimah, Fujairah, Ajman and Umm al-Qaiwain, which stretch along the coast of the Arabian Gulf, and were formed into a federation in 1971. Things have changed rapidly for the bedouin in the Gulf and this book attempts to describe a little of the lifestyle that has been lost.

History

Abu Dhabi: a Portrait   *John Daniels 1974*
Pearl fishing and oil both played an important part in making Abu Dhabi the wealthiest state in the UAE. Daniels describes the background to the formation of the federation and looks at the development projects of the 1970s.

The Trucial States *Donald Hawley 1970*
Hawley deals with the seven states of the
region from their earliest history, through
the arrival of the Arabs and ultimately the
British, and their time as the Trucial States.
He concludes with their formation into the
UAE federation and the withdrawal of the
British. Very useful information on each of
the states, their geography and natural history.

The Gulf States and Oman
Christine Osborne 1977
The author begins by dealing generally with
the birth of the federation, before examining
each state separately.

IRAN

'The start of a journey in Persia resembles
an algebraical equation: it may or may not
come out.' Robert Byron *The Road to
Oxiana* 1937

Anthropology

✔ **Nomad. A Year in the Life of a
Qashqa'i Tribesman in Iran** *Lois Beck
1991*
Beck lived with the Qermezi, a Qashqa'i
tribe, in southwestern Iran for a year in
1970/1. She kept a daily journal documenting
the migratory cycle of these nomadic pastoralists, but also focused her observations on
one man, the group's leader, who selected
pastures and mediated in disputes.

Art and Archaeology

Persian Painting *Basil Gray 1977*
The author believes that the Mongol invasion
actively encouraged the growth of calligraphy and book illustration, the disciplines
which he emphasizes in this book.

**Tribal Rugs: an Introduction to the
Weaving of the Tribes of Iran**
Jenny Housego 1978
An introduction to the nine principal weaving tribes; the short text is accompanied by
black and white photographs.

Persia: an archaeological guide
Sylvia A. Matheson 1972
Obviously now out of date, it is still interesting as a guide to what had been excavated
up until 1972.

Old Routes of Western Iran
Sir Aurel Stein 1940
Stein went on an archaeological journey to

southern and western Iran between 1932
and 1936. The antiquities are described in
detail.

Islamic Painting: a Survey
David Talbot Rice 1971
The book goes up to the eighteenth century
and is mainly devoted to book and miniature
painting. Illustrated with colour and black
and white reproductions.

Persian Lustre Ware *Oliver Watson 1985*
The technique of lustreware is described;
how it is made, the kinds of materials needed
and the different styles. Lists of individual
objects are included.

**The *Shah-namah* of Firdausi: the book
of the Persian kings** *J.V.S. Wilkinson 1931*
Twenty-four illustrations from the *shahnameh* manuscript with an in depth analysis of
their narrative power. There is an introduction by Laurence Binyon on their artistic
importance.

Biography

✔ **Out of Iran**
Sousan Azadi with Angela Ferrante 1991 (1987)
The author grew up in a wealthy Iranian
family, but was thrown into jail after the
Shah was overthrown; she finally managed
to escape with her son over the Zagros mountains into Turkey.

✔ **Death Plus Ten Years. My Life as
the Ayatollah's Prisoner by 'Notorious
British Spy'** *Roger Cooper 1994 (1993)*
Roger Cooper spent over five years in the
notorious Evin prison in Tehran; the story of
how he coped with his imprisonment, not
knowing from one day to the next what was
going to happen to him, makes inspirational
reading.

The Blindfold Horse *Shusha Guppy 1989
(1988)*
Shusha Guppy writes movingly about her
childhood in Persia where she was born and
brought up. The lost life of pre-Ayatollah
Persia is vividly described by using large and
small incidents and she has wonderful recall
for the memories of her own childhood.

✔ **An Iranian Odyssey** *Gohar Kordi
1991*
The author was born in a small Kurdish
village and went blind at the age of four. Her
family then moved to Tehran and she became
involved in the struggle to get an education,
finally becoming the first woman student at
the university.

Fiction

Classical Persian Literature
A.J. Arberry 1958
The chronological development of Persian literature from the ninth to fifteenth centuries by both Iranian and European scholars. The chief poets, Sa'di, Rumi, Hafez and Jami, all have chapters devoted to them.

Sohrab and Rustum *Matthew Arnold*
1853
Based on Ferdousi's original.

The Collected Persian poems: poems from the Persian. *John C.E. Bowen 1976*
Fifty poems with the Persian text and English translations from the major poets of the tenth to fifteenth centuries.

✔ Persian Myths *Vesta Sarkhosh Curtis*
1993
A short, illustrated edition of the most important Persian myths.

Savushun *Simin Daneshvar 1991 (1969)*
About modern Iran. The story follows basic cultural themes and metaphors; sensitive and imaginative, it goes straight to the emotions. 'Savushun' is a pre-Islamic folk tradition from Southern Iran that conjures up hope in spite of everything.

✔ The Legend of Seyavash *Ferdowsi*
Translated by Dick Davis 1992
A section from the Shahnameh, Persia's national epic, which was written by Ferdowsi in the tenth century. The poem combines heroic warfare with psychological and ethical insight and is reputedly the longest poem ever written by one person.

Hāji Aghā. Portrait of an Iranian Confidence Man
Trois Gouttes de Sang *Sadeq Hedayat*
1978

Folk Tales of Ancient Persia *Retold by*
Forough Hekmat 1974
A group of ten folk-tales from Shiraz which had been handed down in the oral tradition.

The Adventures of Hajji Baba of Ispahan *James Morier 1930 (1824)*
Morier was a diplomat in Tehran and wrote this satire on his return to England. It was instantly extremely popular and went into many editions; a faithfully captured portrait of contemporary Persian manners and life could only have been written by someone with a deep understanding of the Orient. The hero is a Persian adventurer, one part good and three parts knave, who is always at the mercy of fortune; the book charts his various adventures and encounters and Hajji Baba is never totally implausible as a character.

Food

✔ The Legendary Cuisine of Persia
Margaret Shaida 1992
A glossy hardback book which explores the long history of Persian cuisine. Disappointingly few colour pictures.

✔ Entertaining the Persian Way
Shirin Simmons 1991 (1988)

General Background

Behind Iranian Lines *John Simpson*
1989 (1988)
Simpson was on the same flight from Paris to Tehran as Khomeini in 1979; he took full advantage of this and his invitation to return to Iran in 1987.

Guides

✔ Odyssey Illustrated Guide: Iran
Helen Loveday 1994

✔ Iran. Travel Survival Kit
David St. Vincent 1992

Touring Iran *Philip Ward 1971*

History

The Legacy of Persia *A.J. Arberry (ed.)*
1968
A summary of Persian history and the many different facets of Persian culture described in a series of articles.

Persia and the Persian Question
George N. Curzon 1892
This is still important as a source book for nineteenth-century Persian history; there was much British interest in the area at the time and the politics of this and other aspects of Persian life are described.

The Pride and the Fall: Iran 1974–1979 *Anthony Parsons 1984*
The author was British ambassador to Tehran from 1973 until 1979; this personal record describes the most interesting period of his diplomatic life.

✔ The Shah's Last Ride
William Shawcross 1989 (1988)
Shawcross starts his book with the Shah's journey into exile in 1979 when he was denied entry into almost every country in the world and had to camp on an island in the

Bahamas. He then analyses the background to the Shah's fall and describes his illness in detail since he was able to talk to many of the doctors who treated him. A comprehensive account of the fall of a dynasty which clearly illustrates the relationship between states and leaders.

A History of Persia   *Sir Percy Sykes   1969 (1915)*
Sir Percy Sykes spent twenty-one years living and travelling in Persia and so was well qualified to write what was to become the definitive history of the country. By the time of the third edition in 1930, Persia had changed dramatically, mainly due to the personality of Shah Riza, the founder of the Pahlavi dynasty. He had ensured that a strong national spirit had been awakened and Persia was finally competing with the west on equal terms, having shaken off the capitulations which had been imposed by Russia. Discoveries at Ur had also taken place.

The English Amongst the Persians, during the Qajar Period, 1787–1921
Sir Denis Wright   1977
Persia was considered immensely important by the British because of her geographical position on the threshold of India; they felt it imperative to protect her from Russian encroachment. This background of Anglo-Russian rivalry with all its activity is described by Wright. [Peter Hopkirk]

✔ **The Persian Expedition**   *Xenophon*
Translated by Rex Warner   1972 (1949)
Xenophon joined Cyrus' army of Greek mercenaries to march into Persia in the fourth century BC. He is observant about what he saw along the way and so we get a very good idea of the people and the countries he and the army passed through including Syria, Kurdestan and Armenia.

Natural History

To Persia for Flowers   *Alice Fullerton 1938*
The author kept a diary of her trip to Iran in 1935 in search of flowers. Twenty-four illustrations accompany the text.

Photography

Persian Landscape: a photographic essay.   *Warwick Ball and Anthony Hutt   1978*
A combination of black and white and colour photographs accompanied by short descriptions in a small format book.

Isfahan, Pearl of Persia   *Wilfred Blunt and Wim Swaan   1974*
Blunt's text concentrates on the Safavid period, but is also a good general background to Isfahan, as he includes earlier and later architecture; the text is accompanied by stunning black and white and colour illustrations.

Travel Literature

Journeys in Persia and Kurdistan
Isabella Bird Bishop   1989 (1891)
Taken from letters which Isabella Bird had written as she was travelling, over a period of two years. She apologizes for the fact that 'they were written in haste at the conclusion of fatiguing marches, and often in circumstances of great discomfort and difficulty'. She describes her actual travels, not wanting to go into any great detail about the antiquities in Persia, as she felt that others had done that adequately.

A Year Amongst the Persians. Impressions as to the Life, Character, and Thought of the People of Persia Received during Twelve Months' Residence in that Country in the Years 1887–1888   *Edward Granville Browne 1926 (1893)*
In his day Browne was the greatest exponent of Persian life and letters; he finally visited Persia, the country of his dreams, in 1887, already speaking the language fluently on his arrival. He had a prodigious memory and was able to recall conversations verbatim, both contributory factors in making this such an interesting book. He was as much a genius in conversation as with the written word and was well-loved by the Persians who paid him many tributes.

✔ **The Road to Oxiana**   *Robert Byron 1992 (1937)*
One of the classic travel books about Persia and Afghanistan. Robert Byron made this journey in 1933–4 and vividly describes the people he met and what he saw. The aim of his journey was to search for the origins of Islamic architecture; I found it very exciting to be in a building in Southern Iran in the 1970s which was then overrun by sheep and to read Byron's lyrical prose describing in marvellous detail the squinches in the roof. [Jeremy Paxman]

✔ **Travels in Persia 1673–1677**
Sir John Chardin   1988
The account of Chardin's second visit to Persia in 1673 which lasted four years. He had a great knowledge of Persia and through him

we see life at the Shah's court and how he had to struggle to get paid for the jewels he had brought with him to sell.

Curzon's Persia   Peter King (ed.)   1986
A interesting selection, biased towards travel, from Curzon's *Persia and the Persian Question* which was originally published in 1892 and has remained a classic. The text is accompanied by photographs which Curzon took with his own precious Kodak.

Through Persia in Disguise
Sarah Hobson   1973
Sarah Hobson was 23 when she travelled to Persia to study designs and crafts. She would not have been able to visit many of the places as a woman, so she disguised herself as a man and was able to go almost wherever she pleased, including a men's theological college in Qum.

✔ **Eastern Approaches**
Fitzroy Maclean (see 'Caucasus')

✔ **Persian Letters**   Montesquieu
Translated by C.J. Betts)   1973
The letters of two Persian travellers in Europe, Montesquieu's first book, was published in 1721; he uses their journey as a backdrop to air his views on every area of human interest.

✔ **Among the Believers**   V.S. Naipaul
1982 (1981)
The first part of Naipaul's Islamic journey is in Iran.

A Tower of Skulls   Gerald Reitlinger   1932
(A Journey through Persia and Turkish Armenia)
A record of three months' 'hurried travel' through Persia and Turkish Armenia in 1930/1. The author does not profess to be an expert on the areas he visits, but he gives good visual descriptions.

Twelve Days   Vita Sackville-West   1928
(An Account of a Journey Across the Bakhtiari Mountains in South-Western Persia)
It was some time after her journey that Vita Sackville-West was able to turn the experiences of her trip into a book. She had travelled to South-West Persia with Harold Nicolson, Gladwyn Jebb, Copley Amory (an American) and Lionel Smith to visit the Bakhtiari, a proud people, who claim that they were the only Persians not conquered by Alexander the Great.

✔ **Adventures in Persia**
Reginald Teague-Jones   1990 (1988)
When the book was published in 1988, the author 'Ronald Sinclair', aged 99, became

famous as the oldest person to publish a first book; however, it was only when he died that his true identity was revealed. For seventy years he had been in hiding from the Russians. This is the old-fashioned account of a journey from Beirut to India made in 1926 in a Model-A Ford.

Lords of the Mountains
Marie Therese Ullens de Schooten   1956
The author, wife of a diplomat, travelled to Southern Persia to meet the Kashkai, a nomadic tribe who had been in Persia since the thirteenth century. The book is the account of her journey and is also interesting archaeologically and anthropologically.

Blind White Fish in Persia
Anthony Smith   1966
Four Oxford students embarked on a journey to Kerman in 1950 with the aim of studying the *qanats* (underground water channels). Their adventures along the way are described here in very readable prose.

✔ **Perseus in the Wind**   Freya Stark   1948
Freya Stark spent several weeks one summer among the mountains of Elburz which separate the Caspian jungle from the Qazvin plain. She considered 'these landscapes as among the most beautiful in the world, and remember long days on stony paths, with the bells of the mules tinkling behind me as they found their steps in valleys yet unmapped, by rarely visited streams'. Most nights she observed the constellation Perseus and named the book after this memory, as she felt 'his stars as a friendliness and a bond in the gaiety of spaces and the cold of night'.

✔ **The Valleys of the Assassins and Other Persian Travels**   Freya Stark
1991 (1936)
This was Freya Stark's first book for which she was given the Burton Memorial Medal by the Royal Asiatic Society. Her journey, which she undertook alone with a guide, was for fun. She went from North-West Luristan to the Valley of the Assassins and to the Throne of Solomon, most of which was in remote and unexplored territory.

The Land of the Great Sophy
Roger Stevens   1971 (1962)
Stevens wrote the book for those living or visiting Persia who were not experts on Asian matters. The first half is background, containing chapters on geography, history, religion and art, while the second part describes his travels throughout the country. Eminently readable although now somewhat out of date.

Ten Thousand Miles in Persia or Eight Years in Iran   *Percy M. Sykes   1902*
The author goes into great detail about everywhere he visited during his long so-journ in Iran. The people are well described and the geography and geology of the towns and provinces are analysed in depth.

Arminius Vambéry. His Life and Adventures   *Written by Himself   1884 (see 'Central Asia –General')*

IRAQ

'The Ark and all the rest become quite comprehensible when one sees Mesopotamia in flood time.' Gertrude Bell, letter to her family, 26th May 1916

Art & Archaeology

Ruined Cities of Iraq   *Seton Lloyd   1942*
A guide to some of the ancient cities of Iraq, including Baghdad, Babylon, Samarra, Nineveh and Ur. Includes an outline of Iraq's history.

✔ **Ur of the Chaldees: a Record of Seven Years of Excavation**
Leonard Woolley   1950
Woolley reconstructs the past daily lives of the people who lived beside the Euphrates and describes the discoveries of the various cities which were found up until the time of Nebuchadnezzar.

Biography

Haji Rikkan, Marsh Arab   *Fulanain
1927 (pseud. S.E. Hedgecock and Mrs Hedgecock)*
Gertrude Bell suggested that this book be written, but died before she had completed her promised foreword. The central figure in the book is meant to portray an accurate picture of Arab tribal life and the changes which occurred after the First World War.

Fiction

✔ **The Last Voyage of Somebody the Sailor**   *John Barth   1992 (1991)*
William Behler is shipwrecked off Sri Lanka while retracing one of Sinbad's legendary voyages; he finds himself marooned in Sinbad's house in medieval Baghdad.

✔ **Murder in Mesopotamia**
Agatha Christie   1981 (1936)
A murder takes place among the members of an expedition to Mesopotamia to excavate the ruins of an ancient city. Poirot happened to be passing through Baghdad and was called in to solve the diabolically clever crime. Written in Mesopotamia while Agatha Christie was accompanying her husband on a dig.

Folk-Tales of Iraq   *E.S. Stevens (ed.)   1931*
Inevitably folk-tales which are passed down verbally, get changed and embellished over the years; this collection of forty-eight fairy-tales is a rich and varied assortment.

Food

✔ **The Baghdad Kitchen**
Nina Jamil-Garbutt   1985

History

✔ **No Friends but the Mountains. The Tragic History of the Kurds**   *John Bulloch and Harvey Morris   1993 (1992)*
The history of the Kurds is traced by two authors who know the area well and their hopes and disappointments, post the Gulf War, are investigated.

The Long Road to Bagdad
Edmund Candler   1919
Three stages of the Mesopotamian campaign: the fall of Kut, the capture of Samarrah and the armistice and surrender of the Turkish Army at Shergat Ali.

Three Kings in Baghdad 1921–1958
Gerald de Gaury   1961
In 1921 Britain renamed the modern state they had established in Mesopotamia, Iraq. The three kings de Gaury writes about are the first king of the new Iraq, Faisal I, his son Ghazi and Ghazi's son Faisal II who died in 1958.

Foundations in the Dust: A Story of Mesopotamian Exploration   *Seton Lloyd
1980 (1947)*
A history of the lives and works of some of the better known archaeologists who worked in the region, such as Austin Henry Layard and Henry Rawlinson.

Iraq   *Stephen Hemsley Longrigg and Frank Stoakes   1958*
A matter-of-fact general introduction to the history, economy, society and politics of Iraq up until 1958; the Iraqi revolution occurred in July 1958 when the book was at proof stage.

✔ **Mesopotamia**   *Julian Reade   1991*
A brief illustrated history.

✔ **Ancient Iraq** *Georges Roux 1992 (1964)*
An accessible and readable account of the early history of Iraq. The book is a compilation of articles originally published in *Iraq Petroleum*.

Iraq Since 1958 from Revolution to Dictatorship *Marion Farouk-Sluglett and Peter Sluglett 1987*
A political and economic history of Iraq which begins with an introduction to Iraq before the 1958 revolution and continues in chronological fashion to chart the rise of Saddam Husain in 1970 and the social, political and economic policies since then.

Loyalties: Mesopotamia 1914–1917 *Arnold Wilson 1969 (1930)*
A personal account of the events leading up to the British occupation of Iraq; Wilson was acting British Civil Commissioner in Mesopotamia. He also wrote *Mesopotamia: a Clash of Loyalties 1917–1920* (1921)

Photography

Iraq: Land of Two Rivers *Gavin Young 1980*
A photographic record of the landscape and people of Iraq which shows that, despite enormous industrialization, the Iraqis are proud of their past.

Travel Literature

From Amurath to Amurath *Gertrude Bell 1911*
A description of Gertrude Bell's extensive travels in Mesopotamia; she concentrates on the archaeological history of Babylon and Assyria.

The Letters of Gertrude Bell *Florence Bell (ed.) 1927*
The second volume of Gertrude Bell's letters was written from Baghdad, where she went after Cairo in 1916, and during the time that she was involved in the founding of the national museum in 1923.

✔ **The Tigris Expedition** *Thor Heyerdahl 1980*
Heyerdahl built a boat of reeds in the marshes of Southern Iraq and sailed down the Tigris to the Arabian Gulf and to the sea, in search of the routes which he believed the ancient Sumerians must have used 5,000 years ago. Descriptions of the building of the boat and the lives and customs of the Marsh Arabs (although the people who actually built the boat had been brought from the highlands of South America!) The *Tigris* was ceremonially burnt at the end of the journey.

✔ **Come, Tell Me How You Live** *Agatha Christie Mallowan 1990 (1946)*
The famous crime writer's light-hearted and often funny account of the time she spent in Syria and Iraq in the 1930s, with her archaeologist husband, Sir Max Mallowan. She met her husband-to-be, who was then assistant to the Woolleys, on a visit to Ur; they were soon married and she threw herself into the life of an archaeologist playing a very practical role. She wrote the book not as a task but as 'a labour of love'.

✔ **A Reed Shaken by the Wind** *Gavin Maxwell 1994 (1957)*
(A Journey through the Unexplored Marshlands of Iraq)
In 1956 Gavin Maxwell accompanied Wilfred Thesiger to the marshlands of Iraq. He describes the people he met, his experiences during his travels and how he acquired an otter named Mijbil.

Escape from Baghdad *Carl Raswan 1938*
When the Royal Commission from London were about to announce their decision in regard to Palestine, Raswan who had lived for many years among the Bedouin, decided to go behind the scenes and see for himself what was happening.

✔ **Baghdad Sketches** *Freya Stark 1992 (1937)*
Eight of the short essays and sketches were written as the result of a visit to Iraq in 1937; the rest tried to capture what life was like in Baghdad in 1931. By then a veneer of westernization was settling over Baghdad, the Caliph's City, and Freya Stark found that by 1937 this had dramatically increased.

✔ **Riding to the Tigris** *Freya Stark 1959*
A description of her travels in the Hakkiari and Zab Valleys in Iraq.

✔ **The Marsh Arabs** *Wilfred Thesiger 1964*
A book about the fast disappearing people who live in the marshes in Iraq, around the junction of the Tigris and Euphrates. Thesiger spent eight years living among them and visited practically every small village; the book describes in interesting detail his love for the people and his knowledge of the area. Many of the floating islands on which the Marsh Arabs lived were man-made, their houses were made of reeds and the economy was based largely on herds of water buffalo. One of the many groups of people who Saddam Husain has now virtually eliminated.

Return to the Marshes *Gavin Young* 1977
Gavin Young was introduced to the marshes
of Southern Iraq by Wilfred Thesiger in the
1950s; here he describes how much their
lives had changed by the time he returned in
the 1970s and also writes about their background and history. He calls it 'a memorial to
my Marsh Arab friends'.

ISRAEL

'The word Palestine always brought to my
mind a vague suggestion of a country as
large as the United States. I do not know
why, but such was the case. I suppose it
was because I could not conceive of a small
country having so large a history.' Mark
Twain *The Innocents Abroad* 1869

Art and Archaeology

✔ **A Guide to the Archaeological Sites
of Israel, Egypt and North Africa**
Courtlandt Canby 1990 (see 'North Africa')

✔ **The Holy Land**
Jerome Murphy-O'Connor 1992 (1980)
An archaeological guide from the earliest
times up to 1700 and includes Jewish underground systems, Roman temples and Byzantine and Crusader buildings. Fairly detailed
but very accessible.

**Archaeological Encyclopedia of the
Holy Land** *Avraham Negev (ed.)* 1972
Over 600 entries, many illustrated, covering
the Holy Land and its history from the earliest times.

Fiction

✔ **Children at the Gate**
Lynne Reid Banks 1988 (1968)
A Jewish-Canadian divorcee is living alone
in poverty in the Arab quarter of Acre;
through an Arab friend she re-establishes
herself and finds happiness. Lynne Reid
Banks also wrote *Defy the Wilderness*, set in
Jerusalem, and *An End to Running*, about
life on a kibbutz.

Penguin Book of Hebrew Verse
T. Carmi (ed.) 1981
An anthology with parallel texts dating from
biblical times to the present day.

✔ **See Under: Love** *David Grossman*
1991 (1989)
A wide ranging imaginative novel which
tackles the worst horrors of the twentieth

century: 'A brave and moving attempt by an
outstandingly talented writer to redefine
love, having looked the Facts of Death full in
the face.' (Clive Sinclair, *The Independent*)

The Little Drummer Girl *John Le Carré*
1983
A spy-novel about the Israeli–Palestinian
conflict.

✔ **The Hill of Evil Counsel** *Amos Oz*
1993 (1976)
Three stories, a mixture of history and narrative, which take place in Jerusalem during
the last days of the British Mandate. Novels
by Amos Oz include *My Michael* 1991(1968),
a love story set in Jerusalem before Suez, and
A Perfect Peace 1993 (1985), in which Yona-
ton Lifshitz leaves his kibbutz and marriage
to start a new life.

The Penitent *Isaac Bashevis Singer* 1983
A rich businessman gives up his lifestyle,
goes to Israel and marries a rabbi's daughter.

✔ **The Mandelbaum Gate** *Muriel Spark*
1967 (1965)
Barbara Vaughan visits Jerusalem and
meets a diplomat, Freddy Hamilton; she ignores his warnings that she might be arrested because of her Jewish blood and
promptly disappears in Jordan.

Exodus *Leon Uris* 1958
A blockbuster novel about Palestine and
Zionism.

✔ **Absence of Pain** *Barbara Victor* 1990
(1988)
Maggie Sommers is a journalist in the Middle
East; she had assured herself that she
wanted nothing more to do with love, but
then meets a married Israeli general, Avi
Herzog. 'Stark, witty, raw realism that
leaves you gasping for air.' (*Washington Post*)

General Background

To Jerusalem and Back *Saul Bellow*
1976
Saul Bellow's personal impressions on his
journey to Jerusalem.

✔ **Against the Stranger**
Janine di Giovanni 1994 (1993)
A weaving together of the lives and deaths of
Arabs and Israelis since the Palestinian uprising in 1987: 'An excellent primer on what
it is like to live in one of the lousiest places
on earth'. (GQ)

✔ **In the Land of Israel** *Amos Oz* 1983
Amos Oz looked at his country as a tourist,
in order to get to the bottom of the fears,

hopes and prejudices of his fellow countrymen.

The Slopes of Lebanon Amos Oz 1991 (1990)
A collection of pieces by Amos Oz who is increasingly writing non-fiction. The *Washington Post* said of him 'Countries need writers as their voices of conscience; few have them. Israel is one of the few. It has Amos Oz . . . ' This selection contains, among others, Oz's thoughts on the Israeli president's visit to Germany, Claude Lanzmann's film *Shoah: An Oral History of the Holocaust* 'the most powerful film I have ever seen. It is a creation that transforms the viewer,' and the Lebanon War.

Guides

✔ **Baedeker's Historical Palestine**
1985
The reprint of the classic Baedeker which was published in 1912.

✔ **Kibbutz Volunteer** John Bedford 1990 (1978)
A guide which tells you about kibbutzim, where they are and how to apply to them.

✔ **Berlitz Discover Israel** 1993

✔ **Blue Guide Jerusalem** 1989

✔ **Discovery Guide to Jordan and the Holy Land** Diana Darke 1993

✔ **Israel. The Rough Guide** Shirley Eber and Kevin O'Sullivan 1989

✔ **Israel. Insight Guide** 1992

✔ **The Heart of Jerusalem**
Arlynn Nellhaus 1988
Aimed at short and long-term visitors.

✔ **Guide to the Holy Land** Theoderich
1986 (1897)
A reprint of a guide which was written for pilgrims in about 1172.

✔ **Israel. Travel Survival Kit**
Neil Tilbury 1992 (1989)

✔ **Let's Go Greece, Israel and Egypt**
1995
Updated annually.

History

O Jerusalem Larry Collins and Dominique Lapierre 1972
The book is based on interviews and is the account of the 1948 siege of Jerusalem and the War of Independence.

✔ **Personal Witness** Abba Eban 1993 (1992)
The history of Israel as seen through the eyes of Abba Eban who has always been close to the centre of what has happened since the foundation of the state.

✔ **Imperial Israel** Michael Palumbo 1992 (1990)
A well researched account of the history of the occupation of the West Bank and Gaza.

Religion

✔ **The Dead Sea Scrolls Uncovered**
Robert Eisenman and Michael Wise 1993 (1992)
A complete translation and interpretation of fifty key documents which were withheld for thirty-five years. They show what was happening in Palestine at the dawn of Christianity.

Travel Literature

Disraeli's Grand Tour: Benjamin Disraeli in the Holy Land 1830–51
Robert Blake 1982
Based on the diaries that Disraeli wrote during his tour of the Holy Land.

✔ **Winner Takes All. A Season in Israel** Stephen Brook 1991 (1990)
The combination of part travel and part background history and politics makes this an ideal book to take on a trip to Israel, or indeed to read as an introduction to the country.

✔ **Jerusalem. City of Mirrors**
Amos Elon 1990 (1989)
A biography of Jerusalem which charts the history of the city with its violent conflicts and religious wars and shows how these conflicts are reflected in the life of the city today.

✔ **Travels with Myself and Another**
Martha Gellhorn 1991 (1978) (see 'East Africa', 'China' and 'Caribbean')
In Eilath, Martha Gellhorn came across a group of hippies; she has a wonderful ear for the conversations she had with them as to why they were travelling: 'Three words sufficed for the experience of travel: great, beautiful, heavy.'

In the Steps of the Master H.V. Morton
1984 (1934)
Somewhat dated travelogue, but nonetheless interesting.

Jerusalem Colin Thubron 1969
A history of the city and a look at why it became so important to so many different

people, as well as an account of Thubron's own time there. 'The best evocation of that magical city I have ever come across.' (Jeremy Paxman)

JORDAN

'Match me such marvel save in Eastern clime
A rose-red city –"half as old as time"!'
J.W. Burgon *Petra* 1845

Art and Archaeology

The Antiquities of Jordan
Gerald Lankester Harding 1967 (1959)
An invaluable guide to the history and archaeological sites of Jordan. Begins with a general history and continues with site-by-site surveys.

Jawa: Lost City of the Black Desert
Svend W. Helms 1981
This short lived, fourth millenium BC city, which only lasted for one generation, was able to function in the arid black desert of NE Jordan because of its complex hydro-technology. The book demonstrates the reconstruction of the city.

General Background

✔ **Jewels of the Kingdom. The Heritage of Jordan** *Peter Vine* 1987
An illustrated book divided into the Past, Natural History, Traditions, Art and Artists, and Modern Jordan.

Guides

✔ **Discovery Guide to Jordan and the Holy Land** *Diana Darke* 1993

✔ **Jordan: An Insight Guide** 1994

✔ **Jordan and Syria. Travel Survival Kit** *Hugh Finlay and Damien Simonis* 1993

✔ **Petra. A Guide to the Capital of the Nabataeans** *Rami G. Khouri* 1986
A concise and comprehensive guide.

✔ **Petra. A Traveller's Guide**
Rosaly Maqsood 1994

Jordan: a MEED practical guide
Trevor Mostyn (ed.) 1983
Now out of print and somewhat out of date, nevertheless useful for background information for business and other travellers.

✔ **An Insight and Guide to Jordan**
Christine Osborne 1981
Aimed at the general traveller, with a detailed section on history and a, by now out of date, section of practical hints on accommodation and travel.

History

Uneasy Lies the Head
HM King Hussein of Jordan 1962
King Hussein writes about the ten-year period between 1951, when his grandfather was assassinated until 1961, when he married. It is interesting to read his account of Glubb Pasha's dismissal in 1956 and of the particularly turbulent period between 1956 and 1960.

The Brink of Jordan   *Charles Johnston*
1972
The author was British ambassador between 1956 and 1960 – a time of endless coups, assassinations and plots. He has great knowledge of the area and writes with insight about those troubled times

The Hashemite Kings   *James Morris* 1959
Morris' book is more concerned with the history of the area and its relationship with Britain between 1916 and 1958, than the individual Hashemite kings, although he does write about several of the Jordanian monarchs in detail. He became interested in the area after representing the *Manchester Guardian* at a press conference in Amman at which King Hussein announced with tears in his eyes that his cousin King Feisal II had been assassinated.

Caravan Cities   *Michael I. Rostovtzeff* 1932
The ruined cities of Petra and Jerash which both featured in the caravan trade are described here and their importance on the trade route is assessed.

✔ **The History of the Crusades**
Steven Runciman   Vol.2 1987 (1952)
The second volume in the trilogy, *The Kingdom of Jerusalem and the Frankish East 1100–1187*, starts with the foundation of the Kingdom of Jerusalem and ends with its reconquest by Saladin. It contains information about the crusader period in trans-Jordan after the fall of Jerusalem.

✔ **The Modern History of Jordan**
Kamal Salibi 1993
A political history of Jordan which shows how the poor and sparsely populated country became one of the most successful in the Middle East.

Leisure

✔ **Treks and Climbs in the Mountains of Rum and Petra, Jordan**
Tony Howard   1987
Line drawings and brief notes about trekking and climbing in Jordan.

Natural History

Portrait of a Desert: the story of an expedition to Jordan   *Guy Mountfort   1965*
One of the aims of the expedition was to find out about the environmental situation in Jordan; the findings suggested the creation of three national parks. There are descriptions of birds and animals.

Photography

✔ **Jerash and the Decapolis**
Iain Browning   1982
Jerash is the best preserved city of the Decapolis; its history, architecture and early explorers are described here and the text is accompanied by many photographs.

Petra   *Iain Browning   1989 (1973)*
Browning describes the importance of Petra on the trade routes, its history as the Nabatean capital, its early explorers and later scientific ones and the significance of the six major architectural periods. The text is accompanied by many photographs and line drawings.

✔ **High Above Jordan**   *Jane Taylor   1990 (1989)*
Aerial photographs of Jordan.

✔ **Petra**   *Jane Taylor   1993*
A large photographic book with ample text.

Travel Literature

The Letters of Gertrude Bell
Florence Bell (ed.)   1927
The first desert journeys that Gertrude Bell undertook were into Jordan; she visited Petra in 1900 and the first of her two-volume collection of letters is about this trip.

The Vanished Cities of Arabia
Mrs Steuart Erskine   1925
Descriptions of the lost cities of Petra, Jerash and the Decapolis, in the days when very little archaeological exploration had taken place.

✔ **The Rob Roy on the Jordan**
John Macgregor   1904
The author went in a canoe down the River Jordan to the Dead Sea. [John Keay]

The Lovely Land: the Hashemite Kingdom of Jordan   *Ethel Mannin   1965*
A personal and readable account of a trip to Jordan in the 1960s.

LEBANON

'At Baalbec, as at other eastern ruins, a traveller must luxuriate on the pleasures of imagination, for he will get no luxury more substantial.' John Carne *Letters from the East* 1830

Biography

An Arab Tells His Story: A Study in Loyalties   *Edward Atiyah   1946*
The author was born in Lebanon, although he was educated in the West; he writes movingly about the changes that have occurred for Lebanese Christians since the end of the Ottoman Empire at the beginning of this century.

Lady Hester Stanhope: Queen of the Desert   *Virginia Childs   1990*
Lady Hester spent most of her life in Syria and Lebanon. She was extremely independent and was very concerned about the welfare of the people of the countries in which she lived. She died in the Lebanon in 1839.

Holding On   *Sunnie Mann   1990*
Sunnie Mann wrote this book during her husband's two-year disappearance; it is a moving story of what it was like to live in post-Second World War Beirut, the changes that the 1975 war brought and the struggle learning to cope with her husband's absence.

Fiction

Death in Beirut   *Tawfiq Yusuf Awwad   1976*
A young Shi'i Muslim girl from the south of Lebanon goes to study in Beirut; set against the rising tension in Lebanon at the time.

✔ **The Return to Beirut**   *Andrée Chedid   1989 (1985)*
Set in Beirut in 1975, when Lebanon is on the brink of civil war, an American girl, Sybil, meets her grandmother, Kalya, for the first time; Kalya recalls through a series of flashbacks, times she spent with her own grandmother.

✔ **A Woman of Nazareth**
Hala Deeb Jabbour   1992 (1989)
Set in Beirut in the 1960s and 1970s, the
story of a Palestinian woman in exile and her
struggles to come to terms with the limita-
tions of a traditional life.

✔ **Little Mountain**   *Elias Khoury*
Translated by Maria Tabet   1990 (1989)
Set in Beirut during the civil war in 1975–6,
the novel examines how society disintegrates
during a conflict, in a mixture of surrealism
and reality.

The Story of Zahra   *Hanan al-Shaykh   1986*
The story of a young girl from the south of
Lebanon; part of it is set among the Lebanese
community in West Africa, but it finishes
during the Lebanese civil war.

Food

✔ **Food for the Vegetarian.**
Traditional Lebanese Recipes
Aidda Karaoglan   1992

✔ **A Taste of Lebanon. Cooking Today**
the Lebanese Way   *Mary Salloum   1992*
The first book devoted entirely to Lebanese
cooking. Over 200 recipes including pita
bread, yogourt, hommous, tabouli, baklava
and burghul.

General Background

Beirut Spy   *Saïd K. Aburish   1990 (1989)*
Much of the intrigue and gossip in post-war
Beirut took place in the bar of the Hotel
Saint-Georges, until it was blown up in 1975.
The man who was general manager in the
1960s said of it 'a unique, once-a-century
happening. I felt as if my clients were running the Middle East, occasionally the world.'
Aburish recounts much of what happened
there but holds back that which he believes
is still not safe to tell.

✔ **An Evil Cradling**   *Brian Keenan   1993*
(1992)
The harrowing account of Brian Keenan's
four-and-a-half years in captivity at the
hands of Shi'ite militiamen.

The Slopes of Lebanon   *Amos Oz   1991*
(1990) (see 'Israel')

Guide

Touring Lebanon   *Philip Ward   1971*
Wildly out of date, but apart from some
French guides this is about the only one

available in English; it is still of use for the
descriptions of sites and monuments.

History

Syria and Lebanon   *Robin Fedden   1965*
A very readable history of post-Second World
War Syria and Lebanon.

✔ **Pity the Nation**   *Robert Fisk   1991*
The veteran Middle East reporter's account
of the war in Lebanon and the troubled years
that followed its outbreak. Fisk analyses how
the Lebanon is enmeshed with the Israeli–
Palestinian conflict.

Lebanon: the Fractured Country
David Gilmour   1984 (1983)
Gilmour traces the conflicts in the Lebanon
back to their origins, with carefully researched historical analysis and first-hand
experience of the fate of the country.

A Short History of Lebanon
Philip K. Hitti   1965
Begins with ancient Lebanon, Syria and Palestine and continues through the history of
the Phoenician, Roman, Byzantine, Moslem,
Crusader and Ottoman eras, up until the
nineteenth century.

Natural History

The Birds of Britain and Europe with
North Africa and the Middle East
Hermann Heinzel, Richard Fitter and John Parslow
1979 (see 'Middle East –General')

✔ **Flowers of the Mediterranean**
Oleg Polunin and Anthony Huxley   (see 'Turkey')

Photography

Baalbek   *Friedrich Ragette   1980*
The history of Baalbek which was known to
the Ancient Greeks as Heliopolis is described
and illustrated. It was the centre of worship
of the Sun God cult and later had Roman,
Byzantine and Arab additions.

Religion

✔ **The Prophet**   *Kahil Gibran   1991 (1926)*
Although Gibran emigrated to the USA, he
was born in the Lebanon.

Travel Literature

The Nun of Lebanon: the Love Affair of Lady Hester Stanhope and Michael Bruce *Ian Bruce (ed.) 1951*
When this book appeared Lady Hester Stanhope's letters had only just been discovered. Apart from telling a wonderful story the letters give interesting insights into nineteenth century Lebanon and Syria.

Letters from Syria *Freya Stark 1942*
Written to her mother and friends after her arrival in the Middle East for the first time; the book begins with letters from Lebanon.

✔ **The Hills of Adonis** *Colin Thubron 1987 (1968)*
The account of a walking trip into the Lebanese mountains in 1967.

SYRIA

'Most perfect of medieval fortresses (and model for every sandcastle ever built). Peter Wilsher *The Sunday Times* 30 December 1979 [About The Crac des Chevaliers]

Art and Archaeology

Palmyra *Iain Browning 1979*
A survey of Palmyra which became famous as a trading centre in 106 AD; Browning describes many of the later travellers to the site including Lady Hester Stanhope who was there in 1813. Well illustrated with colour photographs.

Biography

In Aleppo Once *Taqui Altounyan 1969*
The writer was the granddaughter of Dr Alam Altounyam who was one of the founder's of Aleppo's main hospitals.

Lady Hester Stanhope: Queen of the Desert. *Virginia Childs 1990 (see 'Lebanon')*

Asad of Syria: The Struggle for the Middle East *Patrick Seale 1988*
A biography of Asad which shows what the world looks like from the seat of power in Damascus.

Fiction

✔ **Said the Fisherman**
Marmaduke Pickthall 1986 (1903)
The story of a corrupt Muslim fisherman who goes to Damascus to seek his fortune in the summer of 1860 at the time of a massacre of Christians by Muslims and Druze; Said takes advantage of this and abducts the daughter of a Christian merchant. He makes his fortune selling carpets and after many intrigues finally meets his death whilst upholding his faith. Pickthall's contemporaries wrote of his work: ' . . . in imagination he goes native. And that thoroughly,' D.H. Lawrence: ' . . . the only contemporary English novelist who understands the nearer East,' E.M. Forster. And ironically H.G. Wells wrote: ' I wish I could feel as certain about my own work as I do of yours, that it will be alive and interesting people fifty years from now.'

Food

✔ **The Art of Syrian Cookery**
Helen Corey 1992 (1962)
Over 250 Syrian and Lebanese recipes including kibby, shish-kebab and stuffed vine leaves.

General Background

Syria *Tabitha Petran 1972*
A detailed introduction to the geography, history, economy and politics of Syria.

Guides

Syria. A History and Architectural Guide *W. Ball 1995*

✔ **Monuments of Syria** *Ross Burns 1994 (1992)*
Invaluable guide to the historical sites of Syria, arranged alphabetically and accompanied by maps and plans. Essential for anyone interested in Syria.

✔ **Jordan and Syria. Travel Survival Kit** *Hugh Finlay and Damien Simonis 1993*

History

Syria: A Short History *Philip K. Hitti 1959*
Much of the book is about the Arab Revolt and the establishment of the French Mandate.

Mirror to Damascus *Colin Thubron 1986 (1967)*
The history of Damascus from Biblical times until the revolution in 1966. Although James Morris wrote 'Damascus is not a sophisticated city. Those westerners who do not sub-

scribe to the brittle charm of its Arab quarters are likely to find it something of a hick town', Thubron manages to find it and describe it as a fascinating place and calls his book 'simply work of love'.

Natural History

✔ **Flowers of the Mediterranean**
Oleg Polunin and Anthony Huxley   (see 'Turkey')

Photography

✔ **Syria in View**   Michael Jenner   1986
Chapters on Syria's early past, the Aramaeans, Phoenicians, Greeks and Romans, Christianity, the monuments of Syria, the Umayyads and the Dawn of Islam and the legacy of the crusades. Well illustrated.

Syria: Land of Contrasts   Peter Lewis
1980
A guide to the main sites of Syria, accompanied by many photographs.

Travel Literature

Ibn Battuta. Travels in Asia and Africa 1325–1354   (see 'North Africa –Algeria and Sahara')
Ibn Battuta came from Tangier to Syria in 1325 and describes Aleppo, Antioch and Damascus.

From Amurath to Amurath
Gertrude Bell   1924 (see 'Iraq')

The Desert and the Sown   Gertrude Bell
1985 (1907)
Gertrude Bell's life was dominated by the Arab world; she was brave, had fantastic stamina and was a good linguist. She undertook archaeological excavations, but in 1915 at the outbreak of war she was asked by the British government to join the Arab Bureau in Cairo to gather intelligence to mobilize the Arabs against Turkey. In 1916 she went to India, then to Basra and after the war to Baghdad where she founded the national museum in 1923. She was a great admirer of Lady Anne Blunt, wanting to follow her footsteps into unknown areas of Arabia. *The Desert and the Sown* is an account of her journey into the Syrian interior (which in those days comprised the present day Syria, Lebanon, Jordan, Israel and the occupied West Bank and Gaza strip).

Travels in Syria and the Holy Land
John Lewis Burckhardt   1822
The Swiss explorer, Burckhardt, lived in

Aleppo while he was preparing for his major expeditions and during that time he travelled widely throughout Syria.

Syria and Lebanon   Robin Fedden   1965
A very readable travelogue of post-Second World War Syria and Lebanon in which the author describes the major sites and gives their potted histories.

✔ **Come, tell me how you live**
Agatha Christie Mallowan   1990 (1946) (see 'Iraq')

Letters from Syria
Freya Stark (see 'Lebanon')

TURKEY
'I have fallen a hopeless victim to the Turk; he is the most charming of mortals and some day, when I have a little more of his language, we shall be very intimate friends, I foresee.' Gertrude Bell, letter to her family 21 April 1905

Anthropology

Everyday Life in Ottoman Turkey
Raphaela Lewis   1971
Interesting insights into what life was like during the days of the Ottoman Empire.

Art & Archaeology

✔ **Aegean Turkey**   1989 (1966)
✔ **Turkey's Southern Shore**   1989 (1968)
✔ **Turkey Beyond the Maeander**
1989 (1971)
✔ **Lycian Turkey**   1989 (1978)
The definitive series of archaeological guides to south-wast Turkey; all include maps and plans.

✔ **The Antiquities of Constantinople**
Pierre Gilles   1988 (1729)
Gilles visited Constantinople in 1544 when it was the largest and wealthiest city in the western world; his book tries to reconstruct the city in the age of Justinian as well as telling us what it was like in the sixteenth century.

✔ **A History of Ottoman Architecture**   Godfrey Goodwin   1992
A comprehensive guide to Ottoman architecture covering the whole of Turkey.

✔ **Caves of God. Cappadocia and its Churches**   Spiro Kostof   1989 (1972)
A guide and explanation to the hundreds of

monasteries and churches in Christian Cappadocia.

✔ Early Christian and Byzantine Architecture   Richard Krautheimer   1986 (1965)

A wide ranging and overall view of the history and changing character of Early Christian and Byzantine architecture; in the Pelican History of Art series.

Ancient Turkey – A Traveller's History of Anatolia   Seton Lloyd   1992 (1989)

The author was head of the British Archaeological Institute in Ankara and has written an indispensable book on the ancient sites and civilizations of Turkey.

✔ Byzantine Style and Civilization
Steven Runciman   1990 (1975)

Runciman defines and describes eleven centuries of art in the Byzantine world culminating with the jewelled mosaics which aimed 'to increase the understanding of the divine beyond the finite limits of the human mind'.

✔ Turkey. A Traveller's Historical and Architectural Guide   James Steele   1990

Illustrated with plans and colour photographs.

✔ Islamic Art   David Talbot Rice   (see 'Middle East – General')

A good far-reaching introduction to the subject.

Biography

Atatürk: the Rebirth of a Nation
Lord Kinross   1990 (1964)

A very readable account of Atatürk's life which gives a clear picture of the birth of the Turkish Republic. 'By far the most thorough study of Atatürk in English and an absorbing biography in its own right.' (*The Times*)

✔ Portrait of a Turkish Family
Irfan Orga   1990 (1950)

The author was born into a prosperous family under the Sultans, but with the advent of the First World War, the family was ruined and Turkey transformed. Irfan Orga finally came to London in 1941 and wrote the moving story of his family's survival.

✔ Scenes from an Armenian Childhood   Vahan Totovents   1980

The author grew up in a town which lay on the old Roman road from Byzantium to Babylon; his account of his childhood in the 1880s is delightful, but has an added poignancy in that we know what happens to the area.

Fiction/Poetry

George Beneath a Paper Moon
Nina Bawden   1975

A mixture of comedy, love story and thriller set between England and Turkey.

Greenmantle   John Buchan   1916

An exciting story which is about the secret service east of Constantinople; the grand climax is set in Erzurum in Eastern Turkey. (Peter Hopkirk)

✔ Murder on the Orient Express
Agatha Christie   1990 (1933)

Although mostly about the journey to Turkey, there are some scenes set in Turkey itself.

The Fall of an Eagle   Jon Cleary   1964

A thriller set in eastern Turkey.

The Life of the Party   Maureen Freely   1985

Set in Istanbul in 1969, the story takes place around an American college.

Count Belisarius   Robert Graves   1970 (1938)

An historical novel about Belisarius, a cavalry commander and Christian, who was born in 500 AD and for whom the centre of the world was Constantinople.

✔ Stamboul Train   Graham Greene   1975 (1932)

A spy thriller set aboard the Orient Express which crosses Europe from Ostend to Constantinople.

America, America   Elia Kazan   1962

A Greek boy in Constantinople tries to save enough money from his carpet business to get to America.

✔ Mehmed My Hawk   Yasar Kemal   1992 (1955)

Set in Anatolia as are its sequels: *They Burn the Thistles* and *The Lords of Akchasaz: Murder in Ironsmith's Market*. *The Sea-Crossed Fishermen* is set in a fishing village near Istanbul where an old man is trying to save dolphins.

✔ The Book of Dede Korkut
Geoffrey L Lewis (ed.)   1974

The national epic of Turkey; a collection of twelve stories set in the heroic age of the Oghuz Turks.

✔ Aziyade   Pierre Loti   1989 (1927)

A tale of romance and intrigue in nineteenth-century Ottoman Turkey. Loti vividly evokes a vanished world, as Lafcadio Hearn wrote: 'Constantinople and the romantic Golden

Horn have never been portrayed with such elegance'.

✔ **The Towers of Trebizond**
Rose Macaulay 1956
The book opens with a much quoted sentence: '"Take my camel, dear" said my Aunt Dot, as she climbed down from this animal on her return from High Mass.' The story is about a group of people who set out with a camel to explore the possibilities of a proposed Anglican mission to Turkey. Two of the party vanish into Soviet Russia, causing a scandal.

✔ **The Prizegiving** *Aysel Özakin 1988 (1980)*
The author now lives in Germany, but in this novel written in Turkey before she left, she questions the institution of marriage. Nuray goes to Ankara to receive a prize for her first novel, but she is haunted by disturbing memories, discovering that prizes are not always what they seem.

✔ **Under a Crescent Moon**
Daniel de Souza 1989
Vignettes from prison by a jailed foreigner; remarkable for its optimism and lack of bitterness.

Julian *Gore Vidal 1976 (1954)*
Based on the life of the Emperor Julian, Vidal has stayed close to the facts found in the three volumes of his letters and essays which have survived. Julian attempted to stop Christianity and revive Hellenism ensuring that he kept cropping up in odd places throughout history. Much of the novel takes place in what is modern-day Turkey.

Food

✔ **The Art of Turkish Cooking**
Neset Eren 1993 (1969)

✔ **Nevin Halici's Turkish Cookbook**
1989
A selection of regional dishes from all over Turkey.

General Background

The Owl's Watchsong *John A. Cuddon*
Life in Istanbul in the 1950s. [Colin Thubron]

Guides

✔ **Turkey. The Rough Guide**
Rosie Ayliffe, Marc Dubin and John Gawthrop 1994 (1991)

✔ **Turkey. A Travel Survival Kit**
Tom Brosnahan 1993 (1985)

✔ **Discovery Guide to Eastern Turkey and the Black Sea Coast** *Diana Darke 1990*

✔ **Guide to Aegean and Mediterranean Turkey** *Diana Darke 1989*
Diana Darke acknowledges her debt to George Bean as a primary source at the beginning of the book, which is an easy-to-read and useful guide.

✔ **Everyman Guide Istanbul** *1993*

✔ **Cadogan Guide Turkey** *Dana Facaros and Michael Pauls 1993 (1986)*

✔ **Fodor's Turkey** *1993*

✔ **Blue Guide Istanbul** *John Freely 1987*

✔ **The Companion Guide to Turkey**
John Freely 1989 (1979)

✔ **Introduction to Turkey. An Odyssey Guide** *Gilbert Horobin 1991*

✔ **Insight Guide Istanbul** *1991*

✔ **Insight Guide Turkey** *1993*

✔ **Insight Guide Turkish Coast** *1992*

✔ **Istanbul. A Traveller's Companion**
Laurence Kelly 1989
An anthology of selected writings about Istanbul past and present with various aspects of the city and giving a feeling for it during all the different periods of history.

✔ **Strolling through Istanbul**
Hilary Sumner-Boyd and John Freely 1987
The classic and invaluable guide for walking around the city. [Colin Thubron]

✔ **Imperial Istanbul: Iznik–Bursa–Edirne** *Jane Taylor 1989*
A very detailed guide to the four imperial cities.

History

✔ **The Voyage of the Argo**
Apollonius of Rhodes Translated by E.V. Rieu 1971
The account of Jason's voyage along the Black Sea coast.

✔ **The Campaigns of Alexander**
Arrian Translated by Aubrey de Selincourt 1971
Even though this was written 400 years after Alexander the Great's death it remains probably the most reliable account of his character and achievements. Arrian himself had been a military commander.

✔ **The Alexiad of Anna Comnena**
Anna Comnena   Translated by E.R.A. Sewter   1969
A history of the reign of the Emperor Alexius
I by his daughter, a Byzantine princess who
was one of the first, if not *the* first woman
historian; it includes an account of the first
crusade from 'the other side'.

✔ **Chronicles of the Crusades**   *Joinville*
and Villehardouin   Translated by M.R.B. Shaw
1963
The two French chronicles were written by
soldiers who took part in the Crusades. Villehardouin writes a straightforward account
of the Fourth Crusade and Joinville's *Life of
Saint Louis* shows his close attachment to
the king.

**The Ottoman Centuries. The Rise and
Fall of the Turkish Empire**
Lord Kinross   1977
A thorough all-encompassing book about the
rise of the Turkish Empire with its changing
fortunes and boundaries and its subsequent
fall, abolition of the sultanate and declara-
tion of a republic in 1923.

The Emergence of Modern Turkey
Bernard Lewis   1968 (1961)
A thorough and interesting book which is
mostly about the hundred years between
1850 and 1950 and which describes the emergence of a new Turkey from the decay of the
old. The first part is a chronological history
and the second examines four aspects of this
change: the transformation of the corporate
sense of identity and loyalty among the
Turks, the transformation of the theory and
practice of government, of religion and the
cultural life and of the economic and social
order.

✔ **Gallipoli**   *Alan Moorehead   1967 (1956)*
'Essentially the great question remains: Who
will hold Constantinople?' (Napoleon). Until
as late as August 1914 it was by no means
obvious that Turkey was going to go into the
First World War on the German side; the
background to Gallipoli is examined by
Moorehead along with details of the campaign itself.

✔ **Byzantium: the Early Centuries**
John Julius Norwich   1990 (1988)
A narrative history about the five formative
centuries and beginnings of Byzantium and
the Byzantine empire. Full of detail and yet
very readable: 'He is brilliant . . . He writes
like the most cultivated modern diplomat
attached by a freak of time to the Byzantine
court, with intimate knowledge, tactful
judgement and a consciousness of the surviving monuments.' (*The Independent*)

War and Revolution in Asiatic Russia
Morgan Philips Price   1918
'A powerful and moving account of the war in
eastern Turkey, Persia and the Caucasus in
1915–16 by the *Manchester Guardian* correspondent, with Russian armies fighting the
Turks. Includes vivid and evocative descriptions of eastern Turkey in the terrible grip of
winter and enchantment of spring.' (Peter
Hopkirk)

✔ **The Secret History**   *Procopius*
Translated by G.A. Williamson   1981 (1966)
Procopius who lived in the sixth century AD
was the official historian to the emperor;
however, after he had written the official
history, he wrote this 'Secret History' which
is full of salacious gossip and tales of the
murky happenings at the courts of Justinian
and Theodora.

✔ **The Fall of Constantinople 1453**
Steven Runciman   1992 (1965)
Western Christendom was unprepared for
the fall of Constantinople in 1453 after a
siege which lasted several weeks; the plight
of the city had been neglected, whereas for
the Turks it meant that the survival of their
empire was ensured. The classic book on the
subject.

✔ **A History of the Crusades**
✔ **Vol.1 The First Crusade and the
Foundation of the Kingdom of
Jerusalem**
✔ **Vol.2 The Kingdom of Jerusalem
and the Frankish East 1100–1187**   *1990
(1952)*
✔ **Vol.3 The Kingdom of Acre and the
Later Crusades**   *Steven Runciman   1978
(1954)*
The classic trilogy of books on the Crusades.
Volume 1 starts at the beginning, through
the preaching of the First Crusade up to the
triumphant establishment of the Kingdom of
Jerusalem. The main theme of volume 2 is
warfare and tells the story of the Frankish
states of Outremer from the accession of King
Baldwin I to the reconquest of Jerusalem by
Saladin. Volume 3 describes the revival
through the Third Crusade of the Frankish
Kingdom of Jerusalem and its fall a century
later with the accompanying degeneration of
Crusading ideals.

✔ **A Traveller's History of Turkey**
Richard Stoneman   1993
A short and readable history of the region
from Prehistory until the present day; the
book includes an historical gazetteer, a chronology of major events, historical maps and
famous battles.

Armenia: The Survival of a Nation
Christopher Walker   1980
'From the earliest period to the present hour,
Armenia has been the theatre of perpetual
war.' (Edward Gibbon *The Decline and Fall
of the Roman Empire*) The dispersal of Armenians world-wide has an ancient precedent,
although this 'ëspiurk' has not on the whole
been voluntary, but has been characterized
by invasion, massacre and misrule. Christopher Walker looks sympathetically at their
history.

✔ **The Ottomans**   *Andrew Wheatcroft   1993*
A reinterpretation of the Ottomans and their
culture and a look at the inner life of the
Ottoman world as seen through Western
eyes.

✔ **Turkey. A Modern History**
Erik J. Zürcher   1994 (1993)
A new comprehensive and scholarly guide.

Leisure

✔ **Trekking in Turkey. A Lonely
Planet Trekking Guide**   *Marc Dubin and
Enver Lucas*
Both long and short walks which cover much
of Turkey.

✔ **Turkey and the Dodecanese
Cruising Pilot**   *Robin Petherbridge   1985*
Practical facts on the harbours and anchor-
ages with plans and charts.

✔ **The Ala Dag. Climbs and Treks in
Turkey's Crimson Mountains**
O.B. Tuzel   1993

Natural History

✔ **Flowers of the Mediterranean**
Oleg Polunin and Anthony Huxley   1987 (1965)
Western Turkey is included in this illus-
trated guide to over 700 plants.

✔ **Mediterranean Wildlife. The Rough
Guide**   *Pete Raine   1990*
Where to see birds, plants and other wildlife.
The first half describes the species and the
second half is arranged under area by
country.

Photography

✔ **Splendours of the Bosphorus.
Houses and Palaces of Istanbul**
Chris Hellier and Francesco Venturi   1993
A lavishly illustrated book depicting the
houses on the Bosphorus and showing many
architectural details.

✔ **Turkey**   *Roland and Sabrina Michaud   1986*
A well illustrated photographic book.

Religion

✔ **A Time to Keep Silence**
Patrick Leigh Fermor   1988 (1957)
In his book about religious orders and re-
treats Patrick Leigh Fermor visits the Rock
Monasteries of Cappadocia.

Travel Literature

On Horseback through Asia Minor
Frederick Burnaby   1985 (1877)
Burnaby travelled on a Great Game mission
by horse in the winter of 1876.

✔ **A Traveller on Horseback in
Eastern Turkey and Iran**
Christina Dodwell   1992 (1987)
Christina Dodwell travelled from Eastern
Turkey to Cappadocia, Iran and Pakistan by
horse; on her way back she went up to the
Russian border at Mount Ararat.

✔ **Journey to Kars**   *Philip Glazebrook*
1985 (1984)
Intrigued by all the ancient travellers to Turkey, Philip Glazebrook made his own trip to
eastern Turkey, following their routes
through the ruined cities of Asia Minor.

✔ **On Foot to the Golden Horn. A
Walk to Istanbul**   *Jason Goodwin   1993*
Although this book records Goodwin's journey through Eastern Europe, since Istanbul
was his aim, it is included here.

✔ **The Histories**   *Herodotus   c.460 BC*
'I wonder if you ever took a look at Herodotus
– which is a wonderful travel book. It was the
only book I carried with me right through the
war (and I still have some of the rags to which
it was reduced).' (Norman Lewis)

My Travels in Turkey   *Denis Hills   1964*
Wanderings in and around Turkey between
1955 and 1962. Unusually for the time, he
travelled into the lesser known eastern provinces and in his words 'I have tried to present
Turkey in her true colours, not as a mere
appendage of Istanbul and the classical coastal districts but as a country of countless
small towns and villages scattered over a
great area.'

✔ **The Scholar and the Gypsy. Two
Journeys to Turkey, Past and Present**
James Howard-Johnston and Nigel Ryan   1992
This joint book uses two very different ap-
proaches to the same journey which started
in Trebizond and ranged over remote country

up to the Iranian and Soviet borders. They repeated their experience the following year going into the interior of western Turkey.

Europa Minor   Lord Kinross   1956
A series of journeys made between 1947 and 1954 which ranged from Antioch and the Syrian frontier in the South-east to Adrianople and the Greek frontier in the North-west. Observant and readable.

✔ **The Crossing Place. A Journey Among the Armenians**   Philip Marsden   1994 (1993)
Philip Marsden visited Armenian communities throughout the Middle East, the old Soviet Union and Eastern Europe before arriving in Armenia itself. He quickly succombed to the beauty of Ararat and recognizing the Armenians' passion for their language quotes Mandelstam: 'These are people who jangle the keys of their language even when they are not using them to unlock any treasures'.

Secrets of the Bosphorus
Henry Morgenthau   1918
The US ambassador's account of the dramatic and important events in Constantinople in World War I. [Peter Hopkirk]

East of Trebizond   Michael Pereira
Pereira's travels between the Black Sea and Northeast Anatolia during the 1960s. [Peter Hopkirk]

Ionia – A Quest   Freya Stark   1954
Freya Stark travelled around the western coasts of Asia Minor during the autumn of 1952 visiting fifty-five ruined sites which she describes with a mixture of history and romance; the only tourist she met during that whole trip was in Pergamum. [Colin Thubron] *The Lycian Shore* (1956) is the account of a single journey by sea along the Asia Minor coast in a boat. [Colin Thubron] She also wrote *Alexander's Path* (1991 (1958)) which traces the route Alexander took through Turkey, from Caria to Cilicia, on his way to defeat Darius.

The Innocents Abroad   Mark Twain.
(see 'Egypt')
Many interesting observations about Istanbul.

YEMEN

'Aden should mean oven. Only the camels seemed baked enough to suit it.' Henry Adams, journal letter to Elizabeth Cameron. 29 September, 1891

Autobiography

The Uneven Road   Lord Belhaven   1955
The author was a British officer in Aden. He visited San'a in 1933–34.

Fiction

Treacherous Road   Simon Harvester   1967
A spy novel set between Yemen and Egypt.

✔ **The Long Lost Journey**
Jennifer Potter   1991 (1989)
In 1910 Elinor Grace, an archaeologist, left Aden for Hodeidah, with James Fergusson, to try and discover the truth about the Queen of Sheba's legendary capital at Mareb. The expedition was ill-fated from the beginning; the intrigue has been erased from official files, but Jennifer Potter fills in the gaps: '*The Long Lost Journey* . . . has the compelling force of a nightmare . . . ' (*The Guardian*)

General Background

Farewell Arabia   David Holden   1966
At least half of this book is about the Yemen; it was written at the time when the Yemen entered the twentieth century from the twelfth!

Qat in Yemen   Shelagh Weir   1990
A good introduction to daily life in the Yemen today.

Guides

✔ **Yemen. Travel Survival Kit**
Pertti Hamalainen   1991 (1988)

✔ **Yemen. Insight Guide**   1992

✔ **Yemen. A Pallas Guide**   Peter Wald   1995
An acclaimed and scholarly guide translated from the German. Very clear and fully illustrated with maps, diagrams and many plates.

History

✔ **The Two Yemens**   Robin Bidwell   1983
A history of the Yemen Arab Republic and the People's Democratic Republic of Yemen since the Europeans arrived in the sixteenth century.

Arabia Without Sultans   Fred Halliday   1974
The book has about 180 pages devoted to the recent history of the Yemens.

The Yemen: Imams, Rulers and Revolutions *Harold Ingrams* *1963*
Harold Ingrams was the British Resident Adviser in the Western Aden Protectorate and writes predominantly about Anglo–Yemeni issues.

The View from Steamer Point
Charles Johnston *1964*
The author was three years in Aden between 1960–63, as Governor and High Commissioner. During this time Aden was merged into the Federation of South Arabia.

A History of Arabia Felix or Yemen
Sir Robert Playfair *1970 (1859)*
When Aden, which was described by Ibn Batuta as 'a large city without either seed, water, or tree', became a British possession, there was a sudden renewed interest in the history of the Yemen. Playfair collated the notes which he had made during a long residence in Arabia, starting his work from the beginnings of Christianity as at the time of his writing there was no connected history of the Yemen extant.

Arabian Assignment *David Smiley* *1975*
The second part of Smiley's book deals with his time in the Yemen when he supported the guerillas in their country's fight against the Egyptians in the early 1960s. The UN chose to ignore this invasion, so it is interesting to learn what the situation was like.

Natural History

South Arabian Hunt *R.B. Serjeant* *1976*
An interesting study of the origins and meaning of the ritual ibex hunt, using anthropological fieldwork, and archaeological, epigraphical and literary evidence.

Photography

✔ **Yemen Rediscovered** *Michael Jenner* *1983*
A limited amount of text, but on the whole a well illustrated and good introduction to the Yemen and the Yemenis.

Arabia Felix: the Yemen and its People
Pascal Maréchaux *1979*
Stunning photographs, mostly colour, with ample captions of the Yemen Arab Republic.

San'a – an Arabic Islamic City
R.B. Serjeant and Lewcock *1983*
Vast, expensive and rare, this is the ultimate book on the Yemen, which was published by the World of Islam Festival Trust.

Seen in the Hadramaut *Freya Stark* *1938*
Photographs taken by Freya Stark accompanied by interesting and perceptive captions.

Travel Literature

Island of the Dragon's Blood
Douglas Botting *1958*
An account of the expedition to Socotra under the auspices of the Oxford University Exploration Club.

A French Doctor in the Yemen
Claudie Fayein *1958*

Arabia Felix: the Danish Expedition of 1761–67 *Thorkild Hansen* *1964*
A readable account of the Danish expedition in which everyone lost their lives except for Carsten Niebuhr who then wrote about his experiences.

✔ **A Journey through the Yemen. Some General Remarks upon that Country** *Walter Harris* *1985 (1893)*
A mixture of the political history of the time and a journey through the Yemen, which Harris so enjoyed, despite the hardships, that he wrote 'My recollections of the country are ones that I shall always treasure, in spite of the dangers and sickness, in spite of long marches and days in prison, the Yemen will always be for me, Arabia Felix.'

Aden to the Hadramaut
D. Van Der Meulen *1947*
This journey in Southern Arabia was undertaken by the author in the 1930s.

Travels Through Arabia, and Other Countries in the East *M. Niebuhr*
1792   Translated by Robert Heron
Carsten Niebuhr, one of the first European travellers, was the only survivor in the ill-fated Danish expedition to Egypt and the Yemen which reached Hodeida in 1762. He writes interestingly about the everyday life and flora and fauna that he came across. His story is recounted in *Arabia Felix* by Thorkild Hansen (q.v.).

Arabian Peak and Desert: Travels in Al-Yaman *Ameen Rihani* *1930*
The author was told by a Yemeni he met in New York that it was impossible for a foreigner to travel in the Yemen; firstly the British in Aden would never grant permission and secondly if permission were granted, being there would lead to almost certain death. Nevertheless Rihani managed to travel throughout the Yemen and on reaching San'a was not disappointed: 'No, San'a is not disenchanting. Unlike other

cities, the nearer one gets to it the more powerful is its spell. Beautifully, uniquely situated, its atmosphere is like an Arab poet's fancy, crisp and vigorous.'

Complete Works, Selected Letters
Arthur Rimbaud   Edited and translated by Wallace Fowlie   1975 (see 'Ethiopia' and 'Somalia')
Several of Rimbaud's letters complaining about his life in Aden are printed in this parallel text.

In the High Yemen   *Hugh Scott   1947 (1942)*
A good background book to the Yemen. Scott was a naturalist and this account of his travels from Aden into the Yemen and to San'a and Hodeida is full of interesting information.

✔ The Southern Gates of Arabia
Freya Stark   1990 (1936)
Freya Stark followed the Incense Route inland from the southern shores of Arabia to Tarim in the Hadhramaut. For centuries relays of Bedouin and camels had taken 'incense of Arabia and Africa, tied pearls and muslins from Ceylon and silks from China, Malacca tortoiseshell and spikenard from the Ganges ... and from India, diamonds and sapphires, ivory and cotton, indigo, lapis lazuli, and cinnamon and pepper above all,' to sell in northern markets. [Colin Thubron]

✔ A Winter in Arabia   *Freya Stark   1991 (1940)*
Freya Stark returned to the Hadhramaut in November 1937 and travelled through the desert throughout that winter; her perception of people and objects is acute and often very funny. She writes 'The archaeologist was feverless in the morning and packed our collected pots, and now alas! is in bed again with a temperature. The pots are so depressingly ugly that a prolonged contemplation of them would make anyone ill.'

Arthur Rimbaud in Abyssinia
Enid Starke   1937 (see 'Ethiopia' and 'Somalia')
For the last ten years of his life, Rimbaud was a trader on the Red Sea coast, probably dealing in arms. He was as ambivalent about Aden, where he often went, as he was about Africa and the rest of his life. He wrote to his mother and sister in France, 'Aden is the most boring place in the world, after, however, the one where you live.' (22 September 1880) He felt he was like a prisoner, trapped, only earning six francs a day and thus unable to afford to leave.

A Modern Pilgrim in Mecca, and a Siege in Sanaa   *A.J.B. Wavell   1912*
The second part of this book is an account of Wavell's visit to Hodeidah and Sanaa in 1911 which was at the time when Yemen was under Turkish rule.

Central Asia

GENERAL

Art and Archaeology

✔ The Art and Architecture of Islam
650–1250   *Richard Ettinghausen and Oleg Grabar   1991 (1987) (see 'Middle East')*

✔ Buddhist Art and Architecture
Robert E. Fisher   1993
All the Buddhist schools and their art are included in this well illustrated introduction to the subject.

✔ The Arts and Crafts of Turkestan
Johannes Kalter   1984
A well illustrated introduction to the varied and colourful arts and crafts of Turkestan. The area, which is a combination of arid steppes and fertile ground, was influenced by many different cultures and has produced a wealth of unique items.

On Central Asian Tracks   *Aurel M. Stein (1964)*
A summary of Stein's work in Central Asia.

✔ Islamic Art   *David Talbot Rice   1993 (1975) (see 'Middle East')*

Ancient Arts of Central Asia
Tamara Talbot Rice   1965
A general survey of Central Asian art beginning with the nomads from the first millenium BC and including Soghdia, Ferghana and Chorasmia, Bactria and North West India (until Islamic times), East Turkestan in the Roman and Buddhist periods and Armenia, Georgia and Caucasian Albania in early Christian times. Well illustrated throughout.

Autobiography/Biography

Beyond Bokhara *Garry Alder 1985*
The life of William Moorcroft, Asian Explorer
and Pioneer Veterinary Surgeon 1767–1825.
William Moorcroft had been much neglected
until this biography appeared; he made journeys in Central Asia in 1811 and 1812 and in
1819 he received long awaited permission
from the British army to make his 'Great
Journey' which lasted from 1819–1825. The
purpose of the journey was to go in search of
'horses to improve the breed within the British Provinces or for military use'. He started
in northern India and passed through Ladakh, Leh, Srinagar, Peshawar, Kabul, Bamian, Mazar-i-Sharif, Balkh, Karshi before
finally arriving in Bokhara. William Moorcroft died in mysterious circumstances on his
way back to India.

Bokhara Burnes *James Lunt 1969*
A biography of Sir Alexander Burnes (1805–
41), an officer with the East India Company
who travelled widely in Central Asia before
his death in Kabul.

**Ney Elias, Explorer and Envoy Extra-
ordinary in High Asia** *Gerald Morgan
1971*
Ney Elias (1844–97) went to China, crossed
the Gobi Desert from the Great Wall of China
to Novgorod and travelled widely in South
and Central Asia. He also explored the
Pamirs, the Oxus, Badakshan and Balkh.

Fiction

The Lotus and the Wind *John Masters
1956 (1953)*
Although Robin Savage, the chief character
in this novel, is a good soldier, he is also a
loner; when he is accused of cowardice he
undertakes a mission to remedy the rumour.
The mission, to do with the secret service of
British India, takes place in 1880 and is set
in the wild border country of Central Asia.

Food

✔ **The Complete Asian Cookbook**
Charmaine Solomon 1993 (see 'South East Asia')

General Background

✔ **Between Marx and Muhammad**
Dilip Hiro 1994
An analysis of the changing face of Central
Asia which looks at the role that Russia will
play in the future of the new republics and
the contrast of the fundamentalist régimes
with the secular democracy of Turkey.

Guides

✔ **Karakoram Highway. The High
Road to China. A Travel Survival Kit**
John King 1993 (1989)

✔ **Central Asia. The Practical
Handbook. A Cadogan Guide**
Giles Whittell 1993
Turkmenistan, Uzbekistan, Tajikistan, Kir-
ghizstan, Kazakhstan, the Karakoram High-
way and Western China.

History

The Golden Road to Samarkand
Wilfrid Blunt 1973
A well-illustrated book following the journeys of travellers including Alexander the
Great, Aurel Stein, Hsuan-tsang, Marco
Polo, Ibn Battuta and Babur who, although
travelling through Central Asia at very different times, all found it alluring and all left
fascinating accounts.

✔ **The Great Game** *Peter Hopkirk 1992
(1990)*
The secret agents of both Britain and Russia
were involved in a great struggle in Central
Asia during the last century; this became
known as the Great Game. Peter Hopkirk's
exciting book tells the story of how the two
great powers vying with each other for supremacy employed both espionage and treachery to achieve their ends. Compulsive
reading. 'A wonderful tale of derring-do
among the spies sent out to try to win Afghanistan' (Jeremy Paxman) ✔ *On Secret
Service East of Constantinople* (1994) is the
sequel to *The Great Game* and is an equally
enthralling account of the German and Turkish plots, in 1914, to incite violent revolutionary uprisings against the British in India
and the Russians in Central Asia. It is the
true story of John Buchan's *Greenmantle*
(q.v.).

The Dream of Lhasa *Donald Rayfield
1976*
The life of the Russian explorer Nikolay
Przhevalsky (1839–88) who made four expeditions through Mongolia, Chinese Central Asia and Northern Tibet. He discovered
the Mongolian horse which is named after
him and as a botanist he discovered so much
that his collections are still being analysed.

Natural History

Beyond the Caspian   *Douglas Carruthers*
1949
Douglas Carruthers, who travelled before
World War I, recorded everything that he
saw that appealed to him in Nature – birds,
animals, forests, flowers, deserts and the climate, with enthusiasm and love. Unusually
for the time, he was allowed to travel freely
north of the Oxus for a considerable length of
time ensuring that we have a complete picture of the natural history of the region.

Photography

To the Back of Beyond   *Fitzroy Maclean*
1974
An illustrated companion to Central Asia
and Mongolia which includes material from
some of the many journeys the author made
in the area; a good general overall survey of
Central Asia.

✔ **Mirror of the Orient**   *Roland and*
Sabrina Michaud   1992 (1980)
Colour photographs are juxtaposed with reproductions of central Asian miniatures providing an insight into the past and yet
showing the continuity of life in the region.

✔ **Visions of a Nomad**   *Wilfred Thesiger*
1993 (1987)
A selection of Thesiger's black and white
photographs of Africa, the Arab World and
Asia.

Travel Literature

✔ **The Way of the World**
Nicolas Bouvier   1992 (1985)
In 1953 the Swiss artist and writer, Nicolas
Bouvier set off in an old Fiat across Yugoslavia, Greece, Turkey, Iran, Afghanistan and
Pakistan. When the book was eventually
published it became a cult travel book, but
has only recently been translated into English. The English edition has an introduction
by Patrick Leigh Fermor who says 'He has all
the gifts that come to a traveller's help, his
wide erudition, rooted in the classics . . . the
capacity to admire and assess. Passionate
curiosity, appropriate seriousness . . . '

✔ **The Road to Oxiana**
Robert Byron (see 'Iran')

✔ **In Xanadu**   *William Dalrymple   1990*
(1989)
Dalrymple travelled from Jerusalem to Xanadu and Kubla Khan's palace, crossing Asia
by a variety of transport. His approach is

both scholarly and adventurous and at times
can be very amusing; his descriptions of
Kashgar which mix history with the present-
day reality of aging hippies are extremely
well observed.

✔ **Danziger's Travels**   *Nick Danziger*
1993 (1987)
Nick Danziger travelled widely throughout
forbidden areas of Asia, often disguised as a
wandering Muslim. He went through Iran,
Afghanistan, Pakistan, Xinjiang (including
the TaklaMakan Desert), Tibet, Bhutan and
the heart of China.

My Life as an Explorer   *Sven Hedin   1926*
Sven Hedin wrote many books about his explorations in Asia but this is a compilation of
all his adventures and therefore gives an
overall view of his life. As a boy he had read
prodigiously the books of Jules Verne, Fenimore Cooper, Livingstone, Stanley and Franklin and had known from an early age that
he wanted to follow in their footsteps and
become an explorer himself. His journeys
took him to Meshed, Bokhara, Samarkand,
the Pamirs, Tibet (where he was taken
prisoner) and all over Central Asia.

✔ **Central Asia. A Traveller's**
Companion   *Kathleen Hopkirk   1993*
The book is arranged alphabetically by place
and under each travellers and writers past
and present and their journeys are described
and quoted from. Certainly a 'must' as a
companion on any present-day journey to
Central Asia.

✔ **The Travels of Sir John Mandeville**
Translated by C.W.R.D. Moseley   1983
(see 'Middle East')

✔ **Heart of Asia**   *Nicholas Roerich   1990*
(1929)
Nicholas Roerich, artist, writer, philosopher,
educator, archaeologist, visionary, philosopher and peacemaker was also an explorer
who spent much time journeying through
Central Asia visiting monasteries and meeting lamas. 'Roerich's vision is a pantheistic
hymn to a union of man and nature.' (*The
New York Times*)

✔ **Goodnight, Mister Lenin**
Tiziano Terzani   1994 (1993)
Terzani was sailing down the Amur in 1991
when he heard the news about Gorbachev; he
proceeded to travel through Siberia, across
Central Asia and to the republics of the Caucasus listening to the people who were everywhere proclaiming 'Communism is dead'.

✔ **The Lost Heart of Asia. Journey Beyond Samarkand**   *Colin Thubron   1994*
Colin Thubron travels to the newly emergent countries of Central Asia searching for their fragmented identity. A classic travel book in the best sense; the sympathetic combination of history, people and a 6,000-mile journey is engrossing.

Between Oxus and Jumna
Arnold J. Toynbee   1961
A journey which took place between the Rivers Oxus and Jumna; Toynbee never crossed either river but was constantly crossing the Indus flowing in between them. Among the places he visited were: Lahore, Peshawar, Jaipur, Jodhpur, Kabul, Kandahar, Herat, Bamian, Quetta and Karachi.

Arminius Vambéry His Life and Adventures   *Written by Himself   1884*
In his autobiography Vambéry begins with his childhood, how he developed an interest in language and continues with a resumé of all his travels to Turkey, Persia and Central Asia; he ends up with his appointment as Professor of Oriental Languages in Hungary.

Travels in Central Asia
Arminius Vambéry   1864
Vambéry was born in Hungary in 1832; from his boyhood he took a great interest in linguistics and became intrigued by the reciprocal relationships of languages. It was this interest in the peoples and their customs and languages which led him to travel through Central Asia from Teheran across the Turkoman Desert to Khiva, Bokhara and Samarkand. He travelled in disguise on this very dangerous journey.

AFGHANISTAN

'One feels that perhaps Afghanistan has struck the mean for which Asia is looking.'
Robert Byron *The Road to Oxiana* 1937

Anthropology

The Kaffirs of the Hindu Kush
George Scott Robertson   1896
The author was a British medical doctor and the British agent in Gilgit. He carried out pioneering fieldwork in 1889–91 in unexplored Kafiristan, spending almost a year with the Kafirs, having first glimpsed the area through 'a translucent cloud-film'; it remains an important study of the people of the region, now known as Nuristan. He set out to discover all that he could about the

people, their religion, laws, clothing, women, feuds, funerals and sport.

Fiction

Plain Tales of the Afghan Border
John Charles Edward Bowen (ed.)   1982
A collection of stories told to a serving British officer at the end of the British Raj.

The Hero of Herat   *Maud Diver   1924 (1912)*
Set at the time of the First Afghan War and subtitled 'a frontier biography in romantic form', this is a more or less true rendition of the life of Major Eldred Pottinger who was present, in a heroic role, at the siege of Herat (but whose journals of that time are unfortunately lost). Pottinger was extremely self-effacing which made the author's task difficult, but Sir Henry Lawrence wrote: 'India, fertile in heroes, has shown since the days of Clive no man of greater or earlier promise than Eldred Pottinger. Yet hero as he was, you might have sat for weeks beside him at table and never discovered that he had seen a shot fired.'

✔ **Flashman**   *George Macdonald Fraser   1986 (1969)*
The adventures of Flashman as a reluctant secret agent in Afghanistan who belonged to the exclusive company of Lord Cardigan's Hussars; the novel combines humour and historical accuracy making it eminently readable.

Salang   *Sandy Gall   1989*
A novel based on the struggle between the Mujahedeen and the Soviet army; an SAS officer and a Soviet defector are on a secret mission to blow up the Salang tunnel.

A Vizier's Daughter   *Lillias Hamilton   1900*
(A Tale of the Hazara War)
The author was court physician to Abdur Rahman, the Amir of Afghanistan, but she states in her introduction that every character is drawn from a model and that it should therefore be an accurate description of Afghan life. Lillias Hamilton got to know the Afghans 'as intimately as one can ever know a people so far removed from us in thought and education' and it is therefore a fascinating insight into the life of the time.

Dust on the Paw   *Robin Jenkins   1986 (1961)*
Nurania, Afghanistan, is a backward country on the borders of Russia with both Russia and America aiming to dominate it. The novel deals with the problems of mixed marriage. Western values are contrasted

with Eastern tradition and the role of women is examined.

✔ **The Far Pavilions** *M.M. Kaye 1978*
The end of this novel takes place in Afghanistan where the hero takes part in the actual historical events which led to the Second Afghan War.

✔ **The Man Who Would Be King**
Rudyard Kipling 1895
A short story supposedly based on the exploits of Colonel Alexander Gardner who was meant to have travelled in Kafiristan.

Caravans *James Michener 1963*
An American girl disappears in Afghanistan; an American official goes to find her and has to overcome numerous obstacles in his search.

✔ **Afghan Stories** *Oleg Yermakov 1993 (1991)*
The author is a Russian who served in Afghanistan during the war there; he uses the war as a brooding backdrop for his rather bleak stories.

Food

✔ **Afghan Food and Cookery**
Helen Saberi 1986
The author lived in Afghanistan for ten years and married into an Afghan family. She went on to cook these dishes in England and adds practical advice for western cooks. Some of the dishes included are: aush-e-asli (pasta, yogourt and meatballs), qabili pilau uzbeki (uzbek rice with carrots and raisins) shola goshti (sticky rice with meat) and baqlawa (sweet pastry with nuts).

General Background

✔ **Zinky Boys. Soviet Voices from a Forgotten War** *Svetlana Alexievish 1992 (1990)*
A million Soviet troops were engaged in the war in Afghanistan between 1979 and 1989, but the new Soviet society continues to reject the memory of the war; this book, which created great controversy when it was published in the USSR, presents, in a non-judgemental way, the words of the men and women who were affected by the war.

History

An Account of the Kingdom of Caubal, and its Dependencies in Persia, Tartary and India
Mountstuart Elphinstone 1972 (1815)
The author spent a year at the King of Kabul's court gathering information for the British government; the mission was 'in a style of great magnificence' in order to please the King who was 'known to be haughty'. Since it was not feasible for him to visit all the places he wrote about, he used the expertise of surveyors and geographers in the vicinity; the result is a book packed with interesting facts and information. [Geoffrey Moorhouse]

Kabul Catastrophe. The Retreat of 1842
Patrick Macrory (1966)
An acclaimed account of the British retreat from Kabul when sixteen thousand soldiers, camp-followers, women and children perished, leaving Surgeon Brydon as sole survivor of General Elphinstone's army. George MacDonald Fraser reputedly used this as his spur to creating Flashman. This book was originally published as *Signal Catastrophe*.

Every Rock, Every Hill *Victoria Schofield*
(see 'Pakistan')

Lords of the Khyber. The Story of the North-West Frontier *André Singer 1984*
A survey of the history and events which took place on the North-West frontier, an area that has always attracted heroes and romance. Singer establishes a setting for what has happened recently in Afghanistan by looking at some of the Pushtun, British, Sikh and Russians who spent time there.

A History of Afghanistan *Sir Percy Sykes 1940*
The author, who went on to become a distinguished diplomat, first went to Central Asia in the 1890s and had taken a keen interest in Afghan affairs. At the time of publication this was the first complete history of Afghanistan; published in two volumes its aim was to supply British officials and the British public with accurate information.

Photography

✔ **Afghanistan** *Roland and Sabrina Michaud 1990 (1980)*
One hundred and four beautiful photographs of Afghanistan, most of which were taken before the Russian invasion in December 1979.

✔ **Horseman of Afghanistan**   *Roland and Sabrina Michaud   1988*
Exciting photographs showing the game of Buzkashi played by Afghan horsemen to celebrate special occasions.

✔ **Caravans to Tartary**   *Roland and Sabrina Michaud (see 'Central Asia – General')*
Many photographs of the Kirghiz peoples of Afghan Turkestan.

✔ **Desert, Marsh and Mountain**
Wilfred Thesiger   1979
Thesiger travelled in the Hazarajat in Central Afghanistan and in Nuristan in the north-east, during the 1950s and 1960s. Numerous black and white photographs.

Travel Literature

✔ **The Road to Oxiana**
Robert Byron (see 'Iran')

✔ **Danziger's Adventures**
Nick Danziger   1993 (1992)
In Nick Danziger's second volume of adventures he returns to Kabul after the Soviet withdrawal and finds the Mujahedeen attacking it; he later returns to try and find homes for many abandoned children.

✔ **Danziger's Travels**   *Nick Danziger 1993 (1987)*
A chunk of this book is about Afghanistan; Danziger travelled with the Mujahedeen from Herat to Quetta.

Afghanistan: Agony of a Nation
Sandy Gall   1988
Sandy Gall made three trips to Afghanistan to report on the war; the book is an account of his last trip which was across the Hindu Kush to meet the guerilla leader Ahmed Shah Masud less than 100 miles from the Soviet border.

Afghanistan   *John C. Griffiths   1967*
Although the author gives an account of his travels in Afghanistan, emphasizing the extraordinary hospitality he received, he starts with events that occurred in 1747 which he argues typify the treachery, brutality and intrigue which run throughout Afghan history and also mark a watershed in Afghan development.

Under a Sickle Moon   *Peregrine Hodson 1986*
The author travelled through north-eastern Afghanistan in the summer and autumn of 1984. The book is an account of the journey taken from his diary and tape-recordings. It is a personal narrative which includes many meetings with ordinary people.

✔ **The Wind Blows Away Our Words**
Doris Lessing   1987
Doris Lessing who had been involved for many years in Afghan Aid flew to Pakistan in 1986 to interview refugees and Mujahedeen leaders to find out their views on the war; she also talked to the women and discovered their very different attitudes and sufferings.

✔ **The Light Garden of the Angel King**   *Peter Levi   1984 (1972)*
Peter Levi uses his classical background as the theme for this book. Afghanistan has been the crossroads for so many different cultures and peoples, that travelling through it, looking for clues and influences makes a fascinating search. This was Levi's first trip to Asia, but Bruce Chatwin who was also on the trip had been before.

✔ **The Cruel Way**   *Ella Maillart   1986 (1947)*
Ella Maillart set out for Afghanistan from Paris in 1939 to find 'the secret of harmonious living' with her friend Christina, who was trying to kick drug-addiction and was looking for a personal cure. They drove through Italy, Yugoslavia, Bulgaria, Turkey and Iran; as well as being an interesting travel document of the time the book looks at the problems of travelling with a fellow European: 'When a girl is on her own, she can travel easily. She gets taken in by people and looked after, for nomads have good hearts. If there's a couple, however, they form a unity and people leave you alone. You are two Europeans, isolated.'

The Narrow Smile. A Journey back to the North-west Frontier   *Peter Mayne 1955*
Peter Mayne, who had worked in India before Independence and spoke Pashto, returned to the North-West Frontier border and travelled to Quetta, Peshawar, over the Khyber Pass, into Swat and to Kabul. His account is written in a very approachable style.

✔ **A Short Walk in the Hindu Kush**
Eric Newby   1981 (1958)
Eric Newby was working in the rag trade in London when he set off for the Hindu Kush; his book has now become a travel classic. It is adventurous and funny but also describes the magnificence of the scenery he travels through. [John Keay]

✔ **The Afghan Amulet** *Sheila Paine*
1994 (see 'Middle East')

Among the Wild Tribes of the Afghan Frontier *T.L. Pennell 1909*
Pennell was a medical missionary who spent sixteen years on the North-West Frontier of India. Many of his patients came from across the border in Afghanistan.

A Hitch or Two in Afghanistan
Nigel Ryan 1983
Nigel Ryan travelled behind the Russian lines in Afghanistan between August and October 1982. Before leaving he admits that he would have had difficulty finding Afghanistan on the map, but when Sandy Gall asked him to accompany him on the journey he went with alacrity. The resulting book makes interesting reading.

The Minaret of Djam *Freya Stark 1970*
Freya Stark's travel diary of a journey from Kabul, through the centre of Afghanistan to Herat and Kandahar. She records what she sees, the history of the country and what she learns from the people she meets en route.

A Personal Narrative of a Journey to the Source of the River Oxus by the Route of the Indus, Kabul, and Badakhshan *John Wood 1841*
The author accompanied Sir Alexander Burnes on his mission to Afghanistan and wrote rough notes about the journey which he later turned into this book trusting that it would 'not be unacceptable to the public'. As well as surveying the area of the river, the purpose of the journey was to establish trade links.

CAUCASUS - AZERBAIJAN, ARMENIA AND GEORGIA

'Nobility is cheap in Georgia. There is only one rank, and that is prince.' John Foster Fraser *Round the World on a Wheel* 1899

'And at day dawn, they looked eastward, and midway between the sea and the sky, they saw white snowpeaks hanging, glittering sharp and bright above the clouds. And they knew that they were come to Caucasus, at the end of all the earth: Caucasus the highest of all mountains, the father of the rivers of the east.' *Heroes* Kingsley

Autobiography/Biography

✔ **A Captive of the Caucasus**
Andrei Bitov 1992
Bitov writes that Russians visit the Caucasus with a sense of homecoming, recognizing the landscapes described by Lermontov, Pushkin and Tolstoy. In the first memoir *Lessons of Armenia*, Bitov explores the Russians relationship with the Caucasus and the idea of homeland and in the second, *Choosing a Location* he describes his journey through Soviet Georgia.

✔ **Lermontov. Tragedy in the Caucasus** *Laurence Kelly 1983 (1977)*
A popular biography of Lermontov the soldier, painter and poet. Lermontov had been taken to the Caucasus as a child by his grandmother and was much affected by the exoticism and natural beauty he found there; later on, during his military career, he was twice exiled to the Caucasus, eventually being killed, in a duel, in 1841 aged 26.

Fiction

The Golden Fleece. Tales from the Caucasus *1971*
A collection of fifteen folk tales from Georgia, Armenia and Azerbaijan.

✔ **The Gate at the End of the World**
Philip Glazebrook 1990 (1989)
'The Gate at the End of the World', in the Caucasus, marked the boundaries of Europe for the Roman Empire; during the Crimean War the British under Sir Daniel Farr and with the assistance of Captain Vinegar, joined the Turks and Russians who were all fighting for control of the area. 'A good, chunky, upmarket historical novel with plenty of classical allusion.' (*Preview*)

✔ **A Hero of Our Time**
Mikhail Lermontov 1966 (1840)
Written between 1838–40, Lermontov's only novel; it consists of five stories, each complete in itself. It was a landmark in Russian literature, being the first psychological novel to be published and was the inspiration for Tolstoy, Dostoyevsky and Chekhov. [Laurence Kelly]

Sketches of Russian Life in the Caucasus *By a Russe (many years resident amongst the various mountain tribes) 1853*

Zarya. A Tale of the Caucasus
Dixon Scott 1911
A love story with much action set in the Caucasus. Whistler arrives in the 'city of his dreams', Théba, in the Caucasus, as a young

correspondent in a firm in which his brother also works. He falls in love with Zarya and has a succession of adventures as a result.

✔ The Cossacks　Leo Tolstoy　1862
Tolstoy, influenced by Rousseau, describes the attempt of a young Russian disenchanted with civilization to 'return to nature'. The experiment fails, but he (Olenin) finds a certain peace with himself. Turgenev regarded *The Cossacks* as 'the finest and most perfect production of Russian literature'.

Food

✔ The Classic Cuisine of Soviet Georgia　Julianne Margvelashvili　1991
As well as recipes the book shows how history, tradition and people reflect the food of Soviet Georgia.

✔ Russian Food: All the Peoples, all the Republics　Jean Redwood　1989
Includes food from Transcaucasia: Georgia, Armenia and Azerbaijan.

General Background

✔ Georgia. A Rebel in the Caucasus
Peter Nasmyth　1992
The author visited Georgia over a period of five years, observing the great changes that were taking place in this area where Islam meets Christianity and which has been called 'Russia's poetic homeland'.

Guide

✔ Introduction to the Georgian Republic. An Odyssey Guide
Roger Rosen　1991

History

✔ The Sabres of Paradise
Lesley Blanch　1960
Shamyl, Imam of Daghestan, lived between 1796 and 1871. Although he is not much remembered in the West today, in his time he captured the West's imagination; his bravery was infectious and while English ladies sewed bunting for his flag, questions about Britain's commitments in the Caucasus were asked in the House of Commons. Lesley Blanch's very lively biography of Shamyl is extremely readable.

War and Revolution in Asiatic Russia
Morgan Philips Price　1918 (see 'Turkey')

✔ On the Edge of Europe. Mountaineering in the Caucasus　Audrey Salkeld and José Luis Bermudez　1993
The Caucasus form the natural boundary between Europe and Asia; after the great age of Alpine exploration, mountaineers turned to climbing in the Caucasus as new and unexplored territory. This history of climbers such as Freshfield, Dent, Mummery, Schulze, Merkl and Bauer would be useful for anyone planning a climb in the Caucasus as well as being interesting reading.

✔ Armenia. The Survival of a Nation
Christopher J. Walker　1990 (1980)

Leisure

✔ Classic Climbs in the Caucasus
Friedrich Bender　1992 (1991)
A guide for mountaineers which includes eighty of the finest routes.

Travel Literature

Prometheus Unbound　Aeschylus　1978
Of the fragments that have survived, three relate to the travels of the Titans to the Caucasus.

✔ Claws of the Crab. Georgia and Armenia in Crisis　Stephen Brook　1993 (1992)
Stephen Brook arrived in Georgia on the brink of civil war; his book is a mixture of that war, but also of the parallel life that was going on – banquets and meetings with poets and politicians.

Adventures in the Caucasus
Alexandre Dumas　1962 (1859)
Dumas had spent the summer of 1858 travelling across Imperial Russia after which he went on to visit Caucasia. He was completely undeterred by the fact that the whole country was at war; for thirty years the Russians had been trying to subdue the fiercely independent mountain tribesman led by the king-priest Shamyl who was finally arrested in 1859. Dumas' zest for living and for new situations, people and places is very evident from this book.

✔ A Dry Ship to the Mountains
Daniel Farson　1994
Daniel Farson went down the Volga and across the Caucasus, following in his father's footsteps and aiming to cross the Klukhor

Pass which his father had attempted in 1929 (see *Caucasian Journey* below)

Caucasian Journey Negley Farson 1988 *(1951)*
Negley Farson and his companion (who insisted on walking rather than riding) set out from Moscow for the Caucasus in 1929 during the Russian Revolution. Before the Soviets were able to tame the inhabitants of the Caucasus, many diverse people lived there including a German enclave, Tartars and Mongolian aristocrats. Farson travelled widely as a journalist, but had a constant fight against alcoholism and guilt; at one point he admitted himself to an asylum in Switzerland, but the doctor said to him 'Keep your conflicts. It is better for you not to be a normal man.'

A Vagabond in the Caucasus. With Some Notes of His Experiences Among the Russians Stephen Graham 1911
Stephen Graham had taught himself Russian and eventually determined to live there having worked there for a while as a freelance journalist. He writes that after he had made this decision 'My life as a wanderer began. I might say my life as a tramp began, for I never worked again.'

✔ **Eastern Approaches** Fitzroy Maclean 1991 *(1949)*
'A heady tale of high adventure and politics, superbly told, set in the Caucasus, Central Asia, Persia and Yugoslavia. It had a powerful effect on me as a young subaltern of 19 (and doubtless on many others of my generation) and first set my feet in the direction of Tashkent and Tbilisi, Kashgar and Kabul. I must have given away more copies of this magical book than of any other I have read.' (Peter Hopkirk)

To Caucasus. The End of all the Earth Fitzroy Maclean 1976
An illustrated companion to the Caucasus and Transcaucasia which has chapters on history, life today, people, food and drink, buildings and scenery. A good overall survey.

Across the Caucasus Michael Pereira 1973
Pereira travelled through remote parts of the Caucasus writing a very readable book which combines personal travel anecdote and history; there are many myths attached to this region, which in ancient times stood on the periphery of the known world. Pereira describes the characteristics and heritage of the indigenous people while acknowleging their debt to the Romans, Greeks, Persians, Arabs, Turks and Russians.

✔ **Please Don't Call it Soviet Georgia** Mary Russell 1991
The author had thought of her trip to Georgia as a 'jaunt' since she was used to visiting places of conflict. Ironically by the time she had planned her journey, Georgia was also suffering from conflict and when she came to write the book many changes had occurred. She travelled all over the area meeting and staying with local people.

✔ **The Jason Voyage** Tim Severin 1986 *(1985)*
The legend is that Jason and his band of Heroes set sail from Greece in search of the Golden Fleece. Their journey took them across the Aegean Sea, through the Bosphorus and into the Black Sea. In Cochis, proven to be famous in classical times for its gold production, Jason found the Golden Fleece and his future wife, Medea. At Vani, up the Rhioni River in Georgia, many gold objects have been found. Tim Severin reconstructed Jason's journey on a boat called the *Argo*.

CHINESE CENTRAL ASIA

Guides

✔ **Introduction to the Silk Road. From Xi'an to Kashgar. An Odyssey Guide** Judy Bonavia 1992 *(1988)*

History

The Silk Road L Boulnois 1966 *(1963)*
Silk was apparently first seen by the Romans on the war-banners of the Parthians in 53 BC, but it soon became very familiar to the Romans. By 14 AD the Senate had to restrict its use to women, banning men from using it, as it would 'dishonour' them. Boulnois' book charts the history of silk and the silk road in a fascinating manner.

✔ **Foreign Devils on the Silk Road** Peter Hopkirk 1991 *(1980)*
A highly readable account which pulls together the adventures and race of all the explorers who made archaeological raids on the Silk Road, including Aurel Stein, Sven Hedin, Von Le Coq, Paul Pelliot, Count Otani and Langdon Warner. A very good introduction to the area.

Travel Literature

✔ **The Gobi Desert**
Mildred Cable with Francesca French   1984 (1942)
The two authors and Francesca French's sister, Evangeline (Eva), were missionaries who had met in Shanxi province in 1901 and whose friendship lasted until their deaths fifty years later. They spent twenty years with the China Inland Mission, dressed in Chinese clothes and became the first Western women to cross the Gobi, which they did five times during twelve years' tending the sick and spreading the gospel. A real love of the desert shines through this book despite their encounters with brigands and sandstorms.

✔ **News from Tartary**   *Peter Fleming   1936*
One of the reasons Peter Fleming made the journey was to find out what was happening in Sinkiang or Chinese Turkestan; it had been eight years since a traveller had crossed the region. The second reason was simply because he wanted to travel. He wrote in the foreword: 'The trouble about journeys nowadays is that they are easy to make but difficult to justify.' He remarks that the reason that he and 'Kini (Ella Maillart) got on so well on the journey was that she had a certain friendly contempt for him and he had a sneaking respect for her. A very interesting account of the events in Chinese Central Asia.

✔ **An English Lady in Chinese Turkestan**   *Lady Macartney   1985 (1931)*
Lady Macartney was the wife of the British Agent who later became the Consul General in Kashgar from 1890 until 1918. Catherine Macartney married in 1898 and spent a total of seventeen years in Chini Bagh their house in Kashgar. The couple were renowned for their hospitality and much respected; the book describes their day-to-day life in this remote outpost during a very important epoch.

Forbidden Journey. From Peking to Kashmir   *Ella Maillart   1937*
The account of the journey which Ella Maillart took with Peter Fleming from Peking to Kashmir via Sian, Lanchow, Khotan, Kashgar and Hunza in 1935. She had dreamed of getting to China all her life and had finally persuaded the editor of a French newspaper that she should make the trip. Especially interesting to read this in conjunction with Peter Fleming's *News from Tartary*.

✔ **Calling from Kashgar. A Journey through Tibet**   *Rod Richard   1991 (1990)*
The author begins his journey in China and travels through Western Tibet to Kashgar. He meets many pilgrims on the way to Mount Kailas.

✔ **From Heaven Lake**   *Vikram Seth   1990 (1983)*
Vikram Seth, a keen observer, hitch-hiked through Chinese Central Asia and Tibet to Nepal, seeing much that would not have been seen by anyone else at the time. A delightful book; he writes engagingly and convincingly about his journey.

✔ **The Antique Land**   *Diana Shipton   1987 (1950)*
The author's husband, Eric Shipton, was the last British Consul-General in Kashgar where they spent two years. This is a lively account of their lives there and it is interesting to compare it with earlier accounts, such as that by Lady Macartney.

Ruins of Desert Cathay   *M. Aurel Stein   1912*
Stein's personal narrative of his explorations in Central Asia and westernmost China which he undertook in the years 1906–1908 under the orders of the Government of India. In 1907 he had come across a rock chapel which had been walled up for around 900 years; from these caves he brought back twenty-four cases 'heavy with manuscript treasures rescued from that strange place of hiding, and five more filled with paintings, embroideries, and similar remains of Buddhist art'. Many remained unopened for years in the vaults of the British Museum.

Sand-Buried Ruins of Khotan
M. Aurel Stein   1903
This was Stein's first public book; he wrote it as a popular account for the general reader of the journey he carried out in 1900–1 under the auspices of the Government of India. He set out from Kashmir and travelled to Khotan on the Yurung-kash River in the south of the Taklamakan Desert where he explored the ancient remains in the region.

✔ **Journey to Turkistan**   *Eric Teichman   1988 (1937)*
In 1935 Teichman left the British Embassy in China and travelled by motor truck and pony, through Mongolia and Chinese Turkistan, on a special mission to Urumchi to establish contact with the new régime and to discuss the restoration of trade.

✔ **Buried Treasures of Chinese Turkestan**   *Albert Von Le Coq   1987 (1928)*
An account of the activities and adventures

of the second and third German Turfan expeditions which were led by Von Le Coq. The object of the expeditions was to collect paintings and art objects and take them back to Germany; they were packed into cases and sent to Berlin. The second expedition accrued 103 cases, each weighing an average of about 270lb and the third gathered 128 cases.

The Long Old Road in China
Langdon Warner 1926
The 'Long Old Road' goes between the northern desert and the Tibetan ranges via Sian, Lanchow and Suchow. In Langdon Warner's day it took ten weeks' steady cart travel from Peking to the Sinkiang border and a further three months to India. When he finally saw the caves at Tun Huang 'there was nothing to do but gasp'. He then spent a further ten days quite unable to leave the caves and unable to do any critical study. His descriptions of what he saw are immediate and alive.

✔ The Heart of a Continent
Francis Younghusband 1984 (1896)
Younghusband first had a taste for travelling in the Himalayas when he had had a few months leave from his regiment stationed in the Punjab. He subsequently spent the summer of 1885 at Simla reading about Yarkand and Kashgar and was invited on a long journey by H.E.M. James of the Indian Civil Service who 'walked into my house and asked me if I would go a journey with him. Nothing was said as to where we should go; but to go a journey anywhere was enough for me, and of course I said "yes".'

RUSSIAN CENTRAL ASIA – KAZAKHSTAN, KIRGHSIA, TAJIKISTAN, TURKMENISTAN AND UZBEKISTAN
'Death has no repose
warmer and deeper than the Orient sand
. . .
For lust of knowing what should not be known
We make the Golden Journey to Samarkand' (James Elroy Flecker)

Biography

✔ From the Steppes to the Savannah
Barbara Porajska 1990 (1988)
The author was living comfortably in Poland at the outbreak of war; she was shipped to Soviet Central Asia on a truck and stayed

there for two years, before eventually being reunited with the rest of her family in a refugee village in Uganda.

Fiction

The White Steamship   *Chingiz Aïtmatov 1972*
Aïtmatov was born in a small Kirghizian settlement in the foothills of the Tien Shan mountains; he writes about the harsh climate, rugged mountains and parched steppes in *The White Steamship*. *Farewell Gul'sary* (1970) is the story of Tanabai and his horse Gul'sary, in the Kirghiz Republic in Soviet Central Asia; it is about the present-day descendants of the nomad farmers in the very west, close to the border of the Kazakh Republic. Also *The Day Lasts More than a Hundred Years* (1983), a science fiction novel set in Kajakistan; *The Time to Speak Out* (1988), *The Place of the Skull* (1989) and *The Cranes Fly Early* (1983).

The Golden Journey to Samarkand
James Elroy Flecker 1913
A collection of poems inspired in Flecker's words by the 'Moslem East'.

✔ Mission to Samarkand   *Felix Godwin 1964*
The landscape, terrain, dangers and people described in this novel, set in Soviet Central Asia and Sinkiang, are all based on fact. Much of his material came from Gustav Krist and Herbert Wood.

✔ Samarkand   *Amin Maalouf 1992*
Omar Khayyam arrives in Samarkand and is recognized as a ribald poet. There are descriptions of eleventh-century Central Asian courts, bazaars and lives of mystics; there is much about Sufi mysticism.

Tamberlane the Great
Christopher Marlowe c. 1587
An exciting play full of wonderful language about Tamberlane's lust for power.

Timour the Tartar, or the Iron Master of Samarkand-by-Oxus   *John Oxenford and Shirley Brooks 1860*
A play in six scenes which was first performed in 1860 and which is set in the fortress and battlements of Samarkand. Timour is betrothed to the Georgian princess Zorilda; before they actually marry there are many plots, sub-plots and intrigues.

Tamerlane   *Edgar Allan Poe 1827*
The hero of Poe's poem has little in common with the historical Tamberlane, but it was written when he was in his teens at a time

when Oriental themes were popular. It deals with human love and the only likely reference to Tamerlane is:
'The pageantry of monarchy
And the deep trumpet-thunder's roar
. . . telling
Of human battle . . . '

General Background

✔ **Samarkand and Bukhara**
John Lawton 1991
An illustrated introduction to the area which includes much history.

Guide

✔ **USSR. Travel Survival Kit**
John Noble and John King 1991

History

The Decline and Fall of the Roman Empire Edward Gibbon 1978 (1776–88)
Chapter LXV of Gibbon's work is about the elevation of Timour or Tamerlane to the throne of Samarkand and his subsequent conquests in Persia, Georgia, Tartary, Russia, India, Syria and Anatolia. Gibbon then writes about Timour's Turkish war, which led to the defeat and captivity of Bajazet, and finally his death aged 70 in 1405 AD.

✔ **Setting the East Ablaze. On Secret Service in Bolshevik Asia** Peter Hopkirk 1986 (1984)
The story of the Bolshevik attempt to 'set the east ablaze' with the doctrine of Marxism between the wars. Lenin wanted to liberate the whole of Asia, beginning with British India; this led to a shadowy and undeclared war. Peter Hopkirk's book is like an exciting spy story.

Tamerlane. The Earth Shaker
Harold Lamb 1929
An easy-to-read biography and history of Tamerlane and his times. Lamb also discusses the Tamerlane of myth and how he kindled the imagination of European poets and writers such as Marlowe, Milton (Satan reflects the legendary Tamerlane by having his great trumpets summoning the armed host to battle in oriental splendour) and Pierre Bergeron whose *Voyages en Tartarie* contains much accurate information about the Tartar and Muhammadan peoples.

✔ **The Rise and Rule of Tamerlane**
Beatrice Forbes Manz 1991 (1989)
A biography of Tamerlane and an analysis of

his methods of control over both nomad and settled peoples and the relationship between the two. The author examines Tamerlane's career and shows how immensely powerful he was, ultimately changing the world in which he lived.

The Age of Tamerlane. Warfare in the Middle East c.1350–1500 David Nicolle 1990
A book written for children, but with clearly laid out and interesting text.

Travel Literature

✔ **Red Odyssey** Marat Akchurin 1992
Akchurin, a Muscovite, travelled through the outlying republics of Kazakhstan, Uzbekistan, Turkmenia and Azerbaijan as the Soviet Union was breaking up. He sees old friends, meets new ones and describes the history of the region.

✔ **Mission to Tashkent** F.M. Bailey 1992 (1946)
In 1918 Bailey was an agent in charge of a small mission which was sent to Kashgar, from where he almost immediately departed for Tashkent. He had some extraordinary adventures which he recounts here; at one point he passed himself off as an Albanian soldier clerk in the Serbian army who had been sent to Russia to help with the Serbian Volunteer Corps. He was even sent by the Bolshevik secret police to arrest himself. During all his hazardous exploits he kept a list of the butterflies he saw. [Peter Hopkirk]

A Ride to Khiva Fred Burnaby 1983 (1876)
Burnaby, the strongest man in the British army, left his regiment in 1875 and set out on horseback for Khiva because 'the Government at St Petersburg had given an order that no foreigner was to be allowed to travel in Russian Asia, and that an Englishman who had recently attempted a journey in that direction had been turned back by the authorities. I have, unfortunately for my own interests, from my earliest childhood had what my old nurse used to call a most 'contradictorious' spirit, and it suddenly occurred to me, why not go to Central Asia?' His swashbuckling character, which led him into many adventures, can be imagined from the portrait of him in the National Portrait Gallery by J.J. Tissot.

Through Khiva to Golden Samarkand
Ella R. Christie 1925
Ella Christie travelled beyond the Caspian because she wanted to fill in the blank spots on the map to her own satisfaction and be-

cause she was lured by the names of Bokhara and Samarkand. She mostly travelled alone and gives good descriptions of the places she passed through

Russia in Central Asia *George Curzon*
1889
The author's travels by the recently constructed Transcaspian railway into Tsarist Central Asia. An assessment of the Russian threat to British India, but containing much local description. A seminal work. [Peter Hopkirk]

✔ **Journey to Khiva** *Philip Glazebrook*
1993 (1992)
Philip Glazebrook travelled through Russian Central Asia – Bokhara, Samarkand, Khiva and the River Oxus, following in the steps of both British and Russian travellers of the last century.

Alone Through the Forbidden Land
Gustav Krist 1938
(Journeys in disguise through Soviet Central Asia in pursuit of a love of adventure.)
No foreigner was allowed into Soviet Central Asia, so Krist with his love of adventure disguised himself and travelled throughout the region. Most of the Europeans who had visited Bokhara in the nineteenth century had been secret agents, also in disguise; most never returned.

A Person from England and other Travellers to Turkestan *Fitzroy Maclean*
1958
An account of some of the agents, official and unofficial, military and civilian, who have penetrated Central Asia over the last 100 years. Joseph Wolff, Arminius Vambéry, George Curzon, Januarius Aloysius MacGahan (an American), General Skobelyov, Edmund O'Donovan, Charles Stoddart, Joseph Kastamuni (F.M. Bailey's disguise as an Albanian) and Enver Pasha are all included.

Turkestan Solo *Ella Maillart 1935*
On this journey made in 1933, which started in Moscow and went to Kazalinsk, Tashkent, the Tien Shan Mountains, Samarkand and Bokhara, Ella Maillart got as far as the border to Chinese Central Asia. It made her a confirmed traveller and having seen the border she determined to go back: 'The nomad's life enthralls me. Its restlessness pursues me: it is as much part of me as of the sailor.'

✔ **Apples in the Snow**
Geoffrey Moorhouse 1991 (1990)
Geoffrey Moorhouse started his journey on the Soviet Union's border with China and continued through the mountains, steppes and deserts of Central Asia before arriving at

Tamberlane's tomb in Samarkand: 'Moorhouse is one of the great travellers; everywhere attuned to past and present, to the uneasiness and muted discords of the people about him, to the mundane, the ridiculous and the extraordinary beauties of Central Asia.' (*The Guardian*)

Hunted. Through Central Asia.
P.S. Nazaroff 1932
Nazaroff was a mining engineer who travelled extensively throughout the Caucasus and Urals; after he had settled in Tashkent he opened copper, silver and coal mines. He was multi-talented and introduced many Western European flowers and fruits into Turkestan. He was also a geologist, mineralogist, chemist, ornithologist, taxidermist, sportsman and archaeologist. He was ringleader of an anti-Bolshevik plot which was foiled. An account of his hair raising adventures on the run.

The Land of Timur. Recollections of Russian Turkestan *A. Polovtsoff 1932*
The book starts with a Persian distich:
'Shirazee (ah, the rogue!) take my heart in your hand!
For one mole on your cheek I would gladly give up
Both Bokhara and Samarcand.'
This memoir, written many years after the author had left the area, is about the time he had spent in Samarkand, Bokhara and Mazanderan – a personal and descriptive account of that 'Paradise on Earth'.

Turkistan. Notes of a Journey in Russian Turkistan, Khokand, Bokhara and Kuldja *Eugene Schuyler 1876*
By the American consul-general to St Petersburg. The classic study of the region. [Peter Hopkirk]

✔ **The Spy Who Disappeared**
Reginald Teague-Jones 1991 (1990)
Captain Teague-Jones, a British intelligence officer, was forced to change his name and 'disappear' after he was accused of the murder of twenty-six Baku Commissars. It was assumed that he was long dead; but when 'Ronald Sinclair' died, aged 99, in 1988 the truth finally emerged.

TIBET

'The centre of high snow mountains,
The source of great rivers,
A lofty land,
A pure land.' (ninth-century Tibetan poet)

Anthropology

The People of Tibet   *Sir Charles Bell*   1928
Sir Charles Bell, who knew Tibet well, writes about the whole spectrum of society: nobility, traders, nomads, peasants, beggars and robbers. There are also chapters on how the Tibetans live. Bell also wrote *Tibet, Past and Present* (1924) and *The Religion of Tibet* (1931). All three are classic scholarly studies.

✔ **The Renaissance of Tibetan Civilization**   *Christoph von Fürer-Haimendorf* 1990
The story of Tibetan refugees who fled their country with nothing and yet have managed to maintain their culture in exile.

Art and Architecture

The Art of Tibet   *Pratapaditya Pal*   1969
The catalogue of an Asia House Gallery exhibition (the author has also compiled one for the Los Angeles County Museum). A cross-section of art, both sacred and everyday, well illustrated with ample text.

The Tibetan Carpet   *Philip Denwood*   1974
How to make Tibetan carpets and the materials used; well illustrated with 24 colour plates and 83 black and white illustrations.

✔ **Ceremonies of the Lhasa Year**
Hugh Richardson   1993
Old photographs and fascinating text about the many ceremonies which used to take place in Lhasa.

✔ **A Cultural History of Tibet**
David Snellgrove and Hugh Richardson   1968
A scholarly survey of Tibetan culture from its pre-Buddhist origins, through the schisms between the different sects and up until the Chinese invasion in 1959.

Autobiography/Biography

Portrait of the Dalai Lama
Sir Charles Bell   (1946)
Broader than the title suggests. [Peter Hopkirk]

✔ **Freedom in Exile: the autobiography of His Holiness the Dalai Lama of Tibet**   *Tenzin Gyatso, fourteenth Dalai Lama* 1990
Includes the early life of the Dalai Lama in Tibet before he fled to India after the Chinese invasion. It is written with wisdom and compassion and is an inspiration.

✔ **Daughter of Tibet. The Autobiography of Rinchen Dolma Taring**
1986 (1970)
The author was born into one of the oldest families in Tibet, but was educated in Darjeeling, learning to write and speak English. Covers the fifty years leading up to 1959 and the flight of the Dalai Lama.

✔ **Tibet is My Country**
Thubten Jigme Norbu   1986 (1960)
The autobiography of Thubten Jigme Norbu, brother of the Dalai Lama, told to Heinrich Harrer. Jigme Norbu was recognized as a reincarnated lama and trained as a monk but moved to Lhasa when his younger brother was found to be the new Dalai Lama. In 1950 he was exiled to America where he married and works for the Tibetan cause.

✔ **Memoirs of a Political Officer's Wife in Tibet, Sikkim and Bhutan**
Margaret D. Williamson   1987
The Williamsons married in 1933 in Sikkim and during the short time they had together, before Frederick Williamson died in Lhasa in 1935, they made three tours of duty through the Himalayas. She writes: 'In a sense, that brief period was my life . . . '

Fiction

The Superhuman Life of Gesar of Ling
Alexandra David-Neel, Lama Yongden   1959
This epic has been described as the *Iliad* of Central Asia. Many of the exploits of the hero, Gesar of Ling, whereby he triumphs over evil, are probably based on historical fact.

Lost Horizon   *James Hilton*   1933
A plane crashes in Tibet and the passengers find themselves in a Tibetan lamasery – Shangri-la.

Lama. A Novel of Tibet
Frederick R. Hyde-Chambers   1984
The story, which is closely allied to fact, takes place between February 1956 when there was great unease in Tibet about the Chinese occupation in the west of the country, and March 1959 when the Dalai Lama fled and Tibet entered a dark age, worse than anyone had envisaged; many ill omens occurred in-

cluding earthquakes and the birth of twin-headed animals. There is an epilogue and prologue written in 1983.

Tibetan Folk Tales   *Frederick and Audrey Hyde-Chambers   1981*
A collection of over thirty legends and folk tales.

Folk Tales of Tibet   *W.F. O'Connor   1990 (1979)*
A collection of fifteen folk tales which O'Connor collected from many different sources during the two years he spent in Tibet.

Food

✔ **Food in Tibetan Life**   *Rinjing Dorje 1987 (1985)*
The author, who now lives in the USA, worked as a cook in a Buddhist monastery as a boy.

General Background

✔ **In Exile from the Land of Snows**
John F. Avedon   1985 (1979)
An excellent and sympathetic introduction to what has happened in Tibet; it demonstrates the extraordinary and indomitable spirit that the Tibetans have shown in their struggle against the Chinese.

Guides

The Tibet Guide   *Stephen Batchelor   1987*
The author is a Tibetan speaker and an expert in Tibetan Buddhism; the combination ensures a wealth of worthwhile information.

✔ **Tibet Guide. A Pilgrimage Guide. A Moon Guide.**   *Victor Chan   1994*

✔ **Tibet. A Travel Survival Kit**
Robert Strauss   1992 (1986)

The Power Places of Central Tibet: The Pilgrim's Guide   *Keith Dowman   1988*
Based on a nineteenth-century guide for Tibetan pilgrims, with descriptions of 170 monasteries, temples, sacred caves, lakes and mountains with information about their location, religious significance and relics.

✔ **Insight Pocket Guide: Tibet, Lhasa to Kathmandu**   *1993*

History

✔ **Bayonets to Lhasa**   *Peter Fleming 1992 (1961)*
An account of the Younghusband expedition

to Lhasa in 1903/4 in which Tibetan isolation came temporarily to an end, due to a treaty formulated by Younghusband which paved the way for Anglo-Tibetan friendship. However this was no straightforward event and because of adverse intervention from Whitehall the whole mission nearly failed.

✔ **Trespassers on the Roof of the World.**   *Peter Hopkirk   1991 (1982)*
Tibet was forcibly opened to foreigners in the nineteenth and twentieth centuries; here Peter Hopkirk describes the race for Lhasa which took place with missionaries, soldiers and explorers from nine different countries all competing to get there.

Tibetan Civilization   *R.A. Stein   1972*
A comprehensive survey of Tibetan civilization which is divided into five main sections: Habitat and Inhabitants, Historical Survey, Society, Religion and Customs, and Art and Letters. Much of what had been written about Tibet up until this time had either been too personal or too specialized, so this contribution from a celebrated French scholar was particularly welcome.

Tibet: its history, religion and people
Thubten Jigme Norbu and Colin Turnbull   1972
A Tibetan's view of the history, culture and religion of Tibet; an interesting contrast to the many Western accounts.

✔ **The Pundits: British Exploration of Tibet and Central Asia**   *Derek Waller 1990*
Derek Waller covers the period between 1863–93 when the British used many native explorers and spies to fill in the gaps on the map to the north of British India. Their records on the whole were far more detailed and accurate than their western counterparts.

Leisure

✔ **Trekking in Tibet. A Traveler's Guide**   *Gary McCue   1991*
The only guide that deals exclusively with trekking in Tibet. Includes how to pre-plan the trip and treks, as well as the pilgrimage to Mount Kailas.

✔ **Trekking in Nepal, West Tibet and Bhutan**   *Hugh Swift   1989*
All the principal trekking routes in Western Tibet are covered; includes much practical advice on clothing and equipment and a glossary of Tibetan terms.

Photography

✔ **Kailas on Pilgrimage to the Sacred Mountain of Tibet** *Russell Johnson and Kerry Moran 1989*
One hundred and sixteen photographs of the pilgrims and the landscape around Mount Kailas.

✔ **Tibet. Reflections from the Wheel of Life** *Photographs by Thomas L. Kelly Text by Carrol Dunham and Ian Baker 1993*
A photographic journey through the Tibetan wheel of life from birth through midlife to death and rebirth.

✔ **Tibet** *Kevin Kling 1990 (1985)*
Kevin Kling had access to many forbidden places when her husband was in Tibet on official business. She took advantage of this and the resulting book of ninety-six photographs contains many hitherto unphotographed landscapes.

✔ **Tibet: the Lost Civilisation**
Simon Normanton 1988
A well illustrated introduction to the history of Tibet seen through the writings and illustrations of early visitors such as Sir Charles Bell, Edmund Candler and Heinrich Harrer.

Religion

✔ **Magic and Mystery in Tibet**
Alexandra David-Neel 1984
During her travels Alexandra David-Neel met and was enthusiastically received by many mystics. She learnt a great deal about telepathy and psychic phenomena, much of which is related here.

✔ **The Tibetan Book of the Dead**
W.Y. Evans-Wentz (ed.) 1960
One of the great sacred books of the world which was considered not only as a guide for the dying but also for the living. In Tibet it is read or recited at the time of death; it says much about the science of death, life after death and rebirth.

Travel Literature

✔ **A Mountain in Tibet** *Charles Allen 1991 (1982)*
Mount Kailas, considered by both Hindus and Buddhists to be the holiest mountain on earth, is in the very west of Tibet. Close by are the sources of four mighty rivers: the Ganges, the Indus, the Sutlej and the Tsangpo-Brahmaputra. Few outsiders had penetrated this area behind the Western Himalayas; Charles Allen tells of those who succeeded.

✔ **Flight of the Wind Horse: a Journey into Tibet** *Niema Ash 1992 (1990)*
Niema Ash travels for enjoyment; this enthusiasm pervades the book even though she sees much which is depressing. She writes in a lively manner about incidents she witnessed giving a portait of Tibet today.

✔ **Inside the Treasure House: A Time in Tibet** *Catriona Bass 1992 (1990)*
The author spent over a year teaching in Tibet in the mid-80s; she has written an easy-to-read account of her everyday life in Lhasa in 1986 when things seemed to be improving for the Tibetans and there seemed to be reason for optimism; after she left the Chinese again began to shoot people in Lhasa.

✔ **A Stranger in Tibet: the Adventures of a Zen Monk** *Scott Berry 1991 (1990)*
A biography of the Japanese Buddhist, Ekai Kawaguchi, who reached Lhasa dressed as a Chinese doctor in 1901. He stayed there for some time having several audiences with the thirteenth Dalai Lama; there are debates as to whether or not he was a British spy – Berry thinks not, but he was shocked by much of what he found in Lhasa including the sexual infidelity of Tibetan women; these accounts, joined with his reports of Russian activities in Lhasa probably paved the way for the Younghusband Expedition.

✔ **First Russia, then Tibet**
Robert Byron 1985 (1933)
Byron contrasts post-revolutionary Russia with pre-industrial Tibet, both of which he knew fairly well and which he describes lucidly.

Point of Departure *James Cameron 1980 (1967)*
A chapter on Tibet and the Dalai Lama.

The Fire Ox and Other Years
Suydam Cutting 1940
An account of Cutting's journey on which he collected many objects for the Newark Museum.

✔ **My Journey to Lhasa. The Personal Story of the only White Woman Who Succeeded in Entering the Forbidden City** *Alexandra David-Neel 1988 (1927)*
Alexandra David-Neel had sought solitude and had had a desire to travel from childhood; as an adult she studied Oriental philosophy and comparative religion and managed to manoeuvre a meeting with the Dalai Lama in Kalimpong in 1912. After she

had visited Tibet she felt that here at last was the place she had dreamt of from childhood and as a result made many trips, meeting many high lamas before finally reaching Lhasa.

✔ Alone Through China and Tibet
Helena Drysdale 1986
The author travelled to Lhasa from Xian following a route similar to that which Alexandra David-Neel had taken years earlier. She describes in detail a sky-burial which she must have been one of the few westerners to have witnessed in recent years.

Captured in Tibet *Robert Ford (1957)*
A fine book by a brave man.

✔ Seven Years in Tibet *Heinrich Harrer* *1988 (1953)*
Probably one of the best known and most widely read books about Tibet; in 1943 Harrer, who had been interned by the British in India during the war, escaped from India and made his way to Lhasa. He won the confidence of the Tibetans and stayed there for seven years.

✔ Travels in Tartary and Thibet
Abbé Huc 1987 (1850) (see 'Mongolia')
The Abbé Huc was a Lazarist missionary who travelled, dressed as a lama, throughout Tartary and Thibet from 1844 to 1846. He and his companion, Gabet, met many Tibetans and learnt much about Tibetan Buddhism before finally reaching Lhasa.

Salween *Ronald Kaulback 1938*
Ronald Kaulback had first entertained the possibility of exploring the Salween River when he had been close to it with Kingdon Ward in 1933. The basin of the Salween River lies in South-Eastern Tibet and the aim of the journey he later undertook was to explore the Ngagong Chu valley, the Salween-Brahmaputra watershed and the upper part of the Salween, eventually trying to discover its source.

Tibetan Marches *André Migot 1955*
Migot travelled through Eastern Tibet in

1946/7, starting from Hanoi and ending up in Peking. He failed to reach Lhasa but visited Kantze, Derge and Jyekundo; he is sympathetic to Tibetan Buddhism and visited many monasteries on his journey.

✔ Heirs to Tibet. Travels Among the Exiles in India *Andrew Powell 1992*
Andrew Powell visited Tibet in 1987 and two years later made a pilgrimage through India and Nepal to find out by talking to a cross-section of Tibetan refugees through an interpreter, to what extent they were preserving their traditional culture. An interesting survey.

Diary of a Journey through Mongolia and Tibet in 1891 and 1892
William Woodville Rockhill 1894
Rockhill spoke both Chinese and Tibetan, ensuring that the detailed anthropological information in his books is accurate. He collected everyday objects on his journeys, many of which he gave to the Smithsonian Institution and which are illustrated in the text.

✔ Shambhala *Nicholas Roerich 1990* *(1930)*
Shambala appears as the mythic land in Western mythology, while in the East it is seen as both a physical place and the dawning of a new era of enlightenment. Roerich travelled through Tibet at the turn of the century and wrote about the Tibetan art and desert cities that he came across.

✔ From Heaven Lake
Vikram Seth (see 'Chinese Central Asia')

The Sacred Mountain: Travellers and Pilgrims at Mount Kailas in Western Tibet and the Great Universal Symbol of the Sacred Mountain *John Snelling* *1983*
Snelling explains the significance of Mount Kailas to the different religions which consider it their sacred mountain. He also documents both pilgrims and explorers who travelled to Kailas.

Indian Sub-Continent

GENERAL

Art, Archaeology and Architecture

The Rise of Civilization in India and Pakistan *Raymond and Bridget Allchin* *1982*
The development of Indian culture is traced from its roots in the paleolithic era through the rise and fall of the Indus Valley civilization, to the spread of Indo-Aryans and the emergence of the first city states in the early Buddhist period.

✔ **The Art and Architecture of the Indian Subcontinent** *J.C. Harle* *1990 (1986)*
Sculpture, architecture and painting of the whole sub-continent are included in this extremely useful book. The sections are: Early Indian Art, The Gupta Period, The Post-Gupta Period, The Later Hindu Period, South India, Painting, Indo-Islamic Architecture, Sri Lanka and Nepal. The text is full of illustrations and line drawings and there is a comprehensive bibliography at the back. [Geoffrey Moorhouse]

✔ **Great Monuments of India: Bhutan, Nepal, Pakistan and Sri Lanka. An Odyssey Guide** *Shobita Punja* *1994*

Autobiography/Biography

✔ **Autobiography of a Yogi**
Paramahansa Yogananda *1993 (1950)*
Yogananda was the first great Indian master to live in the West and to introduce thousands to yoga. His autobiography has been much acclaimed worldwide.

✔ **India Seen Afar** *Kathleen Raine* *1990*
The concluding volume in Kathleen Raine's autobiography, in which she reflects on the profound significance of Indian philosophy and wisdom.

General Background

✔ **Traveller's Literary Companion to the Indian Subcontinent**
Simon Weightman (ed.) *1994*

Hobson–Jobson: A Glossary of Colloquial Anglo-Indian Words and Phrases, and of Kindred Terms, Etymological, Historical, Geographical and Discursive
Colonel Henry Yule *1985 (1886)*
A delightful etymological discussion of Anglo-Indian words which show the complex symbiosis which East and West imposed on each other. There are interesting articles on durians, curry, tiffin and chintz as well as elephants, Elephanta and Bombay. [Geoffrey Moorhouse]

Guides

A Handbook for Travellers in India, Pakistan, Nepal, Bangladesh and Sri Lanka *L.F. Rushbrook Williams (ed.)* *1982*
This twenty-second edition of the 'Murray's' guide to India, originally published in 1859, was the last. For many years it was the only worthwhile guide and is certainly still worth buying second-hand if possible.

✔ **India Handbook** *1995 Published by Trade and Travel*
Includes Bhutan, Sri Lanka and the Maldives.

History

✔ **Heaven's Command** *1979 (1973)*
✔ **Pax Britannica** *1979 (1968)*
✔ **Farewell the Trumpets** *1987 (1978)* *James Morris*
The three volumes in James Morris' trilogy chart the course of the British Empire up until its decline. *Heaven's Command* describes the rise of the empire until its apogee in 1897, *Pax Britannica* describes the Empire at its moment of climax in 1897 and *Farewell the Trumpets* depicts the decline of the empire until the death of Sir Winston Churchill in 1965.

A Historical Atlas of South Asia
Joseph Schwartzberg (ed.) *1978*
[Geoffrey Moorhouse]

Natural History

✔ **The Book of Indian Birds** *Salim Ali and Dillon Ripley 1979*
The two authors are considered to be the founders of research into South Asian birds. Abridged from the 10-volume *Handbook of the Birds of India and Pakistan*, it is useful for the whole of the Indian Sub-continent and is practical and compact. [Geoffrey Moorhouse]

✔ **Indian Hill Birds** *Salim Ali 1987 (1949)*
Three hundred species of bird are described and many are illustrated in colour.

✔ **Birds of the Indian Subcontinent**
M. Woodcock 1984 (1980)

Travel Literature

Letters from India Describing a Journey in the British Dominions of India, Tibet, Lahore and Cashmere During the Years 1828, 1829, 1830, 1831 Undertaken by Order of the French Government *Victor Jacquemont 1979 (1834)*
Jacquemont was 'travelling naturalist' to the Museum of Natural History in Paris; he wrote lengthy descriptions of the specimens he collected, but also irreverent letters to his family and friends, who included Stendhal and Merimee, back in France. He died from an abcess on the liver in 1832 in Bombay, but his letters which had been privately circulated before his death were soon published to great acclaim.

✔ **Full Tilt** *Dervla Murphy 1991 (1965)*
Dervla Murphy fulfilled a childhood dream when she made a six-month bicycle journey of 3,000 miles across Europe, through Persia, Afghanistan and Pakistan and into India. The journey was fraught with danger and difficulty yet it is the warmth of the people she met which emerges.

Horned Moon *Ian Stephens 1953*
An account of a journey through Pakistan, Kashmir and Afghanistan.
'There's tempest in yon hornèd moon,
And lightening in yon cloud.' (Allan Cunningham)
The Horned Moon is the symbol of Islam; this is the description of a journey made during the spring and summer of 1952, an interesting time, just after the break-up of the British Empire in India.

HIMALAYAS – GENERAL
'As the dew is dried up by the morning sun, so are mankind's sins at the sight of Himalaya.' Puranas

Art and Archaeology

Himalayan Art: Wall-painting and sculpture in Ladakh, Lahaul and Spiti, the Siwalik Ranges, Nepal, Sikkim and Bhutan *Madanjeet Singh 1968*
The main bulk of the book, which is well illustrated, is devoted to this area of Northern India. Ample text describes the context in which the art was created.

General Background

✔ **The Himalayan Kingdoms: Nepal, Bhutan and Sikkim** *Bob Gibbons and Bob Ashford 1987 (1983)*
A basic introduction to the climate, geography and natural history of the three Himalayan Kingdoms; however, the emphasis is very much on Nepal.

Guide

✔ **India's Western Himalaya. Insight Guide** *1992*

History

The Gilgit Game *John Keay 1979*
The Explorers of the Western Himalayas 1865–95.
Today Gilgit is an administrative centre for northern Pakistan; it has always been strategically important because this is where the frontiers of India, China, Russia, Afghanistan and Pakistan meet. *The Gilgit Game* is the story of how, when and by whom this area was explored and exploited.

✔ **When Men and Mountains Meet**
John Keay 1981 (1977)
A history of the explorers of the Western Himalayas between 1820–75; the intrepid people such as Joseph Wolff, Victor Jacquemont and Alexander Gardener who actually managed to get to the Himalayas, a seemingly impenetrable barrier, were extraordinarily resilient; John Keay with his knowledge of the region brings them very much alive.

Natural History

✔ **Man-Eaters of Kumaon**   Jim Corbett
1992 (1944)
Ten stories about tracking and shooting man-eaters in the Himalayas at the beginning of this century. There is much incidental information on the flora and fauna of the area.

✔ **Himalayan Enchantment**
Frank Kingdon-Ward   *1990*
An anthology of Kingdon-Ward's best writing which combines his botanical activities with his geographical interest. He mostly travelled in the remote corner of the Himalayas where Assam, Burma, China and Tibet meet; it was through his writings that we know most of what we do about the flora, fauna, geology, climate and ethnology of the region. Included here are extracts from the following books: *The Land of the Blue Poppy, The Mystery Rivers of Tibet, In Farthest Burma, The Riddle of the Tsangpo Gorges, Plant Hunting on the Edge of the World, Plant Hunter in Tibet* and *Return to the Irrawaddy.*

✔ **Concise Flowers of the Himalaya**
Oleg Polunin and Adam Stainton   *1988*
Intended as a field guide, this is an extremely useful book to use in India, Nepal and Pakistan. Each entry has a scientific description and there are many colour photographs and line drawings.

Photography

Mountains of the Gods   Ian Cameron
1984
An account of the exploration of the Himalayas by Hindu pilgrims, Alexander the Great and present-day climbers.

✔ **Himalaya. Encounters with Eternity**   Ashvin Mehta and Maurice Herzog
1991 (1985)
Seventy-seven colour photographs of the scenery and people of Kashmir, Ladakh, Himachal Pradesh, Garhwal-Almora, Nepal, Sikkim and Darjeeling.

Travel Literature

✔ **Beyond the Limits. A Woman's Triumph on Everest**   Stacy Allison   *1994*
(1993)
Stacy Allison was the first American woman to climb Everest.

Point of Departure   James Cameron   *1980*
(1967)
One of the chapters in this autobiography is about Kalimpong and the Himalayas.

Where Three Empires Meet   E.F. Knight
1903 (1894)
Knight visited Ladakh with Captain Bower and joined Colonel Durand's expedition in Gilgit against the Hunza-Nagas; in his day the three great empires, Russia, China and Great Britain, met near Gilgit on the 'Roof of the World'. A classic book which narrates his travels in Kashmir, Western Tibet, Gilgit and the adjoining countries.

Abode of Snow   Kenneth Mason   *1987*
(1955)
This classic book contains descriptions of the mountains as well as a history of exploration and climbing expeditions up to 1954.

Peaks and Lamas   Marco Pallis   *1942*
(1939)
A compilation of different journeys made between 1933 and 1936 to Ganges and Satlej, Sikkim and Ladakh. Includes much about Tibetan art.

Stones of Silence: Journeys in the Himalaya   George B. Schaller   *1980*
George Schaller spent six years exploring the Himalaya studying the wildlife and looking for potential national parks; there is much about the animals he saw (one of the journeys is the subject of Peter Matthiesen's *The Snow Leopard* q.v.), but also as he says himself in the mountains 'one becomes an explorer in an intellectual realm as well as in the physical one, and the following pages include some of my lonely thoughts born of windswept mountain passes'.

✔ **The Seven Mountain Travel Books**
H.W. Tilman   *1991*
An anthology of Tilman's climbing books which includes *Nepal Himalaya.*

BHUTAN
'Nepal, Bhutan, Sikkim, Three Pendants on India's Himalayan necklace.' Ved Mehta
Portrait of India 1970

Art and Archaeology

Himalayan Art: Wall-painting and Sculpture in Ladakh, Lahaul and Spiti, the Siwalik Ranges, Nepal, Sikkim and Bhutan   Madanjeet Singh
1968
Bhutan's art history did not begin until the

fifteenth century, but since then it has developed a rich religious art which reflects the faith and ideals of the monks and the people. About thirty pages are devoted to Bhutan.

Guides

✔ **Introduction to Bhutan. An Odyssey Guide** *1993*

✔ **Trekking in Nepal, West Tibet and Bhutan** *Hugh Swift 1989*
About twenty pages on Bhutan are tacked on to the end of this book, nevertheless it contains some useful information about trekking routes.

History

Bhutan. The Early History of a Himalayan Kingdom *Michael Aris 1979*
The author was private tutor to the Royal Family of Bhutan and as a result spent five years in the country teaching, exploring, translating and studying. The book concentrates on early texts and is very scholarly, being a revised version of his thesis.

✔ **Bhutan and the British**
Peter Collister 1987
A history of 200 years of Anglo-Bhutanese relations; since much of the contact was through official missions, many diaries, letters and records have been drawn on in the writing of this book, which includes accounts of the travels of John Claude White, George Bogle, Alexander Hamilton and Samuel Turner.

Natural History

✔ **Field Guide to the Birds of the Eastern Himalayas** *Salim Ali 1977*
There are descriptions of 536 birds, 366 of which are illustrated in colour and the text describes their status and habitats.

Photography

✔ **Views of Medieval Bhutan. The Diary and Drawings of Samuel Davis 1783** *Michael Aris 1982*
Samuel Davis was a lieutenant in the Bengal Army who was appointed by Warren Hastings to join Samuel Turner's mission to Bhutan and Tibet as draftsman and surveyor.

Bhutan. Land of Hidden Treasure
Text by Blanche Olschak Photographs by Ursula and Augusto Gansser 1971
A three-month expedition which covered over 1,000 kilometres; the text provides a good introduction to the culture and art of Bhutan and the eighty colour photographs give a good overall picture of the country.

Bhutan. Land of the Thunder Dragon
Tom Owen Edmunds 1988
Colour photographs of the landscape and scenery of Bhutan as well as sacred artefacts are divided into eight different chapters or themes.

✔ **Bhutan. Kingdom of the Eastern Himalayas** *Guy van Strydonck 1989*
Colour photographs.

Travel Literature

The Thunder Dragon Kingdom. A Mountaineering Expedition to Bhutan
Steven K. Berry 1988
Steven Berry led the first British mountaineering expedition to Bhutan to climb Gangkar Punsum, at 24,770 feet its highest peak. The book is an account of the expedition as well as a description of the country and people.

✔ **Dreams of the Peaceful Dragon. A Journey Through Bhutan**
Katie Hickman 1987
The journey which was made with the photographer, Tom Owen Edmunds, took a year to plan and went from the capital Thimpu to the very east of Bhutan. They travelled mostly on horseback over mountain passes, through villages, impenetrable alpine forests and leech-infested jungles; they were often in country where the people had never seen a foreigner before.

Lords and Lamas. A Solitary Expedition Across the Secret Himalayan Kingdom of Bhutan
Michel Peissel 1970
Peissel started in Hassimara and travelled through Phuntsholing, Chuka, Paro, Thimbu, Tongsa, Tashi Yantse and Tashigang to Sam Druk Dzong Kar over a combination of mule track and road at a time when it was very difficult for foreigners to get visas.

Lands of the Thunderbolt: Sikhim, Chumbi and Bhutan *Earl of Ronaldshay 1923*
The author describes the countries he writes about as having some of the most impressive mountain scenery in the world, but goes on to note that his interest lies mainly in the

people and customs. The book describes his extensive travelling throughout Sikkim.

Sikhim and Bhutan. Twenty-One Years on the North-East Frontier
1887–1908 *J. Claude White 1909*
The author was Political Officer in administrative charge of Sikkim, a post he much enjoyed (although as he makes very clear in the preface he suffered financially as a result!) Afterwards he was put in charge of political relations with Bhutan and so travelled widely throughout the area. When his government service finished he wrote this geographical and historical account of the two countries.

KASHMIR, LADAKH AND ZANSKAR, AND INDIAN HIMALAYAS

'Who has not heard of the Vale of
CASHMERE
With its roses the brightest that earth ever
gave,
Its temples and grottos, and fountains as
clear
As the love-lighted eyes that hang over
their wave?'
Thomas Moore *Lalla Rookh* 1817

Fiction

Ahmed and the Old Lady *Jon Godden*
1976
An English widow travels with a young Indian servant in Kashmir during the Second World War.

✔ Death in Kashmir *M.M. Kaye 1984*
(1953)
The heroine is involved in a plot which has consequences for the whole of the free world.

Guides

✔ Insight Guide India's Western Himalaya *1992*

✔ Kashmir, Ladakh and Zanskar. A Travel Survival Kit *Margret and Rolf Schettler 1989 (1981)*

✔ Trekking in the Indian Himalaya. Lonely Planet Walking Guide
Garry Weare 1991 (1986)

Photography

✔ Zanskar. A Himalayan Kingdom
Olivier Föllmi 1989 (1988)
One hundred colour photographs of the people and landscapes of Zanskar; minimal text.

✔ Kashmir. Garden of the Himalayas *Raghubir Singh 1987 (1983)*
Begins with a preface by Jawaharlal Nehru who described Kashmir 'like the face of the beloved that one sees in a dream and that fades away on awakening', and continues with an introduction and 78 colour plates of people and landscapes by Raghubir Singh.

Travel Literature

The Himalayan Letters of Gypsy Davy and Lady Barrett. Written on Pilgrimage to the High Quiet Places among the Simple People of an Old Folk Tale *Pseudonyms of Robert Lemoyne Barrett and Katherine Barrett, 1927*
A book of a journey or *safar* (pilgrimage) in Ladakh and Baltistan, written in the form of informal letters about the 'high quiet places'.

Kulu. The End of the Habitable World
Penelope Chetwode 1972
Penelope Chetwode had originally ridden into the Kulu Valley with her mother in 1931; on her return to India in 1963, she made the same trip. The book is an account of her second journey, which inevitably includes memories from her first. She also describes the history of Kulu, where at one time Nicholas Roerich (q.v.) lived and which had a variety of English settlers.

Magic Ladakh. An Intimate Picture of a Land of Topsy-Turvy Customs and Great Natural Beauty
'Ganpat' (Major M.L.A. Gompertz) 1928
The book begins with Kipling's sentiment that we each have been 'appointed some particular corner of the world to be our own – some spot which should hold us more than any other'. Ganpat found his corner in the High Snows of the Himalayas and believes that in a previous existence he must have been a pack-animal of the high passes.

✔ A Journey in Ladakh *Andrew Harvey*
1984 (1983)
Andrew Harvey went to Ladakh to visit a Tibetan Buddhist community; his journey is a beautifully described travelogue as well as a spiritual quest: 'Ladakh *is* the land of high passes; my experience of Ladakh and its

people was to be, for me, a pass, into another awareness of reality.'

✔ **Travels in Kashmir**   Brigid Keenan
1990 (1989)
A popular and readable history of the people, places and crafts of Kashmir which draws heavily on the writings of earlier travellers.

✔ **Himalayan Circuit**   G.D. Khosla   1989 (1956)
A journey through the mountainous regions of Kulu, Lahoul and Spiti in the Indian Himalayas. There are many decriptions of the landscape as well as the religion and culture of the isolated communities he meets.

✔ **Where the Indus is Young**
Dervla Murphy   1991 (1977)
Dervla Murphy spent three months travelling through Baltistan (Little Tibet) with her six-year-old daughter Rachel. The whole region is covered by the Karakoram, but in mid-winter they walked and rode through five valleys including the Indus Gorge. They travelled very light and the book is interesting in that it shows how little is needed for survival as well as being enlightening about the area.

✔ **At Home in the Himalayas**
Christina Noble   1991
Christina Noble lived in Manali in the Kullu Valley for nineteen years and speaks Hindi. She was considered a hippy at the beginning (although she never thought of herself as one) and later became a businesswoman, wife and mother. The letters she wrote home to Scotland were cheerful (she did not want to worry her mother), but her journals reveal doubts and fears. The resulting memoir is well observed and highly revealing of life in the Western Himalayas.

Over the High Passes   Christina Noble
1987
Christina Noble spent a year travelling with the self-sufficient migratory Gaddi in Himachal Pradesh. She went with them from the Punjab plains, into Lahoul, the Kullu Valley and Kangra. The book is warmly observed and unsentimental.

✔ **Ancient Futures. Learning from Ladakh**   Helena Norberg-Hodge   1992 (1991)
The author has worked in Ladakh for sixteen years and writes about the so-called 'progress' that she has observed which has produced pollution and divisiveness, inflation and unemployment, intolerance and greed. She argues for a reappraisal of 'development'.

Zanskar: the Hidden Kingdom
Michel Peissel   1979
Peissel travelled to Zanskar when it was extremely hard to get there, so his book reads like an old fashioned adventure story.

✔ **Ladakh. Crossroads of High Asia**
Janet Rizvi   1990 (1983)
Janet Rizvi lived in Leh for a long time so is well qualified to write a book on this interesting mountainous area of Jammu and Kashmir. Leh is known as 'Little Tibet' and is the last outpost of Tibetan civilization, and is therefore Buddhist, but nearly half of the Ladakhis are Muslims and the Muslim/Buddhist mix has produced a unique society.

✔ **Painted Mountains. Two Expeditions to Kashmir**   Stephen Venables   1986
The 1983 expedition was to the unclimbed north face of Kishtwar-Shivlin which was a mixed climb on snow, ice and rock. The 1985 expedition was on the eastern ranges of the Karakoram close to the Indo-Pakistan border in a hostile and remote environment. The two very different expeditions are described in an historical setting.

NEPAL

Anthropology

Nepali Aama: Portrait of a Nepalese Hill Woman   Broughton Coburn   1982
While he was in the Peace Corps, the author lived as a guest of the Gurung woman, south of Pokhara, whom he subsequently wrote about in this delightful book which also has black and white photographs.

✔ **Against a Peacock Sky**
Monica Connell   1993 (1991)
Monica Connell lived as an anthropologist in the Jumla district of Nepal, ten days' walk from the nearest road. Although she was gradually accepted into village life, she always remained an outsider: 'The author has a rare combination of precise observation, humility and a sense of wonder.' (Maggie Gee)

Himalayan Traders. Life in Highland Nepal   Christoph von Fürer-Haimendorf   1975
Material on the Sherpas, the Bhotias, the Thakalis and other peoples from Mustang, Dolpo and Karnali.

Art and Archaeology

✔ **The Art and Architecture of the Indian Subcontinent** *J.C. Harle 1986*
(see 'Indian Sub-continent')
The last chapter is devoted to Nepal.

Art of Nepal: a Catalogue of the Los Angeles County Museum of Art Collection *Pratapaditya Pal 1985*
An illustrated and detailed description of the museum's collection, which is also a very good introduction to Nepalese painting.

Himalayan Art: Wall-painting and Sculpture in Ladakh, Lahaul and Spiti, the Siwalik Ranges, Nepal, Sikkim and Bhutan *Madanjeet Singh 1968 (see 'Himalayas – General')*
Over fifty pages are devoted to Nepal; many colour illustrations accompany the detailed text.

Autobiography/Biography

Man of Everest: the Autobiography of Tenzing told to James Ramsay Ulman *Tenzing Norgay 1955*
The book tells of the difficulties of being transformed from an ordinary sherpa into a celebrity and gives a whole different perspective to the Everest Expedition.

Tiger for Breakfast: the Story of Boris of Kathmandu *Michel Peissel 1984 (1967)*
Boris Lissanevitch, a White Russian refugee, became a legendary figure in Kathmandu where his Royal Hotel was a famous meeting place for Nepalese and foreign visitors. Michel Peissel originally met him when he helped him arrange a trip to Solu Khumbu.

Fiction

Beyond the Mountain *Elizabeth Arthur 1984*
The heroine joins a women's expedition to Nepal, after her brother and husband had died in climbing accidents.

Come Tomorrow *(1980)*
The Red Temple *Mani Dixit* **(1977)**
Two novels published in Kathmandu; the first is the story of a Tamang who serves on the Burma front and gets involved in gem smuggling, and the second is set during the fight of the Khampas in Tibet against the Chinese.

The King Who Rode a Tiger, and Other Tales from Nepal *Patricia Hitchcock 1966*
Twelve illustrated Nepalese folktales.

The Wake of the White Tiger
Daman Shamsher Rana 1984
An historical novel set in 1854–56 during the war with Tibet; not very accurate historically, but full of atmosphere.

Escape from Kathmandu
Kim Stanley Robinson 1990 (1989)
George and Fred who are trekking and enjoying themselves in Nepal find themselves caught up in saving the Great Mysteries of Nepal: they have to rescue a yeti, climb Mount Everest and save Shangri-la.

The Mountain is Young *Han Suyin 1962 (1958)*
Han Suyin attended the coronation of the King of Nepal and uses the background and events as the setting for this love story which was described by the *Daily Telegraph* as 'desperately readable, witty, edgy'.

General Background

The Wildest Dreams of Kew: a Profile of Nepal *Jeremy Bernstein 1970*
Begins with a survey of Nepalese history followed by a description of Kathmandu in the late sixties and an account of a trek to the Everest region.

Guides

✔ **Nepal. Insight Guide** *1992*

✔ **Nepal. The Rough Guide**
David Reed 1993 (1990)

✔ **Nepal. Travel Survival Kit**
Tony Wheeler and Richard Everist 1993 (1990).

History

Nepal *Perceval Landon 1928*
A two-volume history of Nepal, a country which had been closed to outsiders from early times; it was described by Marco Polo as 'wild and mountainous, and is little frequented by strangers, whose visits the King discourages'. By writing the book Landon hoped to present an account of the people as well as the land; 200,000 Gurkhas fought in the First World War and Landon pays tribute to them through his work. As one critic wrote: 'Almost wherever there was a theatre of war Gurkhas were to be found, and everywhere they added to their name for high courage. Gurkhas helped to hold the sodden trenches of France in that first terrible winter and during the succeeding summer. Their graves are thick on the Peninsula, on Sinai, and on the stony

hills of Judea. They fell in the forests of Africa and on the plains of Tigris and Euphrates, and even among the wild mountains that border the Caspian Sea. And to those who know, when they see the map of that country of Nepal, there must always recur the thought of what the people of that country have done for us.'

Leisure

✔ **Trekking in the Nepal Himalaya. Lonely Planet Walking Guide**
Stan Armington 1991 (1979)

✔ **Trekking in Nepal. A Traveler's Guide** *Stephen Bezruchka 1991 (1972)* Detailed and informative guide to trekking throughout Nepal; excellent descriptions of each day's trek and a comprehensive bibliography at the back.

✔ **White Water Nepal. A rivers guidebook for rafting and kayaking**
Peter Knowles and Dave Allardice 1992 Includes many different grades of river-rafting and should be of use to anyone contemplating a river trip as there are over 2,000 kilometres of river descriptions as well as sixty maps.

✔ **Trekking in Nepal** *Toru Nakano 1990 (1985)* The descriptions of the treks are quite good and are accompanied by colour photographs, but maddeningly there is no index.

✔ **The Trekking Peaks of Nepal**
Bill O'Connor 1992 (1989) There are eighteen permitted trekking peaks in Nepal; this book describes them and their camps with some historical background. Rather basic and not much detail about any individual stage.

Natural History

Search for the Spiny Babbler: An Adventure in Nepal *Ripley P. Dillon 1978 (1952)* The travels of an ornithologist in 1948 in search of a bird species; much interesting information on the natural history, as well as descriptions of the country.

Birds of Nepal *Robert L. Fleming 1976* Invaluable field guide to the birds of Nepal, covering over 2,000 species, but unfortunately is only available in Kathmandu.

Plant Hunting in Nepal *Ray Lancaster 1981* An account of an expedition to gather wild

plant seed in eastern Nepal with details of plants found along the route.

✔ **Royal Chitwan National Park Wildlife Heritage of Nepal**
Hemanta R. Mishra and Margaret Jefferies 1991 The official guidebook to the history, geography, geology, people, conservation and animals at Chitwan. There are many endangered species including the Royal Bengal tiger, the Asian one-horned rhinoceros and the Gharial crocodile. The book contais colour photographs of some of the birds, plants and animals.

✔ **Concise Flowers of the Himalaya**
Oleg Polunin and Adam Stainton 1988 (1987) (see 'Himalayas –General')

Stones of Silence: Journeys in the Himalaya *George B. Schaller 1980 (see 'Himalayas –General')*

Photography

✔ **Journey through Nepal**
Mohamed Amin, Duncan Willetts and Brian Tetley 1987 A large photographic book which gives some idea of what the country looks like with illustrations of wildlife, scenery, buildings and people. Scant text.

✔ **The Hidden Himalayas**
Thomas L. Kelly and Carrol Dunham 1987 Photographs of Humal, a territory on the edge of Nepal on the border of Tibet, taken during the different seasons.

Kathmandu: City at the Edge of the World *Thomas L. Kelly and Patricia Roberts 1989* Wonderful photographs are accompanied by essays on culture and religion.

Nepal Rediscovered *Padma Shrestha 1986* A collection of rare photographs of Nepal during the Rana era.

Honey Hunters of Nepal *Eric Valli and Diane Summers 1988* Extraordinary photographs of the acrobatic feats that the Gurung have to employ, to collect honey from beehives.

Religion

✔ **Himalayan Pilgrimage. A Study of Tibetan Religion by a Traveller through Western Nepal** *David Snellgrove 1989 (1981)* The author spent seven months trekking through the remote Tibetan-speaking regions of Nepal in 1956. He began along the border with India, went through Dolpo, Mustang and back into the Kathmandu Valley. David Snellgrove has published much on Buddhism and Himalayan culture; this book combines his expertise in those areas as well as being a descriptive travelogue.

Travel Literature

Annapurna South Face   Chris Bonington
1977 (1971)
An account of the 1970 ascent which was televised. The technicalities are described as well as the actual climb on which one member of the team was killed.

✔ **The Two-year Mountain. A Nepal Journey**   Phil Deutschle   1986
The author was in the Peace Corps in Nepal in the late 70s; his account is written in journal form.

✔ **Annapurna: Conquest of the First 8000 Metre Peak**   Maurice Herzog   1986 *(1952)*
The account of the 1950 French expedition, written by the author in hospital where he was recovering from frost-bite.

High Adventure   Edmund Hillary   1955
As well as the 1953 British Everest expedition, also includes the 1951 British and 1952 Swiss expeditions. Gives a feel for the atmosphere of the climb.

✔ **The Snow Leopard**   Peter Matthiessen
1989 (1978)
Although Peter Matthiessen primarily went in search of the elusive snow leopard in the remote Crystal Mountains to the very north of Nepal, his book is essentially a spiritual search. Inspiring descriptions of the scenery and wildlife make this in Paul Theroux's words 'A beautiful book, and worthy of those mountains he is among'.

The Waiting Land. A Spell in Nepal
Dervla Murphy   1967
Dervla Murphy travelled throughout Nepal, but spent much of her time in Pardi a hamlet in the Pokhara Valley, where she worked in a Tibetan refugee camp. Excellent descriptions of village life and people.

✔ **Travels in Nepal. The Sequestered Kingdom**   Charlie Pye-Smith   1990 (1988)
Charlie Pye-Smith travelled throughout Nepal from Kathmandu to Namche Bazar, down the Kali Gandaki and south to the Terai along the Indian border. He looks at the impact of foreign aid on the country and the

struggle that exists between the traditional way of life and modernization.

The Red Chapels of Banteai Srei And Temples in Cambodia, India, Siam and Nepal   Sacheverell Sitwell   1962 (see 'South East Asia')
Sacheverell Sitwell devotes four chapters to Kathmandu, Patan, Bhatgoan, Swayambunat, Bodnath and Pashupatinat.

✔ **Window onto Annapurna**
Joy Stephens   1988
The author and her husband went to Nepal to supervise a small hydro-electric scheme; they lived in a remote village inhabited by Magars who are of Mongolian origin and who were not at all interested in learning to read or write or having other Western customs thrust at them.

✔ **Everest**   Walt Unsworth   1989
The history of Everest with accounts of all the great expeditions and some of the failures. It tells of the pettiness and incompetence of some of the parties, but this is certainly balanced by the heroism of others.

MUSTANG

Travel Literature

Mustang. A Lost Tibetan Kingdom
Michel Peissel   1968
The author trekked from Pokhara, which he describes as an 'isolated village', but which later became a hippy centre, to Mustang on the Tibetan border, an area which was (and remains) very difficult to get to. The book describes his journey there and what he found when he arrived.

SIKKIM

Art and Archaeology

Himalayan Art: Wall-painting and Sculpture in Ladakh, Lahaul and Spit, the Siwalik Ranges, Nepal, Sikkim and Bhutan   Madanjeet Singh   1968 (see 'Himalayas – General')
Sikkimese art seems to be characterized by freedom of expression; the eighteenth- and nineteenth-century illustrations of folk-art are surprisingly modern.

Autobiography/Biography

Time Change *Hope Cooke* *1982*
An interesting view of the country by Hope
Cooke, an American who became Queen of
Sikkim.

Guide

✔ **Insight Pocket Guide Sikkim,
Darjeeling and Kalimpong** *1993*

Natural History

✔ **Field Guide to the Birds of the
Eastern Himalayas** *Salim Ali* *1977 (see
'Bhutan')*

Travel Literature

**Lepcha Land or Six Weeks in the
Sikhim Himalayas** *Florence Donaldson*
1900
The description of a journey made in 1891
which the author describes as 'a prolonged
picnic in one of the byways of the Himalayas
– where Time still walks on crutches' but the
extended picnic was one with no alcohol for
'At dinner the delicious mountain water was
the only drink, the difficulty and expense of
carrying wine or spirits up the rough roads
being so great . . . '

**Himalayan Village. An Account of the
Lepchas of Sikkim** *Geoffrey Gorer* *1967
(1938)*
Geoffrey Gorer went to Sikkim with John
Morris; he spoke the language when he arrived and spent several months in the village
of Lingthem, population of 176 people, making a record of the lives of the Lepchas (or
Rong as they prefer to be called).

**Living with Lepchas. A Book about the
Sikkim Himalayas** *John Morris* *1938*
The author was an ethnologist who had permission to stay several months in the Talung
Valley, the only remaining purely Lepcha
place in existence; in other parts of Sikkim
the people had already so intermarried with
Tibetans and Nepalis that they had virtually
lost all their tribal consciousness.

**Lands of the Thunderbolt: Sikhim,
Chumbi and Bhutan** *Earl of Ronaldshay*
1923 (see 'Bhutan')

**Sikhim and Bhutan. Twenty-One
Years on the North-East Frontier
1887–1908** *J. Claude White* *1909 (see
'Bhutan')*

Photography

✔ **Sikkim** *Rajesh Bedi* *1989*
A combination of photographs and text. The
photographs show the lush, rich tropical
vegetation of Sikkim, the Buddhist images
and people.

BANGLADESH

'I have never seen so lovely a place to look
at, nor one so loathsome to live in.' John
Beames *Memoirs of a Bengal Civilian* 1961

Autobiography/Biography

Two Under the English Sun *Jon and
Rumer Godden* *1985 (1966)*
The authors left England for Narayanuns in
East Bengal at the outbreak of war in 1914;
these memoirs are an evocation of a time that
is gone. Since children are much indulged in
India, the two sisters immediately felt at
home and 'content as we never were to be
content in our own country'.

Fiction

✔ **Janani** *Shaukat Osman* *1993 (1961)*
Two families of peasant farmers scratch a
living in colonial Bengal and although on the
surface their lives revolve round the harvest-
ing of crops, underneath there are many conflicts.

General Background

✔ **Songs at the River Edge** *K. Gardner*
1991
The author stayed with a family in a small
Bangladeshi village where she lived as a
Muslim woman sharing her life with the vil-
lagers.

Guide

✔ **Bangladesh. A Travel Survival Kit**
Jon Murray *1991 (1985)*

Travel Literature

✔ **On the Brink in Bengal** *Francis Rolt*
1991
A journey through tribal and Bengali villages
along the eastern border of Bangladesh.

INDIA

'India rarely changes and rarely forgets.'
F. Yeats Brown *Bengal Lancer* 1930

Anthropology

The Twice-Born. A Study of a Community of High-Caste Hindus
G. Morris Carstairs 1957
Carstairs spent his childhood in India and spoke Hindi as his first language; his book is a study of the differences which characterize three castes in a remote part of Rajasthan. The author, a doctor and anthropologist, explores the essential differences between Indian and Western personality structure. A fascinating study.

The Tribal World of Verrier Elwin: an autobiography *Verrier Elwin 1964*
Elwin who was greatly influenced by Gandhi spent much of his life studying and writing about the tribal peoples of India. He was influential in shaping the Indian government's policy towards the tribal peoples.

Family Web *Sarah Hobson 1982*
Sarah Hobson spent time with a family in rural Karnataka observing and participating in their customs. Much of the text is the actual discussions and words spoken by the family members about women, family planning, sex, village politics and kinship ties.

My Village, My Life: Portrait of an Indian Village *Prafulla Mohanti 1974*
All aspects of life in an Indian village are discussed: the joint family, economic systems, foods, religions, women, education and the cow. The villagers speak for themselves which makes this a very valuable book.

Art and Archaeology

(for books on Islamic art see 'Middle East')

The Birth of Indian Civilisation. India and Pakistan before 500 BC *Bridget and Raymond Allchin 1968*
A comprehensive survey of the foundations of Indian culture with descriptions of much that is known about the Harappan civilization from archaeological digs: its town planning, sanitation, baths and shops etc. The script has still not been deciphered preventing much further research.

✔ **Hindu Art** *T. Richard Blurton 1992*
A well-illustrated and very accessible book on the origins and development of Hindu art written by the curator of the Department of Oriental Antiquities in the British Museum.

Hindu art has largely been ignored by the West; this book does much to rectify the matter.

✔ **History of Indian and Indonesian Art** *Ananda K. Coomaraswamy (1927)*
A well-illustrated book which covers the whole range of Indian and Indonesian architecture, sculpture, painting and bronzes up until the arrival of the Mughals.

✔ **Indian Art** *Roy C. Craven 1991 (1976)*
A concise but comprehensive survey of Indian art which begins with the artefacts found from the Indus Valley civilization and continues through the ages by describing Buddhist and Hindu art and the Muslim arrival, which eventually led to the painting of Mughal miniatures and the building of the Taj Mahal.

✔ **Penguin Guide to the Monuments of India. Vol.2: Islamic, Rajput, European** *Philip Davies 1989*
Begins with an introduction to the historical and cultural period covered and continues with a gazetteer to the Islamic, Rajput and European monuments arranged by region.

✔ **Mughal Architecture** *Ebba Koch 1991*
A well-illustrated history and guide to gardens, palaces, mosques and other Mughal architecture in India between 1526 and 1858. The author looks at the various influences exerted on the Mughal style by earlier Indian and Persian architecture and also by European paintings and engravings.

✔ **The Hindu Temple** *George Michell 1988 (1977)*
An excellent survey of Hindu architecture as seen through the Hindu temple. The history and symbolism of the temple are explained and illustrated by examples such as Ellora, Elephanta, Khajuraho and Mahabalipuram with their religious, cultural and architectural significance.

✔ **Penguin Guide to the Monuments of India. Vol.1: Buddhist, Jain, Hindu** *George Michell 1990 (1989)*
Begins with an introduction to Indian culture and religion and continues with a gazetteer of the Buddhist, Jain and Hindu monuments throughout India, arranged by region. There is also a useful glossary of architectural terms. [Geoffrey Moorhouse]

✔ **Much Maligned Monsters** *Partha Mitter 1992 (1977)*
A fascinating look at European attitudes to Indian art as seen through the eyes of travellers, antiquarians, orientalists, archaeolog-

ists and the Victorians as well as a reassessment of present-day notions. One of the problems was, and often still is, that Europeans approach Indian art with a preconceived idea, whereas the art should in reality be viewed with new and unbiased eyes.

✔ **Mughal Miniatures** *J.M. Rogers 1993*
A first-rate introduction which is well illustrated.

✔ **The Art and Architecture of India: Buddhist, Hindu, Jain**
Benjamin Rowland 1967
Well-illustrated history of Buddhist, Hindu and Jain art in the Penguin History of Art series.

Annals and Antiquities of Rajasthan
James Tod 1983 (1829)
Extremely detailed survey of buildings, sites and ruins in Rajasthan. [Geoffrey Moorhouse]

✔ **Myths and Symbols in Indian Art**
Heinrich Zimmer 1946
Sadly Zimmer died soon after arriving in the States in 1943, leaving behind many unfinished projects. This book was edited by Joseph Campbell and is a reworking of a lecture course that Zimmer delivered on the interpretation of Indian myths and symbols at Columbia University in 1942.

Autobiography/Biography

✔ **The Autobiography of an Unknown Indian** *Nirad C. Chaudhuri 1991 (1951)*
Chaudhuri, a distinguished scholar, was born in East Bengal in 1897 and finally settled in England in 1970. The book which starts with the first twenty-four years of the author's life in Calcutta, shows an extraordinary understanding of the two different cultures, in fact Naipaul writes of it that it 'may be the one great book to come out of the Indo-English encounter'. [Geoffrey Moorhouse]

E.M. Forster. A Life 1879–1970
P.N. Furbank 1978
Forster wrote many letters home from India and this biography covers his time there in a fair amount of detail. It is also interesting as a background to *A Passage to India*.

✔ **An Autobiography or the Story of My Experiments with Truth**
M.K. Gandhi 1982 (1927–29)
Gandhi held to two firm beliefs during his life – *Ahimsa* (non-violence) and *Satya* (Truth), but as he said 'I have nothing new to teach the world. Truth and non-violence are as old

as hills.' His autobiography describes the practical applications of his beliefs. [Geoffrey Moorhouse]

✔ **An Indian Attachment** *Sarah Lloyd 1992 (1984)*
Sarah Lloyd fell in love with a Sikh and lived with him in a remote rural village for two years. The book is a beautifully written and genuine portrayal of life in an Indian village and yet there is a somewhat calculated feeling about it, which is profoundly disturbing.

Daddyji *Ved Mehta 1979*
The author's father had been educated in Britain and India and as a result did not feel at home in either. Mehta grew up in a north Indian family in the 1930s.

✔ **Thangliena. A Life of T.H. Lewin. Amongst Wild Tribes on India's North-East Frontier** *John Whitehead 1992*
T.H. Lewin, who lived from 1839–1916, was a soldier–administrator in the wild hills of India's north-east frontier. He was also an anthropologist, linguist, writer, artist and musician; he was known affectionately as 'Thangliena' by the Lushai whom he lived among and where he is still well thought of.

Fiction/Poetry

Coolie *Mulk Raj Anand 1980*
Anand was the foremost Indian novelist in the 1930s and 1940s; he tended to choose the disavantaged as his main characters. In Coolie a hill-boy dies of tuberculosis as a rickshaw puller in Simla.

Two Leaves and a Bud *Mulk Raj Anand 1972*
Set in an Assam tea plantation, Anand uses this novel as a protest against British rule in India.

✔ **Afternoon Raag** *Amit Chaudhuri 1994 (1993)*
Beautifully written book about the details of life: 'Again and again, he produces the perfect adjective, the stupendous adverb . . . radiantly exact.' (James Wood *The Guardian*)

✔ **Games at Twilight** *Anita Desai 1982 (1978)*
Eleven short stories set in urban environments, including Bombay, which give a very accurate feeling of the diversity of contemporary life in Indian cities.

✔ **The Village by the Sea** *Anita Desai 1988 (1982)*
Set in a small fishing village near Bombay

and based entirely on fact, Hari and Lila, who have lived in the village Thul all their lives, face the change into adulthood at the same time as industrialization encroaches into the village. Other novels by Anita Desai include: *Clear Light of Day, Cry, the Peacock, Fire on the Mountain, Voices in the City* and *Baumgartner's Bombay*.

All About H. Hatterr
Govindas Vishnoodas Desani   1970 (c.1947)
The 'autobiography' of a Eurasian who arrives in India to search for a philosophy of life which he finds after consulting seven sages. The book was hailed, on publication, as a literary sensation by T.S. Eliot and others.

✔ The Siege of Krishnapur   J.G. Farrell
1990 (1973)
A novel set in 1857 about the siege at Krishnapur: 'What a book. It has everything you could expect to find . . . characters, suspense, military action, romantic attachments, satire, wit, tenderness, philosophy.' (Mary McCarthy)

✔ A Passage to India   E.M. Forster   1989 (1924)
An incident at the Marabar caves between Adela Quested and Dr Aziz forms the central part of this classic novel which is one of Forster's masterpieces. He had obtained much of the material for the novel on his two visits to India as the guest of the Maharajah of Dewas Senior; on each visit he had travelled widely throughout the sub-continent. [Geoffrey Moorhouse, Jan Morris]

✔ Flashman in the Great Game
George Macdonald Fraser   1989 (1975)
This volume of Flashman's adventures deals with his involvement in the Indian Mutiny in 1857. Packed with action – in his role as secret agent, Flashman survived innumerable adventures at Cawnpore and Lucknow and flights from Thuggees and tsarist agents.

The Pilgrim Kamanita   Karl Gjellerup   1911
A novel about the last years of Buddha's life which combines the historical atmosphere of India with an excellent portrayal of the spiritual beauty of Buddhism.

✔ Heat and Dust   Ruth Prawer Jhabvala
1992 (1975)
A bored Olivia runs off with an Indian prince and thus scandalizes the small town of Satipur where she has been living. The story is told through the eyes of her granddaughter who returns fifty years later to find out what really happened. Other novels by Ruth Prawer Jhabvala include: *Esmond in India, The Householder, A Backward Place* and *A*

New Dominion and she has written several collections of short stories including: *A Stronger Climate, How I Became a Holy Mother* and *Out of India*.

The Sheriff of Bombay   H.R.F. Keating
1984
An Inspector Ghote mystery; other books involving Inspector Ghote of the Bombay police include *The Murder of the Maharajah* (1981), *Inspector Ghote Goes by Train* (1972) and *Inspector Ghote Draws a Line* (1979).

The Final Image   Dennis Kincaid   1939
Dennis Kincaid had a real knowledge, understanding and sympathy for India and her people. *The Final Image* is the story of Bhimi, a young girl from an Indian hill village who was married by her drunken father to his creditor, the local money-lender. She is unhappy with her elderly husband, so elopes to the city with her young lover; they struggle to adapt to city life, but their lives end in tragedy. Other novels of India by Dennis Kincaid include *Durbar* (1933) set in the town of Krishnagad at the time of the Dassera Durbar and *Cactus Land* (1934) partly set in Bombay.

✔ Bhowani Junction   John Masters
1987 (1954)
Published in the wake of partition, *Bhowani Junction* evokes the tensions and conflicts which occurred at the birth of modern India.

An Indian Trilogy:
The Deceivers
Nightrunners of Bengal
The Lotus and the Wind   John Masters
1978
Three novels set in India: *Nightrunners of Bengal* is based on facts about the Indian Mutiny.

✔ Tales from Firozsha Baag
Rohinton Mistry   1992 (1987)
Firozsha Baag is an apartment block in Bombay; by the end, the residents and the bustle of Bombay have become very familiar to the reader. Mistry also wrote *Such a Long Journey*.

✔ Waiting for the Mahatma
R.K. Narayan   1990 (1955)
Mahatma Gandhi visits Malgudi and gains an ardent disciple in Sriram who falls in love with Bharati, a loyal Gandhi follower. This book reaches the heart of Indian life like any other of his Malgudi novels which include *The Bachelor of Arts, The Dark Room, The English Teacher, The Financial Expert, The Man-Eater of Malgudi, The Vendor of Sweets, The Painter of Signs* and *A Tiger for Malgudi*. [Geoffrey Moorhouse]

✔ **Midnight's Children** *Salman Rushdie*
1981
India in the first thirty-one years after independence as seen through the eyes of two
people who were switched at birth in Bombay. A poetic and lyrical novel which captures the reality of life in India today.

✔ **The Raj Quartet** *Paul Scott 1985*
(1966–1975)
The four volumes *The Jewel in the Crown*,
The Day of the Scorpion, *The Towers of
Silence* and *A Division of the Spoils* together
form a marvellous panoply of life at the time
of the decline of the British Raj in India.

✔ **A Suitable Boy** *Vikram Seth 1993*
A vast and epic novel, set in the early fifties
just after partition, follows the lives of several families which all intermingle. The
theme of finding a 'suitable boy' for Lata,
runs through the book.

✔ **Selected Poems** *Rabindranath Tagore*
Selected and translated by William Radice 1987
(1985)
Yeats described Tagore as a poet whose work
'stirred my blood as nothing has for years';
this selection demonstrates Tagore's extraordinary diversity and innovation.

Tara. A Mahratta Tale
Captain Meadows Taylor 1863
Captain Meadows Taylor was asked to portray the events from 1657 as fiction for *Black-
wood's Magazine*. He declined at the time but
later wrote a long saga: *Tara, Ralph Darnell*
and *Seeta* representing three epochs in Indian history. *Tara* is the history of the
Mahrattas and continues to 1757 when they
were the most powerful state in India. *Ralph
Darnell* is from 1757 and portrays the Black
Hole. *Seeta* covers the fulfilment of the
prophecy that the Indian company should
come to an end.

Call the Next Witness *Philip Woodruff*
1948 (1945)
A picture of village life in Northern India set
in 1935; it was not written as a conventional
detective story because the way of dealing
with criminals in India was very different
from the usual detective fiction. It takes an
immense length of time to bring each witness
to court and therefore the story of each witness has to be told within the main story. All
based on fact.

The Wild Sweet Witch *Philip Woodruff*
1947
Philip Woodruff worked in Garwhal in
Northern India for many years. His novel is
set in this region with its unique hills and
people and is divided into three parts: *The*

Uprooting set in 1875, *The Uprooted* in 1923;
part three was published in 1938. Many of
the incidents are based directly on his own
experiences.

Food

✔ **Mahdur Jaffrey's Indian Cookery**
Madhur Jaffrey 1982
Easy to follow recipes which accompanied
the television programme.

✔ **A Taste of India** *Madhur Jaffrey 1985*
Easy to follow recipes from all over India.

✔ **Indian–Jewish Cooking**
Mavis Hyman 1992
A collection of recipes from the Jews of India
especially those who came from Syria and
Iraq. The author collected recipes from In-
dian Jews in Bombay, Calcutta and Cochin.

✔ **Indian Cookery** *Dharamjit Singh 1970*
Probably the best overall guide to the extreme variety of Indian cookery.

General Background

✔ **Calcutta. The Living City**
Sukanta Chaudhuri (ed.) 1990
The first volume is a compilation of Calcutta's past, while the second concentrates on
the present and future. Over fifty articles are
accompanied by nearly 1,000 illustrations.
Extremely useful for anyone who wants in-
depth knowledge.

✔ **The Dance of Siva**
Ananda K. Coomaraswamy 1985 (1924)
Fourteen essays on Indian art and culture
written by Coomaraswamy whose knowledge
of Indian culture, philosophy, religion and
language remains unexcelled. Coomaraswamy understood the West so that his essays aimed at westerners are extremely
illuminating and essential reading for those
who want to begin to understand the complexities of Indian culture.

✔ **City of Djinns. A Year in Delhi**
William Dalrymple 1994 (1993)
Dalrymple delves into Delhi's past unear-
thing many layers of history as well as re-
counting what life is like in the New Delhi of
today.

**Hindu Manners, Customs and
Ceremonies** *Abbé J.A. Dubois 1959 (1897)*
The Abbé Dubois spent the whole of his life
in the Deccan and Madras Presidency, as an
unprejudiced missionary; he was both a
Sanskrit and Tamil scholar and gives an

unbiased account of what he learnt about Hindus and Hinduism. [Geoffrey Moorhouse]

Banaras. City of Light   Diana L. Eck
1984 (1983)
Good descriptions of Varanasi and its religious significance and a thorough introduction to Hindu cosmology.

✔ **City of Joy**   Dominique Lapierre   *1991*
(1985)
An account of the city of Calcutta which concentrates on Mother Teresa, an unknown Polish Catholic priest, Stephen Kovalski, and Max Loeb, an American physician, all of whom have dedicated their lives to helping the poor. A compulsive pot-boiler.

✔ **The Speaking Tree**   Richard Lannoy
1974 (1971)
A study of Indian culture and society with chapters on art, the family, social structure, thought and Gandhi. An enlightening and instructive book which is very thought-provoking. [Colin Thubron]

✔ **Karma Cola**   Gita Mehta   *1991 (1980)*
A very perceptive, if somewhat cynical, look at the West's desire for eastern spirituality. Gita Mehta wittily describes the many charlatans, and occasional genuine guru, she found in India.

✔ **Portrait of India**   Ved Mehta   *1993*
(1970)
Ved Mehta's impressions of India from the Himalayas in the north to the arid Tamil Nadu in the south. He writes about villages, cities, religion, people from all walks of life, so that we get a real feeling for the rich diversity of the country. [Colin Thubron]

✔ **Calcutta. The City Revealed**
Geoffrey Moorhouse   1983 (1971)
An illuminating book about the city past and present, rich in anecdote and history. Kipling called Calcutta 'The City of Dreadful Night', but Geoffrey Moorhouse finds much that is heart-warming in the human spirit within the city.

✔ **Beyond the Dragon's Mouth**
Shiva Naipaul   1985 (1984)
Several articles in this collection are about India.

✔ **The Overcrowded Barracoon**
V.S. Naipaul   1984 (1972)
A whole section in this collection is devoted to India.

✔ **City of Gold. The Biography of Bombay**   Gillian Tindall   *1992 (1982)*
Gillian Tindall, a novelist and historian, describes the richness of Bombay's history, es-

pecially its architecture. The title comes from two sources: many people came to Bombay in search of their fortunes, but many died. Their bodies were laid in a place called Sonapur, which means 'City of Gold' – there is an Indian saying which says to die is to be turned into gold. [Colin Thubron]

Guides

✔ **India. The Rough Guide**
David Abrams, Harriet Podger, Devdan Sen and Gareth Williams

✔ **Cadogan Guide India**   Frank Kusy
1993 (1987)

✔ **India. A Travel Survival Kit**
Hugh Finlay, Geoff Crowther, Bryn Thomas and Tony Wheeler   1993 (1981)

✔ **Insight Guide Calcutta**   *1991*

✔ **Insight Guide Delhi, Jaipur, Agra**
1991

✔ **Insight Pocket Guide New Delhi**
1991

✔ **Insight Guide Rajasthan**   *1992*

✔ **Delhi and Agra. A Traveller's Companion**   Michael Alexander (ed.)   *1987*
An anthology concentrating on Delhi and Agra which includes extracts as diverse as Tamerlane's account of the sack of Delhi in 1398 to E.M. Forster's description of his 'beloved Rajah of Dewas' in *The Hill of Devi* in 1921.

✔ **Louise Nicholson's India Companion**
Louise Nicholson   1991 (1985)
An updated and expanded edition of *India in Luxury*, this guide includes Pakistan for the first time. A well-informed book which gives you great confidence and the feeling that the author really knows her subject which she imparts with enthusiasm.

✔ **India. A Literary Companion**
Bruce Palling   1992
An anthology of impressions of India which is divided into categories such as arrival, climate, religion, village India, Maharajas and departure. The extracts vary from Mark Twain's enthusiastic 'This is indeed India! The lands of dreams and romance, of fabulous wealth and fabulous poverty, of splendour and rags . . . of genii and giants' to the seventeenth-century traveller Peter Mundy's gruesome descriptions 'Women were seen to roast their children . . . A man or woman no sooner dead but they were cut in pieces to be eaten.' A collection such as this

would certainly benefit a traveller to the sub-continent.

✔ Introduction to Museums of India
Shobita Punja 1991
Begins with a short overview of the cultural history of India from the Indus Valley Civilization up until the present day and then continues with an illustrated guide to museums throughout India.

The Traveler's Key to Northern India
Alistair Shearer 1983
Introduction to the major religions – Hinduism, Buddhism and Islam and their chief religious sites. [Geoffrey Moorhouse]

✔ Gujarat, Daman, Diu   *Philip Ward*
1994

✔ Rajasthan, Agra, Delhi   *Philip Ward*
1989

✔ Western India: Karnataka, Bombay, Maharashtra   *Philip Ward 1991*
Detailed information on the chosen areas.

History

✔ Plain Tales from the Raj. Images of British India in the Twentieth Century
Charles Allen (ed.) 1976 (1975)
Around seventy British men and women who had lived in India talk about their experiences. This was originally a series of immensely popular radio programmes skilfully woven together by Charles Allen.

✔ The Wonder that Was India
A.L. Basham 1982 (1954)
An excellent overall introduction to Indian life and thought, up until the coming of the Muslims. There are chapters on Prehistory, History, the State, Society, Everyday Life, Religion, the Arts, and Language and Literature. It is addressed to the ordinary reader who has an interest in India without knowing much about it. [John Keay, Geoffrey Moorhouse]

Freedom at Midnight   *Larry Collins and Dominique Lapierre 1975*
An easy-to-read and dramatic book about partition and the events leading up to it. It concentrates on the tumultuous period from New Year's Day 1947 until February 1948. There are also portraits of Nehru, Gandhi, Jinnah and Mountbatten.

The Ganges in Myth and History
Steven G. Darian 1978
A comprehensive account of the cultural importance of the Ganges; Darian uses examples from archaeology, art, religion, mythology, literature and folklore to show how the Ganges came to occupy such a central place in Hindu life.

✔ The Great Moghuls
Bamber Gascoigne 1991 (1971)
An extremely good and well researched survey of the Great Moghuls with interesting text and beautiful photographs. The first six Great Moghuls who ruled India for nearly two hundred years from 1526–1707 were Babur, Humayun, Akbar, Jahangir, Shah Jahan and Aurangzeb. During their reigns a wealth of buildings (including the Taj Mahal) and paintings were produced.

✔ The Great Mutiny India 1857
Christopher Hibbert 1988 (1978)
An extremely readable and well researched book about the Indian Mutiny, including detailed anecdotes which help to enliven the tragic episode.

The Grand Rebel. An Impression of Shivaji, Founder of the Maratha Empire   *Dennis Kincaid 1937*
A study of the founder of the Maratha state whose memory inspired the rise of modern Hindu nationalism and who is revered in the same way as Frederick the Great by the Germans and Garibaldi by the Italians.

The Men Who Ruled India: The Founders   *1963 (1953)*
The Guardians   *Philip Mason 1963 (1954)*
The first volume starts with the Moghuls in 1600 and continues until the mutiny; the second volume begins in 1858 and goes up to the end of British rule in 1947. The emphasis in these books is on the actual men and what they were like and how they felt and thought rather than on their policies; some are obscure, others famous. As Philip Woodruff (q.v.) the author wrote several novels about his time in India. [Geoffrey Moorhouse]

✔ The Discovery of India
Jawaharlal Nehru 1989 (1946)
An attempt to delve into India's national personality by looking at her past and by following the cultural pattern which has maintained a continuity throughout its history. [Geoffrey Moorhouse]

✔ A History of India. Vol.1   *1990 (1966)*
✔ A History of India. Vol.2   *Romila Thapar and Percival Spear 1990 (1965)*
These two volumes of Indian history cover the whole period from the origins in the Indus Valley up until the post-Nehru period. The first volume goes as far as the coming of the Mughals and the second volume handles the Mughal and British periods. Although not intended for the expert these volumes are

fairly detailed and give a good general overall view.

Natural History (see 'Indian Sub-continent – General, Natural History')

✔ **Insight Guide Indian Wildlife** *1992*

Photography

✔ **Sadhus. The Holy Men of India**
Rajesh Bedi 1991
Ample text accompanies these photographs of esoteric monastic orders.

✔ **The Colours of India** *Barbara Lloyd 1988*
Barbara Lloyd takes a different colour as the theme of each chapter and demonstrates the immense variety within each, by a selection of relevant photographs. An original way to look at a country.

✔ **Mirror of India** *Roland and Sabrina Michaud 1990*
By using photographs on one side of the page and comparing them with painting or sculpture on the other, thus contrasting the old and the new, the Michauds' book of 175 colour illustrations gives an excellent view of Indian civilization.

✔ **Taj Mahal photographs**
Jean-Louis Nou 1993
Photographs of the Taj Mahal in detail accompanied by historical and explanatory text by Amina Okada and M.C. Joshi.

✔ **Khajuraho** *Raghu Rai 1992*
Detailed photographs of the erotic sculpture at the temple at Khajuraho.

✔ **The Ganges** *Raghubir Singh 1992*
The Ganges in different places and moods.

✔ **Rajasthan. India's Enchanted Land** *Raghubir Singh 1989 (1981)*
Satyajit Ray writes a foreword to this book which has an introduction and 80 photographs of buildings, peoples and festivals throughout Rajasthan, by Singh.

Religion

✔ **The Bhagavad Gita** *Translated by Juan Mascaro 1962*
One of the most important Indian texts; it tells the story of Krishna and Arjuna and their big battle. [Geoffrey Moorhouse]

Buddhism: its essence and development *Edward Conze 1975 (1951)*
The major developments in Buddhism are traced from their origins to the Tantric period; the book usefully begins by placing Buddhism in the context of world religions.

✔ **The Jains** *Paul Dundas 1992*
An up-to-date and comprehensive guide to Jainism.

✔ **The Marriage of East and West**
Bede Griffiths 1983 (1982)
Bede Griffiths, a Benedictine monk, lived in Southern India for nearly forty years in a community modelled on a Hindu ashram. This inspiring book shows what a success the mix between Hinduism and Christianity can be.

✔ **Buddhism** *Christmas Humphreys 1990 (1951)*
A good general overall history, introduction and guide to Buddhism by Christmas Humphreys, a Senior Prosecuting Council at the Old Bailey and Circuit Judge, who founded the Buddhist Society in London in 1924.

✔ **Hindu Myths** *Wendy O'Flaherty (ed.) 1975*
As Wendy O'Flaherty writes in her introduction to this collection of seventy-five seminal Hindu myths: 'Every Hindu myth is different; all Hindu myths are alike.' The paradox is very evident from this selection.

✔ **Hinduism** *K.M. Sen 1961*
A general introduction to the complexities of Hinduism, a religion unique in that it had no founder, but evolved from a combination of the Indus Valley culture with its emphasis on the female principle, and the nomadic Aryan invaders with an emphasis on the male principle.

✔ **The Upanishads** *Translated by Juan Mascaro 1965*
A selection from twelve Upanishads, spiritual treatises written in Sanskrit between 400–800 BC. [Geoffrey Moorhouse]

Travel Literature

✔ **Hindoo Holiday** *J.R. Ackerley 1983 (1932)*
J.R. Ackerley's extremely funny account of the journal he kept while he was companion to the Maharajah of Chokrapur in the 1920s. It shows the irony, absurdity and farce of Indian life, as well as the extreme richness of the ancient culture.

✔ **Memoirs of a Bengal Civilian**
John Beames 1990 (1961)
Beames was in India from 1858 until 1893; this lively narrative is about his time as a district officer from 1875 to 1878 and was written for his family rather than for publication. The memoirs give an extraordinarily vivid description of life in India at the time and were only discovered when Beames' grandson was sifting through papers for Philip Mason.

✔ **An Indian Summer** *James Cameron 1987 (1974)*
'When he describes the sounds and smells and characters and inevitable encounters of India he is unparalleled . . . It is his ability to come to terms with India's seething confusion which makes the descriptive passages required reading for a newcomer to the country.' (*Times Literary Supplement*). An invaluable introduction.

✔ **India File. Inside the Subcontinent**
Trevor Fishlock 1989 (1983)
Trevor Fishlock was the *Times* correspondent in India for which he won a citation that his writing 'reflects a deep understanding of the country combined with descriptive powers of a high order'. This is a detailed portrayal of the India he witnessed as he travelled around.

✔ **The Hill of Devi** *E.M. Forster 1965 (1953)*
Forster made two trips to India in 1912 and 1921 as private secretary to the Maharajah of Dewas Senior; this book largely consists of letters he wrote home to his mother, but he also collected much material for his later novel *A Passage to India* (q.v.).

✔ **Chasing the Monsoon**
Alexander Frater 1991 (1990)
In 1987 Alexander Frater followed the monsoon from Cape Comorin in Southern India to Cherrapunji in Bangladesh. The book was described by Melvyn Bragg as 'an exuberant rollercoaster of a book'; it is witty and amusing as well as being very informative.

✔ **Jesting Pilate. The Diary of a Journey** *Aldous Huxley 1994 (1926)*
Vivid and evocative impressions of many places in India including Taxila, Srinagar, Amritsar, Jodhpur, Udaipur, Fatehpur Sikri and Agra where the Taj disappoints him: 'I am always a little uncomfortable when I find myself unable to admire something which all of the rest of the world admires – or at least is reputed to admire. Am I, or is the world the fool?'

✔ **Into India** *John Keay 1973*
An extremely readable short introduction to India. In the space of 200 pages John Keay manages to describe much of the extraordinary diversity which any traveller would find.

✔ **Goddess in the Stones** *Norman Lewis 1991*
Norman Lewis travelled in Orissa, a part of India which had been described by early travellers but which was off the modern-day beaten track.

✔ **An Area of Darkness** *V.S. Naipaul 1968 (1964)*
V.S. Naipaul was born in Trinidad and it was not until 1964 that he went to India, an experience which shocked him. However his stay led to him producing a very perceptive and soul-searching book. [Stephen Brook, Paul Theroux]

✔ **India. A Million Mutinies Now**
V.S. Naipaul 1991 (1990)
'It is literally the last word on India today, witness within witness, a chain of voices that illustrates every phase of Indian life . . . Something like love enters the narrative – a real feeling for the land and its people' wrote Paul Theroux in the *Literary Review* about Naipaul's most recent book on India.

✔ **Slowly Down the Ganges**
Eric Newby 1983 (1966)
The description of a 1,200-mile journey down the Ganges which Eric Newby made with his wife. Newby states that he 'loves rivers', but when he embarked on this journey it had been twenty years since he had seen the Ganges. They started at Hardwar where the sacred river enters the plain and followed it by boat, bullock cart and bus to where it flows into the Bay of Bengal.

✔ **The Shortest Journey** *Philippa Pullar 1984 (1981)*
After achieving success in the West, Philippa Pullar realized that she wanted something more from life and went on a journey of discovery to India. She writes amusingly about her various encounters with gurus and eventually comes to the conclusion that the way to freedom is within oneself.

✔ **Travels on My Elephant**
Mark Shand 1992 (1991)
The author bought an elephant, Tara, and proceeded to ride her for 600 miles across India, from Konarak on the Bay of Bengal along dusty back roads to the elephant market in Sonepur.

The Red Chapels of Banteai Srei And Temples in Cambodia, India, Siam and Nepal   Sacheverell Sitwell   1962 (see 'Nepal' and 'South East Asia')
There are four chapters devoted to Delhi, Agra, Fatehpur Sikri, Jaipur, Udaipur, Bombay, Aurangabad, Ajanta and Ellora.

Monsoon Morning   Ian Stephens   1966
A portrait of India from 1942–44 when a Japanese invasion was feared. Ian Stephens was editor of *The Statesman* newspaper which was published simultaneously in Calcutta and Delhi – at the time an extraordinary technological feat; his view of India is therefore from a very interesting angle.

✔ **No Full Stops in India**   Mark Tully   1992 (1991)
Mark Tully was born in India and worked there for the BBC for many years; his knowledge is therefore almost unparalleled among foreigners and his sympathy and understanding are apparent through all of these ten essays.

✔ **Third-Class Ticket**   Heather Wood   1984 (1980)
A rich landowner left some money to the inhabitants of a small Bengali village, in order that they might 'see all of India'. Heather Wood accompanied them on some of their journey by third-class train and presents the experience through their eyes.

GOA

'It is a fine Citie, and for an Indian Towne very faire.' Ralph Fitch 1583–91 *Purchas his Pilgrimes* 1625

General

✔ **A View of the World**   Norman Lewis   1987 (1986)
An essay about Goa is included in this collection of journalism.

✔ **Window on Goa. A History and Guide**   Maurice Hall   1992
The first part of the book contains chapters on Goa's history, churches, temples, mosques, houses; villages and towns. The second part is a guide to the important and not so well-known sites. Well illustrated with colour photographs.

Hayit Guide Goa. Practical Travel A–Z   1994
Short but useful.

✔ **Goa**   J.M. Richards   1982
A general background book to Goa which pulls together its diverse architecture and culture. Portuguese rule did not end until 1961 after nearly 450 years so the vibrant culture which exists today is a mixture of Indian and Portuguese tradition.

✔ **Visitor's Guide India: Goa. A Moorland Guide**   Christopher Turner   1994

SOUTHERN INDIA

'When I had seen Madura I felt that I had at last seen a temple of Babylon in all its glory, and understood what the worship of Apis might have been in Egypt.' Wilfred Scawen Blunt *Ideas About India* 1885.

Food

✔ **A Cook's Tour of South India**   Vimla Patil   1991 (1988)
Both everyday and festive recipes from Andhra Pradesh, Karnataka, Kerala and Tamil Nadu.

Fiction/Poetry

✔ **Water**   Ashokamitran   1993 (1971)
It is 1969 and there is a bad drought in Madras; Jamuna is struggling to hold her life together, but is overcome by despair.

Mahabalipuram   Louis MacNeice   1948
'A monochrome world that has all the indulgence of colour,
A still world whose every harmonic is audible,
Largesse of spirit and stone;'

Guides

✔ **Cadogan Guide India: South India**   1994

✔ **Insight Guide South India**   1992

✔ **South India: Tamil Nadu, Kerala, Goa**   Philip Ward   1992

✔ **Visitor's Guide India: Goa. A Moorland Guide**   Christopher Turner   1994

Photography

✔ **Kerala. The Spice Coast of India.**   Raghubir Singh   1986
Colour photographs which show the many

different aspects of Kerala from the coast to the hinterland.

Religion

✔ **Hidden Journey** *Andrew Harvey 1994 (1991)*
Andrew Harvey first met his teacher, Mother Meera, in Southern India. This is the account of that meeting and of his spiritual struggles. A moving and brave book.

Travel Literature

✔ **Deccan Tamasha** *Robin Brown 1993*
Southern India by motorcycle.

✔ **Om. An Indian Pilgrimage**
Geoffrey Moorhouse 1993
Geoffrey Moorhouse spent three months travelling throughout Southern India in 1992. He had riveting conversations with a wide range of people, but it is his spiritual quest and encounters with gurus and in ashrams which make this observant book hang together.

✔ **On a Shoestring to Coorg. An Experience of Southern India**
Dervla Murphy 1976
This was the first trip outside Europe that Dervla Murphy made with her then five-year-old daughter Rachel. Coorg was once the smallest province of British India and lies between the Malabar Coast and the Carnatic. It is mountainous with dense forests, paddy fields and coffee plantations; they wander around on foot and by public transport and many new horizons are opened up through a five-year-old's eyes.

Ooty Preserved: a Victorian Hill Station in India *Mollie Panter-Downes 1967*
A delightful book about those families who could not bring themselves to live anywhere other than Ooty.

✔ **Three-Quarters of a Footprint. Travels in South India** *Joe Roberts 1994*
Much praised on publication, this book is a perceptive look at Southern India today, as well as having much background on the history and religion.

Kerala. A Portrait of the Malabar Coast *George Woodcock 1967*
Kerala was not created as an Indian state until 1956; it is the second smallest state and was the first democratically to elect a communist government. Woodcock travelled

throughout Kerala for three months observing its uniqueness.

PAKISTAN
'Lahore is one of the greatest Cities of the East . . . ' William Finch *Journal* 1610, in *Purchas his Pilgrimes* 1625

Art and Archaeology

The Birth of Indian Civilisation
Bridget and Raymond Allchin 1968
(see 'India – Archaeology')

The Indus Civilization
Mortimer Wheeler 1968
Mortimer Wheeler was one of the chief archaeologists digging in the Indus Valley. In this book he discusses the finds, and describes the life and art of the Indus Valley or Harappan civilization much of which was deduced from what he found.

Autobiography/Biography

✔ **Daughter of the East** *Benazir Bhutto 1990 (1988)*
Benazir Bhutto's autobiography about her childhood, education at Radcliffe and Oxford and subsequent politicization, gives an illuminating account of her determination and vision for Pakistan.

Fiction/Poetry

Black Mirrors *Farukh Khalid 1987*
The events in the lives of the people who live in a run-down hotel in Lahore.

✔ **Kim** *Rudyard Kipling 1987 (1901)*
'First whet my appetite for the Great Game – and still does. Although about a child, it is not really a children's book. Alas, many adults don't read it because they think it is.' (Peter Hopkirk) [Also nominated by Geoffrey Moorhouse]

Kingdom's End and Other Stories
Saadat Hasan Manto 1987
Manto wrote many short stories set during the period of partition. He died in 1955.

The Penguin Book of Modern Urdu Poetry *Mahmood Jamal (ed.) 1986*
A cross-section of twentieth-century Urdu poets, many of whom are still writing.

✔ **Shame** *Salman Rushdie 1984 (1983)*
A novel which can be read on many different levels: fable, history or fiction. It teems with

people and imagery and is highly instructive about Pakistan while being full of black humour.

The Bride *Bapsi Sidhwa 1983*
Set at the time of partition – the old world clashes with the new.

Guides

✔ **Insight Guide Pakistan** *1992*

✔ **Pakistan. A Travel Survival Kit**
John King and David St Vincent   1993 (1981)

Pakistan Handbook *Isobel Shaw 1989*
Isobel Shaw lived in Pakistan and has therefore written an extremely well-informed guidebook which includes maps, a trekking guide, historical and background information, descriptions of the sights as well as practical information on hotels and restaurants etc.

History

The Pathans *Olaf Caroe 1958*
The author was governor of the North-West frontier province up until independence; this is an excellent general history to the region.

The Lion River *Jean Fairley 1975*
The Indus River is alleged to rise in Lake Manasarowar in western Tibet which is also the source of the other three great rivers of northern India. Known as the Lion River because of its wildness, the book describes the history, geography and people of the region that the Indus runs through: Alexander, the Huns, Mongols, Afghans, Hindus and Buddhists all passed along the Indus.

Every Rock, Every Hill *Victoria Schofield*
1987 (1984)
A Plain Tale of the North-West Frontier and Afghanistan.
An easy-to-read history of the North-West frontier province, which became part of Pakistan, and Afghanistan, from the time of Alexander until the present day.

Leisure

✔ **Trekking in Pakistan and India**
Hugh Swift 1990
Covers the whole of the mountain country of Northern Pakistan and is of use to both experienced and inexperienced trekkers. There are maps and illustrations throughout.

Natural History

✔ **Concise Flowers of the Himalaya**
Oleg Polunin and Adam Stainton   1988 (see
'Himalayas – General')
Although not specifically on the flora of Pakistan, there are enough examples for it to be of use.

Photography

✔ **Journey through Pakistan**
Mohamed Amin, Duncan Willetts and
Graham Hancock 1982
Glossy photographs showing the diversity of the country from the mountainous north to the port of Karachi and the beaches of the south.

Travel Literature

✔ **The Golden Peak. Travels in Northern Pakistan** *Kathleen Jamie 1993*
(1992)
The acute observations and original way of looking at things make this journey through Northern Pakistan by the Scottish poet, Kathleen Jamie, well worth the read.

The Tigers of Baluchistan
Sylvia A. Matheson 1967
Sylvia Matheson worked in the Political Intelligence Department of the Foreign Office, in the Psychological Warfare Branch, as a journalist in Italy and India, as an archaeologist in Afghanistan and lived among the Bugtis, the 'tigers of Baluchistan', in Western Pakistan for five years. She had one of the tribe's warriors as her bodyguard and with him travelled all over the region including areas normally barred to foreigners.

The Narrow Smile. A Journey Back to the North-West Frontier *Peter Mayne*
1955 (see 'Afghanistan')

✔ **To the Frontier** *Geoffrey Moorhouse*
1992 (1984)
Geoffrey Moorhouse's journey through Sind, Baluchistan and the Punjab and through the Khyber Pass to the border with Afghanistan and into the Hindu Kush gives a wonderful background to the area which, combined with personal anecdote, conveys a powerful impression. [John Keay]

✔ **Among the Believers** *V.S. Naipaul*
1982 (1981) (see 'Iran')
Naipaul's journey through Islamic countries includes a large section on Pakistan.

✔ **The Afghan Amulet**   *Sheila Paine*
1994 (see 'Middle East – General')

On Alexander's Track to the Indus: personal narrative of explorations on the North-West Frontier of India
Aurel M. Stein   1929
The emphasis is on the Buddhist period of North-West Frontier history, although he combines his travel with history and archaeology.

SRI LANKA

'There is so much vegetable luxuriance in Ceylon, that even the marrow in people's bones is vegetable marrow. My!' Edward Lear, letter to Lord Carlingford, 28 March 1875

Art and Architecture

The Arts and Crafts of India and Ceylon   *Ananda K. Coomaraswamy   1964*
The major and minor arts of Sri Lanka.

Autobiography/Biography

✔ **Running in the Family**
Michael Ondaatje   1984 (1982)
An evocative, poetic book which is partly autobiographical. Ondaatje was born into a family in Ceylon which was a mixture of Dutch, Tamil and Sinhalese; here he describes, through a series of sketches and asides, his exotic and unorthodox family.

An Autobiography   *1880–1911*
Leonard Woolf
Leonard Woolf was a civil servant in Ceylon until he left to marry Virginia. During his time there he became increasingly disillusioned with British imperialism. A very interesting portrayal of what life was like.

Fiction

Boomerang   *Mark Bartholomeusz   1983*
Interesting in that it explores the practice of the occult and exorcism in Sri Lanka which are not often written about in English.

✔ **The Scorpion Fish**   *Nicolas Bouvier*
1987 (1981)
A novel set on 'the Island' and narrated by a historian who is ill and therefore extremely vulnerable to the magic which is present. He gets hold of a book about Indian insects, which interweaves with the insects in his room. Bouvier had himself spent a lonely and reflective time in Ceylon and wrote this book which George Steiner describes as a 'dark sparkling little masterpiece'.

The Fountains of Paradise   *Arthur C. Clarke   1979*
In his foreword Arthur C. Clarke states that 'The country I have called Taprobane does not quite exist, but is about ninety percent congruent with the island of Ceylon (now called Sri Lanka)'. The novel is about the master engineer Vannevar Morgan whose project is the building of a space elevator, to launch men and materials outside the earth's atmosphere, from a sacred mountain (Adam's Peak) in Taprobane.

✔ **Monkfish Moon**   *Romesh Gunesekera*
1993 (1992)
Nine haunting stories set in Sri Lanka which give a compelling picture of the country. This is Gunesekera's first book; the style is deceptively simple, but the content and feelings show a remarkable depth. ✔ *Reef* (1994) is narrated by a young man called Triton who goes to Colombo to work as a servant and cook for the wealthy Mr Salgado. His recipes become more and more exotic. Eventually he is taken to London by his boss.

One Last Mirror   *Andrew Harvey   1985*
A novel set in Sri Lanka which makes use of the *Dhammapada*, a collection of sayings of the Buddha and the principal scripture for Buddhists in Sri Lanka.

The Winds of Sinhala   *Colin de Silva   1982*
Set in the second century BC, this is a romantic rendition of the story of King Dutugamunu.

Grass for My Feet. Vignettes of Village Life in Sri Lanka   *Jinadasa Vijayatunga*
1970 (1935)
Probably the best known work of fiction of a Sri Lankan writing in English; it evokes the calmness of village life.

Lay Bare the Roots
Martin Wickramasinghe   1968 (1940)
About a boy growing up in village Sri Lanka and how he deals with all the changes going on around him. The author is one of Sri Lanka's best known writers.

The Village in the Jungle
Leonard Woolf   1981 (1913)
Through this novel, written in London, Leonard Woolf tried to live vicariously the lives of the people he had met and known during his seven years in the Ceylon Civil Service. [Paul Theroux]

General Background

✔ **Only Man is Vile. The Tragedy of Sri Lanka**   *William McGowan   1993 (1992)*
The author has lived and travelled in Sri Lanka extensively over several years. This compelling book focuses on the problems and struggles which are facing the country – nationalistic, racial and religious.

✔ **Places**   *Jan Morris   1984*
One essay in this collection is on Sri Lanka.

Guides

✔ **Insight Guide Sri Lanka**   *1992*

✔ **Sri Lanka. A Travel Survival Kit**
John Noble, Susan Forsyth and Tony Wheeler   1993 (1980)

History

Golden Tips   *H.W. Cave   1901 (1900)*
Ceylon's tea industry played an important part in world commerce extremely quickly; this interesting and readable account of how and why this happened goes into detail without becoming too technical.

An Historical Relation of Ceylon
Robert Knox   1911
Robert Knox was captured with his father during a voyage for the East India Company in 1660 to Cottiar to get a replacement mast for his ship. He was held for twenty years but his father died after only a year in captivity. This book which contains his autobiographical notes was found in the Bodleian Library.

The Story of Ceylon   *E.F.C. Ludowyk   1967*
Ceylon is traced from its part-legendary beginnings, through the development of the ancient civilization, to the Portuguese and Dutch administrations, to the 150 years of British rule and events post-independence up until 1967.

History of Sri Lanka   *K.M. de Silva   1981*
One of the first in-depth histories to cover post-independence Sri Lanka and therefore bring it more or less up-to-date. Although it starts with ancient Sri Lanka there is much about the period of British rule.

Natural History

The Reefs of Taprobane. Underwater Adventures Around Ceylon
Arthur C. Clarke   1957
Arthur C. Clarke has lived for many years in Sri Lanka where one of his great interests is diving. In this book he describes some of the wrecks and the marine life around the island.

A Guide to the Birds of Ceylon
George Morrison Henry   1971
Four hundred species are described and illustrated in this well-known work.

Photography

Island: Ceylon   *Roloff Beny   1971 (1970)*
A magnificent book of illustrations; the text is mainly drawn from other writings on Ceylon.

Religion

Medusa's Hair. An Essay on Personal Symbols and Religious Experience
Gananath Obeyesekere   1981
The author spent a sabbatical year in Sri Lanka in 1978/9. In his preface he writes that he was much more relaxed and open to experience than he would have been in 'the somewhat unreal ethos of La Jolla, California'. A fascinating book, since as a native Sri Lankan, who had continued to make regular visits to his country, he was able to probe the nature of the inner lives of many people.

Travel Literature

Eight Years' Wanderings in Ceylon
S.W. Baker   1855
Eight years of wanderings throughout the island created a 'love for this beautiful island which can only be equalled by my affection for Old England'. Baker was interested in seeing the natural resources as well as looking at its former relics.

The Treasure of the Great Reef
Arthur C. Clarke   1964
The account of a treasure trove found in a wreck off the coast of Sri Lanka in 1961. As Arthur C. Clarke says at the beginning of the book the chances of finding an unplundered shipwreck with treasure intact are very remote: 'But miracles sometime happen, especially to those who are prepared for them. In the spring of 1961, on the old Spice Route to India, one happened to us.'

Two Happy Years in Ceylon
Constance Gordon-Cumming   1892
The author wrote that these two years were the happiest of her life and since 'it was all play and no work', she had ample time to make copious notes about what she did and saw.

MALDIVES

Guides

✔ **Guide to the Maldives**
Lydia J. Cuthbertson   1994
A small guide which lists the various resorts
and has colour photographs.

✔ **Introduction to the Maldives. An
Odyssey Guide**   *Kirsten Ellis   1993 (1991)*

✔ **Spectrum Guide to Maldives**
Compiled by Camerapix   1993

✔ **Maldives and Islands of the East
Indian Ocean. Travel Survival Kit**
Robert Willox   1993 (1990)

Natural History

**Common Reef Fishes of the Maldives 1
and 2**   *Charles Anderson and Ahamed Hafiz
1987 and 1989*
Basic but very useful colour-illustrated
guides, for snorkellers and divers with labels
in English, Maldivian, German, French and
Japanese, to the most commonly seen reef
fishes.

**Land of a Thousand Atolls: A Study of
Marine Life in the Maldive and
Nicobar Islands**   *Irenaus Eibl-Eibesfeldt
1965*
The author was part of the Hans Hass expedition to the Indian Ocean in 1957. A yacht
was equipped as a marine biological research
station and the scientists on board visited the
Red Sea, the Maldives, Ceylon and the Nico-
bars.

Photography

✔ **Journey through Maldives**
*Mohamed Amin, Duncan Willetts and
Peter Marshall   1993*
A large and lavishly illustrated book.

Travel Literature

✔ **The Travels of Ibn-Battuta A.D.
1325–1354** *(see 'North Africa')*
Ibn Battuta visited the Maldives and Ceylon
before sailing to China on a junk.

The Maldive Mystery   *Thor Heyerdahl
1986*
A statue of a male figure with elongated
earlobes is found in the Maldives which, as
an Islamic state, had for years successfully
repressed any notion of a pre-Moslem past;

but Heyerdahl searched for and discovered
many statues and a sixth-century temple.

INDIAN OCEAN ISLANDS

'The Injian Ocean sets an' smiles
So sof', so bright, so bloomin' blue;
There arn't a wave for miles and miles
Excep' the jiggle from the screw.'
Rudyard Kipling *For to Admire* 1894

Fiction/Poetry

✔ **The Arabian Nights
Entertainment**   *Translated by
Richard Burton   1975 (1880)*
The seven voyages of Sinbad reveal the vi-
sions people had in the eighth century of the
Indian Ocean.

✔ **The Rain Forest**   *Olivia Manning   1991
(1974)*
Set on Al-Bustan, an island in the Indian
Ocean.

History

✔ **The Dutch Seaborne Empire
1600–1800**   *Charles R. Boxer   1977 (1965)*
A detailed account of the Dutch mercantile
influence worldwide, with many references
to the Indian Ocean area.

Pirates of the Eastern Seas 1618–1723
Charles Gray   1971 (1933)
An account of piracy in the Indian Ocean;
pirate crews from Réunion, the Comoro Islands, Mauritius and Madagascar preyed on
ships engaged in trade with India and the
spice-producing islands of East Asia.

The Indian Ocean   *Alan Villiers   1952*
Descriptions of Madagascar, Ceylon and the
Kerguélen islands with many anecdotal
stories and accounts of the boats that ply the
ocean such as Arab dhows and Chinese
junks.

Travel Literature

✔ **The Travels of Marco Polo**
Ronald Latham (ed.)   1982
Chapters 6, 7 and 8 deal with Marco Polo's
voyage across the Indian Ocean on his return
from China.

✔ **Darwin and the Beagle**
Alan Moorehead   1969
Darwin's diary which he kept on board the
Beagle records the landings he made on the

Cocos (Keeling) Islands, and at Mauritius and Bourbon Islands (Réunion) in the Indian Ocean.

✔ **The Sinbad Voyage**   Tim Severin   1982
The voyage was undertaken to find out whether Sinbad had really sailed from Arabia to China in the ninth century. A 'boom' was built in Oman according to contemporary shipbuilding specifications and the crew lived and ate like sailor's in Sinbad's time.

ANDAMAN ISLANDS AND NICOBARS

'These people have not any acquaintance with any other people, neither have they trade with any, but live onely of such Fruites as those Ilands yeeld.' Caesar

Frederick, *Indian Observations* c.1567, in *Purchas his Pilgrimes* 1625

Fiction

✔ **Persistent Rumours**   Lee Langley   1993
Set in the Andamans.

History

The Fire Ox and Other Years
Suydam Cutting   1947 (1940)
On pp. 247–64, the author gives a description of the Andaman Islands and the islanders' way of life. He went to this penal colony established by the British to do research for the American Museum of Natural History.

Far East

GENERAL

Fiction/Poetry

✔ **Pacific Nightmare**   Simon Winchester   1993 (1992)
A highly plausible novel about the possibilities of a third world war in the Far East.

Food

✔ **A Taste of the Far East**
Madhur Jaffrey   1993 (see South East Asia)

✔ **The Complete Asian Cookbook**
Charmaine Solomon   1993 (see 'South East Asia')

General Background

✔ **A Traveller's Guide to Asian Culture**   Kevin Chambers   1989
A potted history and background to the countries of Asia.

Pliny the Elder. Natural History a Selection   *Translated by John F. Healy   1991*
(see 'Africa– General')
Pliny the Elder (AD 23–79) collected together over 20,000 facts from 2,000 earlier texts making his work the major source for ancient

beliefs about agriculture, architecture, astronomy, geography, metallurgy and zoology. 'The first human beings we come to are the people called the Chinese, who are well known for a woollen substance obtained from their forests.'

Guides

✔ **North-East Asia on a Shoestring**
Robert Storey   1992
Includes: China, Hong Kong, Japan, Macau, Mongolia, North Korea, South Korea and Taiwan.

History

✔ **East Asia. From Chinese Predominance to the Rise of the Pacific Rim**
Arthur Cotterell   1993
A history of most of the countries of Asia, which ranges from the earliest times up to the present day.

Travel Literature

✔ **In Xanadu. A Quest**   William Dalrymple   1990 (1989) (see 'Central Asia')
A journey across Central Asia.

✔ **Danziger's Travels** Nick Danziger
1993 (1987)
Danziger was the first foreigner to cross from Pakistan into the closed western province of China. An exciting journey.

✔ **The Travels of Sir John Mandeville**
translated by C.W.R.D. Moseley 1983 (see 'Middle East')
Mandeville served with the Great Khan and visited Cathay.

CHINA

'China? There lies a sleeping giant. Let him sleep! For when he wakes he will move the world.' Attributed to Napoleon.

Anthropology

Chinese Women Speak Dymphna Cusack
1958
Dymphna Cusack who died in 1981 was an Australian writer who spent seven months travelling through China in the 1950s interviewing and talking to thousands of Chinese women from peasants to a Manchu princess. When it was published the Chinese themselves hailed it as a 'classic'.

Art and Archaeology

✔ **Imperial China. (Architectural Guides for Travellers Series)**
Charis Chan 1991
A survey of the palaces, temples, tombs and parks of China. The buildings are set in their historical context and the philosophical ideas behind them are explained.

✔ **The Chinese House** Ronald G. Knapp
1990
The architecture of a Chinese house which shows that, beyond the design, aesthetics and materials, great attention is paid to cosmology and folk beliefs. Well illustrated.

✔ **Chinese Painting** T.C. Lai 1992
A small book in the 'Images of Asia' series, with colour and black and white illustrations, which explains the creative process of Chinese painting through the ages and its technical applications.

✔ **The Ming Tombs** Ann Paludan 1991
This concise book explains, with many illustrations, Chinese burial practices, architecture, *fengshui* and the symbolism attached to the thirteen tombs of the Ming Dynasty which ruled China from 1368 to 1644.

Ancient China. Art and Archaeology
Jessica Rawson 1980
The development of Chinese art is traced here in its historical context, accompanied by photographs and line drawings.

✔ **The British Museum Book of Chinese Art** Jessica Rawson (ed.) 1992
Descriptions of Chinese silk, porcelain, calligraphy, jade, bronze, lacquer, cloisonné and glass with illustrations mostly taken from the British Museum's own collection.

✔ **The Art and Architecture of China**
Laurence Sickman and Alexander Soper 1991 (1956)
A very good introduction and survey of 4,000 years of Chinese art in the Pelican 'History of Art' series. Full of black and white illustrations and drawings.

✔ **Chinese Art** Mary Tregear 1991 (1980)
A short, comprehensive well-illustrated survey of China's visual arts.

Autobiography/Biography

A Higher Kind of Loyalty Liu Binyan
1990
Liu Binyan was one of China's best known journalists; in the 1950s he was labelled a 'rightist' by Mao and sent to the countryside; in 1987 he was 'named' by Deng Xiao Ping and expelled from the Communist Party for 'twisting the truth'. This wide-ranging collection of pieces covers many years of work and gives a good indication of life under Mao and after.

Madame Sun Yatsen Jung Chang and
Jon Halliday 1986
Soong Li married Dr Sun Yatsen, founder of the new Republic, in 1915 at the age of twenty two; although her sister was married to Chiang Kai-shek, she remained critical of him for the rest of her life eventually becoming honorary president of the Communist party.

✔ **Wild Swans. Three Daughters of China** Jung Chang 1993 (1991)
An extremely moving account of three generations of Chinese women which shows the harrowing life that people were subjected to and the extraordinary resilience they showed. [Jonathan Mirsky, Colin Thubron]

Life and Death in Shanghai Nien Cheng
1986
A horrifying account of life in China by a remarkably brave, British-educated woman who was denounced as a class enemy in 1966. [Colin Thubron]

✔ **Ancestors. 900 Years in the Life of a Chinese Family** *Frank Ching 1989 (1988)*
Frank Ching's first traceable ancestor was Qin Guan, an eleventh-century poet; he traces his family roots back over 1,000 years, giving a very personal feel to Chinese history.

Son of the Revolution *Liang Heng and Judith Shapiro 1983*
Liang Heng was born in 1954 in central China where he grew up to be a Red Guard during the Cultural Revolution. Eventually he fell in love with and married an American who is the co-author of this book.

The Death of Woman Wang
Jonathan D. Spence 1979
The biography of ordinary people, from original sources, who lived in Shandong in the seventeenth century.

✔ **Hermit of Peking. The Hidden Life of Sir Edmund Backhouse**
Hugh Trevor-Roper 1993 (1976)
Hugh Trevor-Roper was unexpectedly given Backhouse's memoirs in Basel in 1973. He found them to be a wonderful mixture of fact and fantasy and was so intrigued by what he read about Backhouse's exploits in China that he started rummaging through Foreign Office files; the truth turned out to be even more amazing than the original memoirs, as he discovered that Backhouse was a massive swindler, forger and confidence trickster.

Fiction

Anthology of Chinese Literature from Earliest Times to the 14th Century
Cyril Birch (ed.) 1967
A good and comprehensive survey of the poetry, philosophy, drama, biography and fiction of China.

✔ **The Wallet of Kai Lung**
Ernest Bramah 1986 (1900)
The first in the series of Kai Lung books which tells of a wandering story-teller who entertains his audiences with epic tales of heroism and gallantry.

✔ **The Ginger Griffin** *Ann Bridge 1985 (1934)*
Ann Bridge sets her novel in North China drawing extensively on her life in diplomatic circles. As she had to give her novels to the Foreign Office for vetting there is nothing in them which might cause offence.

✔ **Peking Picnic** *Ann Bridge 1989 (1932)*
Ann Bridge was a diplomat's wife who spent time in Peking. The picnic in the novel takes place at a temple which provides both the setting for romance and for violence in the form of hostage taking by bandits. The novel won the 1932 *Atlantic Monthly* Prize.

The Haunted Monastery
The Chinese Maze Murders
Robert Van Gulik 1977 (1961 and 1957)
Fictional detective novels, with accurate historical backgrounds, of the renowned Judge Dee, a historical magistrate of seventh-century T'ang China.

Family *Ba Jin 1972 (1931)*
Ba Jin is one of China's most well-known novelists. *Family* is the first part of a celebrated trilogy. He was born into a wealthy family in 1904 and here attacks the family feudal system. He was much influenced by Turgenev.

Man's Estate *André Malraux 1975 (1933)*
Malraux was a member of the revolutionary committee which witnessed the doomed Communist rising in Shanghai in 1927. This novel arose from those experiences; in it, the characters try to transcend the 'human condition' through different methods: sex, opium, gambling and terrorism. His writing was described by J.B.Priestley: 'from his genuine poetic creation . . . his ruthless interpretation of reality in terms of his private myth of revolutionary tragic contemporary man'.

✔ **René Leys** *Victor Segalen 1990 (1974)*
Set in Peking at the fall of the Chinese empire, the narrator becomes obsessed with the secrets of the imperial palace; he meets René Leys, a young Belgian, who teaches him Mandarin and gradually reveals some of the secrets.

Rickshaw: the Novel Lo-T'o Hsiang Tzu *Lao She Translated in 1980*
A young boy from the country wants nothing more than to buy his own rickshaw, but he is dogged by misfortune. Full of psychological insight.

Teaching Little Fang *Mark Swallow 1991 (1990)*
A novel set in 1988/9.

Monkey. A Journey to the West
Translated by Arthur Waley 1979
The translation of Wu Chengen's sixteenth-century adaptation of the legend of the Monk Tripitaka and his companions Monkey, Piggy and Sandy who went to India. The legend is based on the true-life pilgrim Xuan Zang who brought back many Buddhist scriptures to the Tang court. *Monkey* combines beauty with absurdity and profoundity with nonsense.

The Water Margin *David Weir 1979 (1978)*
David Weir's adaptation of an epic ancient Chinese myth; Wu Sung killed a tiger on his way home and became a hero known as the Tiger Slayer, but because, as the I-Ching teaches, everything changes, he soon became a bandit and joined an outlaw band whose aim was to depose the puppet emperor.

✔ **Death of a Blue Lantern**
Christopher West 1994
A crime novel set mainly in Beijing with much of the action taking place in the old quarter of Chongwen.

✔ **The Ginger Tree** *Oswald Wynd*
(see 'Japan')

✔ **The Story of the Stone: The Dream of the Red Chamber** *Cao Xueqin*
Translated 1973–1986) Vols 1-3 by David Hawkes Vols 4 and 5 John Minford
Translated in five volumes in English, this Chinese classic was unfinished at the author's death in 1763. It gives an extraordinary insight into Chinese civilization.

The Wounded. New Stories of the Cultural Revolution 77–78 *Lu Xinhua et al. Translated by Geremie Barmé 1979*
A collection of eight short stories, which although flawed by their limited subject matter and lack of depth of character, are historically important for showing what was written as a result of the cultural revolution.

✔ **Red Sorghum** *Mo Yan 1994 (1993)*
Three generations of a Chinese family are torn apart by fratricidal violence.

Food

✔ **The Good Food of Szechwan**
Robert A. Delfs 1983 (1974)
The book takes you through the methods of cooking and includes a comprehensive list of Chinese ingredients..

✔ **Classic Food of China** *Yan-Kit So 1992*
A celebration of China's diverse cuisine by Britain's foremost Chinese cookery writer. Three thousand years of Chinese culinary history is included as well as 150 recipes.

General Background

Seeds of Fire *Geremie Barmé and John Minford 1989*
A collection of pieces, by China's long-suppressed dissident voices, which was published early in 1989, prophetically predating Tiananmen Square. [Jonathan Mirsky]

✔ **City of Lingering Splendour. A Frank Account of Old Peking's Exotic Pleasures** *John Blofeld 1989 (1961)*
John Blofeld arrived in Peking in 1934 and spent 'three exquisitely happy years' there, finding a city which was still full of old traditions.

✔ **The Chinese. A Portrait**
David Bonavia 1989 (1980)
David Bonavia spoke fluent Chinese and had travelled extensively throughout the country and was well qualified to write this penetrating account of all aspects of the Chinese and their lives.

✔ **The Moon Year. A Record of Chinese Customs and Festivals**
Juliet Bredon and Igor Mitrophanow 1927
The preface demonstrates just how unfamiliar the Chinese way of life was to foreigners, by describing how the 'needle is put over the thread instead of the thread through the needle, and the carpenter pulls his plane towards him instead of pushing it away'. This fascinating book attempts to unravel and explain some of the many Chinese customs, legends, traditions and superstitions.

✔ **Peking** *Juliet Bredon 1982 (1919)*
The author, who was born in Peking and spent most of her life there, wrote what was to become the definitive book on Peking; it provides both an historical as well as personal approach. It was originally published by Kelly and Walsh in Shanghai and had been extremely hard to get hold of until its reissue.

The Good Earth *Pearl S. Buck 1960 (1931)*
Pearl Buck was brought up in China as the daughter of medical missionaries; her mother trained her to write down everything she saw and felt and due to this early training she was able to write this well-observed book about the Chinese peasants or 'voiceless ones' who cultivate the land.

✔ **China: Alive in the Bitter Sea**
Fox Butterfield 1982
Fox Butterfield was the first *New York Times* correspondent allowed to live in Beijing since 1949. His keen observation and ability to speak Chinese ensure a penetrating analysis.

✔ **Tiananmen** *Michael Fathers and Andrew Higgins 1989*
The authors were both in Peking reporting for *The Independent* during the Tiananmen massacre. They propose that the massacre

was both cynical and calculated, designed to terrify the people into submission; many firsthand accounts ensure this book's immediacy.

The Chinese – Portrait of a People
John Fraser 1981
Fraser arrived in China in 1977 soon after the Cultural Revolution. He travelled widely during the two years he spent there as correspondent for the *Toronto Globe and Mail*.

Fanshen William Hinton 1970
The American William Hinton lived in a Chinese village during the revolutionary period in Chinese agriculture. The book is an interesting social document of life at village level during this time. *Shenfan* (1980) is the sequel he wrote on his return a few years later.

Chinese Shadows Simon Leys 1978 (1974)
A book which was revolutionary when it was published in that, unlike other foreign writers at the time who tended to whitewash the Cultural Revolution, Leys gets to the truth of what had really happened, finally demystifying China.

Chinese Lives Zhang Xinxin and Sang ye 1989
A series of interviews with ordinary Chinese people which brings the country, people and history alive.

Guides

✔ **Introduction to China. An Odyssey Guide** Charis Chan 1992

✔ **Beijing Walks** Don J. Cohn and Zhang Jingqing 1992
Six walking tours around Beijing.

✔ **Introduction to Beijing** Don J. Cohn 1992

✔ **Handbook for China** Carl Crow 1986 (1933)
This was the standard reference/guide book to China between the wars when China began to be more accessible to foreigners. Although obviously much of the information can now only be read for interest, there is much which is still relevant.

✔ **Fodor China** (undated)

✔ **China. A Travel Survival Kit**
Robert Storey, Chris Taylor and Clem Lindenmayer 1994 (1984)

✔ **Odyssey Illustrated Guide to Sichuan** May Holdsworth 1993

✔ **The China Guidebook 1993–94**
Fredric M. Kaplan, Julian M. Sobin and Arne J. de Keijzer 1993
800 pages of information. Proper names in the text have Chinese characters as well as pin-yin which is very useful.

✔ **All About Shanghai. A Standard Guidebook** H.J. Lethbridge 1986 (1934)
A guide that was written during the glamourous heyday of Shanghai describing its bars, dancing academies, clubs and merchant houses.

✔ **In Search of Old Shanghai** Pan Ling 1985 (1982)
An ideal guide for anyone wanting to find out how and why Shanghai became such a fascinating and cosmopolitan city. There are descriptions of what Shanghai was like in the past: how it looked and how it felt.

✔ **Odyssey Illustrated Guide Shanghai**
Lynn Pan, May Holdsworth and Jill Hunt 1992

✔ **Beijing. A Lonely Planet City Guide**
Robert Storey 1994

✔ **In Search of Old Nanking** Barry Till 1984 (1982)
A guide which is useful both for visiting Nanking today and for offering an insight into the hundred historical sites to be found in the city.

✔ **Blue Guide China** Frances Wood 1992

History

✔ **The Last Emperor** Edward Behr 1988 (1987)
In 1908 Pu Yi was enthroned as China's Last Emperor. He was treated as a god during his childhood and so when he was eventually expelled from the Forbidden City he found it hard to cope with the realities of life and squandered his fortune in trying to regain his throne.

✔ **Cultural Atlas of China**
Caroline Blunden and Mark Elvin 1983
A large format book divided into three parts: Space (geographic and demographic context), Time (a survey of Chinese culture from Peking Man until the present) and Symbols and Society (a thematic coverage of aspects of China's culture).

The Great Within Maurice Collis 1941
A look at the interaction between China and Europe from the seventeenth to twentieth centuries, which is prefaced by a survey of Chinese history; the book is addressed to the

general reader and is an interesting interpretation.

✔ China. A Concise Cultural History
Arthur Cotterell 1988

A reassessment of Chinese civilization in the context of China's role in the world today. Arthur Cotterell divides the book into three major periods: Pre-Imperial (up until 221 BC), Imperial (221 BC to 1912 AD) and Post-Imperial (from 1912 onwards). He writes about well known individual figures such as Confucius (551–479 BC), Lao Zi (c.570–490 BC), the founder of Daoism, and modern ones such as Mao and Sun Yat Sen as well as many lesser known Chinese sages and politicians.

The Tiger of Ch'in Leonard Cottrell 1962
How Chinese civilization began and how it developed in comparison with European and Western Asian cultures.

✔ China this Century Rafe de Crespigny 1993
The future of China in the wake of the Tiananmen massacre is considered by tracing key political, social, and economic events in China's recent history.

✔ The Siege at Peking Peter Fleming 1959
An account of the Boxer Rebellion in 1900; much of the information was gathered from records, both verbal and written, left by the participants from the eleven countries who were besieged in the Legations. Peter Fleming looked upon the assembling of this book like the fitting together of a jigsaw puzzle.

Daily Life in China on the Eve of the Mongol Invasion 1250–1276
Jacques Gernet 1962 (1959)

A survey of life in southern China under the Song dynasty and its capital Hangzhou, which at the time was the largest and richest city in the world. The book uses many and varied sources: local gazetteers, letters and anecdotes.

Chinese Civilization Marcel Granet 1950 (1930)
The book is divided into sections called 'Traditional History', 'The Chief Data of Ancient History', 'The People of the Plains', 'The Foundation of the Chieftainships', 'The Seigniorial Town' and 'Society at the Beginning of the Imperial Era'. Granet concludes by suggesting that the absence of intimacy is the dominant feature of family organization but the relations of society are governed by an exclusive use of decorum.

✔ The Tyranny of History W.J.F. Jenner 1994 (1992)
An analysis of the roots of China's crisis, which go deep into the autocratic traditions of its past.

Modern China Edwin M. Moise 1986
A non-academic and readable account of China in the twentieth century.

✔ Escape with Me Osbert Sitwell 1984 (1939)
The second half of Sitwell's book is devoted to China; he lived in Peking for four months visiting the Forbidden City daily, seeing its aspect change from winter to full summer and absorbing its atmosphere.

China Correspondent Agnes Smedley 1984
Agnes Smedley was in China in the 1930s as a correspondent for the *Manchester Guardian*. She got to know both Mao Tse T'ung and Chou En Lai when she worked as a medic for the Red Army.

Red Star Over China Edgar Snow 1968 (1938)
The American Edgar Snow had spent seven years in China as a journalist when, in 1936, the Chinese Communists had completed their successful escape from Southeast China to the Northwest and wanted to tell their story to the outside world. He was in the perfect position to write the book of what was happening; he spent four months with Mao Tse-tung and recorded Mao's own story of the revolution. Much of what he wrote turned out to be prophetic.

✔ The Memory Palace of Matteo Ricci
Jonathan D. Spence 1988 (1985)

The Jesuit Matteo Ricci had left Italy and Counter-Reformation Europe in 1577 and arrived in Ming China via India in 1583. He stayed in China until his death in 1610. The book is interesting about missionary life as well as life in China at the time.

✔ The Search for Modern China
Jonathan Spence 1991 (1990)

Modern China is extremely complex; its history is also as rich and strange as that of anywhere. In this large book Spence does much to elucidate the present by drawing on the past. 'History at its best . . . all in the vivid, accessible style for which the author is well known.' (*Washington Post Book World*) [Jonathan Mirsky]

✔ **The Dragon Empress: the Life and Times of Tsu-hsi Empress Dowager of China 1835–1908** *Marina Warner 1992 (1972)*
A marvellous description and character analysis of the Empress Tsu-hsi who was obsessed with ritual and ceremony and had a passion for power, intrigue, cruelty and extravagance, at the same time having a great love for gardens and painting. Parallel with her life was the decline of the Chinese empire and the fall of the Ch'ing Dynasty.

The Long March *Dick Wilson 1977 (1971)*
A well researched and readable account of this epic march.

Natural History

South China Birds *Harry R. Caldwell and John C. Caldwell 1931*
This was one of the first serious books about birds to appear in China and contains descriptions and illustrations of nearly 550 types of bird found in Fukien, Kwangtung, Kiangsi, Kiangsu and Chekiang provinces.

Plant Hunting in China. A History of Botanical Exploration in China and the Tibetan Marches *E.H.M. Cox 1945*
So many of the plants that we take for granted in the West today, originally came from China; this very readable account, aimed at the general reader and gardener, presents facts with explanations and criticisms.

✔ **The Natural History of China** *Zhai Ji, Zheng Guangmei, Wang Huadong and Xu Jialin 1990*
A large-format book with many photographs and chapters on geography, forests, rivers, lakes and sea coasts, mountains, grasslands, deserts and conservation.

The Chinese Garden: History, Art and Architecture *Maggie Keswick 1978*
The history of the Chinese garden and its influence on Chinese society and how that influence spread to Western civilization. Well illustrated with examples from Chinese landscape painting.

A Naturalist in Western China with Vasculum, Camera and Gun – Being Some Account of 11 Years Travel, Exploration and Observation in Remote Parts of the Flowery Kingdom *E.H. Wilson 1986 (1913)*
Wilson was collecting seeds and plants for Kew on his expeditions through Hubei, Sichuan and across the Sino-Tibetan border.

He also recorded an immense amount of facts about natural history, culture and customs.

Philosophy

✔ **I Ching. The Book of Changes** *Translated by Richard Wilhelm*

The Analects *Confucius*
Tao Te Ching *Lao Zi and Mencius*
Three classic texts which can be read in good modern translations.

✔ **The Soul of China** *Amaury de Riencourt 1989 (1958)*
Very good on philosophy, despite being somewhat jargon-ridden; especially good when he is not wearing his philosopher's hat.

✔ **The Art of War** *Sun Tzu*
'In peace prepare for war, in war prepare for peace' wrote Sun Tzu in the fifth century BC; the book has remained a classic and merited the following description by James Clavell: 'I truly believe that if our military and political leaders in recent times had studied this work of genius, Vietnam could not have happened as it happened; we would not have lost the war in Korea (we lost because we did not achieve victory); the Bay of Pigs could not have occurred; the hostage fiasco in Iran would not have come to pass; the British Empire would not have been dismembered; and, in all probability, World Wars I and II would have been avoided . . . '

Photography

✔ **Han Suyin's China** *Photographs by Mike Langford and Geoff Mason 1987*
Eighty colour photographs accompany Han Suyin's text. The book claims to concentrate on 'out of the way' places, but rather ominously includes Tibet as part of China.

✔ **The Great Wall of China** *Daniel Schwartz 1990*
Daniel Schwartz travelled over 15,000 miles to produce this book of over 150 duotone photographs. There is text: *The Wall and the Books* by Jorge Luis Borges.

Religion

Buddhism in China *Kenneth Chen 1973*
Chen traces the origin of Buddhist thought in China, the influence of India, Tibet and Japan and shows the development of the many different schools.

The Monastery of Jade Mountain
Peter Goullart 1961
Peter Goullart had to leave Russia because of the Revolution and spent the following thirty years in China where he eventually became a practising Taoist. The author attempts to define Taoism by writing about his life.

Three Ways of Thought in Ancient China *Translated by Arthur Waley 1939*
Extracts from Zhuang Zi, Mencius and Han Fei Zi, three very important early Chinese thinkers.

Travel Literature

✔ **Journey to a War** *W.H. Auden and Christopher Isherwood 1986 (1939)*
In 1937 Auden and Isherwood were commissioned by Faber to write a book about 'the East'. Since the Sino-Japanese War broke out in August of that year, they decided they would go and investigate it. The book combines text from their diaries and poems, including Auden's sonnet sequence *In Time of War*.

✔ **The Yangtze Valley and Beyond. An Account of Journeys in China, Chiefly in the Province of Sze Chuan and Among the Man-Tze of the Somo Territory** *Isabella Bird Bishop 1985 (1899)*
Isabella Bird embarked on this expedition to the Yangtze River and remote north-west China when she was sixty-four years old, having previously written to her publisher, John Murray, ' . . . I am too old for hardships and great exertions now'. She showed enormous strength of character by denying herself 'the pleasure of reading any of the recent literature on China' before she had written her book! She was never happier than when travelling, something which shines through her writing but she confounded her doctor who wrote: 'The invalid at home and the Samson abroad do not form a very usual combination, yet in her case the two ran in tandem for many years.'

✔ **The Chinese Smile** *Nigel Cameron 1990 (1958)*
It is interesting to read an account of China written in the 1950s just after the Communists had come to power. There was great enthusiasm and hope both within China and without.

Wanderings in China
C.F. Gordon Cumming 1886
Constance Gordon Cumming travelled from Hong Kong to Canton where 'with many nervous qualms' she climbed up the scaffolding on the new Roman Catholic cathedral which was being built, and admired the view. She then proceeded to travel throughout China recording details of Chinese dinner parties and temple theatres in great detail.

✔ **A Traveller in China**
Christina Dodwell 1987 (1985)
Christina Dodwell travelled to many of the remoter parts of China by all kinds of transport, including her own inflatable canoe. She is extremely adaptable and seemingly fearless.

Manchuria: the Cockpit of Asia
Colonel P.T. Etherton 1932
During the earlier part of this century, Manchuria, which was rich in natural resources, became the focus of world attention. It was part of China and yet outside China proper and Japan, the United States, Soviet Russia and Britain were all interested in it. This is an account of the land, its resources and international relations.

✔ **News from Tartary** *Peter Fleming 1994 (1936)*
An account of the author's journey from Peking to Kashmir in 1935.

✔ **One's Company. A Journey to China** *Peter Fleming 1983 (1933)*
Peter Fleming's account of a journey through Russia and Manchuria to China during which he met many Chinese and Japanese officials and even the puppet Emperor Henry Pu Yi.

✔ **Travels with Myself and Another**
Martha Gellhorn 1991 (1978) (see 'East Africa', 'Caribbean' and 'Israel')
Martha Gellhorn went with her UC (Unwilling Companion) to China in 1941.

Forgotten Kingdom *Peter Goullart 1955*
Peter Goullart got himself sent to Likiang in Yunnan in the far west of China as an employee of the Chinese government in order to promote co-operatives. He was greeted with suspicion and due to his Taoist training was able to deal with the problems he encountered.

✔ **China to Me** *Emily Hahn 1987 (1944)*
In 1935 the American Emily Hahn set off on a world tour which ended up by her staying in the Far East for nine years. She spent five years in Shanghai and co-founded the magazine *Candid Comment*, she wrote a biography of the Soong sisters, fell in love and had a daughter. *China to Me* is a lively account of those years before and during the Second World War.

✔ **Japan. China. A Journal of Two Voyages to the Far East**
Nikos Kazantzakis   1982 (1935) (see 'Japan')

✔ **The Early Arrival of Dreams. A Year in China** *Rosemary Mahoney   1993 (1992)*
The author spent a year teaching at Hangzhou University just before the Tiananmen massacre. Her students were desperate to learn as much about the west as possible and by her telling she was able to learn much about what life was like under a repressive régime.

✔ **On a Chinese Screen**
W. Somerset Maugham   1922
Somerset Maugham writes that 'until age mitigated my wanderlust, I liked to travel. I liked the sensation it gave me of freedom from responsibility.' He wrote *On a Chinese Screen* as the material for a book from a journey he took in China in 1920, making notes of the people and places that excited his interest, thinking of them as useful in the future for stories or novels. When he came to reread them he was struck by their freshness and so put them into book form.

✔ **Very Strange Feeling. A Chinese Journey** *Jan Morris   1992 (1984)*
In the collection Journeys.

✔ **An Australian in China. Being the Narrative of a Quiet Journey Across China to Burma** *G.E. Morrison   1895*
The author, dressed as a Chinese, found the journey up the Yangtze River as far as Chungking to Western China, the Chinese Shan States and Kachin Hills to the frontier of Burma 'easy and pleasant'. He admits that he 'went to China possessed with the strong racial antipathy to the Chinese common to my countrymen, but that feeling has long since given way to one of lively sympathy and gratitude . . .'

✔ **Marco Polo. The Travels** *Penguin Classic Edn   Translated by Ronald Latham   1958*
Marco Polo, who was born in 1254, accompanied his father and uncle on their second journey to China in 1271. He then spent twenty years travelling in the service of Kublai Khan. It is thought that he also went to India and Burma, but since his *Travels* were not written until many years later when he met a romance-writer Rustichello of Pisa in prison in Genoa, there is much debate as to what was fact and what was fantasy.

China's Sorrow. Journeys Around the Yellow River *Lynn Pan   1985*
The account of three trips to the valleys of the Yellow River, a river which has had so much influence on China's history and civilization. The author had left China as a child and thus, as an emigrée, was allowed access to places normally denied to the Chinese.

Iron and Silk *Mark Salzman   1987 (1986)*
The author went to study martial arts in China, loved the country and managed to see a side of it few foreigners are able to.

✔ **The Empty Throne** *Tony Scotland   1994 (1993)*
Much more than a straight travel book; Tony Scotland goes in search of the heir to the Empty Dragon throne, making this an exciting detective story as well as an exploration into what makes the Chinese tick.

Battle Hymn of China *Agnes Smedley   1944 (1943)*
Agnes Smedley, born in the South-west of the United States, had been imprisoned in New York for her political beliefs, before going to China. She became very involved in Chinese politics and friends with most of the leading Chinese of the day.

The Long Revolution *Edgar Snow   1972*
Edgar Snow, who covered events in China for many US publications, made his last visit there in 1970–1. He spent six months gathering impressions of the life there and the changes that had occurred.

✔ **Riding the Iron Rooster: by Train Through China** *Paul Theroux   1989 (1988)*
Theroux spent a year travelling by every conceivable kind of train throughout China, observing his travelling companions in razor sharp detail. His honesty about his blatant curiosity is refreshing – many people would like to, or in fact do, do the things he does without ever admitting to them.

✔ **Behind the Wall** *Colin Thubron   1988 (1987)*
Colin Thubron is a perceptive traveller who writes beautiful prose; without being in any way pretentious, he manages to teach us an enormous amount about the country and its people. [Patrick Marnham, Jan Morris]

✔ **Maiden Voyage** *Denton Welch   1986 (1943)*
The author ran away from school aged sixteen and joined his father, a businessman, in Shanghai. The book was written years later but is about the many adventures and experiences he had while he was in China in the 1930s, including one occasion when he went on a trip into the Interior to Kai-feng Fu to buy bronzes and china with a friend of his father's.

✔ **Journey to the Middle Kingdom**
Christopher West   1994 (1991)
Christopher West, a musician, travelled to China, fulfilling a life-long ambition; he writes unpretentiously about philosophy and people.

HONG KONG

'Hong Kong for all the world like some Spanish or Italian town with its white terraces, and coloured venetians, nestling in masses of dark green foliage at the foot of the bare rugged peak.' Harry de Windt
From Pekin to Calais by Land 1889

Art and Archaeology

Fan Kwae Pictures: Paintings and Drawings by George Chinnery and Other Artists in the Collection of the Hongkong and Shanghai Banking Corporation *G.H.R. Tillotson   1987*
Beautifully reproduced paintings from the Hongkong and Shanghai Bank's impressive collection. *Fan Kwae* means 'foreign' and other artists reproduced here, along with informative text, are: Auguste Borget, W.J. Huggins and Thomas and William Daniell. However, some little known Chinese artists are also represented.

Autobiography/Biography

✔ **Myself a Mandarin: Memoirs of a Special Magistrate** *Austin Coates   1975*
An amusing account of the author's experiences as a magistrate in the New Territories.

Fiction/Poetry

Hiroshima Joe *Martin Booth   1985*
The story of a prisoner-of-war who survived the Japanese camps and subsequently returned to Hong Kong.

Noble House *James Clavell   1984 (1981)*
Set in 1963, the struggle for power between the rival leading houses in Hong Kong involves the CIA, the KGB and the People's Republic of China.

✔ **Taipan** *James Clavell   1989 (1966)*
Dirk Struan, the 'Tai-Pan', head of the most powerful trading company in the east in the 1840s was determined to turn the barren island of Hong Kong into a rich and exotic part of the empire and he saw the opium run as the quickest way to achieve this.

✔ **The Road** *Austin Coates   1987 (1959)*
The story of Richard, a district officer, who sees trying to build a road on a remote island near Hong Kong as a challenge; his wife Sylvia sees it as a threat to their already complicated marriage and the people on the island see it as an end to their way of life.

Dynasty *Robert Elegant   1978 (1977)*
An epic story about the Sekloongs, China's merchant princes who are 'flamboyant, sensual, wily [and] unimaginably rich'. One of the sons marries an English woman and within a generation the family is torn apart by hatred.

✔ **The Honourable Schoolboy**
John Le Carré   1981 (1977)
A spy story featuring George Smiley which moves between London, Hong Kong, Phnom Penh, Vientiane and other places in South East Asia.

The World of Suzie Wong *Richard Mason* 1957
A well-known film was made from this book of a western painter meeting and falling in love with a bar girl.

✔ **The Painted Veil**
W. Somerset Maugham   1978 (1925)
Maugham was sued after the publication of this novel for allegedly using real people as characters in his book.

✔ **An Insular Possession** *Timothy Mo* 1987
An historical novel set in Hong Kong before its acquisition by the British.

✔ **The Monkey King** *Timothy Mo   1991 (1978)*
A Portuguese Chinese marries for money and then attempts to improve his status within the family. Like the Monkey King of Chinese legend he is a born survivor with many hidden inner resources.

A Many Splendoured Thing *Han Suyin* 1952
Han Suyin had completed her medical studies in London before returning to Hong Kong with her child; much of this autobiographical novel was written just after the Communist takeover of China. When it was published many people thought that this romantic novel was an accurate portrayal of life in Hong Kong.

Food

✔ **Fragrant Harbour Taste. The New Chinese Cooking of Hong Kong**
Ken Hom   1991 (1989)
The new cuisine of Hong Kong brings innovative ideas to old recipes.

General Background

Borrowed Place, Borrowed Time: Hong Kong and its Many Faces
Richard Hughes   1976 (1966)
Richard Hughes was a journalist in Hong Kong for many years; this portrait of the life and politics there is entertainingly written.

✔ **Hong Kong: Epilogue to an Empire**
Jan Morris   1993 (1988)
An excellent introduction to Hong Kong. Jan Morris tries to establish its unique and peculiar identity by writing about the history, politics and economics with great appreciation and understanding.

Guides

✔ **Hong Kong and Taiwan. American Express Guide**   *Fred S. Armentrout and Ann Williams   1992*

✔ **Hong Kong and Macau. The Rough Guide**   *Jules Brown and Helen Lee   1993*

✔ **Insight Guide Hong Kong**   *1993*

✔ **The Hong Kong Guide 1893**
Introduction by H.J. Lethbridge   1986 (1893)
Originally published by Kelly and Walsh for the many thousands of visitors to Hong Kong. It contains history as well as suggested itineraries and excursions.

✔ **A Visitor's Guide to Historic Hong Kong**   *Sally Rodwell   1991*
A look at the history of Hong Kong from its stone age up to the present day. An interesting and well illustrated book.

✔ **Hong Kong, Macau and Canton. A Travel Survival Kit**   *Robert Storey   1992 (1978)*

✔ **A Times Bartholomew Guide Hong Kong, Singapore and Macau**   *1989*

History

✔ **An Illustrated History of Hong Kong**   *Nigel Cameron   1991*
Even in 1958 G.B. Endacott thought that it was necessary to begin a book on Hong Kong with the words 'Hong Kong is a British colony situated on the South-east coast of China'; it is a measure of its dramatic change of status that less than half a century later no such introduction would be necessary; this book gives the history of pre-industrial and industrial Hong Kong.

Foreign Mud: Being an Account of the Opium Imbroglio at Canton in the 1830's and the Anglo-Chinese War that Followed   *Maurice Collis   1946*
A rather romanticized, but nonetheless very readable, account of the Opium Wars. Although he has invented dialogue he writes well about the people and history of the time.

✔ **The Private Life of Old Hong Kong. Western Women in the British Colony 1841–1941**   *Susanna Hoe   1991*
Very little has been written about the western women who lived in Canton and Hong Kong after it became a colony. The book looks at women from all strata of society: governors' wives, missionaries, teachers, doctors and prostitutes.

Half-Crown Colony. A Hong Kong Notebook   *James Pope-Hennessy   1969*
James Pope-Hennessy's grandfather was a Governor of Hong Kong. This was his reason for writing the book, but he admitted that although he was fairly intrigued by it, he did not find himself very attuned to it.

The Opium War through Chinese Eyes
Arthur Waley   1958
Commissioner Lin Tse-hsü was sent by the Chinese Emperor to suppress the opium trade in Canton; this eventually led to the occupation of Hong Kong by British military and naval action.

✔ **Beyond Lion Rock: the Story of Cathay Pacific Airways**   *Gavin Young   1988*
The rise of Cathay Pacific as a major airline for Hong Kong and its incorporation into the Swire group, is a fascinating story and Gavin Young makes it far more interesting than most company histories.

Natural History

✔ **Twelve Hong Kong Walks**
Derek Kemp   1985
A description of twelve off-the-beaten-track walks, one for each month of the year, concentrating on the plants and flowers. There are maps, pen and wash drawings and colour photographs.

✔ **A Field Guide to the Birds of South-East Asia** Ben King, Martin Woodcock and E.C. Dickinson 1976 (1975) (see 'South East Asia')
This volume includes birds found in Hong Kong.

Photography

✔ **Hong Kong. The Colony that Never Was** Alan Birch 1991
The book is divided into four sections: 'Where the Sun Never Sets: Hong Kong 1841–1941', 'The Rising Sun: Hong Kong During the Japanese Occupation 1941–45', 'A Place in the Sun: Hong Kong's Struggle for Survival 1946–66' and 'Sunset in the East: Hong Kong Returns to China 1967–97.' The book is full of photographs, both old and new.

MACAU

Biography

Chinnery: the Man and the Legend
Robin G. Hutcheon and Geoffrey W. Bonsall 1975
Chinnery spent most of the time between 1825 and 1852 in Macau; there are many colour plates which include scenes of Macau.

Fiction

Macau Daniel Carney 1986
A novel of fantasy and adventure which has Macau as its backdrop.

✔ **City of Broken Promises**
Austin Coates 1988 (1977)
A novel set in Macau from 1780–1798 which is based on the life of Martha Merop (1766–1828) who came with the house of Thomas Kuyck van Merop when he arrived in Macau. She had been sold into prostitution at the age of thirteen, but went on to become a trader in her own right and one of the richest women on the China Coast.

General Background

Thrilling Cities Ian Fleming 1964
From the series that Ian Fleming wrote for *The Sunday Times* in 1959/60. Macau forms the second chapter of the book and Fleming writes about the gambling at the Hotel Central and his lunch with Dr Pedro José Lobo, the notorious gold smuggler.

✔ **Macau** Cesar Guillen-Nunez 1984
A general introduction to Macau with an emphasis on architecture, art, history and geography; the author works in the Museum in Macau and has written this small volume in the 'Images of Asia' series.

Guides

✔ **Hong Kong and Macau. The Rough Guide** Jules Brown and Helen Lee 1993

✔ **Odyssey Illustrated Guide Macau** Shann Davies 1993

✔ **Hong Kong, Macau and Canton. A Travel Survival Kit** Robert Storey 1992 (1978)

History

✔ **Macau and the British 1637–1842: prelude to Hong Kong** Austin Coates 1988 (1966)
Macau became a Portuguese colony in 1557, eighty years before the British came to the region. It was not until Robert Morrison arrived in the nineteenth century that British influence increased. This book describes how the British developed their power with the opium trade and gun-ships.

A Macau Narrative Austin Coates 1987 (1978)
A narrative history of early Portuguese settlement on the China coast.

Foreign Mud Maurice Collis 1946 (see 'Hong Kong')
Includes a description of Macau in the 1830s.

The Great Within Maurice Collis 1941 (see 'China')

Travel Literature

✔ **The Grand Peregrination. Being the Life and Adventures of Fernao Mendes Pinto** Maurice Collis 1990 (1949)
Macau is mentioned in this book in relation to Pinto's fourth journey to Japan as he visited Portuguese bases in the Pearl River delta during 1555.

JAPAN

'It is so strange to be in a clean land, and stranger to walk among dolls' houses. Japan is a soothing place for a small man.'
Rudyard Kipling *From Sea to Sea* 1889

Anthropology

The Chrysanthemum and the Sword. Patterns of Japanese Culture
Ruth Benedict 1977 (1946)
A study of Japanese habits of thought and emotion and of the pattern into which these habits fall; there are chapters on the Japanese in the War, children and their relationships with their parents, order and hierarchy, the Japanese conception of virtue and self-discipline. A remarkably useful book for learning to understand the Japanese.

A Japanese Village – Suye Mura
John F. Embree 1946
A description based on direct observation of the life of a Japanese village community which gives an original insight and angle into Japanese civilization. The book is dedicated to the memory of Keisuke Aiko who had the first motor transport in the village, a motorcycle, and who was tragically killed when he collided with a train one evening.

Art and Archaeology

Japan Before Buddhism *J.E. Kidder* 1959
An overall view of Japanese prehistory and protohistory which describes the origins of each successive culture, its continental contacts and the unique features of its life. Many illustrations and line drawings.

Japanese Crafts *John Lowe* 1983
A survey of Japanese crafts including wooden combs, fans, brushes, incense, floor mats, paper lanterns, bamboo flutes, sweetmeats and raw fish. Well illustrated with ample text.

The Folk Art of Japan *Hugo Munsterberg* 1958 Published in Japan
A well-illustrated book with interesting text about the toys, pottery, baskets, lacquer ware and sculpture which continued to flourish despite Japan's move to industrialization.

✔ Japanese Art *Joan Stanley-Baker* 1991 (1984)
A good, well-illustrated introduction in the Thames and Hudson 'World of Art' series.

✔ The Art and Architecture of Japan
Robert Treat Paine and Alexander Soper 1974 (1955)
In the Pelican 'History of Art' series; part one is devoted to painting and sculpture and part two to architecture. The book is full of line drawings and is an invaluable introduction to Japanese art of all disciplines.

Biography

✔ Madame Chrysanthemum
Pierre Loti 1985 (1920)
An autobiographical novel about the temporary marriage of a French lieutenant and his geisha; it was the first Western romance to be set in Japan and was at the forefront of the vogue for Japanese things which swept the West. It was the inspiration for Puccini's *Madame Butterfly*.

Fiction/Poetry

The Bonsai Tree *Meira Chand* 1983
Kate falls in love with a Japanese man, Jun, whom she meets in London. She is warned that she shouldn't marry him because he is bound to change when he returns to Japan; she ignores the warning and has an idyllic first year living near Holland Park. Nothing prepares her for the reality of their eventual return to Japan.

The Gossamer Fly *Meira Chand* 1979
Hiroko, a new maid, enters the lives of a family – an English mother who had a nervous breakdown and had to be sent back to England, her powerful Japanese husband and two children, a son and daughter. Hiroko is both cruel and sexy and persuades the father and son that she can be the surrogate wife; the daughter sees what is happening and feels that she must destroy her.

✔ Shogun *James Clavell* 1991 (1975)
A blockbuster historical novel set in sixteenth-century medieval Japan; the large cast of characters includes war-lords, Jesuits, geishas, samurai and a shipwrecked Elizabethan. Full of violence, action and suspense.

✔ Sachiko's Wedding *Clive Collins* 1991 (1990)
An interesting look at a modern Japanese woman; despite having been a rebel against tradition all her life, Sachiko's wedding was arranged by a marriage-broker as a dynastic union and gives her no cause for celebration.

✔ Silence *Shusako Endo* 1988 (1967)
Described by Graham Greene as 'one of the

finest novels of our time', this powerful book which examines truth, Christianity and self-knowledge is profoundly moving. Shusako Endo has also written: *Foreign Studies, The Samurai, Stained Glass Elegies, The Sea and Poison, Wonderful Fool, Volcano* and *When I Whistle*.

✔ **Mona Lisa Overdrive** William Gibson
1989 (1988)
A science fiction 'cyberspace' novel in which Japan becomes a metaphor for the future; Japanese slang, customs and technology are heavily featured as in *Necromancer*, another novel in the same genre.

✔ **An Artist of the Floating World**
Kazuo Ishiguro 1987 (1986)
At the end of the Second World War an aging painter, Masuji Ono, looks back over his life and career: 'An exquisite novel' (*The Observer*).

✔ **Snow Country**
✔ **Thousand Cranes** Yasunari Kawabata
1986 (1956/9)
Kawabata, one of the greatest of modern Japanese writers who won the Nobel Prize for literature in 1968, writes with great sensitivity, subtlety and intensity; *The Snow Country* [Stephen Brook] is set in the remote northern mountains of Honshu and is the story of the love of a local geisha and a man from Tokyo, while *Thousand Cranes* is about the tea ceremony. Other works by him include *The Master of Go, The Old Capital, Beauty and Sadness* and *The Sound of the Mountain*

The Custom House Francis King 1964
(1961)
A novel full of lust and love which shows the violence behind the seemingly calm veneer of Japanese life.

The Japanese Umbrella and Other Stories Francis King 1964
A collection of short stories set in Japan which do much to capture how foreigners feel and react to the country.

The Ninth Netsuke James Melville 1986
(1982)
One of a crime series set in modern Japan; the superintendent's wife finds an unusual netsuke at the scene of a murder which everyone seems desperate to get hold of. It is clearly crucial evidence of something, but of what?

✔ **Death in Midsummer and Other Stories** Yukio Mishima 1971 (1966)
C.P. Snow described Mishima as 'A most beautiful writer of prose – clear, eloquent, visual . . . Mishima's characters are observed with one of the sharpest of eyes and with maximun chill'. This collection of ten short stories range from death and homosexuality to the spiritual emptiness of post-war Japan. His other works include: *After the Banquet, Confessions of a Mask, Forbidden Colours, The Sailor Who Fell from Grace with the Sea* and the tetralogy *The Sea of Fertility*, part of which was completed the morning before his suicide.

✔ **A Wild Sheep Chase** Haruki Murakami
1991 (1989)
A metaphysical comedy by one of Japan's best-selling authors; a nameless copywriter follows a mutant sheep creating an entertaining allegorical yarn.

✔ **Fire from the Ashes** Kenzaburo Oe (ed.)
1985
A collection of short stories by Japanese authors, of differing ages, about Hiroshima and Nagasaki, but as the editor says in the introduction they are also 'highly significant vehicles for thinking about the contemporary world'.

✔ **Bicycle Days** John Burnham Schwartz
1990 (1989)
A first novel which underlines the vast differences between Western and Japanese life. A young American has a brief and rocky encounter with both the social and business worlds of modern Japan; one of the things which clearly emerges is the lack of respect in relationships between men and newly liberated women.

✔ **The Tale of the Genji**
Murasaki Shikibu 1976 Translated by Edward G. Seidensticker
A long romance which describes the court life of Heian Japan during the tenth century. It was probably all written by a court lady known as Murasaki Shikibu, her real name is not known. The tale covers almost three-quarters of a century and is about the life and loves of the nobleman known as 'the shining Genji'.

✔ **A Death in Tokyo** Guy Stanley 1989
(1988)
A fairly gripping detective story set in and around Tokyo.

✔ **The Makioka Sisters**
Junichiro Tanizaki 1983 (1957)
Tanizaki lived in Tokyo until the earthquake of 1923 when he moved to the region of Kyoto–Osaka, a region he lovingly recreates as the setting for *The Makioka Sisters*. It is the story of the extinction of a great family

through pride and is fused with nostalgia for the past.

✔ **The Ginger Tree** Oswald Wynd 1990 (1977)
A young Scottish girl sails to China to marry a British military attaché there; she horrifies the rather straight-laced community by embarking on an affair with a Japanese soldier and is subsequently rejected by her husband and family, eventually moving to Japan.

Food

✔ **Japanese Cooking. A Simple Art**
Shizuo Tsuji 1990 (1980)
A comprehensive and authentic book about Japanese cooking, with an introduction by M.F.K. Fisher.

General Background

✔ **A Japanese Mirror. Heroes and Villains of Japanese Culture**
Ian Buruma 1985 (1984)
Ian Buruma looks at the popular heroes of films, comics, theatre and television as the archetypes of 'the Japanese as they imagine themselves to be, and as they would like themselves to be'. He provides examples and also analyses the many paradoxes to be found in Japanese society.

✔ **The Death of an Emperor. Japan at the Crossroads** Thomas Crump 1991 (1989)
In 1946 the Emperor Hirohito became the first Japanese Emperor in over 2,000 years to renounce his status as a 'living god'; this book is an exploration of the relationship between the Japanese and their emperor; his role in the Second World War and the question of war crimes is also examined.

✔ **Traveller's Literary Companion to Japan** Harry Guest 1994 (see equivalent to South and Central America under 'Central America')

✔ **Writings from Japan. An Anthology**
Lafcadio Hearn 1988 (1984)
Lafcadio Hearn, 'that demon of a Japan-lover', was born in 1850 in Levkas, was brought up in Dublin and arrived penniless in the United States aged nineteen. He went to Japan, which he was never to leave, in 1890 via New Orleans and the French West Indies. He married a Japanese woman and eventually took Japanese nationality and a Japanese name, Koizumi Yakumo, although he never attempted to learn the language. This collection of his writings is divided into three parts 'Recollections', 'Reflections' and 'Relations'; they range from 'My First Day in the Orient' to 'In a Japanese Garden' and 'The Japanese Garden'.

✔ **The Japanese** Joe Joseph 1994 (1993)
The author was Tokyo correspondent for *The Times* and so has a particular insight into Japanese institutions and customs: 'One of the funniest travel books I've ever read. Witty, percipient and always spot-on.' (Simon Hoggart)

Tokyo James Kirkup 1966
James Kirkup had lived in Tokyo for some time when he wrote this book about the complex city; he describes the social, economic, religious, architectural and artistic facets and devotes a chapter to the Noh theatre.

✔ **Into Japan** John Lowe 1986 (1985)
John Lowe first went to Japan in 1967 and returned many times, travelling all over the country and living for a while as a Zen monk. This introduction to the country is perceptive and very readable; the author draws on many of his own experiences and is often very funny.

✔ **The Land of the Rising Yen**
George Mikes 1973 (1970)
George Mikes looks at familiar and not so familiar things with a refreshing curiosity and from an original angle and perspective; the resulting book is easy to read and instructive.

✔ **The Japanese Today**
Edwin Reischauer 1988
An excellent general background to Japanese society which has recently been revised.

The Kimono Mind Bernard Rudofsky 1965
Described as an informal guide to Japan and the Japanese, Rudofsky's book takes an idiosyncratic look at some of the many Japanese institutions and conventions. [Colin Thubron]

Guides

✔ **Tokyo. Bartholomew World Travel Guide** 1991

Fodor Japan (undated)

Fodor Tokyo (undated)

✔ **Japan. An Insight Guide** 1992

✔ **Tokyo. Insight City Guide** 1991

✔ **Introduction to Japan. An Odyssey Guide** Alan Booth 1991 (1988)

✔ **Tokyo City Guide** *Judith Connor and Mayumi Yoshida*
Contains invaluable information for residents and visitors to Tokyo. Large sections on shopping and eating.

✔ **Exploring Kamakura. A Guide for the Curious Traveler** *Michael Cooper 1981 (1979)*
Kamakura is only an hour from Tokyo, but is situated on Sagami Bay and is surrounded by mountains; it is sometimes known as a mini-Kyoto and being small has a charm of its own.

✔ **Old Kyoto. A Guide to Traditional Shops, Restaurants and Inns**
Diane Durston 1986
All the more interesting and traditional sights in Kyoto. Well illustrated.

✔ **How to Live and Work in Japan. A Practical Guide for Expatriates**
Aaron Hoopes 1992
The author has lived and worked in Japan for many years and in this useful guide describes how to understand and adapt to the Japanese way of life; he gives practical advice on documents, opening bank accounts, Japanese law, customs, health care and education.

✔ **Japan for Kids. The Ultimate Guide for Parents and Their Children**
Diane Wiltshire Kanagawa and Jeanne Huey Erickson 1992
An extremely useful guide for families both living in and visiting Japan. It lists planetariums, petting zoos, magicians, toy museums and aquariums.

✔ **New Japan Solo** *Eiji Kanno and Constance O'Keefe*
A well-laid out guide with 193 maps, train timetables, much other detailed information and place names in Japanese characters.

✔ **Good Tokyo Restaurants** *Rick Kennedy*
A cross-section of 100 of Tokyo's restaurants both Japanese and western.

✔ **Cadogan Guide Japan**
Richard Lloyd Parry 1994

✔ **Japan. A Travel Survival Kit**
Robert Strauss, Chris Taylor and Tony Wheeler 1991

✔ **Tokyo. A Lonely Planet City Guide**
Chris Taylor 1993

✔ **Japanese Capitals. A Cultural and Artistic Guide to Nara, Kyoto and Tokyo** *Philip Ward 1985*
A practical guidebook to the successive capitals of Japan. As much emphasis is put on

how to see the cities to their best advantage today, as on their historical past.

✔ **Japan Unescorted. A Practical Guide to Discovering Japan On Your Own** *James K. Weatherly 1992 (1986)*
How to discover Japan away from the tour groups; it suggests where to stay and what to eat.

✔ **Jobs in Japan. The Complete Guide to Living and Working in the Land of Rising Opportunity** *John Wharton 1991*
The book, which is written in a very chatty manner, lists grants, scholarships and over 400 English schools, many of which hire foreign teachers.

History

✔ **The Deer Cry Pavilion. A Story of Westerners in Japan 1868–1905**
Pat Barr 1968
The Meiji era began in 1868 when the young Emperor Matsuhito came to the throne; from 1870 onwards many westerners arrived in Japan to help build a modern industrialized state. Pat Barr has drawn on the accounts of many of the doctors, missionaries, soldiers, diplomats, scientists and engineers who left behind firsthand accounts of their lives and achievements. The book looks at what was happening throughout the whole country.

✔ **The Japanese Achievement**
Hugh Cortazzi 1990
A detailed yet readable and wide-ranging survey of Japanese history and culture.

Everyday Life in Traditional Japan
C.J. Dunn 1969
A very instructive book, full of line drawings, which give you a good sense of what life must have been like in traditional Japan.

✔ **Three Came Home** *Agnes Keith 1989 (1948)*
Agnes Keith was captured by the Japanese in Borneo in 1942. Although forbidden to do so, she managed to keep a diary on scraps of paper and later wrote this remarkable, courageous and balanced book about her ordeal.

The Nobility of Failure. Tragic Heroes in the History of Japan *Ivan Morris 1980 (1975)*
A tragic hero is an important figure in Japan – generally it is someone who has seen good fortune, but falls, despite courage and determination and often dies by his own hand. Ivan Morris starts with Yamato Takeru in the fourth century and includes the melancholy prince Arima whose death was full of

court intrigue, Amakusa Shiro who led a revolt of Japanese Christians, and concludes with the kamikaze fighters of the Second World War.

The World of the Shining Prince. Court Life in Ancient Japan *Ivan Morris* 1985 *(1964)*
Ivan Morris uses *The Tale of Genji* as a frame of reference, i.e. the Japanese Heian period from c.950–1050 AD. He describes the political, social and daily court life with its cult of beauty, in fascinating detail; as Guy Wint wrote in *The Observer* 'He manages to make this strange world thinkable'.

Japan. A Short Cultural History
G.B. Sansom 1987 (1931)
A classic one-volume history of Japanese culture, art, literature and religion from prehistory to the latter part of the nineteenth century. The author shows how Japan's cultural heritage was intricately bound to her political and social development.

Japanese Inn *Oliver Statler* 1985 (1961)
A social history of 400 years in Japan traced through the people who went to the Minaguchi-ya inn on the Tokaido road; from the travellers and guests who passed through the inn you get an excellent idea of the characters and mood of Japanese history.

✔ A History of Modern Japan
Richard Storry 1990 (1960)
The last 100 years in Japan have seen an immense amount of change. Storry looks particularly at the effect the Western intrusion has had on Japan and the mixture of old and new which still exists today.

✔ A Traveller's History of Japan
Richard Tames 1993
A concise, convenient and easy-to-read history which also includes charts and essays on major events, Buddhism, food and drink and national holidays and festivals.

Leisure

✔ Exploring Kiryu Ashio and Nikko. Mountain Walks in the Land of Shodo Shonin *Michael Plastow* 1992
Shodo Shonin was an ascetic and sage who centuries ago roamed the mountain areas and walks described in this book. Gives information about the local flora and fauna as well as places to stay.

✔ Day Walks Near Tokyo
Gary d'A. Walters 1989 (1988)
Twenty-five walks around Tokyo have been selected for their diversity and serenity.

They include beaches, mountains, rivers and lakes; all are free from crowds and yet none is more than an hour or so from Tokyo.

Natural History

✔ A Birdwatcher's Guide to Japan
Mark Brazil 1987
A small book which is a guide to 60 birdwatching sites throughout Japan. The site is described and assessed and a comprehensive list of birds that can be seen there is listed by season; information about how to get there with maps is included.

✔ National Parks of Japan
Mary Sutherland and Dorothy Britton
Includes many photographs but also practical information and maps about the national parks. The flora and fauna are also described.

✔ A Field Guide to the Birds of Japan
Wild Bird Society of Japan   Illustrated by Shinji Takano   Available from Scottish Ornithologists' Club
A guide which follows the Peterson system of indicating field marks, range maps and which gives detailed descriptions. Best birdwatching sights in Japan are listed.

Photography

✔ Wooden Temples of Japan
Peter Popham 1990
Photographs of temples, divided by area and accompanied by ample text.

Religion

✔ The Way of Zen *A.W. Watts* 1990 *(1957)*
Alan Watts wrote the book after many years of studying Zen art and literature and meeting many teachers and students.

Travel Literature

✔ On the Narrow Road to the Deep North *Basho   Translated by Nobuyuki Yuasa*
Basho was born near Kyoto in 1644, moving to Tokyo in 1667 where he continued to write verse. Eventually he became a recluse, relying on the hospitality of temples and fellow poets when he travelled. He was a Zen Buddhist.

Unbeaten Tracks in Japan. An Account of Travels in the Interior Including Visits to the Aborigines of Yezo and the Shrine of Nikko
Isabella Bird Bishop 1984 (1880)
Isabella Bird was advised to leave England for health reasons in 1878; she went to Japan to find 'those sources of novel and sustained interest which conduce so essentially to the enjoyment and restoration of a solitary health-seeker' and found 'its interest exceeded my largest expectations'. Even though she was travelling during the Meiji period in Japan, it was the feudal and remote Japan which appealed to her. She wrote a series of fascinating and observant letters to her sister from the remote island of Hokkaido where she spent time with the Aino, the original inhabitants of the archipelago.

The Roads to Sata. A 2000-Mile Walk Through Japan *Alan Booth 1986 (1985)*
Alan Booth walked from the northernmost tip of Hokkaido to Sata in the very south; the journey took him 128 days and by staying at *ryokan* (country inns), he saw many sides of Japanese life. He was often insulted but also received much hospitality along the way.

✔ **On the Narrow Road to the Deep North. Journey into a Lost Japan**
Lesley Downer 1989
Lesley Downer, inspired by the pilgrimage that the poet Basho had made in 1689, decided to follow in his footsteps. She had already lived in Japan for five years and spoke Japanese, so her journey, mostly on foot, to this underdeveloped part is an interesting look at Japan behind its industrialization.

✔ **A Circle Round the Sun. A Foreigner in Japan** *Peregrine Hodson 1993 (1992)*
Hodson, who speaks fluent Japanese, was a banker by day and a writer by night while he lived in Tokyo. His aim was to try and find *kokoro*, the heart of Japan.

✔ **The Lady and the Monk. Four Seasons in Kyoto** *Pico Iyer 1992 (1991)*
Pico Iyer returned to Kyoto to spend a year there. He finds it full of contradictions; the old and the new are together everywhere: monks on motorcycles watch TV games, modern high-tech buildings are side by side with lily ponds and paper lanterns. Throughout the book, his affair with Sachiko, who is married to a businessman, acts as a gauge to his feelings and understanding of the country.

✔ **Japan. China. A Journal of Two Voyages to the Far East**
Nikos Kazantzakis 1982 (1938)
When Kazantzakis went to China and Japan in 1935 he kept a diary of his explorations. He visited Kobe, Tokyo and Kyoto at a time when Japan was arming for war. In the prologue to this book Kazantzakis writes: 'When I close my eyes to see, to hear, to smell, to touch a country I have known, I feel my body shake and fill with joy as if a beloved person had come near me'.

✔ **Pictures from the Water Trade**
John David Morley 1986 (1985)
The author totally immersed himself in Japanese life for several years; he learnt calligraphy and visited the night-time world of the 'water trade' with its brothels, nightclubs and bars. However it is through his falling deeply in love that we really see how much of an enigma Japan is to the west. [Jan Morris]

✔ **A Superficial Journey through Tokyo and Peking** *Peter Quennell 1986 (1932)*
In 1932 Peter Quennell spent a year in Tokyo and Kyoto (and made a visit to Peking); he writes that the book is 'a kind of travel film, a sequence in which image suggests image'.

✔ **The Inland Sea** *Donald Richie 1978 (1971)*
Donald Richie lived in Japan for many years and was sometime film critic for *The Japan Times*. This book, which he wrote while sailing the Inland Sea, is a reflection on the total Japanese experience and is very instructive about the country being ' . . . a fascinating and subtle blend of travel book and autobiography'. (Christopher Isherwood)

✔ **Low City, High City** *Edward G. Seidensticker 1983*
The history of the city of Tokyo is traced from 1867 to 1923: the Edo period up until the great earthquake.

Bridge of the Brocade Sash. Travels and Observations in Japan
Sachaverell Sitwell 1959
The author had always been fascinated by Japan and Japanese art. He describes his first visit in 1958 which took him to Tokyo and then to Kyoto, a city which exceeded all his expectations. He describes Sumo wrestling, cormorant fishing, painting, pottery and textiles.

Japanese Pilgrimage *Oliver Statler 1984 (1983)*
An account of a walking tour of the Shikoku pilgrimage circuit, created by Kobo Daishi who lived from 774 until 835. He is revered

as a saint, a deity and a miracle worker and the people who make the pilgrimage, which is very demanding and takes two months to complete, believe that Kobo Daishi walks beside them succouring their needs.

✔ **Underground in Japan** Rey Ventura 1992
A young Filipino's story of arriving in Japan and having to live under conditions of exile and secrecy; a vivid account of an underground society where the fear is always of getting caught.

KOREA

Art and Archaeology

Arts of Korea Chewon Kim and Lena Kim Lee 1974
A large-format book which covers sculpture, paintings, bronzes and jade. Full of black and white and colour illustrations and ample text.

Fiction/Poetry

The Living Reed Pearl S. Buck 1966 (1963)
The story of a close-knit family who dedicate themselves to saving their homeland in Korea. 'The Living Reed' is the eldest son of the patriarch who goes into exile; through his experiences we see what was happening in China and Manchuria in the 1920s and 1930s.

✔ **The House of Twilight** Yun Heung-gil 1989
The first collection in English from one of the best known young Korean writers. The stories include some set in the Korean War (when the author was a child) and others set in contemporary Korea.

✔ **A Korean Century, River and Fields. Poems** Ku Sang Translated from Korean by Brother Anthony of Taizé) 1991
Ku Sang was born into a Catholic family in Seoul, grew up in what is now North Korea, studied in Japan and later fled to the South before the Korean War. The poetry is simple yet rich.

✔ **The Book of Masks** Hwang Sun-won 1989 (1976)
A collection of fourteen 'searing psychological' short stories.

Food

✔ **Flavours of Korea**
Marc and Kim Millon 1991
The first Korean cookbook to be published in Britain. The recipes include: miyokguk seaweed soup, chongol Korean meat and vegetable hot pot and paesuk pear punch.

Guides

✔ **Korea. A Travel Survival Kit**
Geoff Crowther and Choe Hyung Pun 1991 (1988)

Fodor Korea (undated)

✔ **Insight Guide to Korea** 1992

✔ **South Korea Handbook**
Robert Nilsen 1988

✔ **Seoul. A Lonely Planet City Guide**
Chris Taylor 1993

History

✔ **An Account of the Shipwreck of a Dutch Vessel on the Isle of Quelpaert, together with a Description of the Kingdom of Corea** Hendrick Hamel 1920 (1668)
The survivors of the ship *Sparrowhawk* which was wrecked in 1653 were imprisoned in Seoul for twelve years. They finally escaped to Japan and eventually wrote this book which became a bestseller; it was the first account of Korea to reach Europe.

A New History of Korea Ki-baik Lee
Translated by E.W. Wagner 1984
An accurate account of Korean history up until 1960. Published in Seoul.

The Origins of the Korean War
Peter Lowe 1986
A readable account of the war between 1950 and 1953.

✔ **At the Court of Korea**
William Franklin Sands 1987 (190?)
Sands was a young American diplomat who was sent to Japan in the early 1890s and subsequently transferred to Korea. There he became the king's chief adviser and wrote these rather unorthodox diplomatic memoirs which reveal much about what was happening in the country at the time.

Natural History

The Birds of Korea Pyong-o Won 1971
Published in the Far East.

Photography

Korea *Jean-Claude and Roland Michaud* 1981
Eighty-five full-page colour photographs of the landscape and people of Korea.

Religion

Korea Buddhism
Korea Buddhism Chogye Order 1986
Photographs of many of the temples and descriptions of Buddhism and the lives of monks. Published in Korea.

Shamanism – The Spirit World of
Korea *Chai-shin Yu and R. Guisso (eds.)* 1988
A scholarly account of Korea's original religion which is still practised today, despite the advent of the more sophisticated religions of Buddhism and Confucianism. Published in USA

Travel Literature

Korea and Her Neighbours. A Narrative of Travel, with an Account of the Recent Vicissitudes and Present Position of the Country
Isabella Bird Bishop 1898
Isabella Bird made four visits to Korea between 1894 and 1897 and had access to sources of information and was allowed into the confidence of the King and Queen in a manner denied all other foreigners. She wrote 'My first journey produced the impression that Korea is the most uninteresting country I ever travelled in'. However due to the rapid changes that were taking place she developed 'an intense interest in it'. So little was known about Korea at the time that when she asked her 'educated friends' to guess where it was not one 'came within 2000 miles of its actual latitude and longtitude', their answers ranging from the Equator, the Black Sea and the Mediterranean.

Point of Departure *James Cameron* 1980 (1967)
A chapter on Korea and references to the Korean War.

Corea or Cho-Sen. The Land of the Morning Calm *A. Henry Savage-Landor* 1895
Savage-Landor spent several months in Korea; his book is a description of the manners and customs of the people.

Korea. A Walk Through the Land of Miracles *Simon Winchester* 1988
Simon Winchester set out from the honeymoon island of Cheju, off the southern tip of Korea and walked over 300 miles north to the capital, Seoul. Korea is full of contrasts and Winchester observed fishing villages, mass marriages, Buddhist monasteries and industrial cities. A good introduction.

MONGOLIA

'Outer Mongolia . . . is such *terra incognita* that Tibet is practically Coney Island by comparison.' John Gunther *Inside Asia* 1939.

Biography

✔ **Genghis Khan. Conqueror of the World** *Leo de Hartog* 1989 (1979)
Analyses how Genghis Khan was able to unite the primitive Mongol tribes of the Siberian steppes and organize them into an efficient army capable of invading Europe. It shows how he exploited the contemporary world situation of the time.

Fiction/Poetry

Modern Far Eastern Stories
Chong-wha Chung (ed.) 1978
Three of the stories in this collection are Mongolian, translated by Charles Bawden.

✔ **Chinese Whispers** *Robert Sproat* 1989 (1988)
A fictional and original approach to the story of Temujin the Shepherd, later to become Christopher Marlowe's Tamburlaine who late in his life was ennobled as Genghis Khan. Sproat brings Temujin's world vividly alive.

General Background

✔ **Mongolia Today** *Shirin Akiner (ed.)* 1991
A collection of essays, by Mongolian experts, on different aspects of the country today: articles include David Morgan on the *Problems of Writing Mongolian History*, Charles Bawden *Mongolia and the Mongolians: An Overview* and Krystyna Chabros on *The Decorative and Applied Art of Mongolia, Traditional and Contemporary.*

✔ **White Months Return. Mongolia Comes of Age** *Guy Hart* 1993
Part political commentary, but also a survey of various aspects of the Mongolian way of life.

Guide

✔ **Mongolia. A Travel Survival Kit**
Robert Storey 1993

History

✔ **The Modern History of Mongolia**
C.R. Bawden 1989 (1968)
Bawden links Genghis Khan's Mongol Empire to Mongolia today in a thorough history of the area. The cultural unity among Mongolians ensured their survival as a distinct entity despite their fragmentation under the Manchus.

✔ **The Lost Country** *Jasper Becker 1993 (1992)*
The author travelled from Peking across the centre of Asia to Leningrad, meeting people who helped him piece together Mongolian history, from the West's first penetration of the area 100 years ago to the White Russian General who, in 1921, wanted to launch a Genghis Khan-like destruction of Bolshevik Russia. He visited Mongolia five times.

The Mongol Empire *Peter Brent 1976*
A straightforward and illustrated history of the Mongol conquests and their empire.

The Devil's Horsemen: the Mongol Invasion of Europe *James Chambers 1988*
The Mongol campaign against Europe which began in 1221.

✔ **Storm from the East** *Robert Marshall 1993*
The history of the Mongol Empire from Genghis Khan to Khubilai Khan, which shows that when the East confronted the West, the West's Eurocentric view was shattered for ever.

✔ **The Mongols** *D. Morgan 1990*
A very good introduction to the medieval Mongols (from the twelfth to the fourteenth centuries) and to their military, religious and economic affairs. The book has an extremely comprehensive bibliography.

Natural History

The Przevalsky Horse *Sándor Bökönyi 1974*
The Polish traveller, Colonel N.M. Przevalsky, found the remains of the wild horse which was named after him in the 1880s. This book describes the characteristics of the horse, its origins, habitat and diet.

Photography

✔ **Mongol Costumes**
Henny Harald Hansen 1994 (1993)
Descriptions of all the different clothes worn in Mongolia, how they're made and their history.

Travel Literature

✔ **The Way to Xanadu**
Caroline Alexander 1993
Caroline Alexander, inspired by Coleridge's poem *Kubla Khan*, went in search of Xanadu. People have argued for years as to where Coleridge got the idea for his poem. Was it just an opium reverie? What literature had he read? What we do know is that his writing was interrupted by a man from Porlock . . . In this book Caroline Alexander tells of her quest across three continents in search of the source of the inspiration.

A Tour in Mongolia *Beatrix Bulstrode 1920*
When Beatrix Bulstrode was refused a passport in Peking to go to Mongolia at a time when the Chinese were fighting the Mongols, she set off regardless and went to Urga via Siberia. She describes her trip, the state of Mongolia at the time and attempts to analyse the Mongol character, which, according to David Fraser *Times* correspondent in Peking at the time was 'particularly instructive'.

Men and Gods in Mongolia
Henning Haslund 1935
The author was on active service with Sven Hedin's Central Asiatic Expedition from 1927–30. Each member of the expedition was encouraged to write about their own personal experiences; this is Haslund's contribution.

**Tents in Mongolia (Yabonah).
Adventures and Experiences Among the Nomads of Central Asia**
Henning Haslund 1934
The Danish author was involved in an expedition in 1923 with Carl Krebs which involved, among other things, the possibility of resettling several thousand Danish dairy farmers from Siberia to Mongolia as their farms in Siberia had been confiscated by the Bolsheviks.

✔ **Travels in Tartary, Thibet and China during the years 1844–5–6**
Abbé Huc 1987 (1850)
Huc and his companion Gabet were Lazarist priests who were sent to find out about the Buddhist peoples of Inner Asia. Huc gives very good descriptions of nineteenth-century life in Inner Mongolia.

Mongol Journeys *Owen Lattimore* *1941*
The record of a vanishing way of life and an
assessment of what the author, an acknowledged expert on the region, saw at the time
was going to happen. He wrote in his introduction: 'What both of us [i.e. he and his wife]
thought about most was not the past, happy
as our share of it was, but the future and the
chance that we may visit again a free Mongolia and a free Mongol people. We are sure
the time will come.' Owen Lattimore also
wrote *Nomads and Commissars: Mongolia
Revisited* (1962) about his visit there in 1961
when he decided that Mongolia was a prosperous country in which the people liked
their close relationship with the Soviet
Union.

**The Land of Genghis Khan. A Journey
in Outer Mongolia** *Rene MacColl* *1963*
In 1962 Rene MacColl flew with a group of
journalists, posing as tourists, to Ulan Bator,
capital of the Mongolian People's Republic
and then travelled throughout the country,
which one of his fellow travelling companions
described as 'the most horrible Communist
country that I have ever been to'.

✔ **The Last Disco in Outer Mongolia**
Nick Middleton *1993 (1992)*
Nick Middleton made two trips to Outer
Mongolia and managed to go to some very
remote places; the emphasis is on the huge
cultural differences that exist between Outer
Mongolia and the West.

Beasts, Men and Gods
Ferdinand Ossendowski *1923*
Ossendowski had been living in Siberia when
the Russian revolution suddenly caught up
with him; he travelled to Mongolia where he
exchanged his gold wedding ring for a Soyot
horse and moved throughout the country recording what he saw; he was particularly sensitive to the religious life and mysteries of the
area.

✔ **Marco Polo. The Travels**
*Penguin Classic Edn   Translated by
Ronald Latham   1958 (see 'China')*

✔ **In Search of Genghis Khan**
Tim Severin *1992 (1991)*
Tim Severin travelled with six Mongol companions in an attempt to follow in the footsteps of Genghis Khan and his armies; they
went through remote and inhospitable territory, encountering shamans and lamas.
Much has not changed, including the annual
outbreak of the Black Death which still exists
today among the horse herders.

TAIWAN

'Formosa is a noble Island, and produces
many valuable Commodities, as well for the
Sustenance of Mankind as for Pleasure and
Luxury.' Alexander Hamilton *A New
Account of the East Indies* 1727.

Anthropology

Among the Headhunters of Formosa
Janet B. Montgomery McGovern *1922*
The author was in Formosa for two years
between 1916 and 1918 and wrote this book
for the general reader rather than for the
specialist anthropologist. In the fifty years
before the book was written, the aboriginal
population of Taiwan had declined by 15 per
cent, a state of affairs which had accelerated
from the time of the arrival of the Japanese
in 1895.

Fiction/Poetry

China Gate *William Arnold* *1983*
Set in Taiwan in the late 1950s, the novel
shows how a hard working youth can rise
from the underworld.

**The Unbroken Chain: An Anthology of
Taiwan Fiction since 1926**
Joseph S.M. Lau (ed.) *1983*
Includes all the thematic and stylistic trends
in Taiwanese fiction; it begins with work by
mainland Chinese refugees and includes fiction from the 'native soil' movement of the
1970s.

Exiles at Home: Short Stories
Ch'en Ying-chen *1986*
A collection of representative short stories by
one of Taiwan's best known writers. He deals
with poverty and ethnic inequality and
champions the underdog.

General Background

Island China *Ralph Clough* *1978*
The politics and economics of present-day
Taiwan from the viewpoints of its neighbour-
ing countries and the United States.

**From Far Formosa. The Island, its
People and Missions**
George Leslie Mackay *1896*
The author spent twenty-three years as a
missionary in Taiwan and got to know the
island well on his travels. Written with
rather too much missionary zeal, but owing
to the shortage of material on Taiwan, it
might be worth looking at.

Guides

✔ **Insight Guide Taiwan** *1992*

✔ **Taiwan. A Travel Survival Kit**
Robert Storey   1990 (1987)

History

The Island of Formosa Past and Prsent. History, People, Resources and Commercial Prospects. Tea, Camphor, Sugar, Gold, Coal, Sulphur, Economical Plants and other Productions *James W. Davidson   1903*
The author was US consul in Formosa; he decided to write the book because he discovered there was very little on the island written in English; much of the research is the result of what he found during the eight years spent there.

Formosa. A Study in Chinese History
W.G. Goddard   1966
A history of Formosa from its beginnings up until the sixties. The author looks closely at the fact that it is a 14,000 square mile island and the effect that that had on its history.

Photography

✔ **Images of Taiwan** *Daniel Reid*
Large coffee-table book published in Hong Kong.

✔ **Taipei** *Published by Times edns*
Good photographs and an interesting text.

Travel Literature

Through Formosa. An Account of Japan's Island Colony *Owen Rutter   1923*
Formosa became Japanese at the end of the nineteenth century, so when the author travelled through the island, which was then virtually unknown to foreigners, it had only been Japanese for around thirty years. He marvels at the economic growth which had occurred during that period.

South East Asia

GENERAL

Art and Archaeology

✔ **Oriental Architecture** *Mario Bussagli   1989 (1981)*
The second half of the book is devoted to the architecture of Indonesia and Indochina and is well illustrated with photographs and plans of buildings.

Handwoven Textiles of South-East Asia *Sylvia Fraser-Lu   1988*
A beautifully illustrated study which shows the variety of South East Asia's textiles. It begins with an historical overview and introduces the materials, equipment and weaving techniques.

✔ **Silverware of South-East Asia**
Sylvia Fraser-Lu   1990 (1989)
An interesting and well illustrated little book documenting the history and tradition of silverware in South-East Asia. Silversmithing in the area used influences from Europe and neighbouring countries producing some unique items.

✔ **The Art of South-East Asia**
Philip Rawson   1990 (1967)
Includes all art forms from architecture to miniature bronzes and is full of illustrations. The text is easy to read and gives a comprehensive overall view of art in Cambodia, Vietnam, Thailand, Laos, Burma, Java and Bali.

Biography

André Malraux: the Indochina Adventure *Walter G. Langlois   1966*
Malraux was in Indochina in 1924–25; he made friends with young intellectuals and was put on trial for taking pieces of sculpture from a temple in Cambodia. There is much about the colonial life at the time.

Fiction

✔ **The Rescue** *Joseph Conrad   1950 (1920)*
Sailing among the islands of the Eastern

Archipelago, Captain Tom Lingard is called upon to rescue an English yacht which has become stranded on a sandbank. The beautiful independent Mrs Travers is on board and the book becomes a story of love and choice.

✔ Far Eastern Tales
W. Somerset Maugham 1993
A collection of short stories set in Malaya and Singapore.

Short Stories W. Somerset Maugham
Somerset Maugham wrote many stories set in South East Asia, including *Mabel and Masterton* (Burma), *The Yellow Streak*, *The Force of Circumstance*, *Flotsam and Jetsam*, *Footprints in the Jungle*, *The Book-Bag*, *The Back of Beyond*, *P. & O. The Outstation*, *Neil MacAdam*, (Malaysia), *The Four Dutchmen* (Singapore), *A Marriage of Convenience*, *Princess September* (Thailand), *Mirage* (Vietnam).

Food

✔ A Taste of the Far East
Madhur Jaffrey 1993
Recipes from Thailand, Vietnam, Korea, Malaysia, Japan, Hong Kong, the Philippines and Indonesia.

✔ The Complete Asian Cookbook
Charmaine Solomon 1993
Recipes from India and Pakistan, Sri Lanka, Indonesia, Malaysia, Singapore, Burma, Thailand, Cambodia, Laos, Vietnam, the Philippines, China, Korea and Japan.

General Background

✔ Early Maps of South-East Asia
R.T. Fell 1988
A small book in the Oxford 'Images of Asia' series which focuses exclusively on the work of European map-makers.

✔ Traveller's Literary Companion to South-east Asia 1994

Guides

✔ Insight Guide South East Asia 1992

✔ South East Asia Handbook
Carl Parkes 1990

✔ South-East Asia on a Shoestring
Tony Wheeler 1992

✔ Thailand and Burma Handbook
1995 Published by Trade and Travel

History

Brother Enemy. The War After the War Nayan Chanda 1988 (1986)
A history of Indochina since the fall of Saigon in 1975. Chanda, who was the Indo-China correspondent of the *Far East Economic Review* and who covered the fall of Saigon, describes the roots of the regional conflict between China and Vietnam and gives fascinating insights into the beginnings of the Khmer Rouge genocide.

✔ Red Brotherhood at War Grant Evans and Kelvin Rowley 1990 (1984)
An account of events in Indo-China since 1975 which explains why a Communist victory did not lead to a peaceful period in the area. The complex politics and events are skilfully untangled and explained. .

✔ A History of Southeast Asia
D.G.E. Hall 1981 (1955)
The standard work on South East Asia; the area is first treated as a whole and then broken down into different countries.

Southeast Asia. An Illustrated Introductory History Milton Osborne 1988 (1979)
An overall potted history of South East Asia from the earliest times until today. An easy-to-read introduction to the area.

In Search of SouthEast Asia: A Modern History David Joel Steinberg (ed.) 1987
Invaluable for an understanding of modern South East Asian history; the book identifies unifying themes that have shaped the history of the region as a whole.

Natural History

✔ SouthEast Asia Wildlife. Insight Guide 1991
Indonesia, Malaysia, Philippines, Singapore and Thailand.

✔ Mammals of South-East Asia
Earl of Cranbrook 1991 (1987)
A short illustrated introduction to the mammals of South-East Asia, in the Oxford 'Images of Asia' series.

✔ A Field Guide to the Birds of South-East Asia Ben King and Edward C. Dickinson Illustrated by Martin W. Woodcock 1993 (1975) .
All 1,198 of the species identified up until 1971 in Burma, Malaysia, Thailand, Laos, Cambodia, Vietnam and Hong Kong are included. The listings give the English name and scientific name, identification, range

and habitat. Black and white and colour illustrations.

✔ **Fruits of South East Asia** *J. Piper*
1989
Fruits of the region as used in cooking, medicine, handicrafts and rituals.

✔ **A Garden of Eden: Plant Life in South-East Asia** *W. Veevers-Carter* *1986*
A small but useful book in the 'Images of Asia' series; a different type of plant is surveyed in each chapter and there are excellent line drawings and illustrations.

Religion

For books on Buddhism, Islam and Hinduism see 'India' and 'Middle East'.

Travel Literature

Little China: the Annamese Lands
Alan Houghton Brodrick *1942*
The author writes with a very colonial attitude, nonetheless there are interesting observations on archaeology and royal ceremonies.

✔ **God's Dust** *Ian Buruma* *1989*
A Modern Asian Journey.
Buruma travels to Burma, Thailand, the Philippines, Malaysia, Singapore, Taiwan, South Korea and Japan and tries to leave aside the clichés attached to each country by the west, in order to get to the core of what Asia is really like today. He is fairly optimistic.

✔ **Crossing the Shadow Line. Travels in South-East Asia** *Andrew Eames* *1988*
(1986)
As a recent graduate from Cambridge where he had done a thesis on Conrad, Andrew Eames spent two years travelling through South East Asia. He visited the Thai hill tribes, a Lao refugee camp, and travelled through Malaysia and Singapore.

✔ **All the Wrong Places. Adrift in the Politics of the Pacific Rim** *James Fenton* *1988*
James Fenton seems to have been in an extraordinary amount of places at extremely dangerous times and wrote this part personal memoir, part travelogue from hot-spots all over South East Asia. He was one of the last journalists in Saigon and was in the Philippines when Corazon Aquino took power.

✔ **Bali and Angkor** *Geoffrey Gorer* *1987*
(1936)
Gorer went on a three months' trip to Sumatra, Java, Bali, Thailand and Cambodia in the early 1930s. His interest was in trying to interpret the role that art and religion played in the life of the Balinese and the Khmers.

✔ **Ways of Escape** *Graham Greene* *1980*
A collection of essays many of which are set in South East Asia. Greene was in Vietnam during the last days of the French and describes that period and the people with whom he comes into contact in his inimitable way. He also writes about Malaya which he found boring in comparison.

Jesting Pilate. The Diary of a Journey
Aldous Huxley *1985 (1926)*
Aldous Huxley travelled from India to California through Burma, Malaya, Java, Borneo, the Philippines, China and Japan. His descriptions are refreshingly iconoclastic; he had a very double-edged view of Brtitish imperial power: it certainly existed but at the same time he saw how tenuous it was.

✔ **A Dragon Apparent** *Norman Lewis*
1982 (1951)
Travels in Cambodia, Laos and Vietnam. Makes poignant reading now as the last forty years have seen South East Asia wracked by war. Lewis is therefore writing about countries which no longer exist in their former state. But there is still much which is the same and he writes so vividly about his journey and the people he meets that it is no wonder the book has become a classic on the area.

Silk Roads. The Asian Adventures of Clara and André Malraux *Axel Madsen*
1990
Malraux was born in 1901 and he missed being called up to fight in the First World War; after the war, like many of his contemporaries, he wanted to prove himself by seeking danger. He and his wife, who were married on a dare to scandalize their elders, set off for Southeast Asia in search of adventure. Clara, being Jewish, was particularly sympathetic to the grievances of the people in Cambodia, Laos and Vietnam whereas André's reaction to the paternalism of French colonialism was one of principle. This first trip to Southeast Asia was to feature prominently in many of their works for the rest of their lives.

✔ **The Travels of Sir John Mandeville**
Translated by C.W.R.D. Moseley 1983 (see 'Middle East')
Mandeville apparently got to Java, if indeed he ever left his library.

✔ **The Gentleman in the Parlour**
W. Somerset Maugham 1930
Maugham set out to write a straightforward account of his journey to Burma, Cambodia, Vietnam and Thailand. While reading Hazlitt on the Irrawaddy he came across the phrase 'The Gentleman in the Parlour' which he immediately lit on as the name for a travel book. He mixed descriptions of the sites and the people he met with comments on the nature of writing and humanity. An enthusiastic and perceptive account of an area of SE Asia which has changed out of all recognition.

✔ **Travels in Siam, Cambodia and Laos 1858–1860** *Henri Mouhot 1992 (1864)*
Mouhot was responsible for popularizing Angkor, not discovering it, as is often claimed. Although he was at times very colonial in his thinking, he was an enthusiast and his book remains easy-to-read; the 1989 reprint is full of fine illustrations, many of which he sketched himself as he travelled.

✔ **Among the Believers** *V.S. Naipaul 1982 (1981) (see 'Iran')*
Naipaul travels through Malaysia and Indonesia.

✔ **Tiger Balm. Travels in Laos, Vietnam and Cambodia** *Lucretia Stewart 1992*
One of the very few books written recently about former French Indo-China. Lucretia Stewart experiences the loneliness and frustration of the lone traveller whose almost every move is watched by some authority, but who nevertheless manages to produce an interesting, sensitive and informed book about the area.

✔ **The Land of the White Elephant. Sights and Scenes in Burma, Siam, Cambodia, and Cochin-China (1871–2)**
Frank Vincent 1988 (1873)
Frank Vincent was an American writer with wide interests whose chief objective in travelling in Indo-China was to see the temples of Angkor which Henri Mouhot had only written about thirteen years before this book was published. A lively account.

✔ **In Search of Conrad** *Gavin Young 1991*
Gavin Young follows Conrad by sea, land and river, powerfully evoking his world with reference to his books and to his life. Gavin

Young slips easily backwards and forwards from the nineteenth century to the present, showing both what has changed and what has stayed the same.

BURMA

Art and Archaeology

✔ **Oriental Architecture** *Mario Bussagli 1989 (1981)*
About twelve pages are devoted to the architecture of Pagan and Prome.

✔ **The Art of South-East Asia**
Philip Rawson (see 'South East Asia –General')

✔ **Pagan. Art and Architecture of Old Burma** *Paul Strachan 1989*
Ample text and well illustrated in colour and black and white. Deals with the rise of the dynasty at Pagan, the temple and stupa and the early, middle and late periods.

Buddhism: Art and Faith
Wladimir Zwalf (ed.) 1985
The catalogue of a joint British Library/British Museum exhibition held in 1985/6 which gives detailed descriptions of the 400 items which were exhibited, with emphasis on Buddhist art and faith.

Biography

✔ **Aung San of Burma: a Biographical Portrait by His Daughter**
Aung San Suu Kyi 1991
A clear and concise biography of Aung San (1915–47), Burma's national hero and independence leader.

✔ **Freedom from Fear And Other Writings** *Aung San Suu Kyi 1991*
A collection of pieces by the Nobel Laureate, written before her house arrest, which reflects her beliefs, hopes and fears for her country and her people.

Into Hidden Burma. An Autobiography *Maurice Collis 1953*
Maurice Collis returned to Burma rather reluctantly in 1919, as he had decided he wanted to be a writer rather than a civil servant; but as he admitted, he was 'fond of Burma' and realized that the life style there would give him ample time to write.

The Changing of Kings: Memories of Burma 1934–1949 *Leslie Glass 1985*
The author was a member of the Indian Civil Service in prewar Burma and became head

of the Burmese section of the Far Eastern Bureau, returning to Burma as oriental secretary in the British Embassy. His affection for Burma and the Burmese is evident.

The Road Past Mandalay. A Personal Narrative *John Masters 1962 (1961)*

John Masters wrote of this book that it 'tells of experiences shared with scores of millions, not yet middle-aged, who fought in war, have loved, have known separation and discomfort and danger. My story is not unique and I am not a hero, and I have written this narrative because I believe that many of you will recognise in it parts of your own life, and know that in writing of myself I have written, also, of you and for you.'

Grandfather Longlegs. The Life and Gallant Death of Major H.P. Seagrim *Ian Morrison 1947*

The subject of the book was a young Englishman who became a great leader among the Karen, tribespeople living in the mountain ranges to the east of Burma; he was finally captured and executed in 1944. The author never met him personally but was so impressed by what he heard that he decided to gather together all possible information.

The Life and Murder of Henry Morshead: A True Story from the Days of the Raj *Ian Morshead 1982*

The author's father was based in Maymyo as director, Burma Circle, of the Survey of India. He was murdered in the Burmese jungle in 1931 under mysterious circumstances; fifty years later his son returns to try and solve the mystery.

✔ Helen of Burma: the Autobiography of a Wartime Nurse *Helen Rodriguez 1988 (1983)*

The author was the daughter of a Scottish nurse and a Portuguese surgeon who was born and brought up in Burma. She stayed on in Taunggyi as a matron when the Japanese invaded, surviving both internment and torture.

✔ Burman in the Back Row: Autobiography of a Burmese Rebel *Aye Saung 1989*

An account of the author's time growing up from 1962 to 1988 under the rule of Ne Win. From being a rural schoolboy he became a Marxist rebel and was imprisoned for four years, finally escaping to Thailand where he started a rebel movement in exile. Published in Thailand.

✔ The Burma of 'AJ' *A.J.S. White 1991*

The author was in the Indian Civil Service from 1922–1937 and Secretary-General of the British Council from 1940–1947. His memoirs are an interesting account of the British in Burma between the wars as he served in outlying districts, as well as the Secretariat in Rangoon.

Fiction/Poetry

Burmese Folk Tales *Htin Aung 1954*

A collection of seventy Burmese folk tales, with explanatory notes, divided into four sections: animal tales, romantic tales, wonder tales and humorous tales. Many were recorded from the oral tradition of villagers between 1933 and 1937.

The Purple Plain *H.E. Bates 1947*

A novel set in Burma in the 1940s. Forrester was a pilot whose wife had been killed by a bomb in London and as a result he had given up all desire to live. But against the backdrop of war, romance flourishes and characters who start out by being incompatible are thrown together and learn to live with each other. *The Jacaranda Tree* (1949) is also set in Burma.

She Was a Queen *Maurice Collis 1937*

An historical novel set at the end of the Pagan empire.

Siamese White *Maurice Collis 1940 (1936)*

Mergui or Mergen is situated in the extreme south of Burma (although in 1687 when this event takes place it belonged to Siam). Samuel White was a sailor and merchant who sailed to Madras in 1675 meeting his wife on the voyage out; he eventually went to Mergui and became involved in a big drama. Collis many years later was in charge of the administration at Mergui for three years; while he was there he heard so much about the violence and fraud in which White, Francis Davenport and Anthony Weltden were involved that when he returned to London he immersed himself in the India Office Library to find out all he could.

Khyberie in Burma: the Adventures of a Mountain Pony *Colin Metcalf Dallas Enriquez 1939*

A children's story about a hill pony belonging to a captain of the Burma Military Police.

I Fall on Grass *Ian Gordon 1952*

An adventurous novel set in the Kachin Hills in 1946.

✔ The Lacquer Lady *F. Tennyson Jesse 1990 (1929)*

In the 1880s Fanny Moroni leaves her British school and returns to Mandalay, where she is swept into court life and becomes the favourite of the Burmese Queen.

✔ **Barrack-room Ballads and Other Verses** Rudyard Kipling 1989 (1892)
Kipling wrote several poems associated with Burma: *Mandalay*, *The Grave of the Hundred Dead* and *The Ballad of Boh Da Thone*.

The Coffin Tree Wendy Law-Yone 1983
A childhood in Burma is followed by a difficult transition to New York.

The Living Lotus Ethel Mannin 1956
An Anglo-Burmese girl becomes separated from her parents during the Japanese occupation of Burma and is rescued by a Burmese family. After the war she is reunited with her English father but finds the lure of Burma and Buddhism too strong.

✔ **Burmese Days** George Orwell 1989 (1934)
Set when the British were ruling in Burma; Flory, a white timber merchant, befriends Dr Veraswami, a black enthusiast for Empire who needs help, since his downfall is being plotted. The novel describes both indigenous corruption and imperial bigotry.

Burmese Proverbs Hla Pe 1962
A collection of 496 Burmese proverbs which show different aspects of Burmese life; well described and introduced.

The Next Best Thing John Ralston Saul 1986
The theft of art treasures from the temples of Pagan and smuggling on the Burma–Thailand border.

Harp of Burma Michio Takeyama 1966 (1946)
A very moving novel about a harp-playing Japanese soldier who decides to stay behind in Burma as a Buddhist monk in order to bury the scattered bones of his fellow soldiers. It was made into a ferociously moral film by Kon Ichikawa in 1956.

The City of Gems Joanna Trollope 1981
Real and fictional characters merge in this historical novel set in Mandalay in the period 1879 to 1885.

Food

✔ **The Best of Burmese Cooking**
Aung Aung Taik 1993
Burmese cuisine blends elements from China, India and Thailand. Over 150 recipes.

General Background

✔ **True Love and Bartholomew. Rebels on the Burmese Border**
Jonathan Falla 1991
The author spent a year in Burma with the Karens, one of Burma's minority peoples. The book is a portrait of the Karen people with chapters on music, food, love, military hierarchy, women and mercenaries as well as being an account of life among the rebels in today's Burma.

✔ **A View of the World** Norman Lewis 1987 (1986)
In this collection of journalism there is an essay entitled *Rangoon Express*.

✔ **Outrage** Bertil Lintner 1990 (1989)
Bertil Lintner, who knows Burma well, writes about the recent events in Burma, having interviewed survivors and eye-witnesses of the 1988 massacre.

✔ **The Burman: His Life and Notions**
Shway Yoe (Sir J.G. Scott) 1989 (1882)
Full of cultural information by a nineteenth-century British colonial official who spent nearly thirty years in Burma. His descriptions are very evocative and are useful in trying to understand the Burma of today.

Guides

✔ **Myanmar. Burma. Insight Guide**
1992

✔ **Burma. A Bradt Guide**
Nicholas Greenwood 1993

✔ **Mandalay and Other Cities of the Past in Burma** V.C. Scott O'Connor 1907
O'Connor was a British colonial officer who describes in detail twelve Burmese cities and temple sites: Mandalay, Ava, Amarapura, Sagaing, Tagaung, Pagan, Prome, Sri Ksetra, Po-u-daung, Thaton, Pegu and Mergui.

✔ **Thailand, Indochina and Burma Handbook** 1995 Published by Trade and Travel

✔ **Myanmar (Burma). A Travel Survival Kit** Tony Wheeler and Joe Cummings 1993

History

A History of Modern Burma
John F. Cady 1958
A standard history of Burma from the eighteenth century up until the mid-fifties. It mainly relies on Western source materials.

Last and First in Burma 1941–1948
Maurice Collis
Collis describes the six-and-a-half years in which the British lost Burma; during this time Burma was invaded by the Japanese in 1942, the British army withdrew over the mountains to India, the Japanese were defeated in 1945 and Aung San, the Burmese national leader achieved the liberation of his country before being assassinated.

Beyond the Chindwin: Being an Account of the Adventures of Number Five Column of the Wingate Expedition into Burma
Bernard Fergusson   1962 (1945)
An account of Wingate's first overland expedition into Burma in 1943 written by the Column's commander in order to sort out his impressions and experiences.

The Story of Burma   *F. Tennyson Jesse*
1946
A short look at the problem of Burma and an outline of the people, politics, religion and history; much of what the author described had been destroyed by the Japanese invasion.

✔ **Burmese Nationalist Movements 1940–1948**   *U Maung Maung   1989*
The author, a former brigadier in the Burma Army, was close to many of the leading political figures of his day. In this book he interviews many of them.

✔ **To the River Kwai. Two Journeys 1943, 1979**   *John Stewart   1988*
The author was taken prisoner of war and was one of the very few survivors of the Sonkurai camp, the worst on the Burma–Siam railway. Since he spoke Japanese he was used as an interpreter; the book attempts to understand what was happening, which was crucial for survival. He returned in 1979 to reflect on the past.

✔ **Sand Against the Wind. Stilwell and the American Experience in China 1911–1945**   *Barbara W. Tuchman*
1981 (1970)
An extremely accessible and easy-to-read history which contains much about Burma in the war. The American army officer General Stilwell's involvement in China spanned the years of revolution, civil war and invasion by the Japanese.

Natural History

Burma's Icy Mountains   *F. Kingdon-Ward*
1949
Kingdon-Ward made four expeditions into the mountains at the sources of the Irrawaddy; he was aware that he only skimmed the surface of the flora since the region to the very north of the country is one of the richest for its size in the whole of South East Asia. He knew more about the birds and mammals because, as he writes, there are fewer of them.

Elephant Bill   *J.H. Williams   1982 (1950)*
'Elephant Bill' was the name by which the author was known throughout Burma where he spent more than twenty years in the jungle living and working with elephants and their riders in the teak forests. When the Japanese army invaded Burma, Williams brought forty-five elephants and over sixty refugee women and children to safety over precipitous mountain tracks; a task which has been compared to Hannibal's crossing of the Alps.

Photography

In Search of Burma   *Caroline Courtauld*
1984

✔ **Burmah. A Photographic Journey 1855–1925**   *Noel F. Singer   1993*
A collection of old photographs.

Religion

The Soul of a People   *Harold Fielding Hall*
1898
A sympathetic portrayal of the Burmese and their religion. Unusually for his time the author's aim was to learn as much as he could about Buddhism from direct personal contact, observation and conversation with the Burmese. The book was immensely popular when it was published.

Travel Literature

✔ **Back to Mandalay. An Inside View of Burma**   *Gerry Abbott   1990*
The account of an English couple's experiences of teaching in Mandalay; they arrived when everything was, on the surface, calm but they were aware of a growing unrest which eventually led, in 1988, to the brutal bloodbath and clamping down on students, many of whom fled to the jungle.

The Grand Peregrination: Being the Life and Adventures of Fernao Mendes Pinto   *Maurice Collis   1990 (1949)*
Pinto was a sixteenth-century Portuguese whose travels in Burma are described on pages 166–228. Collis considered his literary

and historical work 'a masterpiece which enlarges by transcending truth'.

The Land of the Great Image: Being Experiences of Friar Manrique in Araken   Maurice Collis   1953
Friar Manrique was a Portuguese missionary in Arakan between 1629–37. Manrique's vivid descriptions of the Arakanese court are enriched by the fact that Collis knew Arakan well.

✔ Golden Earth   Norman Lewis   1991 (1952)
Norman Lewis by dint of sheer persistence, managed to travel throughout Burma, even though at the time much of the countryside was under the control of insurgent armies. He developed a great love of Burma and her people. [Colin Thubron]

✔ Land of Jade: A Journey Through Insurgent Burma   Bertil Lintner   1990
Lintner spent eighteenh months, mostly on foot, travelling through northern Burma from the Naga Hills to Kachin State and the Golden Triangle. On his journey he interviewed many of the insurgents who have been fighting a civil war for the last forty years.

The Gentleman in the Parlour
W. Somerset Maugham (see 'South East Asia – General')

✔ Borderlines. A Journey in Thailand and Burma   Charles Nicholl   1989 (1988) (see 'Thailand')

✔ Forgotten Land. A Rediscovery of Burma   Harriet O'Brien   1991
Harriet O'Brien spent some time in Burma when she was growing up and then returned and travelled widely throughout the country as one of the few foreign correspondents allowed to do so. She travels from Mandalay to Rangoon and up to the Thai border, trying to analyse and work out why Burma is suffering from so much repression today.

Canoe to Mandalay   Major R. Raven-Hart 1939
Raven-Hart took canoe trips on many rivers throughout the world; in Burma he built his canoe in situ and set out from Myitkyina, on the Irrawaddy in the north of the country near the Chinese border. Although many of his observations are predictable for the time, he is perhaps more sensitive than many: 'I suppose I must get it off my chest sooner or later: I liked the Burmese.'

✔ The Great Railway Bazaar
Paul Theroux   (1975)
Paul Theroux takes the Mandalay Express

from Rangoon to Mandalay and then the local to Maymyo and Naung-Peng.

✔ A Narrative of the Mission to the Court of Ava in 1855; together with the Journal of Arthur Phayre Envoy to the Court of Ava, and Additional Illustrations by Colesworthy Grant and Linnaeus Tripe   Henry Yule   1968
Henry Yule (1820–1889) was appointed secretary to Arthur Phayre's 1855 mission to Burma and in this capacity reported in seven chapters all the mission's proceedings. He was a careful observer and also did numerous pen and ink drawings.

CAMBODIA

Art and Archaeology

Trends in Khmer Art   Jean Boisselier   1989
Detailed descriptions of Khmer sculptures with line drawings explaining their significance and symbolism. Translated from French, but unfortunately only available in Asia.

✔ Angkor. An Introduction
George Coedès   1963 (1943)
A revised edition of a collection of eight lectures which the author delivered in Hanoi. The theme is a general introduction to the background of Angkor and an explanation of their historical and religious setting. In 1907 the Ecole Française d'Extrême-Orient had started cleaning, restoring and studying the monuments in earnest enabling the author a first-hand acquaintance with them.

✔ Oriental Architecture   Mario Bussagli 1989 (1981)
Many black and white illustrations of Angkor and Banteai-Srei.

✔ The Art of South-East Asia
Philip Rawson (see 'South East Asia –General')

Biography

Cambodian Witness   Someth May   1988 (1986)
It is important not to forget the atrocities that occurred in Cambodia and this personal witness makes painful but necessary reading. It is a testimony to the human spirit and its resilience in the face of horrific odds.

Fiction

The Downfall of the Gods
Sir Hugh Clifford 1911
The author had spent many solitary days wandering around the ruins of Angkor Wat and with the 'magic still upon me', he decided to try and piece together the history of what happened to the once mighty civilization of the Khmer Empire. *The Downfall of the Gods* is the resulting rather overwritten but evocative novel.

The Royal Way *André Malraux 1935 (1930)*
Malraux went to Indo-China in 1923 and was arrested for taking some fine Khmer sculptures from the temple of Banteai-Srei near Angkor Wat. The first half is based on the events leading up to this episode, but in the second half Malraux draws on literary, historical and legendary sources. Unfortunately this novel is extremely hard to find in English.

General Background

When the War Was Over. The Voices of Cambodia's Revolution and Its People
Elizabeth Becker 1986
An account of the Cambodian revolution which explains who the Khmer Rouge are, how they fit into their country's history and into the Communist movement, and why they imposed such destruction on their own people. Much of this book is original research and took seven years to write; it is presented as a narrative and through the voices of witnesses that the author interviewed.

Road to Cambodia *James Fenton*
A piece in *Granta Travel Writing* 10 (1984).

Guides

Angkor. Guide Henri Parmentier
Henri Parmentier 1959/60
The best guide book to Angkor, now hard to find, was written in English and French.

✔ A Guide to Phnom Penh
Robert Philpotts 1993 (1992)
A rather basic, but quite useful guide.

✔ Cambodia. Travel Survival Kit
Daniel Robinson and Tony Wheeler 1992

✔ Vietnam, Laos and Cambodia Handbook 1995 *Published by Trade and Travel*

History

Angkor and the Khmers
Malcolm MacDonald 1987 (1958)

The Ancient Civilization of Angkor
Christopher Pym 1968
A popular history in which the author reconstructs the lives of the Khmers from evidence found in the ruins of Angkor. He uses archaeological research as well as a study of the Cambodian people to evoke the Khmer past.

✔ Sideshow *William Shawcross 1986 (1979)*
Kissinger, Nixon and the Destruction of Cambodia.
In 1968 Cambodia was a relatively peaceful and prosperous country, yet by the mid-seventies it lay in ruins. William Shawcross has investigated the American involvement in the destruction of Cambodia and uncovered a mass of corruption and deceit.

Photography

✔ Angkor. The Hidden Glories
Michael Freeman and Roger Warner 1990
A large photographic book with many colour pictures of the buildings, ruins, sculptures and friezes of Angkor; the better known sites are included alongside lesser known ones. Ample text accompanies the photographs.

✔ Cambodia. A Portrait *Photography by Tim Hall Text by John Hoskin 1992*
The book starts with some historical photographs and continues with photographs of Angkor, Phnom Penh, the people and their traditions. Although it refers rather obliquely to the past, there is no feeling of the horror that Cambodia suffered.

✔ Angkor: the Serenity of Buddhism
Marc Riboud 1993 (1992)
Seventy-five black and white photographs and a descriptive essay by Riboud as well as pieces on Cambodia's recent history by Jean Lacouture and Jean Boisselier.

Travel Literature

Little Vehicle *Alan Houghton Brodrick 1948*
Full of fascinating and useful information about Cambodia and Laos based on a journey made in 1939. There is much on the ancient Khmers who were followers of the Mahayana school of Buddhism and also on contemporary Buddhism in Cambodia which follows the Hinayana school (hence the title 'Little Vehicle', meaning Hinayana Buddhism). He refers to Cambodia as 'this earthly paradise'

– ironic, knowing what has happened since then.

Avenue to the Door of the Dead
Harold Elvin 1961
The author cycled 3,000 miles from Bombay to Angkor Wat. He started by crossing India, with an Indian companion; from Madras he took a boat to Penang, cycled up to Chiang Mai in Northern Thailand, back to Bangkok and across to Cambodia and eventually to Siem Reap and Angkor Wat. He describes the journey, mixing it with history and anecdotes.

Siam *Pierre Loti 1902*
Loti's book entitled *Siam* is mostly about Angkor Wat. He had dreamt about the ruins of Angkor from childhood and finally visited them in 1901. His descriptions are rather excessive and flowery but you certainly get a feeling for the magnificence and grandeur of the place, since Loti immerses himself in the enchantment and history of the ruins.

✔ **Angkor** *Malcolm Macdonald 1958*
An easy-to-read and entertaining book about Angkor and the Cambodians with 112 photographs by Loke Wan Tho.

Henri Mouhot's Diary. Travels in the Central Parts of Siam, Cambodia and Laos During the Years 1858–61 *Abridged and edited by Christopher Pym 1966*
It was Henri Mouhot who popularized the ancient Khmer civilization for the western world; although previous explorers had mentioned the temples, for some reason the public's attention was not fired until Mouhot's journal of his discoveries was published posthumously in the west.

The Road to Angkor *Christopher Pym 1959*
The aim of this journey on foot which started in Binh-Dinh in South Vietnam, was to seek traces of a twelfth-century Khmer road which had once linked Angkor with the capital of Champa.

✔ **Escape with Me. An Oriental Sketchbook** *Osbert Sitwell 1984 (1939)*
Sitwell wrote his book from the 'visual and sensual angles, rather than from those of knowledge and learning', so although he spent much time at Angkor he only describes the few monuments that were particularly important to him.

Red Chapels of Banteai-Srei. And Temples in Cambodia, India, Siam and Nepal *Sacheverell Sitwell 1962*
One chapter is devoted to the temples of Banteai-Srei (only very recently reopened to the visitor), but the book is worth finding for its chapters on Angkor Wat, the Bayon and other temples in the Angkor complex. Sacheverell Sitwell compares the temples to other masterpieces which helps put them into context.

INDONESIA – GENERAL

Art and Archaeology

✔ **Oriental Architecture** *Mario Bussagli 1989 (1981)*
Colour and black and white illustrations and a good general introduction to the temples of Bali and Java.

✔ **History of Indian and Indonesian Art** *Ananda K. Coomaraswamy (1927) (see 'India')*

✔ **Indonesian Batik. Processes, Patterns and Places** *Sylvia Fraser-Lu 1989 (1986)*
A short, illustrated and very informative guide in the Oxford 'Images of Asia' series.

✔ **The Kris. Mystic Weapon of the Malay World** *Edward Frey 1988 (1986)*
The kris is the weapon which symbolizes the Malay world; its origins are mysterious, it is credited with supernatural powers and it is a status symbol for its owner.

✔ **Indonesian Textiles**
Michael Hitchcock 1991
Better known textiles decorated with batik and ikat are described and illustrated, as well as lesser known fabric traditions such as supplementary weft. Hitchcock examines the survival of the traditional designs and their continued importance to the people.

✔ **The Art of South-East Asia**
Philip Rawson (see 'South East Asia –General')

Fiction/Poetry

Monkeys in the Dark *Blanche D'Alpuget 1982 (1980)*
A young Australian journalist takes a job in Jakarta just when President Sukarno is about to be overthrown; Sukarno warns people that without him they will be 'monkeys in the dark'. Alexandra, the young journalist has an affair with Maruli Hutabarat, a poet and party activist; her loyalties are divided but she ends up being betrayed by both her own and her lover's societies. Very revealing about Australians who live and work in Indonesia.

✔ **The Outlaw and Other Stories**
Mochtar Lubis 1991 (1987)
Most of the short stories in this collection deal with moral questions which arise from the social conditions in Indonesia. 'Lubis is brilliant at the vignette, the uncanny eye for detail, the momentary flash of intuition.' (Michael Smithies *The Bangkok Post*)

Food

✔ **Indonesian Food and Cookery**
Sri Owen 1986 (1976)
Sri Owen was born in Sumatra and has lived and travelled throughout Indonesia. She has lived in the West for a long time and has much experience of cooking Indonesian food here.

Guides

✔ **Indonesia, Malaysia and Singapore Handbook 1995** *Trade and Travel*

✔ **Indonesia. Insight Guide** *1992*

✔ **Indonesia Handbook** *Bill Dalton 1991 (1977)*
'But for long Highland winters I think I prefer a really meaty guidebook and they come no juicier than Bill Dalton's *Indonesia Handbook*. No book, except perhaps the ABC Flight Guide (another favourite), makes the exotic seem so readily accessible and so inexhaustible. Dalton also seems to be issuing a challenge. He makes you want to find the atoll that escaped him.' (John Keay)

✔ **Indonesia. Travel Survival Kit**
Robert Storey et al. 1992 (1986)

History

The Dutch Seaborne Empire
1600–1800 *C.R. Boxer 1977 (1965)*
An interesting history which puts the Dutch conquest and empire into the context of the time. 'The United Netherlands in the seventeenth century is one of the miracles of world history. A tiny people of 2 million, disunited in religion and by intense provincial loyalties, won independence from the mighty empire of Spain. Within a generation it became a leading naval and colonial power, which also set the pace for Europe in the arts and sciences . . . But the Golden Century lasted barely 100 years. The Netherlands in the 18th century became a third rate power, Dutch culture became cosy and provincial. Professor Boxer's fascinating and vividly written book presents us with all the paradox

of a high civilisation built on exploitation, greed and hypocrisy.' (Christopher Hill *New Statesman*)

✔ **Indonesia: Land Under the Rainbow** *Mochtar Lubis 1990 (1987)*
A popular history of Indonesia which originally appeared in Dutch. It aims to present highlights of history through Indonesian eyes.

Leisure

Underwater Indonesia. A Guide to the World's Greatest Diving. A Periplus Guide *Kal Muller 1992*
Colour photographs, up-to-date travel information, maps, reef ecology, site conditions, local geography and history.

Natural History

✔ **South East Asia Wildlife. Insight Guide** *1991*
Information and illustrations on the following parks: Sumatra Parks, Ujung Kulon National Park, Mount Gede-Pangrango National Park, Bromo-Tengger National Park, Baluran National Park, Bali Barat National Park, Komodo National Park, Dumoga-Bone National Park and Bunaken Marine Park.

✔ **The Malay Archipelago**
Alfred Russel Wallace 1991 (1869)
Wallace spent eight years in Malaysia and Indonesia between 1854 and 1862, recording important data on the flora, fauna and peoples of the area in four field journals. He collected 125,660 specimens and his contribution to the natural history world is immense. This became one of the most important nineteenth-century travel and natural history books and remains eminently readable today.

Photography

✔ **Indonesia. A Voyage Through the Archipelago** *1990*
Photographs by forty-five of the world's leading photographers to commemorate the forty-fifth anniversary of the proclamation of independence in 1989.

✔ **Over Indonesia** *Photographs by Rio Helmi and Guido Alberto Rossi Text by Michael Vatikiotis 1992*
Aerial photographs show the immensity and diversity of the archipelago.

Indonesians. Portraits from an Archipelago *Ian Charles Stewart* *1988 (1983)*
A large photographic book which includes portraits of the people as well as landscapes and traditional crafts.

Travel Literature

✔ **The Head-Hunters of Borneo. A Narrative of Travel up the Mahakkam and Down the Barito. Also Journeyings in Sumatra** *Carl Bock* *1985 (1881)*
Carl Bock was a Norwegian naturalist and explorer who was commissioned to make a collecting expedition to Sumatra by Lord Tweeddale and was also asked to go to the little explored West Borneo by the Dutch colonial authorities.

✔ **Islands of Indonesia** *Violet Clifton* *1991 (1927)*
Violet Clifton travelled through the islands of Indonesia in 1912 visiting Java, Sumatra, Nias, Mentawai and Enggano, the Celebes, Sumbawa, Lombok and Bali. She travelled on horse or by foot staying overnight with her husband in government rest houses.

✔ **An Empire of the East** *Norman Lewis* *1993*
Norman Lewis travels through Aceh in North Sumatra primarily to look at the rich vegetation, but gets caught up in an insurrection; he manages to get into East Timor during a lull in the fighting and learns about Yali stone age tribes in Irian Jaya. He has a marvellous art of telling things the way they are, encouraging the reader to become as incensed or as delighted as he is.

Through the Malay Archipelago *Emily Richings* *n.d. (pre-1904)*
The author travelled to Java, the Celebes, Borneo, the Moluccas, the Solo-Bessir Isles, Sumatra, Krakatau and ended up in Penang. The writing is somewhat flowery, nevertheless she has interesting observations.

BALI

Art and Architecture

✔ **Oriental Architecture** *Mario Bussagli* *1989 (1981) (see 'Indonesia– General')*

✔ **Balinese Paintings** *A.A.M. Djelantik* *1990 (1986)*
A concise overview of the field of Balinese

paintings. In the Oxford 'Images of Asia' series.

Dancing Shadows of Bali *Angela Hobart* *1987*
Shadow theatre is a revered art form in Bali; a mythical story is told while shadow puppets are projected on to a screen. Performances are given in villages, chiefly to men. This book is illustrated with line drawings and photographs.

The Art and Culture of Bali *Urs Ramseyer* *1977*
The idea of art as such does not exist in Balinese, since as Covarrubias wrote 'Everybody in Bali seems to be an artist'. This is an illustrated survey of the many different art forms found in Bali: pottery, sculpture, kris making, temples, ritual artefacts and dance and drama.

Dance and Drama in Bali *Beryl de Zoete and Walter Spies* *1982 (1938)*
A beautiful and thorough book about the dances, legends and mythology of the Balinese. It was compiled as the result of a trip during which Beryl de Zoete spent six months studying dance in countries which still retained a background of Hindu culture.

Autobiography/Biography

Revolt in Paradise *K'tut Tantri* *1960*
An account of life on Bali in the 1930s and the post-World War II Indonesian revolution, by an American woman who was adopted by a Rajah and suffered at the hands of the Japanese.

Fiction

✔ **A Tale from Bali. The Powerful Account of a Holocaust in Paradise** *Vicki Baum* *1992 (1937)*
Vicki Baum visited Bali in 1935 and met an old Dutch resident who gave her some papers, including the draft of a novel on which she subsequently based this book. It tells of an historical event known as 'Puputan' (the End) when the wreck of a Chinese ship was allegedly looted; it ends with the battle of Badung when many Balinese charged the Dutch guns.

✔ **Twin Flower** *G.E.P. Collins* *1992 (1934)*
Fiction cum autobiography about a white man who decides 'to break away from the white man's East, suddenly and completely'. Good descriptions of the life, culture and traditions of Bali.

Food

✔ **The Food of Bali** *Heinz von Holzen and Lother Avsana 1993*
A small well-illustrated book.

General Background

Trance in Bali *Jane Belo 1960*
The ritual of trance in Bali Hindu ceremonies.

Island of Bali *Miguel Covarrubias 1986 (1937)*
The classic book about Bali's people and civilization. Covarrubias, who was Mexican and was Professor of Art History in the National School of Anthropology in Mexico City, was chiefly known as a painter and caricaturist when he first went to Bali. However he was an intelligent traveller and a serious student. The combination of these qualities enabled him to penetrate deeply into the spirit of dance, theatre, music, religion, sexual customs and family life and to write this invaluable book.

✔ **Bali. Sekala and Niskala. Essays on Society, Tradition and Craft**
Fred B. Eiseman 1992 (1990)
A hefty and worthwhile general introduction to the country for the serious visitor. In two volumes.

The Balinese *Hugh Mabbett 1985*
Anecdotes, observations and impressions of Bali and Balinese life.

✔ **A House in Bali** *Colin McPhee 1991 (1944)*
A young American composer went to Bali to study music after hearing recordings of gamelan music. Although this account of his life in Bali has a particular emphasis on music, there are many descriptions of what it was like to live in Bali just before the Pacific War.

✔ **The Night of Purnama**
Anna Mathews 1983 (1965)
In 1963 Bali's long-extinct volcano, Gunung Agung, started erupting. The disaster which continued for six months was witnessed by the author and her husband.

✔ **The Last Paradise. An American's 'Discovery' of Bali in the 1920s**
Hickman Powell 1991 (1930)
Hickman Powell was an American journalist who arrived in Bali in the late 1920s. He describes the inhabitants, customs, beliefs and attitudes.

Guides

✔ **Insight Guide Bali** *1991*

✔ **Introduction to Bali. An Odyssey Guide** *Suzanne Charlé 1991 (1990)*

✔ **Bali. Island of the Gods. A Periplus Guide** *Eric Oey (ed.) 1990*

✔ **Cadogan Guide Bali** *Anthony Mason and Felicity Goulden 1989*

✔ **Bali and Lombok. Travel Survival Kit** *Tony Wheeler and James Lyon 1992 (1984)*

History

Bali – A Paradise Created *Adrian Vickers 1989*
A look at Balinese history and development – from the image that has been created of it in the west, as a tourist destination, beginning with the mass of travellers in the 1930s until the present day.

Natural History

Flowers of Bali. A Periplus Guide
Fred B. Eiseman 1988

✔ **The Birds of Java and Bali**
Derek Holmes and Stephen Nash 1991 (1989)
Descriptions, colour illustrations and checklists of the 433 species of bird which are endemic to Indonesia – of which some 30 are endemic to Java and Bali. In the Oxford 'Images of Asia' series.

JAVA

Anthropology

✔ **Life in the Javanese Kraton**
Aart Van Beek 1990
The Kraton is the Sultan's palace, the cultural and mystical epicentre of Java. The author describes the history of the Sultanates of Solo and Yogyakarta and explores the religious and cultural symbolism associated with the palace buildings.

Art and Architecture

Oriental Architecture *Mario Bussagli 1989 (1981) (see 'Indonesia – General')*

✔ **The Temples of Java**
Jacques Dumarcay 1991 (1986)
A short and useful book on all the main

Hindu and Buddhist monuments in Central and East Java built between the seventh and fifteenth centuries. Although the temples obviously had a strong Indian influence, they were also uniquely Javanese. It shows how the temple building was abandoned when Islam arrived from India.

Autobiography/Biography

Letters of A Javanese Princess
Raden Adjeng Kartini 1976 (1911)
Kartini was born in 1879 and because of her battle for the emancipation of women became known as 'the first feminist of the east'. 'Conditions, both in my own surroundings and in those of others around me broke my heart, and made me long with a nameless sorrow for the awakening of my country.' Her letters show how she achieved her aims; she died aged twenty-five after the birth of a son.

Fiction

✔ **Victory** Joseph Conrad 1989 (1915)
Heyst believes he can avoid suffering by cutting himself off from people; but his life changes when he rescues a young girl from the clutches of the evil innkeeper Schomberg and takes her off to his island retreat. A powerful and complex novel about love and relationships. Some of it is set in Surabaya.

The Year of Living Dangerously
C.J. Koch 1978
Set in 1965 when Jakarta is waiting for the explosion of the abortive revolution which left half a million people dead. The Western journalists who are there to cover the events get caught up in the tension and fear.

✔ **Twilight in Djarkata** Mochtar Lubis 1991 (1963)
A penetrating look at social and political life in Jakarta at the beginning of the 1960s which shows the dark currents of poverty, corruption and vice.

✔ **The Ponsonby Post** Bernice Rubens 1991 (1977)
Hugh Brownlow becomes UN liaison officer in Java; his enthusiasm annoys the local ex-pats, that is until two people die.

✔ **This Earth of Mankind**
✔ **Child of all Nations**
✔ **Footsteps**
✔ **House of Glass** Pramoedya Ananta Toer
This quartet of novels, set in the Indonesia of Dutch colonialism, was written as a result of the author's political imprisonment between 1965 and 1979. All his books have been banned in Indonesia, despite the fact that they are best sellers. [John Keay]

General Background

✔ **Javanese Panorama** H.W. Ponder 1990 (1942)
H.W. Ponder became more and more intrigued with Java the longer she lived there: '. . . the last word about it is never said. You may live there for years, with eyes and ears open to all around you; you may leave and return only to find surprising and fresh discoveries awaiting you round every corner. Java is one of those rare places with which familiarity never breeds contempt, and added knowledge brings no disillusion.' This is a collection of impressions of her life there in the 1930s.

Guides

✔ **Insight Pocket Guide Jakarta** 1992

✔ **Insight Guide Java** 1993

✔ **Insight Pocket Guide Yogyakarta** 1991

✔ **Borobudur** Jacques Dumarcay 1991 (1978)
A small but comprehensive illustrated guide which puts Borobudur into its historical, religious and architectural setting. In the Oxford 'Images of Asia' series.

✔ **Periplus Guide Java** 1994

✔ **Yogyakarta. Cultural Heart of Indonesia** Michael Smithies 1986
Yogyakarta was founded in the eighteenth century near to many previous capitals. It is now a university city in which Smithies lived for two years. He describes the history of the city, the monuments around it and its people and their customs.

History

Javanese Culture Koentjaraningrat 1989 (1985)
A comprehensive study of the Javanese and their society. It starts with the general historical background to Javanese society and culture and then goes into more detail about peasant life, urban culture, religion and values and beliefs.

The History of Java
Thomas Stamford Raffles 1978 (1817)
One of the main reasons that Raffles wrote this lengthy history of Java was to publicize

his activities in Java, thereby contrasting the benevolence of his own measures with the 'tyrannical and rapacious policies' of the Dutch colonial régime. It is fairly heavy going, especially since much extraneous material was included, but it is well informed and was published with many beautiful illustrations and aquatints.

Natural History

✔ **The Birds of Java and Bali**
Derek Holmes and Stephen Nash   1991 (1989)
(see 'Bali')

Photography

✔ **Borobudur: A Prayer in Stone**
Jacques Dumarcay and Soekmono   1990
A large and lavishly illustrated book and essay on Borobudur.

Travel Literature

✔ **Rambles in Java and the Straits in 1852** *'Bengal Civilian' (Charles Walter Kinloch)*
1987 (1853)
The author travelled, with his wife, to recuperate from an illness. His observations are tart, but perceptive; they found the travelling difficult complaining about the food and climate: Singapore was 'too hot and depressing' and 'Dutch cooking . . . is disgusting'.

✔ **An Artist in Java** *Jan Poortenaar   1989 (1928)*
The description of a journey made by a Dutch artist, his wife and daughter through Java in the 1920s. Most of the time was spent in Java, but they also visited Madura, Bali, Sulawesi, Kalimantan and Sumatra.

SUMATRA

Biography

✔ **Tropic Fever. The Adventures of a Planter in Sumatra** *Ladislao Székely   1984 (1937)*
A semi-autobiographical book about a planter's life in Sumatra at the turn of the century. The book enraged the Dutch colonial authorities when it was published since the author observed that the Western plantations 'had not really done the natives a particular favour', and he writes about the brutality of the system.

Fiction

✔ **Coolie** *Madelon H. Lulofs   1987 (1932)*
Ruki, a Javanese, is an indentured labourer on a Dutch-owned rubber plantation in Sumatra who gambles away the small amount of money left to him from his wages. The book caused a sensation in Holland when it was published, as it was considered to be a criticism of Dutch colonial policy in Indonesia.

✔ **Rubber** *Madelon H. Lulofs   1987 (1933)*
A novel about the stultifying lives of the Dutch who were managing the rubber estates in Sumatra in the 1920s. It is semi-autobiographical and one of the characters says: 'Don't you understand how terrible it is? Always to be in this house with nothing around me except this dreadful rubber.'

Guide

✔ **Periplus Guide Sumatra** *1991*

History

✔ **The History of Sumatra**
William Marsden   1975 (1783)
The first detailed account of Sumatra to appear in an European language, it was an immediate success when it was published. He sought to establish 'a regular series of authenticated facts' and to describe 'things as they exist, rather than to display the powers of a creative imagination'.

Natural History

✔ **The Birds of Sumatra and Kalimantan** *Derek Holmes and Stephen Nash   1990*
Descriptions of 148 species from the two islands. There are colour illustrations and information on their plumage, behaviour, habitat and distribution. In the Oxford 'Images of Asia' series.

Travel Literature

✔ **Hunting the Gugu. In Search of the Lost Ape-Men of Sumatra** *Benedict Allen 1990 (1989)*
The legendary lost ape-men of Sumatra are thought to be the missing link in man's evolution; Allen, following folktales, goes in quest of them with an aboriginal guide, but discovers that they are angry and can no longer be appeased by traditional gifts of tobacco.

✔ **Flowering Lotus. A View of Java in the 1950s** *Harold Forster* *1989 (1958)*
Harold Forster became the first lecturer in English at Gadja Mada University in Yogjakarta; he and his wife stayed for four years and travelled round meeting people and studying the culture.

KALIMANTAN

Fiction

✔ **Almayer's Folly** *1992 (1895)*
✔ **An Outcast of the Islands** *1989 (1900)*
✔ **Lord Jim** *1989 (1900)*
✔ **The Rescue** *Joseph Conrad* *1950 (1920)*
All of these were partly set in Kalimantan, although mainly around the coastal areas.

General Background

The Pagan Tribes of Borneo
Charles Hose and William McDougall *1966 (1912)*
A description of the physical, moral and intellectual conditions observed by Charles Hose who was a divisional resident and member of the supreme council of Sarawak.

Guide

✔ **Indonesian Borneo: Kalimantan. Periplus Guide** *Kal Muller* *1990*

Natural History

Quest for a Zoo Dragon
David Attenborough *1957*
Although much of the research was done in the Malaysian part of the island the results apply to the Indonesian part too.

✔ **The Birds of Sumatra and Kalimantan** *Derek Holmes and Stephen Nash* *1990 (see 'Sumatra')*

Travel Literature

A Stroll Through Borneo *James Barclay* *1980 (see 'Sabah')*

✔ **The Headhunters of Borneo**
Carl Bock (see 'Indonesia – General')

✔ **Stranger in the Forest** *Eric Hansen* *1994 (1988)*
Hansen trekked for seven months with Punan guides, trying to get to places that were marked 'unknown' on the map.

World Within *Tom Harrisson (see 'Sarawak')*

✔ **Into the heart of Borneo**
Redmond O'Hanlon *1984 (see 'Sarawak')*

✔ **Through Central Borneo. An Account of Two Years' Travel in the Land of the Head-Hunters Between the Years 1913 and 1917** *Carl Lumholtz* *1991 (1920)*
Lumholtz was a Norwegian explorer and scientist who travelled through the little known interior of Central Borneo between 1913 and 1917. He already had an international reputation as an ethnographer, zoologist and explorer, having travelled extensively in Mexico, Central America and Australia, before going to Borneo; he died in 1922 before completing his research work on Borneo.

SULAWESI

General Background

Dance Quest in the Celebes *Claire Holt* *1939*
The standard work on dance of the area.

Guide

✔ **Periplus Guide Sulawesi and the Celebes** *Toby Alice Volkman and Ian Caldwell (eds.)* *1990*

Natural History

The Poison Tree: Selected Writings of Rumphius on the Natural History of the Indies *E.M. Beekman* *1981*
Rumphius wrote superb descriptions of tropical plants, minerals, shells and fish. Known as 'the blind seer of Ambon', Rumphius located the poisonous Upas tree in Tana Toraja in the seventeenth century: 'The tree grows there on bald mountains. The soil beneath it is barren and singed. The only thing that lives under it is a horned snake that cackles like a hen and by night has fiery eyes.' By the nineteenth century the tree had become a grotesque vision to the Europeans; Belloc includes it in one of his verses:
'U for the Upas tree, which casts a blight,
On those who pull their sisters' hair, and fight.'

Travel Literature

✔ **Not a Hazardous Sport** *Nigel Barley*
1989 (1988)
Nigel Barley, an anthropologist from the Museum of Mankind in London, having been advised by an insurance company that 'anthropology is not a hazardous sport' set off for Sulawesi as he had been told: 'You will go to Sulawesi. If anyone asks why, you will explain it is because the children have pointed ears'. He writes very amusingly about the time he spent in Tanatoraja; while he was there he persuaded four carvers to come to England to build a traditional rice barn at the Museum of Mankind.

Tidemarks ... *H.M. Tomlinson   1925 (1924)*
(see 'Moluccas')

✔ **Six Moons in Sulawesi** *Harry Wilcox*
1989 (1949)
Like many people after the war Harry Wilcox wanted to leave Europe: 'Like millions of others I wanted to escape for a while from the post-war world and the twentieth century; unlike those others, I did escape.'

MOLUCCAS

Fiction

The Ten Thousand Things
Maria Dermout   1983
Nature is combined with murders and ghosts; much of her material is taken from Rumphius 'the blind seer of Ambon', who described the natural history so well.

Guide

✔ **Periplus Guide Spice Islands, the Moluccas** *Kal Muller   1990*

Natural History

The Poison Tree: Selected Writings of Rumphius on the Natural History of the Indies *E.M. Beekman   1981 (see 'Sulawesi')*

Travel Literature

Ambon, Island of Spices *Shirley Deane 1979*
Shirley Deane was a schoolteacher in Ambon and writes about the many strange and supernatural things that happened to her.

Tidemarks: Some Records of a Journey to the Beaches of the Moluccas and the Forest of Malaya in 1923 *H.M. Tomlinson   1925 (1924)*
An entertaining account of a journey just after the First World War through the islands of Indonesia.

IRIAN JAYA

Guide

✔ **Indonesian New Guinea. Irian Jaya. A Periplus Guide** *Kal Muller   1990*

Travel Literature

✔ **Poisoned Arrows** *George Monbiot   1989*
The author managed to bluff his way into the restricted tribal territories of remote Irian Jaya.

✔ **Into the Crocodile Nest** *Benedict Allen*
(see Papua New Guinea)

✔ **Skulduggery** *Mark Shand and Don McCullin   1987*
Irian Jaya is still largely unexplored being marked on the map as 'Relief Data Incomplete'. Three British adventurers 'go exploring' and write about their exploits.

LAOS

Art and Archaeology

✔ **Oriental Architecture** *Mario Bussagli 1989. (1981)*
A small section on Laos with a few illustrations.

✔ **The Art of South-East Asia**
Philip Rawson (see 'South East Asia —General')

Biography

✔ **In a Little Kingdom** *Perry Stieglitz 1990*
Stieglitz went to the lycée in Vientiane on a Fulbright grant in 1959. He later returned as a cultural attaché and married Princess Moune, Prince Souvanna Phouma's daughter. Autobiographical, but interesting about the politics of the time.

Fiction

The Honourable Schoolboy
John Le Carré 1978 (1977) (see 'Hong Kong')

The Ugly American William J. Lederer and
Eugene Burdick 1958
A political novel set in the imaginary country
of Sarkhan; it is a critique of US policy and
activities in Indo-China and the rest of Asia.
The point is made that the majority of Americans make no attempt to understand the
local people or to learn the language, hence
the word 'ugly' and those who do, generally
have their advice ignored.

The Brinkman Desmond Meiring 1964
Set in Laos in 1959/60 – offers a simplified
version of the complex political events of the
time.

The Paradise Eater John Ralston Saul
1989(1988)
Set between Bangkok and Vientiane, a thriller packed with sex, drugs, political intrigue
and life in the sleazy underworld. Good on
the atmosphere in Vientiane.

Food

**Traditional Recipes of Laos: Being the
Manuscript Recipe Books of the Late
Phia Sing, From the Royal Palace at
Luang Prabang** Alan Davidson and
Jennifer Davidson (eds.) 1981
Phia Sing was the royal chef at Luang Pra-
bang; the 124 recipes are accompanied by
introductory material on Lao eating habits,
culinary terms, equipment and ingredients.

General Background

✔ **A View of the World** Norman Lewis
1987 (1986)
Festival in Laos is one of the essays in this
collection of journalism.

✔ **The Ravens. Pilots of the Secret
War of Laos** Christopher Robbins 1989 (1987)
The Ravens were the volunteer pilots who
flew through heavy gunfire over the Ho Chi
Minh trail, with no uniform, on top secret
missions identifying targets and calling in
air-strikes. The casualty rate was enormous,
yet both the Americans and North Vietnamese denied they had any troops in Laos;
this account shows what happened.

Laos: Beyond the Revolution
Joseph J. Zasloff and Leonard Unger (eds.) 1991
A serious examination of the issues faced by
the government of Laos since the revoluti-
nary takeover in 1975. There are sections on

politics, economics, society; external relations and US policy towards Laos is put in
historical perspective.

Guides

✔ **Laos. Travel Survival Kit**
Joe Cummings 1994

✔ **Vietnam, Laos and Cambodia
Handbook 1995** Published by Trade and Travel

History

✔ **Laos. Politics, Economics and
Society** Martin Stuart-Fox 1986
An interesting but somewhat heavy book in
the Marxist régime series; it is ideal as a
reference book for background information.
The author knows the country well having
lived and worked there.

Travel Literature

**Temples and Elephants: Narrative of a
Journey of Exploration Through Upper
Siam and Lao** Carl Bock (1884) (see
'Thailand')

Little Vehicle Alan Houghton Brodrick
(see 'Cambodia')

✔ **A Dragon Apparent** Norman Lewis
1982 (1951) (see 'South East Asia –General')

**River Road to China: the Mekong
Expedition 1866–1873** Milton Osborne
1975
The expedition travelled along the Mekong
looking for a navigable route into South West
China. Previous travellers had not ventured
north of Vientiane; the book includes long
extracts translated from the accounts of explorers.

MALAYSIA

Art and Archaeology

✔ **The Kris. Mystic Weapon of the Malay World** *Edward Frey* *1988 (1986) (see 'Indonesia')*

Autobiography/Biography

Abdullah bin Kadir. The Hikayat Abdullah. Autobiography of Abdullah bin Abdul Kadir 1797–1854 *Translated by A. Hill* *1985*
The author was a clerk to Raffles and wrote his diaries during the most formative years of South East Asian history.

Fiction

No Harvest But a Thorn *Shahnon Ahmad* *1972*
First published in Malay in 1966, the novel is set in the remote village of Banggul Derdap and tells the story of a family's desperate struggle for existence and of their religious faith.

✔ **The Long Day Wanes** *Anthony Burgess* *1981 (1972)*
Originally published under the title *The Malayan Trilogy*, Anthony Burgess' trilogy is a brilliant evocation of life in post-war Malaya. Burgess was education officer in the Colonial Service, so the story is written from first-hand knowledge and is extremely funny.

✔ **Saleh: A Prince of Malaya**
Hugh Clifford *1989 (1926)*
Set in the State of Pelesu (a thinly disguised Pahang) around 1900 when it has just come under British administration. Saleh, a Malay Prince, has been educated in England, but finds himself at the forefront of a rebellion against British rule and is eventually shot dead.

✔ **Lord Jim** *Joseph Conrad* *1989 (1900)*
Jim is first mate on a ship that is about to sink; he takes the cowardly way out and jumps overboard. His guilt and its consequences combine to make this 'One of the world's literary masterpieces' (Cedric Watts). When it was first published, the *Manchester Guardian* wrote 'It is a book to make the world wider and deeper, a piece of life . . .'

✔ **The Shadow Line** *Joseph Conrad* *1986 (1917)*
A young and inexperienced sea captain on his first command finds his ship becalmed in the tropics and his crew smitten with fever. By wrestling with his conscience he crosses the 'shadow-line' between youth and adulthood. The book was written during the First World War and was Conrad's attempt to open men's eyes to the meaning of war through art.

Turtle Beach *Blanche d'Alpuget* *1981*
A young and ambitious journalist goes to Malaysia to report on the refugee crisis; through a series of encounters she is thrown into both professional and personal conflicts.

✔ **The Soul of Malaya** *Henri Fauconnier* *1990 (1931)*
An autobiographical novel, said to be one of the best books written by a foreigner about Malaya. The author was a planter in Malaya and the jungle dominates the book: 'These Malays are interesting. So is the jungle. Trees, nothing but trees. A monotonous country. One enters it . . . and finds the enchanted forest.'

Scorpion Orchid *Lloyd Fernando* *1976*
A novel set in Malaya in the early 1950s as it moves towards independence. Also *Green is the Colour*.

The Return *K.S. Maniam* *1981*
The author is a Tamil and his writing is powerful and descriptive. Also *In a Far Country* and *Plot, the aborting, parablames and other stories* (1989).

Blood and Tears *Keris Mas* *1984*
Twenty short stories by one of the best known contemporary Malay writers; he writes about ordinary people and their reactions to the changes around them.

Maugham's Malaysian Stories
W. Somerset Maugham (selected by Anthony Burgess) *1969*
Six of Maugham's Malaysian stories are included here: *The Vessel of Wrath, The Force of Circumstance, The Door of Opportunity, The Four Dutchmen, P. & O.* and *A Casual Affair*.

. . . And the Rain My Drink *Han Suyin* *1973 (1956)*
Set in Malaya during the Emergency.

✔ **The Consul's File** *Paul Theroux* *1982 (1977)*
A collection of short stories, including *The Flower of Malaya, The Butterfly of the Laruts, The Johore Murders* and *The Last Colonial* set in Malaysia.

The Virgin Soldiers *Leslie Thomas* *1967*
A novel about the lives of the British soldiers

who were conscripted to fight in Malaya in the early 1950s.

Food

✔ **Malaysian Cookery** *Rafi Fernandez 1985*
Malaysia has three main native cuisines: Malay, Indian Malaysian and Chinese Malaysian. There are recipes from each.

✔ **Penang. Nyonya Cooking. Foods of My Childhood** *Cecilia Tan 1992 (1983)*
Penang Nyonya food combines many tastes, making a distinctive cuisine; the author was born and raised in a Penang Baba household and here collects together many of the recipes she grew up with.

General Background

✔ **Malay Poisons and Charm Cures**
John D. Gimlette 1991 (1915)
The author practised Western medicine in Kelantan, became friendly with the local medicine men and learnt about the drugs they used. When he wrote the book very little was known about traditional Malay medicine; now that there is a renewed interest in the subject, Gimlette's book remains interesting.

Guides

✔ **Insight Pocket Guide Kuala Lumpur**
1992

✔ **Insight Pocket Guide Malacca** *1992*

✔ **Insight Guide Malaysia**

✔ **Insight Pocket Guide Penang** *1992*

✔ **Indonesia, Malaysia and Singapore Handbook 1995** *Trade and Travel*

✔ **Illustrated Guide to the Federated Malay States 1923**
Cuthbert Woodville Harrison
This is a reprint of the fourth edition which describes the Malay Peninsula from north to south. It provides 'Notes for Travellers' ('no one need hesitate to bring his feminine belongings with him, nor need the ladies expect to be called upon to rough it') 'Hints for Motorists' and chapters on Big Game Shooting, Museums and Mining.

✔ **Malaysia and Singapore. The Rough Guide** *Charles de Ledesma, Mark Lewis and Pauline Savage 1994*

✔ **Introduction to Malaysia. Odyssey Guide** *Wendy Moore 1991 (1990)*

✔ **Malaysia, Singapore and Brunei. Travel Survival Kit** *Tony Wheeler, Hugh Finlay, Peter Turner and Geoff Crowther 1991 (1982)*

History

Taming the Jungle. The Men Who Made British Malaya *Pat Barr 1977*
Biographies of the people who served in British Malaya at the end of the last century, including Clifford, Maxwell, Swettenham and Weld.

The Jungle is Neutral
F. Spencer Chapman 1950 (1949)
Colonel Chapman was posted to Malaya in 1941 and tells the story of the British in Malaya. The tough conditions that the army had to endure in the jungle are described in a very British way; Chapman himself was often ill from fever, on one occasion being unconscious for seventeen days. A tale of survival and endurance.

A Short History of Malaysia, Singapore and Brunei *C. Mary Turnbull 1988 (1980)*
A readable history which starts 50,000 years ago and continues to the present day. She writes about the geography, people and economy of each country and analyses the major issues.

Natural History

✔ **South East Asia Wildlife. An Insight Guide** *1991*
Information on the following parks: Kuala Selangor, Templer and Taman Negara National Park. It also describes the flora and fauna of Penang, Langkawi, the Cameron Highlands, Fraser's Hill, Tioman, Endau-Rompin and Mount Pulai and has an article on marine turtles.

Malaya. An Account of Its People, Flora and Fauna *Major C.M. Enriquez 1927*
A survey of the archaeology, geography and history of Malaya (including Borneo) with chapters on the flora and fauna.

Photography

✔ **Over Malaysia** *Photographs by*
Guido Alberto Rossi   Text by Kee Hua Chee   1992
Aerial photographs taken by Rossi who is a
keen flier.

Travel Literature

✔ **The Golden Chersonese** *Isabella Bird*
1990 (1883)
Isabella Bird's trip to the Malay States in
1879 was 'unexpected and hastily-planned'.
She went just as the British were beginning
to impose their new colonial order; she gives
us vivid glimpses of this society as well as
much about the country and people she met.

Camping and Tramping in Malaya.
Fifteen Years' Pioneering in the
Native States of the Malay Peninsula
Ambrose B. Rathborne   1984 (1898)
A lively account written in the nineteenth
century about colonial personalities and the
working conditions of the day.

✔ **Glimpses into Life in Malayan**
Lands *John Turnbull Thomson   1991 (1864)*
John Turnbull Thomson was a surveyor in
Malaya from 1838–1841 and a government
surveyor in Singapore from 1841–1853. He
wrote the book many years later in New
Zealand, but his youthful adventures in the
jungles and swamps of Peninsula Malaya are
vivid. As a Malay speaker he writes 'I had
free and unfettered access to the confidence
and sympathies of the people'.

✔ **Six Years in the Malay Jungle**
Carveth Wells   1991 (1925)
The young Carveth Wells was posted to Malaya surveying routes for railways and roads
in Kelantan and Kedah; his book is unpreten-
tious and describes his recipe for gin sling as
well as to how to cook a four-course dinner in
fifteen minutes.

BRUNEI

The Bornean Sultanate of Brunei was under
British protection from 1888 until 1984
when it achieved independence. Many of
the books included in the section on
Sarawak are therefore relevant to Brunei
too.

Fiction

You Want to Die, Johnny!
Gavin Black (pseud. Oswald Wynd)   1979 (1966)
An adventure novel about an importer–ex-
porter who gets involved in organized crime
and intrigue. The setting is the imaginary
Sultanate of Bintan which is in fact Brunei.

Fuel for the Flame: a Novel Set in the
Orient *Alec Waugh   1960*
The novel is set on an imaginary island,
Karak (Borneo) in the South China Sea and
a kingdom (Brunei) which has British consu-
lar assistance, but which is independent of
Westminster. The King welcomes back his
son who returns with his future English wife;
however the local Communists are determined to destroy both the monarchy and
British rule. There are many references to
oil, government and modern colonialism.

Guides

✔ **Periplus Travel Guide to East**
Malaysia and Brunei *Wendy Hutton (ed.)*
1993
Guide to Sabah, Sarawak and Brunei.

History

A Short History of Malaysia,
Singapore and Brunei *C. Mary Turnbull*
1981 (1980) (see 'Malaysia –General')

SABAH

General

A Stroll Through Borneo *James Barclay*
1980
A long trip, by foot and by boat through
Sarawak, Sabah and Kalimantan in Indonesia.

✔ **Among Primitive Peoples in**
Borneo. A Description of the Lives,
Habits and Customs of the Piratical
Head-Hunters of North Borneo, With
an Account of Interesting Objects of
Prehistoric Antiquity Discovered in
the Island *Ivor H.N. Evans   1990 (1922)*
Ivor Evans spent most of his career as a
museum curator in Peninsula Malaya but
was posted to British North Borneo (now
Sabah) in 1910 and decided to devote the rest
of his life to studying the culture and people
of that country. He stayed there until he died
in 1957.

Guides

✔ **Insight Pocket Guide Sabah, Borneo** *1992*

✔ **Periplus Travel Guide East Malaysia and Brunei** *Wendy Hutton (ed.) 1993*
Guide to Sabah, Sarawak and Brunei.

SARAWAK

Anthropology

✔ **Natural Man. A Record from Borneo** *Charles Hose 1988 (1926)*
Hose was recruited into the Sarawak Civil Service as a cadet officer in 1884. He became a keen naturalist and anthropologist. Here he describes the customs, beliefs, arts, crafts, creeds, superstitions and morals of the people of North Borneo. He is not entirely reliable, but always very readable.

✔ **In Borneo Jungles. Among the Dyak Headhunters** *William O. Krohn 1991 (1927)*
Krohn, a forensic surgeon from Chicago, was asked to go to Borneo to collect ethnological specimens for the Natural History Museum. He spent much time with the Dyaks and his book is a fascinating account of their home life, spirit world, character, sports, arts, feasts, ceremonies and their renowned head-hunting.

Borneo People *Malcolm Macdonald 1956*
The author, the son of Ramsay MacDonald, was Governor General of Malaya and British Borneo in 1946 and Commissioner-General, Southeast Asia from 1948–1955. He often visited the Land Dayaks, the Ibans, the Kayans, the Kenyahs, the Melanaus, Malays and Chinese. This is a personal account of his observations.

✔ **The Pagans of North Borneo** *Owen Rutter 1985 (1929)*
All aspects of the lives of the Dusun and Murut peoples are discussed: social organization, arts, trade, headhunting and war, folklore and beliefs and ceremonies.

Biography

Ten Years in Sarawak *Charles Brooke 1866*
Based on the journals of Brooke who was Rajah of Sarawak from 1852 to 1863.

✔ **My Life in Sarawak** *Margaret Brooke, The Ranee of Sarawak 1992 (1913)*
Margaret Brooke arrived in Sarawak as Charles' young bride in the early 1870s. She was instantly curious about everything around her and writes: 'I wanted to know about the country, and asked questions, but no satisfactory answer could be obtained, and I was gently made to understand that I had better find things out for myself . . . The extraordinary idea which English people entertain as to an insuperable bar existing between the white and coloured races . . . appeared to me absurd and nonsensical.'

✔ **Queen of the Headhunters** *Sylvia Lady Brooke, Ranee of Sarawak 1990 (1970)*
A fascinating if somewhat appalling account of the last Ranee's colonial rule.

Fiction/Poetry

Maugham's Borneo Stories *W. Somerset Maugham 1976*
Six of Maugham's Borneo stories are collected together here: *The Yellow Streak*, *The Outstation*, *Before the Party*, *Flotsam and Jetsam*, *Neil MacAdam* and *Virtue*.

Guides

✔ **Periplus Travel Guide East Malaysia and Brunei** *Wendy Hutton (ed.) 1993*
Guide to Sabah, Sarawak and Brunei.

History

✔ **The White Rajahs of Sarawak** *Robert Payne 1990 (1960)*
Three generations of the Brooke family ruled in Sarawak as benevolent despots for over a century. The first was James Brooke who according to Payne was the only man who 'succeeded in coming from the West and making himself king over an Eastern race and founding a dynasty which lasted for a hundred years'. The second was Charles Brooke, James' nephew and the third, Vyner Brooke, Charles' son, who had to bring Sarawak into the twentieth century.

The White Rajahs. A History of Sarawak from 1841–1946 *Steven Runciman 1960*
The book was written at the suggestion of the British Government in Sarawak, which allowed Runciman access to its archives, although he stresses that it is not an official

history. He traces the 100 years of economic development under the Brooke family.

Natural History

✔ **Wanderings in the Great Forests of Borneo** *Odoardo Beccari* 1989 (1904)
A description of Borneo before it came into contact with the modern world and at a time when James Brooke's rule was ending. Beccari was a botanist and the book is an excellent record of the tropical plants in his detailed notebooks and diaries.

✔ **The Gardens of the Sun: or a Naturalist's Journal on the Mountains and in the Forests and Swamps of Borneo and the Sulu Archipelago**
F.W. Burbidge 1989 (1980)
The main object of the journey was to collect new plants in Sarawak, Labuan and Sulu; however, Burbidge has a keen naturalist's eye and vividly describes what he sees on his journeys.

Mulu. The Rain Forest
Robin Hanbury-Tenison 1980
An account of the expedition to the Mulu area of north-east Sarawak, designated a national park, which took place in 1977/8 under the auspices of the Royal Geographical Society and the Sarawak government.

✔ **Orang-Utan** *Barbara Harrisson* 1987 (1962)
The Harrisson's house in Kuching, Sarawak, became a reception centre for baby orangutan when they lived there in the 1950s. The aim was to return them eventually to the jungle, but the animals had become so domesticated that this was thought to be impractical; they were therefore given to various zoos. A charming read.

✔ **The Field-Book of a Jungle-Wallah**
Charles Hose 1985 (1929)
A description of 'shore, river and forest life in Sarawak' by Hose who was one of Charles Brooke's most distingushed officials.

The Birds of Borneo *Bertram E. Smythies*
Revised by the Earl of Cranbrook 1981 (1960)
A descriptive list of the 549 species of birds in Borneo with many colour plates. The first part is devoted to man's relationship with birds; as the author writes 'there is probably no other part of the world where birds and men are more intimately intermixed than in Borneo'.

Travel Literature

A Stroll Through Borneo *James Barclay*
1980 (see 'Sabah')

✔ **Borneo Jungle. An Account of the Oxford University Expedition of 1932**
Tom Harrisson (ed.) 1988 (1938)
The Oxford Exploration Club team which went to Borneo in 1932 consisted of John Ford, C.H. Hartley, Tom Harrisson, Patrick Synge and Edward Shackleton; the book is a collection of articles by each of them.

World Within. A Borneo Story
Tom Harrisson 1959
Tom Harrisson led the hill tribes of Borneo to war and stayed on afterwards to bring them back to peace; he then became curator of the famous Sarawak museum. This book describes Borneo's remote interior and what happened when parachutists appeared out of the sky.

✔ **Wild People** *Andro Linklater* 1993 (1990)
Andro Linklater was meant to be writing for Time–Life Books about the 'wild' Iban; when he discovered that the Iban had outboardmotors and t-shirts, Time–Life were horrified; this is the resulting, very different, book that he wrote.

✔ **Into the Heart of Borneo**
Redmond O'Hanlon 1984
An extremely funny acount of a journey which O'Hanlon made with James Fenton to the mountains of Batu Tiban. He knows a lot about the great Victorian natural historians and his descriptions of the flora and fauna are excellent. [Jeremy Paxman]

PHILIPPINES

Anthropology

Thirty Years with the Philippine Head-Hunters *Samuel E. Kane* 1934
The memoirs of the first American governor of Ifugao. The dotty, salacious and remarkably open thoughts and experiences of an American colonialist.

The Gentle Tasaday. A Stone Age People in the Philippine Rain Forest
John Nance 1976 (1975)
The Tasaday were a tribe of only twenty-eight people who lived in the Philippine rain forest and who apparently had no contact at all with the outside world until 1962. The author was one of the anthropologists who

went to live with and photograph them; he became utterly captivated by them.

Fiction/Poetry

✔ **The Ghosts of Manila**
James Hamilton-Paterson 1994
A compulsively readable novel set in a Manila which tourists do not generally see.

Tropical Baroque: Prose and Poems
Nick Joaquin 1979
Short stories, plays and poetry by a writer much revered in the Philippines.

Noli Me Tangere *José Rizal 1961 (1886)*
A book, rare in that it started a revolution, written by an idealist who trained as a priest and began the idealist tradition of Philippino nationalism; he was executed by firing squad in 1896 ensuring his place as both hero and martyr in the Philippino annals. The book is an irreverent satire on the last years of the Spanish colonial régime in the Philippines. [John Keay]

Scent of Apples: A Collection of Stories *Bienvenido N. Santos 1979*
A collection of stories about Filipino 'old-timers' in America; Santos himself was exiled to America during the war and he writes about the problems and isolation felt by exiles with great sensitivity.

✔ **Awaiting Trespass (A Passion)**
Linda Ty-Casper 1986 (1985)
There is a wake in Manila for the aging playboy Don Severino Gil which becomes the setting for a social satire. There is much speculation as to why his coffin is sealed . . . *Awaiting Trespass* was not published in the Philippines for political reasons.

The Peninsulars *Linda Ty-Casper 1964*
A novel set in Manila just prior to the British occupation in 1762, which evokes both time and place. 'Peninsulars' were Spanish-born Spaniards who looked down on the Philippine-born Spaniards known as 'insulars'.

✔ **Wings of Stone** *Linda Ty-Casper 1986*
Johnny Manalo, a Filipino who has lived in the United States for many years, returns home in 1984 during the lead up to elections. He has been away for so long that he is unable to grasp the pervasive corruption that has consumed everything and everyone. The novel continues until 1986 when in an almost bloodless revolution the people took to the streets and declared their own government.

Food

✔ **The Philippine Cookbook**
Reynaldo Alejandro 1985 (1982)
Classic Philippine food adapted for the use of western kitchens and ingredients.

General Background

✔ **The Snap Revolution** *James Fenton 1986*
James Fenton happened to be in the Philippines at the time of the 'snap election' in February 1986, which ultimately broke the Marcos régime. His pieces were published as a Granta special within two months of Marcos' flight.

Bare Feet in the Palace
Agnes Newton Keith 1955
Vignettes of Philippine life as seen in Manila, Baguio and Mindanao in the 1950s when Ramon Magsaysay as president invited the public to his palace after his inauguration.

Guides

✔ **Insight Guide Philippines** *1992*

✔ **Introduction to the Philippines. An Odyssey Guide** *Evelyn Peplow 1991*

✔ **Philippines. A Travel Survival Kit**
Jens Peters 1991 (1981)

History

A Short History of the Philippines
Teodoro Agoncillo 1975
A useful, if somewhat personal, history published in the Philippines.

The Philippine Story *David Bernstein 1947*
A readable summary of Philippine history and politics with an emphasis on the American period, the problems of independence and the aftermath of war.

✔ **Little Brown Brother** *Leon Wolff 1991 (1960)*
Within months of Philippine independence being proclaimed in 1898, the Philippines faced a fresh challenge: America's desire to establish sovereignty over them. In early 1899 there was an insurrection during which 230,000 were killed – 225,000 of them Filipinos. *Little Brown Brother* describes how it came about, and its long lasting consequences.

✔ **Old Manila** *Ramon Ma. Zaragoza 1990*
Manila was founded by the Spanish in 1571
and immediately became very important as
a trading port. It was fortified by the Spanish
and the inner city, known as Intramuros,
became a cosmopolitan blend of cultures but
was destroyed by the Japanese in the Second
World War. This small book in the Oxford
'Images of Asia' series is the history of Manila
both past and present.

Leisure

The Diver's Guide to the Philippines
*David Smith, Michael Westlake and
Porfirio Castaneda 1982 Published in Hong Kong*
Descriptions of the attractions and facilities
of the Batangas, Apo, Palawan and central
Visayan diving areas. 'The Philippines contains what must be the largest collection of
superb diving sites of any nation in the
world.'

Natural History

✔ **South East Asia Wildlife. An Insight
Guide** *1991*
Illustrations and information on Mount Apo
National Park, Iglit-Baco National Park, St
Pauls National Park, Mount Isarog National
Park, Quezon National Park, Mount Can-
laon National Park and Mount Pulog Na-
tional Park.

Photography

Philippines *Richard Z. Chesnoff Photographs
by Larry Secrist and Jeffrey Aas 1980*
Many visually sharp yet subtle landscapes.

Travel Literature

✔ **Playing With Water**
James Hamilton-Paterson 1988 (1987)
An extraordinarily moving and evocative
book, which combines the story of the auth-
or's life fishing for survival on the remote
Philippine island of Tiwarik, with a journey
of inner exploration. 'Unforgettable . . . The
Philippine landscape and these remote islanders are crystalline and at the same time
mysterious, the writing itself superb.' (Ronald Blythe). 'A classic travel book . . . entirely original: at once astringently and
gorgeously written . . . Everyone in despair
at contemporary literature should read it.'
(Andrew Harvey). Highly recommended.

**Filipinescas. Travels in the
Philippines Today** *James Kirkup 1968*
Kirkup had lived for many years in South-
east Asia, writing this book over a period of
six years and seven long visits. He describes
the history, which is heavy with the failure
of both western and oriental imperialism,
and the great natural beauty of the islands.

SINGAPORE

Biography

Raffles *Maurice Collis 1988 (1966)*
At the age of fourteen Thomas Stamford
Raffles became a clerk in the East India
Company's headquarters in London; his diligence soon attracted attention and led to
his appointment as assistant to the Chief
Secretary in Penang; several posts later led
to his founding of Singapore for which he was
knighted. He was, however, treated shabbily
by the East India Company and on his retirement revived his interests in history, linguistics and botany. In 1825 he founded the
London Zoological Gardens but sadly died
the following year at the age of forty-five.

Fiction/Poetry

✔ **Tanamera** *Noel Barber 1982 (1981)*
The novel moves from British-ruled Malaya,
through the Japanese occupation, to the
birth of a nation; it centres round the British
heir John Dexter who falls in love with Julie
Soong, daughter of Singapore's richest family. Their love was forbidden and had far
reaching consequences.

✔ **Lord Jim** *Joseph Conrad 1989 (1900)*
(see 'Malaysia')

✔ **The Shadow Line** *Joseph Conrad 1986*
(1917) (see 'Malaysia')

✔ **The Singapore Grip** *J.G. Farrell 1982*
(1978)
The novel is set in Singapore on the eve of the
Japanese invasion; it is extremely well researched (it must be one of the few novels to
have a bibliography) and was described by
the *The Observer* as 'brilliant, complex, richly
absurd and melancholy'.

✔ **Saint Jack** *Paul Theroux 1976 (1973)*
Jack who hangs out at the bar at the Ban-
dung Club started off as the youngest member there and ends up as an almost
permanent fixture. He has been variously a
sailor, ship's chandler and pimp and proudly

proclaims that he can offer 'anything you want, anything at all'.

Food

✔ **The Best of Singaporean Cooking**
John Mitchell 1991
A well-illustrated book with a selection of Singapore's 'favourite recipes'.

Guides

✔ **Singapore. Insight City Guide** 1989

✔ **Singapore. Insight Pocket Guide**
1991

✔ **Indonesia, Malaysia and Singapore Handbook** 1995 Trade and Travel

✔ **Introduction to Singapore. An Odyssey Guide** Irene Hoe 1991 (1989)

✔ **Singapore. Lonely Planet City Guide** Peter Turner 1994 (1991)

History

The Singapore Story. From Raffles to Lee Kuan Yew Noel Barber 1978
The book is divided into four parts: 'the unknown island' 1819–1941; 'the end of the myth' 1941–45, 'the road to independence' 1945–65 and 'an experiment in living' 1965–78.

✔ **Main Fleet to Singapore**
Russell Grenfell 1987 (1951)
An account of naval actions of the last war with personal testimonies from most of the principal British commanders. The loss of Malaya is described as well as the sinking of the *Prince of Wales* and the *Repulse*.

✔ **Old Singapore** Maya Jayapal 1992
The history of the city of Singapore from about 1819–1914. The author states that, frustratingly, most of the accounts were written by Europeans giving a somewhat one-sided view of what was happening.

✔ **1907 Handbook to Singapore**
G.M. Reith 1986 (1907)
A guide for the visitor with 'a few hours to a few days to spend in the town'. It combines history, walks and drives, flora and fauna and climate etc.

A History of Singapore 1819–1975
C. Mary Turnbull 1977
A scholarly but readable overview of the history of Singapore in nine chapters. A good bibliography.

Natural History

✔ **South East Asia Wildlife. An Insight Guide** 1991
Illustrations and information on Bukit Timah Nature Reserve, the Botanic Gardens and Sungei Buloh Bird Sanctuary.

✔ **Songbirds in Singapore**
Lesley Layton 1991
Songbird ownership in Singapore is extremely important; the relationship that builds up between the owner and his bird is both complex and dynamic.

Plants and Flowers of Singapore
Ivan Polunin 1987
A very well-illustrated book on the flora of Singapore which underlines its reputation as a 'garden city'. The background of the setting and vegetation is discussed as well as man's influence and the Botanic Gardens. Published in Singapore.

Travel Literature

✔ **The Duke of Puddle Dock. In the Footsteps of Stamford Raffles**
Nigel Barley 1991
Nigel Barley goes in search of the complex character Stamford Raffles who died in penury in London and who had been jokingly named 'The Duke of Puddledock' by his aunt. He follows his tracks from Malacca to Java, Bali and Singapore intrigued to discover the legacy that Raffles left.

✔ **Rambles in Java and the Straits in 1852** 'Bengal Civilian' 1987 (1853) (see 'Java')

✔ **Glimpses into Life in Malayan Lands** John Turnbull Thomson 1991 (1864) (see 'Malaysia')

THAILAND

Art and Archaeology

Thai Painting Jean Boisselier 1976
An interesting look at Thailand's visual art forms in temples and elsewhere; they are put in context by reference to the religious scriptures and folk stories. There is an excellent bibliography on Thai and related art and religious themes. Well illustrated.

✔ **Oriental Architecture** Mario Bussagli 1989 (1981)
Some of the lesser known temples in Thailand are illustrated in black and white.

A Concise History of Buddhist Art in Siam *Reginald Le May   1962 (1938)*
A well-illustrated description of the temples and sculptures of Thailand from the first millenium AD until the sixteenth century.

✔ **The Art of South-East Asia**
Philip Rawson (see 'South East Asia –General')

Biography

Letters from Thailand *Botan   1986 (1970)*
Tan Suang wrote 'letters' to his mother in China over a period of 20 years. We see the changes that happen to him and his eventual collapse.

Consul in Paradise: 69 years in Siam
W.A.R. Wood   1965
Wood was the permanent consul in Chiang Mai who stayed and made his home there.

Fiction

In the Mirror *Edited and translated by Benedict R.O'G. Anderson and Ruchira Mendiones 1985*
A collection of stories and political writings during the American era in Thailand (1955–1976). A new and well-educated intelligentsia emerged as the result of the massive American presence; these translations and critiques by Anderson, Professor of Government and Asian Studies at Cornell University, show some of what emerged.

The Bridge on the River Kwai
Pierre Boulle   1978 (1952)
The book from which the film was made is set in a prisoner-of-war camp beside the River Kwai; the Japanese army made the prisoners, both officers and men, build a bridge for the railway over the river.

King Rat *James Clavell   1962*
The author was a prisoner-of-war in Changi which the Japanese set up after the fall of Singapore in 1942; the story tells of how the prisoners dealt with the conditions of deprivation and claustrophobia.

✔ **The Bangkok Secret** *Anthony Grey 1990*
A woman journalist is intent on solving the mystery of Thailand's King Rama VIII; she seeks clues to his murder and to the death of her father. During her search she gets into much personal danger.

✔ **Rice Without Rain** *Min Fong Ho   1989 (1986)*
A fast-moving story set in Bangkok.

A Single Pilgrim *Norman Lewis   1954*
An Englishman chooses to go to Thailand on a dangerous assignment rather than to return to his marriage in England.

✔ **The Seal of Tammatari. A Novel of Thailand Past and Thailand Present 1688–1987** *J.C. Shaw   1985*
A well researched novel which starts 300 years ago and which is seen through the eyes of Sydney Paston in Ayuthya. This is followed by the diary of a crippled girl today who lives near Chiang Mai. Is her beautiful friend Tari, a reincarnation of a past princess?

✔ **Behind the Painting and Other Stories** *Siburapha   1990*
Siburapha was the pseudonym of Kulasp Saipradit who lived from 1905–1974. He wrote popular romantic novels at the beginning of his career, but was imprisoned from 1952–57 for his political views eventually seeking asylum in China. This collection includes *Behind the Painting* written in 1937 and three post-war stories.

✔ **Jasmine Nights** *S.P. Somtow   1994*
In 1963 a twelve-year-old Thai boy, called Mr Little Frog, has been left with his three maiden aunts on his family estate in Bangkok. He refuses to believe he is Thai, only speaking English and secretly calling himself Justin. Within the story are woven the American civil rights movement and Kennedy's assassination.

✔ **The Politician and Other Stories**
Khamsing Srinawk   1991 (1973)
Twelve satirical short stories about the superstition, greed and gullibility of the peasant trying to come to grips with the modern world.

A Child of the Northeast
Kampoon Boontawee   1988
This sentimental award-winning novel is set in a village in the north-east of Thailand in the 1930s. Good descriptions of local folklore and customs.

Food

✔ **The Taste of Thailand**
Vatcharin Bhumichitr   1991 (1988)
A very good introduction to the history, preparation and eating of Thai food.

General Background

People of the Sun. Encounters in Siam *John Blofeld 1960*
Blofeld considers and writes about many different Thai people: monks, farmers, artists, professors and students, mountain tribes, women and wives and mistresses. The book won the approval of Prince Chula Chakrabongse who agreed to write the foreword.

✔ **Swimming to Cambodia**
Spalding Gray 1987
The actor's account of his time in Thailand on location for the filming of *The Killing Fields*.

Siam *Norman Lewis*
In *Granta Travel 26* (1989).

✔ **Thai Ways and More Thai Ways**
Denis Segaller
Two books which are published in Thailand about Thai traditions and customs.

✔ **Thailand. The Last Domino**
Richard West 1991
An honest attempt to discover the real Thailand; what lies under the skin of what we see on the surface? West writes about Thailand's relationships with other countries and why it failed to become the last domino in the spread of Communism.

✔ **The Kingdom of the Yellow Robe. A Description of Old Siam** *Ernest Young 1986 (1898)*
The author lived in Siam for several years and here writes a comprehensive survey of the domestic and religious rites of the people.

Guides

✔ **Bangkok. Insight Guide** *1992*

✔ **Phuket. Insight Pocket Guide** *1992*

✔ **Thailand. Thomas Cook Travellers Series** *1993*

✔ **Bangkok Handbook. A Moon Publication** *Michael Buckley 1992*

A Guide to Thailand *A. Clerac*
The author was French ambassador to Thailand and wrote what is probably the best guide to Thailand in French. It was translated into English but is extremely hard to get hold of.

✔ **Bangkok. Lonely Planet City Guide** *Joe Cummings 1992*

✔ **Thailand. Travel Survival Kit**
Joe Cummings 1992

✔ **Thailand and Burma. The Traveller's Guide**
Richard Doring, Stefan Loose, Ursula Spraul-Doring and Renate Ramb 1988

✔ **Everyman Guide Thailand** *1993*

✔ **Thailand. The Rough Guide**
Paul Gray and Lucy Ridout 1992

✔ **Introduction to Thailand. An Odyssey Guide** *John Hoskin 1991 (1990)*

✔ **Cadogan Guide Thailand**
Frank Kusy 1991 (1988)

✔ **Koh Samui and Environs. An Odyssey Illustrated Guide** *Dan Reid 1992*

✔ **Old Bangkok** *Michael Smithies 1986*
A short but interesting look at the early development of Bangkok.

✔ **Introduction to Chiang Mai and Northern Thailand. An Odyssey Guide** *Luca Invernizzi Tettoni 1992 (1989)*

✔ **Thailand, Indochina and Burma Handbook** *1995 Published by Trade and Travel*

History

✔ **Journal of an Embassy to the Courts of Siam and Cochin China**
John Crawfurd 1969 (1828)
The author was sent on a mission to Siam, by the government in British India, in 1822; although not much was achieved at the time, the enterprise set the scene for the important treaty of 1855. Crawfurd's observations of contemporary life are interesting.

The Devil's Discus *Rayne Kruger 1964*
An analysis of the events surrounding the death of King Ananda in 1946 when he was still a minor. The book does not come to any conclusion, but was banned in Thailand and is extremely rare as many copies were destroyed.

✔ **The English Governess at the Siamese Court** *Anna Leonowens 1989 (1870)*
Anna Leonowens was engaged by the King of Siam as a governess in 1862. She was young and adventurous but often did not agree with the King who said to her 'Mam, you are one great difficulty'. This is the book which in-

great difficulty'. This is the book which inspired the film *Anna and the King of Siam* and the musical *The King and I*.

✔ **A Physician at the Court of Siam**
Malcolm Smith   1985 (1957)
The author was appointed physician to the court of Siam and as a result was one of the few Europeans to have access to the inner sanctums of the royal palace.

Jim Thompson. The Legendary American of Thailand   *William Warren*
1988 (1970)
Thai silk is now famous throughout the world; the industry was started by the American Jim Thompson, an ex-OSS man who disappeared in the Cameron Highlands in Malaysia in 1967. No trace of him has ever been found. William Warren's book is a fascinating account of life in Thailand and the mysterious Thompson and his fabulous art collection.

Thailand. A Short History
David K. Wyatt   1982
A good general, comprehensive and clearly written introduction and history with many interesting details. An excellent discursive bibliography.
Descriptions, and both photographic and sketched scenes of domestic and religious life in Siam at the end of the last century.

Leisure

✔ **A Trekkers' Guide to the Hilltribes of Northern Thailand**   *John R. Davies*
Short but well-informed book about the culture of the hill-tribes as well as some practical information on walking and language.

Natural History

✔ **South East Asia Wildlife. An Insight Guide**   *1991*
Includes the following articles and illustrations on wildlife in Thailand: The Asian Elephant, Huai Kha Kheng, Khao Yai National Park and Wat Phai Lom.

Thailand: the Kingdom Beneath the Sea   *Ashley J. Boyd and Collin Piprell*
Tips on good diving areas and accounts of diving expeditions, as well as photographs and identification of fish and coral. Published in Thailand.

✔ **A Field Guide to the Flowering Plants of Thailand**   *Patrick D. McMakin*
1988
The book, aimed at the amateur, is divided

into seven different kinds of plant community: garden plants and trees, forests, sub-alpine forests, coastal, freshwater marshes, wild flowers and tropical. There are many colour photographs and descriptions of the plants. Published in Thailand.

Photography

✔ **Peoples of the Golden Triangle. Six Tribes in Thailand**   *Paul and Elaine Lewis*
1984
The six tribes described and illustrated are the Karen, Hmong, Mien, Lahu, Akha and Lisu. Each has its own language, dress, religion and historical background; the book examines each tribe and its customs and is extremely well illustrated with a wealth of colour photographs.

Nest Gatherers of Tiger Cave   *Eric Valli and Diane Summers   1990*
A large format book about the birds' nest gatherers of southern Thailand. The authors scaled the heights with the gatherers to get some sensational photographs.

✔ **Living in Thailand**   *William Warren*
Photographs by Luca Invernizzi Tettoni   1989
Large book with illustrations of traditional Thai houses and furnishings.

Religion

✔ **The Buddha**   *Michael Carrithers   1990*
(1983)
A short book in the 'Oxford Past Masters' series which describes the life of the Buddha and lucidly explains the development of Buddhist thought.

Travel Literature

Temples and Elephants: The Narrative of a Journey of Exploration Through Upper Siam and Lao   *Carl Bock   1986*
(1884)
The account of a fourteen-month journey from Bangkok to the north of Thailand and into Laos. There are many descriptions of rural and court life, although he writes about the 'difficulty of extracting any information from the Siamese, and still more from the Laosians, who hate the sight of a foreigner'.

✔ **Teak-Wallah. The Adventures of a Young Englishman in Thailand in the 1920s**   *Reginald Campbell   1986 (1935)*
The book begins with a description of the author's journey out to Thailand by ship, and continues with vivid descriptions of the

northern Thai countryside where he had been sent to inspect the teak forests

Avenue to the Door of the Dead
Harold Elvin 1961 (see 'Cambodia')

✔ **Borderlines. A Journey in Thailand and Burma** Charles Nicholl 1989 (1988)
Charles Nicholl went to Thailand on a kind of pilgrimage after being moved by the words of a Buddhist monk he saw on television. He has many extraordinary experiences on his journey, which include going to the Golden Triangle and into Burma; he writes with irony, humour and sensitivity.

✔ **Thailand. The Lotus Kingdom**
Alistair Shearer 1989
Alistair Shearer spends much of each winter travelling round South and South East Asia. His book describes what the visitor might see on a visit but also attempts to get behind the superficialities and seeming contradictions of this Buddhist society so recently thrust into the twentieth century.

The Red Chapels of Banteai-Srei And Temples in Cambodia, India, Siam and Nepal Sacheverell Sitwell 1962
The book which takes in much of South Asia, begins with Bangkok and the Temple of the Emerald Buddha.

VIETNAM

Art and Archaeology

✔ **Oriental Architecture** Mario Bussagli 1989 (1981)
The book ends with a short piece, and black and white photographs of Vietnam.

✔ **The Art of South-East Asia**
Philip Rawson (see 'South East Asia –General')

Biography

A Rumour of War Philip Caputo 1988(1977)
Caputo, a young college graduate, served with the Marines in Vietnam and later returned as a journalist. His reminiscences, probably typical of many other young men, many of whom were killed, do much to show us the heartbreaking and terrifying reality of war.

Fiction

Blue Dragon, White Tiger Tran Van Dinh

✔ **The Lover** Marguerite Duras 1985(1984)
Set in the early 1930s, the autobiographical novel which tells the story of a young French girl and her Chinese lover evokes pre-war IndoChina with passion and intensity. Their different races present huge problems and the hatred generated tears her family apart. Duras won the Prix Goncourt with her novel which was written fifty years after the events described.

✔ **The Quiet American** Graham Greene 1955
Set in Saigon in the fifties, Graham Greene's novel about Alden Pyle, who was in Vietnam on a secret mission, has become a classic. Pyle's involvement with Phuong, a beautiful Vietnamese woman, who had left the English journalist Fowler for him, is a masterful account of the meeting of two cultures.

✔ **Saigon** Anthony Grey 1983 (1982)
Joseph Sherman was drawn back to Saigon by Lan, a Vietnamese beauty he could never forget during the five decades beginning in 1925. He was there when a million coolies rose up against the French, when the Legion took its last bloody stand at Dien Bien Phu and during the American involvement.

The Cry of Vietnam Thich Nhat Hanh 1971
Fourteen powerful poems which condemn the injustice of the Vietnam War. The author left Vietnam in the late 1960s having been unsuccessful in establishing a non-violent social action movement.

Going After Cacciato Tim O'Brien 1988
Tim O'Brien fought in Vietnam where he was awarded seven medals. *Going After Cacciato* is an excellent novel about the Vietnam war.

✔ **Under the Starfruit Tree. Folktales from Vietnam** Told by Alice M. Terada 1989
This collection of folk tales is divided into four categories: foibles of man and quirks of animals, tales from the highlands and the lowlands, the spirit world and food, love and laughter.

✔ **Army Blue** Lucian K. Truscott 1991 (1990)
At the height of the Vietnam war in 1969, Lieutenant Blue is being held in a military prison in Saigon charged with cowardice and desertion; however, it is all a frame-up since he has stumbled on a sensational scandal.

Food

✔ **Simple Art of Vietnamese Cooking**
Binh Duong and Marcia Kiesel   1991
Vietnamese cuisine reflects the influence of many cultures: Chinese, French, Indian, Indonesian, Dutch and Portuguese, yet it remains distinctive, using a unique variety of herbs, vine leaves and aromatic grasses.

General Background

✔ **Ridding the Devils. Vietnam Revisited**   *Frank Palmos   1991 (1990)*
In 1968 during the Tet offensive Frank Palmos, a war correspondent, was ambushed in Saigon by the Viet Cong. His four colleagues were killed, but by playing dead he survived. Twenty years later he was asked to return; *Ridding the Devils* is an account of how he comes to terms with his own and others' horrendous experiences.

✔ **Two Cities. Hanoi and Saigon**
Neil Sheehan   1992
In 1989 Neil Sheehan returned to Vietnam and visited Hanoi and Saigon. In Hanoi he talked to soldiers and politicians and in Saigon he is besieged by memories as he goes in search of former acquaintances.

Night in Vietnam   *Colin Thubron*
A piece in *Granta Travel Writing 10* (1984).

✔ **Vietnam at the Crossroads**
Michael C. Williams   1992
A Chatham House paper on the future of Vietnam; both economically and politically the country is at a turning point. The paper discusses the transition to a market economy and the pressures that that has brought to bear on the country's political, social and economic systems.

Saigon Dreaming   *Tela Zasloff*
An article in *Granta Travel 26* (1989).

Guides

✔ **Vietnam. An Insight Guide**   *1991*

✔ **Guide to Vietnam. A Bradt Guide**
John R. Jones   1990 (1989)

✔ **Vietnam Travel Survival Kit**
Daniel Robinson and Robert Storey   1993 (1991)

✔ **Vietnam, Laos and Cambodia Handbook**   *1995   Published by Trade and Travel*

History

Fire in the Lake   *Frances Fitzgerald   1989 (1972)*
Subtitled 'The Vietnamese and the Americans in Vietnam', the book, which won the Pulitzer Prize, examines why the Americans could never have won the Vietnam War. Fitzgerald was the first person to write about the war from the Vietnamese as well as the American point of view . . .

✔ **Dispatches**   *Michael Herr   1979 (1977)*
A unique and disturbing journal about war. Herr conveys the terror of combat and the frightening truth that there are many men who love war. Although this is about Vietnam, the fear and death that he writes about could be true of any war.

✔ **Vietnam. A History**   *Stanley Karnow   1991 (1983)*
The definitive history of the events leading up to and the actual Vietnam War. Many secret documents were used to compile the book and Karnow interviewed French, American, Vietnamese and Chinese diplomats and military. Well researched and easy-to-read.

✔ **The Tunnels of Cu Chi. A Remarkable Story of the Vietnam War**   *Tom Mangold and John Penycate   1986 (1985)*
The story of the secret tunnels which played such an important part in the Vietnam War. Few people knew of the bloody battles that were fought underground in the claustrophobic tunnels between the Viet Cong guerrillas and the American 'Tunnel Rats'.

✔ **A Bright Shining Lie**   *Neil Sheehan   1989 (1988)*
Seen through the eyes of an American Colonel, John Paul Vann, *A Bright Shining Lie* encapsulates everything that was most disturbing about the Vietnam War. Vann was passionate about the military but was also idealistic; he had to leave the army but returned to Vietnam as a civilian and gained enormous power. If you only read one book about the War, this should be it, it is compulsive reading.

Natural History

✔ **A Field Guide to the Birds of South-East Asia**   *Ben King and Edward C. Dickinson   Illustrated by Martin W. Woodcock (see 'South East Asia – General')*

Photography

Vietnam Inc. *Philip Jones Griffiths 1971*
Jones Griffiths was in Vietnam as a Magnum photographer and produced this invaluable collection with an intelligent text.

Travel Literature

Intimate Letters from Tonquin
Marshal Lyautey 1932
These letters were written, not for publication, between 1894 and 1896 when Lyautey was unexpectedly appointed to the Headquarters Staff of the Army of Occupation in Tonquin:
'Some of us are writers and some of us are fighters,
But here is a writer and a fighter both.'

✔ The Great Railway Bazaar
Paul Theroux (1975)
Paul Theroux makes two train trips in Vietnam during the war: from Saigon to Bien Hoa and from Hué to Da Nang.

A Voyage to Cochin China *John White*
1972 (1824)
The author was an American naval officer who spent nearly three months in Saigon in 1819 looking at the possibility of opening up trade contacts. He describes the clothes, food, climate and hygiene and the people he met.

✔ Romancing Vietnam *Justin Wintle*
1991
The author spent three months in Vietnam in 1989–90; the narrative concentrates on his own frustrations and difficulties to the detriment of finding out what the country and people were really like.

AUSTRALASIA AND THE PACIFIC

Australasia and The Pacific

GENERAL

'The Pacific licks all other oceans out of hand.' Robert Louis Stevenson, letter to W.E. Henley October 1879

✔ **Pacific Destiny** *Robert Elegant 1991 (1990)*
Robert Elegant was Asia correspondent for *The Los Angeles Times* and *Newsweek* for over thirty years; this is an in-depth study of the countries of the Pacific Basin: Australia, the Philippines, Singapore, Hong Kong, Taiwan, Korea, China and Japan. He analyses each nation in turn and includes personal anecdotes from his travels.

Rethinking the Pacific *Gerald Segal 1990*
Segal maintains that the Pacific has never had and never could have a common destiny and that thinking of it as a separate region does not make sense. It is important in that large parts of the area have become increasingly relevant in global patterns of ideology, security and trade.

AUSTRALIA

'Earth is here so kind that just tickle her with a hoe and she laughs with a harvest.' Douglas William Jerrold *A Man Made of Money* 1849

Anthropology

Triumph of the Nomads *Geoffrey Blainey 1983 (1976)*
Shows how successful the aborigines were in adapting to Australia's climate and natural resources, thus demolishing the myth that they were 'primitive'.

Art and Archaeology

✔ **Aboriginal Art** *Wally Caruana 1993*
An illustrated background and introduction to the rich and complex beliefs expressed in aboriginal art. In the Thames and Hudson 'World of Art' series.

The Art of Australia *Robert Hughes 1970 (1966)*
A look at Australian painting from the early settlement days until 1964. Robert Hughes was probably the first critic who looked at Australian art as a force in its own right – there was inevitably a conflict between the desire for independence in Australian vision and the obsessive influence of European and American models.

Autobiography/Biography

✔ **Daisy Bates in the Desert** *Julia Blackburn 1994*
A biography combining fact and fiction about the life of the eccentric Daisy Bates.

A Fortunate Life *A.B. Facey 1981*
A very moving autobiography of an Australian orphan and his experiences at Gallipoli. He shows enormous resilience and courage in this straightforward account.

People in Glass Houses. Growing up in Government House *Adelaide Lubbock 1978 (1977)*
Sir Arthur Stanley arrived in Melbourne as Governor of Victoria in 1914; his wife sent many letters home, which are combined with his daughter's memories for this book.

Tall Poppies *Susan Mitchell 1983*
Profiles of ten successful Australian women, all from differing backgrounds and nationalities.

✔ **My Place** *Sally Morgan 1991 (1987)*
Sally Morgan wanted to find out about her ancestry and eventually discovers the mystery of her aboriginal identity; her quest eventually sparks responses from her mother and grandmother who tell their own stories. A powerful and direct book.

✔ **Joseph Banks. A Life** *Patrick O'Brian 1988 (1987)*
Sir Joseph Banks the botanist, explorer and President of the Royal Society, accompanied Captain Cook to Australia and was later instrumental in establishing Kew Gardens. This biography draws on much previously unpublished material.

Fiction/Poetry

Tirra Lirra by the River *Jessica Anderson 1984 (1978)*
An evocative book which follows an old woman's recollection of her troubled life as she returns from Britain to her childhood home in Brisbane.

✔ **Oscar and Lucinda** *Peter Carey* *1990*
(1989)
A rich and complex novel which filled Angela
Carter 'with a wild, savage envy'. It is, at the
same time as being a love story, a many-
layered novel, historically interesting about
Australia and also relevant to today. Other
books by Peter Carey include *The Tax Inspector* (1991) and *Illywhacker* (1985).

✔ **The Songlines** *Bruce Chatwin* *1988*
(1987)
Remarkable and original; the kind of book
which one is very reluctant to finish. 'I have
a vision of the Songlines stretching across the
continents and ages; that wherever men have
trodden they have left a trail of song; and that
these trails must reach back, in time and
space, to an isolated pocket in the African
savannah, where the First Man shouted the
opening stanza of the World Song, "I am!"'

Make Me Rich *Peter Corris* *1985*
Other crime novels by Peter Corris, set in
Sydney include: *Man in the Shadows* (1988),
West Graves (1993), *The January Zone*
(1987), *The Greenwich Apartments* (1986),
The Big Drop and Other Cliff Hardy stories
(1985).

My Brilliant Career *Stella Miles Franklin*
1983 (1954)
An autobiographical tale of bush life which
was an immediate success when it was published at the turn of the century. Discouraged
by her failure to get further novels published,
but determined not to become a housewife in
the bush, Stella Miles Franklin went to
America in 1906 and stayed there until 1915,
although missing 'the aroma of the gumleaf
and the perfume of the wattle blossom'. She
did not return to Australia for good until
1927. She died in 1954.

Postcards from Surfers *Helen Garner*
1989
A collection of short stories. Also *Monkey
Grip* a story of obsession, love and heroin
addiction in inner-city Melbourne.

The Transit of Venus *Shirley Hazzard*
1980
Two sisters from Australia emigrate to London during the 1950s.

✔ **Capricornia** *Xavier Herbert* *1989 (1938)*
An epic saga of the prejudices and brutality
encountered by half-castes in northern Australia.

The Chant of Jimmie Blacksmith
Thomas Keneally *1980 (1972)*
A story, based on fact, about the son of an
aboriginal mother and white father who
wanted to be treated as an equal by white
men, but who was humiliated and abused by
them. Finally he took to violence after which
there was no turning back.

✔ **Kangaroo** *D.H. Lawrence* *1981 (1923)*
A partly autobiographical novel in which
Lawrence examines politics and power. A
young couple leave post-war Europe for Australia where they meet Kangaroo, leader of a
political group called the Diggers. The power
struggle within their marriage is akin to
Lawrence's relationship with his wife Frieda,
to whom he endlessly tried to prove that the
basis of marriage is not perfect love, but
perfect submission of the wife to the husband. [Jan Morris]

**The Penguin Book of Australian
Verse** *(1972)*
**The Penguin Book of Modern
Australian Verse** *Harry Heseltine (ed.)*
(1981)
Both books have interesting introductions
which give an overview of the subject.

✔ **Picnic at Hanging Rock** *Joan Lindsay*
1967
A group of schoolgirls go for a picnic to Hanging Rock; they get caught up in elemental
Australia and the day turns in to a disaster;
a disclaimer at the front of the book an-
nounces that the readers must decide for
themselves whether or not this is fact or
fiction.

Johnno *David Malouf* *1976 (1975)*
Sleazy wartime Brisbane of the 1940s and
the 1950s with its pubs and brothels, are both
evoked in David Malouf's novel which is also
a fine character study between the two main
figures.

✔ **The Penguin Best Australian Short
Stories** *Mary Lord (ed.)* *1991*
Dating from the nineteenth century up until
the present day. Included in the collection
are works by: William Astley, Marcus
Clarke, Patrick White, Elizabeth Jolley,
Peter Carey and Janette Turner Hospital.

**The Man from Snowy River and other
Verses** *A.B. Paterson* *1984 (1895)*
Andrew Barton Paterson was born in 1864
near Orange in New South Wales; he became
a solicitor and his first collection of poems
The Man from Snowy River was published to
instant success in 1895, being described by
the London *Literary Yearbook* as 'without
parallel in colonial literary annals'. He left
the legal world to become the Boer War corre-
sponent for the *Sydney Morning Herald*,
later writing the words to 'Waltzing Matilda'.
This collection of poems by 'Banjo' Paterson

opens with the famous *Man from Snowy River*. The poem gives a real feeling of the landscape:
'He sent the flint stones flying, but the pony kept his feet,
He cleared the fallen timber in his stride,
And the man from Snowy River never shifted in his seat –
It was grand to see that mountain horseman ride.
Through the stringy barks and saplings, on the rough and broken ground,
Down the hillside at a racing pace he went;
And he never drew the bridle till he landed safe and sound
At the bottom of that terrible descent.'

Fortunes of Richard Mahoney
Henry H. Richardson 1929 (1917)
A trilogy comprising *Australian Felix*, *The Way Home* and *Ultima Thule* which follows the fortunes of one man, but shows the development of Australia.

✔ The Tree of Man *Patrick White 1961 (1955)*
The story of a man and woman who make their home in the outback; as their children grow up and the wilderness begins to disappear, many changes occur. Other novels by Patrick White, who was the first Australian to win the Nobel Prize for Literature, include *Voss* (1957) [Stephen Brook] *Riders in the Chariot* (1961) [Paul Theroux] and *The Eye of the Storm* (1973). He also published three collections of short stories *The Burnt Ones* (1964), *The Cockatoos* (1974) and *Three Uneasy Pieces* (1988).

Food

✔ A Good Plain Cook. An Edible History of Queensland *Susan Addison and Judith McKay 1985*
A collection of plain simple recipes set in an historical background.

✔ Stephanie's Australia
Stephanie Alexander 1991
Well-illustrated book which is arranged by state. As well as producing recipes the author talked to food producers and restaurant owners.

✔ Wine Atlas of Australia and New Zealand *James Halliday 1991*
A large well-illustrated book about the wine-growing districts of Australasia. Each section is introduced with a brief summary of the distinguishing features and history of the region and also the wine styles and wines.

General Background

The Passing of the Aborigines: a Lifetime Spent Among the Natives of Australia *Daisy Bates 1966 (1938)*
Daisy Bates, an Englishwoman, spent forty years living among and defending the aborigines in the west and southern regions of Australia, mostly on the rim of the Nullarbor Plain. When her husband died she sold her property and went to live in a tent to be available to the aborigines and their needs. They named her Kabbarli, grandmother; they came to her with their problems and she went to them when they were sick and dying. She was created a CBE.

Outback *Thomas Keneally 1984*
The history, geology and aborigine culture of the Northern Territory.

✔ Nothing if Not Australian *Jan Morris*
About Canberra, in the collection *Locations* 1993 (1992).

✔ Over the Bridge *Jan Morris*
'An Australian Journey' in the collection Journeys 1992 (1984).

✔ Sydney *Jan Morris 1993 (1992)*
The history and background of a beautiful and complex city. George Melly writes: 'elegantly written, affectionate but unsentimental, Jan Morris's book literally covers the waterfront'.

✔ A Secret Country *John Pilger 1992 (1989)*
Pilger in his usual controversial form has written 'a moving account of the abuse of human rights in Australia, all the more valuable because it is written by an Australian writer'. (Graham Greene).

Guides

✔ Melbourne. Lonely Planet City Guide *Mark Armstrong 1993*

✔ Victoria. Travel Survival Kit
Mark Armstrong 1993

✔ Berlitz Travellers Guide Australia *1993*

✔ Discover Australia *Ken Bernstein 1993*

✔ Australia. The Rough Guide
Margo Daly, Anne Dehne, David Leffman and Chris Scott 1993

✔ American Express Cities of Australia *Tony Duboudin and Brian Courtis 1992 (1987)*

✔ **Australia. Travel Survival Kit**
Hugh Finlay etc. 1992 (1977)

✔ **Fodor Australia and New Zealand 1995**

✔ **Australia and New Zealand. Traveller's Survival Kit** *Susan Griffith and Simon Calder 1992 (1988)*

✔ **Insight City Guide Melbourne** *1989*

✔ **New South Wales and the ACT. Lonely Planet** *1994*

✔ **Cadogan Guide Australia** *Nick Lush 1988*

✔ **Introduction to Australia. An Odyssey Guide** *Carl Robinson 1991*

✔ **Sydney. Lonely Planet City Guide**
Barbara Whiter 1991

History

The Tyranny of Distance: How Distance Shaped Australia's History
Geoffrey Blainey 1982 (1966)
The influence of isolation on Australia's history; how the vast distances both between Europe and Australia and within Australia itself were far more influential in its development than had previously been acknowledged.

✔ **The Road to Botany Bay** *Paul Carter 1988 (1987)*
A completely new way of looking at the early pioneering years in Australia; the acts of settlement, the explorers and travellers and the acts of possession and dispossession. Passages from contemporary texts are used throughout the book giving interesting insights into the way the early pioneers thought and planned: 'All crossings, intersections, and abuttings of roads should be made at right-angles for the obvious reason of facilitating the turning from one road to the other or the more speedily crossing.' (T.L. Mitchell)

A Short History of Australia
Manning Clark 1986 (1963)
Based on the author's five-volume history of Australia; a very personal and often provocative work which speaks through the personalities of individuals. He begins with the aborigines and the coming of white men and traces the progress of Australian history up until 1986.

For the Term of His Natural Life
Marcus A.H. Clarke 1970 (1874)
An account of the penal settlement at Port Arthur which was modified to appease people's sensibilities, because of the inhuman behaviour there.

✔ **Kings in Grass Castles** *Mary Durack 1985 (1959)*
Patsy Durack, an eighteen-year-old immigrant, led a pioneering family who were fleeing famine stricken Ireland in 1853, from Sydney through New South Wales to Queensland and finally to North Western Australia. Written by his grand-daughter, it draws on contemporary sources and mentions Australian pioneers and politicians. An excellent portrayal of the tough and resilient pioneers.

To Be Heirs Forever *Mary Durack 1976*
The story of Eliza Shaw who came from Leicestershire to a pioneer settlement in Western Australia. She never returned to England but wrote many letters to her friends there; she discovered that the new colony was nothing like the paradise which had been promised, but struggled on and eventually triumphed over the elements. Her relatives in England had kept her letters and sent them to Perth where they were discovered by Mary Durack.

✔ **The Fatal Shore** *Robert Hughes 1988 (1987)*
An immensely readable yet scholarly history which traces the fate of those who were transported to Australia between 1787 and 1868. Packed with information it is an extremely moving description of the horrors of the journey and the conditions on arrival. A convict ballad from c.1825 goes:
'The very day we landed upon the Fatal Shore;
The planters stood around us, full twenty score or more;
They ranked us up like horses and sold us out of hand,
They chained us up to pull the plough, upon Van Diemen's Land.'

Australian Dreaming: 40,000 Years of Aboriginal History *Jennifer Isaacs 1980*
A standard text for aboriginal studies looked at through myths and legends.

✔ **Coopers Creek** *Alan Moorehead 1963*
The story of the ill-fated Burke and Wills expedition from Victoria, through New South Wales and South Australia to Queensland in 1860/1. The atmosphere and characters and the harshness of the landscape are all well evoked.

✔ **The Fatal Impact. An Account of the Invasion of the South Pacific 1767–1840** *Alan Moorehead 1985 (1966)*
Three examples of white man's first contact

with the inhabitants of the Pacific: Tahiti, Australia and the south polar regions. Moorehead follows Captain James Cook's voyages, since Cook was nearly always the first on the scene and seemed to understand what was going on at the time and what the future consequences would be.

Lion and Kangaroo. Australia: 1901–1919. The Rise of a Nation
Gavin Souter   1978 (1976)
An interesting period in the development of Australia as a Commonwealth. It describes its birth, infancy and youth from the Federation until the end of the Great War during which time most of Australia's national institutions came into being.

Leisure

✔ **Bushwalking in Australia. Lonely Planet Walking Guide**   John Chapman and Monica Chapman   1992 (1988)

✔ **South West Tasmania**   John Chapman   1990 (1979)
Walks and climbs.

✔ **100 Walks in New South Wales**
Tyrone T. Thomas   1992 (1977)

✔ **120 Walks in Victoria**
Tyrone T. Thomas   1990 (1975)

Natural History

✔ **Insight Guide Great Barrier Reef. Queensland Coast**   1991

✔ **A Field Companion to the Butterflies of Australia and New Zealand**   Bernard D'Abrera   1984
Coloured illustrations and short descriptions of the butterflies of Australasia.

✔ **A Field Guide to Australian Birds**
Graham Pizzey   1980
More than 700 birds are illustrated.

✔ **Reader's Digest Book of the Great Barrier Reef**   1986
A large-format, well-illustrated and descriptive book.

✔ **Field Guide to the Birds of Australia**   Ken Simpson and Nicolas Day   1986
The authors claim that every bird species of Australia is illustrated in over 2,000 painted images on 128 colour plates. Clear distribution maps are given alongside each entry which describes the bird and its habitat etc. Very clear and practical.

✔ **Islands of Australia's Great Barrier Reef. A Travel Survival Kit**
Tony Wheeler   1990

✔ **The Great Barrier Reef. A Guide to the Islands and Resorts**   Arne and Ruth Werchick   1988

Photography

A Day in the Life of Australia: March 6th 1981   1981
The first (and the best) in the Day in the Life of . . . series: 100 of the world's leading photo-journalists were commissioned to capture on film one day in the life of Australia.

Kakadu. Looking After the Country – the Gagudju Way   Stanley Breeden and Belinda Wright   1989

Travel Literature

✔ **Feet of Clay. Her Epic Walk Across Australia**   Ffyona Campbell   1991
Ffyona Campbell's mission was to walk across every continent and become the first woman to walk around the world. She crossed Australia from Sydney to Perth in ninety-five days, setting a record.

The Ribbon and the Ragged Square
Linda Christmas   1987 (1986)
Linda Christmas, a writer from the *Guardian*, spent nine months travelling round Australia talking to people and observing life in cities, aboriginal settlements, remote mining communities, cattle stations and on the Great Barrier Reef. She wanted to discover who the Australians really are and in her journey debunked many of the myths that have grown up among them.

✔ **Down Home. Revisiting Tasmania**
Peter Conrad   1989 (1988)
Evocative essays of a Tasmanian childhood and a return home after many years' absence; a combination of travel, autobiography and history. Peter Conrad left Tasmania in 1968 and returned twenty years later, discovering much he had previously been unaware of.

✔ **Tracks**   Robyn Davidson   1993 (1980)
In 1977 Robyn Davidson set off from Alice Springs by camel to cross 1,700 miles of desert and bush. She had to contend with learning how to look after camels, and also with the difficulties of being a woman in a very male world.

One for the Road Tony Horwitz 1988
(1987)
Amusingly written book about hitch-hiking
7,000 miles around Australia, written by an
American journalist working in Australia.

✔ **In the Land of Oz** Howard Jacobson
1988 (1987)
Howard Jacobson travelled around Australia
searching out many unusual places; he
writes about them with his entertaining
novelist's eye.

✔ **Finding Connections** P.J. Kavanagh
1991 (1990)
An examination of the author's family history which takes him from Ireland to Tasmania and on to New Zealand. Beautifully
written.

Rum Jungle Alan Moorehead 1953
Alan Moorehead writes about his return to
Australia which he had left in 1936. Some of
the book first appeared in the *New Yorker*.

Australia and New Zealand
Anthony Trollope 1873
Trollope writes about Australia state by
state describing the history, the large towns,
the present position and the future prospects
of each.

More Tramps Abroad Mark Twain 1897
Mark Twain embarked on a lecturing trip
around the world, starting from Paris, where
he had been living and going to America,
across the Pacific to Australia and New Zealand and on to India. Lively descriptions put
Twain's work among the best kind of travel
literature.

NEW ZEALAND

'The day was the perfection of New
Zealand weather, which is the perfection of
all climates – hot, but rarely sultry; bright,
but not glaring, from the vivid green with
which the earth is generally clothed.'
Bishop George Augustus Selwyn, journal
letter, 13 November 1843

Anthropology

The Maoris of New Zealand Joan Metge
1976 (1967)
A history of the Maoris before 1800 and what
happened to them between then and now.
Their culture, daily living, marriage, kinship, descent and descent groups, leadership,
the *Marae* and *Hui*, in today's world are all
described.

Art and Archaeology

**Te Maori – Maori Art From New
Zealand Collections**
Sidney Moko Mead (ed.) 1984

Biography

Station Life in New Zealand
Lady Barker 1973 (1883)
Lady Barker wrote these letters between
1865 when she arrived in New Zealand and
1868 during which time she was married to
a sheep farmer. The letters are descriptive
and give a very good feeling of what life must
have been like there then. She became very
attached to her life and was sad to leave after
three years.

Fiction/Poetry

**Maori Myths and Tribal Legends:
retold by Antony Alpers** 1964
A rewritten, but not retranslated, collection
of myths and legends.

Greenstone Sylvia Ashton-Warner 1966
Maori legend is woven into a story about an
English writer's family. Other novels by the
same author include: *Spinster* (1959) and
Incense to Idols (1960).

The God Boy Ian Cross 1989 (1962)
The narrator, Jimmy Sullivan, tells of the
events which changed his life; he is largely
unaware of the implications, although the
reader knows and this device continues right
through the book. At the start Jimmy thinks
of himself as a 'God boy', but by the end
believes that God has let him down. The
themes are relevant to life in New Zealand
today.

✔ **Faces in the Water** Janet Frame 1992
(1961)
A novel about confinement in mental institutions and the fear that the 'sane' have of the
'mad' and the ensuing fantasy world which
evolves as a result. Other novels by Janet
Frame include *Owls Do Cry* (1961), *A State
of Siege* (1967), *Living in the Maniototo*
(1979) and *The Carpathians* (1985).

Green Dolphin Street Elizabeth Goudge
1944
Historical novel about frontier life.

Maori Girl Noel Hilliard 1963 (1960)
Netta Samuel, an attractive and easy-going
Maori, lives on the North Island. In order not
to disgrace her family she leaves home for the
city. Despite meeting Arthur, a young whar-
fie, she is eventually defeated by city life.

✔ **The Bone People** *Keri Hulme* 1986 (1983)
Set on the South Island beaches of New Zealand, the book combines Maori myth and Christian symbols. Pronounced by some as 'unreadable', but by others as 'unputable downable'.

The Collected Short Stories
Katherine Mansfield 1981 (1945)
Katherine Mansfield was born in Wellington in 1888; she married John Middleton Murry for whom she had written in *Rhythm*. In 1917 she contracted tuberculosis and spent the rest of her life wandering in search of health before dying at Fontainebleau in 1923. The seventy three short stories and fifteen unfinished fragments in this collection form a representative range of Katherine Mansfield's writing.

Photo Finish *Ngaio Marsh* 1943
A murder mystery about an opera singer in New Zealand.

✔ **Monday's Warriors** *Maurice Shadbolt* 1991 (1990)
An historical novel, based on fact, about Kimball Bent of Maine who joined the British army and was sent to fight the Maoris in New Zealand. He deserted to join the Maoris, whom he served as a spy and was adopted by a warrior chief.

Food

✔ **New Zealand. The Beautiful Cookbook** *Tui Flower (ed.)* 1992 (1984)
A large extremely well-illustrated book with short easy to follow recipes.

General Background

✔ **The Fifth Wind. New Zealand and the Legacy of a Turbulent Past**
Robert Macdonald 1989
Robert Macdonald grew up in the Antipodes. 1990 was the 150th anniversary of the signing of the treaty of Waitangi, when the Maoris handed over the sovereignty of their country to the British, in exchange for the guaranteed rights and privileges of British subjects. He decided to go and march with the young Maori as a Pakeha (white person). He examines the background and history to the unrest in the country.

✔ **Letters and Journals**
Katherine Mansfield 1977
Although very little of this collection is about New Zealand, part of a journal which concerns a journey made to the remote parts of the North Island of New Zealand is included and is worth reading for its descriptions of the landscape.

Guides

✔ **Fodor's New Zealand 1995**

✔ **Insight Guide New Zealand** 1992

✔ **New Zealand Handbook** *Jane King* 1992 (1987)

✔ **Nelles Guide New Zealand** 1992

✔ **New Zealand. Travel Survival Kit**
Nancy Keller and Jeff Williams 1994 (1977)

History

The Discovery of New Zealand
J.C. Beaglehole 1969 (1931)
A vivid study of New Zealand's history including the voyages of discovery by the first Polynesians up to the Europeans of the late eighteenth century.

The Exploration of the Pacific
J.C. Beaglehole 1966 (1934)
A history of the Pacific voyages and discoveries made by the great European explorers including: Magellan, Mendana, Tasman, Dampier, Bougainville and Cook.

A History of New Zealand *Keith Sinclair* 1980 (1959)
A good general history of New Zealand, if somewhat out of date. The author looks at the New Zealanders: the Polynesian Moa-hunters, their Maori descendants and the later Europeans.

The Oxford Illustrated History of New Zealand *Keith Sinclair (ed.)* 1990
Comprehensive and readable account of the country's social, political, cultural and economic evolution from the earliest days up until 1989.

Leisure

✔ **Tramping in New Zealand. Lonely Planet Guide** *Jim DuFresne* 1989 (1982)

✔ **Classic Tramps in New Zealand**
Constance Roos 1993
Walks on the North and South Islands.

Natural History

✔ **Collins Guide to the Birds of New Zealand** *R.A. Falla, R.B. Sibson and E.G. Turbott   1987 (1966)*
Around 300 species are described and illustrated.

The New Zealand Sea Shore *John Morton and Michael Miller   1968*
The New Zealand coastline comprises a variety of different climates and structures; the resulting plants and animals are therefore multifarious. Arranged by habitat.

Photography

Homeplaces *Words by Keri Hulme Photographs by Robin Morrison   1989*
Photographs of three coastal areas on the South Island of New Zealand: on the west Okarito, a former goldrush settlement, on the east Moeraki and in the very south Stewart Island.

Travel Literature

✔ **Fragile Eden. A Ride Through New Zealand** *Robin Hanbury-Tenison   1989*
Robin and Louella Hanbury-Tenison explored the North and South Islands of New Zealand by horse, riding through 'some of the most dramatic and exciting country we have ever seen'. However, they also discovered a country in crisis, ridden with debt and serious environmental problems.

PAPUA NEW GUINEA

'On a map, it resembles an obese, gigantic buzzard.' William Manchester *American Caesar* 1979

Anthropology

Sorcerers of Dobu: the Social Anthropology of the Dobu Islanders of the Western Pacific *Reo F. Fortune   1963*
A very detailed study of Dobu, a small island in the D'Entrecasteaux Group of Milne Bay Province. The author was married to Margaret Mead.

Argonauts of the Western Pacific
Bronislaw Malinowski   1978 (1922)
The book was derived from fieldwork undertaken in the Trobriand Islands between 1915 and 1918; it is required reading for most anthropology students.

A Diary in the Strict Sense of the Term *Bronislaw Malinowski   1967*
Malinowski was stranded in Melbourne at the outbreak of the First World War where, as an Austrian citizen, he was in danger of being interned. He persuaded the authorities to allow him to go on field trips to Papua to Mailu and the Trobriand Islands. The diaries which cover the above two expeditions are very personal.

The Sexual Life of Savages in North-Western Melanesia: an Ethnographic Account of Courtship, Marriage and Family Life among the Natives of the Trobriand Islands, British New Guinea *Bronislaw Malinowski 1982 (1932)*
Controversial and much read, Malinowski's book discusses relations between the sexes, the status of women, pre-nuptial intercourse, betrothal, marriage, divorce and widowhood, pregnancy and childbirth, erotic life, morals and incest.

Growing up in New Guinea: a Study of Adolescence and Sex in Primitive Societies *Margaret Mead   1981 (1931)*
Based on fieldwork done in Pere Village, Manus Province in 1928. In the second half of the book, Mead reflects on the educational problems of the Western world in the light of her findings.

Art and Archaeology

Art and Life in New Guinea
Raymond Firth   1979 (1936)
Many old black and white photographs and a limited text about the objects.

Art Styles of the Papuan Gulf
Douglas Newton   1961
Published as an exhibition catalogue in New York, material from every district of the Papuan Gulf. Well illustrated.

Autobiography/Biography

The High Valley *Kenneth E. Read   1966 (1965)*
An autobiographical account of the two years the author spent in the Central Highlands of New Guinea. When he went to live in the village of Susuroka his first sensation was that of 'stepping into the heart of a crystal'. The book is arranged around a series of villagers each one chosen to represent a particular aspect of native life.

Fiction/Poetry

The Crocodile *Vincent Eri   1981 (1970)*
The first novel published by a Papua New
Guinean tells the story of Hoiri Sevese who
goes on a journey to take revenge against the
sorcerers who caused his wife to be eaten by
a crocodile.

Solomons Seal *Hammond Innes   1980*
A rare postage stamp is discovered in England leading the principal character, Roy
Slingsby, to Papua New Guinea. Includes
much about the Bougainville secessionist
movement.

Kundu *Morris L. West   1957*
Includes in its cast of characters a Nazi war
criminal whose wife was a concentration
camp survivor, a sorcerer and the local
priest.

Visitants *Randolph Stow   1981 (1979)*
An attempt to demythologize the Australian
colonialist in Papua New Guinea; portrays
the clash between the two different cultures.

**The Turtle and the Island: Folk Tales
from Papua New Guinea** *Collected by
Donald S. Stokes   1978*
Forty-two stories collected by Stokes when he
was a lecturer in Papua New Guinea.

The Swiss Family Robinson
Johann David Wyss   1909 (1812)
This classic is often subtitled 'The Adventures of a Shipwrecked Family on an Uninhabited Island near New Guinea" Not very
accurate about the local habitat, nevertheless a popular book about a Swiss pastor who
was shipwrecked with his wife and four
children on a tropical island.

Guides

✔ **Papua New Guinea. A Travel
Survival Kit** *Tony Wheeler and Jon Murray
1993 (1979)*

History

New Guinea, the last unknown
Gavin Souter   1963
A balanced look at the British, Dutch, German and Australian experiences in the area,
written by a journalist with *The Sydney
Morning Herald*. Very good descriptions of
the early explorers.

Leisure

✔ **Bushwalking in Papua New
Guinea. A Lonely Planet Walking
Guide** *Yvon Pérusse   1993 (1983)*

Natural History

Birds of New Guinea *Beehler, Pratt and
Zimmerman   1986*
A somewhat bulky field guide.

Wildlife in Papua New Guinea
Eric Lindgren   1975
An overall introduction and survey to the
wildlife of New Guinea. The chapters are
divided into mammals, birds, reptiles, frogs,
insects, spiders and plants.

Photography

**New Guinea (Time-Life 'World's Wild
Places' series)**
The mainland of New Guinea is dominated
by high mountains and their slopes provide
a variety of climatic zones: tropical rain
forest, cool mid-mountain forests, mist
forest, alpine grasslands and rocky summits.
There are over 600 offshore islands which
have many active volcanoes. The photographs include the scenery as well as wildlife.

✔ **Cousteau's Papua New Guinea
Journey** *Jean-Michel Cousteau and Mose
Richards   1989*
Some underwater photographs, but most are
of the landscape and scenery of Papua New
Guinea. Ample text.

Travel Literature

✔ **Into the Crocodile Nest**
Benedict Allen   1989 (1987)
Allen travels through Irian Jaya and Papua
New Guinea in search of the hidden peoples
of the islands. He wanted to find a tribe who
would let him take part in an initiation ceremony into manhood; he was finally allowed
to participate in the ceremonies of the Sepik
tribe.

✔ **The Proving Grounds. A Journey
Through the Interior of New Guinea
and Australia** *Benedict Allen   1992 (1991)*
Allen returns to the village in Papua New
Guinea where he had previously undergone
an initiation ceremony. He spent eight
months travelling across the central mountain ranges and over the Torres Strait by
canoe to Australia.

A Voyage to New Holland
William Dampier   Edited by J.W. Williamson
1939 (1729)
William Dampier sailed from England in 1699 with instructions to explore Australia and the east coast of New Guinea. He was the first to use the term 'New Britain'.

In Papua New Guinea   Christina Dodwell
1985 (1983)
Christina Dodwell travelled from one end of Papua New Guinea to the other on a two-year expedition through the highlands and jungles of the island. She trekked 1,000 miles on a horse and spent four months paddling a dugout canoe down the Sepik River. Her willingness to tackle any situation, however dangerous, means that she not only gains respect from the people she visits but also learns much from them.

Rape of the Fly. Explorations in New Guinea   John Goode   1977
The determination, bitternesss and achievements of the explorers Luigi Maria D'Albertis and Lawrence Hargrave who explored the Fly River in the 1870s.

Wanderings in the Interior of New Guinea   Capt. J.A. Lawson   1875
Everything that Lawson saw was bigger and better – Mount Hercules (a thousand metres higher than Everest, and never seen again), waterfalls larger than Niagara, huge scorpions and the New Guinea tiger.

✔ Under the Mountain Wall
Peter Matthiessen   1989 (1962)
The Kurelu, a Stone Age tribe that has survived into the twentieth century, lives in the Baliem Valley in central New Guinea. Peter Matthiessen went on a 1961 Harvard-Peabody expedition to live with them and wrote about their culture, combining art, anthropology and ethnography.

Patrol into Yesterday. My New Guinea Years   J.K. McCarthy   1963
An exciting book about the first contact made between the erratic and violent Kamea people and episodes from World War 2.

Some Experiences of a New Guinea Resident Magistrate   C.A.W. Monckton
1920
Monckton was a New Zealander who first arrived in New Guinea in 1895; he stayed as a magistrate and writes about his experiences there from 1895 to 1903. He later wrote *Last Days in New Guinea* (1922) which is about the time from 1903 to 1907.

Plumes and Arrows   Colin Simpson   1962
A combination of the three books that Simpson wrote about Papua New Guinea's land, people and explorers. He spent much time there in the 1950s.

PACIFIC ISLANDS
' . . . it is half the planet: this dome, this half-globe, this bulging Eyeball of water, arched over to Asia, Australia and white Antarctica; those are the eyelids that never close; this is the staring unsleeping Eye of the earth; and what it watches is not our wars.'
Robinson Jeffers *The Eye* 1941.

Much of the material on the Pacific is published either in Hawaii or locally. Bear in mind if actually visiting the South Seas you will be able to find much written material there, both fact and fiction.

Anthropology

The Pacific Islanders   William Howells
1973
Who are the people of the Pacific? Where did they come from? How did they get there? The author uses the most recent discoveries of anthropology, archaeology and linguistics to try and answer the questions.

Art and Archaeology

The Arts of the South Pacific
Jean Guiart   1963 ('Arts of Mankind' series)
A large book with 438 illustrations. Guiart, a linguist and ethnologist, disputes the theory that Oceanic art is primitive, by emphasizing its place in society and culture.

An American Artist in the South Seas
John La Farge   1987 (1914)
The American artist John La Farge spent a year painting his way round the Pacific preceding Gauguin; indeed in his time he was better known than Gauguin. He visited Stevenson in Samoa, was adopted by a noble Tahitian family and travelled through Fiji.

Biography

Rascals in Paradise   James A. Michener
1957
A collection of biographies of people who used the Pacific as an area of escape, including: Sam Comstock (a *Globe* mutineer), Coxinga, the first king of Formosa, Walter Gibson, premier and foreign minister of Hawaii, William Bligh, captain of the *Bounty*, Dona Isa-

bel, lady explorer and wife of Mendana, and Will Mariner, boy chief of Tonga.

Fiction

Pacific Tales *Louis Becke* *1987 (1897)*
A collection of eighteen short stories by Becke, an Australian who went to sea aged fourteen; they cover the Marshalls, the Caroline Islands, Tahiti, Samoa and the Gilbert Islands. Becke writes about the islanders and the Europeans, about whom he is pessimistic: freed from their own society they tended to turn to crime and cruelty, foreshadowing the adverse aspects of twentieth-century colonialism.

✔ **South Sea Tales**
W. Somerset Maugham *1993*
A collection of Maugham's short stories set in the South Pacific.

Mardi *Herman Melville* *1982 (1849)*
An allegory about a visit to a fictitious Pacific archipelago.

✔ **Moby Dick** *Herman Melville* *1992 (1851)*
In the chapter entitled 'The Pacific', Melville describes the history of the Pacific and anticipates the future roles of America and Japan. He writes: 'Thus this mysterious, divine Pacific zones the world's whole bulk about; makes all coasts one bay to it; seems the tide-beating heart of earth.'

Tales of the South Pacific
James A. Michener *1949*
A collection of short stories based on the Pacific War – won the Pulitzer Prize.

The Bounty Trilogy *James Norman and Charles Bernard Nordhoff* *1945*
The mutiny, Bligh's escape to Timor and the mutineers' fate on Pitcairn, told here in fictional form.

South Sea Tales *Jack London* *1911*
Eight stories about pearl divers, missionaries and cannibals.

Oceanic Mythology *Roslyn Poignant* *1967*
The myths of Polynesia, Micronesia, Melanesia and Australia are viewed in the context of their relationship with art.

Best Stories of the South Seas
Philip Snow (ed.) *1967*
A good introduction to and survey of Western literature about the South Seas. Included in the volume are stories by: Herman Melville, Robert Louis Stevenson, James Michener, Thor Heyerdahl and Arthur Grimble.

✔ **The Floating Island** *Jules Verne* *1990 (1895)*
A combination of social satire and science fiction. A group of American millionaires are on an island which floats around the Pacific, combining the comforts of home with the excitements of travel. However although the island is technologically perfect with all material cares having been banished, human nature is inevitably flawed and the outcome is a telling parable.

The West Quartet: Four Novels of Intrigue and High Adventure
Morris L. West *1981 (1956/58)*
Three of these novels are set in the South Pacific.

Food

✔ **A Taste of Hawaii. New Cooking from the Crossroads of the Pacific**
Jean-Marie Josselin *1992*
The other Pacific islands share many recipes with Hawaii, especially since many of the fresh ingredients are the same.

General Background

The Letters of Rupert Brooke
Geoffrey Keynes (ed.) *1968*
Brooke wrote from the South Seas during 1913 and 1914 describing Tahiti, Fiji and Samoa. He describes Tahiti as the most ideal place in the world to live and work.

Islands of the South Pacific
Sir Harry Luke *1962*
Luke, who was Governor of Fiji and High Commissioner for the Western Pacific, concentrates on islands in the area bounded by Australia and New Guinea in the west, South America in the east, the equator in the north and the 30th degree of latitude south. It is a general account with an emphasis on the human aspect.

Pacific Islands Vols I–IV. Geographical Handbook Series
Naval Intelligence Division c.1945
Although inevitably somewhat dated, these volumes which were produced for military purposes during the Second World War, are invaluable today for anyone sailing in the Pacific and wanting a good overall view of the peoples, history and geography; they are extremely detailed and contain almost every known fact. Many maps.

✔ **The Pacific** *Simon Winchester* *1992 (1991)*
Simon Winchester spent five years travelling

the length and breadth of the vast Pacific from the West Coast of America to Sarawak, the Philippines and Japan, visiting most of the fifty-six countries that lie around or within it. His thesis is that the Pacific has been and should or could be a coherent whole. He includes much history but also describes how the various diverse countries are coping with the modern world; each chapter looks at a different aspect of the Pacific: Approaches, Connections, Icons, Places in the Basin, Cities on the Rim and the Wave. Twelve useful maps showing different features are at the end of the book.

Guides

✔ **Adventuring in the Pacific. The Sierra Club Travel Guide to the Islands of Polynesia, Melanesia, and Micronesia** *Susanna Margolis 1988*

✔ **South Pacific Handbook** *David Stanley and Bill Dalton 1993 (1979)*

History

The Mutiny of the Bounty
Sir John Barrow 1951 (1831)
Sir John Barrow as Permanent Secretary to the Admiralty had access to unpublished documents relating to the famous mutiny, which took place in 1789 near the Friendly Islands.

The Exploration of the Pacific
J.C. Beaglehole 1966 (see 'New Zealand')

Lost Paradise. The Exploration of the Pacific *Ian Cameron 1987*
When de Bougainville arrived in the Pacific he wrote 'What a country! What a people! I thought I had been transported to Paradise.' Within a century the people of the Pacific Islands had been decimated by deprivation and disease. Cameron examines the excesses of the explorers in this well-illustrated book.

The Golden Haze. With Captain Cook in the South Pacific *Roderick Cameron 1964*
Roderick Cameron decided to visit only the islands that Cook had visited on his two ships, the *Endeavour* and the *Resolution*, following his three voyages by sea and by air. Cameron reminds himself in the introduction not to lose sight of the grand purpose of Cook's journey which was that he had been commissioned to observe an important astronomical event, the transit of the planet Venus. Retracing Cook's footsteps was made easier by the fact that Cook had kept meticu-

lous journals, never playing the hero and priding himself on his love of truth, admitting when discussing Polynesian religious faiths 'I have learned so little, that I hardly dare to talk upon it'.

The Explorations of Captain James Cook in the Pacific as told by Selections of his own Journals 1768–1779 *1971 (1957)*
Cook kept detailed journals of his three expeditions which were not published until 1893, as all records of a voyage were meant to be handed over to the Admiralty. This is a selection from the originals.

✔ **Darwin and the Beagle**
Alan Moorehead 1969
Darwin's voyage on the *Beagle* had an extraordinary impact on him and on the evolution of modern science. This is a popular and readable account of the voyage with many illustrations.

The People from the Horizon: An Illustrated History of the Europeans among the South Sea Islanders
Philip Snow and Stefanie Waine 1979
A well-illustrated book covering Micronesia, Melanesia and Polynesia about the effects of the Europeans on the South Seas and the effect of the South Seas on the Europeans. The different types of Europeans: explorers, traders, whalers, adventurers, missionaries and settlers are all discussed. Fascinating, very readable and with an excellent bibliography.

Voyages of Discovery. Captain Cook and the Exploration of the Pacific
Lynne Withey 1987
Scientific as well as political motives were increasingly important to the European sea expeditions in the second half of the eighteenth century. Cook commanded three round-the-world expeditions between 1768 and 1779 employing the latest scientific techniques. He returned to Europe with accurate maps, specimens and drawings of flora and fauna. Lynne Withey's book attempts to see all sides of the story as she collects together oral traditions and conventional history and anthropology.

Natural History

Quest in Paradise *David Attenborough 1983*
Attenborough describes the natural history, natural beauty and some of the culture and customs of the Pacific including the land

divers of Pentecost and the cargo cults of Vanuatu.

South Pacific Birds *John E. Dupont* *1975*
An illustrated field guide, published in America.

Birds of the South-West Pacific
Ernst Mayr *1978*
The author spent many years in the area and describes sea birds, shore birds, freshwater and land birds in Samoa, Santa Cruz islands, New Caledonia, Vanuatu, Tonga, the Solomon Islands and Micronesia.

A Fragile Paradise: Man and Nature in the Pacific *Andrew Mitchell* *1990*
Andrew Mitchell is Earthwatch Europe's Deputy Director. He journeys through much of the Pacific looking at nature and wildlife and here pleads the cause for the preservation of all endangered Pacific wildlife.

A Field Guide to the Birds of Hawaii and the Tropical Pacific *Douglas Pratt* *1986*
The best book on birds in the Pacific.

Photography

R.L.S. in the South Seas *Introduced and edited by Alanna Knight* *1986*
Stevenson took a camera and magic lantern with him to the South Seas intending to illustrate a history of the area. The few surviving photographs are published in this book with extracts from his letters and essays.

The New Pacific *Michael Macintyre* *1985*
A well-illustrated book which was related to the BBC television series.

Travel Literature

A Lady's Cruise in a French Man-of-War *C.F. Gordon Cumming* *1882*
After leaving Fiji (q.v.), Constance Gordon Cumming was asked to accompany the French commander of a French man-of-war, which had been put at the disposal of the Bishop of Samoa to enable him to visit his far-flung diocese in the South Pacific. They went to Tonga, the Wallis Isles, Easter Island, Samoa and Tahiti.

✔ **Transit of Venus. Travels in the Pacific** *Julian Evans* *1993 (1992)*
Julian Evans eventually succeeds in getting a passage on a boat from Sydney to the Western Pacific; he travels slowly around the islands often being disappointed. Majuro, the capital of the Marshall Islands had been Ro-

bert Louis Stevenson's 'pearl of the Pacific', but Evans found it an 'unspeakable dump'. Acutely observed.

✔ **Voyages and Discoveries in the South Seas 1792–1832** *Edmund Fanning* *1989 (1833)*
Captain Edmund Fanning from Connecticut, unusually for his time, kept a journal of the voyages he made to the Pacific; this is a firsthand detailed account of life aboard ship; how they were rigged and handled and what life was like in the ports of call.

Across the South Pacific *Iain Finlay and Trish Shepherd* *1981*
The account of a voyage across the Pacific by a family of four.

Over the Reefs *Robert Gibbings* *1948*
Episodes around the Pacific including an account of shark fishing in Eua Iki, where although the fishermen often swim out to the sharks in order to lead them back to the boat, none has ever been harmed.

Castaway *Lucy Irvine* *1983*
The now famous book about the British couple who spent a year on the previously uninhabited island of Tuin in the Torres Strait off the northernmost coast of Australia.

A World of Islands *June Knox-Mawer* *1969 (1965)*
The author, whose husband was a Judge in the Pacific, lived in Fiji for many years visiting the Gilbert Islands, the Ellice Islands and Tonga.

The Cruise of the Snark *Jack London* *1986 (1911)*
Jack London summed up his philosophy of forty years of adventurous life with the words 'Life that lives is life successful'. This book, which shows his love for the Pacific, is an account of the cruise of the yacht *Snark* from San Francisco to the South Seas. Among the islands discussed are: Hawaii, Typee, Tahiti, Bora Bora and the Solomons.

✔ **Tuturani. A Political Journey in the Pacific Islands** *Scott L Malcolmson* *1991 (1990)*
Described by Oscar Hijuelos as 'hip, savvy, elegant and funny', Malcolmson's journey round the Pacific, where he interviewed victims of US nuclear testing, investigated an assassination and was present at a civil war in New Caledonia, is an attempt to understand the Pacific Islands today.

Dead Man's Chest *Nicholas Rankin* *1988 (1987)*
Nicholas Rankin followed in Robert Louis

Stevenson's footsteps from Edinburgh to the South Seas via France, America and England and finally into the Pacific, to Hawaii and Samoa. There is much cross-reference and we learn a lot about Stevenson and the way he travelled.

✔ **The Happy Isles of Oceania**
Paul Theroux   1993 (1992)
Theroux travelled from the Solomons to Fiji, Tonga, Samoa, Tahiti, the Marquesas and Easter Island. He paddled his own boat around to remote spots gathering impressions; he is good at getting behind the myths of places and gives an interesting summary of Gauguin in Polynesia; none of Gauguin's paintings shows any colonial influence, even though there had already been sixty years of colonial rule, because Polynesia was to him inviolate.

More Tramps Abroad   *Mark Twain   1897*
(see 'Australia')
'When one glances at a map the members of the stupendous island wilderness of the Pacific seem to crowd upon each other; but no, there is no crowding, even in the centre of a group; and between groups there are lonely wide deserts of sea.'

✔ **Slow Boats Home**   *Gavin Young   1985*
Gavin Young travelled from Hong Kong to London via the Pacific on a number of boats.In each place he visits he tells us about previous travellers and how they were written about in literature and makes many comparisons with life today.

FIJI
'Tahiti was put on the map by Gauguin, Fiji by Qantas and Panam' George Mikes
Boomerang –Australia Rediscovered 1968

Fiction

Fiji: Islands of the Dawn
Leonard Wibberly   1964
Very little has been written about Fiji, although Rupert Brooke, Jack London, Mark Twain, Rudyard Kipling and Somerset Maugham all visited it. Leonard Wibberly's book is about one man's experiences, in an historical context.

Guides

✔ **Fiji. Travel Survival Kit**   *Rob Kay*
1993

✔ **Fiji Islands Handbook**   *David Stanley*
1990

General Background

Places   *Jan Morris   1973*
There is an essay on Fiji in this collection.

History

Lost Cities of Ancient Lemuria and the Pacific   *D.H. Childress   1989*
An archaeological search for lost sites in the Pacific.

A History of Fiji   *R.A.Derrick   1946*
The author was a great authority on Fiji's history.

Matanitu   *David Routledge   1985*
Reputedly the best book on Fiji's history, but only available there.

Natural History

Birds of the Fiji Bush   *Fergus Clunie   1984*
Published by the Fiji Museum, Suva, and only available there.

Travel Literature

At Home in Fiji   *C.F. Gordon Cumming   1901*
Constance Gordon Cumming left for the South Seas in April 1875. Most of the book is in the form of letters and she writes that a cruise in the South Pacific 'has been one of the dreams of my life'. She arrived in Fiji in September 1875 and stayed there, apart from short trips away until October 1876. She includes history and many fascinating legends in her letters. ' I have never once experienced the great heat which many find so trying, and have always found a dress of navy serge and pilotcloth jacket the most comfortable clothing.'

On Fiji Islands   *Ronald Wright   1987*
A blend of travel book, history, anthropology and culture. The author tries to include every aspect of the island and its inhabitants.

NEW CALEDONIA *(Isle of Pines, Loyalty Islands, Belep Islands, Chesterfield Islands)*
'Those people approach nearer the dress of Adam before he sewed the fig leaves together, than any we have seen before.'
William Wales *Journal* 5 September 1774

Guide

✔ **New Caledonia. Travel Survival Kit** *Leanne Logan 1993 (1990)*

Travel Literature

The Golden Cowrie: New Caledonia: its people and places *May and Henry Larsen 1961*
The authors went in an unsuccesful search for the golden cowrie, a shell found in parts of the Pacific. Good descriptions of the islands and islanders of New Caledonia.

VANUATU *(formerly New Hebrides)*

NORTHERN GROUP: *Torres and Banks, Espiritu Santo, Aoba, Maewa*

CENTRAL GROUP: *Pentecost, Ambryn, Malakula, Paama, Epi, Tongoa and Shepherds Efate*

SOUTHERN GROUP or TAFEA ISLANDS: *Tanna, Aniwa, Futuna, Erromango, Anatom*

Anthropology

Footprints on Malakula
Margaret Gardiner 1988
A tribute to Bernard Deacon, a young British anthropologist who worked in Malakula in the 1920s and who whose notes are extremely informative about society there.

Charlene Gourguechon's Journey to the End of the World
Charlene Gourguechon 1977 (1974)
The author lived with traditional tribes in Malakula, Pentecost and Ambrym and has written an extemely readable book.

Savage Civilization *Tom Harrisson 1937*
Many of the customs that Harrisson writes about no longer exist, which makes this particularly interesting.

Fiction

Beachmasters *Thea Astley 1987*
The author draws on the 1980 Santo rebellion.

Guide

✔ **Vanuatu. Travel Survival Kit** *David Harcombe 1991*

History

To Kill a Bird with Two Stones
Jeremy MacClancy 1980
A history which goes right up to Independence, but unfortunately is only available there.

Travel Literature

Isles of Illusion: Letters from the South Seas *R.J. Fletcher 1986 (1923)*
Written under the pseudonym 'Asterisk', the author was sensitive to the islanders, but saw many around him who were not. The average colonist in his day could scarcely read or write whereas he was a well-educated man who hung Beardsley drawings on the walls of his hut in the New Hebrides and had a gift for languages; the brutal life of the plantations depressed and disillusioned him and for this reason he is often considered bitter and intolerant. The book was edited by Bohun Lynch and is in the form of letters sent to him by Fletcher over a period of thirteen years. Moorea near Tahiti is possibly the island he raved about.

They Came for Sandalwood
Dorothy Shinberg 1967
A fascinating study of the nineteenth-century sandalwood trade.

SOLOMON ISLANDS *– Shortland Islands, Treasury Islands, Choiseul, New Georgia Islands, Santa Isabel, Floridal Islands, Russell Islands, Malaita, Guadalcanal, Makira, Rennell, Bellona, Santa Cruz Islands, Ontong Java*

Art and Archaeology

Grass Roots Art of the Solomons – Images and Islands *John and Sue Chick (eds.) 1978*
A detailed and descriptive book about every form of pictorial and sculptural art form found in the Solomons.

Autobiography/Biography

Aloha Solomons *Gwen Cross* *1978*
Gwen Cross lived in the Solomons before the War. Here she describes the dramatic change of life after the Japanese invasion.

Fiction

Beyond the Reef: a Story of Solomon Islands *John David Bee* *1982*
An historical novel about a Japanese war pilot who parachutes into Malaita; despite trying to befriend the islanders, he meets a tragic fate. His son and daughter visit the Solomons and the daughter embarks on a romance with the colonial district officer.

Bring Another Glass *Georgina Seton* *1944*
A period thriller set on islands which strongly resemble the Solomons.

General Background

White Headhunter: the Extraordinary True Story of a White Man's Life among Headhunters of the Solomon Islands *Hector Hothouse* *1989*
A reconstruction of the life of John Renton, a Scotsman who lived in the Solomons from 1868–1875 and whose name is still remembered there.

Guide

✔ **Solomon Islands. Travel Survival Kit** *David Harcombe* *1993 (1988)*

History

The Story of the Solomons
Charles E. Fox *1975*
Fox, a New Zealander, spent sixty-five years as a missionary in the Solomons and writes this history from the viewpoint of the Solomon Islanders.

The Search for the Islands of Solomon 1567–1838 *Colin Jack-Hinton* *1969*
The efforts of the first explorers to discover the Solomons and what happened subsequently.

Travel Literature

Heat Treatment: The Oriental Travels of an Amorous Hypochondriac
Justin Wintle *1990*
A travelogue which ends in the Solomons.

MICRONESIA

Fiction

Japans's Islands of Mystery
Willard Price *1944*
Micronesia is viewed as the crucial stepping stone to Japan in the Pacific War. An American poses as an absent-minded professor in this spy story which gives a good idea of life in Micronesia in the war.

Guides

✔ **Micronesia. A Travel Survival Kit**
Glenda Bendure and Ned Friary *1992 (1988)*

✔ **Micronesia Handbook** *David Stanley*
1992

Travel Literature

A Reporter in Micronesia *E.J. Kahn* *1966*
One of the interesting things about this book is the changes that have occurred since it was written when there were very few tourists and very few planes.

KIRIBATI *(formerly the Gilbert Islands)*

History

The Christmas Island Story *Eric Bailey*
1977
Cook discovered this as an uninhabited island, but it was soon settled by traders and guano prospectors. A Catholic priest, Father Petrics Emmanuel Rougier, bought the island in 1914 and ruled it somewhat eccentrically until his death in 1932.

Treasure Islands: the Trials of the Ocean Islanders *Pearl Binder* *1977*
An exposé of the tragedy of Ocean Island (Banaba). The British Phosphate Company and Commission destroyed Ocean Island by mining phosphate, leaving behind an ecological wasteland. In 1946 the Banaban Islanders were relocated to Rambi Island about 1,600 miles away. There was a trial in London at which the Banaban plaintiffs demanded that Ocean Island be rehabilitated.

Astride the Equator: An Account of the Gilbert Islands *Ernest Sabatier* *1977*
The author was a French scholar priest who was reputedly the only European to really know the Gilbertese. This account of their

history up until the late 1930s is detailed and descriptive and contains a wealth of information on the myths and beliefs of the people as well as the flora and fauna of the islands.

Travel Literature

✔ **A Pattern of Islands** *Arthur Grimble* *1952*
Grimble was British resident commissioner in the Gilberts from 1926–1932; this has become a classic about life in Kiribati during that time.

✔ **Return to the Islands** *Arthur Grimble* *1970 (1957)*
Reminiscences and reflections about the Gilbert Islands.

✔ **In the South Seas** *Robert Louis Stevenson* *(see 'Polynesia')*

PALAU

Fiction

The Day that I Die: a Novel of Suspense *P.F. Kluge* *1976*
Political intrigue set in Palau by a former Peace Corps Volunteer.

Natural History

With their Islands Around them *Kenneth Brower* *1974*
The conservation of Palau's rich biological diversity which was undertaken by Robert Owen, the Chief Conservationist for the Trust Territory and his protegé, John Kochi.

FEDERATED STATES OF MICRONESIA: YAP, TRUK, PONAPE

Travel Literature

A Song for Satawal *Kenneth Brower* *1985 (1983)*
Divided into three parts, each focusing on an islander and his island: a teacher-naturalist on Yap, a navigator from Satawal and a woman, Katherine Kesolei, from Palau who has compiled a history of the islands and people. An original approach.

The Caroline Islands: Travels in the Sea of Little Lands *F.W. Christian* *1899*
The author spent two years in the islands and writes about their culture, language, geography and environment.

A Residence of Eleven Years in New Holland and the Caroline Islands
James F. O'Connell   Edited by Saul H. Riesenberg *1972*
The experiences of a cabin boy on a convict ship who spent six years in New Holland, Australia and stayed for five years on the island of Pohnpei. The author narrated the account to a publisher in 1836 and it was finally published in 1972.

MARSHALL ISLANDS

'So we came to Bikini: a typical Pacific coral atoll, several tiny islands, surrounding a lagoon twenty miles long by ten miles wide.' James Cameron *Point of Departure* 1967

Mutiny on the 'Globe' *Edwin P. Hoyt* *1976 (1975)*
A good account of the relationship between whalers and the local inhabitants of the Marshall Islands after a mutiny on the *Globe*.

POLYNESIA

FRENCH POLYNESIA

SOCIETY ISLANDS: *Tahiti, Moorea, Bora Bora, Huahine*

MARQUESAS, AUSTRALS, GAMBIERS, TUAMOTUS
'The island [Tahiti] to which every voyager has offered up his tribute of imagination.' Charles Darwin *Journal . . . During the Voyage . . . of HMS Beagle 1832–6*

Anthropology

Love in the South Seas *Bengt Danielsson* *1956*
The first systematic examination of the patterns of Polynesian sex and family life. He draws on accounts by anthropologists, explorers, missionaries and merchants and concludes that the West could learn much from the Polynesian approach to sex and family life.

American Indians in the Pacific. The Theory Behind the Kon-Tiki Expedition Thor Heyerdahl 1952
Heyerdahl sets out the facts supporting his theory of Polynesian origins in early America. He draws his evidence from anthropology, geography, linguistics, ethnobotany, somatology, ethnology, mythology and art and shows the striking similarities between the people of the Pacific island world and those of aboriginal America and traces the Caucasian-like elements in Polynesia and in pre-Inca Peru. He concludes that the ancient Polynesians were a 'composite in race, in culture, and in language'.

Art and Archaeology

The Art of Tahiti Terence Barrow 1979
A well-illustrated book which begins with the history of Polynesia and shows art from the Society, Austral and Cook Islands. Among the objects described are wooden sculpture and ceremonial costumes and weapons.

The Polynesians: Prehistory of an Island People Peter Bellwood 1987 (1978)
A history of the archaeology of Polynesian expansion which uses recent research. Bellwood argues that the Polynesians are almost certainly of Indonesian–Philippine origin. The Polynesians had no metals and stopped making pottery about 1,500 years ago, but their wood carvings are made to a very high standard.

Noa Noa Paul Gauguin 1985
A Tahitian journal kept by Gauguin during his first two years on the island; it is a justification for his position as an artist, his infatuation with Polynesian culture and women as well as a bitter rejection of European society. It was the only text he ever wrote that he unequivocally intended for publication, since he considered writing an inferior medium to painting. The 1985 edition contains the original manuscript of Gauguin's *Noa Noa*, with notes, additional stories from *Noa Noa* and many colour plates.

Biography

Pierre Loti: the Legendary Romantic
Lesley Blanch 1983
The biography reveals how much Polynesia affected Perre Loti's writing and thinking. Lesley Blanch discusses the time he spent in the Pacific in 1872 and analyses *The Marriage of Pierre Loti* (q.v.) and writes about his Tahitian lover Rarahu.

The Intimate Journals of Paul Gauguin Paul Gauguin 1985 (1923)
Gauguin completed these journals in the Marquesas three months before his death. He emphasizes the richness of human intelligence and art and paints himself as a 'noble savage' showing a deep empathy for Polynesian culture and a deep suspicion of colonialism.

Fiction/Poetry

Legends of the South Seas
Antony Alpers 1970
Alpers has tried to dispel the myth of the Pacific as the earthly paradise, by reconstructing the legends, myths, folktales and poetry of the Polynesians as they would have been told before Cook's arrival in 1769.

The South Seas Rupert Brooke 1943
(in *The Collected Poems of Rupert Brooke*)
The collection includes *Tiare Tahiti* a poem about his love affair with Mamua a girl from Mataiea, *Waikiki*, *Heaven* and *The Great Lover*.

The Marriage of Loti Pierre Loti 1880
A romantic story about a young French sailor who falls in love with a Polynesian girl named Rarahu.

✔ **The Moon and Sixpence**
W. Somerset Maugham 1919
Somerset Maugham travelled around the Pacific in 1916/7 to research his novel which is a fictional account of the life of Paul Gauguin. The main character is an Englishman who gives up his life in the West to go to Tahiti to pursue his artistic interests.

✔ **Omoo** Herman Melville 1985 (1847)
An account of Melville's observations on Tahiti at the time of the French takeover; the emphasis is on the mutiny of the *Julia*.

✔ **Typee: A Peep at Polynesian Life**
Herman Melville 1985 (1846)
In 1842 Melville deserted from a whaler in the Marquesas; *Typee* is a semi-fictional account of the ensuing months which he spent with the Typee people. Fascinating descriptions of cannibal feasts and pagan rituals.

Faraway J.B. Priestley 1932
Much of this novel takes place on board a ship en route for the Pacific; there are many descriptions of Tahiti when the ship finally arrives there. Faraway is an island, near Tahiti, which is hard to find and which attracts fortune hunters; one of whom is a young Englishman, William, who has a ship board romance with an American woman.

Banana Tourist   *Georges Simenon   1952 (1946) (in the book entitled Lost Moorings)*
The name 'Banana Tourist' is given contemptuously by residents in the South Seas to people who come in search of the simple life. The background is Tahiti and the story, which is full of tension, is of a young idealist and his progressive disenchantment.

Guides

✔ **Tahiti and French Polynesia. A Travel Survival Kit**   *Robert F. Kay   1992 (1985)*

✔ **Tahiti-Polynesia Handbook**
David Stanley   1992

History

Tahiti. A Paradise Lost   *David Howarth   1983*
A readable account of European exploration in the Society Islands and the destruction of traditional Tahitian culture. Howarth divides the book into three parts 'Innocence: 1767–68', 'Trespass: 1769–89' and 'Original Sin: 1796–1842'.

✔ **The Fatals**
Impact   *Alan Moorehead (see 'Australia')*

Travel Literature

Forgotten Islands of the South Seas
Bengt Danielsson   1957
Life in the Marquesas, a group of ten islands known as the 'forgotten islands' because of their remoteness; they are over 600 miles from the capital of French Polynesia, Papeete. The author spent seven years in different parts of Polynesia.

✔ **Fatu Hiva: Back to Nature**
Thor Heyerdahl   1974
In 1936 Thor Heyerdahl aged twenty and his wife went to live on Fatu Hiva, in Eastern Polynesia for a year. It was this experience which led him to develop his interest in the Pacific and his theory that Polynesia could have been settled from America.

✔ **Kon-Tiki: Across the Pacific by Raft**   *Thor Heyerdahl   1990 (1950)*
Six men sailed on a primitive raft from Peru to Polynesia to prove that 'the Pacific islands are located well inside the range of prehistoric craft from Peru'.

A Writer's Notebook
W. Somerset Maugham   1984 (1949)
Maugham kept a notebook from 1892; it is

part autobiographical, part confessional and packed with impressions and observations. He travelled round the Pacific in 1916/17 and it is interesting to read his notes and jottings on that period.

White Shadows in the South Seas
Frederick O'Brien   1919
O'Brien spent a year on the island of Hiva-oa in the Marquesas and here records his day-to-day life, writing the book 'for those who stay at home yet dream of foreign places'.

✔ **In the South Seas being an account of experiences and observations in the Marquesas, Paumotus and Gilbert Islands in the Course of Two Cruises on the Yacht 'Casco' (1883) and the Schooner 'Equator' (1889)**
Robert Louis Stevenson   1987 (1896)
Descriptions of Stevenson's visits to the Marquesas, Gilberts and Tuamotus in 1888–90 which he wrote while living in Samoa. It is now considered a masterpiece of travel literature containing anthropology and autobiography, written in a humorous and unsentimental manner. It was misjudged on publication, partly no doubt because Stevenson saw and bemoaned what the Europeans were doing to the local customs and beliefs of the people of the South Pacific.

COOK ISLANDS

Guide

✔ **Rarotonga and the Cook Islands. Travel Survival Kit**   *Tony Wheeler and Nancy Keller   1989 (1986)*

History

The Cook Islands 1820–1950
Richard Gilson   1980
A rather dry history of the Cook Islands from the time of the first missionaries until just after the Second World War.

Travel Literature

The Island of Desire   *(1944)*
The Book of Puka-Puka   *Robert Dean Frisbie   (1929)*
Frisbie, an American, ran a store on Puka-Puka; the articles he wrote about it originally appeared in *Atlantic Monthly*.

An Island to Oneself *Tom Neale 1975*
(1966)
The author lived by himself for a total of six years on the deserted atoll of Suwarrow. He was supposed to have been so cantankerous that a deserted island was considered the only place he could have survived.

Isles of the Frigate Bird *(1975)*
The Lagoon is Lonely Now *Ronald Syme*
(1978)
A good introduction to the Cook Islands by Syme who travelled round the islands before ending up on Rarotonga.

SAMOA

'In the South Seas the Creator seems to have laid himself out to show what he *can* do.' Rupert Brooke *Letters from America 1913* 1916

Anthropology

✔ Coming of Age in Samoa
Margaret Mead 1932
Margaret Mead, whose book is now very controversial, writes about childhood, adolescence and sex in Samoa and was full of praise for the Samoans because of the way that they treated sex so naturally and pleasurably.

Autobiography/Biography

Tusitala of the South Seas: the Story of Robert Louis Stevenson's Life in the South Pacific *Joseph W. Ellison 1953*
A biography which shows Stevenson's love for Samoa and the effect it had on his life.

Our Samoan Adventure *Fanny Stevenson*
1955
Fanny Stevenson wrote this diary over the three years that she and her husband Robert Louis Stevenson spent on Samoa.

Fiction

Island Nights' Entertainments
Robert Louis Stevenson 1987 (1893)
Stevenson was known as Tusitala or 'Teller of Tales' when he lived on Samoa towards the end of his life. This collection includes three of the best stories from that time.

The Wrecker *Robert Louis Stevenson 1982*
(1892)
Stevenson wrote most of *The Wrecker* in Samoa. He and his stepson Lloyd Osbourne wanted to write a detective thriller disguised

as a 'novel of manners'. A wreck occurs on the uninhabited island of Midway; Dodd, artist turned smuggler, has adventures in San Francisco, Edinburgh, Paris, Sydney, Tahiti, Tehran and Constantinople. He becomes the detective obsessed with the secret of *The Flying Scud* and its ghostly crew and the book succeeds in being about violent crime without criminals.

Sons for the Return Home *Albert Wendt*
1987
A novel about a Samoan boy brought up with discrimination in New Zealand who finds it difficult to adjust to his own culture. Other books by Wendt include *Flying Fox in a Freedom Tree* (1988) which is a collection of short stories about Samoan life, *Pouliuli* 1987 (1977) which depicts the complex values and social organization in Samoan society and *Leaves of the Banyan Tree* (1981 (1980).

Guide

✔ Samoa: Western and American Samoa. Travel Survival Kit
Deanna Swaney 1990

AMERICAN SAMOA *(Pago Pago and Tau)*

Fiction

Black Coconuts, Brown Magic
Joseph Theroux 1983
An American doctor, a Vietnam veteran, returns to his childhood home in the Pacific. The novel shows the changes but also is fairly optimistic that traditional culture has managed to survive.

TONGA *(Friendly Islands)*
'The Women in particular, who are the merriest creatures I ever met.' Captain James Cook *Journal* October 1773

Fiction

Tales of the Tikongs *(1983)*
Kisses in the Nederends *'Epeli Hau'ofa*
(1987)
Amusingly written books by a local author about the coming of age of a small Pacific island called Tiko, which is a thinly disguised Tonga.

Guide

✔ **Tonga. Travel Survival Kit**
Deanna Swaney   1990

History

The Friendly Islanders: a Story of Queen Salote and Her People   *Kenneth Bain   1967*
The author was stationed in the islands and gives a sympathetic account of life there. He describes the unique blend of Western and Polynesian politics.

The Tongan Past   *Patricia Ledyard   1982*
A light and easy-to-read history of Tonga which includes myths and legends. She writes about pre-European Tonga and describes the coming of the Dutch, English, Spanish and French.

An Account of the Natives of the Tonga Islands   *William Mariner   1817*
A comprehensive account of pre-Christian Tonga.

Photography

Tonga   *James Siers   1978*
A small but well-illustrated book full of colour plates showing the outer islands and all aspects of Tongan life.

Travel Literature

Friendly Isles: A Tale of Tonga Utulei, My Tongan Home   *Patricia Ledyard   1956 and 1974*
Written by an American woman who went to Tonga after reading Mariner's early nineteenth-century account of Tonga and stayed and taught for over forty years, meeting and marrying a Scottish doctor.

NORFOLK ISLAND

✔ **An Owl in Paradise**   *Jan Morris   1993 (1992)*
In the collection called *Locations*.

PITCAIRN ISLAND

Fiction

The Mutineer: a Romance of Pitcairn Island   *Louis Becke   1908*
A novel based on the *Bounty* mutiny, which reflects the cultural tensions between the white sailors and the Polynesians. Fletcher Christian is shown as being indifferent and then remorseful before he dies.

A Singularly Unlucky Imposter
Philip Snow (in the collection Best Stories of the South Seas: see 'Pacific Islands – General, Fiction')

History

The Pitcairn Islanders   *Harry L Shapiro   1968*
The author only spent ten days on the island in 1934, but here provides a history of the colony. He looks at the genetic mixture of the islanders by studying five generations of the mutineers' descendants.

EUROPE

Europe - General

GENERAL

'Europe is dangerously close to becoming a mere hyphen between America and Asia.'
C.J. Jung *The Rise of a New World* 1930

Art and Archaeology

An Outline of European Architecture
N. Pevsner 1951 (1943)
A brief outline of architecture as an expression of Western civilization from the ninth to the twentieth century, with descriptions of the building of each period, style and country.

The Realm of the Great Goddess
Sibylle von Cles-Reden 1961 (1960) (see 'Corsica')
An illustrated study of megalithic monuments throughout Europe with an important chapter on Corsica.

Late Baroque and Rococo Architecture C. Norberg-Schulz 1986 (1979)
(see 'Central Europe' and 'Scandinavia')
The transition from Baroque to Rococo in the eighteenth century heralded a free and more organic form of architecture, as architects began to see man more in the context of the natural world. This is reflected in the cities of Prague, Vienna, Würzburg, Paris, Nancy, London, Turin, Rome and Copenhagen.

General Background

The Europeans Luigi Barzini 1983
A look at Europe's history and the events that have made it what it is today, with perceptive comments on the different nationalities.

✔ **The New Europe** Victor Keegan and Martin Kettle (eds.) 1993
Information about the institutions and landmarks of Europe with essays on the problems that have faced and will continue to face it.

Guides

✔ **Europe. The Rough Guide**
Martin Dunford and Jonathan Buckley 1994 (1992)
Includes Turkey and Morocco.

✔ **Europe by Eurail 1994–95** George and LaVerne Ferguson 1993
The eighteenth edition of this useful book

which helps people to make the most of their Eurail passes.

✔ **Fodor's Europe 1995** 1994

✔ **Let's Go Europe 1995** 1995

✔ **The Scientific Traveler. A Guide to the People, Places and Institutions of Europe** Charles Tanford and Jacqueline Reynolds 1992
A guide to the places where the great names in science lived and worked and to places of scientific interest. The branches of science covered include physics, chemistry, biology, the earth sciences, anthropology and astronomy.

✔ **The Which? Guide to Weekend Breaks in Europe** 1993 (1990)
Twenty-one of Europe's most interesting cities.

✔ **Cheap Eats Guide to Europe 1995**
Katie Wood 1993
Thousands of places to eat and shop for food cheaply throughout Europe.

✔ **Europe by Train** Katie Wood and George McDonald 1995
An updated version of 'the inter-railer's bible'.

Leisure

✔ **The Opera Lover's Guide to Europe** John Philip Couch 1991
Covers Austria, Belgium, France, Germany, Great Britain, Holland, Italy, Spain and Switzerland; the book is aimed at the budget-minded and concentrates on the smaller opera venues.

✔ **Waterways of Europe. Insight Guide** 1989

✔ **RAC Camping and Caravanning in Europe** 1993

✔ **The Good Retreat Guide**
Stafford Whiteaker 1994
Over 300 places to find peace and spiritual renewal in Britain, Ireland, France and Spain.

Natural History

✔ **Marshland and Freshwater Birds.
Eggs and Nests** *Jiri Felix 1993 (1975)*
Over 140 painted colour illustrations.

✔ **Sea and Coastal Birds. Eggs and
Nests** *Jiri Felix 1993 (1975)*
Over 135 painted colour illustrations.

✔ **Woodland and Hill Birds. Eggs and
Nests** *Jiri Felix 1993 (1974)*

✔ **Collins Pocket Guide: Grasses,
Sedges, Rushes and Ferns of Britain
and Northern Europe** *R.F. Fitter, A. Fitter
and A. Farrer 1992 (1984)*

✔ **Photographic Field Guide: Birds of
Britain and Europe** *Jim Flegg and
David Hosking 1993 (1990)*
Over 430 bird species are photographed and
described.

✔ **Letts Pocket Guide to Trees**
Pamela Forey 1993 (1990)
A compact identification guide with colour
paintings.

✔ **Letts Pocket Guide to Butterflies**
Pamela Forey and Sue McCormick 1993
A compact identification guide with colour
paintings.

✔ **Letts Pocket Guide to Insects**
Pamela Forey and Cecilia Fitzsimons 1992
A compact identification guide with colour
paintings.

✔ **Letts Pocket Guide to Wild
Flowers** *Pamela Forey and Cecilia Fitzsimons
1990*
A compact identification guide with colour
paintings.

✔ **Collins Pocket Guide: Birds of
Britain and Europe with North Africa
and the Middle East** *H. Heinzel, R.F. Fitter
and J. Parslow 1992 (1972)*
Colour illustrations showing every species, a
description of each and a postage-stamp size
map showing the distribution. The birds are
arranged under family.

✔ **Letts Pocket Guide to Mammals**
Eleanor Lawrence and Ruth Lindsay 1993
A compact identification guide with colour
paintings.

✔ **Letts Pocket Guide to Mushrooms
and Other Fungi** *Eleanor Lawrence and
Sue Harniess 1990*
A compact identification guide which arranges the fungi into their most likely habitats.

✔ **A Field Guide to the Rare Birds of
Britain and Europe** *Ian Lewington,
Per Alström and Peter Colston 1991*
A complete guide to all the rare, accidental
and vagrant birds ever reliably recorded in
Britain and Europe. Over 1,500 illustrations.

✔ **A Field Guide to the Birds of
Britain and Europe**
*Roger Peterson, Guy Mountfort and P.A.D. Hollom
1993 (1954)*
All of the 635 birds of Britain and Europe are
covered, with text about each and maps and
plates for easy identification. Aimed at the
amateur.

✔ **Mushrooms and Other Fungi of
Great Britain and Europe** *Roger Phillips
1981*
Excellent large format book.

✔ **Collins Photoguide to Wild Flowers
of Britain and Northern Europe**
Oleg Polunin 1988 (1986)
Photographs of over 700 plants in colour and
descriptions of 1,750 species.

✔ **A Concise Guide to the Flowers of
Britain and Europe** *Oleg Polunin 1987
(1972)*
192 pages of colour photographs and easy
identification of 1,080 plants.

✔ **Field Guide to the Trees of Britain
and Europe** *Bob Press 1992*
Over 450 species both native and naturalized
are described and illustrated with photographs. There are also line drawings of
leaves and berries.

✔ **A Field Guide in Colour to Wild
Flowers, Ferns and Grasses**
Dr Bohumil Slavik 1993 (1983)
Sixty-four painted colour plates.

Travel Literature

✔ **Sailing Across Europe** *Negley Farson
1985 (1926)*
A six-month voyage which took place in 1925
up the Danube in a twenty-six foot yawl
called *Flame*. Farson, an American, sailed
with his one-woman 'Crew' (who was later to
become his wife), writing about the trip with
great good humour.

Any Souvenirs *George Mikes 1973 (1971)*
(see 'Hungary')
Mikes fled Hungary in 1956; this was an
account of his first trip home in fifteen years.
He was not allowed into Czechoslovakia, but
travelled through Bavaria, Austria, Yugoslavia and Hungary.

✔ **A Grand Tour. Letters and Journeys 1794–96** *J.B.S. Morritt 1985 (1914)*
The author left Yorkshire in 1794, having inherited his father's fortune. He travelled through Greece, Austria, Hungary, Asia Minor and Italy. The book, which was not published until well after his death, consists of letters that he sent to his mother, sister and aunt.

✔ **Europe without Baedeker** *Edmund Wilson 1986 (1947)*
Edmund Wilson, the respected critic, came to Europe just after the war and travelled to Italy, Greece and England, seeing the ruins created by the Second World War. He incurred the wrath of Evelyn Waugh by pouring scorn on the British and saying exactly what he thought of them.

Western Europe

GENERAL

Art and Archaeology

A Concise History of Western Architecture *R. Furneaux Jordan 1969*
A good brief, illustrated introduction in the Thames and Hudson 'World of Art' Library.

Guides

✔ **Mediterranean Europe on a Shoestring** *Mark Balla et al. 1993*

✔ **Western Europe on a Shoestring** *Mark Balla et al. 1993*

✔ **Are You Two . . . Together? A Gay and Lesbian Guide to Europe** *Lindsy Van Gelder and Pamela Robin Brandt 1992*
Fourteen destinations are included: Brighton, Wales, London, Amsterdam, Copenhagen, Berlin, Bavaria, Belgium, Paris, the Loire Valley, Sitges, Mykonos, Capri and Venice.

✔ **Travellers Survival Kit Europe** *David Woodworth 1990 (1976)*

History

✔ **The Mediterranean and the Mediterranean World in the Age of Philip II** *Fernand Braudel 1990 (1949)*
Two volumes which for years have been the classics on the history, societies, economics, politics and personalities and area of the Mediterranean.

Leisure

✔ **Walking Europe from Top to Bottom** *Susanna Margolis and Ginger Harmon 1986*
A Sierra Club book to the Grande Randonnée Cinq (GR5) through Holland, Belgium, Luxembourg, Switzerland and France.

✔ **100 Hikes in the Alps** *Vicky Spring and Harvey Edwards 1992 (1979)*
Walks in Switzerland, France, Italy, Austria, Germany and Liechtenstein.

Natural History

✔ **The Alpine Flowers of Britain and Europe** *Marjorie Blamey and Christopher Grey-Wilson 1979*

✔ **Field Guide to Wild Flowers of Southern Europe** *Paul Davies and Bob Gibbons 1993*
Over 700 colour photographs of 1,200 species in Spain, Portugal, Southern France, Italy and Malta.

✔ **Flowers of the Mediterranean** *Oleg Polunin and Anthony Huxley 1990 (1965)*
Both the coastal zones and the inland and mountainous regions of the Mediterranean are covered in this book which is illustrated with colour photographs.

✔ **Mediterranean Wildlife. The Rough Guide** *Pete Raine 1990*
Covers France, Greece, Italy, Portugal, Spain and Yugoslavia as well as Morocco, Tunisia and Turkey.

Travel Literature

✔ **On the Shores of the Mediterranean**
Eric Newby   1985 (1984)
'Why don't you start at Naples and go clock-wise . . . instead of dashing off in all directions like a lunatic?' suggested Eric Newby's wife, Wanda, before embarking on their Mediterranean journey which took in Italy, the Adriatic, Greece, Turkey, the Levant, North Africa and Spain.

✔ **Lettres d'Un Voyageur**   *George Sand*
Translated by Sacha Rabinovitch and
Patricia Thomson   1987 (1837)
The twelve letters that George Sand wrote between 1834–6 were published as articles. They were written from Venice, Switzerland and France and talk about her lover Musset and her holiday in Switzerland with Liszt in a refreshing and stimulating way.

✔ **Labels**   *Evelyn Waugh   1974 (1930)*
Evelyn Waugh's account of a Mediterranean cruise to Naples, Port Said, Constantinople, Athens and Barcelona. He got under the skin of the places he went to, but said 'I was simply a young man, typical of my age. We travelled as a matter of course.'

ANDORRA

Guide

✔ **Let's Go France 1995**
Includes six pages on Andorra.

AUSTRIA

'I must own I never saw a place so perfectly delightful as the Fauxbourgs of Vienna. It is very large and almost wholly compos'd of delicious Palaces.' (Lady Mary Wortley Montagu, letter to Lady Mar, Sept. 8th 1716

Fiction/Poetry

✔ **The Piano Teacher**   *Elfriede Jelinek*
1989 (1983)
A bleak but compelling novel set in present-day Vienna: '*The Piano Teacher* is a brilliant, bitter wonderful portrait of mother and daughter, artist and lover.' (John Hawkes)

The Man Without Qualities
Robert Musil   1979 (1930–32)
Although not autobiographical in the strict sense, there is no doubt that Ulrich, an aus-tere yet sensual character, is based on Musil himself. The breadth of life and experience that fill the novel make one feel that the action is taking place over many years, when in fact it all occurs in the framework of less than a year, ending on the brink of the First World War. It is the inner states and theories of the characters, especially Ulrich, and their relationships with each other, that make this such a rich work. Musil began his great traditional work in the early 1920s and although it was never finished it is very long.

Food

✔ **Classic Austrian Cooking**
Gretel Beer   1993
A large comprehensive book which claims to be for people who 'really *enjoy* food'.

Guides

✔ **Moorland Visitor's Guide Austria**
Ken Allan   1988

✔ **American Express Vienna and Budapest**   *1992*

✔ **Baedeker's Austria**   *1992*

✔ **Baedeker's Vienna**   *1992*

✔ **Blue Guide Austria**   *1992*

✔ **Thomas Cook Traveller's Vienna**
1993

✔ **Everyman Guide. Vienna**   *1994*

✔ **Insight Guide Austria**   *1992*

✔ **Insight Guide South Tyrol**   *1992*

✔ **Let's Go Austria**   *1995*

✔ **Michelin Green Guide Austria**   *1992*

✔ **Charming Small Hotel Guide Austria**   *Paul Wade and Kathy Arnold (eds.)*
1994

History

✔ **The Fall of the House of Habsburg**
Edward Crankshaw   1992 (1963)
A compelling account of the last decades of the Austro–Hungarian empire. With the fall of the Habsburg monarchy, the old order of Europe disintegrated; Crankshaw puts this in the context of what was happening in Vienna, Imperial Russia, France, Prussia and Italy.

✔ **Danube**   *Claudio Magris   1991 (1986) (see*
'Central and Eastern Europe – General')

✔ **Fin-de-Siècle Vienna** *Carl E. Schorske 1992 (1961)*
Out of the crisis of political and social disintegration at the turn of the century, much modern art and thought emerged: 'A profound work . . . on one of the most important chapters of modern intellectual history.' (Hugh Trevor-Roper *New York Times Book Review*)

Leisure

✔ **Exploring Rural Austria** *Gretel Beer 1990*
A guide which goes to out-of-the-way places.

✔ **Mountain Walking in Austria**
Cecil Davies 1988 (1986)
A guide to the eighteen mountain groups in the Eastern Alps, with 74 walks described fully.

✔ **Hut to Hut in the Stubai Alps**
Allan Hartley n.d.
The Stubai in the Austrian Tyrol are ideal for the novice to mountain walking. The book describes two tours of eight to ten days.

✔ **South Tyrol. Meran Dolomites**
Franz Hauleitner and Henriette Klier 1988 (1986)
A Sunflower guide to easy alpine walks.

✔ **The Kalkalpen Traverse** *Alan Proctor 1986*
A walk through the limestone alps of the Austrian Tyrol from Lake Constance to the Kaisergebirge.

Natural History *(see 'Europe – General')*

Travel Literature

Double Eagle *Stephen Brook 1988 (see 'Central Europe')*
Brook concentrates on the cities of Vienna, Budapest and Prague, the primary cities of the Habsburg empire – which have changed out of all recognition in the seventy odd years since the glittering days of the Habsburgs. His present-day quest is full of delightful surprises.

BELGIUM

'Were any man to ask my advice upon the subject of retirement, I should tell him: By all means repair to Antwerp.' William

Beckford *Dreams Waking Thoughts and Incidents 1783.*

Art and Archaeology

✔ **From Van Eyck to Bruegel**
Max J. Friedlander 1981 (1916) (see 'Netherlands')
A learned account of the early Flemish masters.

✔ **Dutch Painting** *R.H. Fuchs 1978 (see 'Netherlands')*

✔ **Dutch Civilisation in the Seventeenth Century** *J.H. Huizinga (see 'Netherlands')*

Fiction/Poetry

✔ **The Sorrow of Belgium** *Hugo Claus 1991 (1983)*
An important novel which covers in a rich panorama the adolescent years of a Flemish boy in Belgium between 1939 and 1947. The fictional 'Walle' in the book is based on Kortrijk or Courtrai in West Flanders.

✔ **A House in Flanders** *Michael Jenkins 1993 (1992)*
An English boy is sent to the Franco-Belgian border to stay with his French relations in the 1950s. Detailed descriptions of daily life on the great Flanders plain and the contrast between youth and old age are woven together to make this 'A little gem of a book' (*The Sunday Telegraph*)

Food

✔ **A Taste of Belgium** *Rosine De Dijn 1989*
A large book with essays, photographs and recipes.

Guides

✔ **Cadogan Guide Brussels, Bruges, Ghent and Antwerp** *Antony Mason 1994*

✔ **Holland, Belgium and Luxembourg. The Rough Guide** *Martin Dunford, Jack Holland and Phil Lee 1994 (1990)*

✔ **French Entrée 7. Calais, Champagne, Ardennes and Bruges** *Patricia Fenn 1988*

✔ **Blue Guide Belgium and Luxembourg** *Bernard McDonagh 1993 (1920)*

✔ **Michelin Belgique, Grand-Duché de Luxembourg** *(French only)* *1993*

✔ **Michelin Red Guide Benelux 1995**

✔ **Thomas Cook Traveller's Belgium** *1994*

History

✔ **Fatal Avenue. A Traveller's History of the Battlefields of Northern France and Flanders 1346–1945** *Richard Holmes 1993 (1992) (see 'France – North')*

✔ **The Embarrassment of Riches: An Interpretation of Dutch Culture in the Golden Age** *Simon Schama 1991 (1987) (see 'Netherlands')*

Leisure

✔ **Through the Dutch and Belgian Canals** *Philip Bristow 1988*

✔ **A New Guide to the Battlefields of Northern France and the Low Countries** *Michael Glover*
Includes the battlefields at Bastogne, Arnhem, Ypres and Waterloo. A very readable guide to exploring the area.

Natural History *(see 'Europe – General')*

Travel Literature

✔ **An Inland Voyage**
Robert Louis Stevenson 1992 (1878)
Stevenson and his friend, Walter Simpson, took two sail-powered skiffs and cruised from Antwerp to Pontoise. The journey had many drawbacks: the weather was intolerable and they had been tempted to give up were it not for the feeling that he thought 'an easy book may be written and sold, with mighty little brains about it'.

CYPRUS

'History in this island is almost too profuse. It gives one a sort of mental indigestion.'
Robert Byron *The Road to Oxiana* 1937

Art and Archaeology

✔ **Cyprus from the Stone Age to the Romans** *Vassos Karageorghis 1982*
An illustrated introduction to the archaeology of Cyprus.

The Painted Churches of Cyprus
Andreas and Judith Stylianou 1985
A large illustrated book on sixty-two of the Byzantine Troödhos country churches in Cyprus, which until relatively recently were inaccessible except by donkey.

Autobiography/Biography

Makarios *Stanley Mayes 1981*
The author, as a journalist, first met Makarios in the mid-1950s when the Archbishop was passing through London on his way to lobby the United Nations. He later got to know him well and was granted many long interviews with the man who he believed was the only person who 'could have solved the problem which he had done so much to create'.

Guides

✔ **Cadogan Guide Cyprus** *1994*

✔ **Cyprus. The Rough Guide**
Marc Dubin 1993
Includes northern and southern Cyprus.

Historic Cyprus. A Guide to its Towns and Villages, Monasteries and Castles
Rupert Gunnis
The author visited every site on the island during the 1930s.

✔ **Insight Guide Cyprus** *1993*
Includes northern and southern Cyprus.

✔ **Blue Guide Cyprus** *Ian Robertson 1993 (1990)*
Includes northern and southern Cyprus.

✔ **Thomas Cook Travellers Cyprus** *1993*

History

Footprints in Cyprus. An Illustrated History *Sir David Hunt (ed.) 1982*
A well-illustrated and very readable book which covers all of Cypriot history from its origins in the neolithic age up to the present day.

Leisure

✔ **Landscapes of Cyprus** *Geoff Daniel*
1990 (1986)

Travel Literature

Cyprus as I Saw It in 1879
Sir Samuel Baker 1879
Baker's on-the-spot and personal experiences of Cyprus as 'an independent traveller, unprejudiced by political considerations, and unfettered by the responsible position of an official'.

The Orphaned Realm *Patrick Balfour*
1951
To know Cyprus it is necessary to understand the history of the Egyptians, Hittites, Greeks, Phoenicians, Assyrians, Persians, Macedonians, Romans, Byzantines, Franks, Venetians, Turks and British. *The Orphaned Realm* is basically a travel book but does talk about the history and antiquities of the island.

✔ **Yarns of a Cyprus Pilot**
Captain G.V. Clark 1991
The author was a pilot in the colonial service in Famagusta between 1953–1960. He was responsible for guiding many foreign ships in and out of the port. He heard many stories from these sailors and tells them here.

✔ **Bitter Lemons** *Lawrence Durrell 1957*
Durrell was entranced by Cyprus when he first went there in 1953. He bought a house and became a teacher. He later became Press Advisor to the government recording his life and impressions vividly. [Colin Thubron]

✔ **Journey into Cyprus** *Colin Thubron*
1975
Colin Thubron made a 600-mile trek around Cyprus during the last year of its peace. There is much emphasis on the history and Thubron's theme was the survival of Cyprus through eighty centuries of invasion from the mythic times of Aphrodite up to this century.

NORTHERN CYPRUS

Guides

✔ **Guide to North Cyprus. A Bradt Guide** *Diana Darke 1993*

✔ **Northern Cyprus** *John and Margaret Goulding 1992*
An illustrated Windrush Island Guide.

Natural History

✔ **Flowers of Northern Cyprus**
Sonia Halliday and Laura Lushington 1988
Illustrated with many colour photographs.

Travel Literature

The Infidel Sea. Travels in North Cyprus *Oliver Burch 1990*
Northern Cyprus in the mid 1980s, as seen by a sympathetic outsider who looks at the island's rich and colourful past, rather than the politics of the prsent. The author travelled around the north of the island and was shown unfailing hospitality by the Turkish Cypriots.

FRANCE

'France is the most civilised country in the world and doesn't care who knows it.'
John Gunther *Inside Europe* 1938

Art and Archaeology

✔ **A Concise History of French Painting** *Edward Lucie-Smith 1971*
An overall comprehensive, but brief, art reference book in the Thames and Hudson series.

Fiction/Poetry

✔ **Les Misérables** *Victor Hugo 1982*
(1862)
A huge novel with a breadth of vision and compassion which ranges from Paris to Waterloo. A vivid portrait of early nineteenth-century France.

Food

✔ **Mastering the Art of French Cooking** *Simone Beck and Julia Child 1966*
(1961)
Two volumes which were described by Elizabeth David as 'The most instructive book on fine French cooking yet written in the English language'.

✔ **Larousse Gastronomique**
1993 (1984)
Everything you could possibly want to know about French food. An absolute must.

General Background

✔ **France Today** *John Ardagh* *1990 (1982)*
An overview of French culture and people today which examines the profound changes which have taken place.

Writer's France. A Regional Panorama
John Ardagh *1989*
A fascinating book which shows how the regions of France are reflected in her literature; divided into areas with extracts from some of the major authors.

✔ **Mythologies** *Roland Barthes* *1972 (1957)*
An acute analysis of how the ideas of the French emerge in food and wine etc. His *Selected Writings* (1983) (introduced by Susan Sontag) includes essays from his major collections and extracts from his longer works.

✔ **Portraits of France** *Robert Daley*
1992 (1991)
A combination of little known French history, anecdotes and descriptions of the French countryside.

Sons of the Generous Earth *Philip Oyler*
1963
Philip Oyler managed various estates all over France and here writes about the peculiarities of the different regions and characters he encountered in his work.

That Sweet Enemy
Christopher Sinclair-Stevenson *1987*
A personal view of France, the French and French history by an Englishman who knows the country well.

✔ **The French** *Theodore Zeldin* *1984*
A series of interviews with a cross-section of French people about what moves them and what makes them tick.

Guides

✔ **The Historic Country Hotels of France. A Select Guide** *Wendy Arnold*
1988.
A well-illustrated guide to thirty hotels with individual personality and character.

✔ **France. The Rough Guide** *Kate Baillie and Tim Salmon* *1992 (1986)*

✔ **Bartholomew Guide: France on Back Roads** *1991 (1986)*

✔ **Wild France. A Traveller's Guide**
Douglas Botting (ed.) *1992*
Chapters on Brittany and Normandy, The Northeast, The Alps, Central France, the Loire and Burgundy, the Pyrenees, the Atlantic Coast, the Eastern Mediterranean and Corsica and the Western Mediterranean.

✔ **The Gîtes Guide. French Farm and Village Holiday Guide** *1994*
Over 1,200 gîtes which can be booked directly.

✔ **Guide to B. and B.'s of Character and Charm in France 1993/4** *1993*
A selection of 382 'special' 'maisons d'hôte de charme' throughout France.

✔ **Guide to Hotels and Country Inns of Character and Charm in France 1993/4** *1993*
Published by 'Rivages', this guide is well established in France; hotels vary in prices, but each of the 491 selected has something special about it.

✔ **The Which? Guide to Camping in the South of France and the Dordogne** *Fizz Fieldgrass* *1991*
Over 200 hand-picked and inspected campsites.

✔ **Let's Go France 1995**

✔ **Michelin Green Guide France** *1991*

✔ **Michelin Red Guide France 1995**

✔ **France. Travel Survival Kit**
Daniel Robinson and Leanne Logan *1994*

✔ **France. The Versatile Guide**
Emma Stanford *1994*

History

✔ **The Identity of France** *Fernand Braudel*
Vol.1 *History and Environment* (1989 (1986))
Vol 2. *People and Production* (1991 (1986))
Braudel attempts to explain the essence of France with a 'brilliant evocation of landscape, of sea and river, of village and town, of work and poverty and of trade and war'. [book jacket] In his final book 'Braudel sheds light on every aspect of France, from every conceivable angle'. (Joanna Kilmartin *The Observer*) A brilliant, wide-ranging and comprehensive sweep through France.

✔ **The French Revolution** *Richard Cobb and Colin Jones (eds.)*
A collection of well-illustrated essays about the French Revolution. Also *Promenades*, an historian's appreciation of modern French literature.

✔ **A History of Modern France**
Alfred Cobban *1965 (1957)*
Vol. 1: 1715–99, Vol. 2: 1799–1871 and Vol 3: 1871–1962. A complete and easy-to-read history.

✔ **A Traveller's History of France**
Robert Cole   1992 (1988)
A very brief history of France aimed at the traveller who wants to know more than can be found in the average guide.

✔ **Scum of the Earth** *Arthur Koestler*
1991 (1941)
Koestler was living in the South of France writing *Darkness at Noon* when war broke out. He was imprisoned when he arrived in Paris and was lucky not to have been handed over to the Nazis for torture. His book about France at war is a powerful and searching story.

The Sun King *Nancy Mitford   1983 (1966)*
A re-creation of the life and times in which Louis XIV lived; good descriptions of how Versailles was turned from a hunting lodge into a magnificent palace. Well illustrated.

✔ **Flight to Arras** *Antoine de Saint-Exupéry*
1987 (1942)
A classic story of war in which Saint-Exupéry tells how he was sent on a reconnaissance flight in a damaged plane over German-occupied France in 1940.

✔ **Citizens** *Simon Schama   1989*
A chronicle of the French Revolution which Richard Cobb described in *The Times* as 'The most marvellous book I have read about the French Revolution in the last fifty years' and Bernard Levin wrote in *The Sunday Times*: 'He has chronicled the vicissitudes of that world with matchless understanding, wisdom, pity and truth, in the pages of this huge and marvellous book'.

✔ **A Distant Mirror** *Barbara Tuchman*
1978
A very readable history of the calamitous fourteenth century which was beset by plagues, wars and crusades, but was also an age of chivalry, illuminated chronicles and Books of Hours and Gothic cathedrals.

Leisure

✔ **Through the French Canals**
Philip Bristow   1991 (1970)
Thirty-nine routes are described and illustrated, including through-routes between the English Channel and the Mediterranean.

✔ **Walking in Northern France**
Martin Collins   1987
Walks in Hautes-Vosges, the Ardennes, the Forêt D'Orient and Pays D'Othé, Ile-de-France, Pays de Caux, Suisse Normande and Brittany.

✔ **Cruising French Waterways**
Hugh McKnight   1991 (1984)
Arranged by area: Pas-de-Calais, Somme and the North; Seine and Champagne; Franche Comté, Alsace, Lorraine and the Ardennes; Brittany and the Loire Country; Burgundy and Bourbonnais; the Atlantic Coast; the Rhône Valley, Gascony and Languedoc. Describes the locks and fuelling points and also the regions and history. Invaluable.

✔ **Wining and Dining in France**
Robin Neillands   1990
Compiled in association with Logis de France.

✔ **Cycling France. The Best Bike Tours in all of Gaul** *Jerry H. Simpson   1992*
Route descriptions and special maps for cyclists.

✔ **The Food Lover's Guide to France**
Patricia Wells   1988 (1987)
Divided by region, the guide includes all the main shops, restaurants and markets in the area: 'A must-have for every food lover'. (*Bon Appetit*)

Natural History *(see 'Europe – General')*

Photography

✔ **The French Château. Life. Style. Tradition** *Christiane de Nicolas-Mazery and Jean-Bernard Naudin   1991*
Photographs of thirteen châteaux at different times of year and on different occasions.

✔ **The Most Beautiful Villages of France** *Dominique Repérant   1993 (1990)*
Lavishly illustrated with ample text.

Travel Literature

✔ **Hills and the Sea** *Hilaire Belloc   (1906)*
Hilaire Belloc explored the following areas on foot: Provence, Languedoc and the Pyrenees observing all the while and having 'certain thoughts and admirations'.

✔ **White Horses Over France**
Robin Hanbury-Tenison   1990 (1985)
Robin Hanbury-Tenison and his wife ride some horses from the Camargue to Cornwall.

✔ **A Little Tour in France** *Henry James*
1987 (1900)
Enthusiastic tour of France from Tours around the château country and the Midi.

Henry James wrote with contagious enjoyment about what he saw.

✔ Travels Through France and Italy
Tobias Smollett 1981 (1766)
Most of Smollett's journey took place in France, although he did make a short Italian tour between September and November 1764. It is highly readable. Smollett is a wonderful raconteur, although he acquired the reputation of being 'the most atrabilious, ill-humoured British traveller' ever to cross the Channel. He was vilified in the streets of Nice and Sterne's *Sentimental Journey* (q.v.) was written largely as a riposte to Smollett, whom he called 'the learned SMELFUNGUS'.

✔ A Sentimental Journey Through France and Italy *Laurence Sterne 1938 (1768)*
The journey never progresses beyond Versailles, but the book enjoyed enormous popularity throughout Europe.

PARIS
'Nobody who has not lived intimately in and with Paris can appreciate the unique savour of that word *femmes*.' Arnold Bennett *Paris Nights* 1913

Art and Architecture

✔ A Guide to the Impressionist Landscape *Patty Lurie 1990*
A series of day trips from Paris to the sites of great nineteenth-century paintings. Many colour illustrations and maps.

✔ The Guide to the Architecture of Paris *Norval White 1991*
Fifty-eight walking tours covering more than 2,000 buildings, monuments, bridges and parks.

Autobiography/Biography

✔ A Girl in Paris *Shusha Guppy 1992 (1991)*
The author went to study French at the Sorbonne when she was seventeen; at first not speaking a word of French, she found herself rooms on the Left Bank and gradually became enamoured of Paris.

✔ A Moveable Feast *Ernest Hemingway 1977 (1964)*
Hemingway's memoirs of his life as a young unknown writer in Paris in the 1920s.

✔ Tropic of Cancer *Henry Miller 1978 (1934)*
The wild and erotic side of Paris in the 1930s. Colin MacInnes writes: 'a great prophetic book; a warning of what deadens life, an affirmation that it can yet be lived, though with extreme difficulty in an age whose sterile non-cultures seek to thwart all mainsprings of fertility.'

Journals 1917–1974 *Anais Nin 1976 (1966)*
Anais Nin lived near Paris in the 1930s – and met, among others, Henry Miller, Antonin Artaud and Otto Rank: 'An extraordinary book . . . its egoism is redeemed, raised to a high standard of art, by an extremely subtle sensibility, expressed in a prose style of astonishing beauty.' (Sir Herbert Read)

✔ Down and Out in Paris and London
George Orwell 1989 (1933)
In the late twenties Orwell spent a period living among the tramps and drunks of both Paris and London. 'Written with so much simple force . . . the result is curiously beautiful.' (Compton Mackenzie)

Fiction

✔ Old Goriot *Honoré de Balzac 1991 (1835)*
Wonderfully detailed descriptions of both affluence and squalor in the Paris of the 1820s. ✔ *Cousin Bette* (1847) is the story of the Hulot family who had risen to eminence under Napoleon I, but who were left vulnerable in the bourgeois money-oriented Paris of the 1840s.

To the End of the World *Blaise Cendrars 1956*
An elderly Parisian actress has an affair with a deserter from the Foreign Legion.

Chéri *Colette 1973 (1920)*
This and *The Last of Chéri* chronicle the rise and fall of the handsome Chéri who was brought up in the world of Paris courtesans before the First World War and whose amorous education was left to a talented older woman. Also by Colette *The Vagabond* (1911).

✔ A Tale of Two Cities *Charles Dickens 1991 (1859)*
Set in Paris and London during the 1789 French Revolution, the exciting story and well-shaped plot tell how private individuals coped with the great upheavals of the time; their particular fictional lives set against an historical background.

✔ **Sentimental Education**
Gustave Flaubert   1976 (1964)
A detailed reconstruction of Paris life in the 1840s and the story of a young man's romantic attachment to an older woman.

Les Misérables   Victor Hugo   1982 (1862)
(see 'France – General')
Montfermeil, near Charles de Gaulle airport, was where the terrible Thénardiers had their inn.

✔ **The Ambassadors**   Henry James   1986 (1903)
Mostly set in Paris. Strether is sent to 'rescue' Chad from what his mother assumed was the corrupt life he was leading.

✔ **Maigret**   Georges Simenon
Good descriptions of many of the seedier parts of Paris in most of the Maigret crime novels.

✔ **The Mysteries of Paris**   Eugene Sue   1988 (1842/3)
Sue conjures up a fantastical world rich in melodrama and unusual characters. He writes with a mixture of socialism, sentimentality and sadism.

✔ **Perfume**   Patrick Suskind   1987 (1985)
An extraordinary novel, set in eighteenth-century Paris, which uses the sense of smell as its main theme.

✔ **Nana**   Emile Zola   1973 (1880)
Set in the Second Empire, the story of the rise and fall of a courtesan; part of Zola's twenty-novel saga *The Rougon-Macquarts: the Natural and Social History of a Family under the Second Empire*.

General Background

✔ **Paris**   Julian Green   1991 (1983)
A parallel text of evocations and memories of Paris from the turn of the century.

✔ **The Crazy Years. Paris in the Twenties**   William Wiser   1990 (1983)
The exhilarating period in Paris when so many writers, musicians, dancers and painters converged on the city. Illustrated with black and white photographs.

Guides

✔ **The Historic Hotels of Paris**
Wendy Arnold   1990
Descriptions and photographs of thirty special French hotels.

✔ **Paris. The Rough Guide**   Kate Baillie and Tim Salmon   1993 (1987)

✔ **The Woman's Travel Guide Paris**
Catherine Cullen   1993

✔ **The Companion Guide to the Country Round Paris**   Ian Dunlop   1986 (1979)

✔ **Everyman Guide: Restaurants of Paris**   1994

✔ **Eyewitness Travel Guide Paris**   1993

✔ **Paris. Cadogan City Guide**
Dana Facaros and Michael Pauls   1993

✔ **French Entrée 11. Paris**
Laurence Phillips   1993

✔ **Insight Guide Paris**   1993

✔ **Let's Go Paris 1995**

✔ **American Express Guide Paris**
Christopher McIntosh and Eileen Townsend Jones   1993 (1983)

✔ **Paris. A Helm French Regional Guide**   Vivienne Menkes-Ivry   1991

✔ **Michelin Green Guide Euro Disney Resort**   1992

✔ **Michelin Green Guide Île-de-France**   1990

✔ **Michelin Green Guide Paris**

✔ **Blue Guide Paris**   Ian Robertson   1992

✔ **The Time Out Guide Paris**   1994 (1990)

✔ **Paris Step by Step**   Christopher Turner   1991
Descriptions of 250 locations throughout Paris. Full of clear maps.

✔ **Paris Access Guide**
Richard Saul Wurman

Leisure

✔ **Paris Chic. The Parisian's Own Insider Shopping Guide**   Dominique Brabec and Églé Salvy   1993 (1992)
Over 1,000 shops arranged by type.

✔ **Walks in Gertrude Stein's Paris**
Mary Ellen Jordan Haight   1988
Five half-day tours which take in the bohemian Paris of 1900–1940.

✔ **Paris Bistros**   Robert and Barbara Hamburger   1992 (1991)
A guide to 100 bistros in Paris.

✔ **Paris. A Literary Companion**
Ian Littlewood 1987
Arranged under area, the book celebrates the
writers who lived and worked in Paris by
following their lives through buildings and
streets.

✔ **The Food Lover's Guide to Paris**
Patricia Wells 1994 (1984)
Crammed with restaurants, shops and mar-
kets.

✔ **Walks Round Paris. Footpaths of
Europe Series** 1991
A guide to 600 kilometres of footpaths of the
Île-de-France.

Photography

✔ **Atget's Paris** Eugène Atget 1993 (1992)
A small chunky book with over 800 black and
white photographs by Eugène Atget who
lived in Paris in the late nineteenth and early
twentieth century.

✔ **Philips: Paris. Architecture,
History, Art** Ian Littlewood 1992

Paris John Russell 1983
A large and updated version of Russell's previous book in praise of Paris. Lavishly illustrated and written with feeling and soul, the
book brings together all the different streams
and strands of Paris.

NORTHERN FRANCE –
CALAIS TO CHAMPAGNE

'It is a strange, mongrel, merry place, this
town of Boulogne.' W.M. Thackeray *The
Paris Sketch Book* 1840

Fiction

✔ **The Quest of the Absolute**
Honoré de Balzac 1989 (1834)
Balthazar Van Claës was born at Douai in
1761 and although he was educated in Paris,
he returned to Flanders and made a good
match. However, his world was turned up-
side down when an impoverished visiting
Polish gentleman came to Douai and talked
about his ambitions of finding 'The Absolute';
this became Balthazar's passion and led to
his eventual ruin. A great study in obsession.

Under Fire Henri Barbusse (1916)
A powerful novel about the 1914–18 war;
Barbusse who was half English and half
French was a pacifist at the outbreak of war,
but enlisted and kept a diary of life in the

trenches; when he was wounded he turned it
into a novel which won the Prix Goncourt in
1917.

✔ **What Maisie Knew** Henry James
(1897)
Maisie was entranced by the colourful life of
the port of Boulogne.

✔ **Germinal** Emile Zola 1991 (1885)
The thirteenth volume in Zola's epic saga; the
events all take place, in different years, in the
month of Germinal (21 March–19 April). He
used the region near the Belgian border because the miners came out on strike there in
February 1884 and he wanted to write about
a strike, as the best way of providing a violent
clash between capital and labour.

Guides

✔ **The Gateway to France: Flanders,
Artois and Picardy** James Bentley 1992
(1991)
The chapter headings are as follows: The
Opal Coast, The Riches of the Pas-de-Calais,
The Poetry of the Somme, Exploring the
Charms of the Aisne, The Frontier with Bel-
gium and Approaching Paris.

✔ **French Entrée 6. Boulogne, Pays
d'Opale and Picardy** Patricia Fenn 1993
(1987)

✔ **French Entrée 7. Calais,
Champagne, Ardennes and Bruges**
Patricia Fenn 1988

✔ **Michelin Green Guide Champagne
(Ardennes)** 1993 (French only)

✔ **Michelin Green Guide Flanders,
Picardy and the Paris Region** 1993

History

✔ **Fatal Avenue. A Traveller's History
of the Battlefields of Northern France
and Flanders 1346–1945** Richard Holmes
1993 (1992)
A history and guide to a region which over
the years has seen an excessive amount of
bloody conflict.

Leisure

✔ **Paris to Boulogne. Footpaths of
Europe** 1990
A guide to 880 kilometres of footpaths
through the countryside of northern France.

Travel Literature

Chantemesle *Robin Fedden 1950*
Memories of a childhood house whose 'ghosts
to me were real, stirring the curtains, moving
in and out of the rooms as easily as the bees'.
The area was crammed with history and he
describes the famous people who had lived
there.

ALSACE-LORRAINE AND FRANCHE-COMTÉ

'The plain of Alsace is to me one of the
pleasantest anywhere, so genially
productive, so well cultivated, and so
cheerful, yet with the Vosges and the Black
Forest and the Alps to hinder its being
prosaic.' Matthew Arnold, letter to Miss
Arnold, 25 June 1859

Fiction

✔ **Scarlet and Black** *Stendhal 1974
(1830)*
A reflection of life in France after Waterloo:
through the life and loves of Julien Sorel we
see the rich and the poor, the Royalists and
the Liberals and the Jesuits and the Jansen-
ists.

Food

✔ **A Taste of Alsace** *Sue Style 1990*
Landscape and food photographs with the
odd recipe.

Guides

✔ **Alsace** *James Bentley 1988*
A narrative guide which describes the food
and drink of the region as well as its history
and what to see in the towns and countryside.

✔ **Alsace. Insight Guide** *1990*

✔ **Alsace. The Complete Guide**
Vivienne Menkes-Ivry 1991
The author knows the region well and has
written a complete and comprehensive guide
of its history, cuisine and wines as well as
descriptions of the towns and landscape.

✔ **Michelin Green Guide Alsace
Lorraine. Vosges** *1992 (French only)*

✔ **Michelin Green Guide Jura**
1992 (French only)

✔ **Visitor's Guide France: Alps and
Jura. A Moorland Guide** *Paul Scola 1993
(1990)*

Travel Literature

Small Boat to Alsace *Roger Pilkington 1961*
Pilkington sailed to Alsace on his boat the
Commodore across the Netherlands, through
the Ardennes, up the Moselle gorge and
across the upper Moselle to Lorraine,
through the Vosges watershed and down towards the Alsatian plain.

NORMANDY/BRITTANY

'One is haunted by the name Plantaganet
there. The moment one enters Anjou,
from which the family came, the broom
begins, and Brittany seems all in flower
with it, the furze mixed.' Matthew Arnold,
letter to his mother, 8 May 1859

Art and Architecture

Megalithic Brittany *Aubrey Burl 1985*
A detailed guide to the prehistoric sites of
Brittany.

Autobiography/Biography

The Ruskins in Normandy *J.G. Links
1968*
Subtitled 'A Tour in 1848 with Murray's
Hand-book'. Although Ruskin later disap-
proved of Murray's guides because they 'encouraged the traveller to see too much, rather
than only what he could understand and
remember', in 1848 he was delighted to take
with him the then new guide to France,
packed with invaluable information. Mr Ruskin senior, John and Effie all kept accounts
of this trip to Normandy and it is fascinating
to compare their observations with the Murray's guide. Although Murray detested Calais, Ruskin loved it: 'Calais, the busy – the
bustling – the – I had almost said beautiful,
for beautiful it was to me . . . See Calais and
you can see no more . . . It is a little France.'

Pigtails and Pernod *Simona Pakenham
1961*
As a child, in the 1920s, Simona Pakenham
was taken across the Channel to Normandy
about six times a year. She developed a great
love of Dieppe and recounts her earliest
memories.

Fiction

✔ **Les Chouans** Honoré de Balzac 1972
(1829) (Brittany)
A romantic story about the Royalist Chouan rebellion which took place just after the Revolution. Balzac was greatly influenced by Scott's approach to the serious historical novel and with this story of romantic passion and adventure, most of which takes place in Fougères, Balzac did much to establish the genre in France.

✔ **Flaubert's Parrot** Julian Barnes 1985
(1984) (Normandy)
A novel which weaves its way in and out of the life of Flaubert and provides us with the most extraordinary details: a 'stunning combination of French provincial wisdom and tortured British self-analysis'. (*Books and Bookmen*)

✔ **Ripening Seed** Colette (1923)
Colette wrote this story of adolescents on holiday, discovering their sexuality and finding out about sex, near St Malo.

Bouvard and Pécuchet
Gustave Flaubert (Normandy)
A village betweeen Caen and Falaise is where two people retire to practise the sciences of the time.

✔ **Madame Bovary** Gustave Flaubert
1992 (1857) (Normandy)
The quintessential 'first modern novel', which takes as its theme French bourgeois life in Rouen. Emma, a brilliantly portrayed bored housewife, leaves her husband, Charles Bovary, for the mercurial Rodolphe and a desperate love affair – in the fictional Yonville-l'Abbaye, probably the village of Ry. *A Simple Heart*, (in *Three Tales*) also set in Normandy, is the life of a pious and devoted servant girl.

Strait is the Gate André Gide (1909)
Set in Cuverville where Gide had lived and where he married his cousin Madeleine. The novel has some autobiographical elements but his real life was not as gloomy as the fiction.

✔ **The Cathedral** J.K. Huysmans 1989
(1898)
Durtal converts from satanism to Roman Catholicism; this enraged French Catholics who tried to get the book banned. Has been described as the best guide book to Chartres Cathedral and its publication in England did much to rekindle Gothic art and architecture.

Pêcheur d'Islande (Iceland Fisherman) Pierre Loti 1961 (1886)
Loti got to know Brittany as a junior naval officer and set his novel about the terrors of death at sea in the deep-sea fishing port of Paimpol and at Porseven on the north coast.

✔ **Selected Short Stories**
Guy de Maupassant Roger Colet (ed.) 1971
De Maupassant loved Normandy and its coast and Rouen and the surrounding countryside features in many of his stories which were mostly published in the 1880s.

✔ **In Remembrance of Things Past**
Marcel Proust (1913–1927)
Proust's great continuous novel was originally published in eight parts. 'Balbec' is Cabourg on the Normandy coast, where Marcel first met Albertine on the beach in front of the Grand Hôtel.

La Nausée Jean-Paul Sartre 1982 (1938)
(Normandy)
A relentlessly gloomy description of living, set in Le Havre ('Bouville'), about the alienation of personality and the mystery of being, and Sartre's first lengthy description of existentialist philosophy. George Steiner wrote of Sartre: 'The importance of the man will not only prove to reside in works like *Nausea* which is a masterpiece, but in the example of trying to live rationally, day in day out.'

General Background

Memoirs François-René de Chateaubriand
Translated by Robert Baldick (1965)
Chateaubriand was born in St Malo, but moved as a child to a gloomy and foreboding château north of Rennes which he hated and which he graphically describes in his memoirs.

Selected Letters Madame de Sévigné 1982
Madame de Sévigné, born in 1626, was married to a Breton nobleman who died when she was only 25 leaving her a château in eastern Brittany. She wrote many lively letters to her daughter, complaining about the rather grand life she was expected to lead. She is considered, with the exception of Voltaire, the greatest letter-writer in French literature. Her letters were all written to a limited amount of people and thus go into the fascinating minutiae of daily life.

Guides

✔ **Landscapes of Brittany**
Rodney Ansell 1993
Seven car tours, 42 long and short walks and
22 picnic suggestions.

✔ **Brittany. A Helm French Regional
Guide** *Frank Victor Dawes 1989*

✔ **Everyman Guide Brittany** *1994*

✔ **French Entrée 5: Brittany**
Patricia Fenn 1991

✔ **French Entrée 9: Normandy**
Patricia Fenn 1993 (1991)

✔ **Footpaths of Europe: Coastal
Walks: Normandy and Brittany** *(1989),*
✔ **Normandy and the Seine** *(1989)*
✔ **Walking Through Brittany** *(1989)*
This series is translated from the French and
features the Grande Randonée.

✔ **Insight Guide Brittany** *1992*

✔ **Insight Guide Normandy** *1994*

✔ **Blue Guide Normandy** *John McNeill
1993*

✔ **Michelin Green Guide Brittany**
1991

✔ **Michelin Green Guide Normandy
Cotentin** *1993*

✔ **Michelin Green Guide Normandy –
Seine Valley** *1993*

✔ **The Companion Guide to
Normandy** *Nesta Roberts 1986 (1980)*

✔ **Visitor's Guide France: Brittany. A
Moorland Guide** *Richard Sale 1993*

✔ **Brittany and Normandy. The
Rough Guide** *Greg Ward 1992 (1987)*

✔ **The Which? Guide to Brittany and
Normandy** *1993*
Includes touring, walking, camping and
beach holidays.

History

Six Armies in Normandy *John Keegan
1982*
A military history which combines personal
anecdote with official accounts of what happened.

Sixty Miles from England
Simona Pakenham 1967
An account of the English at Dieppe between
1814 and 1914. At the beginning of the nine-
teenth century, with Napoleon on his way to
Elba, there were no foreign residents in
Dieppe, but 100 years later the town was
swarming with them.

Photography

✔ **Brittany. Philip's Travel Guide**

Travel Literature

✔ **Mont Saint Michel and Chartres**
Henry Adams 1986 (1904)
By using the architecture, sculpture and
stained glass of both Mont Saint Michel and
Chartres, Adams begins a meditative journey across time and space into the medieval
imagination.

THE LOIRE

'One of the most wonderful rivers in the
world, mirroring from sea to source a
hundred cities and five hundred towns.'
Oscar Wilde, letter to George Lewis
Junior, November 1880

Fiction

Eugénie Grandet *Honoré de Balzac 1992
(1833)*
Balzac set *Eugénie Grandet* at Saumur in
Anjou; it is the story of how stifling life can
be in a small French provincial town.

✔ **Le Grand Meaulnes** *Alain-Fournier
1986 (1913)*
Alain-Fournier mixes two areas, Sologne and
Epineuil, for the setting of his delightful
rural novel, which is certainly part autobiographical. His detailed and loving descriptions of the buildings, landscape and people
have changed little today.

✔ **In Remembrance of Things Past**
Marcel Proust (1913–27)
'Combray' was the name Proust gave the
market town of Illiers, south-west of Chartres.

✔ **Gargantua and Pantagruel**
Rabelais 1979 (1532/34)
An exuberant and exaggerated chronicle of
the adventures of two giants with caricatures
depicting the church hierarchy, schools and
universities, theologians, lawyers and philosophers and the feeling of two ages merging:
the new age of humanism and the previous
fixed world order of schoolmen.

✔ **The Devil's Pool** *George Sand 1966 (1846)*
George Sand loved the Berry and her family château at Nohant where she eventually settled and became the very popular châtelaine. She wrote about the dignity of manual labour, contrasting rural life favourably with the artificiality of city dwelling.

✔ **The Earth** *Emile Zola 1980 (1887)*
Zola's novel about the peasantry, whom he portrays as nasty and brutish, in his vast epic, is set in the Beauce and concentrates on a family called Fouans.

Guides

✔ **Châteaux of the Loire. Architectural Guides for Travellers** *Marcus Binney 1992*

✔ **The Visitor's Guide to France: The Loire. A Moorland Guide** *Norman Brangham and Michael Dean 1990 (1985)*

✔ **The Loire. An Eperon French Regional Guide** *Arthur Eperon 1992*

✔ **French Entrée 8. The Loire** *Patricia Fenn 1990 (1989)*

✔ **Michelin Green Guide Châteaux of the Loire** *1991*

Travel Literature

Notes from an Odd Country
Geoffrey Grigson 1984 (1970)
Geoffrey Grigson made his second home in Trôo a French village near the River Loir (*sic*), on the edge of Touraine. Divided into seasons the book describes the happenings and records in detail the natural history of each, while interjecting wicked asides.

BURGUNDY
'Watrish *Burgundy*.' William Shakespeare *King Lear* c. 1605/6

Autobiography/Biography

✔ **My Mother's House and Sido** *Colette 1980 (1922)*
A lyrical portrait of Colette's mother and the Burgundy countryside into which she was born in 1873. She grew up in a house overflowing with dogs, cats and children, all of which played an important part in her later fictional creations.

Fiction

Clochemerle *Gabriel Chevallier 1993 (1936)*
Chevallier who was a journalist in Lyon used to take holidays north-west of Villefranche. He was so amazed by rural French life that he wrote a bucolic comedy satirising 1920s Beaujolais village life.

My Brother Jack *Alphonse Daudet (1868)*
An autobiographical novel; Daudet was born in Nîmes, but soon moved to Lyon like Daniel, the hero of the novel.

✔ **Days of Anger** *Sylvie Germain 1993 (1989)*
Set at the beginning of the century in the forests of Morvan, Sylvie Germain's acclaimed novel tells of feuding families and the importance that the forest, with all its secrets, plays in their lives.

Guides

✔ **Burgundy. An Eperon French Regional Guide** *Arthur Eperon 1992*

✔ **Burgundy. Insight Guide** *1992*

✔ **Michelin Green Guide Burgundy** *1992*

✔ **Burgundy. Blue Guide** *Ian Ousby 1992*

Travel Literature

✔ **Long Ago in France** *M.F.K. Fisher 1993 (1991)*
M.F.K. Fisher arrived in Dijon in the 1920s and discovered a wealth of pleasures and tastes previously unknown to her: 'M F K Fisher is a poet of the appetites'. (John Updike)

✔ **Burgundy** *John Flower 1994*
An introduction to all aspects of Burgundy including descriptions of the three great monasteries, Fontenay, Cîteaux and Cluny, which did much to ensure Burgundy's role at the heart of Christianity.

POITOU-CHARENTES AND THE ATLANTIC COAST
'La Rochelle . . . from the moment I entered . . . I perceived to be a fascinating little town, a most original mixture of brightness and dullness.' Henry James *A Little Tour in France* 1882

Fiction

Lost Illusions Honoré de Balzac 1837
Excellent descriptions of life in the provincial town of Angoulême which Balzac uses to emphasize the theme of the opposition between Paris and the provinces.

The Three Musketeers Alexandre Dumas 1991 (1843/4)
A swashbuckling romance which takes place in the 1620s at the court of Louis XIII and in which the Musketeers, Athos, Porthos, Aramis and their companion d'Artagnan are engaged in a battle with Richelieu. Descriptions of the 1627 siege of La Rochelle.

Moderato Cantabile Marguerite Duras 1968 (1958)
A novel, mostly in dialogue, about obsession; a man and a woman, Chauvin and Anne Desbaresdes, both fascinated by a *crime passionel* have concentrated and intense meetings in a café which has a seaside setting. Made into the film *Seven Days . . . Seven Nights*, directed by Peter Brook with Jean-Paul Belmondo and Jeanne Moreau.

Dominique Eugène Fromentin 1969 (1863)
A romantic semi-autobiographical novel.

Thérèse François Mauriac 1927
Mauriac was much influenced by the forests in the Landes which he makes extremely oppressive in his novel. The unhappy Thérèse is married to an awful brute who she tries to poison. *The Desert of Love* is set in Bordeaux and is about a doctor and his son who are both obsessed by the same woman.

The Voyage Charles Morgan 1987 (1940)
Barbet Hazard is a wine-grower who revels in his simple rural existence. He meets and falls in love with Thérèse Despreux from the bright lights of Paris.

General Background

✔ **Essays** Michel de Montaigne Translated by M.A. Screech 1991)
Montaigne, having travelled widely, spent the last twenty years of his life in his château, near Bordeaux, writing his *Essays*.

Guides

✔ **Aquitaine. An Eperon French Regional Guide** Arthur Eperon 1991

✔ **Michelin Green Guide Berry Limousin** 1990 (French only)

✔ **Michelin Green Guide Poitou, Vendée, Charentes** (French only)

✔ **South West France: Aquitaine, Gascony, the Pyrenees. A Helm French Regional Guide** Andrew Sanger 1990

Travel Literature

✔ **In the Vine Country** E.O. Somerville and Martin Ross 1991 (1893)
A tour of the Médoc country where the authors experience the wine harvest and stay in a grand château.

Ways of Aquitaine Freda White 1968
Aquitaine was the name given by the Romans, meaning Land of Waters; Freda White writes engagingly about the Cher, the Indre, the Lower Vienne, the Creuse and the Gartempe, the upper Vienne, Poitou, the Charentes, Saintonge and the seashore.

DORDOGNE/CEVENNES/LOT

'Lascaux is the Parthenon of prehistory.' Cyril Connolly, Dordogne in *Ideas and Places* 1953

Fiction

Jacquou le Croquant E. Le Roy Ladurie 1945
Set in the forest of Barade, west of Montignac in about 1830 when there was a peasant uprising against a cruel feudal landlord.

Near Périgord Ezra Pound 1914
Ezra Pound made a particular study of troubadours and in this poem tells of a troubadour's love for Lady Maent in her castle. Based on Bertran de Born's *Dompna, puois de mi no us cal*.

✔ **The Swimming-Pool Season**
Rose Tremain 1992 (1985)
English ex-patriate life in a village near Périgueux; after the collapse of a swimming pool business, the Kendals go to live in a quiet village. Larry Kendal soon has an idea for the most exotic swimming pool ever, while his wife has been summonsed to Oxford and her dying mother.

Food

✔ **A Taste of Périgord** Helen Raimes 1991
The Périgord has one of the richest regional cuisines of France. The author has lived

there for twelve years and has collected recipes over that period.

Guides

✔ **The Companion Guide to Gascony and the Dordogne** Richard Barber 1991 (1977)

✔ **Dordogne and Corrèze. An Eperon French Regional Guide** Arthur Eperon 1991

✔ **Lot (Quercy). An Eperon French Regional Guide** Arthur Eperon 1990 (1989)

✔ **Michelin Green Guide Dordogne (Périgord-Quercy)** 1991

Leisure

✔ **Walks in the Cevennes. Footpaths of Europe series** 1991

Photography

✔ **The Dordogne. Philip's Travel Guide** Stephen Brook Photographs by Charlie Waite 1992 (1986)

Travel Literature

✔ **Footsteps** Richard Holmes 1986 (1985) Holmes follows Stevenson's journey through the Cévennes and is according to Michael Holroyd 'The most romantic of contemporary biographers and probably the most revolutionary in spirit and form.'

The Generous Earth Philip Oyler 1950 Oyler wrote about his love for the Dordogne and its food, wine, churches and villages long before the British invasion. He appreciated the vitality and integrity of the Dordogne valley and emphasizes the importance of the sound agriculture to the local people.

✔ **A House in the Sunflowers. Summer in Aquitaine** Ruth Silvestre 1992 (1990) Ruth Silvestre and her family fell in love with a house in the Lot-et-Garonne. The book tells the story of their search for it, their discovery of it and the years they spent restoring it.

✔ **Travels With a Donkey in the Cevennes** Robert Louis Stevenson 1992 (1879) The account of Stevenson's trip through the Cevennes with his recalcitrant donkey, Modestine.

✔ **Three Rivers of France** Freda White 1962 The three rivers are the Dordogne, the Lot and the Tarn which all rise in the Massif Central and run westwards to the Atlantic. The book describes the country and the history which they run through.

A Village in the Cevennes Heather Willings 1979 The author moved to a remote part of the Cevennes after seven years in Paris and found a rich and flourishing way of life.

PYRENEES *(see also 'Spain – Pyrenees')*

'Africa begins at the Pyrenees' Alexander Dumas, attrib. before 1870

Fiction

✔ **Fiesta** Ernest Hemingway 1955 (1927) *(see 'Spain – Pyrenees')*

Ramuntcho Pierre Loti 1897 Loti fell in love with the Basque country; *Ramuntcho* is the story of a young shepherd who was also a smuggler and his love for a local girl, whose mother puts her into a convent.

✔ **The Song of Roland** Translated by Dorothy Sayers French epic written at the end of the eleventh century which has an account of the famous ambush near Roncesvalles.

Guides

✔ **The Pyrenees. An IGN Touring and Leisure Guide** 1991

✔ **Landscapes of the Pyrenees. A Sunflower Book** Paul Jenner and Christine Smith 1990

✔ **The Pyrenees. The Rough Guide** Paul Jenner and Christine Smith 1994 (1990)

✔ **Michelin Green Guide Pyrénées Aquitaine. (Côte Basque)** 1992 *(French only)*

✔ **Michelin Green Guide Pyrénées Roussillon (Albigeois)** 1992 *(French only)*

History

✔ **The Return of Martin Guerre** Natalie Zemon Davis 1985 (1983) A man returns from the wars saying he is the long lost husband of a woman in the village and claiming his property and his wife. A strange and haunting story which takes place in Artigat in the Pyrenees.

✔ **Montaillou** E. Le Roy Ladurie 1990 (1978)
Records from the Inquisition of the Cathar peasants of the eastern Pyrenees in the fourteenth century: 'A fascinating sociological study of medieval life. But it is also far more. It is a Chaucerian gallery of vivid medieval persons.' (Hugh Trevor-Roper *The Sunday Times*)

Leisure

✔ **Walks and Climbs in the Pyrenees**
Kev Reynolds 1983 (1978)
A general guide which covers the most spectacular walks.

Travel Literature

The Pyrenees Hilaire Belloc 1928 (1909)
Belloc's book was written when he was a young man to provide a general knowledge of the Pyrenean mountains for travellers, 'in the old days of peace, "before ever the sons of Achaia came to the land".' Much about the make-up and physical nature as well as practical advice for the traveller.

The Enchanted Mountains
Robin Fedden 1962 (see 'Spain')
An evocative narrative about the Aigües-tortes region of the Pyrenees.

A Book of the Basques Rodney Gallop
1930
A picture of the Basque race, character, traditions and achievements:
'Two thousand years ago a swarm of Romans Came to make war on the Basque Country. The sturdy Cantabrians made answer to them:
We would rather die than submit!
Even to-day their words are not forgotten.' (Piarres Dibarrart)

North of the Pyrenees Henry Myhill 1973
Covers the Garonne and the Pyrenean parts of French Catalonia which today comprises the Landes, Pyrénées-Atlantiques, Hautes-Pyrénées, Gers and Ariège; and much of Gironde, Lot-et-Garonne, Haute-Garonne and Pyrénées-Orientales; an area shaped by rivers, all of which run north from the Pyrenees.

The French Pyrenees John Sturrock 1988
Interesting and detailed book about the Pyrenees going from west to east in a 250 mile journey; the book was conceived because of the author's 'excessive liking for travelling in southern France, and a great liking for mountains'.

LANGUEDOC

'There is nothing more pleasing to a traveller – or more terrible to travel-writers, than a large rich plain.'
Laurence Sterne *Tristram Shandy*, Vol. VII 1765

Fiction

High Are the Mountains Hannah Closs
1945
A novel set between the years 1206–9; the detail does not pretend to be historically exact, but the story culminates with the historic siege of Carcassonne and includes Montségur, a citadel of the Albigenses where Catharism was practised.

Guides

✔ **The Cadogan Guide to the South of France** Dana Facaros and Michael Pauls 1994

✔ **The Companion to the South of France** Archibald Lyall 1987 (1963)

Photography

Languedoc. Philip's Travel Guides
James Bentley   Photographs by Charlie Waite
1991 (1987)

Travel Literature

✔ **An Englishman in the Midi**
John P. Harris 1991
Life in a small village in the Languedoc; the talks were broadcast on BBC Radio 4.

✔ **Small Boat in the Midi**
Roger Pilkington 1989
Roger Pilkington had spent many years sailing around the Midi and here describes his voyages.

West of the Rhone Freda White 1964
The Languedoc, Roussillon and the Massif Central.

MASSIF CENTRAL

Guides

✔ **Auvergne and the Massif Central. A Helm French Regional Guide**
Rex Grizell 1989

✔ **Michelin Green Guide Auvergne**
1991 (French only)

✔ **Michelin Green Guide Gorges du Tarn, Cévennes, Languedoc** 1994
(French only)

Leisure

✔ **Walks in the Auvergne** 1989
In the Footpaths of Europe series.

✔ **Pathmaster Guides. The Auvergne**
Maurice Turner 1992

Travel Literature

West of the Rhone Freda White 1964
The Languedoc, Roussillon and the Massif Central.

THE ALPS
'Nothing is more delightful than fine weather in the Alps; but as a general rule, the next thing to it is bad weather in the Alps.' Leslie Stephen *The Playground of Europe* 1871

General Background

✔ **Pig Earth** John Berger 1988 (1979)
John Berger lived for several years in a simple peasant community in Upper Savoy; in a series of tales he describes the very hard lives that the local farmers led up until the 1970s.

Wars I Have Seen Gertrude Stein 1945
When Gertrude Stein finally had to leave Paris in 1943, she went to live on the upper Rhône, west of Annecy. This book describes life under the German occupation.

Guides

✔ **Michelin Green Guide Alpes du Nord (Savoie-Dauphiné)**
1992 (French only)

✔ **Michelin Green Guide Alpes du Sud (Haute-Provence)** 1992 (French only)

✔ **Visitor's Guide France: Alps and Jura. A Moorland Guide** Paul Scola 1993 (1990)

Leisure

✔ **Pathmaster Guides: Haute Savoie**
Norman Buckley (1990) and **Dauphiné**
Ilona Bellos and Hugh Morison (1991)

✔ **Walking the GR5: Modane to Larche** 1990
In the 'Footpaths of Europe' series

Travel Literature

A Tramp Abroad Mark Twain 1982 (1898)
(see 'Germany', 'Italy', 'Switzerland')
Twain went to Chamonix and gives a hilarious description of his ascent of Mont Blanc 'by telescope'.

RHONE VALLEY AND PROVENCE
'Provence . . . the land where the silver-grey earth is impregnated with the light of the sky.' Henry James *A Little Tour in France* 1882

Art and Archaeology

✔ **Letters from Provence**
Vincent van Gogh 1992 (1990)
A selection of his letters illustrated with his paintings, drawings and sketches.

Autobiography/Biography

✔ **My Father's Glory**
✔ **My Mother's Castle** Marcel Pagnol
1991 (1960)
Two volumes of childhood memoirs told by Pagnol, a boy from the city. He spent glorious summer days exploring the Provençal countryside and manages to capture the way children think and react to events with enormous clarity and delight.

Fiction

Letters from My Windmill
Alphonse Daudet 1984 (1866)
Rural life in the late nineteenth century in

the Crau, a part of Provence for which Daudet had a passionate attachment.

✔ **The Avignon Quintet**
Lawrence Durrell 1992
Monsieur, Livia, Constance, Sebastian and *Quinx* – about the Nazi occupation of Avignon and the surrounding countryside.

✔ **The Rack** A.E. Ellis 1979 (1958)
Uhle, a small town in the Haute Savoie, is the site of a TB sanatorium; the intensity of the feelings and emotions of the incumbents in this enclosed neurotic world makes this an extraordinarily powerful and moving book.

Mistral's Daughter Judith Krantz 1988 (1982)
A glittering story about three generations of women which begins in the Paris of the 1920s and moves to New York.

Jean de Florette
Manon des Sources Marcel Pagnol 1962
Stories of Provençal peasants and their greed for water; the film was written by Pagnol before the book.

Fortune of the Rougons Emile Zola 1985 (1872)
The first volume in Zola's monumental work *Les Rougon-Macquarts* which occupied him for twenty years and was about a family living through the ups and downs of the Second Empire; this is set in Aix-en-Provence (Plassans) during the 1851 rebellion.

Food

✔ **A Taste of Provence** Carey More and Julian More 1988
Landscape photographs and simple recipes accompanied by a chatty text.

Guides

✔ **Provence and the Côte D'Azur. The Rough Guide** Kate Baillie 1992 (1990)

✔ **Visitor's Guide France: Provence and Côte d'Azur. A Moorland Guide**
Norman Brangham and Richard Sale 1993 (1990)

✔ **Everyman Guide: Provence** 1995

✔ **The Rhône Valley and Savoy. A Helm French Regional Guide**
Rex Grizell 1991

✔ **Insight Guide Provence** 1993

✔ **A Guide to Provence** Michael Jacobs 1989 (1988)
Essays on the history and culture of Provence with a gazetteer of the region.

✔ **French Entrée 13. Provence**
Peter King 1993

✔ **Companion Guide to The South of France** Archibald Lyall 1987 (1963)

✔ **Michelin Green Guide Provence** 1991

✔ **Michelin Green Guide Vallée du Rhône** 1989 (French only)

✔ **Provence. A Travelscapes Book**
Francis Pagan 1991
A narrative guide book.

Leisure

✔ **Footpaths of Europe: Walking the GR5: Larche to Nice** 1990

✔ **Eating Out in Provence and the Côte d'Azur** Edward Roch 1992
A guide to over 220 local restaurants.

Photography

✔ **Provence. Philip's Travel Guides**
John Flower Photographs by Charlie Waite 1992 (1987)

✔ **Sketchbook from Southern France**
Sara Midda 1990
Delightfully illustrated, crammed with notes and drawings.

Travel Literature

✔ **A Spell in Wild France** Bill and Laurel Cooper 1993 (1992)
The Coopers have taken a Dutch barge through France (described in their book *Watersteps Through France*) and arrive outside the town of Aigues-Mortes in the Camargue in time for winter.

Two Towns in Provence M.F.K. Fisher 1964
Aix-en-Provence and Marseilles. M.F.K. Fisher was drawn back again and again to the area and with her special knowledge and love of food has written an informative and delightful book. [Colin Thubron]

✔ **Perfume from Provence**
Lady Fortescue 1993 (1935)
In the early 1930s it was cheaper to live in France than in England, one of the reasons which encouraged Winifred Fortescue and her husband to settle in Provence.

✔ **Sunset House** Lady Fortescue 1993 (1937)
The author moved to Provence in the early

1930s where she and her husband converted an old stone farm house called the Domaine. After her husband died, she stayed on in the area, somewhat unhappily until she found a small house which she transformed into 'Sunset House'.

✔ **French Dirt. The Story of a Garden in the South of France** Richard Goodman *1992 (1991)*
The author fell in love with his garden in the South of France: 'Oh No, not another Englishman in Provence living like a native. But Oh Yes, and what's more he's got M.F.K. Fisher to commend it: than which there can be no greater accolade.' (*Daily Mail*)

✔ **Aspects of Provence**
James Pope Hennessy *1988 (1952)*
An account of the history, people and architecture of inland Provence.

✔ **Toujours Provence** Peter Mayle *1992 (1991)*
A continuation of the best seller.

✔ **A Year in Provence** Peter Mayle *1990 (1989)*
I don't think anything need be said about this bestseller.

✔ **Next Time Round in Provence**
Ian Norrie *1993*
The lesser known bits of Provence such as the Vaucluse and Bouches-du-Rhône where the author has a house.

Village in the Vaucluse Laurence Wylie *1974 (1957)*
An American sociologist's study of the hill village of Roussillon, near Avignon. A detailed and absorbing book showing how village life changed and is changing.

COTE D'AZUR

'I went to Hyères and St. Tropez, both of which were bosh.' Edward Lear, letter to Lady Waldegrave, 11 December 1866

Autobiography/Biography

✔ **Jigsaw** Sybille Bedford *1990 (1989)*
An autobiographical novel about growing up in 'the unfashionable part of the Côte d'Azur: Sybille Bedford's evocation of the South of France in the 1920s offers a celebration of affordable pleasures and painterly descriptions written under the great spell of Mediterranean life.' (Chris Petit *The Times*)

Fiction

Point of Departure Jean Anouilh *1951*
A play about a meeting at a train station which leads to an encounter in a squalid hotel in Marseille.

✔ **The Green Hat** Michael Arlen *1991 (1924)*
A good evocation of the atmosphere of the 1920s and fashion for verbal smartness and rebellion.

✔ **Jericho** Dirk Bogarde *1992*
The writer William Caldicott is contemplating divorce when he gets the key to his brother's house in a remote French village. Very good descriptions of small-town French life.

Collected Stories Colette *1985 (1983)*
Colette lived in St Tropez between 1925–39 and some of the stories in this collection are set there.

The Rock Pool Cyril Connolly *1936*
Connolly's only novel was banned in England on grounds of obscenity.

The Count of Monte Cristo
Alexandre Dumas *1990 (1844–46)*
A story of revenge that begins and ends in Marseille; the young sailor Dantès is arrested on his wedding day and imprisoned, after escaping he determines to find the treasure of Monte Cristo. Thackeray wrote: 'began to read Monte Cristo at six one morning and never stopped till eleven at night'.

✔ **Tender is the Night** F. Scott Fitzgerald *1968 (1939)*
Dick Diver, a psychiatrist by training, is married to the beautiful and rich Nicole whom he met as a patient in a Zurich clinic. His life seems increasingly empty to him in the corrupt society to which they belong. Full of romance and emotion; set on the Riviera in the 1920s.

✔ **The Collected Short Stories**
Katherine Mansfield *1981 (1945)*
Katherine Mansfield lived for a while on the Riviera pre-war and some of her seventy-three short stories are set there.

The Three Fat Women of Antibes
W. Somerset Maugham
One of only two short stories Maugham wrote about the South of France, the other being *The Facts of Life*. In *Collected Short Stories* vol.1, 1990.

Bonjour Tristesse Françoise Sagan *1978 (1954)*
Françoise Sagan's first novel is set on the Esterel coast; Raymond and Cécile, father

and daughter, lived amicably enough until Raymond decides to remarry.

General Background

✔ **Côte d'Azur. Inventing the French Riviera** Mary Blume 1992
The author describes how the Côte d'Azur developed into a fantasy playground for the rich and famous. Well illustrated with many previously unpublished photographs.

Guides

✔ **Provence and the Côte d'Azur. The Rough Guide** Kate Baillie 1992 (1990)

✔ **Visitor's Guide France: Provence and the Côte d'Azur** Norman Brangham and Richard Sale 1993 (1990)

✔ **Cadogan Guide Southwest France** Dana Facaros and Michael Pauls 1994

✔ **Insight Guide Côte d'Azur and Monaco** 1992

✔ **French Entrée 10. The South of France** Peter King and Patricia Fenn 1992

✔ **The Companion Guide to the South of France** Archibald Lyall 1987 (1963)

✔ **Michelin Green Guide French Riviera (Côte d'Azur)** 1993.

Leisure

✔ **Eating Out in Provence and the Côte d'Azur** Edward Roch 1992
A guide to over 220 local restaurants.

Travel Literature

Travels in the South of France
Stendhal 1971
Stendhal recorded his trip to the South of France in 1838 in notebooks; much can be learnt about the customs of nineteenth century France from his observations.

CORSICA

Art and Archaeology

The Realm of the Great Goddess
Sibylle von Cles-Reden 1961 (1960)
An illustrated study of megalithic monu-

ments throughout Europe with an important chapter on Corsica.

Biography

His Majesty of Corsica Valerie Pirie 1939
A biography of Theodor von Neuhof, King Theodore, a now legendary figure of whom there is little trace in Corsica, although the Moor's head still appears on the Corsican flag as a lasting memento to his reign.

Guides

✔ **The Corsican High Level Route. Walking the GR20** Alan Castle 1992 (1987)

✔ **Blue Guide Corsica** Roland Gant 1992

✔ **Insight Guide Corsica** 1993

✔ **Visitor's Guide: France, Corsica. A Moorland Guide** Jutta May Revised by Hedley Alcock 1993 (1987)

✔ **Michelin Green Guide Corse** 1993 (French only)

✔ **Landscapes of Corsica. A Sunflower Guide** Noel Rochford 1993 (1988)

✔ **Corsica. The Rough Guide** Theo Taylor 1994

History

Columbus's Isle Joseph Chiari 1960
The author explores the possibility that Columbus might have been born on Corsica.

Travel Literature

An Account of Corsica James Boswell 1955 (1768)
Contained in *Boswell on the Grand Tour*. Boswell's account of his journey round the island and his visit to Pasquale Paoli.

✔ **Granite Island** Dorothy Carrington 1984 (1971)
Dorothy Carrington spent a great deal of time in Corsica and was bewitched by it. She writes about the archaic beliefs of rural Corsica as well as the architecture and scenery.

Journal of a Landscape Painter in Corsica Edward Lear 1870
Difficult to find, but Lear's account with his engravings was one of the first books on Corsica.

✔ **Time Was Away** *Alan Ross and John Minton   1989 (1948)*
Alan Ross and John Minton travelled to Corsica in 1947: 'Poetic, personal, the pungent effect of travel on keen senses.' (V.S. Pritchett *New Society*)

GERMANY

'To be an Englishman is in Germany to be an angel –they almost worship you.' S.T. Coleridge, letter to Thomas Poole, 26th October 1798

Art and Archaeology

✔ **German Cathedrals** *J. Baum   1956*
A large format book with many black and white illustrations and minimal text.

Bauhaus *Frank Whitford   1984*
An accessible history of this explosive and innovative era which lasted from 1919 until 1933. Whitford traces the ideas behind the conception of the Bauhaus and describes its teaching methods. In the Thames and Hudson 'World of Art' library.

The Weimar Years: A Culture Cut Short *J. Willett   1984*
The distinctive new culture which was established by the Weimar Republic from the roots of the Modern Movement was cut short by the rise of Hitler in 1933. A well-illustrated book with informative captions.

Autobiography/Biography

✔ **The Past is Myself**
Christabel Bielenberg   1990 (1968)
The British author was married to a German and spent the war in Germany as a German citizen. A very moving account of those years.

Fiction/Poetry

✔ **The Lost Honour of Katharina Blum** *Heinrich Böll   1978 (1974)*
A woman's life is ruined as a result of intrusion by the press and her brief involvement with a terrorist.

Threepenny Novel *Bertolt Brecht   1983 (1934)*
Brecht adapted Gay's *Beggar's Opera* into first the *Threepenny Opera* and later the *Threepenny Novel*, but set it around 1900, with deals involving the Boer War.

Auto da Fé *Elias Canetti   1978 (1946)*
The extraordinary story of Peter Kien, a distinguished scholar who lived in Germany between the wars, his illiterate and grasping housekeeper Therese and the thuggish Nazi-like concierge, Benedikt Pfaff: 'Savage, subtle, beautifully mysterious . . . one of the few great novels of the century.' (Iris Murdoch)

The Riddle of the Sands *Erskine Childers 1902*
An exciting story about the secret service which is accurately set among the Frisian Islands. 'I keep on going back to Erskine Childer's *The Riddle of the Sands*, not for its plot, which is only just this side of infantile, but for its wonderful descriptive passages about navigating the Frisian Islands.' (Jonathan Raban)

The Sorrows of Werter
Johann Wolfgang von Goethe   Translated by Daniel Malthus   1991 (1779)
Malthus' translation was the one known and praised by Goethe; we can feel its sense of period, something a more modern translation would lack; this gives it a rightful sense of gravitas. *Werter* was influential when it was published, officers in the army becoming concerned by possible 'suicides from love' among members of the Guard; it was also much read by Napoleon, who discussed the work with Goethe, and took it with him to St Helena.

✔ **The Tin Drum** *Gunter Grass   1989 (1959)*
A bitter and impassioned political novel; a study of the German character between the years 1925 and 1955 as seen through the eyes of a dwarf, Oskar Matzerath.

✔ **Grimm's Tales** *Jakob and Wilhelm Grimm*

Fatherland *Robert Harris   1992*
A Cold War novel in which Germany has conquered Europe and the Soviet Union.

The Glass Bead Game *1987*
Narcissus and Goldmund *(1930)*
Steppenwolf *(1929)   Hermann Hesse*
The Glass Bead Game is a vast utopian novel, *Narcissus and Goldmund*, about two very different monks, is set in medieval Germany and *Steppenwolf* is about schizophrenia and is 'a savage indictment of bourgeois society'. (*The New York Times*)

Tales of Hoffmann
Ernst Theodor Amadeus Hoffmann   Translated by R.J. Hollingdale   1982 (1815–19)
Hoffman was a lawyer by day, but at night became a fantasist with a leaning to the

freakish and weird. Most of his stories have been in print continuously since they were first published. This collection includes his most famous including *Mademoiselle de Scudery*, *Doge und Dogaressa* and *Rat Krespel*.

✔ **Buddenbrooks** Thomas Mann (1957 (1902)
Written when Mann was only 26, *Buddenbrooks* charts the decline of a German family at the end of the last century. It is considered Mann's masterpiece and was banned and burned by Hitler.

✔ **The Adventures of Baron Münchausen** Rudolph Erich Raspe 1989 (1785)
A spoof travelogue in which the author borrowed freely from the classics, medieval literature and fairy stories.

✔ **All Quiet on the Western Front** Erich Maria Remarque 1991 (1929)
Written by a soldier in the Kaiser's army, this was one of the finest novels to have come out of the First World War.

Food

✔ **The New German Cookbook** Jean Anderson and Hedy Würz. 1993
Over 230 contemporary and traditional recipes from all over Germany.

✔ **German Baking Today** Dr. Oetker 1987
Well-illustrated recipes.

General Background

✔ **Germany and the Germans** John Ardagh 1991 (1987)
A contemporary account of the country and its people, history, politics and psyche, updated to include post-unification.

✔ **The Germans** Gordon A. Craig 1991 (1982)
The German identity seen through a broad historical perspective; Craig examines the paradoxes of the German character by looking at religion, money, literature, democracy and nationalism.

✔ **Krauts!** Granta 42 1992
An issue dedicated to Germany and the Germans with pieces by Heinrich Böll, Ian Buruma, Günter Grass and Martha Gellhorn among many others.

Guides

✔ **Baedeker Germany** 1992

✔ **Cadogan Guide Germany** Rod Bolt 1994

✔ **German Country Inns and Itineraries** Karen Brown 1994 (1980)

✔ **Let's Go Germany and Switzerland** 1995

✔ **Germany. The Rough Guide** Gordon McLachlan 1992 (1989)

✔ **Michelin Green Guide Germany** 1993

✔ **Michelin Red Guide Deutschland** 1995

History

A History of Germany 1815–1985 W. Carr 1991 (1969)
To understand the power and political influence of Germany today, it is necessary to understand its past – particularly the period from the Congress of Vienna in 1815. This is considered the best single-volume survey of the subject.

✔ **A Concise History of Germany** Mary Fulbrook 1993 (1991)
A concise history from the early middle ages up to the present day which aims to be a guide to the broad sweep of developments in Germany over the last thousand years.

The Rise and Fall of the Third Reich William Shirer 1991 (1960)
Shirer was an American journalist who was in Germany during the Nazi period and was present at the Nuremburg trials; he had access to the secret German archives which were captured intact by the Allies.

✔ **The Germania** Tacitus Translated by H. Mattingly 1948 (98 AD)
Concise analyses of each warlike German tribe which show remarkable presience.

The Last Days of Hitler Hugh Trevor-Roper 1987 (1947)
A reconstruction of the last days of the Third Reich. Hugh Trevor-Roper, as an intelligence officer, was given the task of uncovering step by step the last weeks of Hitler's life: 'This is an incomparable book, by far the best written on any aspect of the second German war: a book sound in its scholarship, brilliant in its presentation, a delight for historians and laymen alike. No words of praise are too strong.' (A.J.P. Taylor *New Statesman*)

A Train of Powder *Rebecca West 1984 (1955)*
Includes Rebecca West's account of the Nuremburg trials, commissioned by the *Daily Telegraph*. Her sharp and illuminating journalism is at its best here.

Natural History *(see 'Europe – General')*

Photography

✔ **Germany** *Ivan Ivanji 1991*
A cross-section of colour photographs from throughout the country.

✔ **Germany. A Photographic Journey** *1994*
Published by Ziethen.

Travel Literature

✔ **A Visit to Germany, Italy and Malta, 1840–1841** *Hans Christian Andersen 1985*
Andersen travelled through Germany to the castle at Breitenburg, to Nuremburg, Munich and the Tyrol.

✔ **Vanishing Borders** *Michael Farr 1993 (1991) (see 'Poland' and 'Czech Republic')*
The author was the *Daily Telegraph* correspondent in East Germany before and after the revolutions and was able to travel around reporting on crucial meetings and observing daily life.

Deutschland: A Winter's Tale
Heinrich Heine 1986 (1843)
A travelogue in verse describing Heine's journey from exile in Paris to Hamburg mid-late nineteenth century; its first aim was satirical, Heine attacked Germany's antiquated institutions and its contemporary culture, especially the Romantic obsession with an idealized Middle Ages; its second aim was ideological, but its third aim was a lightness and a determination not to get bogged down by the earnestness of the first two aims.

✔ **A Time of Gifts** *Patrick Leigh Fermor (see 'Central and Eastern Europe')*

A Tramp Abroad *Mark Twain 1982 (1898) (see 'France', 'Italy')*
There is a fair amount about Germany at the start of this witty, poetic and informative book. Twain delighted in travelling slowly (a train that approached speeds of 45 mph was far too fast), so we can really absorb and

reflect on his writings about a Europe that no longer exists.

NORTHERN GERMANY

Guides
'I have seen the famous Cathedral,[Cologne] which is a fine building, but not half finished, and as such, an uncomfortable sight, for it looks like a broken promise to God.' Thomas Hood *Up the Rhine* 1840

✔ **Visitor's Guide: Northern Germany. A Moorland Guide** *Grant Bourne and Sabine Körner-Bourne 1993*

✔ **Prestel Guide: Museums in Cologne** *1992*
A guide to twenty-six collections.

RHINELAND

Guides

✔ **Insight Guide The Rhine** *1992*

✔ **Visitor's Guide Germany: Rhine and Mosel. A Moorland Guide** *John Marshall 1992*

Photography

✔ **The Rhine. A George Philip Travel Guide** *James Bentley*

Travel Literature

✔ **To the End of the Rhine** *Bernard Levin 1991 (1987)*
Bernard Levin follows the Rhine from the Alps through to Holland observing the art, architecture, music, politics and people en route.

SOUTHERN GERMANY

Guides

✔ **Baedeker Guide Stuttgart** *1987*

✔ **Visitor's Guide Southern Germany. A Moorland Guide** *Grant Bourne and Sabine Körner-Bourne 1991*

BAVARIA

'Bavaria is too humid, too green and lush, and mountains *never* move – they are *always* there. They go all different tones and colours – but still, they are always there. D.H. Lawrence, letter to A.W. McLeod, May 1913

Fiction

✔ **In a German Pension**
Katherine Mansfield   1964 (1911)
Katherine Mansfield's first collection of short stories are set in Bavaria.

✔ **A Model Childhood**   *Christa Wolf   1988 (1976)*
A fictionalized autobiography about growing up in Bavaria in the 1930s, in a Nazi family.

Guides

✔ **Bavaria. A Guide for the Civilized Traveller**   *James Bentley   1990*
A narrative travel guide.

✔ **Thomas Cook Travellers Guide Munich and Bavaria**   *1994*

Leisure

✔ **Walking in the Black Forest**   *Fleur and Colin Speakman   1990*

Photography

✔ **Bavaria. A Photographic Journey** *1993*
Published by Ziethen.

EASTERN GERMANY

Guides

✔ **A Guide to Eastern Germany**
James Bentley   1994 (1993)
Each chapter focuses on a major town and then tours the surrounding countryside.

✔ **Insight Guide Dresden**   *1992*

BERLIN

'We like our Berlin immensely –an ugly place it must be to anyone who comes to it hipped or solitary, or what is worse, with a disagreeable companion. But, to make a very novel quotation –'the mind is its own place' and can make a pretty town even of Berlin.' George Eliot, letter to John Chapman, 9th January 1854

Fiction

Winter: A Berlin Family 1899–1945
Len Deighton   1987
Saga of a Berlin family's fortunes from the First World War to the collapse of the Third Reich. Len Deighton also wrote *Funeral in Berlin* a spy-thriller set in Cold War Berlin.

✔ **Pentimento**   *Lillian Hellman   1979 (1973)*
Lillian Hellman's memoirs contain *Julia*, a fictionalized account of one of her friends who were caught up in the Berlin resistance.

✔ **Mr Norris Changes Trains**   *1987 (1935)*
✔ **Goodbye to Berlin**
Christopher Isherwood   1993 (1939)
Christopher Isherwood lived in Berlin for four years and his novels clearly evoke the feeling during the time of the rise of the Nazis.

✔ **The Innocent**   *Ian McEwan   1990*
Set in 1950s Berlin, a post office worker is caught up in Cold War espionage: 'To call *The Innocent* a spy novel would be like calling *The Lord of the Flies* a boy's adventure yarn . . . the plot crackles like thin ice with dread and suspense . . . it ensures McEwan's major status.' (John Carey *The Sunday Times*)

General Background

✔ **Berlin. The Biography of a City**
Anthony Read and David Fisher   1994
The history past and present and the future of Berlin, from its rise as an outpost on the fringe of the Holy Roman Empire to becoming a big and powerful city.

✔ **Berlin: Coming in From the Cold**
Ken Smith   1991 (1990)
Ken Smith watched what was happening in the streets of Berlin in the months after the wall came down.

✔ **The Berlin Diaries of Marie 'Missie' Vassiltchikov 1940–45**   *1991 (1985)*
The author was a white Russian emigré who was caught in Germany with her family at the outbreak of war. A courageous woman, she became involved in the Resistance eventually having to flee from Vienna before the advancing Red Army.

Guides

✔ **Cadogan City Guide Berlin**
Andrew Gumbel   1991

✔ **Berlin. The Rough Guide**   Jack Holland
and John Gawthrop   1993 (1990)

✔ **Slow Walks in Berlin. A Visitor's
Companion**   Michael Leitch   1993
Twenty-two walks around the city.

Travel Literature

Zoo Station   Ian Walker   1988 (1987)
A lively and well informed account of Berlin
in the late 1980s when the two faces of east
and west were so different from each other.

GIBRALTAR

'It . . . is suggestive of a 'gob' of mud on the
end of a shingle.' Mark Twain *The Innocents
Abroad* 1869

Guide

✔ **Discover Gibraltar**   Terry Palmer   1990
(1987)
A very brief guide to the history and sites.

History

Gibraltar   José Pla   1955
The history of Gibraltar and the reasons for
the claims on it.

Travel Literature

A Journey to Gibraltar   Robert Henrey
1945 (1943)
Most of the journey is spent getting to Gibraltar via Portugal and Spain.

GREECE

'It is the only place I ever was contented
in.' Lord Byron, letter to Edward John
Trelawney 15 June 1823

Art and Archaeology

✔ **Greek Art**   John Boardman   1989 (1964)
A very good concise introduction in the
Thames and Hudson 'World of Art' series.

✔ **Greek Art. Its Development,
Character and Influence**   R.M. Cook
1976 (1972)
An examination of the aesthetic canon which
was created by Classical and Hellenistic
Greek art.

✔ **Greek Architecture**   A.W. Lawrence
1983 (1957)
A well-illustrated introduction to Greek
architecture in the Pelican 'History of Art'
series.

Art of the Byzantine Era
David Talbot Rice   1963
An illustrated and good introduction to an
art which was essentially Christian and controlled by the Church, but which at the same
time contained a degree of abstraction in its
relationship to nature while being very complex. It covers the long period from 550 to
1450.

✔ **A Handbook of Greek Art. A Survey
of the Visual Arts of Ancient Greece**
Gisela M.A. Richter   1987 (1959)
Well-illustrated book arranged according to
subject matter, from the tenth century BC up
to the Hellenistic period.

✔ **Hellenistic Sculpture**   R.R.R. Smith
1991
A concise introduction with 387 illustrations
in the Thames and Hudson 'World of Art'
series.

Biography

✔ **Eleni**   Nicholas Gage   1989 (1983)
Eleni Gatzoyiannis was tortured and shot in
a Greek mountain village in 1948 for helping
her children escape the Communist guerrillas during the Greek Civil War; her son
eventually arrived in America and became
an investigative reporter for *The New York
Times*. This is the story of his search and
reconstruction of those events.

Classics

✔ **The Histories**   Herodotus   Translated by
Aubrey de Sélincourt   1972 (1954) (see 'Turkey')

✔ **The Odyssey**   Translated by E.V. Rieu
1991 (1946),
✔ **The Iliad**   Homer   Translated by Martin
Hammond   1987
The Odyssey tells of Odysseus' return to
Ithaca from the Trojan war and his various
escapades before his eventual reunion with
his wife Penelope. *The Iliad*, an epic poem,
tells of the critical events in the last year of

the Trojan War which determined the fate of Troy.

✔ **The Guide to Greece** Pausanias
Translated by Peter Levi 1979 (1971)
The first volume is to Central Greece and the second to Southern Greece. Pausanias was a doctor from Asia Minor who spent ten to twenty years travelling through Greece in the second century AD. He describes buildings, tombs and statues and gives much mythological, religious and historical background to what he saw. Peter Levi revisited the sites and has written a detailed accompanying commentary.

✔ **The Age of Alexander** Plutarch
Translated by Ian Scott-Kilvert 1977
Agesilaus, Pelopidas, Dion, Timoleon, Demosthenes, Phocion, Alexander, Demetrius and Pyrrhus are the subjects of Plutarch's Nine Greek Lives which was written in the first century AD and which charts history from the collapse of Athens to the rise of Macedonia. *Plutarch on Sparta* (translated by Richard J.A. Talbert) 1988 is about the lives of Lycurgus, Agis and Cleomenes and does much to explain the society of Sparta.

✔ **History of the Peloponnesian War**
Thucydides Fifteen extracts translated by M.G. Dickson 1991
The Peloponnesian War fought between Athens and her allies and Sparta and hers, lasted from 431–404 BC. Thucydides, an Athenian, decided early on that he was going to be meticulous about the chronology of it. The extracts chosen here include the bloody conflict in Corfu.

✔ **The History of My Times** Xenophon
Translated by Rex Warner 1979
Xenophon was born in Athens about 430 BC, but having served under Cyrus in his revolt against the King of Persia, was exiled to Scillus. He began to write there; his *History* should not be considered accurate, but it does give a good feeling for the time.

Fiction/Poetry

Collected Poems C.P. Cavafy Translated by Edmund Keeley and Philip Sherrard 1984 (1968)
Cavafy lived in Alexandria for most of his life; his work, which is now extremely well thought of, was not much favoured during his lifetime; this is a complete collection of 174 Cavafy poems.

✔ **The Seventh Garment**
Eugenia Fakinou 1991 (1983)
Three generations of women tell the stories

of their lives from the war of Independence to the colonel's junta.

✔ **The Greek Myths**
Robert Graves (2 vols.) 1990 (1955)
Robert Graves retells the Greek legends of gods and heroes in nearly 200 sections, covering the creation myths, the legends of the birth and lives of the great Olympians, the Argonaut voyage, the tale of Troy and the Theseus, Oedipus and Heracles cycles.

The Heroic Age Stratis Haviaras 1985
Fictionalized autobiography about growing up in Greece in the 1940s. *When the Tree Sings* (1980) is a novel which was described in *Publishers Weekly* as 'Stunning . . . This is a beautifully written novel – spare and poetic without ever becoming precious; terrifying without ever stooping to melodrama.'

✔ **Zorba the Greek** Nikos Kazantzakis
1971 (1953)
' . . . He has created in Zorba one of the great characters of modern fiction. Zorba re-flects Greek exhilaration at its best. Zorba, pure in feeling, makes havoc of monks, scholarship and the life of withdrawal . . . ' (*The Times Literary Supplement*). Other books by Kazantzakis include *Christ Recrucified* (1954), *Report to Greco*, *Freedom and Death* (1956) and *The Fratricides*.

✔ **The King Must Die** Mary Renault
1993 (1967)
Through her re-creation of the myth of Theseus, the boy-king of Eleusis, Mary Renault brings alive the world of ancient Greece. Her other books include ✔ *Fire from Heaven* (1972) – set during the wars between Athens and Sparta, ✔ *The Last of the Wine* 1990 (1956) – about Alexander's boyhood and ✔ *The Mask of Apollo* about Nikeratos the gifted tragic actor from the fourth century BC who travels through Greece with a company of players.

✔ **Collected Poems 1924–1955**
George Seferis Translated by Edmund Keeley and Philip Sherrard 1986 (1967)
A parallel text of almost all Seferis' work.

Food

✔ **Greek Food** Rena Salaman 1993 (1983)
This recently reissued classic demonstrates the variety of Greek food through recipes and anecdotes.

Guides

✔ **American Express Pocket Guide Athens and the Classical Sites** *1992*

✔ **Blue Guide Greece** *Robin Barber 1990 (1987)*

✔ **Greece. The Rough Guide** *Mark Ellingham et al 1992*

✔ **Everyman Guide: Athens and the Peloponnese** *1995*

The Traveller's Key to Ancient Greece *Richard G. Geldard 1990 (1989)* A guide to the sacred places of Ancient Greece.

✔ **Greece. Travel Survival Kit** *Rosemary Hall 1994*

✔ **Groc's Candid Guide The Peloponnese** *Geoffrey O'Connell 1993*

✔ **Byzantine and Medieval Greece: Churches, Castles and Art** *Paul Hetherington 1991* A short history of Byzantine and Medieval Greece is followed by descriptions of the various buildings.

✔ **Insight Guide Greece** *1992*

✔ **The Companion Guide to Mainland Greece** *Brian de Jongh 1989*

✔ **Let's Go Greece and Turkey 1995**

✔ **Michelin Green Guide Greece** *1991*

✔ **Greece. The Versatile Guide** *Paul Strathern 1994*

History

✔ **A Traveller's History of Greece** *Timothy Boatswain and Colin Nicolson 1989* A basic history with a gazetteer of the major events.

✔ **Pelican History of Greece** *A.R. Burn 1982 (1965)* Aimed at the general reader with little prior knowledge of Greek history; begins with Crete, Mycenae and the Heroic Age and finishes with the demise of ancient Greece.

Early Greek Travellers and the Hellenic Ideal *David Constantine 1984* An introduction to the most important and interesting men who went to Greece and wrote accounts of their journeys. It also discusses the idea of Greece held by the travellers and their contemporaries. [Colin Thubron]

✔ **A Concise History of Greece** *Richard Clogg 1992* From the late eighteenth century to the present day.

✔ **The Search for Ancient Greece** *Roland and Françoise Etienne 1992 (1990)* An excellent small introduction in the Thames and Hudson 'New Horizons' series.

✔ **The World of Odysseus** *M.I. Finley 1979* An overview of ancient Greece with chapters on Homer, bards and heroes, wealth and labour, home and community and morals and values.

✔ **The Greeks** *H.D.F. Kitto 1991 (1951)* Kitto elaborates on the theme that the Greeks evolved 'a totally new conception of what human life was for'. Raymond Mortimer wrote in *The Sunday Times* that it was 'The best introduction I have ever read to Ancient Greece. The author's liveliness of mind and style has enabled him to make a mass of information appetizing and digestible.'

✔ **Alexander the Great** *Robin Lane Fox 1986 (1973)* An easy-to-read yet erudite life of Alexander the Great whose empire at his death, aged thirty-two, stretched from Greece to India and covered two million square miles: 'I do not know which to admire most, his vast erudition, his exact scholarship or his imaginative grasp of so remote and complicated a period and such a complex personality'. (*The Sunday Times*)

✔ **Byzantium: the Early Centuries**
✔ **Byzantium: the Apogee** *John Julius Norwich (see 'Turkey')*

✔ **The Fall of Constantinople 1453**
✔ **Byzantine Style and Civilization** *Steven Runciman (see 'Turkey')*

✔ **Modern Greece** *C.M. Woodhouse 1991 (1968)* Covers the period from Constantine's foundation of Constantinople in 324 AD up until 1990.

Leisure

✔ **Trekking in Greece. A Lonely Planet Walking Guide** *Marc Dubin 1993*

✔ **The Mountains of Greece. A Walker's Guide** *Tim Salmon 1986* Detailed descriptions of hiking routes and background information about mountain life.

Natural History

✔ Flowers of Greece and the Aegean
Anthony Huxley and William Taylor   1989 (1977)
Almost 500 colour photographs and 77 line drawings.

Flowers of Greece and the Balkans. A Field Guide   Oleg Polunin   1987 (1980)
Almost 3,000 species of flowering plants are named and described with 80 colour plates containing 483 photographs.

Photography

✔ Vanishing Greece   Photographs by Clay Perry   Introduction by Patrick Leigh Fermor   1991
A selection of varied colour photographs.

✔ Greece. A Pictorial Journey   1993
Published by Ziethen.

Travel Literature

The Flight of Ikaros   Kevin Andrews   1984 (1959)
The account of an archaeologist's life in rural Greece during and in the aftermath of the civil war; Andrews went to study medieval fortresses, but ended up writing this extremely readable book about modern Greek peasant life.

The Station   Robert Byron   1949 (1928)
Byron travelled to Mount Athos in his early twenties with two friends, David Talbot Rice and Mark Ogilvie-Grant. He hoped to discover the soul of Greece there through the 'one living articulate [Byzantine] community [preserved] by a fabulous compound of circumstances, into the present time'.

Travels to Jerusalem and the Holy Land through Egypt
Viscount de Chateaubriand   1835
Chateaubriand wrote this as a memoir of a year in his life rather than as a book of travels; he went to the East to complete a circle of studies. He spent a long while in Greece, visiting many of the islands before moving on to Turkey and the Holy Land. He combines much ancient history with his contemporary observations.

Deep into Mani   Peter Greenhalgh and Edward Eliopoulos   1985
Interesting to read this account of the Mani written twenty-five years after Patrick Leigh Fermor's book. The authors had spent over 30 years exploring the area, so knew it extremely well.

Journals of a Landscape Painter in Greece and Albania   Edward Lear   1988 (1851)
The witty account of two journeys in autumn 1848 and spring 1849; the Grecian part was to Epirus and Thessaly in the spring of 1849.

✔ Mani   1984 (1958)
✔ Roumeli   1983 (1966)
Patrick Leigh Fermor
Two of the best books on Greece today, they are full of scholarship and anecdotes about the history and gradual demise of many rural communities with superb descriptions of the countryside. 'Patrick Leigh Fermor's Mani is a near-perfect travel book: magnificently evocative not only of the remote region he describes but of all Greek culture.' (Colin Thubron)

✔ The Hill of Kronos   Peter Levi   1980
A beautifully written and evocative book about the landscape and buildings pre and during the colonels' junta. Levi is attracted to Greece not only by the intellect but by senses and emotions too; this 'love affair', combining his classical knowledge with his feelings makes for an exceptional book.

✔ The Colossus of Maroussi
Henry Miller   1991 (1941)
Miller visited Greece with Lawrence Durrell in 1939, after a friend of his in Paris had described it in 'paint' like terms; in his book he manages to capture the essence of Greece: 'Colossus was written from some other level of my being. What I like about it is that it's a joyous book, it expresses joy, it gives joy.'

An Affair of the Heart   Dilys Powell   1973 (1957)
Three journeys to Greece: the first in 1945, just after the war, the second in 1953, during the civil war and the third in 1954 when she joined an archaeological and diving expedition on Chios.

GREEK ISLANDS – GENERAL

Fiction

The Magus   John Fowles   1967 (1966)
Nicholas Urfe leaves London to work as a school-master on a lonely Greek island. He see this as an escape from his life in England, but is totally unprepared for what happens to him when he meets Maurice Conchis, a rich, cosmopolitan psychic.

Guides

✔ **Cadogan Guide Greek Islands**
Dana Facaros   1993 (1979)

✔ **Insight Guide Greek Islands**   1992

Photography

The Greek Islands   Lawrence Durrell   1984
(1978)
Over 100 photographs accompanied by Durrell's text.

Travel Literature

✔ **A Journey Through the Aegean
Islands**   George Galt   1988 (1982)
Galt visited many of the Aegean islands both large and small, well-known and not so well-known.

CORFU AND THE IONIAN ISLANDS

'A very clean and rather attractive town. It reminded me of Brighton.' Evelyn Waugh Diary 9 January 1927

Guides

✔ **Cadogan Guide The Greek Islands:
Ionian**   1994

✔ **Corfu, Paxos and Antipaxos. Greek
Island Series**   Lorna Chaplin   1992

✔ **Corfu. A Windrush Island Guide**
Nigel Coleman and Conrad Mewton   1991

✔ **Landscapes of Corfu. A Sunflower
Guide**   Noel Rochford   1992 (1987)

✔ **Landscapes of Paxos. A Sunflower
Book**   Noel Rochford   1990

Photography

✔ **Corfu. The Garden Isle**   Presented by Spiro Flamburiari   1994
A huge, well-illustrated book of houses, interiors, landscapes, artefacts and people.

Travel Literature

✔ **My Family and Other Animals**
Gerald Durrell   1977 (1956)
An hilarious book about Durrell's childhood on Corfu with his 'family and other animals' which included toads, tortoises, bats, butter-

flies, scorpions, glow-worms and octopuses among others.

✔ **Prospero's Cell**   Lawrence Durrell   1983
(1945)
A guide to the landscape and manners on the island of Corfu.

The Ionian Islands   Arthur Foss   1969
The book is divided into six parts: Zakynthos, Cephalonia, Ithaka, Levkas, Corfu and Paxos.

ARGO-SARONIC

Guide

✔ **Groc Candid Guide: Mainland
Argo-Saronic and Sporades Islands.
Including Spetses and Skiathos**
Geoffrey O'Connell   1988

CYCLADES

Guides

✔ **Cadogan Guide The Greek Islands:
Cyclades**   1994

✔ **Ios, Santorini and the South East
Cyclades. Greek Island Series**
Lorna Chaplin   1989

✔ **North West Cyclades. Greek Islands
Series**   Lorna Chaplin   1987

✔ **The Central Cyclades. Greek Island
Series**   Bill Taylor   1987

Travel Literature

**The Cyclades, or Life Among Insular
Greeks**   James Theodore Bent   1881
Despite its publication date this is still the best account of island customs and folklore.

RHODES AND THE DODECANESE

'Rhodes, where history lies sleeping.' Freya Stark Beyond Euphrates 1951.

Guides

✔ **Cadogan Guide The Greek Islands:
Dodecanese**   1994

✔ **Insight Pocket Guide Rhodes** *1992*

✔ **Groc Candid Guide: Rhodes and the Dodecanese Islands**
Geoffrey O'Connell 1988 (1985)

Travel Literature

✔ **The Voyage of Argo**
Apollonius of Rhodes Translated by E.V. Rieu 1971 (1959)
Written in the third century BC this is the only account we have of Jason's voyage in quest of the Golden Fleece. It was treated with derision when it was first published but the second version was acclaimed by the Rhodians.

✔ **Reflections on a Marine Venus**
Lawrence Durrell 1978 (1952)
'The marine Venus' is a statue found by sailors in their nets at the bottom of Rhodes harbour and which much appealed to Durrell, who thought of her as the 'presiding genius' of the place. He was assigned to Rhodes as an information officer in 1945.

EAST AND NORTH AEGEAN ISLANDS

Guides

✔ **Landscapes of Samos. A Sunflower Guide** *Brian and Eileen Anderson 1989*

✔ **North Aegean Islands. Greek Island Series** *John Fawsett 1989 (1984)*

✔ **Insight Pocket Guide Aegean Islands – Mykonos and Santorini** *1994*

✔ **Groc's Candid Guide Samos and NE Aegean Islands** *Geoffrey O'Connell 1987*

SPORADES AND EVIA

General Background

Portrait of a Greek Mountain Village
Juliet du Boulay 1979 (1974)
The author built up a very personal relationship with the villagers in Ambéli in Evia; as a woman she saw village life from a particular perspective and was able to record in detail the habits and customs of a dying village community. *'Portrait of a Greek Mountain Village* ranks with John Campbell's study of northern Greek shepherds as one of

the two best books written about Greece in this century.' (Peter Levi *Times Literary Supplement*)

Guide

✔ **Groc Candid Guide: Mainland Argo-Saronic and Sporades Islands. Including Spetses and Skiathos**
Geoffrey O'Connell 1988

Travel Literature

✔ **An Island Apart** *Sara Wheeler 1993 (1992)*
Evia is the second largest island in Greece, yet it remains largely unspoilt. Sara Wheeler spent five months travelling through the island; speaking fluent Greek she was able to totally involve herself in island life. 'Warm hearted and highly informative . . . Wheeler demonstrates Fermor-like fascination for, and understanding of, Hellenic rural life.' (*The Daily Telegraph*)

CRETE
'The people of Crete unfortunately make more history than they can consume locally.' 'Saki' (H.H. Munro) *The Jesting of Arlington Stringham* 1911

Art and Archaeology

✔ **Palaces of Minoan Crete**
Gerald Cadogan 1980 (1976)
A clearly laid out guide to the palaces and grand town and country houses which discusses their significance in the context of the lives of the Minoan people.

✔ **The Archaeology of Crete**
J.D.S. Pendlebury 1979 (1939)
A serious account, with notes and plates, from the earliest times to the Roman Age.

The Villa Ariadne *Dilys Powell 1973*
The story of British archaeology in Crete based on the villa at Knossos where all the British archaeologists stayed.

The Last Lemon Grove *Jackson Webb 1977*
A very atmospheric book by an American who was living a hermetic and solitary life in Paleohóra. His Cretan neighbours helped him build a house and advised him on his planting; he became very involved in his life there which became entwined with theirs, yet maintained an inevitable detachment en-

abling him to write a book which Dilys Powell described as having a 'unique quality. I have read no other book quite like it . . . He belongs, really belongs, to the Crete of now.'

Fiction

See Nikos Kazantzakis: 'Greece – General'

Ill Met by Moonlight W. Stanley Moss
1985 (1950)
An account of the adventurous capture of General Kreipe in Crete in April 1944; he was driven past over twenty of his own guard posts with a hidden British soldier pressing a gun into his side. Moss, along with Patrick Leigh-Fermor (q.v.) was there. Made into a successful film.

✔ **The King Must Die** Mary Renault
1993 (1958) (see 'Greece – General')
The epic of Theseus whose famed enemy is the half-bull, half-man Minotaur.

✔ **Officers and Gentleman**
Evelyn Waugh   1986 (1955)
Includes an account of the Battle for Crete and the evacuation and flight.

General Background

Crete. Its Past, Present and People
Adam Hopkins   1977
A very good introduction to Cretan history and society, beginning with Homer. Hopkins discusses all the major archaeological sites, but also writes about contemporary Crete.

The Great Island Michael Llewellyn Smith
1973 (1961)
A background and introduction to Crete with much about the folk tradition, which aims to place Crete in its proper place in Greek history and thus is not about Minoan civilization and archaeology.

Guides

✔ **The Visitor's Guide Crete. A Moorland Guide** Fiona Bulmer   1990

✔ **Blue Guide Crete** Pat Cameron   1993

✔ **Crete. The Rough Guide** John Fisher
1992 (1988)

✔ **Sunflower Guides: Landscapes of Eastern Crete** (1991)
✔ **Landscapes of Western Crete**
Jonnie Godfrey and Elizabeth Karslake   (1991)

✔ **Insight Guide Crete** 1992

✔ **Groc Candid Guide Crete**
Geoffrey O'Connell   1987

History

✔ **Crete: the Battle and the Resistance** Antony Beevor   1992 (1991)
A lively history with much about the characters involved. 'Excellent . . . an arresting account of the whole war on Crete, including the ghastly experiences of the Cretans under German occupation.' (John Keegan *The Sunday Telegraph*)

The Bull of Minos Leonard Cottrell   1969
(1953)
Easy-to-read account of the discoveries of Schliemann and Evans including the Palace of the Sea-Kings at Knossos.

Travel Literature

The Cretan Journal Edward Lear
The diary of Lear's trip to Crete in 1864. The reprint had excellent colour reproductions of his sketches and watercolours.

Travels in Crete Robert Pashley   1970
(1837)
An interesting account by a nineteenth-century British traveller who spent the summer of 1833 in the Ionian Islands, Albania and Greece and who in the winter of the same year left Malta for Crete; he spent a year writing up his book of travels in Crete which is detailed, but nonetheless readable.

The Cretan Runner George Psychoundakis
1978 (1955)
Translated by Patrick Leigh Fermor; the author was a guide and message-runner for the British and the resistance during the invasion of Crete.

ITALY
'Italy is my Magnet.' Lord Byron, Letter to Annabella Milbanke, 20 April 1814.

Art and Archaeology

✔ **Civilisation of the Renaissance in Italy** Jacob Burckhardt   Translated by S.G.C. Middlemore   1990 (1860)
Shortly after its publication, Burckhardt's

interpretation of the Renaissance period between Dante and Michelangelo became extremely influential and is now regarded as one of the classics of nineteenth-century historical writing.[Colin Thubron]

✔ **History of Italian Renaissance Art**
Frederick Hartt 1987 (1970)
A large and worthwhile introduction to this huge subject published by Thames and Hudson and well illustrated with colour and black and white plates.

✔ **Early Renaissance** *Michael Levey 1977 (1967)*
Levey shows the early Renaissance preference for sober, logical and harmonious art, which was, nevertheless true to experience. Well illustrated with black and white photographs.

✔ **An Architect in Italy**
Caroline Mauduit 1988
'This is a lovely book, observant, informative, elegant, true' writes Hugh Casson in the foreword and indeed the wash drawings of buildings and the text that accompanies them are delightful.

✔ **The Architecture of the Italian Renaissance** *Peter Murray 1988 (1969)*
From Romanesque to Palladio. In the Thames and Hudson 'World of Art' series.

✔ **Art of the Renaissance** *Peter and Linda Murray 1989 (1963)*
A mixture of 251 colour and black and white photographs are included in this general introduction in the Thames and Hudson World of Art series.

✔ **Mannerism** *John Shearman 1977 (1967)*
Mannerism was the style that came between the Renaissance and the Baroque in the sixteenth century; it was self-consciously 'stylish', but its flamboyance is again appreciated today.

✔ **Lives of the Artists** *Giorgio Vasari Translated by George Bull 1987*
An abridgement in two volumes of the first real work of art history, about Vasari's predecessors and contemporaries.

Classics - Ancient

✔ **Selected Works** *Cicero Translated by Michael Grant 1971*
Cicero lived from 106–43 BC and was the greatest of Roman orators, being elected consul for 63.

✔ **Sixteen Satires** *Juvenal Translated by Niall Rudd 1992*
Juvenal began publishing in about 112 AD, under the bloody Domitian and went on until 130 AD under Hadrian. His attacks on the vices and excesses of Imperial Rome have been much used by writers including Ben Jonson, Dryden and Dr Johnson who described his writing as 'a mixture of gaiety and stateliness, of pointed sentences and declamatory grandeur'.

✔ **Stories of Rome** *Livy Translated by Roger Nichols 1982*
A selection of stories with linking narrative and commentary which give an account of the early history of Rome.

✔ **Meditations** *Marcus Aurelius Translated by Maxwell Staniforth 1964*
Marcus Aurelius wrote his *Meditations* during the campaign against the barbarians 121–180 AD.

✔ **Metamorphoses**
✔ **Erotic Poems** *Ovid Translated by Peter Green 1982*
Ovid was exiled from Rome in 8 AD by order of the Emperor Augustus, due in part to the alleged obscenity of *Ars Amatoria*, a sophisticated and witty guide to 'sexual siege warfare'.

✔ **The Aeneid** *Virgil Prose translation by David West 1990*
Inspired by Homer and was in turn an inspiration for Dante and Milton. Through Aeneas, the legendary survivor of Troy and father of the Roman race, we can see every facet of human life.

Classics - Italian

✔ **The Decameron** *Giovanni Boccaccio Translated by Guido Waldman 1993 (c.1351)*
One hundred short stories set in Florence during the Black Death of 1348; ten young noblemen and women, who have escaped the plague, tell each other stories in a villa outside the city.

✔ **Autobiography** *Benvenuto Cellini 1970 (c.1560)*
Self-centred record of the sculptor and master goldsmith's career. He began his *Autobiography* in Florence in 1558 and his own heroic opinion of himself makes this a sparkling autobiography.

✔ **The Divine Comedy** *Dante Alighieri Translated by Laurence Binyon 1947 (c.1321)*
Little is known of Dante's life: his family were impoverished city noblemen and three

major events in his life affected him deeply –
the death of Beatrice, his banishment from
Florence and the collapse of Henry VII's Italian campaign; he pursued the cult of Ideal
Love, was a philosopher and scholar, refor-
mer and prophet but was first and foremost
a poet and his great work is a poetic look at
the moral scheme of God's creation.

✔ **The Prince** *Niccolò Machiavelli*
Translated by Robert M. Adams   1992 (1513)
The famous treatise on statecraft which did
much to form foreigners' preconceptions of
the country.

✔ **The Betrothed** *Alessandro Manzoni*
1972 (1827)
Renzo and Lucia, the hero and heroine of
Manzoni's masterpiece, have to flee from the
villainous Don Rodrigo and their peaceful
village into an Italy which, in the early seventeenth-century, is under foreign domination
and is at the mercy of petty noblemen.

✔ **Selections from the Canzoniere**
Petrarch   Translated by Mark Musa   1985 (1470)
Petrarch dealt with worldly fame, a driving
force in his life, and with secular love, making him known as the first modern poet.
Although born in Arezzo, Petrarch and his
family moved to Avignon in 1312; he became
a diplomat, classical scholar and poet laureate but makes no mention of his Italian
poetry in his *Letter to Posterity*, wanting to
be remembered as a scholar and lover of
classical antiquity writing in Latin.

Fiction/Poetry

The Quality of Light *Ann and*
Michael Caesar (eds.)   1993
An anthology of contemporary Italian
writers.

✔ **If on a Winter's Night a Traveller**
Italo Calvino   1992 (1981)
An extremely imaginative and ingenious al-
legorical and witty book. Calvino also wrote
✔ *Adam, One Afternoon*, (1992) *Castle of
Crossed Destinies, Invisible Cities, Difficult
Loves* and *Mr Palomar*.

✔ **The Name of the Rose** *Umberto Eco*
1992 (1980)
A labyrinthian detective story set in a monastery: 'The late medieval world, teetering on
the edge of discoveries and ideas that will
hurl it into one more recognisably like ours,
its thought, its life-style, its intense political
and ecclesiastical intrigues . . . its steamy
and seductive currents of heresy of thought
. . . all these are evoked with a force and a wit
that are breathtaking.' (*Financial Times*)

✔ **The Talented Mr Ripley**
Patricia Highsmith   1976 (1956)
The action in this study of a schizophrenic
murderer moves all over Italy.

✔ **If This Is a Man** *Primo Levi   1979 (1958)*
Levi's book about his arrest by the Fascists
and his transportation to a concentration
camp, where he was one of the sole survivors,
is free from self-indulgence and recrimina-
tion. In *The Truce* which is about his journey
home to his native Turin, there is a hesitant
note of hope.

✔ **The Conformist** *Alberto Moravia   1983*
(1952)
Above all Marcello wishes to conform; he
marries and joins the Fascist Government as
a secret agent, but through his pursuit of
normality is relentlessly drawn into murder,
betrayal and death.

✔ **Confessions of Zeno** *Italo Svevo   1982*
(1923)
Svevo used Freud's methods as a framework,
albeit ironically, in this novel in which an
analyst publishes a book to annoy his patient; the theme is an addiction to cigarettes
and every 'last cigarette' is recalled.

✔ **Memoirs of Hadrian**
Marguerite Yourcenar   1986 (1954)
As Hadrian was dying he wrote a long vale-
dictory letter to Marcus Aurelius explaining
his philosophy about ruling the far-flung
Roman Empire.

Food

✔ **Italian Food** *Elizabeth David   1989*
(1954)
The book which revolutionized the English
kitchen

✔ **The Classic Italian Cookbook**
Marcella Hazan   1981 (1973)
'The best book on Italian cooking published
to date in this country,' (Philippa Davenport
The Standard). Also *The Second Classic Ita-
lian Cookbook* and *Marcella's Kitchen*.

General Background

✔ **The Italians** *Luigi Barzini   1968 (1964)*
Barzini, an Italian, manages to get to the real
core of Italy and the Italians by cutting
through the familiar clichés: 'He hits his
nails on the head with bitter-sweet vitality.'
(*The Observer*)

Italian Labyrinth *John Haycroft   1985*
Haycroft knew the country extremely well
and has written an entertaining portrait of

contemporary Italy seen against the background of its history.

✔ **The Mirror Maker** Primo Levi 1993 (1986)
A collection of articles, stories and poems which Levi wrote during his time at La Stampa.

Italia, Italia Peter Nichols 1975 (1973)
The author was the *The Times* correspondent in Italy and wrote this perceptive and authoritative account in the 1970s.

✔ **The New Italians** Charles Richards 1994
The author was in Rome for the *Independent* and here takes a perceptive look at the Italians today.

✔ **The Moro Affair and the Mystery of Majorana** Leonardo Sciascia 1991 (1978)
A recreation of the Red Brigade's kidnap, trial and murder of Aldo Moro and also of the disappearance of the Sicilian physicist, Ettore Majorana, in 1938.

✔ **Getting it Right in Italy**
William Ward 1990
How to live in and understand contemporary Italy. Full of anecdote and interest about what to wear at various functions, how to buy a house or flat and how to get rid of unwanted admirers. But it is much more and presents useful advice and information on Italy and the Italians.

Guides

✔ **Baedeker Guide Italy** 1993

✔ **Italy. The Rough Guide** Ros Belford, Martin Dunford and Celia Woolfrey 1993 (1990)

✔ **Cadogan Guide Italy** Dana Facaros and Michael Pauls 1994

✔ **Fodor Italy 1995**

✔ **Italy. The Versatile Guide** Leslie and Adrian Gardiner 1994

✔ **Italy. Travel Survival Kit** Helen and John Gillman 1993

✔ **Italy by Train** Tim Jepson 1993
A guide for the independent rail traveller to Italy. Routes but not timetables.

✔ **Karen Brown's Italian Country Bed and Breakfasts** 1993 (1992)

✔ **Karen Brown's Italian Country Inns and Itineraries** 1993 (1985)

✔ **Italy. A Grand Tour for the Modern Traveller** Charles Fitzroy 1992 (1991)
Divided into area, each section contains a general introduction, specific walks and expeditions; there is an emphasis on the art and the author mentions places to eat en route.

✔ **Insight Guide Italy** 1992

✔ **Let's Go Italy 1995**

✔ **Michelin Green Guide Italy**

✔ **Michelin Red Guide Italy 1995**

History

✔ **The Decline and Fall of the Roman Empire** Edward Gibbon (Penguin edition abridged and edited by Dero A. Saunders) 1981 (1776-88)
Gibbon's massive, rich and ironic work which can be said to have 'something special in it for everyone' begins with the age of Antonines (C2 AD) and finishes with the demise of the empire in the West with the Fall of Constantinople in 1453 AD. Gibbon's definition of history as 'little more than the register of the crimes, follies and misfortunes of mankind' is evident throughout the narrative.

✔ **A History of Contemporary Italy. Society and Politics 1943–1988**
Paul Ginsborg 1990
An account of the profound economic, social and demographic changes that overtook Italy after the war.

✔ **A Traveller's History of Italy**
Valerio Lintner 1989
The development of Italy from prehistoric times until today told as a simple straightforward history.

The Caesars Allan Massie 1988 (1983)
A witty account of the lives of the Caesars which questions many of the established myths, but which has Augustus emerging as the sanest and most balanced Caesar.

✔ **History of the Italian People**
Giuliano Procacci 1991 (1968)
Professor Procacci pinpoints 1000 AD as the time when European supremacy began to take root and traces Italy's progression within its European context, through the communes of the eleventh century to the birth of the European Renaissance and the two world wars.

Leisure

✔ **Eating Out in Italy** Diane Seed 1989
A personal selection of over 150 restaurants, with colour illustrations by Robert Budwig which capture the warmth of Italy and her food.

Natural History (see 'Europe – General')

Photography

✔ **The Classic Italian Garden**
Judith Chatfield 1991
A paperback full of colour photographs illustrating gardens and their houses.

✔ **Discovering the Hill Towns of Italy**
Paul Duncan 1990
History, photographs and social life of the hill towns all over rural Italy.

✔ **Traditional Houses of Rural Italy**
Paul Duncan 1993
Houses from Tuscany, Umbria, Lombardy, the Veneto, Emilia-Romagna and Liguria.

✔ **The Italian Garden** Photographs by Geoffrey James Essay by Robert Harbison 1991
Black and white photographs.

Italian Villas and Gardens Georgina Masson 1959
A large and beautifully illustrated book with black and white photographs. Divided regionally: Liguria and Piedmont, Lombardy, Venetia, Emilia, the Marche, Tuscany, Lazio and the Kingdom of Naples. Also *Italian Gardens*. [Colin Thubron]

✔ **Italian Gardens** Charles A. Platt 1993 (1894)
Black and white photographs and plans by the great garden designer Charles Platt.

Travel Literature

Pictures from Italy Charles Dickens 1989 (1846)
Dickens wrote a series of letters from Italy to friends which were published in the *Daily News* and eventually became *Pictures from Italy*. He wrote anecdotal and amusing pieces from Parma, Modena, Bologna, Venice, Verona, Mantua, Pisa, Naples, Siena, Rome and Florence. [Jan Morris]

To Noto or London to Sicily in a Ford
Duncan Fallowell 1989
A witty, idiosyncratic and off-beat drive

through France and Italy with Noto in Sicily as the final destination.

✔ **Italian Journey** Wolfgang Goethe 1970 (1788)
Goethe's interest in the classical world led him to Italy in 1786; during his trip he kept a journal and wrote many letters which form the basis of his *Italian Journey*.

Italian Hours Henry James 1987
Henry James made several journeys to Italy during the 1870s, recorded in twenty-two 'notes' about the history, art, architecture and people.

✔ **D.H. Lawrence and Italy**
D.H. Lawrence
Lawrence's three books about Italy collected together: *Sea and Sardinia* 1989 (1923) *Twilight in Italy* and *Etruscan Places*.

A Traveller in Italy H.V. Morton 1984 (1964)
A journey through Lombardy, Emilia, Veneto and Tuscany, written in a somewhat dated style, but nonetheless illuminating.

✔ **Love and War in the Apennines**
Eric Newby 1983 (1971)
Eric Newby was captured in Sicily in 1942; he escaped from the prison camp before the Germans arrived and was helped by the local schoolmaster's daughter, Wanda, who later became his wife. Very funny accounts of Newby's attempts to melt into the local Italian background.

✔ **Travels through France and Italy**
Tobias Smollett 1981 (1766) (see 'France')

Rome, Naples and Florence Stendhal

A Tramp Abroad Mark Twain 1982 (1898)
(see 'France', 'Germany', 'Switzerland')
Twain travelled to Milan, Venice and Florence.

NORTHERN AND CENTRAL ITALY - GENERAL

'How glorious that Cathedral is! worthy almost of standing face to face with the snow Alps; and itself a sort of snow dream by an artist architect, taken asleep in a glacier!' [Milan Cathedral] Elizabeth Barrett Browning, letter, 1851

Autobiography/Biography

✔ **The Road to San Giovanni**
Italo Calvino 1993
A book of five parts which is the closest that Calvino came to writing an autobiography.

Fiction

✔ **The Garden of the Finzi Continis**
Giorgio Bassani 1992 (1965)
A nostalgic novel set in Ferrara in the Jewish community during the Fascist period: 'A poignant and exquisitely sensitive piece of work . . . the reader will remember it for a long time.' (Richard Church)

✔ **Seminar on Youth** *Aldo Busi 1988 (1984)*
A young peasant from northern Italy becomes a homosexual prostitute in Milan and Paris.

Devil in the Hills *Cesare Pavese 1978 (1954)*
Set in and around Turin; a group of young people are getting to know the city its environs and themselves.

✔ **The Charterhouse of Parma**
Stendhal 1976 (1839)
Stendhal adapted the theme from a sixteenth-century work and set it in the time of Waterloo at the intrigue-filled small court of Parma.

Guides

✔ **Cadogan Guide The Italian Lakes**
1994

✔ **Cadogan Guide Northwest Italy**
Dana Facaros and Michael Pauls 1992 (1990)

✔ **Visitor's Guide Northern Italy. A Moorland Guide** *Amanda Hinton 1992*

✔ **Blue Guide Northern Italy. From the Alps to Rome** *Alta Macadam 1991*

Leisure

✔ **Walking in the Dolomites**
Gillian Price 1991

Photography

✔ **Philip's Travel Guides Lombardy. The Italian Lakes** *John Flower Photographs by Charlie Waite 1990*

Travel Literature

Alps and Sanctuaries of Piedmont and the Canton Ticino *Samuel Butler 1986 (1881)*
Butler waxes lyrical about Handel and Shakespeare and writes: 'it is always a pleasure to me to reflect that the countries dearest to these two master spirits are those which are also dearest to myself, I mean England and Italy' and 'I have chosen Italy as my second country, and would dedicate this book to her as a thank-offering for the happiness she has afforded me.'

✔ **Italian Journeys** *Jonathan Keates 1992 (1991)*
Over a period of twenty years Jonathan Keates wandered around northern Italy visiting off-beat places: 'Unquestionably the finest book of its genre to appear in many years. Radiating intelligence and vivacity, it is a performance that anyone seriously interested in Italy would be unwise to miss.' (*The Spectator*)

The Surprise of Cremona
Edith Templeton 1955
Unconventional observations on Cremona, Parma, Mantua, Ravenna, Urbino and Arezzo.

FLORENCE AND TUSCANY

'In the distant plain lay Florence, pink and gray and brown, with the rusty huge dome of the cathedral dominating its center like a captive balloon, and flanked on the right by the smaller bulb of the Medici chapel and on the left by the airy tower of the Palazzio Vecchio; all around the horizon was a billowy rim of lofty blue hills, snowed white with innumerable villas.' Mark Twain *Autobiography* (1892) 1924

Art and Architecture

**Medieval Tuscany and Umbria.
Architectural Guides for Travellers**
Anthony Osler McIntyre 1992

Autobiography/Biography

Images and Shadows *Iris Origo 1970*
Iris Origo's biography about her life in Tuscany in the 1930s.

Fiction

✔ **Halcyon** *Gabriele D'Annunzio 1988
(1903)*
Poems, mostly set on the Tuscan coast, which express D'Annunzio's respite from public life (and his distaste for it) written in a happy region where 'there was no other cross except that of the poles suspended over the flood in a miracle of gold'.

✔ **Romola** *George Eliot 1980 (1863)*
Set during the upheavals in fifteenth-century Florence at the time of the expulsion of the Medici and the ascendancy and fall of Savanarola. Heavy going, but George Eliot herself wrote of it: 'There is no book of mine about which I more thoroughly feel that I swear by every sentence as having been written with my best blood.'

✔ **A Room With a View** *E.M. Forster
1990 (1908)*
Set in Florence among a group of tourists and expatriates; Forster writes about the English abroad ironically, but also sympathetically.

✔ **Where Angels Fear to Tread**
E.M. Forster 1976 (1905)
Monteriano, based on San Gimignano, is where some English ladies go to look at frescoes and where one falls in love with an Italian youth called Gino.

✔ **Innocence** *Penelope Fitzgerald 1987
(1986)*
Set in Tuscany in very true-to-life surroundings where things often do not turn out as expected: 'Penelope Fitzgerald's *Innocence* seems to me to be about real people undergoing interesting experiences, more real and more interesting than most biographies, and it carried absolute conviction as to time and place. What more could one ask of a novel?' (J.G. Links *Spectator Books of the Year*)

World So Wide *Sinclair Lewis 1951*
A story of Americans in Italy which was finished at Sir Harold Acton's house outside Florence.

✔ **Summer's Lease** *John Mortimer 1988*
A bickering family rents a villa in Tuscany for the summer. The character of the father, Haverford Downs, makes, in Ruth Rendell's words, the novel 'superb'.

✔ **Death in Springtime** *Magdalen Nabb
1984 (1983)*
This and many other titles including *Death in Autumn* 1986 (1985) are thrillers set in Florence. Excellent on the Italian background.

Prince of Foxes *S. Shellabarger 1973 (1948)*
An inspirational historical novel set in Renaissance Italy.

General Background

✔ **Florence. The Biography of a City**
Christopher Hibbert 1993
A readable examination of the artistic heritage of Florence, which although somewhat bulky would also make an ideal companion and guide.

Siena: A City and Its History
Judith Hook 1979
Mainly about the medieval heyday of Siena, in relationship to its great art and architecture; the nature of Sienese civilization explains why it is like it is today and makes it a good contemporary portrait.

✔ **The Stones of Florence and Venice Observed** *Mary McCarthy 1972 (1956)*
'The Florentines invented the Renaissance, which is the same as saying they invented the modern world – not, of course, an unmixed good,' writes Mary McCarthy in her interpretation of modern-day Florence.

✔ **A Small Place in Italy** *Eric Newby
1994*
Eric and Wanda Newby bought a small derelict farmhouse on the borders of Northern Tuscany and Liguria in 1967; their account of its renovation is by turns funny and affectionate.

Tuscany: An Anthology *Laura Raison
1984*
An exploration of Tuscany through the eyes and words of the many foreign visitors.

Guides

Florence: A Traveller's Companion
Harold Acton 1986

✔ **A Guide to Tuscany** James Bentley
1988 (1987)
Chapters on the art and literature of the Florentines followed by a gazetteer.

✔ **The Companion Guide to Florence**
Eve Borsook 1988 (1966)

✔ **Tuscany and Umbria. The Rough Guide** Jonathan Buckley, Tim Jepson and Mark Ellingham 1994 (1991)

✔ **Cadogan Guide Siena, Florence, Pisa** 1994

✔ **Cadogan Guide Tuscany, Umbria and The Marches** 1994

✔ **Everyman Guide Florence** 1993

✔ **American Express. Florence and Tuscany** Sheila Hale 1992 (1983)

✔ **Insight Guide Tuscany** 1993

✔ **A Literary Companion to Florence**
Francis King 1991

The Companion Guide to Tuscany
Archibald Lyall 1973

✔ **Blue Guide Florence** Alta Macadam
1991

✔ **Blue Guide Tuscany** Alta Macadam
1993

✔ **Florence and Tuscany. A Black's Italian Regional Guide** Laura Raison
1994

History

Paradise of Exiles Olive Hamilton 1974
Olive Hamilton became interested in the history of the British in Tuscany when she bought a house there. She chose to write about the people who interested her most, rather than making it a comprehensive account.

✔ **The Rise and Fall of the House of Medici** Christopher Hibbert 1979 (1974)
A study of the whole family from the rise of the Medici bank in the last half of the fourteenth century to the death of the last Medici Grand Duke in 1737.

Florence, Rome and the Origins of the Renaissance George Holmes 1988 (1986)
A history which places the extraordinary cultural achievements of the early Renaissance in full perspective. Holmes deals with both literary and visual art and shows how the achievements of the great masters were made possible and the effect that Papal patronage had.

The Merchant of Prato Iris Origo 1984 (1957)
Based on the documentation of the fourteenth-century Datini business empire; Francesco di Marco Datini eventually had trading houses in Avignon, Prato, Florence, Pisa, Genoa, Spain and Majorca and his rise to success and riches is all fully recorded, making this a fascinating document.

✔ **The Italian City Republics**
Daniel Waley 1988 (1969)
From the eleventh century onwards many Italian towns achieved independence as political entities; these experiments in self-government were well documented and in the cultural achievements of the medium-sized towns Daniel Waley sees the seeds of the early Renaissance.

Leisure

✔ **Eating Out in Florence and Vicinity** Christopher Cowie n.d.
A personal guide to restaurants and trattorias.

Photography

✔ **The Villas of Tuscany** Harold Acton
Large and lavishly illustrated book with plenty of text.

✔ **Tuscany from the Air** Giuseppe Grazzini
Photographs by Guido Alberto Rossi 1991 (1990)
It is interesting to be able to see the famous towns and cities of Tuscany as a whole, from the air.

✔ **Philip's Travel Guides. Tuscany**
Jonathan Keates Photographs by Charlie Waite
1992 (1988)

Travel Literature

War in Val D'órcia Iris Origo 1985 (1947)
A moving account, in diary form, of Iris Origo's role in the last war – hiding partisans, refugee children and Allied troops in her large farm in Southern Tuscany.

✔ **Within Tuscany** Matthew Spender
1993 (1992)
Spender went to live in Tuscany and has written a book about his experiences which is 'by turns informative, ruminative, funny

and touching' (Emma Tennant *Evening Standard*)

UMBRIA

Art and Architecture

✔ **Medieval Tuscany and Umbria. Architectural Guides for Travellers** Anthony Osler McIntyre 1992

Fiction

✔ **Rat King** Michael Dibdin 1989 (1988)
Aurelio Zen is transferred from a desk job in Rome to take over a kidnapping case. A crime novel set in Perugia.

The Assisi Murders Timothy Holme 1986 (1985)
A thriller set in Assisi; a good-looking Italian policeman, Peroni, lusts after a fellow pilgrim who ends up behind bars accused of shooting her husband and discovers a thirteenth-century mystery.

General Background

✔ **A Valley in Italy. Confessions of a House Addict** Lisa St Aubin de Terán 1994
The author and her family bought a ruined castle without realizing how much work needed to be done on it; five years later she thinks, that it will never be finished, a fact which quite pleases her. This is a riveting and beautifully written account of a house and its new owners.

Guides

✔ **Tuscany and Umbria. The Rough Guide** Jonathan Buckley, Tim Jepson and Mark Ellingham 1993 (1991)

✔ **Umbria, The Marches and San Marino. A Black's Italian Regional Guide** Christopher Catling 1994

✔ **Cadogan Guide Tuscany, Umbria and The Marches** 1994

✔ **Insight Guide Umbria** 1992

✔ **Blue Guide Umbria** Alta Macadam 1993

The Companion Guide to Umbria Maurice Rowdon 1969

Photography

✔ **Philip's Travel Guides. Umbria** Jonathan Keates Photographs by Joe Cornish 1991

Travel Literature

Umbria Michael Adams 1988 (1964)
A general background, particularly good on the early history; when Michael Adams first went to Umbria he was captivated by its beauty and 'something intangible in the atmosphere'; twenty-five years later, although much changed by the advent of mass tourism he thinks that most of the changes have been for the better.

VENICE AND THE VENETO

'When I went to Venice – my dream became my address.' Marcel Proust, Letter to Madame Strauss, c. May 1906 – of 1900.

Art and Architecture

✔ **Palladio** J.S. Ackerman 1991 (1972)
Ackerman sets Palladio in the context of his age and examines each of his buildings in turn.

✔ **The Stones of Venice** John Ruskin Abridged and edited by J.G. Links 1960 (1853)
When the book first came out a reviewer wrote: 'If Mr Ruskin be right, all the architects, and all the architectural teaching of the last three hundred years, must have been wrong.' Ruskin agreed that this was indeed so and nearly 150 years later it is interesting to read what he said.

✔ **A Concise History of Venetian Painting** John Steer 1989 (1970)
A good introduction in the Thames and Hudson 'World of Art' series.

✔ **Palladio and Palladianism** Robert Tavernor 1991
There are 163 black and white illustrations in this introduction to Palladio in the Thames and Hudson 'World of Art' series.

Autobiography/Biography

The Quest for Corvo A.J.A. Symons 1969 (1934)
The biography of Frederick Rolfe, Baron Corvo, a notoriously difficult subject to pin down; he was 'an uncouth, lonely, arrogant genius'.

Fiction

The Desire and Pursuit of the Whole
Frederick Rolfe (Baron Corvo) 1993 (1934)
Frederick Rolfe arrived in Venice in 1908 having been dogged by ill health for several months. As a young man he had tried unsuccessfully to become a priest and had subsequently tried to make a living as a writer and as a painter. He began writing this strange book – his 'Venetian romance', in July 1909. It is the book of a disappointed man, but is nonetheless moving.

Across the River and Into the Trees
Ernest Hemingway 1977 (1950)
In Venice, after the war, a cynical and war-weary American colonel falls passionately in love with a young Italian countess who seduces him with the freshness of her love.

✔ **The Aspern Papers** *1888*
✔ **The Wings of the Dove** *Henry James* 1984 (1902)
The Wings of the Dove begins with a Bronzino portrait in an English country house, which precipitates the fatally ill American heiress, Milly Theale, into going on a European adventure, much of it in Venice and its palaces.

✔ **Death in Venice** *Thomas Mann* 1971 (1912)
On a visit to Venice, Gustav von Aschenbach meets a boy with whose beauty he becomes obsessed. An oppressive and haunting novel.

✔ **The Comfort of Strangers**
Ian McEwan 1982 (1981)
Set in Venice, the story 'has you in its stranglehold from first page to last. Ian McEwan has honed his prose style (always admirably spare) to tell his tale, and with all the skill of an accomplished torturer, he throws the occasional crumbs of comfort, as the tension becomes unbearable, only to snatch them away again within moments.' (Angela Huth *The Listener*)

✔ **A Venetian Theory of Heaven**
William Rivière 1993 (1992)
Francesca Ziani, a student, lodges with her cousin who is married to an Englishman, in a crumbling Venetian palazzo: 'A hymn to beauty . . . The real hero is the city itself, with its dark, thick waters and decaying beauties.'

✔ **Territorial Rights** *Muriel Spark* 1991 (1979)
Good descriptions of Venice where Robert Leaver, a young art historian, goes to escape from his rich admirer, but ends up bumping into his father.

✔ **Stone Virgin** *Barry Unsworth* 1986 (1985)
In 1432, in Venice, a strange and seductive stone virgin was carved, which the sculptor paid for with his life; in the eighteenth century a salacious affair took place in front of the statue and in the 1970s a conservation expert also gets caught up in the web of eroticism surrounding the statue: 'A marvellous novel, beautifully written and compelling to read.' *Daily Telegraph*

✔ **The Passion** *Jeanette Winterson* 1988 (1987)
'A story about history and hero-worship, the plight of women, the pains of soldiering, the violence of youth, and about the sadness of the unfulfillable condition of humanity . . . a book of great imaginative audacity and assurance . . . brilliantly physical (and funny) detail.' (*Times Literary Supplement*)

General Background

✔ **Watermark** *Joseph Brodsky* 1992
An original and quirky book in forty-eight short chapters which recall specific incidents from Brodsky's many visits to Venice.

Guides

✔ **Venice and the Veneto** *James Bentley* 1992
A narrative guide.

✔ **Venice. The Rough Guide**
Jonathan Buckley and Hilary Robinson 1993 (1989)

✔ **Everyman Guide Venice** *1993*

✔ **Cadogan Guide Venice** *Dana Facaros and Michael Pauls* 1994

✔ **The Companion Guide to Venice**
Hugh Honour 1990 (1965)

✔ **Venice for Pleasure** *J.G. Links* 1994 (1966)
The essential and much loved companion to Venice, recently revised: 'Not only the best guide-book to that city ever written, but the best guide-book to *any* city ever written'. (Bernard Levin *The Times*)

✔ **Venice. A Literary Companion**
Ian Littlewood 1991

Venice and its Lagoon *G. Lorenzetti*
An extraordinarily detailed guide which is unfortunately not available in the UK; 'a must' for addicts of Venice.

✔ **Blue Guide Venice** *Alta Macadam* 1989

✔ **Venice. A Traveller's Companion**
John Julius Norwich   1990

History

✔ **Venice. The Biography of a City**
Christopher Hibbert   1990 (1988)
An excellent illustrated history of Venice
which as *The Times* described is 'as captivat-
ing as the city itself'. John Julius Norwich
wrote: 'Everything we could wish to know
about the most magical of cities, presented
with effortless elegance . . . Mr Hibbert has
produced a work worthy to stand alongside
those of Jan Morris, Hugh Honour and J.G.
Links.' (*The Sunday Times*)

✔ **Palladio's Villas**   Paul Holberton   1990
A description of life in the Renaissance
countryside and an exploration of the special
qualities of the Palladian villas. It can be
used as a guide to the area.

✔ **The Venetian Empire**   Jan Morris
1990 (1980)
A reconstruction of the glittering sea-power
of Venice.

✔ **A History of Venice**
John Julius Norwich   1983 (1977)
A large and scholarly history: 'Lord Norwich
has loved and understood Venice as well as
any other Englishman has ever done. He has
put readers of this generation more in his
debt than any other English writer.' (Peter
Levi *The Sunday Times*)

Photography

✔ **Venice**   Photographs by Dorothy Bohm   1992
A mixture of colour photographs.

✔ **Philip's Travel Guides. The Veneto**
Stephen Brook   Photographs by Joe Cornish   1991

✔ **The Ghetto of Venice**   Roberta Curiel
and Bernard Dov Cooperman   1990
Many Jews who were expelled from other
European countries ended up in Venice; this
well illustrated book shows some of the treasures to be found there.

✔ **Travel To Landmarks. Verona**
Sheila Hale   1991
Colour photographs, many showing the
Roman buildings which inspired so much
Renaissance architecture. Ample text.

✔ **Palaces of Venice**   Peter Lauritzen and
Alexander Zielcke   1992 (1978)
The history of forty-five outstanding palaces
with explanations of their construction and
development.

✔ **Charlie Waite's Venice**   1989
Photographs with an emphasis on the details.

Travel Literature

✔ **The Stones of Florence and Venice
Observed**   Mary McCarthy   1972 (1956)
A journey through the alleys and backwaters
of Venice.

✔ **Venice**   Jan Morris   1993 (1960)
An essential companion to Venice which
Geoffrey Grigson described as 'Entertaining,
ironical, witty, high-spirited and apprecia-
tive. Both melancholy and gay, and worldly,
the best modern book about a city that I have
read.' [Colin Thubron] 'Of all the books I have
read about cities, I'd place Jan Morris' *Venice*
easily first, for the brilliance with which it
captures the atmosphere of the Serenissima
through all ages and at every season of the
year. This is one of those books I should most
like to have written myself.' (Geoffrey Moorhouse) 'I think that Jan Morris' book on
Venice remains my undisputed favourite.
Partly due to the skill and sensitivity of the
writing itself, but also because I read it before
I had much experience of travel. All I can say
is it quite brilliantly created an appetite for
the city without ever spoiling the reality of
seeing it for myself.' (Michael Palin)

Italian Neighbours   Tim Parks   1993 (1992)
A very readable account of how an Englishman copes in the Veneto; he learns to accept
what the locals take for granted – thereby
getting to grips with the real Italy.

SOUTHERN AND CENTRAL ITALY – GENERAL

'This region surely is not of the earth.
Was it not dropt from Heaven?' [Naples]
Samuel Rogers *Italy* 1822–34

Autobiography/Biography

✔ **The Story of San Michele**
Axel Munthe   1975 (1929)
Axel Munthe was born in Sweden and became a doctor in Paris at a very young age.
He rebuilt the Tiberian villa of San Michele
on Capri and from there worked among the
poor people he loved. His book was an instant
success and has remained hugely popular
ever since.

Fiction

South Wind *Norman Douglas* *1962 (1917)*
A novel set in Capri, which Douglas calls
Nepenthe; an Anglican bishop, on holiday
from his diocese in Africa stops on the island
and finds his values changed out of all recognition.

✔ **The Island** *Gustaw Herling* *1990 (1967)*
Suffering, solitude and violence to the spirit.
About Capri.

✔ **Christ Stopped at Eboli** *Carlo Levi*
1982 (1945)
Set in a remote region of Basilicata where
Levi was exiled under the Fascists, a world
cut off from history and the state: 'We're not
Christians, Christ stopped short of here, at
Eboli'.

✔ **Arturo's Island** *Elsa Morante* *1991*
(1957)
Arturo grows up on an island near Naples
where he spends his days idling by the sea,
but with the advent of adolescence he
becomes disillusioned: 'One of the most honest statements of its kind ... one of the most
living explorations of growth in human
beings that has been written.' (*Sunday
Times*)

✔ **The Volcano Lover** *Susan Sontag*
1993 (1992)
Based on the lives of Sir William Hamilton,
his wife Emma and Lord Nelson and set
against the backdrop of Vesuvius.

✔ **The Law** *Roger Vailland* *1985 (1957)*
The Law is a cruel game played in southern
Italy which reflects life; everyone is involved:
'*The Law* deserves every reading it will have.
It is and does all that a novel should –
amuses, absorbs, excites and illuminates not
only its chosen patch of ground but much
more of life and character as well'. (*New York
Times*) [Patrick Marnham]

✔ **Anna, Soror** *Marguerite Yourcenar* *1992*
(1982)
Set in the late Renaissance, a tale of inces-
tuous passion in Naples

Guides

✔ **Naples. An Early Guide** *Enrico Bacco*
1991 (1616)
One of the best extant descriptions of the
Renaissance city of Naples.

✔ **Blue Guide Southern Italy**
Paul Blanchard *1990*

✔ **Cadogan Guide The Bay of Naples
and the Amalfi Coast** *1994*

**The Companion Guide to Southern
Italy** *Peter Gunn* *1969*

✔ **South Italy. A Traveller's Guide**
Paul Holberton *1992*
A narrative guide arranged under area.

✔ **Insight Guide The Bay of Naples**
1992

✔ **Northern Lazio. An Unknown Italy**
Wayland Kennet and Elizabeth Young *1990*
Between Tuscany and Rome lies what was
the heartland of the Etruscans; the authors
who know the area well have written a narrative history and guide to this relatively
unknown region.

✔ **Naples and Campania. A Black's
Italian Regional Guide** *Martha Pichey*
1994

History

✔ **Pompeii. The Day a City Died**
Robert Etienne *1992 (1986)*
An excellent well-illustrated history in the
'New Horizons' series.

Travel Literature

✔ **Ramage in South Italy**
Edith Clay (ed.) *1987 (1965)*
Craufurd Tait Ramage, tutor to the sons of
the British Consul in Naples, set off on a
solitary tour of southern Italy in 1828, publishing a book about his journey called *The
Nooks and Byways of Italy* in 1868. It was
much admired by Norman Douglas and has
here been annotated by Edith Clay.

Torregreca. A World in Southern Italy
Ann Cornelisen *1969*
Torregreca is a town in the region of Basilicata in Southern Italy. The author spent
many years with the people admiring their
hard struggle to make a living from the rocks
and clay which make up their world.

Old Calabria *Norman Douglas* *(1915)*
Rambles around southern Italy at the begin-
ning of the century. [Colin Thubron]
[Stephen Brook]

Siren Land *Norman Douglas* *1948 (1911)*
Mostly about Capri and Sorrento and the
hinterland on the Gulf of Salerno where the
Sirens once sang; Douglas delved deeply into
ancient, medieval and modern siren lore, but
also tells us about the emperor Tiberius and
the local ecstatic Sister Serafina.

✔ **Naples 44** *Norman Lewis   1989 (1978)*
Norman Lewis arrived in Naples as an Intelligence Officer attached to the American Fifth Army and after a year there decided that given the chance to be born again, he would choose to be an Italian: 'Here is a book of gripping fascination in its flow of bizarre anecdote and character sketch; and it is much more than that.' (J.W. Lambert *Sunday Times*) 'You'll have lots of Norman Lewis already, I imagine, but could I enter a plea for *Naples'44*? People usually talk about it as one of the classics of World War Two, but it tells you a lot about southern Italy as well as being very funny indeed in places.' (Jeremy Paxman)

✔ **Between Two Seas. A Walk Down the Appian Way** *Charles Lister   1992 (1991)*
Lister was commissioned to walk down the Appian Way from Rome to Brindisi in 1960 for an advance of £50, but because he lost his job on his return the book did not get written for a further thirty years: 'It is full of superstitions, shepherds, witches, ruined castles, with landscapes of buried amphorae, glass and Roman metals . . . Lister is propulsively rude, violently English, misanthropic and bitterly articulate. Never was "local colour" more acidly daubed.' (*The Sunday Times*)

✔ **A Traveller in Southern Italy**
H.V. Morton   1983 (1969)
Morton was persuaded to explore Southern Italy by an Italian friend and travelled through Abruzzi, Campania, Apulia, Basilicata and Calabria on the then newly completed Autostrada del Sole.

✔ **Capri** *Alberto Savinio   1989 (1988)*
A kaleidoscopic fast moving account of Savinio's visit to Capri which was written in 1926, but not published in book form until 1988.

ROME

'I hardly slept the night before I arriv'd there with the thought of seeing it – my heart beat high, my imagination expanded itself, and my Eyes flash'd again, as I drew near the *Porta del Popolo*' David Garrick, letter to George Colman, 24 December 1763.

Art and Architecture

✔ **Bernini** *Howard Hibbard   1976 (1965)*
A general overview of the life and work of Bernini which shows his artistic development and evolution and how enormously im-

portant he was in expressing the spirit of his age.

Fiction

✔ **The Child of Pleasure**
Gabriele D'Annunzio   1991 (1889)
One of the seminal books of the decadent movement; a young count meets and becomes entangled with a woman, expert in perversion.

✔ **Enderby** *Anthony Burgess   1982 (1973)*
Enderby is often to be found in Rome with his glamorous wife . . .

✔ **The Marble Faun** *Nathaniel Hawthorne   1990 (1860)*
Set in Rome. This was the first novel to explore the influence of European cultural ideas on American morality. It is concerned with the nature of transgression and guilt.

✔ **Daisy Miller** *Henry James   1986 (1880)*
Based on a true story of a young American woman who 'picked-up' a good-looking Roman in Switzerland. *Roderick Hudson* is also set in Rome.

✔ **The Voyeur** *Alberto Moravia   1991 (1985)*
The ex-left-wing militant Eduardo has become a professor of French, but lives his life as a voyeur through his quizzical blue eyes, without really ever knowing what is going on under the surface.

✔ **A Violent Life** *Pier Paolo Pasolino   (1959)*
Set in the slums of Rome, the book caused a scandal when it was first published.

✔ **The Late Mattia Pascal**
Luigi Pirandello   1987 (1904)
Pascal travels to Rome under an assumed name leaving his family and gambling debts; he returns to discover that his wife has remarried and so has to eke out his existence as a ghost.

The Conquest of Rome *Matilde Serao   1991 (1885)*
The Neapolitan writer Matilde Serao moved to Rome in 1881, becoming a journalist. She aimed to gain a reputation as an international writer with this novel about unrequited love in the context of the city's social and parliamentary life.

Guides

✔ **The Woman's Travel Guide Rome**
Ros Belford   1993

✔ **Everyman Guide: Rome** *1994*

✔ **Eyewitness Travel Guide Rome**
1993

✔ **Cadogan City Guide Rome**
Dana Facaros and Michael Pauls 1993 (1989)

Companion Guide to Rome
Georgina Masson

✔ **Michelin Green Guide Rome** *1992*

✔ **American Express Guide Rome**
Anthony Pereira and Nick Skidmore 1992 (1983)

✔ **A Literary Companion Rome**
John Varriano 1991

History

✔ **Rome. The Biography of a City**
Christopher Hibbert 1987 (1985)
3,000 years of history told in very readable form.

✔ **The Search for Ancient Rome**
Claude Moatti 1993 (1989)
Packed with nuggets of information and pictures, in the 'New Horizons' series.

✔ **The Twelve Caesars** *Suetonius*
Translated by Robert Graves 1978
The Roman rulers from Julius Caesar to Domitian; much of the material came from eye-witnesses and as well as being an accurate report of the times it is also a racy and vivid account of the domestic lives of the Caesars. 'How about Rome with Suetonius' *Twelve Caesars*, which I always carry with me when away (in Penguin) to help tackle the long misery in airports dependent upon AIR INDIA?' (Norman Lewis)

✔ **Histories** *Tacitus Translated by Kenneth Wellesley 1992*
Tacitus was a barrister/historian and his history, which he wrote thirty years after the event, spans the years 68–96 AD.

Photography

✔ **Philip's Rome. Architecture. History. Art** *James Bentley Photographs by John Heseltine 1991*

✔ **Inside Rome** *Joe Friedman and Marella Caracciolo 1993*
A range of Roman interiors from antiquity to Art Deco.

Travel Literature

A Traveller in Rome *H.V. Morton 1984 (1957)*
In Morton's first book on Italy, he wrote ex-clusively about Rome; despite the dated style it is still worth reading.

SARDINIA
'One of the most neglected spots in Europe.' Arthur Young *Travels . . . [in] . . . France* 1792

Autobiography/Biography

✔ **Cosima** *Grazia Deledda 1991 (1947)*
Grazia Deledda's portrait of herself growing up and attempting to write fiction in the countryside of Sardinia at the end of the last century. Although she had little formal schooling she was inspired by the natural forces and mythology surrounding her.

Fiction

✔ **La Madre (The Woman and the Priest)** *Grazia Deledda 1987 (1920)*
'The interest in "La Madre" lies in the presentation of sheer instinctive life. The love of the priest for the woman is sheer instinctive passion, pure and undefiled by sentiment. The instinct of direct sex is so strong and so vivid, that only the blind instinct of mother obedience, the child instinct, can overcome it.' (D.H. Lawrence). Grazia Deledda also wrote ✔ *Elias Portolu* (1992).

✔ **The Day of Judgement**
Salvatore Satta 1994
Change and decay in Nuoro, Sardinia: 'One of the masterpieces of solitude in modern literature.' (George Steiner)

Guides

✔ **Windrush Island Guide. Sardinia**
Andrew Gravette 1992

✔ **Visitor's Guide Sardinia. A Moorland Guide** *Amanda Hinton 1993*

✔ **Insight Guide Sardinia 1991**

✔ **Insight Pocket Guide Sardinia** *1991*

Travel Literature

✔ **Sea and Sardinia** *D.H. Lawrence 1989 (1923) (see 'Italy – General')*
In 1921 Lawrence travelled from Sicily to the heart of Sardinia with his 'Queen Bee'. The book was described by Anthony Burgess as 'The most charming work he ever wrote'.

SICILY
'Like Sicily extremely – a good
on-the-brink feeling– one hop and you're
out of Europe; nice, that.' D.H. Lawrence,
letter to Lady Cynthia Asquith, Taormina,
25 March 1920

Art and Architecture

Sicilian Baroque *Anthony Blunt* 1968
A thorough, scholarly, yet readable, large
format history of Sicilian Baroque with many
black and white photographs. Blunt's aim
was to 'convey to others some of the pleasure'
which he had obtained from looking at Baroque architecture in Sicily.

Sicily: An Archaeological Guide
Margaret Guido 1968 (1967)
The most important prehistoric and Roman
remains and the Greek cities are described in
ten chapters, working round the island in a
series of routes in an anti-clockwise direction. Clear plans and maps accompany the
text.

Autobiography/Biography

Sicilian Lives *Daniel Dolci* 1981
Dolci moved to Trappeto in the early 1950s;
here he records the lives of the people he met
during the thirty years he spent living and
working with them, in their own words.

✔ **The Last Leopard** *David Gilmour* 1990
(1988)
An excellent life of Giuseppe Tomasi di Lampedusa.

God Protect Me From My Friends
Gavin Maxwell 1957
A biography of the bandit Salvatore
Giuliano.

Fiction

✔ **Bell'Antonio** *Vitaliano Brancati* 1993
(1949)
The most handsome young man in Catania,
Antonio Magnano, is recalled from Rome to
marry into the local bourgeoisie; rumours
start that he is unable to perform his hus-
bandly duties, setting the two families at
daggers drawn. Both very funny and very
sad. Also ✔ *The Lost Years* 1992 (1938)

✔ **Blind Argus** *Gesualdo Bufalino* 1992
(1984)
In the summer of 1951 a young school teacher
pursues one of his students who lives with
her grandfather in a crumbling palazzo. But

since she was already being courted by half
the local population, he stood little chance: 'A
book about an unhappy love-affair is all very
fine if you're up to writing it. Bufalino carries
it off triumphantly.' (Pietro Calabrese *Il
Messaggero*). Other books by Bufalino include *The Plague Sower* and *Night's Lies*.

✔ **The Leopard** *Giuseppe di Lampedusa*
1993 (1958)
In 1860 the old order still reigns in Sicily, but
there are echoes of a new political movement,
with Garibaldi, on the mainland: 'The most
remarkable windfall in contemporary fiction.
It is incontestably a masterpiece.' (John Raymond *The Listener*)

The March of the Long Shadows
Norman Lewis 1987
Set in post-war Sicily against a background
of the Separatist movement and the times of
the bandit Giuliano.

✔ **The Silent Duchess** *Dacia Maraini*
1993 (1990)
Set in the mid-eighteenth century, the novel
is about the Ucria family as seen through the
eyes of the deaf-mute Duchess Marianna: 'It
is brimming with detail, vividly presented in
a style that is abrupt, spiky, and yet luxuriant. Every page presents one with the unexpected. It arouses intense feeling, it
provokes thought.' (Allan Massie *The Scotsman*)

✔ **The Sicilian** *Mario Puzo* 1991 (1984)
A novel based on the real-life of the bandit
Salvatore Guiliano who, defying the corrupt
government in Rome, struggled to feed the
poor in Sicily.

✔ **The Viceroys** *Federico de Roberto* 1989
(1959)
The Viceroys are the great families of the
Sicilian nobility; when one of them dies in the
mid-nineteenth century greed and jealousy
break out.

✔ **Sicilian Uncles** *Leonardo Sciascia* 1986
Also by Sciascia *The Wine Dark Sea*, ✔ *Can-
dido* 1985(1982) and *The Day of the Owl* and
Equal Danger.

✔ **Short Sicilian Novels** *Giovanni Verga*
1984
Also by Verga *Cavalleria Rusticana* and *The
House by the Medlar Tree*.

✔ **Conversation in Sicily** *Elio Vittorini*
1988 (1951)
The narrator ran away from his Sicilian
home to Milan at the age of fifteen. One year
he does not send a card to his mother, hears
from his father who has left her, so revisits
Sicily. A deceptively simple tale.

General Background

✔ **Men of Honour** *Giovanni Falcone* *1993*
Falcone's compelling account of the Mafia before his murder in 1992.

✔ **The Honoured Society** *Norman Lewis 1991 (1964)*
A readable and rightly well-known account of the Mafia in Sicily: 'This book has not a dull moment in it; it is indeed imbued with that quality of *terribilità* which Giuliano himself was said to possess.' (*The Spectator*)

Guides

✔ **Sicily. The Rough Guide**
Robert Andrews and Jules Brown 1993 (1989)

✔ **Baedeker's Sicily** *1993*

✔ **Sicily. A Traveller's Guide**
Paul Duncan 1992
A narrative guide full of history and descriptions,.

✔ **Cadogan Guide Italian Islands**
Dana Facaros and Michael Pauls 1989 (1981)

✔ **Cadogan Guide Malta, Gozo and Comino** *Simon Gaul 1993*
Includes excursions to Sicily.

✔ **Cadogan Guide Sicily** *1994*

✔ **Blue Guide Sicily** *Alta Macadam 1993*

History

✔ **The Golden Honeycomb**
Vincent Cronin 1992 (1954)
Excellent descriptions of Sicily's art, architecture and folklore, written in the form of a quest for the golden honeycomb, which Daedalus is said to have offered to Aphrodite in return for his escape from King Minos of Crete: 'Honey from Hybla' (Patrick Leigh Fermor)

A History of Sicily *M.I. Finlay, D. Mack Smith and C.J.H. Duggan 1968*
An abridgement of the trilogy which was the most comprehensive history of Sicily.

The Normans in Sicily
John Julius Norwich 1992 (1967)
An omnibus version of Lord Norwich's two books: *The Normans in the South* and *The Kingdom in the Sun*, which tell the history of the Normans' dramatic entry into the south of Italy and what they created in Sicily.

✔ **The Sicilian Vespers**
Steven Runciman 1992 (1958)
A history of the Mediterranean world in the latter part of the thirteenth century: 'Superb. It is an intensely dramatic story (the Vespers, like all revolutions, re-shaped history) and he tells it brilliantly.' (*The Tribune*)

Photography/Illustration

Expedition into Sicily
Richard Payne Knight 1986
Knight was a member of the Society of Dilettanti and benefactor of the British Museum. In 1777 he travelled to Sicily and kept a journal which is published here accompanied by sketches by Jakob Philipp Hackert and Charles Gore.

Travel Literature

Sicilian Carousel *Lawrence Durrell 1977*
Durrell took a bus tour round Sicily; at first he baulked at being cooped up with a load of strangers, but gradually they all fell under the spell of the island.

The Ten Pains of Death *Gavin Maxwell 1960 (1959)*
Maxwell went to Sicily to research the life and death of the 'bandit' Giuliano, but became fascinated by Western Sicily with its poverty and very individual people.

On Persephone's Island
Mary Taylor Simetti 1986
The author is an American married to a Sicilian professor; here she tells of a typical year spent on the west of the island.

LIECHTENSTEIN

General Background

Switzerland for Beginners
George Mikes 1975 (1962)
The last chapter in this book is on Liechtenstein.

LUXEMBOURG

✔ **Blue Guide Belgium and Luxembourg** *Bernard McDonagh 1993*

✔ **Michelin Red Guide Benelux 1995**

MALTA

'It is a whole rock cover'd with very little

Earth.' Lady Mary Wortley Montagu, letter to the Abbé Conti, 31 July 1718

Autobiography/Biography

The Moon's a Balloon David Niven 1986 (1971)
David Niven describes some of his time in the army in Malta in a very amusing way.

Fiction

Earthly Powers Anthony Burgess
The life story of Kenneth Marchal Toomey in his final years of sun-drenched idleness in Malta.

The Kappillan of Malta
Nicholas Monsarrat 1973
It was the duty of Father Salvatore, a priest or kappillan, to keep up the spirits of his people during the siege of Malta between 1940 and 1942. The book takes place during a particular six days.

V Thomas Pynchon 1975 (1963)
The search for the mysterious 'V' ranges from New York to Cairo to Alexandria to Malta and along the way a large, varied and eccentric cast of characters is created.

✔ **The Perfect Kill** A.J. Quinnell (1992)
Although this thriller ranges across Europe, it has many scenes set in Gozo.

Food

Recipes from Malta Anne and Helen Galizia n.d.

Guides

✔ **Visitor's Guide Malta and Gozo**
Geoffrey Brown 1993

✔ **Malta, Gozo and Comino. A Windrush Island Guide** Brian Dicks 1991

✔ **Blue Guide Malta and Gozo**
Peter McGregor Eadie 1990

✔ **Cadogan Island Guide Malta**
Simon Gaul 1993

✔ **Insight Guide Malta** 1992

✔ **Landscapes of Malta, Gozo and Comino** Douglas Lockhart and Sue Ashton 1993 (1989)

✔ **Thomas Cook Travellers Guide Malta and Gozo** 1994

History

The Great Siege. Malta 1565
Ernle Bradford 1962 (1961)
In 1565, Suleyman the Magnificent invaded Malta with a fleet of 200 ships and 40,000 men; the ensuing siege was a classic in the history of warfare.

Siege: Malta 1940–1943 Ernle Bradford 1985
Interesting to see how little siege warfare has changed over the centuries.

✔ **Malta. The Thorn in Rommel's Side** Laddie Lucas 1993 (1992)
Between June 1940 and December 1942, because it was strategically so important, Malta was one of the most bombed places on earth. The author was commanding officer of the Spitfire squadron and experienced the daily difficulties first hand.

Travel Literature

✔ **A Voyage in Vain. Coleridge's Journey to Malta in 1804** Alethea Hayter
Coleridge went to Malta in the spring of 1804, when he was thirty-one, in order to restore his health and to refind his muse. Alethea Hayter uses his diary and letters to piece together this crucial period of his life.

Malta Sir Harry Luke 1960 (1949)
Luke was lieutenant governor in Malta between 1930 and 1938 and paints an affectionate picture of the island.

The Journey of Sir Walter Scott to Malta Donald Sultana 1986
Scott was dying when he went to Malta in 1831. Sultana describes his journey in the broad context of Mediterranean and European history and literature, but also relates it more specifically to a wide range of the Waverley novels.

✔ **Labels** Evelyn Waugh 1991 (1930)
A great part of Evelyn Waugh's Mediterranean cruise was spent in Malta.

MONACO

'The casino is all right in its florid, heavy way – but what a chance for an architect, on that site over the sea!' Arnold Bennett *Journal* 26 January 1904

Fiction

Earthly Powers Anthony Burgess (see *'Malta'*)
Parts of this novel are set in Monaco.

Loser Takes All Graham Greene 1955
Two people spend their time gambling and when not gambling thinking about it and adultery.

The Honeymoon Katherine Mansfield
A short story which has Monte Carlo as its background, in the collection *The Dove's Nest*, in *Collected Short Stories* 1981 (1923)

NETHERLANDS

As a nation the most ancient ally, the *alter idem* of England, the best deserving of the cause of freedom and religion and morality of any people in Europe.' Samuel Taylor Coleridge *Table Talk* 15 August 1831

Art and Archaeology

From Van Eyck to Bruegel
Max J. Friedlander 1981 (1916) (see *'Belgium'*)
A learned account of the early Flemish masters, which despite its age still remains the standard work on the subject. There are separate chapters on great masters and on the geography of Netherlandish art and on the style of the sixteenth century.

✔ **Dutch Painting** R.H. Fuchs 1978 (see *'Belgium'*)
An excellent introduction, arranged chronologically and charting the last 500 years.

Dutch Civilisation in the Seventeenth Century J.H. Huizinga 1968
An analysis of life and culture in the Dutch Republic with profound insights into the Golden Age of the United Provinces, which were very different from simultaneous cultural achievements elsewhere in Europe.

✔ **Dutch Art and Architecture 1600–1800** Jacob Rosenberg et al. 1988
An anthology of essays on the art and buildings of the Golden Age, in the Pelican 'History of Art' series, lavishly illustrated with black and white photographs and divided

into four sections: painting 1600–1675, painting 1675–1800, architecture and sculpture.

✔ **Rembrandt** Christopher White 1984
A wide-ranging short introduction to Rembrandt and his work.

Biography

✔ **Lust for Life** Irving Stone 1989 (1934)
A semi-fictionalized, very easy to read, biography of Van Gogh which shows his incessant struggle with poverty, discouragement, madness and despair.

Fiction/Poetry

✔ **The Fall** Albert Camus 1957
Camus spent one day and one night in Amsterdam, but makes great use of what he saw in *The Fall*.

The Riddle of the Sands Erskine Childers (1902) (see *'Germany'*)

✔ **The Mirror of the Sea** Joseph Conrad 1988 (1906)
An openly autobiographical book in which Conrad explores his knowledge of the sea at a time when the great sailing ships were making way for steam.

The Diary of a Young Girl Anne Frank 1954
A clearly written, if gruelling, account of life in the Second World War for the Jews in Amsterdam.

✔ **A City Solitary** (1985)
✔ **Love in Amsterdam** 1984 (1962)
✔ **Cold Iron** (1986)
✔ **Strike Out Where Not Applicable**
Nicolas Freeling
Detective novels, set in Belgium and Holland, with the rebel cop, van der Valk, as their hero.

✔ **The Glass Bridge** Margo Minco 1988
About the Dutch Jews in the last war; the novel sold half a million copies in Holland. A sequel *An Empty House* follows the character back to Amsterdam.

✔ **Rituals** Cees Nooteboom 1992 (1980)
Inni Wintrop tries to kill himself on the day that his wife leaves him, but like everything else he does, as a dilettante, he fails. *In the Dutch Mountains* (1991(1984)) is a seductive tale of illusion which was described by Bernard Levin in *The Sunday Times* as 'the brilliant and original fruit of a deep (and well read) imagination'.

✔ **Hard Rain** *Janwillem van de Wetering*
1987 (1985)
A detective story set in Amsterdam and
which moves into Holland. Very good off-beat
characters.

Food

✔ **The Dutch Table** *Gillian Riley* *1994*
A delightful book which has recipes accompanied by Dutch paintings.

General Background

Holland *Adam Hopkins* *1988*
An interesting and comprehensive introduction with chapters on land and water, the
struggle against Spain, Rembrandt, William
and Mary, Monarchy to Mondrian, Lessons
of War, the Dutch in public and Dutch interiors.

**The Making of the Dutch Landscape.
An Historical Geography of the
Netherlands** *A.M. Lambert* *1985*
Between the first edition in 1971 and the
latest edition a wealth of new material came
to light which the author states meant 'much
less certainty about the past'. Few countries
have been so physically shaped by man as the
Netherlands – over half the land would be
liable to flooding without dikes. Lambert's
scholarly book shows how the landscape was
formed over the centuries.

The Netherlands *Sacheverell Sitwell* *1974*
(1948)
Basic history and updated travelogue which
shows how the Dutch influence on world history was out of all proportion to its size.

Guides

✔ **Baedeker Netherlands** *1992*

✔ **American Express Guide
Amsterdam, Rotterdam and the
Hague** *Derek Blythe* *1992*

✔ **Cadogan City Guide Amsterdam**
Rodney Bolt *1992*

✔ **Amsterdam. The Rough Guide**
Martin Dunford and Jack Holland *1994 (1988)*

✔ **Holland, Belgium and Luxembourg.
The Rough Guide** *Martin Dunford, Jack
Holland and Phil Lee* *1993 (1990)*

✔ **Everyman Guide Amsterdam** *1993*

✔ **Blue Guide Amsterdam** *Charles Ford*
1993

✔ **Blue Guide Holland** *Charles Ford*
1993 (1933)

✔ **Insight Guide the Netherlands** *1991*

✔ **Michelin Green Guide
Netherlands** *1990*

✔ **Michelin Red Guide Benelux 1995**

History

**The Dutch Seaborne Empire
1600–1800** *C.R. Boxer* *1977 (1965)*
'No living scholar has done more to shock us
into awareness of large but neglected episodes in the early history of European expansion . . . No praise can be too high for the
elegance with which [Professor Boxer] has
woven his complex themes into a coherent,
searching, and at times delightful survey,
much of which will be fresh even to students
of the Netherlands.' (*Times Literary Supplement*)

✔ **The Embarrassment of Riches. An
Interpretation of Dutch Culture in the
Golden Age** *Simon Schama* *1991 (1987) (see
'Belgium')*
A mixture of social and cultural history and
much more; the Dutch Republic was an
astonishing phenomenon, a collection of
diverse communities with no shared language who transformed themselves into a
world empire: 'The lightheartedness and energy that characterize the author and his
marvellous book are the finest tribute he
could have paid to the subject of his choice'.
(Anita Brookner *The Observer*)

**The Dutch Republic and the
Civilization of the C17th** *C.H. Wilson*
1968
A concise history in the 'World University
Library' series.

Leisure

✔ **Through the Dutch and Belgian
Canals** *Philip Bristow* *1988*

✔ **Slow Walks in Amsterdam**
Michael Leitch *1990*
Twenty strolls through Amsterdam.

Natural History (see 'Europe General')

Travel Literature

Transatlantic Sketches Henry James
1875
Among the many European sketches is one of Amsterdam.

PORTUGAL

'Wet or fine the air of Portugal has a natural happiness in it, and the people of the country should be as happy and prosperous as any people in the world.'
H.G. Wells A Year of Prophesying 1925

Anthropology

Portugal. A Book of Folk Ways
Rodney Gallop 1961 (1936)
Portugal is very rich in folklore having remained mainly pastoral and agricultural for many years. Even when Gallop was writing in the 1930s he remarked on how difficult it was to find any evidence of traditional folkways, as they were fast disappearing.

Art and Archaeology

The Art of Portugal 1500–1800
R.C. Smith 1968
A learned overview.

Fiction/Poetry

✔ **An Explanation of the Birds**
Antonio Lobo Antunes 1992 (1981)
'A richly imagined work that has all the shifts in perspective we have come to expect from the modern novel. But it is, in essence, the timeless story of a man whose life has come unravelled. And as the story rushes to a close, its central, final act achieves an equally timeless and haunting power.' (*New York Times Book Review*)

The Lusiads Luis Vaz de Camões (Camoens)
1987 (1572)
The poem is about Vasco da Gama and his famous voyage which left Lisbon in 1497. It has been described as 'the first successful attempt in modern Europe to construct an epic poem on the ancient model.' Based on Virgil's *Aeneid*.

✔ **The Following Story** (about Lisbon) Cees Nooteboom 1994 (1991)
A misanthrope wakes to find himself unexpectedly in a hotel room in Portugal; an illustration of differences between physical and platonic love as recalled by memory.

✔ **The Book of Disquiet. A Selection**
Fernando Pessoa 1991
Mainly known as a poet, Pessoa's only prose work shows the workings of a solitary intelligence and literary imagination, evoking the city of Lisbon.

Ballad of Dog's Beach José Cardoso Pires
1986 (1982)
A 'gripping, erotic, fast-paced, highly-intelligent thriller based on a true story of political intrigue in Salazar's Portugal. Step-by-step, Inspector Elias builds up his reconstruction of the events leading to the discovery of the body on the beach; interweaving his own fantasies, suppositions and – eventually – solution.' [book-jacket]

✔ **The Illustrious House of Ramires**
Eca de Queiroz 1993 (1968)
Goncalo Mendes Ramires, a Portuguese aristocrat who lives in his ancestral home in Santa Ireneia, is involved in both literature and politics; through him we get a very clear idea of nineteenth century Portugal. Also by de Queiroz *The Reliquary*, *The Mandarin*, *The Sin of Father Amaro* and *The Maias* (1986).

Baltasar and Blimunda José Saramago
1988 (1982)
Historical novel set at the time of Dom João V and his Austrian Queen Dona Maria Ana Josefa. Baltasar is a soldier, dismissed from the army and Blimunda the daughter of a bewitched and excommunicated woman. Also *The Year of the Death of Ricardo Reis*.

Food

✔ **The Taste of Portugal** Edite Vieira
1989 (1988)
Recipes combined with history, tradition and folklore.

General Background

✔ **The Portuguese: the Land and its People** Marion Kaplan 1991
A very good and accurate general introduction to the country; every aspect of Portuguese life is covered.

Guides

✔ **Portugal. The Rough Guide**
Mark Ellingham, John Fisher, Graham Kenyon and Alice Martin 1994

✔ **Cadogan Guide Portugal**
David J.J. Evans 1992 (1990)

✔ **Cadogan Guide Portugal: The South, Algarve and Lisbon** 1994

✔ **Insight Guide Lisbon** 1992

✔ **Insight Guide Portugal** 1993

✔ **Let's Go Spain and Portugal 1995**

✔ **Michelin Green Guide Portugal**
1989

✔ **Blue Guide Portugal** Ian Robertson
1989 (1988)

✔ **Portugal. A Traveller's Guide**
Ian Robertson 1992
A narrative guide.

History

The Portuguese Seaborne Empire 1415–1825 C.R. Boxer 1991 (1969)
A summary of the vicissitudes and the achievements of the old Portuguese seaborne empire, from the capture of Ceuta from the Moors in 1415 until Portugal's recognition of Brazilian independence in 1825.

The Portugal Story John Dos Passos 1970 (1969)
Subtitled 'three centuries of exploration and discovery', this is an interesting and readable account of Portugal's far-flung and worldwide history.

A New History of Portugal
H.V. Livermore 1976 (1966)
The emphasis is on the history of the nineteenth and twentieth centuries; the Roman, Germanic, Muslim and medieval periods are included, although in a compressed form.

✔ **They Went to Portugal**
Rose Macaulay 1985 (1946)
An anthology of British travellers' writings about and to Portugal. There is a second volume and continuation called ✔ *They Went to Portugal Too* (1990).

Leisure

✔ **Landscapes of Portugal. Algarve. A Sunflower Guide** Brian and Eileen Anderson 1991

✔ **Landscapes of Portugal. Estoril Coast and Costa Verde. A Sunflower Guide** Brian and Eileen Anderson 1991

✔ **Walking in Portugal** Bethan Davies and Ben Cole 1994
A well-researched and up-to-date guide.

Natural History

Flowers of South-West Europe
Oleg Polunin and B.E. Smythies 1988

Photography

Portuguese Gardens Helder Carita and Homem Cardoso 1990
A large illustrated book showing how Portuguese gardens were less influenced by outside forces than the architecture, so that for centuries the gardens remained closely connected to the way of life and imagination of the Portuguese soul.

Travel Literature

The Journal of William Beckford in Portugal and Spain 1787–1788
Boyd Alexander (ed.) 1954
Beckford stayed in Portugal for eight months, having stopped off on his way to Jamaica because he felt seasick. He was ostracized from official functions and English society because of his reputation, but he was introduced to the Queen's favourite, Diogo, the Marquis of Marialva, which put Beckford on a high social footing. He moved on to Madrid in 1787, where he was again caught up in a social whirl and a series of sexual entanglements.

Recollections of an Excursion to the Monasteries of Alcobaca and Batalha
William Beckford Edited by Boyd Alexander 1972 (1835)
An important piece of travel literature which was described by Whibley as 'the masterpiece of his experience and is so far embellished by memory and invention as to seem a work of pure imagination', and by Rose Macaulay as 'For fact-seekers it is tantalizing'.

The Selective Traveller in Portugal
Ann Bridge and Susan Lowndes 1949
Although wildy out of date, this remains a favourite with many people.

The Journal of a Voyage to Lisbon
Henry Fielding   1958 (1755)
Fielding travelled to Lisbon in 1754 for reasons of ill-health and died there on 8th October aged 48. The book shows Fielding's stoicism when suffering from pain and mortal illness as well as having sharp and satirical, yet kindly, observations about the people and places he encountered.

Travels in My Homeland
Almeida Garrett   1987 (1843-46)
First published as a series of articles in a Lisbon weekly magazine. Garrett was described as 'orator and poet, historian and philosopher, critic and artist, jurist and administrator, scholar and statesman'. He had to spend much of his life in exile, in England and France; with this book he combines the genre of the period, travel literature, with speculation on the arts and has as his central theme 'What went wrong with Portugal?'

Portugal and Madeira   *Sacheverell Sitwell 1954*
Sitwell visited Portugal five times between 1926 and 1953 and was taken to out-of-the-way places by Portuguese friends: 'Portugal is one of the most lovely countries of Europe, with its musical pinewoods, its vineyards, and Hesperidean orchards'.

AZORES
'It was the aurora borealis of the frozen pole exiled to a summer land.' (Flores)
Mark Twain *The Innocents Abroad* 1869

✔ **Landscapes of the Azores**
Andreas Stieglitz   1992

MADEIRA
'The climate is so fine that any man might wish it was in his power to live there under the benefits of English laws and liberty.' Sir Joseph Banks *Journal of the Rt. Hon. Sir Joseph Banks* September 1768

General Background

Portugal and Madeira   *Sacheverell Sitwell 1954*
There is only one chapter on Madeira at the start of the book.

Guides

✔ **Madeira. The Complete Guide** *John and Susan Farrow   1990 (1987)*
A good introduction and comprehensive guide.

✔ **Madeira and Porto Santo. A Windrush Island Guide** *Andrew Gravette 1990*

✔ **Landscapes of Madeira** *John and Pat Underwood   1994*

SPAIN
'Spain is not a land of fleshly comforts, or of social sensual civilization. *Oh! dura tellus Iberiae!* – God there sends the meat, and the evil one cooks: there are more altars than kitchens – *des milliers de prêtres et pas un cuisinier.*' Richard Ford *A Handbook of Travellers in Spain* 3rd edn 1855

Art and Archaeology

Moorish Culture in Spain
Titus Burckhardt   1972
An indispensable background book which shows different ways of looking at Islamic buildings in Spain, explaining their significance and the social environment in which they were produced.

✔ **Carolingian and Romanesque Architecture 800–1200** *Kenneth J. Conant 1973 (1959)*
In the Penguin 'History of Art' series.

✔ **Islamic Spain** *Godfrey Goodwin   1991 (1990)*
An architectural guide with descriptions of almost every Islamic building in Spain.

Romanesque Art   *Meyer Schapiro   1977*
An excellent, illustrated survey of Romanesque art and architecture.

Spanish Baroque   *Sacheverell Sitwell   1931*
Includes buildings in Portugal, Mexico and other colonies. It was written as a work of information rather than of criticism and by the author's admission is not easy to read as it is more of a catalogue of names and places.

✔ **In Search of the Firedance: Spain Through Flamenco** *James Woodall   1992*
A history and exploration of flamenco which gets right to the heart of the culture.

Autobiography/Biography

✔ **The Life of Saint Teresa of Avila by Herself** *1957 (1588)*
St Teresa's conversion started at the age of forty when she was utterly transformed by her religious experiences; she maintained an analytical and critical view of ecstasy and a fear of false mysticism. Her *Life* is extremely widely read in Spain.

The Forging of a Rebel
Arturo Barea (see 'Morocco')
An autobiographical trilogy comprising *The Forge* 1984 (1941), *The Track* 1984 (1943) and *The Clash* 1984 (1946). In *The Forge* he goes back to his beginnings 'to the things which I had smelled, seen, touched and felt and which had hammered me into shape'. *The Track* is the shocking account of the Spanish army in Morocco during the Riff War and *The Clash* is about the horrors of the Spanish Civil War and his part in it.

Forbidden Territory *Juan Goytisolo 1989 (1985)*
A painfully honest autobiography (1931–56) of Goytisolo's struggles growing up during the Franco years, involvement with Cuba (where he had relations) and odd 'atavistic reflex action' of wanting to meet those who shared his name, although 'the idea of family has for years ceased to have any meaning for me'.

Dialogue with Death *Arthur Koestler 1983 (1937)*
Koestler was captured and imprisoned by Franco's troops for three months under sentence of death; this is the diary he kept in captivity: 'A vivid picture of the reaction to prison life and to imminent death of a man who was not designed by nature as a criminal and who was too young to die.' (*Times Literary Supplement*)

Franco *Paul Preston 1993*
A huge and penetrating biography of Franco which analyses why he was able to survive for so long.

Fiction/Poetry

The Three-Cornered Hat and Other Stories *Pedro de Alarcon English translation by Michael Alpert 1975*
Ironic nineteenth-century tales about corruption, bureaucracy and absolutism.

Red Doll *Juan Luis Cebrián 1987 (1986)*
A thriller set in the post-Franco years which involves Basque terrorists. Cebrián was editor of *El País* and wrote it during his holidays as a 'book . . . to be read', not to be put down after a few chapters, about love, politics, intrigue and power.

✔ **The Family of Pascal Duarte**
Camilo José 1964 (1942)
Revolving around a meaningless murder and with a sense of a spiritual void, Cela's book, which was published at the same time and has much in common with Camus' *L'étranger*, with its starkness and restraint, has become a classic.

✔ **Don Quixote** *Miguel de Cervantes Translated by Tobias Smollett 1986 (1755)*
Smollett's translation of Don Quixote was out of print for over 100 years; it has been praised by Carlos Fuentes as 'the homage of a novelist to a novelist' and shows why it was known as the first modern novel and the spearhead for European fiction.

Spanish Drums *Harry Chapman 1991*
A thriller about an English woman who enters into a family's life and finds skeletons of the Civil War.

✔ **The Penguin Book of Spanish Verse**
J.M. Cohen (ed.) 3rd edn 1988

Journey of the Wolf *Douglas Day 1988 (1977)*
A Civil War fighter, Rosales, 'El Lobo' returns to his village, from exile in France, forty years after the fighting; his mind fills with the horrors of war and he realizes that he is still an exile, but this time in his native land.

Torquemada *Benito Pérez 1988*
An epic nineteenth-century novel about a vicious Madrid moneylender; comparisons are made with Tomás de Torquemada (1420–98) who was appointed inqisitor general under Ferdinand and Isabella in 1482 and who was noted for his cruelty. Also *Fortunata and Jacinta*.

✔ **Marks of Identity** *Juan Goytisolo 1988 (1966)*
Goytisolo novels which are about Spain's position on the periphery of the western and Islamic worlds were banned throughout the Franco years. *Marks of Identity* expresses an angry and painful struggle – that of a man who has no love for his country, his generation or himself . . . 'whoever is interested in the Spain of today and tomorrow owes it to themselves to read this passionate literary account'. (*Le Monde*). He also wrote ✔ *Landscapes After the Battle* 1987(1983), ✔ *The Virtues of the Solitary Bird* 1991(1988) and ✔ *Juan the Landless* 1975(1990)

✔ **Monsignor Quixote** Graham Greene
1983 (1982)
The character of Monsignor Quixote, who wanders through life with his friend the deposed Communist mayor, is vintage Greene.

For Whom the Bell Tolls
Ernest Hemingway 1965 (1941)
A novel which takes place during only four days of the Spanish civil war, but which feels as if it encompasses the whole of Spain with its scenes of passion between Jordan and Maria and tales of bull-fighting.

Murder in the Central Committee
Manuel Vazquez Montalban 1984 (1981)
An exciting thriller set between Barcelona and Madrid, starring the Catalan gourmand-detective Pepe Carvalho; the general secretary of the Spanish Communist Party is murdered and Carvalho is hired to find his assassin.

✔ **Penguin Parallel Text. Spanish Short Stories** *Jean Franco (ed.) 1966*
A selection of eight short stories which include Borges, Márquez and Cela.

✔ **Desperately Seeking Julio**
Marujo Torres 1991
Extremely readable and successful novel about Julio Iglesias.

Food

✔ **The Food of Spain and Portugal**
Elisabeth Lambert Ortiz 1990 (1989)
An inspiring and practical book which shows the range of Spanish and Portuguese cookery.

✔ **A Season in Spain** Ann and
Larry Walker 1992
An off-the-beaten-track gastronomic tour of 'uncommon encounters with Spanish food and wine'..

General Background

The Soul of Spain Havelock Ellis 1937
Havelock Ellis attempted a completely fresh look at Spain and meditated at leisure about what he had seen.

✔ **Spain. A Portrait after the General**
Robert Elms 1994 (1992)
An idiosyncratic, personal and rather off-beat portrait of Spain which was praised in *The Sunday Times* for its descriptions of bull-fighting.

The Buried Mirror: Reflections on Spain and the New World Carlos Fuentes
1992
An excellent introduction to the history and culture of Spain and its continuing influence on Latin America.

✔ **The Face of War** Martha Gellhorn 1993 *(1959)*
This collection includes Martha Gellhorn's reports from the Spanish Civil War: 'The best prose on its subject written by anybody.' *(New Statesman)*

The Assassination of Federico Garcia Lorca Ian Gibson 1983 (1979)
Lorca, a poet who understood and embraced his country, was murdered on 19th August 1936. For many years the truth about his death was hushed up by the Spanish government, but Gibson has created 'a marvelous piece of detective work . . . [and] a profound examination of the corruption of Spain by fascism'. Stephen Spender *The New York Times Book Review*

✔ **Fire in the Blood** Ian Gibson 1992
Ian Gibson has lived in Spain since 1978 and presents a vivid and sympathetic portrait of contemporary Spain, while at the same time putting it in the context of history.

✔ **The Dangerous Summer**
Ernest Hemingway 1986 (1960)
Hemingway returned to Spain fifteen years after the Civil War and wrote this companion volume to *Death in the Afternoon* (1932): 'No prose can beat Hemingway's for conveying tension . . . *The Dangerous Summer* is Hemingway's valediction to the Spain he loved, his homage to the beautiful and deadly sport which was for him the noblest of all.' *(The Economist)*

✔ **Death in the Afternoon**
Ernest Hemingway 1972 (1932)
Hemingway's account of bullfighting which was described by V.S. Pritchett in *The Listener* as 'The most readable and the most nearly exhaustive account of the contemporary Spanish bullfight that we have'.

✔ **The Spaniards** John Hooper 1993 *(1990)*
Post-Franco Spain as observed by the *Guardian* correspondent. A very good introduction full of insight into the new generation.

Iberia James Michener 1983 (1968)
Longwinded, nevertheless it contains some interesting insights. Volume one is about Badajoz, Toledo, Cordoba, Las Marismas, Seville and Madrid and volume two:

Salamanca, Pamplona, Barcelona, Teruel, Santiago and bullfighting.

Guides

✔ **Baedeker's Spain** *1993*

✔ **Spain. A Literary Companion**
Jimmy Burns 1994

✔ **Spain. The Rough Guide**
Mark Ellingham and John Fisher 1994 (1991)

A Handbook for Travellers in Spain and Readers at Home; Gatherings from Spain *Richard Ford*
Described in the Rough Guide as 'the best guide ever written to any country', Murray's Handbook stayed in print well into this century; Ford wrote wittily and was incredibly knowledgeable about Spain. Very hard to find second-hand. [Jan Morris]

✔ **Cadogan Guide Spain** *Dana Facaros and Michael Pauls 1992 (1987)*

✔ **Insight Guide Spain** *1993*

✔ **Let's Go Spain and Portugal 1995**

✔ **Blue Guide Spain** *Ian Robertson 1991 (1989)*

History

✔ **The Spanish Labyrinth**
Gerald Brenan 1993 (1943)
The social and political background to the Spanish Civil War, and an account of Brenan's own experiences in it.

✔ **Modern Spain 1875–1980**
Raymond Carr 1980
The imposition of nineteenth-century liberal institutions on the very conservative and backward Spanish society caused huge problems, which Carr argues explain much of modern Spanish history.

Spain: The Root and the Flower
John Crow 1975 (1963)
Cultural and social history from Roman Spain up to the present.

✔ **Imperial Spain 1469–1716** *J.H. Elliot 1990 (1963)*
A study of the sudden rise of Spain, its 'Golden Age' and its equally dramatic fall.

✔ **Moorish Spain** *Richard Fletcher 1994 (1992)*
A history of Islam in Spain, a presence which completely transformed western civilization; the scientific and philosophical learning of the Greeks and Persians which had been lost

in Europe, was reintroduced via Spain, changing western European thought.

✔ **Blood of Spain** *Ronald Fraser 1994 (1986)*
Oral and therefore moving accounts of the experiences of over 300 people in the Civil War 1936–39.

Islamic Spain 1250–1500 *L.P. Harvey 1990*
There were two distinct categories of Muslims in Spain – those in the independent Kingdom of Granada and those throughout the rest of Christian Spain. Harvey looks at both groups and underlines the importance of the period at the end of the Middle Ages when Islam was being expelled from Europe.

✔ **Roman Spain** *S.J. Keay 1988*
Well illustrated, definitive guide to Roman Spain, which explains how the many peoples of Iberia were united under the Roman empire from the third century BC onwards.

✔ **The Moors in Spain** *Stanley Lane-Poole 1984 (1887)*
Originally one of the first complete and historically accurate accounts of the period: 'Spain set to all Europe a shining example of a civilized and enlightened State . . . Art, literature and science prospered. Mathematics, astronomy and botany, history, philosophy and jurisprudence were to be mastered in Spain, and Spain alone.'

✔ **A Traveller's History of Spain**
Juan Lalaguna 1990

✔ **The Spanish Civil War** *Hugh Thomas 1990 (1961)*
Huge and comprehensive book which 'traces in scrupulous detail a bewilderingly complicated era'. (*Times Educational Supplement*)

Leisure

✔ **Trekking in Spain. A Lonely Planet Walking Guide** *Marc S. Dubin*

✔ **The Good Retreat Guide**
Stafford Whiteaker 1994
Over 300 places to find peace and spiritual renewal in Britain, Ireland, France and Spain.

Natural History

✔ **Wild Spain** *Frederic V. Grunfeld 1989*
Spanish wildlife arranged under region.

✔ **Collins Guide to the Birds of Britain and Europe** *Heinzel, Fitter and Parslow 1992 (1972)*

✔ **Wildlife Travelling Companion.**
Spain *John Measures 1992*
Precise information on where to go, how to get there and what to see. Well illustrated.

Flowers of the Mediterranean
Oleg Polunin and Anthony Huxley 1990

Photography

✔ **Reflections of Spain** *Barbara Lloyd 1992*
Colour photographs divided thematically.

Travel Literature

A Visit to Spain and North Africa
1862 *Hans Christian Andersen 1975 (1864)*
Andersen spent four months in Spain in 1862, a country he had loved since childhood and which he described as 'The land of enchantment beyond the high Pyrenees'. He always read as much as he could about a country before going there, but although he was a nervous traveller who often imagined he was being laughed at, some of his travel writing does manage to be objective.

The Bible in Spain *George Borrow 1985 (1842)*
A Protestant bible-salesman's account of his travels through the west of Spain, southern Portugal and Tangier, for five years from 1835 to 1840; Borrow, a likeable braggart and egotist, declared that the time was 'the most happy of my existence'. He was often a chameleon, easily slipping into protective guises when necessary and enjoying the situations in which he found himself. A unique portrait of post-Trafalgar Spain.

✔ **The Face of Spain** *Gerald Brenan 1987 (1950)*
Brenan's journey through central and southern Spain in 1949 during Franco's régime. Among the places he visited were Madrid, Cordova, Malaga, Granada, La Mancha, Mérida, Toledo and Aranjuez.

✔ **Spanish Journeys** *Adam Hopkins 1993 (1992)*
Hopkins' in-depth knowledge and love of Spain is evident from the way he enables geography to reflect history and literature and vice versa: 'A staggering feat of scholarship. Hopkins gives a detailed account of Spanish history from the Moorish invasion of 711 up to the death of Franco . . . Journeys across the old territories of Aragón and Castile are enlivened by a rich amalgam of anecdote, impressions and reflections on the

literary and artistic life of Spain.' (Ian Thomson *Independent on Sunday*)

✔ **Between Hopes and Memories: A Spanish Journey** *Michael Jacobs 1994*
Michael Jacobs travelled through every region of mainland Spain, meeting many prominent Spaniards as well as many lesser known poets, eccentrics and mystics. He is well qualified to tackle his subject and sees everything with a discerning eye.

Spain *Nikos Kazantzakis 1983*
Kazantzakis first went to Spain as a reporter before the war and visited Miranda, Salamanca, Toledo, Cordova, Madrid and Seville. He returned later, during the war and wrote about the fighting he saw.

Gatherings from Spain *Richard Ford 1970*
Extracted from the famous Murray's Handbook (q.v.).

✔ **Cities of Spain** *David Gilmour 1992*
A modern cultural portait of Spain; an evocation of history, especially good on Moorish Spain. Cities include Toledo, Cordoba, Santiago de Compostela, Seville, Salamanca, Cadiz, Barcelona, San Sebastian and Madrid.

✔ **As I Walked Out One Midsummer Morning** *Laurie Lee 1990 (1969)*
Lee walked through pre-Civil War Spain from Vigo to Malaga in 1936 accompanied by his violin; rich descriptions of the countryside and people and how it feels to be young and 'on-the-road'.

✔ **Spain** *Jan Morris 1982 (1964)*
Jan Morris' feeling for Spain is apparent in this short but elegant book which was described by Gerald Brenan as 'Perhaps the best general book ever written on Spain'. [Colin Thubron]

A Stranger in Spain *H.V. Morton 1986 (1955)*
Morton reflects on history as he travels through Spain describing the mosque at Cordova, the plains of Andalusia, Castile and the Basque country.

✔ **Farewell Spain** *Kate O'Brien 1985 (1937)*
A series of reminiscences written during the early part of the Spanish Civil War by the novelist and playwright.

✔ **Marching Spain** *V.S. Pritchett 1988 (1928)*
V.S. Pritchett walked 300 miles across Spain in 1927, at a time when the country was still

almost completely isolated. He was greeted throughout with hospitality and courtesy.

The Spanish Temper V.S. Pritchett 1984 (1954)
V.S. Pritchett spent two years travelling through Spain before the Civil War (see *Marching Spain*) and in the early 1950s returned and again travelled throughout weaving together his impressions of people, landscape, history and myth. [Patrick Marnham]

Spain Sacheverell Sitwell 1975 (1950)
The result of many journeys to Spain, the first of which was in 1919 just after the First World War, when Sitwell was an impressionable twenty-year-old. He made over twenty journeys in all and concludes that 'the Spaniards, beyond argument, have been the greatest builders after the Romans'.

Spanish Raggle Taggle Walter Starkie 1973 (1934)
Starkie travelled as a minstrel throughout much of Spain as he felt 'a good dose of Picaresque Spain would be necessary to cure me of my folly'.

PYRENEES/CATALONIA
(see also 'France: Pyrenees')
'It sounds an odd thing to say of eager Catalonia – but it is true – that here, if anywhere in the world, there is peace.'
Hilaire Belloc *Many Cities* 1928

Art and Architecture

✔ **Walks in Picasso's Barcelona**
Mary Ellen Jordan Haight and James J. Haight 1992
Seven walks through the Barcelona of Picasso, Dali, Miró, Rusiñol, Casanovas, Llimona, Carrera, Casals, Gaudi, Sagnier and Domenech.

Autobiography/Biography

✔ **Homage to Catalonia** George Orwell 1986 (1938)
There was a heady feeling about the early days of revolution in Barcelona which was followed by feelings of disillusionment with the factional fighting among the Republicans: '*Homage to Catalonia* is that phoenix, a book which is at the same time a work of first-class literature and a political document of the greatest importance.' (Geoffrey Gorer)

Fiction

✔ **Obabakoak** Bernardo Atxaga 1992 (1991)
A sequence of tales about life in a Basque village by a Basque writer.

✔ **Solitude**
Victor Català (Caterina Albert i Paradis) 5th edn. 1992
An important pre-Civil War Catalan novel about a woman's life and sexual passions in a mountain village.

✔ **Fiesta** Ernest Hemingway 1927 (1955)
Hemingway's first novel; the account of the San Fermin festival in Pamplona.

✔ **The Truth About the Savolta Case**
Eduardo Mendoza 1993 (1975)
Set in Barcelona in 1917 around the Savolta ammunition factory.

✔ **The Time of the Doves** Mercé Roderada
A working-class woman in the Barcelona suburb of Gracia struggles to survive in the post-Civil War years.

✔ **The South** Colm Tóibín 1992 (1990)
Katherine Proctor arrives in Barcelona from Ireland in 1950, hoping to be an artist. She meets a veteran of the Spanish Civil War and they embark on a new life together.

General Background

✔ **Barcelona** Robert Hughes 1993 (1992)
'Destined to become, like E.M. Forster's *Alexandria* and Mary McCarthy's *Venice Observed*, a classic of urban history.' (Nicholas Shrady *New York Times*) Hughes places Barcelona firmly in its Catalan past realizing that that there was little point in describing the new without the old: 'The city is lucky to be commemorated by so formidable a chronicler as Robert Hughes'. (Jan Morris *Los Angeles Times*)

Catalonia. Traditions, Places, Wine and Food Jan Read and Maite Manjón 1992
A combination of background and history and the relatively unknown food and wine of the area.

Guides

✔ **Baedeker Guide Barcelona** 1992

✔ **Baedeker Guide Costa Brava** 1993 (1988)

✔ **Bartholomew Barcelona and Catalonia** *1991*

✔ **Barcelona and Catalunya. The Rough Guide** *Jules Brown 1994*

✔ **Barcelona and Catalonia** *Paul Gogarty 1993*

✔ **Catalonia. A Complete Guide** *Jane and Peter Holliday 1992* Ten routes with maps and plans.

✔ **Insight Guide Catalonia** *1991*

✔ **Blue Guide Barcelona** *Michael Jacobs 1992*

✔ **Landscapes of Cataluña Delta del Ebro and Puertos de Beceite. A Sunflower Guide** *Paul Jenner and Christine Smith 1993*

✔ **The Pyrenees. The Rough Guide** *Paul Jenner and Christine Smith 1993 (1990)*

✔ **Slow Walks in Barcelona** *Michael Leitch 1991*

✔ **Visitor's Guide Spain: Costa Brava to Costa Blanca** *Barbara Mandell 1991*

✔ **Barcelona. A Celebration and a Guide** *Charlie Pye-Smith 1992* An introduction to the past and the present and an informative guide about restaurants and hotels as well as cultural sites.

✔ **Barcelona Step by Step** *Christopher Turner 1991*

✔ **Pauper's Barcelona** *Miles Turner 1992*

History

✔ **Barcelona. A Thousand Years of the City's Past** *Felipe Fernandez-Armesto 1992* 'His portait of the city emphasizes the paradox of its phoenix-like renewals from the ashes of rebellion, defeat and economic catastrophe . . . this opinionated, splenetic, heterodox and ferociously intelligent book is the most eloquent of tributes to Barcelona's maddening otherness.' (Jonathan Keates *The Observer*)

✔ **Barcelonas** *Manuel Vázquez Montalbán 1992 (1990)* An anecdotal history written as an imaginary tour of the city. He is critical of much, especially the values of the new 'Olympic' Barcelona which contrast so strongly with the slums. Very stimulating.

Leisure

✔ **Walks and Climbs in the Pyrenees** *Kev Reynolds 1983 (1978)*

Photography

✔ **Inside Barcelona** *Josep M. Botey Photographs by Peter Aprahamian 1992* One hundred of the finest period interiors of Barcelona.

Travel Literature

The Essence of Catalonia *Alastair Boyd 1988* Good for the history, art and architecture of the region from Barcelona, through Catalonia from the Pyrenean valleys to the Ebro delta. It is a mixture of personal travel book and guidebook which attempts to draw out the influences on a few buildings rather than a comprehensive list of all buildings.

The Romance of the Basque Country and the Pyrenees *Eleanor Elsner 1927* An attempt at explaining the mystery of the Basques is accompanied by a collection of old photographs.

The Enchanted Mountains *Robin Fedden 1962. (see 'France')* An evocative narrative about the Aigüestortes region of the Spanish Pyrenees which combines three journeys made by the author and his wife over three summers.

✔ **Voices of the Old Sea** *Norman Lewis 1985 (1984)* Norman Lewis lived in a remote Catalan fishing village in the 1950s. This record of how life was then, is in stark contrast to what has happened in the area today: 'A marvellous, iridescent epitaph' (*The Times*)

Fabled Shore *Rose Macaulay 1986* Rose Macaulay drove along the Spanish coast in 1949 from Catalonia to the Algarve when the area was still completely unspoilt.

The Spanish Pyrenees *Henry Myhill 1966* Henry Myhill spent seven summers on the Basque coast, accompanying tourists at the weekends, but having the weekdays to himself to explore the surrounding countryside, days which he described as 'golden days, undeserved by anyone over the age of twelve'.

✔ **Catalonia. Portrait of a Nation** *John Payne 1991* Two thousand years of Catalonian history are mingled with the author's personal reminiscences of living in Barcelona as a student.

NORTHERN SPAIN

'The architecture is luxuriant, but its heroic grandeur prevents it from being tiresome and the perfect balance of the decorative motives gives an impression of an almost classic severity. It is like a purple patch in Chapman's Homer.' [Santiago – Cathedral] W. Somerset Maugham *Don Fernando* 1935

Art and Architecture

✔ **The Road to Santiago de Compostela. Architectural Guides for Travellers** *Michael Jacobs 1992 (1991)*

Guides

The Pilgrim Route to Compostela *Abbé G. Bernes, Georges Veron and L. Laborde Balen 1990* A practical guide.

✔ **Visitor's Guide Northern and Central Spain. A Moorland Guide** *Barbara Mandell 1992*

✔ **North-west Spain** *Melissa Shales 1993* Divided into routes which take in all the most important sites.

Leisure

✔ **Picos de Europa. Northern Spain** *Robin Collomb 1983 (1980)*

✔ **Walks and Climbs in the Picos de Europa** *Robin Walker 1993 (1989)*

Photography

✔ **The Pilgrim Route to Santiago** *Brian and Marcus Tate 1987* Photographs of the landscape en route to Santiago.

Travel Literature

✔ **The Way of Saint James. A Pilgrimage to Santiago de Compostela** *James Bentley 1992* Bentley follows the pilgrimage route from Paris via Bourges, Bordeaux, Pamplona, Burgos and Léon.

Grapes and Granite *Nina Epton 1956* One of the few books in English on Galicia, the northwest corner of Spain, which includes the cities of Santiago, La Coruña, Vigo and Pontevedra.

✔ **Spanish Pilgrimage. A Canter to St James** *Robin Hanbury-Tenison 1991 (1990)* Robin Hanbury-Tenison, his wife and son rode on white horses to Santiago.

The Pilgrimage to Santiago *Edwin Mullins 1974* The route of the pilgrimage goes through the Pyrenees; this is a history of the people and places en route to Santiago. The pilgrim in the Middle Ages believed that certain places and objects possessed unusual spiritual powers and one was the better for visiting them; Mullins takes this as a parallel for the tourist today, who visits sites dedicated to 'art' as opposed to those dedicated to God.

✔ **Pilgrim's Road. A Journey to Santiago de Compostela** *Bettina Selby 1994* The intrepid Bettina Selby followed the route to Santiago by bicycle.

MADRID AND CENTRAL SPAIN

'A most excellent air; a pleasant site, but the inhabitants are slovens, and the streets uncleanly kept.' Richard Burton *Anatomy of Melancholy*, 1621

Fiction

✔ **The Disinherited** *Michel del Castillo 1959* Madrid during the Civil War.

Guides

✔ **Baedeker's Madrid** *1992*

✔ **The Companion Guide to Madrid and Central Spain** *Alastair Boyd 1988 (1974)*

✔ **Visitor's Guide Northern and Central Spain. A Moorland Guide** *Barbara Mandell 1992*

✔ **Madrid. A Traveller's Companion** *Hugh Thomas 1988*

Photography

✔ **Philip's Travel Guides. Castile** *James Bentley Photographs by Joe Cornish 1991*

✔ **Philip's Madrid. Architecture. History. Art** *Michael Jacobs Photographs by James Strachan 1992*

Travel Literature

✔ **Journey to the Alcarria**
Camilo José Cela 1990 (1948)
Seven years after the end of the Civil War, Cela decided to go and discover the heart of Spain; he chose the Alcarria in north-east Castile, believing that nothing ever happened there and as such the area would be remarkable for its Spanishness. A nostalgic yet remarkable book.

SOUTHERN SPAIN

'Andalucia's maids
Nurst in the glowing lap of soft Desire.'
Lord Byron *Childe Harold's Pilgrimage* Canto the First 1812

Autobiography/Biography

✔ **Death's Other Kingdom**
Gamel Woolsey 1988 (1939)
Gamel Woolsey went to live near Malaga after her marriage to Gerald Brenan in 1930. In 1936 they woke to find the town ablaze; initially they determined to stay, but their situation became too dangerous as they turned their home into a shelter for local refugees. A moving first-hand experience of civil war.

Food

✔ **The Flavours of Andalucia**
Elisabeth Luard 1991
The author lived in Andalucia for many years and her book has recipes from each of the eight provinces.

General Background

Andalucia *Nicholas Luard 1985 (1984)*
Life in an Andalucian village where the author lived with his wife and family for eight years in the fishing port of Tarifa.

Guides

✔ **Andalucia. The Rough Guide**
Mark Ellingham and Geoff Garvey 1994

✔ **Cadogan Guide Southern Spain. Andalucía and Gibraltar** *Dana Facaros and Michael Pauls 1994 (1991)*

✔ **Lorca's Granada. A Practical Guide** *Ian Gibson 1992 (1989)*
Lorca was born 18 kilometres from Granada in the fertile Vega plain; the Vega formed a background to all his work and this book guides us to all the places in Granada associated with Lorca, including his place of execution: 'If God continues to help me and one day I become really famous, half the celebrity will be due to Granada.' (Lorca in 1929)

✔ **Insight Pocket Guide Marbella. Costa del Sol** *1992*

✔ **Insight Pocket Guide Seville, Cordoba and Granada** *1992*

✔ **A Guide to Andalusia** *Michael Jacobs 1991 (1990)*

The Companion Guide to the South of Spain *Alfonso Lowe 1973*

✔ **The Visitor's Guide Southern Spain and Costa del Sol. A Moorland Guide**
Barbara Mandell 1990

✔ **The Penguin Guide to Seville**
Christopher Turner 1992

Leisure

✔ **Gredos Mountains and Sierra Nevada** *Robin Collomb 1987*
A walking book.

Photography

✔ **Philip's Travel Guides Andalusia**
Hugh Seymour-Davies Photographs by Charlie Waite 1990

Travel Literature

✔ **The Sierras of the South. Travels in the Mountains of Andalusia**
Alastair Boyd 1992
The author lived near Ronda for many years and got to know the sierras well while searching for a house to buy.

✔ **South from Granada** *Gerald Brenan 1987 (1957)*
Brenan lived in the village of Yegen in the Sierra Nevada for many years; he writes about his life there and what Granada was like in the 1920s.

Two Middle-Aged Ladies in Andalusia
Penelope Chetwode 1985(1963)
The second 'middle-aged' lady was Penelope Chetwode's horse, La Marquesa; together they rode around Andalucia searching out the remotest parts of the countryside, enjoying primitive rural inns and people: 'seeing human beings as God made them to be'.

✔ **The Alhambra** *Washington Irving* 1986
(1896)
Irving visited the Alhambra in 1828 and
stayed in the Governor's apartments; he fell
in love with his surroundings and wrote vivid
descriptions and records of its legends.

✔ **A Rose for Winter** *Laurie Lee* 1971
(1955)
Lee's return visit to Andalucia was filled with
as much passion and enthusiasm as before.
The Civil War had changed much, but so
much about Spain had proven indestructible
and this is what he searched for and found.

MAJORCA AND THE BALEARICS

Fiction

The Doll's Room *Lloren Villalonga* 1988
(1956)
The decline of nobility in nineteenth-century
Mallorca was described by the author as 'the
portrait, or, if you wish, the poem of Mallorca.
Of a certain Mallorca, that is: mine'.

Guides

✔ **Landscapes of Menorca. A
Sunflower Guide** *Rodney Ansell* 1990

✔ **Landscapes of Mallorca. A
Sunflower Guide** *Valerie Crespi-Green* 1992

✔ **Entrée to Mallorca** *Patricia Fenn* 1993

✔ **Menorca. A Windrush Island Guide**
John and Margaret Goulding 1990

✔ **Insight Guide Mallorca and Ibiza,
Menorca and Formentera** 1989

✔ **Insight Pocket Guide Ibiza** 1992

Travel Literature

✔ **Not Part of the Package**
Paul Richardson 1993
The account of a year spent in Ibiza, which
gives a very good idea of what tourism is like
in Spain.

A Winter in Majorca *George Sand* 1956
(1855)
George Sand was little liked in Majorca since
she called the Majorcans 'barbarians,
thieves, monkeys and Polynesian savages';
she had tried to get them to become part of
the modern world and to shake themselves
free of their intellectual and moral shackles,

but after three months of persuasion and
example, she had had to admit defeat and
retired permanently embittered.

CANARY ISLANDS

'Ah, Teneriffe!
Retreating Mountain!
Purple of Ages – pause for *you* –
Sunset – reviews her Sapphire Regiment –
Day – drops you her Red Adieu!

Still – Clad in your Mail of ices –
Thigh of Granite – and thew – of Steel –
Heedless-alike – of pomp – or parting
Ah, Teneriffe!
I'm kneeling – still'
Emily Dickinson (untitled) c. 1863

Guides

✔ **Baedeker's Gran Canaria** 1991

✔ **Baedeker's Tenerife** 1991

✔ **Lanzarote. Windrush Island Guide**
John and Margaret Goulding 1993 (1989)

✔ **Insight Guide Gran Canaria,
Lanzarote, Fuerteventura** 1989

✔ **Landscapes of Fuerteventura. A
Sunflower Guide** *Noel Rochford* 1989

✔ **Landscapes of Gran Canaria. A
Sunflower Guide** *Noel Rochford* 1986

✔ **Landscapes of La Palma and El
Hierro. A Sunflower Guide**
Noel Rochford 1993

✔ **Landscapes of Southern Tenerife
and La Gomera. A Sunflower Guide**
Noel Rochford 1994 (1988)

✔ **Landscapes of Tenerife. A
Sunflower Guide** *Noel Rochford* 1989

SWITZERLAND

'I lived in Switzerland among the Alps at twenty six, under a bitter domestic calamity. I found their solitudes soothe me as nothing else would – I have loved solitude more since.' William Beckford, Letter of 1820s, quoted in Cyrus Redding *Memoirs of William Beckford* 1859 – of 1786

Fiction/Poetry

✔ **Hôtel du Lac** Anita Brookner 1993 (1984)
The romantic novelist Edith Hope walks into the rarefied atmosphere of the Hotel du Lac with her modest dreams. Set around Vevey.

The Prisoner of Chillon Lord Byron 1816
Byron's epic poem was inspired by the sojourn of Franois Bonivard in the dungeon of Chillon.

A Pocketful of Rye A.J. Cronin
A young doctor answers an advertisement for a 'British doctor, single and preferably under 30' for the Maybelle Children's Clinic and Holiday Home, in Switzerland. He applies and gets the job, whereupon his adventures start.

✔ **The Manticore** Robertson Davies 1978 (1978)
Part of the Deptford trilogy; in this volume the Canadian David Staunton enters Jungian analysis in Switzerland because of his father's strange death and the manticore is one of the symbols that emerges.

✔ **Daisy Miller** Henry James 1986 (1878)
There are parts set in Switzerland around Lac Léman and Chillon. Winterbourne meets Daisy in a hotel overlooking Lake Geneva and is thrown into a dilemma by her constant flirtation.

✔ **The Magic Mountain** Thomas Mann 1961 (1927)
Set in a sanatorium in the Swiss mountains, the characters are involved exclusively with ill health symbolizing the diseased capitalistic society of pre-war Europe.

Frankenstein Mary Shelley 1933 (1818)
Set mainly around Lake Geneva where she and Shelley were neighbours of Lord Byron; 'it proved a wet, ungenial summer, and incessant rain often confined us for days to the house'. Due to this Byron suggested that they each write a ghost story, this was the result of Mary Shelley's work.

Lenin in Zurich Alexander Solzhenitsyn 1978 (1975)
A compelling psychological portrait of Lenin during the years 1914–1917; starting at the time he was arrested in Cracow and following his subsequent flight to Zurich at the start of the First World War.

Not to Disturb Muriel Spark 1971
Set in Geneva, the book involves various scandals which the characters assume will have the 'whole of Geneva talking'. Funny and gruesome.

✔ **Heidi** Joanna Spyri 1956 (1880)
Children's books set in the Maienfeld region north of the Graubünden capital of Chur. Heidi is forced to live with her solitary grandfather in the Alps. She quickly learns to love him and her new life.

Food

✔ **A Taste of Switzerland** Sue Style 1992
Divided into sections by the kind of food. Photographs.

General Background

Switzerland for Beginners
George Mikes 1975 (1962)
An amusing look at the Swiss and Switzerland which nonetheless conveys much about the country and its people: 'Yes, the whole world loves the Swiss franc; but only the Swiss adore the Swiss centime.'

Switzerland John Russell 1950
A general background book which was written in order to supplement guides. It is divided into areas: Geneva and the Pys de Vaud, Neuchâtel, Berne and the Jura, the Valais, Zurich, Central Switzerland, the Ticino, the Grisons and Basle, St Gall and the Bodensee.

Guides

✔ **Baedeker Switzerland** 1993

✔ **Karen Brown's Swiss Country Inns and Itineraries** Clare Brown and Karen Brown 1993

✔ **Fodor's Switzerland 1995**

✔ **Switzerland. Travel Survival Kit** Mark Honan 1994

✔ **Insight Guide Switzerland** 1993

✔ **Let's Go Germany and Switzerland 1995**

✔ **Michelin Green Guide Switzerland**
1991

✔ **Michelin Red Guide Suisse 1995**

✔ **Blue Guide Switzerland**
Ian Robertson 1992

History

A Short History of Switzerland
E. Bonjour, H.S. Offler and G.R. Potter 1954 (1952)
Descriptions of the country and its people, the origins of the Confederation, the Reformation and counter-reformation, the foundation of the Federal State and what happened during and after the First World War.

Leisure

✔ **Walking Switzerland the Swiss Way** *Marcia and Philip Lieberman 1987*
Five different alpine centres suitable as bases from which to walk.

✔ **Walking Easy in the Swiss Alps**
Chet and Carolee Lipton 1993

✔ **Pathmaster guides: Bernese Oberland** *Maurice and Marion Teal 1990*

Natural History *(see 'Western Europe –General')*

Alpine Flowers of Britain and Europe
C. Grey-Wilson and N. Blamey 1979

✔ **Our Alpine Flora** *E. Landolt and K.M. Urbanska 1989*
480 colour photographs, published by the Swiss Alpine Club.

Photography

✔ **Switzerland a Pictorial Journey**
1993
Published by Ziethen in full colour.

Travel Literature

✔ **Neither Here Nor There** *Bill Bryson*
1992 (1991)
Bryson's humorous sweep through Europe includes Switzerland.

✔ **Southwards to Geneva. 200 Years of English Travellers** *Mavis Coulson 1988*
A portrait of the city of Geneva between the mid-seventeenth and mid-nineteenth centuries where many travellers ended the Grand Tour.

Heidi's Alp *Christina Hardyment*
Christina Hardyment took her family around Europe in a camper-van in search of the origin of fairy tales.

A Tramp Abroad *Mark Twain (see 'France', 'Germany', 'Italy')*
Twain visits Lucerne, Interlaken, Zermatt and Geneva – mostly on foot.

Scrambles Among the Alps in the years 1860–69 *Edward Whymper 1986 (1871)*
Whymper started keeping a diary from his first visit to the Alps in 1860; his repeated attempts to climb the Matterhorn are well chronicled, both by him and others, but there is still something of a mystery surrounding the accident which occurred on 14th July 1865.

(former) YUGOSLAVIA

Fiction/Poetry

Illyrian Spring *Ann Bridge 1935*
At the start of the novel Lady Kilmichael is embarking on the boat-train for Venice, leaving her husband and family behind 'possibly for good'. She has many adventures in Italy and Yugoslavia before eventually returning.

✔ **Garden, Ashes** *Danilo Kiš 1985 (1965)*
Set in Yugoslavia during the Second World War, the semi-autobiographical novel is about Kiš's childhood growing up in the shadow of a brilliant and destructive father.

✔ **The Dawning** *Milka Bajić Poderegin*
1988 (1987)
A family saga set in a province in southern Yugoslavia as it emerged after the collapse of the Turkish and Austro-Hungarian empires and during the lead up to the First World War.

General Background

✔ **A Paper House. The Ending of Yugoslavia** *Mark Thompson 1992*
Mark Thompson travelled throughout Yugoslavia in the late 1980s and wrote this report on the decline and fall of Yugoslavia.

Guides

✔ **Blue Guide Yugoslavia**
Paul Blanchard 1989

✔ **The Companion Guide to Jugoslavia** J.A. Cuddon 1986 (1968)

History

✔ **The Fall of Yugoslavia** Misha Glenny 1993 (1992)
'The best work on the causes, effects and dangers of the latest Balkan crisis . . . It is virtually impossible to imagine a more informed, objective and far-sighted account of a conflict that will, like it or not, affect us all.' (Phil Davison *Independent*)

Natural History

Flowers of Greece and the Balkans. A Field Guide Oleg Polunin 1987 (1980) (see 'Greece')

Travel Literature

✔ **The Impossible Country** Brian Hall 1994
Brian Hall travelled through Yugoslavia in the spring and summer of 1991 as Croatia and Slovenia were seceding and the civil war was beginning.

✔ **Black Lamb and Grey Falcon**
Rebecca West 1993 (1942)
Rebecca West made three journeys to Yugoslavia in 1935, 1937 and 1938; she became so intrigued by the country that she wrote a masterpiece about the history, archaeology, politics, conversations and landscape. An im-

portant book for understanding the present conflicts in the Balkans. [Stephen Brook]

BOSNIA

History

✔ **Bosnia. A Short History**
Noel Malcolm 1994
A clarification of the complex history and a demythologization of the racial, religious and political history of Bosnia which puts the Bosnian war into its true perspective.

SERBIA

Fiction

✔ **White Eagles Over Serbia**
Lawrence Durrell 1993 (1957)
A gripping cold-war spy thriller, based on Durrell's own experiences, about a British secret service agent who was sent out from London to investigate the murder of a colleague.

SLOVENIA

Fiction

✔ **The Day Tito Died** 1993
A collection of contemporary Slovenian short stories by Drago Jančar, Brane Gradišnik, Jani Virk, Lela B. Njatin and Andrej Blatnik.

Central and Eastern Europe

GENERAL

Art and Archaeology

The Wooden Churches of Eastern Europe: An Introductory Survey
D.R. Buxton 1981
Includes churches in Northern Russia, Ukrainian Galicia and Carpathia, the Ukrai-

nian plains, Rumania, Hungary, Yugoslavia, Poland and Czechoslovakia. Well illustrated with black and white photographs.

✔ **Baroque Art and Architecture in Central Europe** E. Hempel 1965
Pelican 'History of Art' Series. The book covers Germany, Austria, Switzerland, Hungary, Czechoslovakia and Poland and is well illustrated. It includes painting and sculp-

ture of the seventeenth and eighteenth centuries and architecture from the sixteenth to the eighteenth century.

Late Baroque and Rococo Architecture
C. Norberg-Schulz 1986 (1979) (see 'Western Europe' and 'Scandinavia')
The transition from Baroque to Rococo in the eighteenth century heralded a free and more organic form of architecture, as architects began to see man more in the context of the natural world. This is reflected in the cities of Prague, Vienna, Würzburg, Paris, Nancy, London, Turin, Rome and Copenhagen.

Fiction/Poetry

✔ **The Glance of Countess Hahn-Hahn (down the Danube)** Péter Esterházy 1994 (1991)
A mixture of novel and travel book about a Central European journey of the imagination down the Danube from Donaueschingen through Ulm, Vienna and Budapest to the Black Sea.

Storm Magazine
A quarterly magazine of new writing from east and west.

Food

✔ **The Food and Cooking of Eastern Europe** Lesley Chamberlain 1989
A collection of recipes and gastronomical history, which incorporates Eastern European cooking from Vienna to Moscow and from the Adriatic to the Baltic.

General Background

✔ **Granta 30. New Europe** 1990
A collection of pieces on central Europe.

✔ **High Hopes. Young Voices of Eastern Europe** Mita Castle-Kanerova (ed.) 1992
Young people from Czechoslovakia, Hungary, Poland, Germany, Romania and Russia talk about their hopes and fears for the future.

✔ **The Uses of Adversity**
Timothy Garton Ash 1989
A collection of journalistic pieces.

✔ **We the People: the Revolutions of 1989** Timothy Garton Ash 1990
Descriptions of all the 1989 revolutions.

✔ **Traveller's Literary Companion to Eastern Europe** Jim Naughton (ed.) 1994

Guides

✔ **Fodor's Eastern Europe 1995**
Hungary, Poland, Romania, Slovakia, the Czech Republic and Bulgaria.

✔ **Eastern Europe. Travellers Survival Kit** Emily Hatchwell and Simon Calder 1994
Estonia, Latvia, Lithuania, Poland, Czech Republic, Slovak Republic, Hungary, Romania, Bulgaria and Albania.

✔ **Insight Guide Eastern Europe** 1993
Russia, Ukraine, Belarus, the Baltic States, Poland, the Czech and Slovak Republics, Hungary, Romania and Bulgaria.

✔ **Eastern Europe on a Shoestring**
David Stanley 1991 (1989)
Eastern Germany, Poland, Czechoslovakia, Hungary, Romania, Bulgaria, Yugoslavia and Albania.

History

The Burden of the Balkans
M. Edith Durham 1905
Edith Durham made six journeys to the Balkans and aimed to give her readers a true idea of the affairs in the Balkan Peninsula. She believed that the troubles between the Turks, thought of as 'Moslem and bad' and the Macedonians 'all Christian and virtuous' were racial not religious.

✔ **The Rebirth of History: Eastern Europe in the Age of Democracy**
Misha Glenny 1990
Eight chapters which mostly focus on the problems of the future.

✔ **History of the Balkans. Twentieth Century** Barbara Jelavich 1991 (1983)
Begins with a discussion of the internal events and developments in Bulgaria, Greece, Montenegro, Romania and Serbia from 1878 and of the Romanian and South Slav nationalities of the Habsburg Empire from 1867. The different routes taken since 1945 are discussed and continue up to 1980.

✔ **Balkan Ghosts. A Journey Through History** Robert D. Kaplan 1993
A political travel book, full of insight into the current crises.

✔ **Danube** Claudio Magris 1991 (1986) (see 'Austria')
A wide-ranging and excitingly original book

about the Danube and the history, philosophy, people, war and politics that occur along its route: 'A splendid book . . . Magris peppers his journey with . . . serendipitous details; they come at us, one after the other, in brilliant abundance . . . *Danube* is not simply a masterpiece of travel; it is an odyssey. From Heraclitus to Baudelaire the river has appeared as a metaphor for life, winding safely from its source to the sea.' (Ian Thomson *Independent*)

Natural History *(see 'Europe – General')*

Travel Literature

✔ **Balkan Hours. Travels in the Other Europe** *Richard Bassett 1990*
Richard Bassett wrote for *The Times* in Eastern Europe and in this book looks at the past and present of the cities he travels through.

Double Eagle *Stephen Brook 1988 (see 'Austria')*
Brook concentrates on Vienna, Budapest and Prague, the primary cities of the Habsburg empire – which have changed out of all recognition in the seventy odd years since the glittering days of the Habsburgs. His present-day quest in the three cities is full of delightful surprises.

Balkan Holiday *David Footman 1935*
A sympathetic traveller who is aware of both the luxuries and hardships of travelling and who describes what he sees in a lively manner.

Curtain Calls. Travels in Albania, Romania and Bulgaria *Leslie Gardiner 1976*
Leslie Gardiner spent fifteen years travelling through the communist lands of Eastern Europe, with the belief that 'human beings the world over are pretty much alike when you get to know them'.

✔ **Berlin to Bucharest. Travels in Eastern Europe** *Anton Gill 1990*
Gill, who speaks many languages, travelled all over Eastern Europe by air, road and rail.

✔ **Brief Spring. A Journey through Eastern Europe** *Iris Gioia and Clifford Thurlow 1992*
As the barriers in Eastern Europe were crumbling Iris Gioia and Clifford Thurlow set out to travel through East Germany, Poland, Czechoslovakia, Hungary, Bulgaria and Romania.

✔ **Stealing from a Deep Place** *Brian Hall 1989 (1988)*
Brian Hall bicycled through Romania, Bulgaria and Hungary, sleeping rough and meeting many people who were unfailingly kind to him.

✔ **Exit into History** *Eva Hoffman 1993*
Shortly after the dramatic events of 1989, Eva Hoffman spent several months travelling through her native Poland and to Czechoslovakia, Hungary, Romania and Bulgaria.

✔ **Between the Woods and the Water** *Patrick Leigh Fermor 1988 (1986)*
The second part of the trilogy describes Leigh Fermor's journey from the woods of Transylvania to the waters of the Danube: 'Even better than everyone says it is.' (Peter Levi) [Laurence Kelly]

✔ **A Time of Gifts** *Patrick Leigh Fermor 1979 (1977)*
The first volume of the projected trilogy in which Leigh Fermor walked from London to Istanbul in the 1930s. In this volume he reaches Hungary; excellent dense descriptions of life in middle Europe: 'I know of no other account of pre-war Europe which conveys so much so powerfully.' (Peter Levi) [Laurence Kelly]

✔ **Stalin's Nose. Across the Face of Europe** *Rory Maclean 1993 (1992)*
A journey from the Baltic to the Black Sea in a Trabant with an aunt and a pig, *Stalin's Nose* was described by William Dalrymple as 'dark, sardonic and brilliant'.

✔ **Once Upon a Time in the East** *Dave Rimmer 1992*
Dave Rimmer moved to Berlin in 1988 and travelled around the eastern bloc as régimes crumbled around him.

✔ **Prejudice and Plum Brandy** *Alec Russell 1993*
The author was *The Daily Telegraph* correspondent for South-East Europe arriving in Romania a few days after the revolution in 1989 with forged papers and travelling throughout the Balkans during a period of intense change.

Dead Puppets Dance *Philip Thornton 1937 (see 'Albania')*

✔ **Lambada Country** *Giles Whittell 1993 (1992)*
Whittell bicycled from the Baltic to the Black Sea on a six-month journey in 1990 when so much was changing throughout Eastern Europe: 'Constructed with the precision of a

very expensive cocktail ... a really good reporter-writer.' (*Financial Times*)

ALBANIA

'Land of Albania! where Iskander rose,
Theme of the young, and beacon of the
                                                wise,
And he his namesake, whose oft-baffled foes
Shrunk from his deeds of chivalrous
                                        emprize.'
Lord Byron *Childe Harold's Pilgrimage* Canto the Second 1812

'Viola: What country, friends, is this?
Capt: This is Illyria, lady.
Viola: And what should I do in Illyria?'

Shakespeare *Twelfth Night*

Autobiography/Biography

One Man in His Time *Xan Fielding* 1990
The biography of Billy MacLean, which has much about his involvement in Albania during the war.

Fiction/Poetry

✔ **Childe Harold's Pilgrimage**
Lord Byron 1813
Byron began writing the poem in Albania in 1809 and his descriptions of Albania were the only ones that the British reader had information on for a long time.

✔ **Chronicle in Stone** *Ismail Kadare* 1987 (1971)
During World War II control of a city, where a small boy lives, passes backwards and forwards from Italians to Greeks; he sees ghosts mingling with the harsh reality of everyday life. Also ✔ *Broken April* and ✔ *The Palace of Dreams*.

Guides

✔ **Albania. A Guide and Illustrated Journal** *Peter and Andrea Dawson* 1989
A rather whimsical guide in prose and pictures.

✔ **Blue Guide Albania** *James Pettifer* 1994

✔ **Albania** *Philip Ward* 1987 (1983)
For a long time the only guide, but now superseded and out of date.

History

The Great Betrayal. The Untold Story of Kim Philby's Biggest Coup
Nicholas Bethell 1984
In 1949 Kim Philby left Southampton for Washington at the same time as nine Albanians who had been specially trained to be guerillas as a counter to Stalin's aggressive moves; they had been betrayed by Philby before they even arrived back in their country. Albania was chosen by the United States and Britain as a secret battleground between west and east.

The Struggle for Scutari
M. Edith Durham 1914
Edith Durham was present in the area, north Albania, where the various powers of Europe were all striving to gain possession. She writes that 'None who have not lived through the past few years on the spot can imagine the fraud, the treachery, the cold-blooded cruelty and brutality with which the various rulers of Europe have striven, each against each, to obtain, by hook or by crook, possession of, or influence over, that little corner of land in the Near East which has been lately the seat of war, and is now the seat of hopeless misery.'

The Eagle Spreads His Claws
Leslie Gardiner 1966
A history of the Corfu Channel dispute and Albania's relations with the west from 1945–1965.

Albanian Assignment *David Smiley* 1985 (1984)
In 1943 Smiley was parachuted behind enemy lines in order to cross into Albania, organize the local resistance and help wage a guerilla war against the Germans and Italians; a task made even more difficult by the fact that the Albanians were on the brink of civil war and far more interested in fighting each other rather than a common enemy.

Albania: The Rise of a Kingdom
Joseph Swire 1929
Swire quotes from Byron's *Childe Harold's Pilgrimage: Canto the Second, Verse LXV*: 'Fierce are Albania's children, yet they lack Not virtues, were those virtues more mature,' to illustrate his belief in the stalwart Albanians and the vicissitudes they had put up with over the previous fifty years.

The History of Albania from its origins to the present day *S. Pollo and A. Puto* 1981

Travel Literature

Illyria Reborn *Dymphna Cusack* *1966*
Dymphna Cusack had wanted to explore Illyria ever since she had heard the name in *Twelfth Night*. She found very little about Albania before she went and was warned by everyone of its potential dangers.

High Albania *M. Edith Durham* *1985 (1909)*
The travel book of Edith Durham's seven years of journeying throughout the Balkans. She describes the mountainous terrain of northern Albania and intersperses it with history, ethnology, religion and politics. She was the first European seen by many of the tribespeople and became affectionately known to them as 'Queen of the Mountain People'.

In the Lands of the Eagle *Paul Edmonds 1927*
Illustrated travels in Montenegro and Albania by a self-styled 'traveller' : 'The tourist travels for amusement, the traveller because of some urge within him which cannot be resisted . . . The traveller, while by no means blind to fine scenery, regards it as an incident . . .'

Two Vagabonds in Albania *Jan and Cora Gordon* *1927*
The authors travelled throughout Albania during the summer of 1925 observing this 'half-Oriental, half-Western community trying to make a state of itself'. Some of their journey was by car and some on horseback.

Travels in Albania and Other Provinces of Turkey in 1809 and 1810
John Hobhouse (Right Hon. Lord Broughton) 1855
Hobhouse left Malta with Byron, both of them deciding to go to 'some port of European Turkey', rather than Smyrna, due to a brig of war passing at the opportune time. Hobhouse gives detailed descriptions of the sites and buildings.

Journals of a Landscape Painter in Greece and Albania *Edward Lear 1988 (1851)*
Two journeys through Greece and Albania in autumn 1848 and spring 1849. His journey to Albania had not been planned ahead; he had been intending to go to Mount Athos, but after discovering that it was closed to visitors as a result of a cholera epidemic he set out for the then unknown Albania.

✔ **On the Shores of the Mediterranean** *Eric Newby*
(see 'Western Europe – General')

Dead Puppets Dance *Philip Thornton 1937*
Philip Thornton started his travels round the Balkans with a visit to Albania, because he was intrigued by the language.

BULGARIA

'They are a fine people with a *passion* for freedom: so great that it made them able to remain 500 years under the Turk and come out pure Bulger at the end.' Freya Stark, letter 24 March 1939 in *The Coasts of Incense* 1953

Art and Archaeology

The Thracians *R.F. Hoddinott 1981*
A good if somewhat technical introduction to the Thracians and their archaeology.

Biography

The Truth that Killed *Georgi Markov 1983*
Markov defected to England, but the authorities were so enraged by the publication of this book that they ordered his murder.

Fiction/Poetry

✔ **The Devil's Dozen** *1990*
A collection of thirteen Bulgarian women poets.

✔ **The Last Rock Eagle** *Blaga Dimitrova 1992*
Blaga Dimitrova is considered to be Bulgaria's finest contemporary poet.

✔ **The Inn at Antimovo**
✔ **Legends of Stara Planina**
Yordan Yovkov 1990 (1989)
These books appeared originally in 1927 and are stories set in the villages and the mountains.

Food

✔ **The Wine and Food of Bulgaria**
Don Philpott 1989
A large-format book, chiefly about wine, with recipes in the back.

General Background

✔ **Bulgarian Voices** *Philip Ward 1992*
A collection of monologues recorded by Bulgarians from all walks of life.

Guides

✔ **Bulgaria. The Rough Guide**
Jonathan Bousfield and Dan Richardson   1993

✔ **Bulgaria. A Travel Guide**
Philip Ward   1989

✔ **Sofia. Portrait of a City**   Philip Ward
1993

History

✔ **A Short History of Modern
Bulgaria**   R.J. Crampton   1993 (1987)
A good introduction which is easy to read,
beginning with pre-modern Bulgaria and the
first Bulgarian empire of 681 AD and continuing to the mid-1980s.

Travel Literature

Gay Bulgaria   Stowers Johnson   1964
Johnson travelled across Bulgaria by Dor-
mobile and was therefore able to go almost
anywhere he wanted; he notes and dismisses
the behaviour and conversations of most
other foreigners.

Bulgarian Background   Bernard Newman
1961
Newman had first visited Bulgaria in 1933
and went back again in 1959 travelling
throughout, having learnt a little of the language.

Donkey Serenade   George Sava   1940
Most of Sava's travelling was along the back-
roads of Bulgaria; he had been much influenced by Robert Louis Stevenson as a
child, and had determined that before he died
he 'would take a nag and investigate some
corner of the earth with the same curiosity
and interest'.

CISS

'When one reflects of the immense
magnitude of this empire, one is lost in the
idea.' Sir N.W. Wraxall A Tour Round the
Baltic 1775

Art and Archaeology

A History of Russian Painting
Alan Bird   1987
Illustrated and with potted biographies of all
the major artists. Bird starts with icons and
continues into the twentieth century. Mostly
black and white illustrations.

Russian Art of the Avant Garde   Edited
and translated by J.E. Bowlt   1988 (1976)
Critical essays on the theory and criticism of
the Russian avant-garde between 1902 and
1934. The anthology includes manifestos, articles and declarations by artists and writers
including Kandinsky, Lissitsky, Malevich
and Rodchenko.

✔ **Moscow Graffiti**   John Bushnell   1990
An illustrated look at the language and sub-
culture associated with the graffiti which
began to appear in Moscow and other cities
in the late 1970s.

Russian Medieval Architecture
D.R. Buxton   1934
Concentrates on Kiev, Novgorovod, Pskov,
Vladimir, Moscow and the wooden architecture of the Ukraine. Includes an account of
the Transcaucasian styles and their influence in the west.

**New Worlds: Russian Art and Society
1900–1937**   D. Elliott   1986
A magazine-style look at what was happening in Russia during the years leading up to
the Revolution and in the aftermath.

**The Russian Experiment in Art
1863–1922**   Camilla Gray   1971
A guide to the many movements in Russian
art. Throughout the period covered by the
book there was the idea of a renewal of art as
a socially active force – sometimes obvious
and sometimes disguised. 256 illustrations
with twenty-one in colour.

✔ **The Art and Architecture of
Russia**   George Heard Hamilton   1983 (1954)
In the Penguin 'History of Art' series. The
book is confined to the area west of the Urals
and is well illustrated with black and white
photographs.

**Russian Art from Neoclassicism to the
Avant Garde**   D.V. Sarabianov   1990
A large illustrated book which looks at Russian art from 1800 to 1917 and helps to elucidate the antecedents of Russian avant
garde painting.

Autobiography/Biography

✔ **Years of Childhood**   Sergei Aksakov
1983 (1858)
Aksakov grew up in eastern Russia on his
father's estate at the close of the eighteenth
century; there was a tension between this life
and the more sophisticated urban life of his
mother, which divided his loyalties, but
which he writes about with an unflinching
honesty and clarity.

✔ **Manuscripts Don't Burn**
Mikhail Bulgakov 1992 (1991)
The life of Bulgakov compiled from diaries
and letters by Julie Curtis.

✔ **The House by the Dvina**
Eugenie Fraser 1991 (1984)
Russia before, during and after the Revolution is delightfully evoked by Eugenie
Fraser who was half Scottish and half Russian; she was brought up in Russia with
occasional visits to Scotland and eventually
made a dramatic escape to Scotland.

✔ **Within the Whirlwind**
Eugenia Ginzburg 1989 (1979)
Into the Whirlwind tells how Eugenia Ginzburg was falsely accused of terrorism during
Stalin's purges. *Within the Whirlwind* narrates how she was sent to work as a nurse,
fell in love with a doctor and how they were
eventually released in 1955.

✔ **My Childhood** *Maxim Gorky 1966
(1913)*
The first volume of Gorky's autobiographical
trilogy which continues with *My Apprenticeship* and *My Universities*. 'One of the most
moving descriptions of boyhood ever written
... Reading it we enter into Russian life as it
really was at the turn of the century, and this
is an unforgettable experience.' (Ronald
Wilks)

The Russian Album *Michael Ignatieff
1988 (1987)*
The history, from diaries and notebooks, of
four generations of a family which had its
roots in St Petersburg. Starting in pre-Revolutionary times at the court of Tsar Alexander III, the family is swept along by the tide
of revolution and exile.

✔ **I Remember** *Fara Lynn Krasnopolsky
1992*
A memoir by a Jewish girl, Hannah, about
village life in pre-Revolutionary Russia.

Rasputin and the Fall of the Romanovs
Colin Wilson 1977 (1964)
A sceptical look at Rasputin, but which was
described by Maria Rasputin his daughter as
'The first real book I have ever come across
that speaks honestly and honourably about
my father, and shows him as an outstanding
man and not as an unscrupulous adventurer
... It is the best book on my father that I have
ever read.'

Fiction/Poetry

✔ **The Little Angel** *Leonid Andreyev 1989
(1915)*
A collection of short stories which with their
deep metaphysical despair struck a chord in
pre-revolutionary Russia and were instantly
popular on publication. Also by Andreyev
✔ *The Red Laugh* 1989 (1905)

Petersburg *Andrei Bely 1983 (1916)*
Anthony Burgess described *Petersburg* as
'the one novel that sums up the whole of
Russia'. It is a masterpiece of suspense which
takes place during several days in the
autumn of 1905.

✔ **Pushkin House** *Andrei Bitov 1990
(1978)*
The hero, Lyova, is born in Leningrad, graduates in the year of Stalin's death, but dies
on the first page of the book: 'Imagine, if you
will, a cross between Bely's *Petersburg* and
Nabokov's *The Gift*, with the dash and gaiety
of Pushkin and the slightly skewed vision of
Gogol, and you will have the flavour.' (John
Banville)

Lenin – The Novel *Alan Brien 1988 (1987)*
Written in the form of a diary by Lenin, a
clever evocation of the man which combines
detailed research with imagination: 'Anyone
wanting to explore the Russian Revolution
and its presiding genius would not be led
astray if the first book they picked up was the
diary Alan Brien has imagined Lenin writing.' (Mark Frankland *The Observer*)

✔ **The Master and Margarita**
Mikhail Bulgakov 1988 (1967)
Part satire, part fantasy; the devil arrives in
Moscow, creates havoc and leaves people
brought out the worst in everybody. The Master and Margarita, the woman he loves, remain undiminished by these exploits.

Honey for the Bears *Anthony Burgess 1963*
A story set in 1950s Leningrad about sexual
discovery and black-marketeering. Paul
Hussey, an antique dealer from Sussex, sails
to Leningrad with his American wife, Be-
linda with the aim of selling drylon dresses.

✔ **The Portable Chekhov**
Anton Chekhov Avrahm Yarmolinsky (ed.) 1977
Twenty-eight of Chekhov's best stories.

✔ **The Brothers Karamazov**
*Fyodor Dostoevsky Translated by
David Magarahack 1982 (1880)*
Dostoevsky's last novel, which he finished
just before he died, concerns parricide, a subject with which he had been fascinated since
childhood, but for which he got the idea while
imprisoned in Siberia. Other works include

✔ *Crime and Punishment,* ✔ *The Idiot,* ✔ *The Gambler* and ✔ *The Devils.*

✔ **From the Reminiscences of Private Ivanov and other Stories** V. Garshin 1988
This collection contains sixteen of Garshin's short stories, almost all he wrote during his short life (1855–88).

✔ **Dead Souls** Nikolai Gogol 1961 (1842)
A businessman buys up the dead 'souls' or serfs whose names still appear on the government census. Writing the novel drove Gogol to madness.

✔ **Doctor Zhivago** Boris Pasternak
Translated by Manya Harari and Max Hayward 1991 (1957)
Set against the background of the Revolution, the story of Yuri Zhivago, his love life and his love of literature. The book was published in Russia in 1987, having originally been published in Italy.

✔ **Eugene Onegin** Alexander Pushkin
Translated by Charles Johnston 1979 (1830) [Laurence Kelly]
A brilliant verse novel, brilliantly translated, about the see-sawing love between Tatyana and the dashing cynical Onegin. Also by Pushkin *Boris Godunov, The Gipsies, The Captain's Daughter* and *The Queen of Spades.*

✔ **The Penguin Book of Russian Short Stories** David Richards (ed.) 1981
A collection of stories by twenty major writers including Pushkin, Gogol, Lermontov, Dostoevsky and Gorky.

✔ **Mother Russia** Bernice Rubens 1992 (1989)
The love story of the daughter of a count and the son of a peasant, set at the turn of the century.

August 1914 Alexander Solzhenitsyn 1990 (1989)
Also *Cancer Ward* (1967), *The First Circle* (1968) and *One Day in the Life of Ivan Denisovich.* Powerful and disturbing books which made a great impact in the west when they were first published.

✔ **And Quiet Flows the Don**
Mikhail Sholokov 1988 (1929)
And Quiet Flows the Don and *The Don Flows Home to the Sea* are the two volumes of Sholokov's great novel, set in a Cossack village, which he wrote on returning to his native Don after years spent in Moscow as a stonemason, house-painter and labourer. ✔ *Virgin Soil Upturned* 1984 (1932) is a novel about

the problems of making Communism work in the deep south of Russia.

✔ **War and Peace** Leo Tolstoy Translated by Rosemary Edmonds 1982 (1869)
This great, epic novel depicts Russian family life with all its strengths and weaknesses during and after the Napoleonic War, as well as being an historical chronicle of the time. Other books by Tolstoy include ✔ *Anna Karenina,* ✔ *The Death of Ivan Ilyich,* ✔ *Childhood, Boyhood and Youth.*

✔ **On the Golden Porch and Other Stories** Tatyana Tolstoya 1990 (1987)
'Magical! . . . A luminous collection . . . Tolstaya is an enormously gifted writer and this volume is a dazzling debut.' (*The New York Times*) Another collection of stories is called ✔ *Sleepwalker in a Fog.*

✔ **Sketches from a Hunter's Album**
Ivan Turgenev 1990 (1852)
Drawn from first-hand observations of the countryside, the sketches make valuable social documents as well as beautiful stories. Also *First Love* (1860), *On the Eve* (1859), *Spring Torrents* 1990 (partly autobiographical), *Fathers and Sons* (1861) and *Virgin Soil* (1877) [Colin Thubron] [Jan Morris]

Food

✔ **Russian Cookbook** Kira Petrovskaya 1992
An easy-to-follow guide to over 200 recipes.

General Background

✔ **Voices of Glasnost** Christopher Cerf and Marina Albee 1990
A selection of letters to the magazine *Ogonyok.*

✔ **Out of Red Darkness. Reports from the Collapsing Soviet Empire**
Trevor Fishlock 1992
As a foreign correspondent Trevor Fishlock travelled all over the Soviet Union and saw at first hand what happened with Gorbachev's attempts at reform.

✔ **The Other Russia** Michael Glenny and Norman Stone 1991 (1990)
Three generations of émigrés from Russia tell the story of why, how and where they fled.

✔ **Moscow! Moscow!** Christopher Hope 1991 (1990)
Hope found much in Moscow in common with South Africa, his homeland. His impressions of the changing and multi-faceted Moscow are unforgettable.

✔ **Russian Voices** Tony Parker 1991
Tony Parker spent five months in Moscow in 1990 recording and interviewing wherever he went; for the first time people seemed to be able to talk without fear.

✔ **Epics of Everyday Life**
Susan Richards 1991 (1990)
Susan Richards had long been fascinated by Russia; she made four journeys to the Soviet Union between 1988 and 1990 observing the major changes and writing an orginal book about them: 'Susan Richards writes . . . about the passions, hopes and hard realities of life for the ordinary Russian citizens whom she befriended. Her book is about despair and ultimately about the triumph of the human spirit in a disintegrating empire.' (Sue Mac-Gregor *Mail on Sunday*) [Colin Thubron]

✔ **The New Russians** Hedrick Smith 1990
Hedrick Smith did not return to the Soviet Union until 1988 when he went to join Reagan's summit meeting with Gorbachev. He was so struck by the changes that were taking place in Gorbachev's Russia that he spent nine months spread over two years travelling over 40,000 miles to find out what it was like in the then 'new' Soviet Union. A fascinating book.

The Russians Hedrick Smith 1977 (1976)
Written in 1975 when the author had just returned to the States after three years of being Moscow Bureau Chief of *The New York Times*. The book won the Pulitzer Prize for its complex and authentic account of life in Russia during the early seventies. Compulsive reading.

Guides

✔ **Hippocrene Language and Travel Guide to Russia** Victoria Andreyeva and Margarita Zubkus 1993

✔ **Baedeker's Leningrad** n.d.

✔ **Baedeker's Moscow** 1991

✔ **Cadogan Guide Moscow and St Petersburg** 1994

✔ **Insight Guide Moscow** 1992

✔ **Insight Guide Russia** 1994

✔ **Insight Guide St Petersburg** 1992

✔ **Moscow. A Traveller's Companion**
Laurence Kelly 1983

St Petersburg: A Traveller's Companion Laurence Kelly 1989 (1981)

✔ **USSR. Travel Survival Kit** John Noble and John King 1991

✔ **Blue Guide Moscow and Leningrad** Evan Mawdsley 1991

✔ **Introduction to Leningrad. An Odyssey Guide** Masha Nordbye 1991

✔ **Introducing Moscow and the Golden Ring. An Odyssey Guide**
Masha Nordbye 1991

✔ **St Petersburg. The Rough Guide**
Dan Richardson and Rob Humphreys 1993

✔ **Where in Moscow** Paul E. Richardson 1993 (1991)
A comprehensive directory to Moscow goods and services with a clear coloured map.

History

✔ **Russia. The Present and the Past**
Edward Acton 1987 (1986)
A chronological history from the ninth century which tries to explain the Soviet Union as it was in the 1980s.

✔ **History of Soviet Russia** E.H. Carr 1953
A history in three volumes.

✔ **Russia. A Concise History**
Ronald Hingley 1993 (1972)]
A brief but informative and well-illustrated history.

A History of the Soviet Union
Geoffrey Hosking 1990 (1985)
A well-researched history of the Soviet political system covering the period from 1917, which shows how power has rarely been devolved from a tightly-knit ruling élite and how that affects both the rulers and the ruled.

The Making of Modern Russia
Lionel Kochan and Richard Abraham 1983 (1962)
A weighty Russian history from the beginnings up until Brezhnev.

✔ **Catherine the Great. A Short History** Isabel de Madariaga 1993 (1990)
A stimulating biography of Catherine which includes in depth detail about the times she lived in: 'De Madariaga's book will be the standard and an essential guide for all students and scholars of Russian and European history of the second half of the eighteenth century.' (Marc Raeff *Journal of Modern History*)

Nicholas and Alexandra Robert Massie 1985 (1967)
A very readable history with much about the

haemophilia of the Romanovs which indirectly brought down the dynasty and the power which Rasputin held at court.

Peter the Great: His Life and Work
Robert Massie 1980
Peter the Great who ruled from 1682–1725 was 'a force of nature', a complex character who was by turn cruel yet tender and arrogant yet dedicated.

✔ A Traveller's History of Russia and the USSR *Peter Neville 1990*
A concise comprehensive history from prehistoric times up to 'perestroika' and 'glasnost'.

✔ Ten Days that Shook the World
John Reed 1977 (1919)
An eye-witness account of the 1917 Bolshevik revolution which contains verbatim reports of speeches by leaders and the chance remark from bystanders.

✔ To the Finland Station
Edmund Wilson 1940
A look at Lenin's place in the Russian revolutionary tradition.

Natural History

The Natural History of the USSR
Algirdas Kynstautas 1987
An overview of the varied natural history of the Soviet Union with 275 colour photographs; the author looks at the distribution of the flora and fauna and continues with a region-by-region survey of the vegetation and wildlife.

The Nature of Russia
John Massey Stewart 1992
The range and diversity of the natural history found in the 22 million sq. km of the former Soviet Union, is immense. This illustrated book looks at the natural history of the various regions.

Photography

Imperial Splendour. Palaces and Monasteries of Old Russia
Prince George Galitzine 1991
Lavishly illustrated book with minimal text of the palaces at Novgorod, Pskov, those in the Golden Ring, Moscow and St Petersburg. He concentrates on three periods – pre-Muscovite, when the building was in timber, the sixteenth and seventeenth centuries and the ascendancy of Muscovy and the final period, the foundation of St Petersburg by Peter the Great.

✔ Old Russian Cities *Vadim Gippenreiter and Alexei Komech 1991*
The photographs of nine cities, carefully taken to avoid modern Soviet architecture.

✔ The Russian Style *Evgenia Kirichenko and Mikhail Anikst 1991*
A broad spectrum of Russian interiors lavishly illustrated with 300 illustrations, 260 of which are in colour. Ample text.

✔ The Wooden Architecture of Russia. Houses, Fortifications, Churches *A.V. and Y.A. Opolovnikov 1989*
Northern Russia and Siberia are the richest areas in the world for buildings made of wood.

✔ Imperial Palaces of Russia
Prince Michael of Greece 1992
A well-illustrated survey of twenty-five of the major palaces in and around St Petersburg, some of which had not been photographed before. The Russian style was unique in that it used Italian, German, British and Russian architects and the Romanovs often wanted the interiors to be 'cosy'.

Travel Literature

✔ First Russia, Then Tibet
Robert Byron 1985 (1933)
A classic travel book written in the 1930s: 'Byron was a scholar, a most courageous traveller, a writer of great diligence and an extremely funny man.' (Jan Morris *Independent*)

In the Communist Mirror
Lesley Chamberlain 1990
One of the last western observers to travel widely throughout the Soviet Union; she creates a varied landscape.

✔ What Am I Doing Here
Bruce Chatwin 1990 (1989)
One of the pieces is about visiting Russia with George Ortiz.

✔ Letters from Russia
Marquis de Custine Translated and edited by Robin Buss 1991 (1843)
When the Marquis de Custine travelled through Russia in 1839, having observed the social, political and religious state of the country, he was filled with foreboding, realizing that Russia's goal was the conquest of the world.

✔ A Russian Journal *John Steinbeck 1994 (1949)*
John Steinbeck and the photographer Robert Capa travelled round the Soviet Union in the

1940s writing about and photographing ordinary people.

✔ **Among the Russians** Colin Thubron
1985 (1983)
Colin Thubron drove around Russia by car when this was still extremely difficult: 'One of the best – and best-written – travel books of recent years.' (Nigel Ryan *Times Literary Supplement*)

Ustinov in Russia Peter Ustinov 1987
Ustinov travelled throughout Russia while making a television documentary; full of history and personal philosophy of what he saw and discovered.

✔ **Journey into Russia**
Laurens van der Post 1965 (1964)
Van der Post managed to get behind the officialdom of Russia and meet hundreds of ordinary people: 'The next best thing to seeing the place for oneself . . . ' (*Guardian*)

SIBERIA AND KAMCHATKA

'In Siberia, 100 miles is ordinary distance, 100 roubles an ordinary sum, but a day without sunshine is extraordinary.' Old Proverb.

Biography

✔ **The Princess of Siberia**
Christine Sutherland 1988 (1984)
The story of Princess Maria Volkonsky, the wife of one of the leaders of the 1825 Decembrist Rising, who travelled over 4000 miles in a Russian winter to join her husband in exile.

Fiction

✔ **Memoirs from the House of the Dead** Fyodor Dostoevsky Translated by Jessie Coulson 1991 (1861/2)
More of an autobiography of Dostoevsky's time spent as a convict in Omsk in western Siberia.

General Background

✔ **The Gulag Archipelago**
Alexander Solzhenitsyn 1988
Solzhenitsyn's masterwork is based on the testimonies of 200 survivors of the camps and prisons of the Gulag. 'What gives the book its value is the sound it gives out; the harsh roar given out by a wise and experienced animal as a warning that the herd is in danger.' (Rebecca West *The Sunday Telegraph*)

The Siberians Farley Mowat 1982 (1971)
Mowat travelled across Soviet Siberia from the Ural Mountains to the Sea of Okhotsk and from the Mongolian border to the Arctic Ocean meeting many Siberians, whom he writes about with understanding and compassion.

Guides

✔ **Irkutsk and Lake Baikal. A Guide**
Mark Sergeyev 1986
Published in Moscow.

✔ **The Trans-Siberian Rail Guide**
Robert Strauss 1993 (1987)
Background facts on Siberia, the Russian Far East and Mongolia, with useful phrases in each language, strip maps of the railway routes, tips for the journey and anecdotes from past travellers.

✔ **Trans-Siberian Handbook**
Bryn Thomas 1994 (1988)
Up-to-date information on how to embark on a trip on the world's longest continuous railway track.

History

✔ **East of the Sun** Benson Bobrick 1993 (1992)
A history of Siberia from its conquest in the sixteenth century through the creation of Stalin's Gulag Archipelago to the break-up of the Soviet Empire at the end of the twentieth century.

Photography

✔ **Kamchatka. Land of Fire and Ice**
Vadim Gippenreiter 1992
Colour photographs of volcanoes and the landscape.

✔ **Baikal. Sacred Sea of Siberia**
Peter Matthiessen Photographs by Boyd Norton 1992
Lake Baikal, the size of Belgium, is the largest freshwater lake in the world, containing one-fifth of the world's fresh water. Peter Matthiessen visited the area in 1990; his diary is produced here.

✔ **The Wooden Architecture of Russia. Houses, Fortifications, Churches** A.V. and Y.A. Opolovnikov 1989
Northern Russia and Siberia are the richest areas in the world for buildings made of wood.

Travel Literature

✔ **Beyond Siberia** *Christina Dodwell* *1994 (1993)*
Christina Dodwell travelled to Kamchatka and learned to herd reindeer, ski frozen rivers and track bears.

✔ **The Big Red Train Ride** *Eric Newby 1989 (1978)*
Eric Newby made the trip from Moscow to Nakhodka in 1977 with three diverse companions and a quantity of vodka: 'The best kind of travel book . . . it awakened frosty demons in me, and memories I had thought forgotten.' (Paul Theroux)

THE BALTIC STATES: ESTONIA, LATVIA, LITHUANIA

'It is inconceivable how few are the wants of the Lithuanian peasants! Their carts are put together without iron; their bridles and traces are generally plaited from the bark of trees, or composed merely of twisted branches.' William Coxes *Travels into Poland, Russia, Sweden etc.* 1792

Autobiography/Biography

Baltic Countdown *Peggie Benton* *1985*
A British diplomat's wife was caught in Riga at the outbreak of World War II.

Fiction

✔ **Professor Marten's Departure**
Jaan Kross *1994*
Professor Marten, an Estonian working for the Russian Empire in the nineteenth century takes a long train journey from Pärnu to St Petersburg and reflects on his life and loves.

Venusberg *Anthony Powell* *1932*
Lushington, who began his career in the city and wanted to be a drama critic, is sent as a special correspondent to Lithuania.

General Background

✔ **The Baltic States. A Reference Book** *1991*
Published in Tallinn by the publishers of the Estonian, Latvian and Lithuanian encyclopedias, the book lists important addresses, 'who's who', and background information such as language and folklore.

The Baltic Experience *Anatol Lieven* *1993*
An interesting background to the cultural, economic and political life of the Baltic.

The Singing Revolution *Clare Thompson 1992*
A British journalist's account of what happened in the Baltics in 1989–90.

Guides

✔ **Scandinavia and Baltic Europe on a Shoestring** *Glenda Bendure et al.* *1993*

✔ **Traveller's Survival Kit Eastern Europe** *Emily Hatchwell and Simon Calder 1994*
Includes chapters on Estonia, Latvia and Lithuania.

✔ **Insight Guide Baltic States** *1993*

✔ **A Guide to the Baltic States**
Ingrida Kalnins *1990*
Written and published by Baltic-Americans at the time when the Baltic states were going through a great transition.

✔ **Baltic States and Kaliningrad. Travel Survival Kit** *John Noble* *1994*

✔ **Estonia. The Guide** *John O'Brien* *1993*
Published in Tallinn.

History

The Baltic Nations and Europe
John Hiden *1991*
Twentieth century history in Estonia, Latvia and Lithuania.

✔ **The Baltic States. Years of Dependence 1940–90** *Romuala Misiunas and Rein Taagepera* *1993 (1983)*
Description and analysis of how the Baltic nations survived fifty years of social disruption.

Photography

✔ **My Lithuania** *Aleksandras Macijauskas 1991*
Black and white photographs.

Travel Literature

✔ **Ticket to Latvia** *Marcus Tanner* *1989*
A journey from Berlin to the Baltic by an indirect and circuitous route, via Potsdam and Erfurt.

MOLDAVIA

Fiction

✔ **My Childhood at the Gate of Unrest** Paul Goma 1990 (1987)
A family live through World War II in a remote Moldavian village that is swallowed up by Stalin's Russia. The father is deported to a Soviet labour camp, leaving the mother to take care of the school and bury all the dead.

UKRAINE

' We passed through the Ukraine, which depressed me in spite of its rich black soil, for I remembered how before the war I had stayed there in the magnificent hospitality of Polish friends, riding, dancing, laughing . . . ' Vita Sackville-West *Passenger to Tehran* 1926

Guide

✔ **Hiking Guide to Poland and Ukraine. A Bradt Guide** Tim Burford 1994

CZECH REPUBLIC

'Prague seemed –it still seems, after many rival cities –not only one of the most beautiful places in the world, but one of the strangest.' Patrick Leigh Fermor *A Time of Gifts* 1977

Art and Archaeology (see
'Eastern Europe – General')

Autobiography/Biography

Prague Farewell H. Margolius Kovaly 1988
The autobiography of the widow of a defendant executed in the 1950s, which starts in the concentration camps of World War II.

Prague Winter N. Martin 1990
Martin grew up in Prague in the 1930s and ended up in a concentration camp before escaping to Canada.

✔ **Dubček** William Shawcross 1990 (1970)
The book begins with the history of Czechoslovakia in 1918 and follows Dubček's life as a courageous leader during the Prague

Spring, his disappearance from public life and his re-emergence in 1989.

Fiction/Poetry

✔ **Utz** Bruce Chatwin 1989 (1988)
A novel about a compulsive porcelain collector in the Jewish quarter of Prague. 'For my money, Chatwin is the greatest stylist writing in England today . . . Not a word is wasted in the telling of this tale. Each sentence is fashioned, polished, and put into place with microscopic care.' (Nicholas Shakespeare *The Daily Telegraph*)

The Labyrinth of the World and the Paradise of the Heart
John Amos Comenius Translated by Matthew Spinka 1972 (1663)
An allegory or description of reality metaphorically depicted, written by Comenius (1592–1670), who had been driven from his home in Moravia by the Thirty Years War and had found refuge on the estates of a nobleman. His work, which faces up to the harsh realities of life, as well as giving the prescription for happiness, is thought of as 'the gem of Czech literature'.

A Stricken Field Martha Gellhorn 1940
An autobiographical novel about an American journalist who arrives in Prague at the time that the Nazis march into Sudetenland.

✔ **The Weeping Woman of Prague**
Sylvie Germain 1993 (1992)
In a ghostly Prague 'the weeping woman' is a symbolic figure of grief, the epitome of suffering and pain; poetry and history are combined in this strange and distressing book.

✔ **The Good Soldier Švejk** J. Hašek
Translated by C. Parrott 1974 (1973)
A rambling story about Švejk who creates havoc in the army in World War I; a little man who takes on bureaucracy and officialdom by a combination of passive resistance, native cunning and insolence.

✔ **I Served the King of England**
B. Hrabal (1989)
A fantasy about a waiter's coming of age, set against the backdrop of modern Czech history. Also by Hrabal *The Death of Mr Baltisberger* (1990) and *Closely Watched Trains* (1990).

✔ **Old Czech Legends** Alois Jirásek 1992
A glorification of the Czech past written in the 1890s.

✔ **The Complete Novels** F. Kafka 1992
The Trial, *America* and *The Castle* are in-

cluded. Other compendiums include *Complete Short Stories* (1983) *Diary* (1969).

✔ **My Companions in the Bleak House** *Eva Kantůrková 1989 (1987)*
The detention cell in a woman's prison outside Prague: 'It will take its place in prison literature as a quiet indictment of human stupidity and a celebration of the spark that somehow survives.' (*Literary Review*)

✔ **Love and Garbage** *I. Klima 1991*
The narrator of the novel has abandoned his work on Kafka and has become a roadsweeper in Prague; he argues with himself about life and finally comes to the conclusion that it is impossible to be an honest writer and an honest lover. ✔ *Judge on Trial* (1991) is an epic novel about those who stayed in Prague after 1968. Also by Klima ✔ *A Summer Affair* (1987) and ✔ *My Golden Trades* (1992).

✔ **The Unbearable Lightness of Being** *M. Kundera 1984*
'There are novels which are tragic, or entertaining, and this one is both. There are very few that give a fresh perspective on existence, and force the reader to reassess his own life and attitudes. Kundera is consistently interesting.' (*The Sunday Times*) Also by Kundera *The Book of Laughter and Forgetting* (1982), ✔ *Immortality* (1991), *The Farewell Party* (1993) and ✔ *The Joke* (1983).

✔ **By Night Under the Stone Bridge** *Leo Perutz 1990*
Historical novel set in the Prague of Rudolf.

✔ **The Piper on the Mountain** *Ellis Peters 1991 (1966)*
A modern-day detective story set in Prague and the Slovak Tatra mountains; the amateur sleuth Dominic Felse makes a detour to Czechoslovakia where his innocent journey becomes deadly.

✔ **The Book of Wishes and Complaints** *Zina Rohan 1992 (1991)*
A young country girl, Hana, moves to the city at the time of the 1968 Prague Spring; she is taken in by the local doctor and his wife (who has recently come from England) and grows up around a mixture of Earl Grey tea and Marxist tracts, eventually fleeing to England.

✔ **The Bass Saxophone** *J. Škvorecký*
Based on Škvorecký's love of jazz; also by Škvorecký *The Cowards, The Swell Season, Miss Silver's Past,* ✔*The Miracle Game* (1990) and *Dvořak.*

Stalin's Shoe *Zdena Tomin 1987 (1986)*
A Czech exile is forced to come to terms with her Stalinist childhood in Prague when she ends up in a remote cottage in North Wales: 'She takes a curious mixture of politics, recent Eastern European history, personal pain, unrequited love, despair, and sheer frivolity, sets them all on a Welsh mountain, exposes the mix to what I can only describe as some kind of incandescent cosmic light, and produces not only brilliant, but an informative and international, novel.' (Fay Weldon)

Food

✔ **The Czechoslovak Cookbook** *Joza Brizova 1965*
Czech food adapted for American kitchens.

General Background

✔ **Open Letters** *Václav Havel 1991*
A series of essays, some of which date back to the mid-1960s. Also by Havel is ✔*Living in Truth* (1989), a collection of six essays by Havel and sixteen testimonies by fellow writers.

The Serpent and the Nightingale *C. Parrott 1977*
The author was appointed Information Officer and First Secretary in the British Embassy in Prague in 1945; he retired from his posting in 1966, going into academic life, writing these memoirs and a biography of Hašek.

✔ **Talkin' Moscow Blues** *J. Škvorecký 1989 (1988)*
Essays on a range of different subjects including jazz, literature, film and politics.

✔ **A Cup of Coffee With My Interrogator** *Ludvik Vaculik 1987*
Essays on life in Czechoslovakia post the 1968 revolution.

Guides

✔ **Prague. A Guide** *Lucy Abel Smith 1991*
A narrative guide with photographs.

✔ **Everyman Guide Prague** *1994*

✔ **The Czech and Slovak Republics. The Rough Guide** *Rob Humphreys 1993*

✔ **Prague. The Rough Guide** *Rob Humphreys 1992*

✔ **Insight Guide Czechoslovak Republics** *1993*

✔ **Insight Guide Prague** *1993*

✔ **Blue Guide Czechoslovakia**
Michael Jacobs 1992

✔ **Cadogan City Guide Prague**
Sadakat Kadri 1993 (1991)

✔ **Prague. Prestel Guide**
Anneliese Keilhauer 1993

✔ **American Express Guide Prague**
Sevan Nisanyan 1993

✔ **Czechoslovakia. A Pallas Guide.**
Sebastian Wormall (ed.) 1992

History

The Story of Prague Count Francis Lützow
1907
An introduction to the city's history.

The Meaning of Czech History
T.G. Masaryk 1974
Masaryk's concept of Czech history was a call to action or an appeal to his nation to whom he wanted to give a national ethic. These writings mostly date from the 1890s apart from a speech he gave on Jan Hus in 1910.

A History of Czechoslovakia since
1945 H.A. Renner 1988
The author was one of the 1968 émigrés; the book goes up to 1987.

The History of the Czechs and
Slovaks R.W. Seton-Watson 1943
Written during the Second World War – a very balanced account.

Photography

✔ **Prague. Architecture, History, Art**
Stephen Brook 1992

Travel Literature

Czechoslovakia John Burke 1976
A workaday travelogue which roams all over the country.

✔ **Vanishing Borders** Michael Farr 1993
(1991) (see 'Poland' and 'Germany')
The author was *The Daily Telegraph* correspondent in East Germany before and after the revolutions and was able to travel around reporting on crucial meetings and observing daily life.

A Wayfarer in Czechoslovakia
E.I. Robson 1929 (1925)
A record of travel with historical observations and drawings which were made on the spot. Robson only travelled through 'the western portion . . . of the new Republic'.

HUNGARY

'Life in Budapest moves to a more rapid rhythm than elsewhere in Europe, as though every moment of the day had unlimited possibilities of emotional excitement.' Walter Starkie *Raggle-Taggle* 1933

Autobiography/Biography

Any Souvenirs George Mikes 1973 (1971)
(see 'Europe –General')
Mikes fled Hungary in 1956; this was an account of his first trip home in fifteen years. He was not allowed into Czechoslovakia, but travelled through Bavaria, Austria, Yugoslavia and Hungary.

✔ **The Undefeated**
George Paloczi-Horvath 1993 (1959)
The author realized that the privileged background and wealth of his family was based on the exploitation of peasants; by the 1930s he had become an active anti-Nazi, fleeing Hungary in 1941. He returned after the war and although he became an ardent Communist, he was arrested, tortured and imprisoned by the Communist régime. He was released in 1954 and escaped to Britain with his wife and child.

Fiction/Poetry

The Hunt Tamás Aczel 1990
An allegorical novel of loyalty and betrayal and truth and falsehood. Set in the early fifties.

Hungarian Folk Tales Val Biro 1992
(1980)
Aimed at children; full of dragons and demons.

And Where Were You, Adam
Heinrich Böll 1978 (1951)
A collection of interwoven semi-autobiographical stories describing the panic-stricken retreat of Hitler's army before the advance of the Red Army and the effects of war on the lives of ordinary people.

The Magician's Garden and Other
Stories Géza Csáth 1983 (1980)
A collection of tormented magic realism stories. Csáth, who was addicted to opium, committed suicide in 1918; there is another collection entitled *Opium and Other Stories*.

Helping Verbs of the Heart
Peter Esterházy 1990 (1985)
An account of a son's grief after his mother's

death: 'It's nearly two weeks since my mother died, and I'd better get to work before the urge I felt so violently during the funeral, the urge to write about her, turns back into the lethargic wordlessness I felt at the news of her death.'

✔ **Under the Frog** Tibor Fischer 1993 (1992)
Hungary between 1944–56. Makes a serious topic funny.

✔ **A Hungarian Romance**
Agnes Hankiss 1992 (1988)
Set in seventeenth-century Transylvania and superficially about a passionate love triangle of two men and a woman, the book in fact looks at a woman's quest for self-identity; Agnes Hankiss, a Jungian analyst, is preoccupied with the 'universal soul' and how the archetype is treated in literature.

Rakóssy Cecelia Holland 1967 (1966)
An historical romance about a shy Austrian princess who was married to a Magyar baron in the sixteenth century. Another historical romance is *Death of Attila* which is about the Huns, Romans and Goths of the Dark Ages.

✔ **The Case Worker** György Konrád 1987 (1974)
Konrád's novels are bleak, dealing with alienation, hypocrisy and madness. Other titles include *The City Builder* and *The Loser*.

In Praise of Older Women
Stephen Vizinczey 1967
The memoirs of a lustful and self-obsessed young man who grows up in refugee camps and in Budapest.

Food

The Hungarian Cookbook
Susan Derecskey 1987
Modern and traditional recipes.

✔ **The Cuisine of Hungary**
George Lang 1985 (1971)
More than just a cookbook, it is also a treatise on Hungarian cuisine.

Guides

✔ **Blue Guide Hungary** Bob Dent 1991
Described by the Rough Guide as having 'a left-wing slant', thereby distinguishing it from other Blue Guides.

✔ **Hungary Travel Survival Kit**
Steve Fallon 1994

✔ **Insight Pocket Guide Budapest and Surroundings** 1993

✔ **Insight Guide Hungary** 1991

✔ **Hungary. The Rough Guide**
Dan Richardson and Charles Hebbert 1992

History

✔ **A History of Modern Hungary 1867–1986** Jörg K. Hoensch 1989 (1988)
A broad, authoritative and accessible account of the political, social and economic history of Hungary from the Compromise in 1867 up until today.

Travel Literature

Raggle-Taggle Walter Starkie 1964 (1933)
Walter Starkie was a professor at Dublin; he wandered round Hungary in the 1920s searching for gypsy music.

POLAND

'The soul of Poland is indestructible . . . she will rise again like a rock, which may for a spell be submerged by a tidal wave, but which remains a rock.' Sir Winston Churchill, speech in the House of Commons, 1 October 1939

Art and Archaeology

The Arts in Poland 1908–89 Edited by Polish Realities
An anthology of essays on all aspects of Polish life.

Autobiography/Biography

✔ **Red Cavalry** Isaac Babel 1961 (1957)
Short stories about the 1919–20 invasion of Poland and the Soviet regiments of horse operating there.

✔ **Winter in the Morning**
Janina Bauman 1986
The author and her family survived the Warsaw Ghetto, but eventually left in 1968. The first volume describes life and death in the ghetto and the second, ✔ *A Dream of Belonging* (1988), is about life in the Communist Party in Poland just after the war and her life in Israel and Britain.

✔ **Scenes from a Disturbed Childhood** Adam Czerniawski 1991
The author's childhood was spent escaping the traumas of the Second World War; he

eventually landed in England having been in Turkey and Palestine.

✔ **A Square of Sky** *Janina David 1992 (1964)*
An amalgamation of two books, *A Square of Sky* and *A Touch of the Earth* which tell of the author's childhood; at the age of nine, from leading a privileged life, her family was sent to the ghetto and life became an unmitigated struggle, full of fear: 'She has the artist's gift for knowing exactly what to say and what to leave out.' (Miriam May *The Observer*)

✔ **Native Realm** *Czeslaw Milosz 1988 (1968)*
An autobiography of Milosz's life before he escaped to the West, which is deeply self-questioning: 'Reading this book has shaken me, in a way I hope it may shake others.' (Richard Holmes *The Times*)

So Many Miracles *Saul Rubinek 1988*
An oral history of what it was like for Jews (including the author's parents) in Nazi-occupied Poland.

A Path of Hope. An Autobiography *Lech Walesa 1987*
Lech Walesa's life from childhood, time in the Gdansk shipyard and up to 1987. Seemingly ghostwritten by a committee.

Fiction/Poetry

A Simple Story *Shmuel Yozef Agnon*
The novel is set among the Jewish communities of the Polish Ukraine.

Short Stories *Shmuel Yozef Agnon (1970)*

✔ **This Way for the Gas Ladies and Gentlemen** *Tadeusz Borowski 1976 (1959)*
Short stories based on experiences at Auschwitz, published in Poland after the war by Borowski who was a concentration camp victim.

✔ **A Personal Record** *Joseph Conrad 1988 (1912)*
Semi-autobiographical and moving account of Conrad's early life in the Russian part of partitioned Poland and how he dealt with being separated from his native country. It also shows his persistent quest to impose a meaning on life.

✔ **A Scrap of Time** *Ida Fink 1989 (1988)*
Describes the Polish gentiles who sheltered the Jews who were striving to escape from concentration camps. *The Journey* 1994 (1990) is the story of two teenage girls who escape from the Jewish ghetto in a small

Polish town in 1942 and spend the rest of the war on the run.

✔ **The Tin Drum** *Günter Grass 1989 (1959)*
A scathing dissection of the years 1925 to 1955 through the eyes of the dwarf, Oskar Matzerath. The 'Danzig Trilogy' which includes *Dog Years* and ✔ *Cat and Mouse* 1989 (1961) is set in Danzig/Gdansk where Grass grew up; the superficial outlandish antics mask the horrors of a countryside torn apart by war.

✔ **The Eighth Day of the Week** *Marek Hlasko 1992 (1956)*
Hlasko puts into words the anger felt by many who grew up after World War II.

Who Was David Weiser? *Pawel Huelle 1991 (1987)*
An enigmatic young Jewish boy is idolized by his contemporaries and disappears.

✔ **Schindler's Ark** *Thomas Keneally 1993 (1982)*
Based on the life of Oskar Schindler who saved thousands of Jews by sheltering them in his factory. Now a Spielberg film.

✔ **Poland** *James Michener 1993 (1983)*
A blockbuster which tells you a lot about Polish history, through the eyes of a tough farmer and of a politician.

The Colour of Blood *Brian Moore 1987*
A thriller set in the 1980s (in an unnamed Poland), which includes church and state. Full of religious plots.

The Palace *Wieslaw Mysliwski 1991 (1970)*
A shepherd, Jacob, remains at a palace which was deserted by both the nobility and peasants at the outbreak of war. His wanderings unravel secrets and become a journey of self-discovery.

✔ **Tales from the Saragossa Manuscript: Ten Days in the Life of Alphonse von Worden** *Jan Potocki 1990 (1814)*
A huge multifarious unfinished Gothic novel set at the beginning of the nineteenth century: '... One of the most beautiful fantastic novels in the whole history of literature.' (Bernard Pivot)

Polonaise *Piers Paul Read 1978 (1976)*
A family saga set partly in Poland; Count Stefan Kornowski has a bankrupt father and dead mother; he is a law student and revolutionary whose life takes him from Warsaw to Paris and the decadent world of the European intellectual.

✔ **The Magician of Lublin**
Isaac Bashevis Singer 1979 (1960)
A novel set in the ghetto of early twentieth-century Poland, which is extremely evocative of a vanished community. Singer left Poland in the 1930s and wrote much, all in Yiddish, so we are dependent on translations some of which include: ✔ *The Family Moskat* 1988 (1950), ✔ *The Slave* 1974 (1962), ✔ *Satan in Goray* 1981 (1958) and ✔ *The King of the Fields* 1990 (1988).

The Beautiful Mrs Seidenman
Andrzej Szczypiorski 1991 (1988)
A Jewish woman uses her looks and intelligence to survive the Nazis, however in 1943 she is denounced to the Gestapo and an unlikely chain of people join together to try and save her: 'Like a pebble dropped cleanly into deep water, *The Beautiful Mrs Seidenman* stirs ripples and echoes around the brief, bleak events that it describes . . . This magnificent novel, excellently translated, is both heart-wrenching and optimistic.' (*The Observer*)

Insatiability *Stanislaw Ignacy Witkiewicz*
1985 (1957)
Complex novel about artistic and intellectual life after a Chinese invasion of Europe.

✔ **Ariadne's Thread. Polish Women Poets** *Translated and introduced by Susan Bassnett and Peter Kuhiwczak 1988*
A selection from eight women poets.

✔ **Young Poets of a New Poland**
Translated by Donald Pirie 1993
Shows the interesting developments in poetry from Poland since the 1980s.

Food

✔ **The Best of Polish Cooking**
Karen West 1991 (1983)
A compilation of traditional Polish cooking for everyday and special occasions.

General Background

The Captive Mind *Czeslaw Milosz 1985 (1953)*
An analysis (with four particular case studies) of why so many Polish artists and intellectuals sold out to Communism after 1945.

Nice Promises *Tim Sebastian 1985*
Tim Sebastian was the BBC correspondent in Poland, arriving in Warsaw in 1979 as the BBC's first East European correspondent; the book gives many insights into life there

at the time, including descriptions of his 'tower of Babel' apartment block, where everyone was a foreigner.

✔ **I Remember Nothing More**
Adina Blady Szwajger 1990
The story of the Warsaw Children's Hospital and the Jewish Resistance where the author worked from 1941 until the liberation of Warsaw by the Soviet Army in 1945 when she became a paediatrician near Lodz.

Guides

✔ **Poland. A Travel Survival Kit**
Krzysztof Dydynski 1993

✔ **Insight Guide Poland** *1992*

✔ **Insider's Guide to Poland's Jewish Heritage** *Joram Kagan 1992*
Historical background and chronological tables which show the history of Polish Jewry through the years up to the Holocaust.

✔ **Poland. The Rough Guide** *Mark Salter and Gordon McLachlan 1993*

✔ **Polish Cities. Travels in Cracow and the South, Gdansk, Malbork and Warsaw** *Philip Ward 1988*

✔ **Poland. A Pallas Guide**
Sebastian Wormall (ed.) 1994

History

The Struggles for Poland
Neal Ascherson 1988 (1987)
Ascherson focuses on twentieth-century Polish history by tracing the political and social events through the restoration of independence in 1918, the Nazi and Soviet occupation, the Warsaw uprising, the creation of the Communist state, the rise of Solidarity and Jaruzelski's coup in 1981.

✔ **The Polish Revolution: Solidarity 1980–82** *Timothy Garton Ash 1991 (1983)*
An eye-witness account and an analysis of what happened after the birth of Solidarity up until 1989.

✔ **The Heart of Europe: A Short History of Poland** *Norman Davies 1986 (1984)*
Although the history begins in 1945, Davies looks back to the past to illustrate his theories.

The Holocaust *Martin Gilbert 1987 (1985)*
Many of the Nazi concentration camps were in Poland; this book describes the role of Poland and what happened to the Jews.

✔ **The Drowned and the Saved**
Primo Levi   1994 (1988)
Primo Levi committed suicide shortly after completing this book dispelling the myth that he forgave the Germans for the horrors of Auschwitz, which he felt guilty about surviving, while so many had perished. His autobiographical books are: *If This Is a Man* and *The Truce*.

✔ **The Polish Way**   Adam Zamoyski   1993 (1987)
A readable and accessible history of Poland up to the 1989 elections: 'Adam Zamoyski's *The Polish Way* is a stunner; a comprehensive history of Poland . . . Clear, calm, beautifully written, its scope is enormous, its story enthralling and its plates magnificent.' (Bernard Levin *The Times*)

Leisure

✔ **Hiking Guide to Poland and Ukraine**   Tim Burford   1994

Travel Literature

✔ **Vanishing Borders**   Michael Farr   1993 (1991) (see 'Germany' and 'Czech Republic')
The author was *The Daily Telegraph* correspondent in East Germany before and after the revolutions and was able to travel around reporting on crucial meetings and observing daily life.

Return to Poland   Denis Hills   1988
Hills was deported from Poland in 1985 as a result of official suspicion as to why he was there; the account of his ordeal is somewhat lacklustre.

ROMANIA
'No country is kinder to the wanderer who has good legs.' Walter Starkie *Raggle-Taggle* 1933

Autobiography/Biography

✔ **Queen of Roumania**   Hannah Pakula   1989 (1984)
Princess Marie of Edinburgh was the granddaughter of Queen Victoria and Tsar Alexander II; she was married off to the Crown Prince of Roumania by her mother: 'Hannah Pakula's enthralling book is like a huge, spicy plum-pudding stuffed with juicy fruits.' (Maureen Cleave *The Standard*)

Fiction/Poetry

✔ **Fantastic Tales**   Mircea Eliade and Mihai Niculescu   1990 (1969)
Three fantastical stories, with differing backgrounds, in parallel Romanian and English texts.

✔ **The Old Man and the Bureaucrats**
Mircea Eliade   1988 (1979)
A satire of the Communist police state: a retired schoolteacher tries to trace the career of one of his pupils; when he is brought in for questioning he manages to spellbind his guards with his tales.

✔ **Youth Without Youth and Other Novellas**   Mircea Eliade   1988
Mythical fantasy camouflaged in everyday reality.

✔ **The Balkan Trilogy**   Olivia Manning   1993 (1960s)
The trilogy is composed of *The Great Fortune*, *The Spoilt City* and *Friends and Heroes* which Olivia Manning wrote as a result of her experiences with her husband, a lecturer for the British Council in pre-war Bucharest. In the novels Guy and Harriet Pringle are forced to leave Rumania for Greece before the advancing German army.

✔ **The Passport**   Herta Müller   1989 (1986)
Surreal tale about a German village in Romania which is caught between the stifling dictatorship of Ceausescu and the temptations of the west.

✔ **Exile on a Peppercorn**
Mircea Dinescu   1990 (1985)
Dinescu is known as the 'angry young man' of contemporary Romanian poetry.

Guides

✔ **Hippocrene Companion Guide to Romania**   Lydle Brinkle   1992

History

Ceausescu's Romania   Julian Hale   1971
A look back at Romania's history and how it relates to Ceausescu's time.

King Carol II   by his grandson, Prince Paul of Hohenzollern-Roumania   1988
An attempt to show the serious side of King Carol II who cared deeply for his country, but who gave up the throne for his mistress, Elena Lupescu, known as Magda.

Leisure

✔ **Hiking Guide to Romania. A Bradt Guide** *Tim Burford 1993*

Travel Literature

✔ **In Another Europe. A Journey to Romania** *Georgina Harding 1991*
In 1988 Georgina Harding cycled through Eastern Europe from Vienna to Istanbul; her book describes in detail the towns, villages and countryside she passed through.

✔ **Transylvania and Beyond** *Dervla Murphy 1993 (1992)*
The indefatigable Dervla Murphy first went to Rumania at the fall of Ceausescu in 1990 and returned in 1991. As in all her travels, she got to the heart of the country and to the people whom she met.

✔ **Roumanian Journey** *Sacheverell Sitwell 1992 (1938)*
Sitwell spent four weeks in Roumania in the 1930s: 'At the first mention of going to Roumania, a great many people, as I did myself, would take down their atlas and open the map. For Roumania, there can be no question, is among the lesser known lands of Europe.'

Scandinavia

GENERAL

Fiction/Poetry

✔ **The Terrors of Ice and Darkness** *Christoph Ransmayr 1992 (1984)*
An amalgam of fact and fiction. The pull of the Arctic dominates this book in which a young Italian becomes obsessed with the Austro-Hungarian Arctic expedition of 1873. He decides to copy their adventure and his story is woven with chronicles of the original expedition.

✔ **Scandinavian Folktales** *Translated and edited by Jacqueline Simpson 1988*
The harsh climate and rugged landscape of Scandinavia is reflected in its very intriguing folklore about supernatural forces and mythical beings.

Food

✔ **Pea Soup Andersen's Scandinavian–American Cookbook** *1988*
Recipes from the popular chain of restaurants.

General Background

✔ **The Sayings of the Vikings** *1992*
The *Hávamál* – the words of wisdom which served as the spiritual provision for the Vikings on their long journeys.

Guides

✔ **Scandinavian and Baltic Europe on a Shoestring** *Glenda Bendure et al. 1993*

✔ **Karen Brown's Scandinavian Country Inns and Manors** *Clare and Karen Brown 1989*
Sweden, Norway, Finland and Denmark.

✔ **Scandinavia. The Rough Guide** *Jules Brown and Mick Sinclair 1993 (1988)*

✔ **Fodor's Scandinavia 1995**

✔ **Frommer's Scandinavia '93–'94**

✔ **Off the Beaten Track Scandinavia** *Margaret and Robin Rogers 1992*

History

✔ **The Vikings** *Johannes Brendsted*
A good general introduction and history of the Vikings.

Scandinavian Mythology *H.R. Ellis Davidson 1982 (1969)*
Who's who in Nordic mythology.

Leisure

✔ **Scandinavian Mountains**
Peter Lennon   1987
A West Col walking, climbing and skiing guide.

Natural History

✔ **Field Guide to Wild Flowers of Britain and Northern Europe**
Bob Gibbons and Paul Davies   1994
Over 720 colour plates and 200 line drawings, from Southern Scandinavia to the Loire Valley and from the Atlantic east to all of Germany.

Travel Literature

✔ **The Viking Voyage. With Gaia to Vinland** Judy Lomax   1992
The ship Gaia followed the Viking route from Norway via Orkney, Shetland, the Faroes, Iceland and Greenland to 'Vinland', the name the Vikings in the Sagas gave to North America.

✔ **Last Places** Lawrence Millman   1992 (1990)
Millman vaguely followed on foot and by boat the Vikings' route from Norway to Newfoundland, the Shetlands, the Faroes, Iceland, Greenland and Labrador.

✔ **A Short Residence in Sweden, Norway and Denmark**
Mary Wollstonecraft   1987 (1796)
The author travelled alone through Scandinavia in 1795, in search of happiness in the remote backwoods. Richard Holmes thinks that this is one of the neglected masterpieces of early English Romanticism.

DENMARK

'What strikes me now most as regards Denmark is the charm, beauty, and independence of the women. They go about freely, sit in cafés together, smoke without self-consciousness.' Arnold Bennett Journal 29 August 1913

Art and Archaeology

✔ **The Bog People** P.V. Glob   1977 (1969)
Iron Age bodies preserved in peat-bogs in northern Europe, especially the Tollund and Grauballe men, found in Denmark: 'The astonishing finds so ably chronicled . . . give us a tantalizing glimpse of life in northern Europe in the first two centuries of our era.' (*Times Literary Supplement*)

Late Baroque and Rococo Architecture C. Norberg-Schulz   1986 (1979)   (see 'Western Europe' and 'Central Europe')
The transition from Baroque to Rococo in the eighteenth century heralded a free and more organic form of architecture, as architects began to see man more in the context of the natural world. This is reflected in the cities of, Vienna, Würzburg, Paris, Nancy, London, Turin, Rome and Copenhagen.

Biography

✔ **Isak Dinesen: The Life of Karen Blixen** Judith Thurman   1984 (1982)
A penetrating biography of Karen Blixen who lived out her life of fantasy by creating Isak Dinesen, thereby recreating herself. She married Baron Bror von Blixen and not his twin, Hans, with whom she was in love, spending thirty years on a Kenyan coffee farm before returning to her native Denmark.

Fiction/Poetry

The Riddle of the Sands Erskine Childers (1902) (see 'Germany')

✔ **Seven Gothic Tales** Isak Dinesen
1979 (1934)
Fantastic, strange, lyrical and weird tales, which are glittering and harsh and give no comfort.

✔ **The Liar** Martin A. Hansen   1986 (1950)
A perceptive novel about the thoughts of a schoolteacher who is living on a small Danish island in the 1950s. The author probes into the mind of Johannes Vig, and it is a 'vindication of religious truth and a farewell to the traditional modes of extended fiction'.

✔ **Miss Smilla's Feeling for Snow**
P. Hoeg   1993 (1992)
A compulsive read, full of suspense, about a woman from Greenland who gets mixed up in a mystery involving a child's death in Copenhagen and which eventually involves her sailing to Greenland.

✔ **The Fairy Tales of Hans Christian Andersen** Naomi Lewis (ed.)   (1835)
Widely read today, the fairy tales were condemned for their 'violence and questionable morals' when they were published.

✔ **Winter's Child** *Dea Trier Mørch* *1986 (1976)*
Modern Denmark as seen through the eyes of women in a maternity ward in Copenhagen. 'When I first decided to write about my experiences, I found to my surprise that birth had been a taboo subject. I tried to find novels dealing with this topic, but apart from very short, idyllic descriptions or terse terrifying reports, I found none. And furthermore, the experience had never been described by the person concerned – always by an outsider.' She also wrote ✔ *Evening Star* 1986 (1982)

General Background

✔ **Either/Or: A Fragment of Life**
Søren Kierkegaard *1992 (1843)*
Musings on life, love and death in nineteenth-century Denmark, published soon after his return from four months in Berlin and written under the pseudonym of a fictitious editor, Victor Eremita. Other works by Kierkegaard include *Repetition* (1843), *Fear and Trembling* (1843), *Philosophical Fragments* (1844), *The Concept of Anxiety* (1844), *Stages on Life's Way* (1846) and *The Sickness unto Death* (1849).

Guides

✔ **Baedeker Copenhagen** *1992*

✔ **The Visitor's Guide to Denmark. A Moorland Guide** *Pat and Hazel Constance* *1991 (1989)*

✔ **Blue Guide Denmark** *W. Glyn Jones and Kirsten Gade* *1992*

✔ **Insight Guide Denmark** *1993*

History

Denmark: A Modern History
W. Glyn Jones *1986*
Concentrates on the twentieth century, but has an outline of what went before.

FAROE ISLANDS

'The houses were all of wood, high-roofed, with little white casements, the rest of the walls being mostly done over with Stockholm tar: every roof was of turf, and fine crops of flowery grass grew on some of them . . . ' [Thorshaven]. William Morris *Journal of Travel in Iceland* 11 July 1871

✔ **The Faroes. The Faraway Islands**
Anthony Jackson *1991*
A good handbook for anyone thinking of travelling to the Faroes.

✔ **The Faroe Islands** *Liv Kjørsvik, Schei and Gunnie Moberg* *1991*
Chapters on nature, geology, geography, politics, folklore, the language, culture and fishing as well as an island by island guide.

GREENLAND

Fiction

✔ **Miss Smilla's Feeling for Snow**
P. Hoeg (see 'Denmark')

Guide

Nagel's Denmark and Greenland *1980*

FINLAND

'A man flying over it (which I have not done) sees, I am told, such a mass of isolated water patches, from very large lakes to mere pools, that the thing looks under a morning summer sun like torn and ragged lace, supposing such lace to be green in colour and stretched over a shining surface of mirror.' Hilaire Belloc *Places* 1942

Autobiography/Biography

Memoirs of Marshal Mannerheim *1954*
Mannerheim (1867–1951) was an important Finnish military leader and conservative statesman who successfully defended Finland against Soviet forces during World War II and who served as Finnish President from 1944–46.

Fiction/Poetry

Harjunpää and the Stone Murders
Matti Joensuu *1986 (1983)*
A Helsinki detective investigates a spate of teenage gang warfare and ends up by having his own child.

The Unknown Soldier *Väinö Linna* *1968 (1954)*
Linna's book aroused much controversy because the soldiers in his book, which takes place during the war between 1940 and 1944,

are shown as men who drink and womanize rather than being 'heroes in white'. He wrote 'I described a group of men that I tried to bring alive so that people could see just what has died'. He contributed much to the speed of development of Finnish society by rejecting chauvinistic ideologies and values and replacing them with ideas of social growth and democracy.

Kalevala *Elias Lönnrot (English selections 1976)*
Lönnrot is a rural doctor who over the years collected local folktales. It is *the* classic in Finnish literature and involves war between the mythical regions of Kalevala and Pohjola over a disputed talisman.

Mika Waltari, another Finnish writer wrote *The Egyptian*, *The Dark Angel* and *The Secret of the Kingdom* 1961 (1959)

Guides

✔ **Insight Guide Finland** *1992*

✔ **Finland. Travel Survival Kit**
Markus Lehtipuu and Virpi Mäkelä 1993

✔ **Visitor's Guide to Finland. A Moorland Guide** *1987*

History

✔ **A Short History of Finland**
Fred Singleton 1991 (1989)
The historical development of the country is traced from its settlement by the Finns in the first millenium AD up until the present.

ICELAND
'Fortunate island,
Where all men are equal
But not vulgar – not yet.' W.H. Auden
Iceland Revisited 1964

Fiction/Poetry

✔ **Men at Axlir** *Dominic Cooper 1992 (1978)*
Based on a true story about the crime of a young girl and her brother which was exploited in the feud between two sheriffs in the eighteenth century.

The Bread of Life *(1987)*
A Quire of Seven *Haldor Laxness (1974)*
Recommended by Jan Morris.

✔ **Njal's Saga** *Translated by Magnus Magnusson and Hermann Pálsson 1960*
This, the greatest of Icelandic sagas, was written by an unknown author in the late thirteenth century and based on historical events in Iceland which had taken place 300 years earlier.

General Background

✔ **Iceland Saga** *Magnus Magnusson 1992 (1987)*
The background to Iceland and its remarkable literature.

Places *Jan Morris 1972*
There is an article on Iceland in this collection.

Guides

✔ **Insight Guide Iceland** *1992*

✔ **Iceland, Greenland and the Faroe Islands. Travel Survival Kit**
Deanna Swaney 1994

History

✔ **The Vinland Sagas: The Norse Discovery of America** *Translated and with an introduction by Magnús Magnússon and Hermann Pálsson 1978 (1965)*
These two medieval Icelandic sagas tell of the tenth-century 'discovery' of North America by Norsemen; they describe how Eirik the Red founded an Icelandic colony in Greenland and how his son, Leif the Lucky made a sailing expedition south.

NORWAY
'Norway is a hard country; hard to know, hard to shoot over, and hard – very hard – to fall down on: but hard to forsake and harder to forget.' J.A. Lees *Peaks and Pines, Another Norway Book* 1899.

Art and Archaeology

Edvard Munch *J.P. Hodin 1972*
A good general introduction with 168 illustrations, 30 in colour. Munch created a 'spiritual climate' and was the initiator of a style of art called 'Expressionism', which deliberately abandoned the rules of Impressionism, in favour of simplification and an awareness of an archetypal imagery.

Autobiography/Biography

Quisling: A Study in Treason Oddvar K.
Hoidal 1989
A long and comprehensive biography of the
famous, many-faceted Norwegian traitor
who collaborated with the Germans during
the war and whose name has become synon-
omous with a person accused of treasonable
cooperation with an outside power.

Fiction/Poetry

✔ **Séraphita** Honoré de Balzac 1989 (1834)
The story revolves round the hermaphrodite
Séraphita who inspires love in everyone she
meets; it is set in eighteenth century Norway
and gives Balzac's love of the supernatural
full reign: 'Never did Balzac approach the
very ideal of Beauty as in this book'. (Theo-
phile Gautier)

The Sleeping Prince Knut Faldbakken
1988 (1971)
A lonely spinster spins a fantasy in her mind
about a sleeping prince. The whole story is
seen from her viewpoint and while we see her
obsessive concern for the minutiae of daily
life, at the same time, as in all Faldbakken's
novels, there is an underlying current of sexuality demanding expression. Other novels
by Faldbakken include *Insect Summer* 1991
(1972), *Adam's Diary* 1989 (1978) and *The
Honeymoon* (1982).

✔ **Hunger** Knut Hamsun 1976 (1967)
Hamsun's novels are deceptively simple but
have sinister undertones. Other titles include *The Wanderer* 1977 (1909), ✔ *Mysteries* 1992 (1971), ✔ *The Women at the Pump*
1992 (1978), *Wayfarers* 1982 (1980), ✔ *Victoria* 1992 (1969) and *Growth of the Soil* 1980
(1917)

Ibsen Plays Henrik Ibsen 1993
Ibsen had a keen ear for contemporary society which comes through in his plays which
include *A Doll's House* and *Hedda Gabler*.
[Jan Morris]

✔ **The Seer and Other Norwegian
Stories** Jonas Lie 1990
The nineteenth-century writer Jonas Lie had
a nature which shifted from light to gloom;
these short stories reveal his darkening vision.

✔ **Tom Reber's Last Retreat**
Øystein Lønn 1992
A businessman's past and complicated pres-
ent.

✔ **Alberta and Jacob** 1980 (1926)
✔ **Alberta and Freedom** (1931)
✔ **Alberta Alone** Cora Sandel (1939)
A trilogy which shows the struggles of a
young woman in an alien environment.

✔ **The Moon is Down** John Steinbeck
1958
The story of men and women patriots on the
coast of wartime Norway. A novel of courage,
defiance and human dignity under stress.

✔ **The Ice Palace** Tarjei Vesaas 1993
(1966)
Two eleven-year-old girls meet; one is about
to reveal a secret which leads to her death;
the other struggles with fidelity to the memory of her friend. A hauntingly beautiful
book.

Food

✔ **A Taste of Norway** Arne Brimi 1987
A cookery book which is based on the best
fresh ingredients found in Norway.

General Background

Guides

✔ **Fodor's Norway** (an undated Fodor
guide) 1993

✔ **Insight Guide Norway** 1992

✔ **Guide to Spitsbergen. A Bradt
Guide** Andreas Umbreit 1991

History

✔ **King Harald's Saga** Snorri Sturluson
Translated by Magnus Magnusson and Hermann
Pálsson
Harald Hardradi of Norway, the most feared
warrior of his time and the last of the Viking
warrior kings, was killed by Harold of England at the Battle of Stamford Bridge in
Yorkshire, in 1066, nineteen days before the
Battle of Hastings. His life was written by
the great Icelandic historian, Snorri Sturluson in the thirteenth century.

✔ **The Norse Atlantic Saga** Gwyn Jones
1986 (1964)
The narrative and descriptive account of the
Norse or Viking voyages of discovery and
westward colonization across the North Atlantic to Iceland, Greenland and the eastern
seaboard of North America.

Photography

✔ **Norway** Michael Tomkinson 1991 Text by Alf R. Bjeicke
Scattered with matt colour photographs.

Travel Literature

Three in Norway Two of Them
1968 (1882)
A classic, written in the manner of *Three Men in a Boat*, which relates the adventures of three English gentlemen on a hunting trip in the Jotunfjeld.

SWEDEN

'Sweden appeared to me the country in the world most proper to form the botanist and natural historian; every object seemed to remind me of the creation of things, of the first efforts of sportive nature. When a country arrives at a certain stage of perfection it looks as if it were made so, and curiosity is not excited.' Mary Wollstonecroft, *Letters Written During a Short Residence in Sweden etc*, 1796

Autobiography/Biography

Bernadotte Alan Palmer 1990
Bernadotte's life was full of contradictions; he was good-looking and so brave as to be almost foolhardy. He started life as a staunch republican, but by 1813 was convinced that constitutional monarchy was the answer and he remained loyal to his wife Désirée Clary despite twelve years of absence. Alan Palmer's biography, although chronological, divides his life into four parts: his military career, his relationship with Napoleon, his election as Prince Royal of Sweden and why he joined a coalition against Napoleon, and his activities as ruler of Sweden.

Fiction/Poetry

✔ **A Burnt Child** Stig Dagerman 1990
(1948)
The reactions and subsequent tensions of a family living in Stockholm to the mother's death. *The Games of Night* are short stories by Dagerman who committed suicide at the age of 31.

✔ **Preparations for Flight and Other Swedish Stories** Robert Fulton 1990
Eight short stories, many of which reflect childhood experiences.

✔ **The Death of a Beekeeper**
Lars Gustafsson 1990 (1978)
A schoolteacher turned beekeeper with a limited time to live keeps a journal: 'This thoughtful and beautifully written novel . . . We cannot fail to be moved.' (Diana Hinds *Independent*)

✔ **My Brother Sebastian** Annika Idström
1991 (1985)
An interesting psychological novel about an eleven-year-old boy who is subjected to cruelty and yet has the determination to survive.

✔ **Merab's Beauty** Torgny Lindgren 1990 (1983)
Short stories from the farming tradition in the north of Sweden. Also *Bathsheba*.

The Dog Star Agneta Pleijel 1991 (1989)
A novel about a young girl approaching puberty.

✔ **The Swedish Cavalier** Leo Perutz
1992 (1936)
Two men meet in a farmer's barn in 1701, one is a thief and the other an army officer on the run. The book 'works excellently as an adventure story, but all the time one is aware of a moral purpose . . . Confirms that Perutz was an uncommonly interesting and powerful writer.' (Allan Massie *The Scotsman*)

Désirée Annemarie Selinko 1953
An historical novel based on Désirée Clary, Napoleon's first love and the wife of Bernadotte.

✔ **Augustus Rex** Clive Sinclair 1993 (1992)
A very funny novel which dwells on Strindberg's many neuroses when he is brought back to life by the devil in the 1960s. 'Brace yourself for a story in which August Strindberg, the Swedish playwright, did not die in 1912 as popularly supposed. Instead, he sold his soul to the Devil . . . Sinclair has always been an offbeat writer . . . always lucid, always original.' (Nicholas Best *Financial Times*)

✔ **Plays** August Strindberg 2 vols 1975
Strindberg was extraordinarily prolific, publishing sixty plays, twelve historical dramas, five novels, short stories and much autobiographical material. Very little has been translated into English.

Guides

✔ **Fodor's Sweden** *1992*
(an undated Fodor guide)

✔ **Insight Guide Sweden** *1992*

✔ **The Visitor's Guide to Sweden. A Moorland Guide** *1987*

History

✔ **Sweden: A Traveller's History**
Eric Elstob   1979
The Swedes have worked out, through observing layers of sediment samples, an exact date for the beginning of their history – 6839 BC. Elstob starts his book at this point at the end of the Ice Age and continues into this century.

United Kingdom

GENERAL

Art and Archaeology

Rings of Stone: the Prehistoric Stone Circles of Britain and Ireland
Aubrey Burl   1980
A survey of many of the stone sites in Britain and Ireland.

✔ **Archaeology of the British Isles**
Andrew Hayes   1993
A good introductory history, illustrated with maps and plans, which contains a gazetteer of sites in England, Wales, Scotland and Ireland.

✔ **The Architectural Heritage of Britain and Ireland**   *Michael Jenner   1993*
Architectural terms well explained and illustrated by pictures of particular buildings and line-drawings. Arranged alphabetically but also well cross-referenced. Very useful.

British Cathedrals   *Paul Johnson   1980*
How and why cathedrals were built and the role of the clergy in their social history.

The Genius of British Painting
David Piper (ed.)   1975
A large-format illustrated book with chapters on the following periods: The Middle Ages by Jonathan Alexander, Tudor and Early Stuart Painting by David Piper, Painting under the Stuarts by Oliver Millar, The Eighteenth Century by Mary Webster, The Romantics by Alan Bird, The Victorians by Alan Bowness and The Twentieth Century by Grey Gowrie.

British Landscape Painting
Michael Rosenthal   1982
An illustrated large-format book which begins with British landscape painting in the Middle Ages and continues up to this century. Rosenthal points out how our detachment this century from the rural environment is unprecedented and how that has affected landscape painting, which by definition needs a deep understanding of the countryside.

Architecture in Britain 1530–1830
John Summerson   1977 (1953)
Beginning with architecture at the court of Henry VIII, this detailed and well illustrated book continues to the post-Waterloo Greek and Gothic revival.

Fiction/Poetry

✔ **Foreign Land**   *Jonathan Raban   1985*
George Grey comes back to England having lived abroad for forty years; of course his 'vision' of England turns out to have been entirely wrong – what he finds is a coldness and hostility he had not anticipated. He plans his escape by boat.

✔ **Humphry Clinker**   *Tobias Smollett*
1966 (1771)
Smollett's last novel, and often considered his best; in a series of letters it relates the adventures of a family as they travel through England and Scotland describing the places they visit with animation and wit.

✔ **Henry Esmond**
William Makepeace Thackeray   1852
A military romance set in eighteenth-century England, which apart from being excellent on the history and warfare of the time, is also acute about human nature and its unchanging rivalries and prejudices.

Food

✔ **British Cookery** Lizzie Boyd (ed.) 1988 (1976)
A very good and comprehensive book with traditional and regional recipes.

✔ **Food Lovers' Guide to Britain**
Henrietta Green 1993
A unique book which has over 600 entries on the finest food producers and the best food shops in England, Scotland and Wales.

General Background

✔ **Whose Cities?** Mark Fisher and Ursula Owen (eds.) 1991
Aspects of city cultures, sub-cultures, public art and economics by a group of novelists and journalists including Paul Bailey, Jeannette Winterson, Margaret Drabble, Ruth Rendell, Tim Hilton and Gillian Reynolds.

✔ **Dictionary of Place Names**
Adrian Room 1993 (1988)
The origins and history of over 4,000 place names in the British Isles.

Guides

✔ **The 1995 Good Pub Guide**
Alistair Aird (ed.) 1993
More than 1,000 pubs are assessed on food, drink and atmosphere.

✔ **English, Welsh and Scottish Country Hotels and Itineraries** June and Karen Brown 1994

✔ **Children Welcome. Family Holiday Guide '95**
Establishments of all kinds which welcome children.

✔ **Farm Holiday Bureau: Stay on a Farm 1995** 1995
Details of over 100 working farms that offer accommodation – both full-board and self-catering.

✔ **Fodor Great Britain 1995**

✔ **Staying Off the Beaten Track in England and Wales 1994** Elizabeth Gundrey 1994
Now in its thirteenth edition, includes around 600 small hotels, houses, inns and farms.

✔ **Hotels and Restaurants of Britain 1995**
Each establishment has a short description and a colour photograph.

✔ **Insight Guide Great Britain** 1992

✔ **Let's Go Britain and Ireland 1995** 1994

✔ **The Which? Guide to Country Pubs** David Mabey (ed.) 1993

✔ **Michelin Red Guide Great Britain and Ireland 1995**

✔ **Blue Guide Victorian Architecture in Britain** Julian Orbach 1987

✔ **The Oxford Literary Guide to Great Britain and Ireland** 1993 (1981)
Hundreds of places connected with literary figures and events.

✔ **Pets Welcome! Holidays for Owners and Pets 1995** 1994
The holiday guide for animal lovers.

✔ **RAC Hotel Guide Great Britain and Ireland 1995** 1993

✔ **Egon Ronay's Cellnet Guide 1995: Hotels and Restaurants** 1993
3,000 establishments in Great Britain and Ireland.

✔ **Les Routiers Guide Britain and the North of Ireland 1995** 1994
Over 1,500 detailed entries listed alphabetically by town with short descriptions.

✔ **The Good Hotel Guide 1995 – Britain and Europe** Hilary Rubinstein (ed.) 1993
A wide range of hotels from grand châteaux to modest bed and breakfasts; includes Turkey and Morocco.

History

The History of the Kings of Britain
Geoffrey of Monmouth 1966 (c.1136)
The purpose of Geoffrey of Monmouth's book was to trace the history of the Britons through 1,900 years, from the mythical Brutus, great-grandson of Aeneas, who supposedly gave his name to the island, to Cadwallader, the last British king, who harassed by plague and famine abandoned Britain to the Saxons in the seventh century AD.

Leisure

✔ **The Good Food Guide 1995**
Tom Jaine (ed.)
Over 1,400 eating places of all kinds, with paragraph-long descriptions and comments, with graded cooking.

✔ **National Trust Handbook 1995** *1995*
Descriptions and opening times of National Trust properties in England, Wales and Northern Ireland.

✔ **Pan/Ordnance Survey Walker's Britain** *1992*
The Complete Pocket Guide to over 240 Walks and Rambles.

✔ **Good Gardens Guide 1995**
Graham Rose and Peter King (eds.) *1993*
Over 1,000 of the best gardens in Britain and Ireland.

✔ **The Good Retreat Guide**
Stafford Whiteaker *1994*
Over 300 places to find peace and spiritual renewal in Britain, Ireland, France and Spain.

Natural History *(For natural history books on Britain see 'Europe– General')*

✔ **Collins Pocket Guide Birds of Britain and Europe with North Africa and the Middle East** *H. Heinzel, R.F. Fitter and J. Parslow* *1992 (1972)*

✔ **A Field Guide to the Rare Birds of Britain and Europe** *Ian Lewington, Per Alström and Peter Colston* *1991*

✔ **Collins Field Guide Birds of Britain and Europe** *Roger Tory Peterson, Guy Mountfort and P.A.D. Hollom* *1993 (1954)*

✔ **Collins Photoguide to Wild Flowers of Britain and Northern Europe**
Oleg Polunin *1988 (1986)*

The History of the Countryside
Oliver Rackham *1989 (1986)*
The fascinating story of Britain's landscape; a marvellous book for dipping into.

✔ **A Field Guide in Colour to Wild Flowers Ferns and Grasses**
Bohumil Slavik *1993 (1973)*
Sixty-four painted colour plates.

✔ **Wildlife Travelling Companion: Great Britain and Ireland**
Martin Walters *1992*
Arranged regionally with advice on what to see in each area.

Travel Literature

✔ **The Kingdom by the Sea**
Paul Theroux *1983*
An account of a three-month journey round Britain by foot, bus and train, to see Britain

and to describe the British in all their aspects.

ENGLAND

'Is there any in the world like it? [English landscape] To a traveller returning home it looks so kind – it seems to shake hands with you as you pass through it.' W.M. Thackeray *Vanity Fair* 1847

Anthology

✔ **England. An Anthology** *Compiled by Richard Ingrams* *1991 (1989)*
An unsentimental anthology which includes poetry and prose of the best writing about England.

Art and Archaeology

✔ **The Cathedrals of England**
Alec Clifton-Taylor *1974 (1964)*
A basic illustrated introduction in the Thames and Hudson 'World of Art' series.

✔ **Shell Guide to English Parish Churches** *Robert Harbison* *1992*
Well illustrated and opinionated guide to the parish churches of England, arranged by region.

A History of English Architecture
Peter Kidson, Peter Murray and Paul Thompson *1979 (1962)*
This concise book begins with the Anglo-Saxon period and continues through the Victorian age up until the present day. It lists 'Famous British Buildings' and is well illustrated with photographs and plans.

The Englishness of English Art
Nikolaus Pevsner *1956*
An expanded and annotated version of the Reith lectures given by Pevsner in 1955. He arranges English art in categories rather than historically and there are chapters on: an introduction, Hogarth, Reynolds, Blake, Constable, the Perpendicular style, the Picturesque and principles of planning.

The Pattern of English Building
Alec Clifton-Taylor *1971*
English domestic architecture, with chapters on all the different materials used.

Fiction/Poetry

✔ **Country Tales** *H.E. Bates* *1992 (1938)*
Twenty-six lyrical stories selected from

various of H.E. Bates's volumes of short stories. They share an understanding and humour of a rural England that no longer exists.

General Background

✔ **Native Land** Nigel Barley 1990 (1989)
The anthropologist, Nigel Barley, who had previously written about the Cameroons and Indonesia, turns his professional eye on his native land . . .

✔ **Les Anglais. Portrait of a People**
Philippe Daudy 1991 (1989)
It is claimed that Daudy is one of 'rare Frenchmen, if not the only one, who can claim to be able to understand and explain the English,' and indeed throughout the book one gets shocks of recognition.

The English J.B. Priestley 1973
A large-format well-illustrated book which takes a critical look at the English temperament as it has developed since the Middle Ages.

Guides

✔ **England. The Rough Guide**
Robert Andrews et al. 1994

✔ **Blue Guide Churches and Chapels: Northern England**
Stephen C. Humphrey (ed.) 1991

✔ **Blue Guide Churches and Chapels: Southern England** Stephen C. Humphrey (ed.) 1991

✔ **England. The Blue Guide** Ian Ousby 1989

✔ **Blue Guide Country Houses of England** Geoffrey Tyack and Steven Brindle 1994

✔ **Where to Stay Bed and Breakfast, Farmhouses, Inns and Hostels: England 1995**
Short descriptions with quality gradings.

History

A Social History of England Asa Briggs
1987 (1983)
By tracing the cultural, economic and political factors that have influenced social history, Asa Briggs shows how the English way of life has changed from the Roman Conquest to the present day.

✔ **A Traveller's History of England**
Christopher Daniell 1991
A concise, yet comprehensive, look at English history. Aimed at the traveller who wants more than a guide book.

Life in the English Country House
Mark Girouard 1978
Lots of wonderful detail about day-to-day life in the English country house.

✔ **The Story of England**
Christopher Hibbert 1992
An introduction to English history. Concise and well illustrated, with useful fold-out date charts.

The Making of the English Landscape
W.G. Hoskins 1977 (1955)
Riveting look at the evolution of the English countryside from pre-Roman times until today. Man has had a profound effect on the countryside for centuries, but great areas of Britain have hardly changed since the time of the Black Death in 1348.

Pelican History of England: Roman Britain S.I. Richmond
Beginnings of English Society
D. Whitelock
English Society in the Early Middle Ages D.M. Stenton
England in the Late Middle Ages
A.R. Myers
Tudor England S.T. Bindoff
Stuart England J.P. Kenyon
England in the Eighteenth Century
J.H. Plumb
England in the Nineteenth Century
David Thomson
England in the Twentieth Century
D. Thomson
The nine-volume Pelican History of England has been reprinted many times.

The Shorter Pepys Robert Latham 1985
Pepys' Diary is unquestionably the best first-hand account of London in the 1660s. This abridgement contains about one-third of the original and has an introduction, chronology, glossary and index.

✔ **The Making of the English Working Class** E.P. Thompson 1980 (1963)
An important book for anyone interested in seeing how British society has evolved.

English Social History G.M. Trevelyan 1944
A survey of six centuries of social history from Chaucer to Queen Victoria. Published in many editions, including an illustrated one.

Leisure

✔ **English Tourist Board: English Castles Almanac** *1992*
Colour photographs and short descriptions of over 100 castles.

✔ **English Tourist Board: English Gardens Almanac** *1992*
Descriptions and photographs.

✔ **The Forestry Trust: Woodlands to Visit in England and Wales 1994**
Descriptions of over 600 woodlands and forests.

✔ **Blue Guide Gardens of England**
Frances Gapper, Patience Gapper and Sally Drury 1991

Natural History

✔ **Reading the Landscape** *Richard Muir 1993 (1981)*
Shows how different facets of the landscape have been created and describes the meanings of field patterns, woodlands, villages, churches, industrial relics and deserted settlements. Well illustrated: 'The book is a delight.' (Ronald Blythe *The Sunday Times*)

Photography

✔ **The Villages of England**
Richard Muir 1992
One hundred and fifty illustrations of different aspects of English village life.

Travel Literature

✔ **A Passage to England**
Nirad C. Chaudhuri 1989 (1959)
When Chaudhuri made his first trip outside India in 1955, he already knew a great deal about England from literature and books; his vision of England was somewhat different from the reality which he writes about wittily.

Rural Rides *William Cobbett 1830*
Cobbett's rides took him through the counties of Surrey, Kent, Sussex, Hants, Berks, Oxford, Bucks, Wilts, Somerset, Gloucester, Hereford, Shrophire, Worcester, Stafford, Leicester, Hertford, Essex, Suffolk, Norfolk, Cambridge, Huntingdon, Nottingham, Lincoln, York, Lancaster, Durham and Northumberland in the years between 1821 and 1832. He was passionately interested in all rural occupations and makes a very good record of what he saw. The first collection of rides was published in 1830; he then made a trip north in 1832.

Tour through the Whole Island of Great Britain *Daniel Defoe 1992 (1724–26)*
An ideal way of discovering what Britain was like in the 1720s; the book was very popular when it was published as Defoe, although not known for his accuracy, was a very competent observer with a keen eye for important and relevant facts. He liked modern buildings, not towns which excelled in the 'tumbledown picturesque', as his real interest lay in the economic and social state of the country.

The Journeys of Celia Fiennes *1947 (from an 1888 ms.)*
Celia Fiennes was the daughter of a Cromwellian colonel who moved freely and easily between social spheres. She started on rounds of visits with a little sightseeing thrown in, but in 1697 began travelling seriously with a journey to the north of England; this was the first of many which were to take her to every English county. Her writing shows her craving for new facts and her enthusiasm for what she sees is infectious. Since she was wholly detached and an independent witness we get an excellent idea of what England was like at the turn of the eighteenth century at a time when there was much social change and many great houses were being built or rebuilt.

English Hours *Henry James 1905*
A collection of essays that illuminate the English character.

✔ **Journeys of a German in England**
Carl Philip Moritz 1983 (1783)
The account of a walking tour in England in 1782 which took in London, Richmond, Eton and Windsor, Nettlebed, Henley, Oxford, Stratford, Matlock, Nottingham and Northampton. Byron Rogers wrote in *The Standard*: 'The writing is so fresh that you are startled when a stage-coach appears'.

In Search of England *H.V. Morton 1984 (1927)*
The first in the series 'In Search of . . . ' Morton travelled through Kent and Hampshire to the West Country, Cornwall and the Welsh borders, up to the Lake District and Gretna Green, across to Newcastle, and south via York, Lincoln, Norfolk, Rutland and Stratford-on-Avon to London: 'He teaches us how to begin to search for that England of which we are so rightly proud and so wrongly ignorant'. (*The Daily Telegraph*)

English Journey *J.B. Priestley 1984 (1934)*
On its publication in 1934, Howard Spring wrote, 'This may come to be regarded as its

author's most important work. It gives a fair and rounded picture of contemporary England which no other writer has equalled.' It is reputed to have influenced political thought in the forties and fifties, but it is the interviews with a varied cast of characters which give it its long life.

Pückler's Progress (see 'Ireland')

✔ **Coasting** Jonathan Raban 1986
Jonathan Raban wanted to see his island home from the sea, so in 1982 he set sail round the British Isles in a thirty-foot ketch. This approach brought out much about his own past as well as about the troubled Britain of the day. A clear and lucid inner and outer journey.

An English Journey Richard West 1981
Richard West started his journey round England in Manchester and went via Liverpool, the Lake District, the North East, Yorkshire and East Anglia, Kent and the South coast, through Winchester, Salisbury, Worcester, ending up in Birmingham.

LONDON

'I think it on the whole the best point of view in the world.' Henry James, letter to Charles Eliot Norton, 13 November 1880

Anthology

✔ **The Faber Book of London**
A.N. Wilson (ed.) 1993
The whole spectrum and diversity of London in prose and verse.

Art and Archaeology

✔ **The Buildings of England: London 1. Cities of London and Westminster**
Nikolaus Pevsner Revised Cherry 1993 (1957)

✔ **The Buildings of England: London 2. South** Nikolaus Pevsner with Cherry 1990 (1983)

✔ **The Buildings of England: London 3. North West** Nikolaus Pevsner with Cherry 1991

✔ **Georgian London** John Summerson 1991 (1945)
Described by the author as 'an outline sketch of the subject from a particular and personal angle', this study of Georgian London has been endlessly reprinted: 'The title gives no idea of the variety of this learned and lively book. It treats not only of Georgian architec-

ture, but of the whole problem of the growth of a city.' (Times Literary Supplement)

✔ **Docklands. Phaidon Architecture Guide** Stephanie Williams 1993 (1990)
Divided into the various districts of docklands, the buildings are analysed and discussed.

Autobiography/Biography

Diary John Evelyn 1818
Good descriptions of court life and society; Evelyn was born in 1620 and was well acquainted with kings, queens, ambassadors and bishops, as well as the London and countryside of the day. He kept his diaries over a period of 56 years in a very small cramped hand, so there is a wealth of information. The diary was not published until 1818.

All Done from Memory Osbert Lancaster 1963
Childhood memories of being brought up in London, some of which was originally published in the Cornhill Magazine.

✔ **Journey Through a Small Planet**
Emanuel Litvinoff 1993 (1972)
A series of autobiographical sketches about the author's turbulent and poverty-stricken childhood in London's East End. His family were persecuted Jews from Russia living in Bethnal Green in the 1920s and 1930s.

Fiction/Poetry

Hawksmoor Peter Ackroyd 1988 (1985)
In 1711 an Act of Parliament was passed to erect seven new Parish Churches in London; the architect, Dyer, worked on the models himself, while across the city builders struggled to achieve his vision. Parallel to this runs a twentieth-century detective story which weaves in and out of history and the area round Spitalfields: 'With consummate formal control, he has created a fictional nightmare, combining the genres of thriller, ghost story and metaphysical tract . . . Its nastiness illuminates modern evil as well as testifying to the author's brave way with the unspeakable.' (Marina Warner The Sunday Times) Also Chatterton

✔ **London Fields** Martin Amis 1990 (1989)
Observations of 'low-life' London: 'London Fields, its pastoral title savagely inappropriate to its inner-city setting, vibrates, like all Amis's work, with the force fields of sinister, destructive energies. At the core of its surreal

fable are four figures locked in lethal alignment.' (Peter Kemp *Sunday Times*)

✔ **The Napoleon of Notting Hill**
G.K. Chesterton 1946 (1904)
Auberon Quin, a Pickwickian gentleman, who can be outrageous in public places is one day chosen to be king.

The Secret Agent Joseph Conrad 1983 (1920)
A spy story which is based on the 1906 anarchist plot to bomb Greenwich. It is a chillingly prophetic examination of terrorism, predating the espionage thriller genre by many years and giving a good portrait of turn of the century London.

✔ **Journal of the Plague Year**
Daniel Defoe 1992
Defoe was a child in 1665 when the plague struck London, but he later used his experiences in a remarkable way for telling fiction in the guise of truth. The book is historically extremely vivid, yet it is most unlikely that Defoe actually witnessed the horrors he later wrote about.

✔ **Our Mutual Friend** Charles Dickens (1864/5)
'But – in the masterpiece line – *the* book for me would have to be Dicken's *Our Mutual Friend*. It is London between hard covers; London in the 1840s . . . London in the 1990s . . . it doesn't matter. If you want the whole texture of a metropolitan city brought alive on the page, read *Our Mutual Friend*. It seems to me to be one of the really majestic achievements in our literature – and for many reasons, not least of which is that it is a distillation of everything that Dickens had known and felt about the city in which he's spent a lifetime.' (Jonathan Raban) Other novels set in London include *Oliver Twist*, *Bleak House* 1986 (1853) in which the interminable suit of Jarndyce v. Jarndyce becomes central to the large cast of characters, *Little Dorrit*, *Dombey and Son* and *The Old Curiosity Shop*.

✔ **The Adventures of Sherlock Holmes** Arthur Conan Doyle 1993 (1892)
The descriptions of London in the gloom and fog are so powerful that many foreigners believe London is always in the midst of a pea-souper. Also ✔ *The Return of Sherlock Holmes* 1993 (1905).

The Diary of a Nobody George and Weedon Grossmith 1968 (1892)
A straight-faced imaginary journal of suburban life in Holloway, which was a very respectable district at the time. Mr Pooter who writes the diary is a City clerk, with an over-developed sense of dignity, which often leads him to the ridiculous.

✔ **The Golden Bowl** Henry James 1983 (1904)
A rich American art collector and his daughter 'collect' a young wife and noble husband, who unbeknownst to them had previously been lovers.

✔ **The Wings of the Dove** 1986 (1902)
Milly Theale arrives in Europe suffering from a grave illness.

Taste for Death P.D. James 1986
A confused and convoluted case starts for Adam Dalgliesh with the discovery of two bodies in the vestry of St Matthew's Church in Paddington.

Night and the City G. Kersh 1946
Set around the clubs of Soho, dated and full of cockney rhyming slang, but astmospheric nonetheless.

Foreign Affairs Alison Lurie 1984
Two American professors are doing research in London.

The World My Wilderness
Rose Macaulay 1950
Some good descriptions of London and docklands.

Absolute Beginners
City of Spades 1984 (1957)
Mr Love and Justice Colin MacInnes 1980 (1960)
The three 'London' novels of Colin Macinnes are about the sub-culture world of teenagers, crooks, policemen, prostitutes and pimps: 'MacInnes knew the underside of London life and conveys its atmosphere with authority'. (Anthony Burgess)

Downriver Iain Sinclair 1991
Many areas of London are described.

The Girls of Slender Means
Muriel Spark 1963
Set in a women's hostel at the close of the Second World War.

The History of Pendennis
William Makepeace Thackeray (1849–50)
Fictionalized autobiography; Arthur Pendennis moves from an 'Oxbridge' university, through his first love affair to London where he becomes a journalist.

The London Embassy Paul Theroux 1984
The experiences of an American diplomat at the Embassy in London.

✔ **Mrs Dalloway** Virginia Woolf 1972 (1925)
Clarissa Dalloway is the wife of a Member of

Parliament; the action takes place during the course of one day on which she is giving an important party.

General Background

Limehouse Days *Daniel Farson 1991*
Subtitled 'a personal experience of the East End', this well illustrated book is interesting about the history and contemporary life in the East End. Also ✔ *Soho in the Fifties* 1993 (1987) which makes a fascinating social document over a period of twenty-five years.

84 Charing Cross Road *Helen Hanff 1978*
The correspondence between the author in New York and a bookshop in London, a place she had never visited but had always wanted to.

London Labour and the London Poor
Henry Mayhew 1965 (1861)
Mayhew was the supreme recorder of mid-nineteenth century urban squalor and his records almost certainly gave impetus to the social amelioration which occurred towards the end of the century. Mayhew was one of seventeen children, running away from Westminster School to India when he refused to be flogged.

✔ **Down and Out in Paris and London** *George Orwell 1982 (1933)*
London and Paris seen from a tramp's point of view.

In Camden Town *David Thomson 1983*
Beautifully written book about living in London and Camden Town in particular. Thomson makes you feel that you know the streets he writes about and if you don't know them you want to walk them with him.

London Journal *Flora Tristan 1980 (1840)*
Flora Tristan was born in Paris in 1803; after an unsuccessful marriage in Paris she arrived in London as a ladies' maid in 1826. She then went to Peru to find her father's family before arriving back in France. She championed the cause of workers and in her *London Journal* criticizes much of what was happening in England although she admired Mary Wollstonecroft and other women writers. She was very enthusiastic about the burgeoning railway system which she saw as a way of transcending national boundaries and eliminating narrow provincialism.

Survey of London *John Stow 1980 (1603)*
One of the greatest antiquaries to write about London; Stow was interested in everything that went on around him, which makes this extremely useful as a source book, being one of the most detailed surveys of a medieval town ever written (1525–1603).

Guides

✔ **The Historic Hotels of London. A Select Guide** *Wendy Arnold 1989 (1986)*

✔ **The New Penguin Guide to London** *F.R. Banks 1990 (1958)*
Has become one of the classic guides to London and is practical and useful.

✔ **London. The Woman's Travel Guide** *Josie Barnard 1994*

The Blue Plaque Guide to London
Caroline Dakers 1982

✔ **Everyman Guide London** *1993*

✔ **Eyewitness Travel Guides: London** *1993*

✔ **London. The Blue Guide** *Ylva French 1994*

✔ **Cheap Eats in London**
✔ **Cheap Sleeps in London**
Sandra A. Gustafson 1994
Good for budget travellers – lengthy descriptions of each establishment.

Walks in London *Augustus Hare 1878*

✔ **American Express: London**
Michael Jackson, Leonie Glass and Fiona Duncan 1993

✔ **Let's Go London 1995**

✔ **Evening Standard London Restaurant Guide 1994** *Fay Maschler 1993*
Arranged alphabetically with long descriptions of each restaurant.

✔ **Michelin London Hotels, Restaurants 1995**

✔ **Nairn's London** *Ian Nairn Revisited by Peter Gasson 1988 (1966)*
Idiosyncratic choice of the best things to see in London.

✔ **Nicholson: London Restaurant Guide** *1994 (1975)*
Over 750 places to eat.

✔ **Fodor's London Companion**
Louise Nicholson 1993 (1988)
An excellent companion for visitors and residents.

✔ **Blue Guide Museums and Galleries of London** *Malcolm Rogers 1991*

✔ **Thomas Cook Travellers London**
1993

✔ **London. A Literary Companion**
Peter Vansittart 1992

History

✔ **Notting Hill and Holland Park
Past** *Barbara Denny 1993*
Fascinating history and social backgrounds to two completely different but adjoining areas.

A History of London *Robert Gray 1979*
An architectural and social history of London.

London: the biography of a City
Christopher Hibbert 1983
A mine of fascinating information about the development of London with maps and photographs.

✔ **A Traveller's History of London**
Richard Tames 1992

✔ **The London Encyclopedia**
Ben Weinreb and Christopher Hibbert 1992 (1983)
Packed with information on London's history and its present. An essential book for anyone with a serious interest in the history of London.

Leisure

✔ **London Walks. A Constable Guide**
Guy Williams 1981

Natural History

The Compleat Angler *Izaak Walton*
(1653)
Walton was born in Stafford, but moved to London where he became acquainted with many eminent people. His seventeenth-century fishing guide, set on the River Lea, London, makes a good companion having both literary charm and human appeal as well as being of practical value.

Photography

✔ **Above London** *Robert Cameron and*
Alistair Cooke 1992 (1980)
A fascinating collection of aerial views.

Travel Literature

In Search of London *H.V. Morton 1988*
(1951)
Morton starts his wanderings in the City where Roman London began and continues westward following the expansions made during the seventeenth and eighteenth centuries: 'A book to explore London with for most of a lifetime.' (*The Spectator*)

SURREY, SUSSEX, KENT, MIDDLESEX

'Though I have now travelled the Sussex Downs upward of thirty years, yet I still investigate that chain of majestic mountains with fresh admiration year by year.' Gilbert White, letter to Daines Barrington, 9 December, 1773 in *The Natural History of Selbourne* 1789

Art and Archaeology

✔ **The Buildings of England: Surrey**
Nikolaus Pevsner with Nairn 1990 (1962)

✔ **The Buildings of England: Sussex**
Nikolaus Pevsner with Nairn 1991 (1965)

✔ **The Buildings of England: Kent,
North East and East**
Nikolaus Pevsner revised Newman 1991 (1969)

✔ **The Buildings of England: Kent,
West and the Weald**
Nikolaus Pevsner revised Newman 1988 (1969)

Fiction/Poetry

✔ **Emma** *Jane Austen 1992 (1816)*
Set mostly in Surrey.

The Orchid Trilogy *Jocelyn Brooke 1981*
(1948-50)
Brooke was born in Kent, and although he went to Oxford, returns to Kent. This book is autobiography intertwined with fiction; the theme is a search for a rare orchid and Brooke has the ability of making botany intelligible to the unbotanical. 'He has an ear for talk; an eye for the beautiful and a sense of the comic. He writes simply and never shows off. Yet he is as subtle as the devil.' (Sir John Betjeman)

✔ **The Canterbury Tales**
Geoffrey Chaucer 1965 (c.1400)
The pilgrimage probably takes place over a period of five days and the pilgrims' tales come from all over Europe. Nevertheless

since the destination is Canterbury it is included in the Kent section.

The Crab-Apple Tree *Richard Church 1959*
After years at sea, Jim Bright returns to his native village in the Kentish Weald to find everything changed, but not as dramatically as when a young Welsh widow arrives. All set against the background of a Kentish year.

✔ **David Copperfield** *Charles Dickens 1966 (1849/50)*
Much of this novel takes place between Kent and Norfolk; Dickens described it as his favourite book: 'But like many fond parents, I have in my heart of hearts a favourite child. And his name is David Copperfield'.

Cold Comfort Farm *Stella Gibbons 1964 (193?)*
An extremely funny book about an orphan who lands up on a strange farm owned by her relations in Sussex. A brilliant satirization of the melodramatic nineteenth-century English novel: 'Novels that are really funny are rare . . . *Cold Comfort Farm* is one of them.' (*New York Times*)

✔ **Brighton Rock** *Graham Greene 1963 (1938)*
Pinkie's attitude to crime was that it was a wonderful release and no other external stimuli were necessary. This sinister character who worships in the house of evil stalks around Brighton.

Of Human Bondage
W. Somerset Maugham 1975 (1915)
Set in Whitstable and Canterbury and based on Maugham's own experiences as an orphan, this is the story of Philip Carey, an orphaned cripple who is searching for life and love.

Guides

✔ **Lunch, Dine, Stay and Visit: Southern England: Dorset, Wiltshire, Hampshire, Sussex** *Joy David 1993*

✔ **Kent. A Pocket Guide**
Frank Victor Dawes 1990

✔ **Hidden Places South East: Surrey, Sussex and Kent** *n.d.*
✔ **Sussex** *n.d.*

✔ **Philip's County Guide Surrey** *1993*

✔ **Philip's County Guide East Sussex**
1993

✔ **Philip's County Guide West Sussex**
1993

✔ **The Companion Guide to Kent and Sussex** *Keith Spence 1989 (1973)*

History

✔ **A Darwen County History of Sussex** *R.J. Armstrong 1978*

✔ **A Darwen County History of Surrey** *Peter Brandon 1977*

✔ **A Darwen County History of Kent**
Frank Jessup 1978

Leisure

✔ **A Guide to the South Downs Way. A Constable Guide** *Miles Jebb 1984*

✔ **A Guide to the Wealdway. A Constable Guide** *John H.N. Mason 1984*

✔ **National Trail Guide: South Downs Way** *Paul Millmore 1990*

✔ **Ordnance Survey Pathfinder Guides: Kent Walks** *(1993)*

✔ **A Guide to the Pilgrims' Way and North Downs Way** *Christopher John Wright 1993 (1971)*

Photography

✔ **The South Downs. Travels Through White Cliff Country** *Michael George 1992*
A collection of colour photographs with short captions.

HERTFORDSHIRE, BEDFORDSHIRE, BUCKINGHAMSHIRE, BERKSHIRE, OXFORDSHIRE, GLOUCESTERSHIRE, NORTHAMPTONSHIRE

'We came to Oxford, a very sweet place . . . Oxford mighty fine place and well seated, and cheap entertainment.' Samuel Pepys *Diary* 9 June 1668

Art and Archaeology

✔ **The Buildings of England: Hertfordshire**
Nikolaus Pevsner revised Cherry   1978 (1953)

✔ **The Buildings of England: Bedfordshire and the County of Huntingdon and Peterborough**
Nikolaus Pevsner   1968

✔ **The Buildings of England: Berkshire**   Nikolaus Pevsner   1993 (1956)

✔ **The Buildings of England: Oxfordshire**   Nikolaus Pevsner with Sherwood   1990 (1974)

✔ **The Buildings of England: Gloucestershire, Cotswolds**   Nikolaus Pevsner revised Verey

✔ **The Buildings of England: Gloucestershire. Vale and the Forest of Dean**   Nikolaus Pevsner revised Verey   1988 (1970)

✔ **The Buildings of England: Northamptonshire**
Nikolaus Pevsner revised Cherry   1985 (1961)

Fiction/Poetry

The Green Man   Kingsley Amis   1970
'The Green Man' is the pub where a local ghost conjures up a nasty thing.

✔ **Mansfield Park**   Jane Austen   1985 (1814)
Mansfield Park is in Northamptonshire. ✔ *Pride and Prejudice* (1813) is mostly set in Hertfordshire.

Zuleika Dobson   Max Beerbohm   1947 (1911)
'It is beauty forgetting to be men. Or rather it is laughter remembering all the graces: laughter holding both its sides – but as the figures do in a Watteau minuet. For if the phrases move in a galliard it is because they do form part of a ballet set in Oxford.' Dixon Scott *Men of Letters* (1916)

The Shooting Party   Isobel Colegate   1980
A pheasant shoot set in Oxfordshire in 1913, in the autumn preceding the outbreak of the First World War: 'It was an error of judgement which resulted in a death.'

Dusky Ruth and other Stories
A.E. Coppard   1975 (1921–28)
Coppard captures the quiet sensuality of rural life and has a sharp eye for detail: 'It is a sparrow's-eye view, sharp, wry, surviving, and not one that can quarrel with the savage economies of the field or the hedgerow.' (Doris Lessing)

✔ **Howard's End**   E.M. Forster   1960 (1910)
Set mostly between Hertfordshire and Shropshire, Forster's novel which has as its theme 'only connect' is about a London-based family which gets drawn into the country by a compelling family.

✔ **Jude the Obscure**   Thomas Hardy   1971 (1895)
Jude is a villager with intellectual aspirations who is trapped in a disastrous marriage. His wife deserts him and he embarks on a course of study for the priesthood; however he is possessed by passion for his married cousin, so his ambitions are thwarted. Much is set in Oxford.

The Prince Buys The Manor
Elspeth Huxley   1983
An African prince sets out to buy a manor house in a Cotswold town.

Three Men in a Boat   Jerome K. Jerome   1982 (1889)
The adventures of three men (not forgetting the dog) who set out on a hilarious voyage on the Thames: 'We agree that we are overworked, and need a rest – A week on the rolling deep? – George suggests the river.'

✔ **Cider with Rosie**   Laurie Lee   1962 (1959)
Adolescence in the Cotswolds in the 1920s: 'Laurie Lee's account of childhood and youth in the Cotswolds remains as fresh and full of joy and gratitude for youth and its sensations as when it first appeared. It sings in the memory.' (*The Sunday Times*)

Mr Pim   A.A. Milne   1930
The dead Mr Pim returns to visit his widow and her new husband. Set in Buckinghamshire.

A Few Green Leaves   Barbara Pym   1980
A woman anthropologist wants to write an article on English village life. Also *Crampton Hodnet* (1985) which is set in North Oxford and although it was published relatively recently, was one of Barbara Pym's first completed novels.

The Gaudy   J.I.M. Stewart   1975
The author is an Oxford don who captures the minutiae of Oxford life.

General Background

✔ **Oxford**   Jan Morris   1987 (1965)
'Few cities have been more loved, loathed, and celebrated', wrote Jan Morris and her

book has now become a classic on all the different aspects of Oxford.

✔ **Oxford Observed. Town and Gown**
Peter Snow 1992 (1991)
Useful for both those who already know and for those who want to get to know Oxford: 'No one should miss this clever, kind, astringent bouquet of a book.' (Brian Aldiss *Oxford Times*)

Lark Rise to Candleford *Flora Thompson 1954 (1945)*
The trilogy of volumes about rural English life in the north-east corner of Oxfordshire; by writing about the minutiae of daily life, Flora Thompson gives us an idea of the larger picture of England at the time. She records every stratum and sub-stratum of village/hamlet society and captures a transitional age, contributing to literature and social history.

Guides

✔ **Gloucestershire. A Pocket Guide**
Carole Chester 1990

✔ **Oxfordshire. A Pocket Guide**
Carole Chester 1990

✔ **Leisure Guide Hertfordshire**
Jon Culverhouse 1989

✔ **Hidden Places of the Cotswolds: Gloucestershire and Wiltshire** *n.d.*
✔ **Thames and Chilterns** *n.d.*
✔ **Oxfordshire, Buckinghamshire and Bedfordshire** *n.d.*

✔ **Lunch, Dine, Stay and Visit: Mid Shires: Northamptonshire, Leicestershire, Rutland, Derbyshire, Nottinghamshire, Lincolnshire and South Humberside** *Joy David 1992*

✔ **Exploring Oxford** *Michael De-la-Noy 1992 (1991)*
A literate guide which bases its information on ten walks through Oxford.

✔ **Insight Guide Oxford** *1992*

✔ **Philip's County Guide Oxfordshire** *1994*

✔ **A Guide to the Churches of Oxfordshire** *Jennifer Sherwood 1989*
Includes every Anglican and Roman Catholic church in the county and city of Oxford, but excludes chapels belonging to colleges and private houses. Arranged alphabetically under place with paragraph-length descriptions about each church.

✔ **Discovering the Cotswolds**
Charles W.J. Withers 1990

History

✔ **A Darwen County History of Northamptonshire** *R.L Greenall 1979*

✔ **A Darwen County History of Hertfordshire** *Tony Rook 1985*

✔ **A Darwen County History of Bristol and Gloucestershire** *Brian Smith and Elizabeth Ralph 1982*

Leisure

✔ **National Trail guide: The Ridgeway** *Neil Curtis 1994 (1989)*

✔ **A Guide to the Thames Path. A Constable Guide** *Miles Jebb 1988*

✔ **Ordnance Survey. Pathfinder Guides: Chilterns and Thames Valley Walks** *1994*
✔ **Cotswold Walks** *1993 (1990)*

✔ **A Guide to the Cotswold Way. A Constable Guide** *Richard Sale 1988 (1980)*

Photography/Illustrated

✔ **Hugh Casson's Oxford** *Hugh Casson 1988*
A delightfully illustrated book to the Oxford colleges.

HAMPSHIRE, WILTSHIRE

'Most pure and piercing the air of this shire [Hampshire]; and none in England hath more plenty of clear and fresh rivulets of troutful water; not to speak of the friendly sea conveniently distanced from London.' Thomas Fuller *History of the Worthies of England* 1662

Art and Archaeology

✔ **The Buildings of England: Hampshire and the Isle of Wight**
Nikolaus Pevsner with Lloyd 1990 (1967)

✔ **The Buildings of England: Wiltshire** *Nikolaus Pevsner revised Cherry 1976 (1963)*

Autobiography/Biography

John Aubrey a Life *David Tylden-Wright*
1991
The author and his family bought a house
next door to the one in which John Aubrey
had been born in 1626 in a corner of north
Wiltshire. He shows 'how interesting a
neighbour and a person Aubrey proved to be'.

Fiction/Poetry

The Spire *William Golding* *1964*
A novel set around the building of a medieval
cathedral spire in a city thinly disguised as
Salisbury. Salisbury's spire was probably
begun in 1334 and the novel takes place
during a period of two years around that
time. There is little story or plot, the interest
coming from the moral and spiritual dilemma of the main protagonist, Dean
Jocelin.

The Bird in the Tree *Elizabeth Goudge*
1940
One of a trilogy which comprises *Pilgrim's
Inn* (1948) and *Heart of the Family* (1953)
about a family who live on the Hampshire
coast and during the war come into contact
with a whole range of different people.

✔ **The Enigma of Arrival** *V.S. Naipaul*
1987
A young Indian comes to England from Trinidad and eventually finds himself a writer in
the countryside round Salisbury, where at
first sight little seems to have changed since
the days of Hardy: '*The Enigma of Arrival* is
a wonderful book in the original sense of the
adjective – a magical book.' (Jan Morris *Independent*)

✔ **Barchester Towers** *Anthony Trollope*
1993 (1857)
The 'Barsetshire' novels are set in and
around Salisbury. *Barchester Towers* is the
second in the series.

General Background

✔ **A Traveller's Companion to the
West Country** *Michael Jenner* *1992 (1990)*
(see 'West Country')
An illustrated book which surveys the West
Country's historical and cultural past. It in-
cludes early monuments and remnants of the
Industrial Revolution as well as the more
obvious buildings. Avon, Cornwall, Devon,
Dorset, Isles of Scilly, Somerset and Wilt-
shire.

✔ **Wight Magic** *Philip Ward* *1990*
Tales of the Isle of Wight and its islanders.

Guides

✔ **Lunch, Dine, Stay and Visit:
Southern England: Dorset, Wiltshire,
Hampshire, Sussex** *Joy David* *1993*

✔ **Hidden Places of the Cotswolds:
Gloucestershire and Wiltshire** and
Hampshire and the Isle of Wight

✔ **Philip's County Guide Hampshire**
1993

History

✔ **A Darwen County History of
Hampshire** *Barbara Carpenter Turner* *1978*

✔ **A Darwen County History of
Wiltshire** *Bruce W. Watkin* *1989*

Leisure

✔ **Ordnance Survey Pathfinder
Guides: Hampshire Walks** *(1993)*
✔ **Isle of Wight Walks** *(1994)*

Natural History

Kilvert's Diary *Rev. Francis Kilvert* *1973*
(1870–79)
A vivid picture of the life of a village clergy-
man and the changing seasons in Wiltshire
and the Welsh border: 'The best picture of
quiet vicarage life in Victorian England that
has yet been given us.' (John Betjeman)

**The Natural History and Antiquities of
Selborne** *Gilbert White* *1901*
Gilbert White was born in Selborne in 1720,
the eldest of eleven children. He took holy
orders in 1747 and although he was given
various parishes, he preferred to live in his
old family house in Selborne. The book has a
peculiar charm which makes it memorable;
it is both learned and simple, practical and
contemplative.

WEST COUNTRY: AVON, SOMERSET, DORSET, DEVON, CORNWALL

'There are more saints in Cornwall than
there are in heaven.' (Cornish proverb)

Art and Archaeology

✔ **The Buildings of England: Somerset North and Bristol**
Nikolaus Pevsner   1990 (1958)

✔ **The Buildings of England: Somerset South and West**
Nikolaus Pevsner   1989 (1958)

✔ **The Buildings of England: Dorset**
Nikolaus Pevsner with Newman   1989 (1972)

✔ **The Buildings of England: Devon**
Nikolaus Pevsner with Cherry   1991 (1952)

✔ **The Buildings of England: Cornwall**   Nikolaus Pevsner revised Radcliffe
1990 (1951)

Fiction/Poetry

✔ **Northanger Abbey**   1965 (1818)
✔ **Persuasion**   Jane Austen   1965 (1818)
Both books were written in Bath and satirize Bath's spa society; neither was published until after her death. ✔ *Sense and Sensibility* (1811) is set mostly in the West Country.

Evelina   Frances Burney   1968 (1778)
A young girl fresh from the provinces is ignorant of the ways of the world. Descriptions of the social life between London and Bristol.

✔ **Lorna Doone**   R.D. Blackmore   1963 (1869)
John Ridd, a yeoman-farmer, lives in Exmoor during the reign of Charles II. His father is killed by the Doone family and he is rescued from them by the young Lorna, whom he in turn intends to rescue and marry.

Except the Lord   Joyce Cary   1953
Set in the 1870s, the Devonshire childhood and young adulthood of Chester Nimmo who became a preacher and politician.

The Rose and the Yew Tree
Mary Westmacott (Agatha Christie)   1986 (1947)
A romantic novel in which Isabella Charteris waited for her cousin Rupert to come back from the war, but instead ended up marrying the ruthless John Gabriel. Set in Cornwall.

Summer of the Royal Visit
Isobel Colegate   1991
A retired teacher returns to near where he was born overlooking Bath; he spends much time in the reference library reading about Victorian Bath and in particular Stephen Collingwood, the curate in charge of the Chapel of St Catherine in whose life he becomes involved.

A Horseman Riding By   R.F. Delderfield
1966
A family saga which begins in 1902 with the return of a young man from the Boer War to a run-down estate in Devonshire. *Green Gauntlet* (1968) continues the saga up until the end of the Second World War.

✔ **The Hound of the Baskervilles**
Arthur Conan Doyle   1993 (1902)
Conan Doyle was given the idea for *The Hound of the Baskervilles* by a friend, Bertram Fletcher Robinson, in Norfolk and subsequently went to Dartmoor to pursue it, where Robinson wrote: 'One of the most interesting weeks that I ever spent was with Doyle on Dartmoor'.

✔ **Tom Jones**   Henry Fielding   (1749)
In 1735 Fielding married and assumed the character of a country squire in East Stour in Dorset. *Tom Jones* was published after the death of his first wife and was extolled by Gibbon in florid prose: 'The successors of Charles V may disdain their brethren in England; but the romance of *Tom Jones* – that exquisite picture of humour and manners – will outlive the palace of the Escurial and the imperial Eagle of Austria.'

The French Lieutenant's Woman
John Fowles   1969

A Victorian love story, set in Lyme Regis, Dorset with modern insights.

✔ **Far From the Madding Crowd**
Thomas Hardy   1993 (1874)
Other novels set in Hardy's native Dorset include *The Mayor of Casterbridge* and ✔ *Tess of the D'Urbervilles* 1971 (1891), a novel full of anguish and suffering. ✔ *The Return of the Native* 1976 (1878) is about Eustacia Vye who lives with her grandfather on 'Egdon Heath' and Clym Yeobright who returns to the heath from Paris and falls in love with and marries her; their relationship is doomed because Clym loves the heath and she hates it.

Bath Tangle   Georgette Heyer   1972
This and *Lady of Quality* are Regency novels set in Somerset.

Penmarric   Susan Howatch   1971
What happens in the life of a brutally selfish man and his children and grandchildren. Historical parallels are drawn between them and Henry II and Eleanor of Aquitaine.

The Black Tower   P.D. James   1987 (1975)
When Adam Dalgliesh arrives to convalesce in Dorset he discovers that his host has died suddenly and this is followed by other mys-

terious deaths. The 'black tower' of the title is on the Purbeck coast of Dorset.

Stalky and Co Rudyard Kipling 1987 (1899)
Nine stories about three naughty schoolboys at Kipling's old school, the United Services College at Westward Ho! in Devon – much criticized for its brutality, but equally praised as the best school story of all.

Frenchman's Creek Daphne du Maurier 1942
Also ✔ *Jamaica Inn* 1976 (1936) in which Mary Yellan discovers that her uncle was leader of a strange bunch of men who induced fear into the neighbourhood; and *My Cousin Rachel* (1952), *The King's General* 1960 (1946) and *Rebecca* (1938).

The Nice and the Good Iris Murdoch 1968
A combination of love story, mystery and sexual comedy set in Dorset.

General Background

Somerset Maxwell Fraser n.d.
A dated but nonetheless useful, informative, illustrated and idiosyncratic book describing the towns and areas of Somerset.

✔ **A Traveller's Companion to the West Country** Michael Jenner 1992 (1990)
(see 'Hampshire')
An illustrated book which surveys the West Country's historical and cultural past. It includes early monuments and remnants of the Industrial Revolution as well as the more obvious buildings. Avon, Cornwall, Devon, Dorset, Isles of Scilly, Somerset and Wiltshire.

Journals Dorothy Wordsworth 1963 (1800–1803)
About The Quantocks in Somerset.

Guides

✔ **Lunch, Dine, Stay and Visit: Devon, Cornwall** Joy David 1993

✔ **Lunch, Dine, Stay and Visit: Somerset, Avon** Joy David 1993

✔ **Lunch, Dine, Stay and Visit: Southern England: Dorset, Wiltshire, Hampshire, Sussex** Joy David 1993

✔ **Discovering Dartmoor and South Devon** Ron and Marlene Freethy 1992

✔ **Discovering Exmoor and North Devon** Ron and Marlene Freethy 1992

✔ **Hidden Places of Somerset, Avon and Dorset**

✔ **Devon and Cornwall**

✔ **Michelin Green Guide West Country** 1994

✔ **The Companion Guide to Devon** Shirley Toulson 1991

History

✔ **A Darwen County History of Dorset** Cecio N. Cullingford 1980

✔ **A Darwen County History of Somerset** Robert Dunning 1983

✔ **A Darwen County History of Cornwall** Ian Soulsby 1986

✔ **A Darwen County History of Devon** Robin Stanes 1985

Leisure

✔ **A Guide to the South Devon and Dorset Coast Paths. A Constable Guide** Roland Gant 1982

National Trail Guides: South West Coast Path:
✔ **Minehead to Padstow** Roland Tarr (1990)
✔ **Padstow to Falmouth** John Macadam (1990)
Falmouth to Exmouth Brian Le Messurier (1990)
✔ **Exmouth to Poole** Roland Tarr (1990)

✔ **Ordnance Survey. Pathfinder Guides: Cornwall Walks** 1991 (1990)
✔ **Exmoor and the Quantocks Walks** 1991 (1990)
✔ **Dartmoor Walks** (1991 (1989)
✔ **Dorset Walks** (1992)

✔ **Ordnance Survey: South Devon and Dartmoor. Landranger Guidebook** 1990

✔ **Ordnance Survey: North Devon, Exmoor and the Quantocks. Landranger Guidebook** 1989 (1985)

✔ **Best Walks in the South-west. A Constable Guide** Richard Sale 1992

Photography

✔ **Wetland. Life in the Somerset Levels** Patrick Sutherland and Adam Nicolson 1991 (1986)
A collection of black and white photographs with ample text describing the Somerset levels which lie between the Mendips and the

Quantocks and border the shores of the Bristol Channel.

Travel Literature

A Book of the West: Cornwall
S. Baring-Gould 1981 (1899)
Baring-Gould emphasized the spirit of a place; this meant that he was not always completely historically accurate, but he caught the atmosphere by starting with the world of the ancient Celtic saints.

✔ **An Unsentimental Journey Through Cornwall** *The Author of 'John Halifax, Gentleman' 1988 (1884)*
A re-issued travel diary of a journey taken by a lady authoress, Mrs Craik, and her two nieces through Cornwall.

✔ **Vanishing Cornwall**
Daphne du Maurier 1981 (1967)
A celebration of Cornwall and all that it has lost with many literary references, reminiscences, history and legends.

Journeys *Jan Morris 1980*
An essay on Wells. *Travels* (1984) has an essay on Bath.

EAST ANGLIA: CAMBRIDGESHIRE, ESSEX, NORFOLK, SUFFOLK

'The Norfolk people are quick and smart in their motions and in their speaking. Very neat and *trim* in all their farming concerns, and very skilful.' William Cobbett *Rural Rides* 24 December 1821

Art and Archaeology

✔ **The Buildings of England: Cambridgeshire** *Nikolaus Pevsner 1991 (1954)*

✔ **The Buildings of England: Essex**
Nikolaus Pevsner revised Radcliffe 1991 (1954)

✔ **The Buildings of England: Norfolk North East and Norwich**
Nikolaus Pevsner 1990 (1962)

✔ **The Buildings of England: Norfolk, North West and South** *Nikolaus Pevsner 1990 (1962)*

✔ **The Buildings of England: Suffolk**
Nikolaus Pevsner revised Radcliffe 1991 (1961)

Fiction/Poetry

✔ **David Copperfield** *Charles Dickens (see 'Kent')*

Sleeping Dogs Lie *Julian Gloag 1980*
A psychological thriller set in Cambridge. *Our Mother's House* (1963) is about a Cambridge psychiatrist and a student who has an unusual phobia.

The Good Listener
Pamela Hansford Johnson 1975
Three men start at Cambridge just after the war.

Death of an Expert Witness *P.D. James 1977*
A biologist is murdered in a small village in East Anglia.

Make Death Love Me *Ruth Rendell 1979*
Two teenage bank robbers and a bank manager are characters in this psychological novel.

Waterland *Graham Swift 1984 (1983)*
A family saga set in the fens of East Anglia: 'Graham Swift has mapped his Waterland like a new Wessex. The tale he tells is at once a history of England, a Fenland documentary, and a fictional autobiography.' (Hermione Lee *The Observer*)

General Background

Akenfield. Portrait of an English Village *Ronald Blythe 1969*
A village in East Anglia described by its inhabitants.

Guides

Lunch, Stay, Dine and Visit: East Anglia *Joy David 1992*

✔ **Hidden Places of East Anglia**

✔ **East Anglia. A Pallas Guide**
P. Sager 1994

✔ **The Companion Guide to East Anglia** *John Seymour 1990 (1970)*

✔ **The Visitor's Guide to East Anglia. A Moorland Guide** *Clive Tully 1990 (1984)*

History

✔ **A Darwen County History of Essex**
A.C. Edwards 1978

✔ **A Darwen County History of Cambridgeshire** *Bruce Galloway 1983*

✔ **A Darwen County History of Norfolk** *Susanna Wade Martins* *1984*

✔ **A Darwen County History of Huntingdonshire** *Michael J. Wickes* *1985*

Leisure

✔ **National Trail Guide: Peddars Way and Norfolk Coast Path** *Bruce Robinson 1992*

Photography/Illustrated

✔ **Hugh Casson's Cambridge** *Hugh Casson 1992* A delightfully illustrated book on the colleges of Cambridge.

✔ **Ruth Rendell's Suffolk** *Photographs by Paul Bowden 1992 (1989)* A selection of Ruth Rendell's favourite places.

CENTRAL ENGLAND: WEST MIDLANDS, LEICESTERSHIRE, LINCOLNSHIRE, DERBYSHIRE, NOTTINGHAMSHIRE, STAFFORDSHIRE, WARWICKSHIRE

' . . . this strange, mountainous, misty, moorish, rocky, wild country . . . the craggy ascents, the rocky unevenness of the roads, the high peaks and the almost perpendicular descents . . . ' Edward Browne *Journal of a Tour in Derbyshire* 1662

Art and Archaeology

✔ **The Buildings of England: Leicestershire and Rutland** *Nikolaus Pevsner revised Williamson 1989 (1960)*

✔ **The Buildings of England: Lincolnshire** *Nikolaus Pevsner with Harris revised Antram 1990 (1964)*

✔ **The Buildings of England: Derbyshire** *Nikolaus Pevsner revised Williamson 1986 (1953)*

✔ **The Buildings of England: Nottinghamshire** *Nikolaus Pevsner revised Williamson 1979 (1951)*

✔ **The Buildings of England: Staffordshire** *Nikolaus Pevsner 1975 (1974)*

✔ **The Buildings of England: Warwickshire** *Nikolaus Pevsner with Wedgwood 1990 (1966)*

Fiction/Poetry

✔ **Burning Leaves** *Don Bannister 1982* A university teacher leaves his work in London to live in a Midlands town.

✔ **Anna of the Five Towns** *Arnold Bennett 1902* Bennett writes about industrial life in the Staffordshire Potteries, but tempers the realism with his own humanity and compassion. *The Old Wives' Tale* (1908) begins and ends in the Five Towns and embraces their history as well as being about two sisters who grow old together. The *Clayhanger Trilogy* (*Clayhanger* (1900), *Hilda Lessways* (1911) and *These Twain* (1916)) was intended to trace the lives of a man and woman from youth to old age. The first volume, about youth, is unquestionably the most successful. Staffordshire had become very prosperous towards the end of the eighteenth century and Bennett who was born in Hanley, although he went to work in a solicitor's office in London and later lived in Paris, saw himself as the historian of life in the Potteries.

✔ **Middlemarch** *George Eliot 1974 (1871–2)* *Middlemarch* describes life in the Midlands, as well as having fine portrait studies of its characters and the development of Dorothea's social awareness, parallel to the awakening of her feelings of love for Will Ladislaw. ✔ *Scenes of Clerical Life* (1858) is a series of tales, *Adam Bede* (1859), set in the Midlands at the turn of the eighteenth century, is about a triangle of three foolish lovers who through their naivety and imprudence fall into a trap of seduction, murder and retribution. ✔ *The Mill on the Floss* 1973 (1860), partly autobiographical, is an exposé of bourgeois values and is thought to be based on Gainsborough in Lincolnshire.

✔ **Sons and Lovers** *D.H. Lawrence 1966 (1913)* The background of the story is the Nottinghamshire coalfield where Lawrence was brought up. The fictional Morel family is closely based on his own; central to the novel is the relationship between Mrs Morel, a strong woman married to a miner, and her third child Paul, who as he grows up finds other women in his life. ✔ *Women in Love* 1967 (1921) is about the relationships of two women, Ursula and Gudron, who live in a

Midland colliery town before the First World War.

Next to Nature Art *Penelope Lively* *1983*
About a 'Creative Study Centre' in the Warwickshire countryside.

Saturday Night and Sunday Morning
Alan Sillitoe *1958*
Nottingham factory life in the 1950s and an angry young man's life in industrial Britain. Saturday night was 'the best and bingiest glad-time of the week', whereas on Sunday morning 'he didn't much care whether he lived or died'. Also *The Widower's Son* (1977) and *Men, Women and Children* (1974).

General Background

✔ **Tales from Two Cities** *Dervla Murphy* *1989 (1987)*
Dervla Murphy went to live in Manningham, Bradford and Handsworth, Birmingham and joined both communities which were at the centre of urban deprivation; 'Tales from Two Cities is not a comfortable read. It is a disturbing, shocking, thought-provoking account of one woman's attempt to share at first hand the experience of the residents . . . of Britain's multi-racial communities.' (Shelley Rohde *Daily Mail*)

Guides

✔ **Lunch, Dine, Stay and Visit: Heart of England: Warwickshire, West Midlands, Worcestershire, Herefordshire, Shropshire, Staffordshire** *Joy David* *1992*

✔ **Lunch, Dine, Stay and Visit: Mid Shires: Northamptonshire, Leicestershire, Rutland, Derbyshire, Nottinghamshire, Lincolnshire and South Humberside** *Joy David* *1992*

✔ **Discovering the Pennines**
Ron and Marlene Freethy *1992*

✔ **Hidden Places of Nottinghamshire, Derbyshire and Lincolnshire**

History

✔ **A Darwen County History of Derbyshire** *Joy Childs* *1987*

✔ **A Darwen County History of Staffordshire** *M.W. Greenslade and D.G. Stuart* *1984*

✔ **A Darwen County History of Nottinghamshire** *David Kaye* *1987*

✔ **A Darwen County History of Leicestershire and Rutland**
Roy Millward *1985*

✔ **A Darwen County History of Lincolnshire** *Alan Rogers* *1985*

✔ **A Darwen County History of Warwickshire** *Terry Slater* *1981*

Leisure

✔ **Best Walks in the Peak district. A Constable Guide** *Frank Duerden* *1991* *(1988)*

✔ **Ordnance Survey. Pathfinder Guide: Peak District Walks** *1991 (1989)*

✔ **100 Walks in Staffordshire** *1992*

✔ **The Peak and Pennines. A Constable Guide** *W.A. Poucher* *1988* *(1966)*

WELSH BORDERS: SHROPSHIRE, HEREFORD AND WORCESTER

'The peculiar flavour of the scenery [Shropshire] has something to do with the absence of evolution; it was better marked in Egypt: it was felt wherever time-sequences became interchangeable.' Henry Adams *The Education of Henry Adams* 1906.

Art and Archaeology

✔ **The Buildings of England: Shropshire** *Nikolaus Pevsner* *1989 (1958)*

✔ **The Buildings of England: Herefordshire** *Nikolaus Pevsner* *1990 (1963)*

✔ **The Buildings of England: Worcestershire** *Nikolaus Pevsner* *1985 (1968)*

Fiction/Poetry

✔ **Howard's End** *E.M. Forster* *1992 (1910)*
Set mostly between Hertfordshire and Shropshire.

A Shropshire Lad *A.E. Housman* *1890–95*
A collection of about twenty poems set in Shropshire; Housman was born in Worcestershire but: 'I had a sentimental feeling for Shropshire because its hills were our western horizon'.

Cast a Long Shadow *Mary E. Pearce 1983*
A blissful marriage set in Worcestershire comes adrift after a horrifying experience.

Precious Bane *Mary Webb 1926*
Farming life and farming people in Shropshire.

Guides

✔ **Lunch, Dine, Stay and Visit: Heart of England: Warwickshire, West Midlands, Worcestershire, Herefordshire, Shropshire, Staffordshire** *Joy David 1992*

✔ **Hidden Places of Hereford and Worcester**

History

✔ **A Darwen County History of Shropshire** *Barrie Trinder 1983*

✔ **A Darwen County History of Herefordshire** *John and Margaret West 1985*

Leisure

✔ **Hereford and the Wye Valley. A Walker's Guide to The Malverns, Herefordshire and the Forest of Dean** *David Hinchliffe 1993*

✔ **National Trail Guide: Offa's Dyke Path North. Knighton to Prestatyn** *1989*
✔ **Offa's Dyke Path South** *Ernie and Kathy Kay and Mark Richards 1989*

✔ **Ordnance Survey. Pathfinder Guide: Wye Valley and Forest of Dean Walks** *1991*

Photography

✔ **Borderlands: Shropshire and Welsh Marches** *Julian Critchley and David Paterson n.d.*
Colour photographs with ample text.

✔ **The Malvern Hills. Travels Through Elgar Country** *Archie Miles 1992*
Colour photographs with small captions.

✔ **The Heart of England** *Robin Whiteman and Rob Talbot 1992*
Colour photographs of Shropshire, Gloucester, the Welsh Borders and Stratford-upon-Avon.

THE NORTHWEST: CHESHIRE, GREATER MANCHESTER, MERSEYSIDE, LANCASHIRE, CUMBRIA, ISLE OF MAN

'I never saw daffodils so beautiful.[Near Ullswater] They grew among the many mossy stones around and about them; some rested their heads upon these stones as on a pillow for weariness; and the rest tossed and reeled and danced, and seemed as if they verily laughed with the wind, that blew upon them over the lake; they looked so gay, ever glancing, ever changing.'
Dorothy Wordsworth *Journal* 15 April 1802

Anthology

✔ **The Lake District. An Anthology**
Compiled by Norman Nicholson 1978 (1977)
'If you seek a bedside book that will give you a lifetime of pleasure, your search is over. Norman Nicholson, the much admired Cumbrian poet, has produced an anthology of sheer magic, brilliantly sectionalised under fells, dales, work, play, lake poets, customs and so on . . . the ideal anthology.' (*Yorkshire Post*)

Art and Archaeology

✔ **The Buildings of England: Cheshire** *Nikolaus Pevsner with Hubbard 1990 (1971)*

✔ **The Buildings of England: Lancashire North** *Nikolaus Pevsner 1991 (1969)*

✔ **The Buildings of England: Lancashire South** *Nikolaus Pevsner 1989 (1969)*

✔ **The Buildings of England: Cumberland and Westmorland** *Nikolaus Pevsner 1988 (1967)*

Fiction

Quiet Life *Beryl Bainbridge 1977*
Set in a village near Southport, the story of a family's strife. *Young Adolf* (1979) evolves out of a diary entry that Adolf Hitler visited Liverpool as a young man.

✔ **Hard Times** *Charles Dickens 1854*
Dickens went to Preston during a strike to get material for this book which is set in a Lancashire mill town in the 1850s. However

he does not seem to be at ease with the characters, not giving himself enough time to get to know the Lancashire characters. There are vivid descriptions of Coketown.

The Bride of Lowther Fell
Margaret Forster 1981
A woman's sister is killed and she becomes responsible for her young nephew with whom she moves to an isolated cottage in Cumbria.

Gold by Gemini Jonathan Gash 1978
A mystery involving Roman coins set in the Isle of Man.

Mary Barton Elizabeth Gaskell 1972 (1848)
Mrs Gaskell was well qualified to write about the excesses and deprivations of Victorian life as she lived near Manchester, which was the symbol of the new industrial age at its best. She sees that it is men's tragic ignorance of each other which is at the root of evil. In contrast ✔ *Cranford* 1976 (1853) is about small town life: 'In the first place, Cranford is in possession of the Amazons; all the holders of houses, above a certain rent, are women'.

General Background

✔ **Wordsworth and the Lake District**
David McCracken 1990 (1984)
Descriptions of Wordworth's Lake District and walks following in his footsteps, which it is possible to do either literally or from an armchair.

Guides

✔ **Discovering Cumbria**
Ron and Marlene Freethy 1991

✔ **Discovering the Pennines**
Ron and Marlene Freethy 1992

✔ **Hidden Places of Lancashire and Cheshire**
✔ **Hidden Places of Cumbria**

✔ **Raw Guide Greater Manchester**
Debbie Ridehalgh and Mike Parker 1991
Basic streetwise guide.

Leisure Guide: Lancashire Alan and Dorothy Sewart 1989

✔ **Visitor's guide: Lake District. A Moorland Guide** Brian Spencer 1993 (1981)

✔ **The Companion Guide to the Lake District** Frank Welsh 1989

History

✔ **A Darwen County History of Lancashire** J.J. Bagley 1976

✔ **A Darwen County History of Cheshire** Dorothy Sylvester 1993

✔ **The Road to Wigan Pier**
George Orwell 1989 (1937)
The effects of the Great Depression on the industrial communities of Lancashire and Yorkshire.

✔ **A Darwen County History of Cumberland and Westmorland**
William Rollinson 1978

Leisure

✔ **Best Walks in the Lake District. A Constable Guide** Frank Duerden 1994 (1986)

✔ **Isle of Man Coastal Path**
Aileen Evans 1991 (1987)

✔ **A Literary Guide to the Lake District** Grevel Lindop 1994 (1993)
Follows five major routes; the author has scoured the area, which he knows well, for all the literary associations, both known and not so well known, that he could find.

✔ **Ordnance Survey. Landranger Guidebook: The Lake District** 1991 (1988)

✔ **Ordnance Survey. Pathfinder Guide: Lake District Walks** 1993 (1989)

✔ **The Lakeland Peaks. A Constable Guide** W.A. Poucher 1992 (1960)

✔ **A Coast to Coast Walk** A. Wainwright 1994 (1973)

✔ **The Pictorial Guides to the Lakeland Fells:** A. Wainwright
Book 1: The Eastern Fells 1992 (1955)
Book 2: The Far Eastern Fells 1992 (1957)
Book 3: The Central Fells 1992 (1958)
Book 4: The Southern Fells 1992 (1960)
Book 5: The Northern Fells 1992 (1962)
Book 6: The North Western Fells 1992 (1964)
Book 7: The Western Fells 1992 (1966)
Wainwright's books are now classic accounts of exploration of the mountains in the English Lake District. All written in his clear hand and profusely illustrated with line drawings, plans and maps. A must for any serious walker.

Photography

✔ **An Illustrated Companion into Lakeland** *Walt Unsworth 1988*
Anecdotes and history as well as photographs.

✔ **Wainwright's Tour in the Lake District. Whitsuntide 1931** *Photographs by Ed Geldard 1993*
In 1931 Wainwright walked, with three friends, 102½ miles round the Lake District, over the Whitsun Holiday. This is a record of his journey.

Travel Literature

✔ **A Walk Around the Lakes** *Hunter Davies 1993 (1979)*
A journey of rediscovery as well as one of familiarity; Hunter Davies found all sorts of new places on his journey which in the text he combines with a Wordsworth narrative.

Journals *Dorothy Wordsworth 1963 (1800–1803)*
Dorothy Wordsworth finally settled into a house in Grasmere with her brother William in 1799. She had an acute sense of nature and De Quincey said of her that 'she was the very wildest (in the sense of the most natural) person that I have ever known'. It is well known that William drew much of the sustenance for his poetry from her. Her *Grasmere Journals* were written between 1800–1803.

NORTH YORKSHIRE, WEST YORKSHIRE, SOUTH YORKSHIRE, HUMBERSIDE
'More than any other in England, Yorkshire retained a sort of social independence of London. Scotland itself was hardly more distinct.' Henry Adams *The Education of Henry Adams* 1906

Art and Archaeology

✔ **The Buildings of England: Yorkshire North Riding** *Nikolaus Pevsner 1985 (1966)*

✔ **The Buildings of England: Yorkshire West Riding** *Nikolaus Pevsner revised Radcliffe 1989 (1959)*

✔ **The Buildings of England: Yorkshire, York and the East Riding** *Nikolaus Pevsner with Hutchinson 1989 (1972)*

Fiction/Poetry

Room at the Top *John Braine 1957*
Small town life in Yorkshire, in which a man has an insatiable lust for power and wealth.

✔ **Wuthering Heights** *Emily Brontë 1963 (1847)*
A passionate story, dominated by the wild Heathcliff, infused with the bleakness and beauty of the Yorkshire moors.

A Month in the Country *J.L. Carr 1984 (1980)*
Two survivors of the Great War meet in the summer of 1920 in the English countryside; they are dealing with their traumas in different ways, but their meeting produces profound feelings for the countryside and history and the rhythms of life.

Sylvia's Lovers *Elizabeth Gaskell 1982 (1863)*
Set during the French Revolutionary wars in the whaling port of Monkshaven in Yorkshire and described by the author as 'the saddest story I ever wrote'. Two men are in love with Sylvia, a bold sailor and a meek man who idolizes her. Against a setting of provincial England where the main fear is of press-gangs, we see Sylvia develop from a wilful girl into a mature woman who has suffered.

A Prodigal Child *David Storey 1983*
Set in Yorkshire before the Second World War, it shows class differences being bridged by artistic abilities.

General Background

✔ **Tales from Two Cities** *Dervla Murphy 1989 (1987)*
Dervla Murphy went to live in Manningham, Bradford and Handsworth, Birmingham and joined both communities which were at the centre of urban deprivation; *'Tales from Two Cities* is not a comfortable read. It is a disturbing, shocking, thought-provoking account of one woman's attempt to share at first hand the experience of the residents . . . of Britain's multi-racial communities.' (Shelley Rohde *Daily Mail*)

Guides

✔ **Lunch, Dine, Stay and Visit: Mid Shires: Northamptonshire, Leicestershire, Rutland, Derbyshire, Nottinghamshire, Lincolnshire and South Humberside** *Joy David 1992*

✔ **Discovering Coastal Yorkshire**
Ron and Marlene Freethy 1992

✔ **Discovering Inland Yorkshire**
Ron and Marlene Freethy 1992

Hidden Places: Yorkshire and Humberside
North Yorkshire
Yorkshire South, East and West

✔ **Visitor's Guide : North York Moors, York and the Coast. A Moorland Guide** *Brian Spencer 1993 (1984)*

✔ **The Which? Guide to Yorkshire and the Peak District** *Martin Wainwright and Tim Locke 1992*

History

✔ **York** *R.K. Booth 1990*
The history and heritage of the city of York. Illustrated.

✔ **The Road to Wigan Pier** *George Orwell*
(see 'Lancashire')

✔ **A Darwen County History of Yorkshire** *Fred Singleton and Stuart Rawnsley 1986*

Leisure

✔ **National Trail Guide: Pennine Way North (Bowes to Kirk Yetholm)**
Tony Hopkins 1990 (1989)
✔ **Pennine Way South (Edale to Bowes)** *Tony Hopkins 1990*

✔ **National Trail Guides:**
✔ **Wolds Way** *Roger Ratcliffe 1992*
✔ **Cleveland Way** *Ian Sampson (1989)*

✔ **Ordnance Survey. Landranger Guidebooks: The Yorkshire Dales and York** *1991 (1989)*
✔ **York and the Moors** *1991 (1988)*

✔ **Ordnance Survey. Pathfinder Guides: North York Moors Walks** *1991 (1990)*

✔ **Yorkshire Dales Walks** *1993 (1989)*

✔ **A Coast to Coast Walk** *A. Wainwright 1994 (1973)*

✔ **A Guide to the Pennine Way. A Constable Guide** *Christopher John Wright 1991 (1967)*

Travel Literature

✔ **A Pennine Journey** *A. Wainwright 1987 (1986)*
Just before the Second World War, Alfred Wainwright set out to walk the Pennines from Settle to Hadrian's Wall and back.

THE NORTHEAST: DURHAM, NORTHUMBERLAND, CLEVELAND AND TYNE & WEAR

'Between our eastward and our westward sea / The narrowing strand / Clasps close the noblest shore fame holds in fee / Even where English birth seals all men free Northumberland.' A.C. Swinburne, 'Northumberland' *A Channel Passage and Other Poems* 1904

Art and Archaeology

✔ **The Buildings of England: County Durham** *Nikolaus Pevsner revised Williamson 1990 (1953)*

✔ **The Buildings of England: Northumberland** *Nikolaus Pevsner revised Grundy et al. 1987 (1957)*

Fiction/Poetry

Tilly *Catherine Cookson 1980*
A poor young girl ends up as mistress of a manor in Durham. Set in Victorian times. *The Black Velvet Gown* (1984), *Pure as a Lily* (1973) and *The Cinder Path* (1978) are all set in Northumberland.

The Ivy Tree *Mary Stewart 1961*
A case of mistaken identity when a Canadian girl is mistaken for a dead heiress. Good descriptions of the Northumberland countryside.

Guides

✔ **Discovering Northumberland**
Ron and Marlene Freethy 1992

✔ **Discovering the Pennines**
Ron and Marlene Freethy 1992

✔ **Hidden Places of Northumberland and Durham**

The New Shell Guide. North East England: Northumberland, Co. Durham, Cleveland and Tyne & Wear   Brian Spencer   1988

History

✔ A Darwen County History of County Durham   Douglas Pocock and Roger Norris   1990

Leisure

✔ Best Walks in Northumberland. A Constable Guide   Frank Duerden   1990

✔ Ordnance Survey. Pathfinder Guide: Northumbria Walks   1991

Photography

✔ Travel To Landmarks: Durham Cathedral   Debra Shipley   Photographs by Angelo Hornak   1990

WALES

'All that I heard him say of it was, that instead of bleak and barren mountains, there were green and fertile ones; and that one of the castles in Wales would contain all the castles that he had seen in Scotland.' James Boswell, quoting Samuel Johnson *Life of Johnson* October 1774

Art and Archaeology

✔ The Buildings of Wales: Powys
R. Haslam   1979

✔ The Buildings of Wales: Clwyd
E. Hubbard   1986

Houses of the Welsh Countryside
Peter Smith   1988 (1975)
The best single book on houses on any country in Europe. A large and comprehensive survey of domestic architecture in Wales from the late Middle Ages to the Industrial Revolution, particularly good on indigenous architecture. Well illustrated with photographs and line drawings.

Autobiography/Biography

The Autobiography of Giraldus Cambrensis   1937
Gerald of Wales lived between 1146 and 1223; his writing exemplified many of the trends of the time and is therefore of particular interest. He was born at Manorbier Castle near Pembroke into the class of Marcher knights of South Wales, studied civil and canon law in Paris, was a fine observer of contemporary political events and a good historian and naturalist. He was, however, very vain and pompous, lacking a sense of humour. His first book on Wales, the *Itinerary*, is in the form of a diary of the tour that he took with Baldwin, Archbishop of Canterbury, to preach the Crusade in Wales to try and persuade Welsh soldiers to join up. Their route was a circular tour of North and South Wales with particular emphasis on the South and St Davids.

I Bought a Mountain   Thomas Firbank
1964 (1940)
The book was a bestseller when it was published and is about the battle with the elements and misadventure of a newcomer who bought a mountain in Snowdonia and tried to build up a sheep farm on it.

Peacocks in Paradise
Elizabeth Inglis-Jones   1950
The creation of a landscape Utopia at Hafod in Cardiganshire in the eighteenth century by Thomas Johnes, a visionary Welsh squire of unimaginable wealth. Hafod became known worldwide as a mountain Paradise, after Johnes had transformed it into a flourishing estate and encouraged agriculture and afforestation as well as building a vast Gothic pile. But tragedy struck both Hafod and Johnes at the height of its fame; the book tells of the rise and fall of this extraordinary man and his creation.

Jackdaw Cake   Norman Lewis   1987 (1985)
Norman Lewis' autobiography covering his early life and extraordinary eccentric aunts living between Carmarthen and Llansteffan in South Wales.

The Two Ladies of Llangollen
Elizabeth Mavor   1976 (1971)
Lady Eleanor Butler and Miss Sarah Ponsonby eloped together in the spring of 1778 and settled in rural bliss in Llangollen, North Wales where they were much admired by the literati and artists of the day.

The South Wales Squires
Herbert M. Vaughan   1988 (1926)
An eccentric and touching description of a class of amiable Anglo-Welsh landowners, a group which used to form the Welsh ascendancy and which no longer exists.

George. An Early Autobiography 1905–1927 Emlyn Williams 1976 (1961)
Emlyn Williams was born in Flintshire, North Wales in 1905; in this volume of autobiography he recalls his early childhood in rural Wales. *Emlyn 1927–1935* 1982 (1973), the second volume, a sequel to *George* is mostly about his life in the theatre.

Fiction/Poetry

✔ **Lucky Jim** Kingsley Amis 1968 (1954)
A celebration of the follies of 1950s British society as personified in Welsh academic life at Swansea University. *Lucky Jim* changed the outlook of a generation. Also *The Old Devils* 1987 (1986), set in the real Carmarthen and Cowbridge, and many fictitious places, in which the characters' main aim is to drink Wales dry and *Take a Girl Like You*.

✔ **On the Black Hill** Bruce Chatwin 1983 (1982)
Rural isolation and its effect on two brothers who lived and farmed a border hill farm all their lives. Very poignant. 'The most refreshing novel I have read this year. He knows intimately the comedies, the tragedies and above all the passions and deceits of toil on the land. Chatwin's people are not victims nor are they resigned . . . This is a very moving yet also often funny book.' (V.S. Pritchett *The Sunday Times*)

My People Caradoc Evans 1987 (1915)
The books of Caradoc Evans were sometimes banned from public libraries and once were even burnt in a public incinerator, because they are stories of greed, lust and hypocrisy among the peasants of West Wales.

Flying to Nowhere John Fuller 1984
A monastic mystery and horror story set on an island off Wales during the Middle Ages.

A Moment of Time Richard Hughes 1930 (1926)
A collection of stories which includes many set in Wales, also *Lochinvarovic* set in Trieste.

A Toy Epic Emyr Humphreys 1958
About three boys who live in Wales but who each belong to a different group of the small society in which they live. *A Man's Estate* 1988 (1955) is the story of Hannah Elis who is thirty-five, unmarried and still living on her mother and step-father's farm in Wales. She yearns for the return of her brother whom she believes will rescue her from her bleak existence. *Natives* (1968) is a collection of varied stories set in Wales.

Starved Fields Elizabeth Inglis-Jones 1929
An upstart Cardigan squire has pretensions to be English; a touching novel set in Cardiganshire about social foibles and pretensions.

The Sleeping Lord David Jones 1992 (1974)
In a collection called *The Selected Works of David Jones*; a poem published just before David Jones' death.

✔ **Classic Welsh Short Stories** Selected by Gwyn Jones and Islwyn Ffowc Elis 1992 (1971)
Includes stories by Kate Roberts, Dylan Thomas, Richard Hughes, Alun Lewis, Caradoc Evans and David Monger.

✔ **How Green Was My Valley** Richard Llewellyn 1991 (1939)
The detailed chronicle of individual lives seen as part of the surrounding mining community and told by the youngest son of the family: 'The strength of this book is in the quietness . . . and in the deep appreciation of everything in life from blackberry pie to the joy of singing.' (Monica Dickens)

The Mabinogion
A condensation of the *Red Book of Hergest*, a fourteenth-century manuscript containing eleven tales of Welsh literature in prose and verse. The *Taliesin*, from a much later manuscript, is also included. The tales divide themselves into four groups: *The Mabinogion* of the four-branches: *Pwyll*, *Branwen*, *Manawyddan* and *Math*. (Mabinog was the term used to describe an aspirant to bardic rank who had to undergo a rigorous literary training.) Two short old-world Welsh tales: *Maxen's Dream* and *Lludd and Llevelys*. Stories of Arthur: *Kilhwch and Olwen*, *Rhonabwy's Dream*, *Lady of the Fountain*, *Peredur* and *Geraint*. The *Taliesin*.

The Shining Pyramid Arthur Machen 1925
Unlike most Welsh writers whose fantasies are realistic, Machen's writing is full of unresolved mystery.

Morte D'Arthur Thomas Malory (1485)
A romance about the life and times of King Arthur set in Caerleon, near Cardiff. Although the historical King Arthur will never be truly defined, Malory's rendition makes him and the places with which he was associated very plausible – a king with faults and thus very human.

The Betrothed Walter Scott 1825
This and *The Talisman* (1825) are tales of the Crusades set in Wales and combined with the

warring between the Welsh and Norman lords of the Marches.

Jones a Gentleman of Wales Twm Teg 1954
It is obvious from this fantastic and funny novel that the anonymous author knew Wales and its customs well and based his characters on real people among the Anglo-Welsh 'ascendancy'.

Portrait of the Artist as a Young Dog
Dylan Thomas 1940
Dylan Thomas' prose has a strong visual appeal; in a *Visit to Grandpa's* in the above work, the description of his grandfather who 'clutched his bag to his side' as he stood on the bridge in Carmarthen is very vivid. He said of his writing: 'Naturally, my early poems and stories, two sides of an unresolved argument, came out of a person who came willy-nilly out of one particular atmosphere and environment'. (i.e. Swansea and West Wales). Also *The Map of Love* (1939), *Under Milk Wood* (1954)

Where Did I Put My Pity? Gwyn Thomas 1946
Gwyn Thomas grew up in industrial South Wales with the pit and chapel, hunger, dole and drama all of which he writes about as if he were talking.

✔ Collected Poems 1945–1990
R.S. Thomas 1993
R.S. Thomas was born in Cardiff in 1913 and was ordained as a priest in 1936. He lived all his life near to nature in rural Wales and was involved in a sustained mystical quest for most of his life. He is considered the outstanding Welsh poet writing in English and also one of the leading religious poets of the century.

Cousin Henry Anthony Trollope 1879
Uncle Indefer Jones, a bachelor, has a property called Llanfeare, 'a country house which looked down from the cliffs over the sea on the coast of Carmarthenshire;' he is unsure to whom to leave it.

A Winter in the Hills John Wain 1970
A university professor visits Wales hoping to learn enough about Celtic studies to go and teach in Sweden.

The Gauntlet Ronald Welch 1958 (1951)
Two boys find a gauntlet, which has the ability to take them into the past, in the hills around Carreg Cennen near Llandeilo in Carmarthenshire. Most of the story is historically and geographically accurate although some names and places have been transposed.

A King Reluctant Vaughan Wilkins 1952
Set in Tenby in 1799, a post-revolutionary mystery about the Dauphin's fate. What was the fate of the prisoner of 'Dragon Castle'? Was that drama linked with the mysterious murder of the banker Petitval and his family whose deaths were hushed up? And what were the true motives of the French expeditionary force, which landed in Wales under the American commander, Colonel William Tate, and who surrendered to an inferior militia?

Tintern Abbey William Wordsworth 1798
Composed just above Tintern Abbey on 13th July 1798: 'No poem of mine was composed under circumstances more pleasant for me to remember than this. I began it upon leaving Tintern, after crossing the Wye, and concluded it just as I was entering Bristol in the evening, after a ramble of four or five days, with my Sister. Not a line of it was altered, and not any part of it written down till I reached Bristol.'

Food

✔ Lamb. Leeks and Lavabread. The Best of Welsh Cookery Gilli Davies 1989
Traditional recipes from the towns and countryside of Wales. Adapted for the modern health-conscious cook.

General Background

The Welsh Wyn Griffith 1950
An attempt at tracing a social pattern among the Welsh by a study of the culture and environment of the people as seen through their philosophy, literature, arts and religious and social codes of behaviour.

The Physicians of Myddvai Translated by John Pugh 1861
An important medieval herbal translated from the Welsh. It was a compilation of learning by many hands and a source of early medical knowledge.

The Oxford Companion to the Literature of Wales Compiled by Meic Stephens 1986

Guides

Companion Guide to North Wales
Elisabeth Beazley and Peter Howell 1975

Companion Guide to South Wales
Peter Howell and Elisabeth Beazley 1977

✔ **Wales. A Pallas Athene Guide**
P. Sager 1991

✔ **Wales. Blue Guide** John Tomes 1992
(1990)

History

A Short History of Wales A.H. Dodd
1977 (1972)
A vivid picture of Welsh life and customs
from prehistoric times to the emergence of
political nationalism in the nineteenth and
twentieth centuries.

Wales: The Shaping of a Nation
Prys Morgan and David Thomas 1984
A general and cultural history of Wales with
an emphasis on the land and the language
and a look at the unusual and rich Welsh
literary tradition.

✔ **A Darwen County History of
Gwynedd** Dorothy Sylvester 1983

✔ **When Was Wales?** Gwyn A. Williams
1991 (1985)
The question of identity has always affected
the Welsh throughout their history. The book
draws on myth, legend and poetry to illustrate this.

Leisure

✔ **The Forestry Trust: Woodlands to
Visit in England and Wales 1994**
Descriptions of over 600 woodlands and
forests.

✔ **National Trail Guides:**
✔ **Offa's Dyke Path North. Knighton
to Prestatyn**
✔ **Offa's Dyke Path South** Ernie and
Kathy Kay and Mark Richards 1989

✔ **Ordnance Survey. Pathfinder
Guides: Brecon Beacons and
Glamorgan Walks** (1994)
✔ **Pembrokeshire and Gower Walks**

✔ **The Welsh Peaks. A Constable
Guide** W.A. Poucher 1987 (1962)

✔ **Best Walks in Southern Wales. A
Constable Guide** Richard Sale 1990

✔ **Owain Glyndwr's Way. A Constable
Guide** Richard Sale 1992

✔ **Wales. A Good Eating Guide**
Roger Thomas 1992
Where to eat, stay and shop for food.

✔ **A Guide to the Pembrokeshire
Coast Path. A Constable Guide**
Christopher John Wright 1993 (1989)

Natural History

Kilvert's Diary Rev. Francis Kilvert 1973
(1870–79)
A vivid picture of the life of a village clergy-
man and the changing seasons in Wiltshire
and the Welsh border: 'The best picture of
quiet vicarage life in Victorian England that
has yet been given us.' (John Betjeman)

Photography

✔ **Wales. The First Place** Jan Morris and
Paul Wakefield 1987 (1982)
A very individual look at Wales with imagin-
ative photography and original prose.

✔ **Wales from the Air** Foreword by Jan
Morris Photographs by Aerofilms
Houses, landscape and towns from the air.
The text is in Welsh and English.

✔ **Snowdonia** W.A. Poucher 1990
A range of photographs of Snowdonia taken
at different seasons of the year.

✔ **Philip's Welsh Borders**
Christopher Somerville
Photographs by John Heseltine 1991

Travel Literature

Wild Wales George Borrow 1977 (1862)
An account of the people, language and scenery of Wales. *Wild Wales* became a classic
travel book with the eccentric Borrow immor-
talizing the 'land of old renown and wonder,
the land of Arthur and Merlin.'

✔ **The Matter of Wales** Jan Morris 1986
(1984)
A celebration of Jan Morris' native country:
'No recent work on Wales has so effectively
captured the smells, sounds and sights of the
past and the present.' (Geraint H. Jenkins
Times Literary Supplement)

In Search of Wales H.V. Morton 1932
A dated but pleasing account of the author's
journey round Wales.

Tours in Wales Thomas Pennant 1883
(1778)
Pennant was born at Downing, Whitford,
near Holywell in Flintshire in 1726. He became a Fellow of the Royal Society and his
British Zoology was well received on publication. He made several journeys to Cornwall,

Ireland, the Isle of Man, England and Scotland, saying he 'was possessed with an active love of travelling' before embarking on his serious travels in Wales. The first part was referred to by Pennant as 'a complete tour of the tamer parts of our country' and includes Flintshire, Hawarden, Chester, Chirk Castle, Whittington and Oswestry. Volume 2 was called 'The Tour in North Wales' and includes Valle Crucis, Mold, Dolgelleu, St Asaph, Denbigh, Bettws y Coed, Snowdonia, Bardseye Isle and Caernarvon. Volume 3 starts in Anglesey and goes to Beaumaris, Holyhead, Bangor, Conwy, Montgomery, Powys, Shrewsbury and Caer Caradoc. He was an acute observer and his narrative is full of historical detail, anecdotes and natural history observations. He also published *Literary Life* 1793.

CHANNEL ISLANDS

'Faire Jersey first of these heere scattred in the deepe, Peculiarlie that boast'st thy double-horned sheepe.' Michael Drayton, Poly-Olbion, *The First Song* 1612

Fiction/Poetry

Last Ditch *Ngaio Marsh* 1977
A university professor on holiday in the Channel Islands becomes involved in drug smuggling.

General Background

✔ **The Channel Islands** *Raoul Lempriere* 1990 (1970)
A good general background and history.

Guides

✔ **Blue Guide: The Channel Islands** *Peter McGregor Eadie* 1989 (1987)

✔ **Insight Guide Channel Islands** 1992

Leisure

✔ **Landscapes of Guernsey with Alderney, Sark and Herm. A Sunflower Book** *Geoff Daniel* 1994

✔ **Landscapes of Jersey. A Sunflower Book** *Geoff Daniel* 1994

SCOTLAND

'Once you get the hang of it, and apprehend the type, it is a most beautiful and admirable little country – fit, for 'distinction' etc., to make up a trio with Italy and Greece.' Henry James, letter to Miss Alice James, 15 September 1878

Anthology

✔ **Scotland. An Anthology** *Douglas Dunn* 1992 (1991)
A collection of history, poetry, nature and fiction sensitively chosen.

Art and Archaeology

Scottish Art 1460–1990 *Duncan MacMillan* 1990
A lavish overview of Scottish art.

Prehistoric Scotland *Ann MacSween and Mick Sharp* 1989
An introductory guide well illustrated with black and white photographs and drawings of the prehistoric sites in Scotland.

Autobiography/Biography

✔ **Dreams of Exile** *Ian Bell* 1992
Good biography of Robert Louis Stevenson which explains his work in the context of his travels and voluntary exile in the South Seas: 'Singular that I should fulfil the Scots destiny throughout, and live a voluntary exile and have my head filled with the blessed, beastly place all the time.' (letter to Sidney Colvin, August 1893)

Brother Scots *Donald Carswell* 1927
Biographies which bring to life a variety of diverse Scots.

✔ **Burns. A Biography of Robert Burns** *James MacKay* 1992
A large and comprehensive biography of Burns who in the nineteenth century was more popular than Shakespeare. There have been more than 2,000 editions of his poems and songs since 1786 and over 900 volumes of biography since 1797.

Charles Edward Stuart. A Tragedy in Many Acts *Frank McLynn* 1988
A large and readable biography which the author spent twelve years researching and consulting around 100,000 individual documents. It claims to be the first comprehensive scholarly biography of 'Bonnie Prince Charlie' ever written.

Fiction/Poetry

The Crow Road *Iain Banks* *1992*
About growing up in Scotland this century; many good descriptions of the landscape mixed with black humour.

The Complete Richard Hannay
John Buchan *1986 (1930)*
The four novels with Richard Hannay are *The Thirty-Nine Steps*, *Greenmantle*, *Mr Standfast* and *The Three Hostages*. Fast-moving stories which range worldwide but the Scottish scenes have a good feeling for the landscape.

✔ **Selected Poetry** *Robert Burns* *1991*
The ploughman and poet, Robert Burns, embodied the pastoral dream that people were seeking in eighteenth-century Europe. This selection of his verse shows his humour, compassion and essential 'Scottishness'.

Mary, Queen of Scotland and the Isles
Margaret George *1992*
A well-researched novel about the life of Mary Queen of Scots.

✔ **Looking for the Possible Dance**
A.L. Kennedy *1994 (1993)*
The difficulties of human relationships: 'Praise the Lord and pass the orchids – a real writer is among us, with a beautiful first novel.' (Julie Burchill)

Magnus Merriman *Eric Linklater* *1934*
An extremely funny book written in prose but with bawdy verse interspersed, about the funny side of Scotland's cultural revival.

The Five Red Herrings *Dorothy Sayers* *1958*
A Peter Wimsey mystery set in a Scottish village.

Kidnapped *Robert Louis Stevenson* *1886*
Set in eighteenth-century Scotland with a great feel for Scottish landscape, history, character and local atmosphere. *The Master of Ballantrae* (1889) is good on characters and very good on Scottish scenery and weather. *Weir of Hermiston* (1896) is based on the life-story of the 'hanging-judge', Lord Braxfield and although unfinished is considered his masterpiece.

Food

✔ **Scottish Cookery** *Catherine Brown* *1993 (1985)*
An invaluable well illustrated working cook book.

✔ **The Scots Kitchen. Its traditions and Lore with Old-Time Recipes**
F. Marian McNeill *1993 (1929)*
A delightful account of eating and drinking in Scotland through the ages with recipes for all the national dishes.

General Background

A Companion to Scottish Culture
David Daiches (ed.) *1981*
Over 300 articles which interpret Scottish culture in the widest sense of the word.

Anatomy of Scotland *Magnus Linklater and Robin Denniston* *1992*
Essays on how institutions and organizations and the law work in Scotland.

Guides

✔ **The Historic Hotels of Scotland**
Wendy Arnold *1988*

✔ **Hidden Places of South and Central Scotland**

✔ **Insight Guide Scotland** *1993*

✔ **Michelin Green Guide Scotland** *1994*

✔ **Scotland. The Rough Guide**
Donald Greig et al. *1994*

✔ **The Which? Guide to Scotland**
Andrew Leslie *1994 (1992)*

✔ **Blue Guide Scotland** *John Tomes* *1992*

History

✔ **A Traveller's History of Scotland**
Andrew Fisher *1990*
A very basic, but concise and readable history of Scotland.

Scotland. A New History *Michael Lynch* *1992 (1991)*
A history which goes right up to 1991 and is a good general overview.

✔ **A History of Scotland** *J.D. Mackie* *1991 (1964)*
The definitive one-volume history of Scotland.

Leisure

✔ **The Hillwalker's Guide to Scotland** *Bruce Sandison* *1993 (1988)*

✔ **Exploring Rural Scotland** *Gilbert Summers 1990*

Photography

✔ **Wainwright in Scotland** *Photographs by Derry Brabbs 1992 (1988)*
A well illustrated book which follows Wainwright's journey from the far north of Scotland, down the west coast to the Southern Highlands.

✔ **Shades of Scotland 1956–1988**
Photographs by Oscar Marzaroli Text by James Grassie 1989
Black and white photographs taken over a period of thirty years.

Travel Literature

Summer in Scotland *Ivor Brown 1952*
Evocative book which captures the essence of the country.

In Search of Scotland *H.V. Morton 1984 (1929)*
A journey throughout the different regions of Scotland which puts the landscape into historical perspective.

EDINBURGH, WEST LOTHIAN AND FIFE

'Stately Edinburgh throned on crags.'
William Wordsworth *The Excursion* 1814

Art and Archaeology

✔ **The Buildings of Scotland: Edinburgh** *John Gifford et al. 1988 (1984)*

✔ **The Buildings of Scotland: Fife** *J. Gifford 1988*

✔ **Edinburgh. Illustrated Architectural Guide** *Charles McKean 1982*

Fiction/Poetry

The Drinking Well *Neil M. Gunn 1946*
Although mostly set in the Grampians there is one section set in Edinburgh before the hero returns to his native Highlands.

The Private Memoirs and Confessions of a Justified Sinner *James Hogg 1983 (1824)*
A complex novel which examines the confession of an Edinburgh murderer from three

view points. Against a background of historical realism, the murderer, a pious young man, uses the Calvinist doctrine of predestination to justify the murder of his brother.

The Prime of Miss Jean Brodie
Muriel Spark 1961
Middle-class life and aspirations in Edinburgh in the 1930s. Miss Jean Brodie has strong ideas about the education of her pupils as well as about her own position.

Guide

✔ **Discovering West Lothian**
William F. Hendrie 1986

History

Edinburgh. Portrait of a City
Charles McKean 1991
A readable look at the development of Edinburgh up to the present day.

Photography

Edinburgh in Focus *Photographs by Marius Alexander Text by Neil Maclean 1992*
A wide range of photographs with minimal text.

✔ **Vanishing Edinburgh** *Alastair J. Durie 1989*
The photographs of George Washington Wilson who worked in the late Victorian and Edwardian age. The contrasting modern photographs are taken by Brian Kiloh.

GLASGOW AND THE CLYDE

'The City of Glasgow I take to be a very fine one –I was astonished to hear it was twice the size of Edinburgh – It is built of Stone and has a much more solid appearance than London.' John Keats, letter to Thomas Keats, 10-14 July 1818

Art and Archaeology

✔ **The Buildings of Scotland: Glasgow** *M. Higgs et al. 1990*

Central Glasgow *Charles McKean, David Walker and Frank Walker 1989*
An architectural look at Glasgow with plenty of photographs.

Autobiography/Biography

Memories of the Gorbals *Jack Caplan*
Stories about growing up as a Jew in the
Gorbals during the 1930s.

Fiction/Poetry

Streets of Stone *Moira Burgess and
Hamish White (eds.) 1985*
An anthology of contemporary Glaswegian
short stories.

Dance of the Apprentices
Edward Gaitens 1948
The story of the Macdonnel family in Glas-
gow between the wars.

✔ **Lanark. A Life in Four Books**
Alasdair Gray 1985 (1981)
A post-modern fantasy about an art student,
set in a thinly veiled Glasgow. Interwoven
tales of Lanark and Duncan Thaw in the
disintegrating cities of Unthank and Glasgow.

No Mean City *Alexander McArthur and
Kingsley Long 1935*
Razor gangs in the slums of Glasgow in the
1930s. The author who lived in the Glasgow
slums had been unemployed for five years
and wrote endless novels to kill time; *No
Mean City* finally satisfied the publishers as
'to the essential truth . . . of slum life in one
section of Glasgow' and was published in
1935, before the author sank back into obscurity.

A Gift from Nessus *William McIlvanney
1968*
A moral story set in 1960s Glasgow. In mythology Deianeira, wife of Hercules, believed
her husband to be in love with someone else,
so she gave him a tunic which was meant to
have the power to restore the wearer's love to
the giver. When Hercules tried to take it off,
his skin came with it. The tunic came from
Nessus.

Swing Hammer Swing! *Jeff Torrington
1993 (1992)*
Contemporary working-class life in Glasgow:
'*Swing Hammer Swing!* is a seriously good
novel. Critics have rightly claimed that he
does for Glasgow what James Joyce did for
Dublin. He writes with an unstoppable energy and deals with large philosophical
issues, but in the street language of puns,
Glasgow vernacular and gallows humour.'
(Stephen Pile *The Daily Telegraph*)

Guides

✔ **Insight Guide Glasgow** *1990*

✔ **Discovering Arran** *Alastair Gemmell
1990*

✔ **Discovering the River Clyde**
Innes Macleod and Margaret Gilroy 1991

History

✔ **An Illustrated Guide to Glasgow
1837** *Maurice Lindsay 1989*
Glasgow recalled and evoked as it was in
1837 at the dawn of a new era, just before it
rose to industrial pre-eminence.

Photography

Glasgow's People: 1956–1988
Oscar Marzaroli
A sympathetic photographic survey.

SOUTHERN SCOTLAND
'This queer compromise between fairyland
and battlefield which is the Border.' H.V.
Morton *In Search of Scotland* 1929

Art and Archaeology

✔ **The Buildings of Scotland: Lothian,
except Edinburgh** *C. McWilliam and
C. Wilson 1980 (1978)*

Fiction/Poetry

✔ **Tales of the Borders** *Michael Brander
1991*
Nineteenth-century Border tales retold and
put into historical context.

Beattock for Moffat
R.B. Cunninghame Graham 1979
In a collection called *Scottish Stories* (1914)
– strong on narrative.

Effie Ogilvie *Margaret Oliphant 1886*
Set in Dumfriesshire; Effie loves her childhood sweetheart who is serving in India, but
her step-mother forces her into an engagement with a tycoon; however he loses his
money and her step-mother changes her
tune.

Old Mortality *Walter Scott (1816)*
The hero of *Old Mortality* is torn between
loyalty to the rebels of the Scottish lowlands
and loyalty to the English king. *The Bride of*

Lammermoor (1819) is set in the seventeenth century. A bride goes insane on her wedding day, being found covered with blood, a fate she only survives for two weeks. *The Heart of Mid-Lothian* (1818) is based on the story of the remarkable Helen Walker, fictionalized as Jeanie Deans, who walked to London to save her sister's life; it examines the nature of Justice.

Guide

✔ **Discovering the Borders 1**
Alan Spence 1992
The eastern part of the Border area.

Leisure

✔ **A Guide to the Southern Upland Way. A Constable Guide** David Williams 1989

NORTHERN SCOTLAND: HIGHLANDS AND ISLANDS

'In the highlands, in the country places,
Where the old plain men have rosy faces
And the young fair maidens,
Quiet eyes.'
Robert Louis Stevenson *Songs of Travel* 1896

Art and Archaeology

✔ **The Buildings of Scotland: Highland and Islands** John Gifford 1992

Autobiography/Biography

A Farmer's Boy John R. Allan 1935
An account of a childhood in the north-east.

✔ **Nairn in Darkness and Light**
David Thomson 1991 (1987)
A mixture of autobiography and history written with the feeling of a great love of the area.

Fiction/Poetry

A Princess of Thule William Black 1873
Much is set in the Outer Hebrides; it contrasts the lives of the islanders with the 'incomers'.

The Jacobite Trilogy D.K. Broster 1984
The three volumes are: *Flight of the Heron* (1925), *Gleam in the North* (1927) and *Dark Mile* (1929). A romantic historical saga set around Jacobite supporters.

My Friend Sashie Jane Duncan 1972
One of a series of books about Reachfar, Jane Duncan's 'country of the mind'. She writes about a very personal Highlands and is concerned with the separateness and the paradoxical interconnectedness of things.

A Scots Quair Lewis Grassic Gibbon
A trilogy, comprising *Sunset Song* (1932), *Claude Howe* (1933) and *Grey Granite* (1934), set in northeast Scotland during the First World War which shows the effect of the soil and the climate on those who live there.

✔ **Highland River** Neil M. Gunn 1991 (1937)
A scientist reflects on his boyhood in the Highlands and especially the river that haunts him. *The Grey Coast* (1926) and *The Lost Glen* (1932) also deal with Highland life and in *The Serpent* (1943) a young man leaves the Highlands to go to Glasgow.

The Silver Darlings Neil M. Gunn 1969 (1941)
Set on the northeast coast of Scotland; the story of the herring fishermen during the years that the industry was in its prime and what happens to the social situation when people are moved to the coast. Full of adventure and insight into human life in the Highlands.

✔ **The Cone-Gatherers** Robin Jenkins 1983 (1955)
During the Second World War, life on a large Scottish estate goes on uninterrupted until the undertones of evil begin to predominate.

Household Ghosts James Kennaway 1961
A decadent squirearchal family on a dairy farm on the Tay near Dundee.

Gillespie J. MacDougal Hay 1914
The novel takes place in Brieston (Tarbert in Argyll) and is about the rise and fall of Gillespie Strang who was determined to become a tycoon and in so doing destroyed his wife and family.

Whisky Galore Compton Mackenzie 1961 (1947)
An amusing novel based on a true story about a ship the ss *Cabinet Minister*, which was bound for America with its cargo of whisky and was wrecked on a Hebridean island during the war.

When Eight Bells Toll Alistair MacLean 1966
An exciting adventure set in the Highlands.

The Bull Calves Naomi Mitchison 1947
A Jacobite novel in which Naomi Mitchison is able to draw on her Haldane forebears.

✔ **Imagined Corners** *Willa Muir 1987 (1935)*
A newly married woman finds herself stulti-fied by the confines of small-town Scottish life; her newly widowed sister-in-law returns from Italy and teaches her much about how to come to terms with life.

The Fair Maid of Perth or Saint Valentine's Day *Walter Scott 1969 (1828)*
An historical novel set at the end of the fourteenth century, when the Scottish king was Robert the Third and Catharine or Kate Glover was known as 'the Fair Maid of Perth'. *Rob Roy* (1818) is set in the eighteenth cen-tury and is about a wild, yet subtle character reminiscent of Robin Hood of the Middle Ages.

Waverley *Walter Scott (1814)*
A story of the Jacobite rebellion of 1745 which reinterprets the manners and customs of a lost Highland civilization.

Summer of the Red Wolf *Morris West 1971*
A writer arrives in the islands in search of spiritual renewal, but finds himself in com-petition over a woman doctor.

General Background

Hebridean Connection *Derek Cooper 1991 (1977)*
An honest and unromantic appraisal of high-land culture. *The Road to Mingulay* (1985) is a view of the Western Isles – each chapter being about a different island.

✔ **Island Voices** *Fiona McDonald 1992*
A wry and perceptive account of the many different kinds of people who live on the He-brides.

Island on the Edge of the World
Charles MacLean 1980
The story of St Kilda, where up until 1930 there was commonly held property and an economy based on agriculture and birds.

✔ **Portrait of Caithness and Sutherland** *James Miller 1985*
A general, rather worthy background book.

Guides

✔ **Discovering Lewis and Harris**
James Shaw Grant 1992 (1987)

✔ **Discovering Angus and the Mearns** *I.A.N. Henderson 1990*

✔ **Discovering Inverness-shire**
Loraine Maclean of Dochgarroch 1988

✔ **Discovering Aberdeenshire**
Robert Smith 1994 (1988)

✔ **Discovering Speyside**
Francis Thompson 1990

✔ **Treasure Islands of the Inner Hebrides. A Traveller's Guide**
C. Wiener 1992
A narrative pocket-sized guide illustrated with maps and black and white photographs. Also in the same series guides to Mull and Skye.

✔ **Discovering The Black Isle**
Douglas Willis 1989

History

Glencoe *John Prebble 1968 (1966)*
A very readable account of the bloody mas-sacre of Glencoe when the Campbells were ordered to slaughter their hosts the MacDo-nalds. John Prebble also wrote: *Culloden* (1961), the story of the battle and its results which led to the destruction of a way of life and the persecution of a people and *The Highland Clearances* 1971 (1963) which con-tinues on from *Culloden* and tells how the Highlanders were deserted and sub-sequently betrayed by their own clan chiefs.

Leisure

✔ **A Guide to the West Highland Way. A Constable Guide** *Tom Hunter 1992 (1979)*

✔ **Ordnance Survey. Pathfinder Guides: Perthshire Walks** *1994*
✔ **Loch Lomond and Trossachs Walks** *(1992)*

✔ **The Magic of Skye. A Constable Guide** *W.A. Poucher 1989 (1949)*

Natural History

Ring of Bright Water *Gavin Maxwell 1965*
The author's relationship with two sea otters on a remote part of the Highland coast.

✔ **Out of the Wild** *Mike Tomkies 1992 (1985)*
Tomkies lives without any mod cons in the Highlands surrounded by wild animals. He was described by *Country Life* as 'a field naturalist of exceptional perception and practical knowledge'.

Photography

✔ **The Cairngorms. The Nature of the Land** *Colin Baxter and Rawdon Goodier 1990*
A book which emphasizes the natural seasons of the land.

✔ **The First Munroist: The Reverend A.E. Robertson: His Life, Munros and Photographs** *Peter Drummond and Ian Mitchell 1993*
The Rev. Robertson was the first person to climb all the Munros (Scottish mountains over 3,000 feet).

✔ **Granite and Green. Above North-East Scotland** *Angus and Patricia Macdonald 1992*
Aerial photographs of castles, cliffs and the Cairngorms.

✔ **The Highlands and Islands of Scotland** *Angus and Patricia Macdonald 1991*
Matt colour photographs with descriptions.

✔ **Barra** *Helen McGregor and John Cooper 1987 (1984)*
Black and white pictures, poetry and prose.

✔ **Skye** *Ann MacSween Photographs by John Cooper 1990*
A comprehensive picture of Skye from its early beginnings to the present.

✔ **The Highlands of Scotland** *W.A. Poucher 1988 (1983)*

✔ **Eigg** *Judy Urquhart and Eric Ellington 1987*
Black and white photographs of Eigg which is both fertile and wooded as well as being beautiful.

Travel Literature

✔ **A Walk to the Western Isles. After Boswell and Johnson** *Frank Delaney 1993*
Delaney retraces Boswell and Johnson's 'Scottish jaunt' from Edinburgh, through Fife to Aberdeen and across to Loch Ness and over to Skye, Raasay and Mull.

✔ **A Journey to the Western Isles of Scotland** *Samuel Johnson (1777)*
✔ **The Journal of a Tour to the Hebrides** *James Boswell 1984 (1785)*
Johnson's and Boswell's books are records of the same journey, to the Western isles and throughout Scotland. Boswell's account is a lively diary of a journey round the Hebrides and other parts of Scotland, undertaken with Samuel Johnson. Boswell did not publish his book until a year after Dr Johnson's death. Both are now published in one volume.

Highland Drove *John Keay 1984*
Every year the cattle used to have to trek around 200 miles to market; John Keay, his wife and other companions followed the old drovers' roads with a herd of cattle.

A Summer in Skye *Alexander Smith 1865*
'Surely one of the most luminous Scottish travel-books ever written . . . memorable descriptions of Stirling, Glasgow, Loch Coruisk.' (*History of Scottish Literature* Maurice Lindsay)

ORKNEY AND SHETLAND

'Those north-western islands, in summer, are neither hot nor cold, having a most wholesome and temperate air, and to yield abundance of corn, even more than sufficient for the inhabitants; which is yearly transported to the firm land and sold.'
William Lithgow *Rare Adventures and Painfull Peregrinations* 1614/32

Anthology

Travellers in a Bygone Shetland. An Anthology *Derek Flinn 1989*
An amazing amount of travellers found their way to Shetland between 1550 and 1850; this is a compilation of extracts from their writings.

Fiction/Poetry

Greenvoe *George Mackay Brown 1972*
Portraits of people centred on one community, the fictional Orkney fishing village of Greenvoe, on the island of Hellya. *Magnus* (1973) is another novel set in Orkney.

General Background

Orkney and Shetland: An Historical, Geographical, Social and Scenic Survey *Eric Linklater 1965*
Although Linklater was born in Wales, he was educated in Scotland and spent most of his life in the Orkneys; his affection for and knowledge of the islands is apparent in this book.

A Calendar of Love *George Mackay Brown 1967*
Both this and *A Time to Keep* (1969) examine the diverse characters on Orkney with an acute sensitivity and understanding. *An Orkney Tapestry* (1969) and *Hawkfall and Other Stories* (1974) are studies in depth of a

community with its rich neolithic, Pict, Norsemen and Scot history.

History

✔ **The Orkney Chronicles 1900 and 1989** *Anne Buxton and Jacqueline McEwan* *1992*
A young woman travelled to Orkney in 1900 and kept a journal of her journey which is historically very interesting. The journal is reprinted along with an account of the present day journey.

Photography

✔ **Portrait of Orkney** *George Mackay Brown* *1988 (1981)*
A personal account with photographs by Gunnie Moberg.

NORTHERN IRELAND
'The Lord in His Mercy be good to Belfast The grief of the exile she soothed as he passed.' Old ballad

Art and Archaeology

✔ **Buildings of Ireland: North Leinster** *A. Rowan* *1993*

✔ **Buildings of Ireland: North West Ulster: Londonderry, Donegal, Fermanagh, Tyrone** *A. Rowan* *1979*

Fiction/Poetry

Shadows on Our Skin *Jennifer Johnston* *1978*
Working-class life in contemporary Derry.

The Lonely Passion of Judith Hearne *Brian Moore* *1993 (1988)*
Set against a bleak Belfast background; Judith Hearne is one of life's losers being poor, unattractive and having no talents. She

practises her religion conscientiously but it has no deep roots and she begins to question the existence of God.

Food

✔ **Gourmet Ireland** *Paul and Jeanne Rankin* *1994*
The authors are Northern Ireland's best-known chefs, their Belfast restaurant, Roscoff, won a Michelin star in 1991.

General Background

The Crack *Sally Belfrage* *1988 (1987)*
All aspects of Belfast communities.

✔ **The Giant's Causeway. A Remnant of Chaos** *Philip S. Watson* *1992.*
The Giant's Causeway which is on the north Antrim coast is remarkable for its volcanic rock formations and its association with the legendary Irish giant, Finn MacCool.

Guides
(Many of the guides to 'Ireland' include Northern Ireland)

✔ **Where to Eat in Northern Ireland 1994**

✔ **Where to Stay in Northern Ireland 1994**

Travel Literature

✔ **A Place Apart** *Dervla Murphy* *1979 (1978)*
Dervla Murphy was determined to try and understand the situation in Ireland and to sort out her opinions and emotions. She cycled throughout Northern Ireland: 'An extraordinarily successful attempt to present Northern Ireland from the inside out, with honesty, sympathy and understanding.' (*The Times Literary Supplement*)

Ireland

General
'The English and the Irish are very much alike, except that the Irish are more so.' James Dunne, in conversation during the Irish troubles, quoted by J.M. and M.J. Cohen *The Penguin Dictionary of Modern Quotations* 1971

Anthology

The English Traveller in Ireland
John P. Harrington 1991
An anthology, covering five centuries, which includes Edmund Campion, Fynes Moryson, William Brereton, Arthur Young and Harriet Martineau.

✔ **Yeats' Ireland. An Illustrated Anthology** *Benedict Kiely 1989*
A selection of Yeats' prose and poetry illustrated with contemporary paintings and photographs.

Art and Archaeology

✔ **Irish Art** *Bruce Arnold 1991 (1969)*
In the Thames and Hudson 'World of Art' series.

The Archaeology of Medieval Ireland
T.B. Barry 1987
Descriptions, illustrations and plans to the earthen and stone castles, moated sites, villages, towns, cathedrals, churches, tower houses, pottery kilns and mills of medieval Ireland.

A Guide to Irish Country Houses
Mark Bence-Jones 1988
A record and short description of the standing, demolished, important and obscure houses, many illustrated with black and white photographs. Originally published as *Burke's Guide to Country Houses volume 1.*

Castles of Ireland *Brian de Breffny Photographs by George Mott 1977*
The castles of Ireland arranged alphabetically.

The Houses of Ireland *Brian de Breffny and Rosemary Ffolliott (sic) Photographs by George Mott 1975*
The houses selected were for the most part those which had changed least; for this reason they are mostly exteriors that are illustrated.

✔ **A Guide to Megalithic Ireland**
J.H. Brennan 1994
There are meant to be around 1200 megalithic sites in Ireland; this guide is full of information about the history, legends and both archaeological and alternative explanations to the monuments.

✔ **The Buildings of Ireland: North Leinster** *Christine Casey and Alastair Rowan 1993*
In the 'Buildings of Ireland' series.

The Architecture of Ireland
Maurice Craig 1982
An illustrated guide to the architecture of Ireland from the earliest times up until 1880.

The Painters of Ireland *Anne Crookshank and The Knight of Glin 1979 (1978)*
This was the first book published which was devoted entirely to the history of painting in Ireland.

✔ **The Watercolours of Ireland. Works on Paper in Pencil, Pastel and Paint. c. 1600–1914** *Anne Crookshank and The Knight of Glin 1994*
The definitive book on Irish watercolours with 400 illustrations.

A Guide to the Georgian Buildings of Britain and Ireland *Dan Cruickshank 1985*
Descriptions of buildings followed by a gazetteer.

✔ **Vanishing Country Houses of Ireland** *The Knight of Glin, David J. Griffin and Nicholas K. Robinson 1989 (1988)*
Many black and white illustrations, with short descriptions of the fast disappearing houses.

A Lost Tradition: The Nature of Architecture in Ireland *Niall McCullough and Valerie Mulvin*
An account of the common buildings of Ireland.

The Noble Dwellings of Ireland
John FitzMaurice Mills 1987
Illustrated with watercolours by the author, who emphasizes unusual details.

✔ **Great Irish Houses and Castles**
Jacqueline O'Brien and Desmond Guinness 1992
A magnificent illustrated book which examines Ireland's architectural heritage.

✔ **North West Ulster** *Alastair Rowan* 1979
In the 'Buildings of Ireland' series.

Exploring the Book of Kells
George Otto Simms 1988
The Book of Kells consists of 680 pages of handwritten text and illustration which was compiled by the monks of ancient Ireland around 800 AD.

Autobiography/Biography

✔ **Walled Gardens. Scenes from an Anglo-Irish Childhood**
Annabel Davis-Goff 1994 (1989)
The author was called home from America to southern Ireland on the death of her father and finds herself back in the world of her Anglo-Irish childhood with a haunting memory of draughty houses, noisy rooks and faded chintzes. 'Vividly entertaining . . . written with a quality of mercy added to the acute perceptions of a child.' (Molly Keane *The Spectator*)

Letters from Georgian Ireland. The Correspondence of Mary Delany 1731–68 *Angélique Day* 1991
Mrs Delany made a great impact and was held in high esteeem for her integrity. King George III and Queen Charlotte met her and were soon asking her advice on questions of morality. She was eventually given a Grace and Favour residence at Windsor.

✔ **James Joyce** *Richard Ellmann* 1983 (1959)
'The greatest critical biography of the century.' (Anthony Burgess)

Oscar Wilde *Richard Ellman* 1987
A large, definitive and fascinating biography.

✔ **Retrospections of Dorothea Herbert 1770–1806** 1988 (1929)
A unique and personal historical record entwined with a tragic love story, which has been described as a 'jewel'.

✔ **Seventy Years Young. Memories of Elizabeth, Countess of Fingall**
Told to Pamela Hinkson 1939
One of the most sensitive and perspicacious commentaries on the decline of the Anglo-Irish world.

✔ **Wheels Within Wheels** *Dervla Murphy* 1981 (1979)
Dervla Murphy's autobiography of her first thirty years: 'An extraordinary book, reflecting an extraordinary woman and one of the great travellers of our time.' (William Trevor)

✔ **Mother Ireland** *Edna O'Brien* 1978 (1976)
Recollections of an Irish childhood linked with a journey and fragments of Irish mythology and history.

An Only Child *Frank O'Connor* 1988 (1979)
O'Connor was born in Cork in 1903 and his father was in the British army. He wanted to educate himself but 'By the time I was fourteen it was clear that education was something I would never be able to afford.' He got caught up in the patriotic fervour of the day, serving with the Republican forces against England and when he was interned he read much.

✔ **A Day in Our Life** *Seán O'Crohan* 1992
The author is the son of Tomás O'Crohan (q.v.) who with Maurice O'Sullivan and others brought the Blasket Islands, off the coast of Kerry, to prominence by writing about the tiny remote community. *A Day in Our Life* is a continuation of the story and tells how the islanders had to move to the mainland and come to terms with the 'modern world'.

✔ **The Islandman** *Tomás O'Crohan* 1991 (1937)
Tomás O'Crohan's (1856–1937) purpose in writing the book about the Blaskets was 'to set down the character of the people about me so that some record of us might live after us, for the like of us will never be again'.

✔ **A Pity Youth Does Not Last**
Mícheál O'Guiheen 1992 (1953)
The author was the last of the poets of the Great Blasket Island and his record of the last days there and evacuation to the mainland are moving and poignant.

✔ **Twenty Years A-Growing**
Maurice O'Sullivan 1992 (1953)
O'Sullivan wrote this book about growing up in the Blaskets, here translated from the Irish, for his own pleasure: 'If the reader laughs at the schoolmistress and the matrons, and is moved by the dream of the butterfly inside the horse's skull – then he is assured of amusement and emotion to come. He is ready to go to the Ventry Races, and to make the great journey from Dingle East . . . to steal out on Hallowe'en and catch thrushes above waves of the living and the dead, and see the Land of the Young in the west . . . This book is unique . . . for here is the egg of a sea-bird – lovely, perfect, and laid this very morning.' (E.M. Forster)

Irish Memories *E. Somerville and M. Ross* 1917
Somerville and Ross lived at a time when the

old semi-feudal personal relationships between landlord and tenant had broken down and the past is remembered with nostalgic regret. This is a collection of letters and reminiscences.

Woodbrook David Thomson 1988 (1974)
Woodbrook, near Sligo, in County Roscommon was the name of the house where David Thomson went as a tutor when he was eighteen and at Oxford. He stayed for ten years and describes the slow magical process of getting to know it and the local people: 'Woodbrook is simply one of the most enchanting books I've read for a long time.' (Seamus Heaney)

Fiction/Poetry

Molloy/Malone Dies/The Unnamable
Samuel Beckett 1979 (1960)
A trilogy of breakdown and glum humour.

Borstal Boy Brendan Behan 1990 (1979)
About his early life in the IRA and in jail.

Light a Penny Candle Maeve Binchy
1992 (1982)
The friendship of two women begins with one's evacuation to Ireland during the Blitz.

The Last September Elizabeth Bowen
1929
Describes life in a Big House during the troubles. Although most of her work is set outside Ireland she also wrote a short story set in Co. Cork called *Summer Night*.

Concerning Virgins Clare Boylan 1990
(1989)
Thirteen short stories.

Traits and Stories of the Irish Peasantry William Carleton (1830–33)
Patrick Kavanagh once claimed on the BBC that Carleton and Joyce were the two big talents of Irish literature. These stories are full of life and humour and are well observed but could do with editing.

Hungry Hill Daphne du Maurier 1983
(1943)
The novel spans the nineteenth century and is partly set in Doonhaven parish where Hungry Hill was 'wild and untrodden, the summit hidden in mist'.

Castle Rackrent Maria Edgeworth 1800
Maria Edgeworth is remembered as the instigator of Irish regional fiction; *Castle Rackrent* has as its complete title '*An Hibernian Tale: Taken from the Facts, and from the Manners of the Irish Squires, before the year 1782*', was published anonymously and has

as its ironic narrator Thady Quirk. It is a complex novel; the first part is about Sir Patrick Rackrent, his son Sir Murtagh and his younger brother Sir Kit; the second part is solely about Sir Conolly (Condy) Rackrent, a vague cousin. Other works by Maria Edgeworth set in Ireland are *Tales of Fashionable Life* (1809), *The Absentee* (from the second series of *Tales of Fashionable Life* (1812)) and *Ormond* (1817).

The Two Chiefs of Dunboy J.C. Froude
1891
Subtitled an Irish romance of the last century, the famous historian starts his novel in France where naturalized Irish exiles are living.

✔ **The Penguin Book of Irish Folktales** Henry Glassie (ed.) 1993 (1987)
One hundred and twenty-five Irish tales from a wide selection of literary sources.

The Deserted Village Oliver Goldsmith
1770
Goldsmith's poem, which is considered a minor classic, has excellent descriptions of the country round Lissoy. It expresses a nostalgic regret for his childhood and a genuine love of the countryside.

✔ **Loving** Henry Green 1992 (1945)
Set in a wealthy English household in rural Ireland during the Second World War and told from the point of view of the servants.

Langrishe, Go Down Aidan Higgins 1966
Three middle-aged spinsters live in a decaying house.

✔ **The Christmas Tree** Jennifer Johnston
1989 (1981)
Constance Keating has returned to her family home in Ireland to die. She replays the fragments of her past.

✔ **A Portrait of the Artist as a Young Man** James Joyce 1960 (1916)
An intense book with the exalted Stephen Dedalus as hero, set against an impressionistic background of an Irish Catholic upbringing: 'By far the most living and convincing picture that exists of an Irish Catholic upbringing. The technique is startling . . . A most memorable novel.' (H.G. Wells) Joyce worked on the early chapters of ✔ *Ulysses* 1972 (1922) in Zurich; it became immediately famous when it was published in Paris by Sylvia Beach of Shakespeare and Co. *Finnegan's Wake* (1939) is on one level the story of a publican from Chapelizod near Dublin, but it exists on so many levels and is so full of archetypes and layers that it is still imperfectly understood.

Good Behaviour Molly Keane 1988 (1981)
An aristocratic Anglo-Irish family are sinking into decay, and because of the rituals of 'good behaviour' are unable to come to terms with their passions and feelings. ✔ *Time After Time* is set in Durraghglass, a mansion in Southern Ireland; three sisters and a brother have their lives interrupted by a visitor from Vienna. Molly Keane also wrote under the name M.J. Farrell; other books include: *Rising Tide* (1937), *Full House* (1935) and *Loving and Giving* 1993 (1988) [Jan Morris]

Cal Bernard MacLaverty 1988 (1982)
Also *Lamb* 1991 (1980). Both are novels about what happens to love in a crisis; one is about the IRA and another about a Christian Brother.

✔ **Catholics** Brian Moore 1992 (1972)
Set in the west of Ireland; Father Kinsella, a new ecumenical Catholic priest is sent to bring the Abbot of Muck into line; their confrontation is interesting in that they are both in their separate ways agnostic. Good on the loss of faith. Also ✔ *The Mangan Inheritance* 1992 (1979).

Irish Melodies Thomas Moore (1808–1834)
Moore is chiefly remembered for *Irish Melodies* published in ten parts between 1808 and 1834. They have become part of the history of Irish nationalism, due in part to their eighteenth-century background.

The Country Girls Edna O'Brien 1960
A lively and amusing novel.

At Swim-Two-Birds Flann O'Brien 1960 (1939)
A complicated book which only sold 244 copies when it was first published; on the first page there are three separate and strange beginnings, but it is funny and rewarding. His publishers refused to publish *The Third Policeman* (1967) saying it was too fantastic, so it was only published after his death.

Collected Stories Frank O'Connor 1975
Collection Two (1964) is a mixture of new and already published stories. Also *Guests of the Nation* which is political fiction.

✔ **True Believers** Joseph O'Connor 1992 (1991)
Short stories in which reality meets romanticism. *Cowboys and Indians* (1991).

A Nest of Simple Folk Sean O'Faolain 1933
Set in Southwest Ireland and about three generations of a family from 1854 to 1916 and how they move from the country to the town to the city.

The Short Stories of Liam O'Flaherty 1937
Simple, authentic short stories about nature and local people.

Experiences of an Irish R.M.
E. Somerville and M. Ross
Collections of stories which were published as *Some Experiences of an Irish R.M.* (1899) and *Further Experieces of an Irish R.M.* (1908), many of them are about hunting. R.M. means Resident Magistrate, someone, often an outsider, who was appointed to dispense justice in an Irish town. The hero of these stories is a Major Yeates of Irish extraction, educated in England and having served in India. In Ireland he felt 'civilisation seemed a thousand miles off' and spent much of his time feeling lonely. *The Real Charlotte* 1990 (1894) is a sharply satirical novel.

The Crock of Gold James Stephens 1978 (1912)
Fable about two philosophers who lived in the centre of a pine wood called Coilla Doraca; they were married by women who were incensed at having had their questions answered correctly in order that they could pinch the men in bed.

The Playboy of the Western World J.M. Synge 1907
Set near Belmullet and around the villainy of the men of Mayo; Synge not only describes Ireland as she was but adds how he would have liked her to have been. Many of Synge's ideas came from stories he heard in Aran and as he was wandering through the provinces.

✔ **The Memoirs of Barry Lyndon Esq.**
William Makepeace Thackeray 1984 (1844)
Set in the second half of the eighteenth century, the fictional autobiography of a rogue whom the reader is encouraged to distrust from the very beginning. Barry Lyndon was born into the petty Irish gentry and after a disastrous love affair volunteered for the British army.

The South Colm Toibin (see 'Spain')

The Quiet End of Evening Honor Tracy 1972
Set on Inishnamona, the Isle of Turf, in the West of Ireland, where 28-year-old Sabina Boxham has gone to live. The inhabitants have blown up the rocky neck that joins them to the mainland in order to get world attention focused on their plight, but in doing so they have cut themselves off from their main source of income – tourism. Excellent de-

scriptions of a laid back life. Also *The Ballad of Castle Reef* (1979) and *In a Year of Grace* (1979).

Fools of Fortune William Trevor 1983
An idyllic childhood is shattered by the Irish uprising.

✔ **The Landleaguers** Anthony Trollope 1991 (1883)
An Englishman, Philip Jones, buys the estates of Ballintubber and Morony in a part of 'distant and wild' Ireland where his son converts to Catholicism. Also set in Ireland *The Macdermots of Ballycloran* (1847) and *The Kellys and the O'Kellys* (1848).

✔ **Selected Poetry** W.B. Yeats 1991
Yeats always thought of Sligo as his real home and his relationship with it was a microcosm of his relationship with Ireland. Yeats rediscovered and remade the Irish tradition and became a great and innovative poet while remaining a romantic.

Food

✔ **Simply Delicious Recipes**
Darina Allen 1992 (1989)
Recipes by the owner of the Ballymaloe Cookery school.

General Background

Escape from the Anthill Hubert Butler 1985
A collection of brilliant and quixotic essays, many about Ireland. Also *The Children of Drancy* (1988) and *Grandmother and Wolfe Tone* (1990).

The Irish World E. Estyn Evans etc. 1977
The history and cultural achievements of the Irish people. Well illustrated and wide-ranging.

Visions and Beliefs in the West of Ireland Isabella Augusta Gregory 1920
A collection, compiled with Yeats over twenty years, of folklore and a study of the supernatural.

Ancestral Voices. The Big House in Anglo-Irish Literature
Otto Rauchbauer (ed.) 1992
A collection of interpretations and essays which brings together the work of Maria Edgeworth, Charles Lever, George Moore, Somerville and Ross, W.B. Yeats, Elizabeth Bowen, Molly Keane and William Trevor among others.

Guides

✔ **Baedeker's Ireland** 1992

✔ **The Berkeley Budget Traveler's Handbook Great Britain and Ireland 1995**

✔ **Cadogan Guide Ireland**
Catharina Day 1991 (1986)

✔ **Ireland. The Rough Guide**
Sean Doran, Margaret Greenwood and Hildi Hawkins 1992

The Green Guide for Ireland
John Gormley 1990
A guide which covers all green issues including pollution, forestry, waste, transport, education and political parties, arranged under subject.

✔ **Insight Guide Ireland** 1992

✔ **Let's Go. The Budget Guide to Ireland 1995**

✔ **Michelin Green Guide Ireland** 1992

✔ **Ireland. A Moorland Guide** 1993
Larger format than the other Moorland guides.

✔ **Ireland. Travel Survival Kit**
John Murray, Sean Sheehan and Tony Wheeler 1994

✔ **Exploring Rural Ireland**
Andrew Sanger 1993 (1989)

Around the Edge of Ireland
Debra Shipley and Mary Peplow 1990
A good and easy-to-use guide about coastal Ireland.

✔ **Thomas Cook Travellers Ireland** 1994

History

The Making of Modern Ireland 1603–1923 J.C. Beckett 1966
Concise and readable – certainly helps explain the complex history.

Twilight of the Ascendancy
Mark Bence-Jones 1987
The old land-owning families of Ireland, known as the Ascendancy, lost most of their political power towards the end of the 1870s, at the same time as their economic foundations began to collapse due to agrarian unrest. An entertaining chronicle about these twilight years.

✔ **The Celts. First Masters of Europe**
Christiane Eluere 1992
Concise, well-illustrated and packed with nuggets of information.

Modern Ireland 1600–1972 Roy Foster
1989 (1988)
Masterful, scholarly, detailed and somewhat complex analysis of Irish history: 'Only superlatives will suffice. Roy Foster has given us the best single-volume history of modern Ireland of our time. No one who claims to be educated can leave it unread.' (Ronan Fanning *Irish Independent*)

The Green Flag Robert Kee 1989
A three-volume history of Irish nationalism: Vol. 1: *The Most Distressful Country* (1976), Vol. 2 *The Bold Fenian Men* (1976), Vol. 3: *Ourselves Alone* (1976).

✔ **Ireland. A History** Robert Kee 1993
(1980)
A book written to accompany the television series: 'History is indeed a difficult prison to escape from, and the history of Ireland is as difficult as any.'

✔ **A New History of Ireland** Edited by
T.W. Moody etc.
The seminal history of Ireland in nine volumes.

✔ **A Traveller's History of Ireland**
Peter Neville 1992
Concise and easy to read.

A Concise History of Ireland Maire and
Conor Cruise O'Brien 1972
A worthwhile illustrated history of Ireland.

The Great Hunger. Ireland 1845–1849
Cecil Woodham Smith 1987 (1962)
The harrowing story of the great potato famine.

Leisure

✔ **The Historic Hotels of Ireland**
Wendy Arnold 1989

✔ **Walking Ireland's Mountains**
David Heiman 1994
A brief guide for hill walkers which includes eighty one-day looped walks and fifty easier ones.

✔ **Best Irish Walks** Joss Lynam (ed.) n.d.

✔ **The Good Retreat Guide**
Stafford Whiteaker 1994
Over 300 places to find peace and spiritual renewal in Britain, Ireland, France and Spain.

Natural History

✔ **Wildlife Travelling Companion Great Britain and Ireland**
Martin Walters 1992
Arranged regionally; it gives advice on what to see in each area.

Photography

✔ **AA Images of Ireland** 1992
Colour-brochure type pictures of Ireland.

✔ **Castles of Ireland** Brian de Breffny
Photographs by George Mott 1992 (1977)
Arranged alphabetically, many illustrations and ample text.

✔ **Ireland. Philip's Travel Guides**
Max Caulfield Photographs by Joe Cornish 1993

✔ **Ireland Through the Ages**
Michael Jenner 1992
An illustrated survey of a cross-section of buildings and sites from all over Ireland.

In Ruins. The Once Great Houses of Ireland Photographs by Simon Marsden Edited
and with text by Duncan McLaren 1980
Evocative black and white photographs.

✔ **The Irish Village** Photographs by
Robin Morrison 1986
Colour photographs with small textual commentaries by Christopher Fitz-Simon.

Travel Literature

✔ **Brendan Behan's Island. An Irish Sketch Book** Drawings by Paul Hogarth
1990 (1962)
A delightful combination of reminiscence, verse and anecdote.

✔ **The Western Island** Robin Flower
1992 (1944)
Robin Flower was a frequent visitor to the Great Blasket Island at the beginning of the century when 150 people lived there; they befriended him and he was made very welcome.

✔ **Now and In Time To Be. Ireland and the Irish** Thomas Keneally 1992 (1991)
Keneally, who is of Irish descent, made a journey around Ireland which is rich in observation and insight.

Jaunting Through Ireland Roy Kerridge
1991
Kerridge had long wanted to visit Ireland and does so in this idiosyncratic and amusing tour through every county.

In Search of Ireland H.V. Morton 1984 (1930)
A haphazard car journey around Ireland, into Leinster, south to Cork and Kerry, to Galway and into Ulster from Donegal.

✔ **Round Ireland in Low Gear**
Eric Newby 1988 (1987)
Eric and Wanda Newby went to Ireland by bicycle in the autumn of 1985 'to enjoy ourselves'. Their trip was full of minor disasters and a major amount of rain; both related with humour.

Irish Miles Frank O'Connor 1947
Also *Leinster, Munster and Connaught*. Two excellent travel books.

Pückler's Progress. The Adventures of Prince Pückler-Muskau in England, Wales and Ireland as told in His Letters to His Former Wife 1826-9
1987 (1830)
Pückler divorced his adored but penniless wife and came to England in search of an heiress; during the two years he was away he wrote to Lucie, his former wife every day, describing in minute but bigoted detail, life in the great country houses and the hardships of travel (he was a hypochondriac) in Britain and Ireland. He failed to find a rich wife, returned home and published his letters in four volumes. Although the reaction to them was mixed, he immediately became famous and was able to move into a house with Lucie whom he never again left.

✔ **Stones of Aran: Pilgrimage**
Tim Robinson 1990 (1986)
An extremely perceptive account of Ireland: '*Stones of Aran*, which deserves to take all the prizes it possibly can, warms cold geology into fervent life. Robinson's chosen form . . . is wholly irresistible.' (Jonathan Keates *The Observer*)

✔ **Far Green Fields** Bernard Share (ed.)
1992
An anthology of extracts of 1,500 years of travel writing by Irish writers.

✔ **The Road to Roaringwater**
Christopher Somerville 1994 (1993)
In 1991 Christopher Somerville walked the 700 miles from Malin Head in the north of Ireland to Cape Clear Island in Roaringwater Bay: 'He has an uncanny ability to make the countryside come alive, whether it is the isolated hills of Donegal, the remote mountains of northern Mayo or the magic of the Burren.' (*Irish Times*)

✔ **The Coast of West Cork**
Peter Somerville-Large 1991 (1972)
An exploration by bicycle of the ragged coastline of West Cork. From Bantry Bay to *Leitrim* (1974) is a journey in search of O'Sullivan Beare. *Cappaghglass* (1985) is a book about the port and market town on the west of Ireland which is set in spectacular surroundings.

The Grand Irish Tour
Peter Somerville-Large 1985 (1982)
A narrative which roams throughout Ireland during a year's journey: 'Marvellous . . . describes to me afresh a landscape I thought I knew.' (Edna O'Brien *The Observer*)

✔ **The Aran Islands** J.M. Synge 1992 (1907)
A record of Synge's visit to the islands when he was gathering folklore for his plays. It is an exploration of an island community with wonderful descriptions of the ascetic beauty as well as being informative about Synge.

The Island of the White Cow: Memories of an Irish Island Deborah Tall 1985
As an American student, Deborah Tall fell in love with an Irish poet and went to live on a remote island with him between 1972–77. She chronicles the changing year in island life and her growing understanding of the people.

✔ **An Irish Sketchbook**
William Makepeace Thackeray 1990 (1842)
A detailed account of a four-month tour of Ireland in 1842. Although Thackeray was very much the Englishman abroad, he paints a vivid picture of Ireland.

✔ **Ireland. Travelscapes** John Watney
1989
A journey and guided tour round Ireland with anecdotes and history.

A Tour in Ireland Arthur Young 1780
The description by the English agriculturist Arthur Young, still remains a useful source of information on the economic affairs of the day. His informants were the local resident gentry and nobility; he approved of industry and the development of capital.

DUBLIN

'The most hospitable city I ever passed through.' Mary Wollstonecraft, *Letters Written During a Short Residence in Sweden etc.* 1796

Art and Archaeology

✔ **Dublin 1660–1860** *Maurice Craig* 1992 (1942)
A readable book about the architecture of the 'classical tradition' in Dublin. Two centuries of building are traced and the author looks at what was happening on the political, literary and social scenes.

Autobiography/Biography

Bowen's Court
Seven Winters *Elizabeth Bowen* 1984 (1942)
In *Seven Winters* Elizabeth Bowen describes her Dublin childhood, through the eyes of a child. *Bowen's Court* is the history of ten generations of her Anglo-Irish family and house, Bowen's Court, in County Cork from the Cromwellian settlement up until 1959.

Fiction/Poetry

✔ **The Journey Home** *Dermot Bolger* 1991 (1990)
Set in Dublin: 'All 1990s life is there – drink, drugs . . . political corruption, all the words which have been repeated so often now that they have lost their power to shock. Here, they shock.' (*Irish Times*)

Down All the Days *Christy Brown* 1970
An autobiographical novel by the severely disabled Christy Brown who gives his account of a large Dublin working-class family; the smells and scenery of Dublin in the 1940s and 1950s are captured brilliantly.

The Ginger Man *J.P. Donleavy* 1962 (1956)
A story about youth and despair and estrangement but also very much about Dublin. *The Beastly Beatitudes of Balthazar B* (1968).

✔ **Dubliners** *James Joyce* 1973 (1914)
Dubliners, fifteen short stories, was written in response to Joyce being offered one pound each for simple stories with an Irish background for a farming magazine. Publication was delayed because the printers objected to the frequent mention of real places and people (as well as to the use of the word 'bloody').

✔ **The Last of the High Kings**
Ferdia Mac Anna 1992 (1991)
A novel about contemporary Dublin which is full of optimism: 'It is very funny, not just in its comic set pieces, but also in its satirical but utterly loving inspection of that holy unit, the family.' (Jennifer Johnston)

✔ **The Red and the Green** *Iris Murdoch* 1967 (1965)
An Anglo-Irish family in Dublin during Easter week, 1916. Two cousins find themselves on opposite sides; a tale of hatred and heroism.

The Charwoman's Daughter
James Stephens 1979 (1912)
We follow Mary Makebelieve, who lived with her mother in a dingy house in a Dublin back street, from girlhood through adolescence.

Guides

✔ **AA Pocket Guide to Dublin**
1992 (1988)

✔ **A Walk Around Dublin**
Vincent Caprani 1992
An exploration of Dublin through her characters, history, haunts, nooks and crannies.

✔ **American Express: Dublin**
Polly Devlin 1993

✔ **Frommer's Dublin '93-'94**

✔ **Insight City Guide Dublin** 1989.

✔ **Dublin. Lonely Planet City Guide**
Tony Wheeler 1993

Leisure

✔ **Dublin. A Travellers' Companion**
Selected and introduced by Thomas and Valerie Pakenham 1988

POLAR REGIONS

Polar Regions

ARCTIC including GREENLAND, ARCTIC CANADA AND ALASKA

'Polar exploration is at once the cleanest and most isolated way of having a bad time which has been devised . . . It is more lonely than London, more secluded than any monastery, and the post comes but once a year'. (Apsley Cherry-Garrard)

Anthropology

Living Arctic: Hunters of the Canadian North Hugh Brody 1987
An account of the native peoples of arctic and subarctic Canada by a sociologist and anthropologist who knows them and their country well.

The People's Land: Eskimos and Whites in the Eastern Arctic
Hugh Brody 1975
A description of how the whites eroded the Eskimos' way of life. They came as furtraders and missionaries and stayed on as administrators bringing their suburban world with them.

The Snow People Marie Herbert 1973
The author and her husband, Wally Herbert spent over a year with the Thule Eskimos in north-west Greenland.

Eskimos Wally Herbert 1976
A short introduction to the Eskimo people.

✔ **Arctic Dreams. Imagination and Desire in a Northern Landscape**
Barry Lopez 1986
Magical descriptions of the Arctic landscape and the animals and peoples who live there. 'But this is also a book about dreams, about why people have gone to the Arctic and what they have found: the sixth century Irish monks searching in open, single-masted boats for the Isles of the Blessed; Elizabethan sailors in search of a North-West passage trapped in winter darkness in implacable ice; Cook and Parry obsessed with reaching the Pole; what were they really in pursuit of? And today what are we to make of this land?' (dust jacket) [Colin Thubron]

The Last Kings of Thule Jean Malaurie 1982
The Thule Eskimos live in northeast Greenland; the author spent over a year with them

learning the language and carrying out scientific research.

Art and Archaeology

Eskimo Art Cottie Burland 1973
An illustrated look at Eskimo art from the earliest times to the present day.

Autobiography/Biography

My Life as an Explorer Roald Amundsen 1927
Amundsen's first great achievement was to navigate the Northwest Passage in 1903–6. In 1926 he flew over the North Pole.

✔ **Nunaga: Ten Years Among the Eskimoes** Duncan Pryde 1985 (1971)
An autobiographical account of the author's time spent among the hunters and traders of the Canadian Arctic.

Nansen the explorer Edward Shackleton 1959
A short biography of Nansen which concentrates on his arctic expeditions.

Fiction/Poetry

The Great Alone Janet Dailey 1986
An epic novel set in the seventeenth century which begins with the arrival of Russian fur traders in the Aleutians.

The Call of the Wild Jack London 1960 (1903)
A domestic dog has to discover the ways of the wilderness while pulling sleds across Alaska during the Gold Rush.

Anna's Book George Macbeth 1983
Fiction based on fact; Nils Strindberg (the nephew of the writer) accompanied Andrée on his ill-fated balloon trip in 1907 which ended in disaster. The story is told by Anna Charlier who was Strindberg's pupil.

Bear Island Alistair MacLean 1971
MacLean uses an Arctic setting for this typical thriller. *Night Without End* (1960) is set in Greenland and *Ice Station Zebra* (1956) is a Russian–American cold-war adventure.

The Vinland Sagas: the Norse Discovery of America and Erik's Saga
Translated by Magnus Magnusson 1968
Two mediaeval Icelandic sagas; one tells of

the founding of a colony on the west coast of Greenland by Eric the Red.

✔ **Paradise Lost** John Milton 1642
The Arctic was mythologized by Milton in Paradise Lost: 'nature breeds, Perverse, all monstrous, all prodigious things Abominable, inutterable, and worse
Than fables yet have feigned or fear conceived,
Girgons and Hydras, and Chimaeras dire'.

✔ **Samson Agonistes** John Milton 1671
Although the Arctic summer days lasted twenty-four hours, the winter was 'dark, dark, dark . . . without all hope of day'.

The Snow Walker Farley Mowat 1978
A white man intrudes on a remote Eskimo community and describes what he sees in a series of short stories.

✔ **Due North** Mitchell Smith 1994 (1992)
A woman's husband dies in Alaska and for a while she struggles on alone there before being equally traumatized by a return to the big city.

General Background

Greenland Michael Banks 1975
A general introduction and survey.

The Arctic World Fred Bruemmer 1985
Essays on the people, animal and plant life of the seven countries in the Arctic.

Guides

✔ **Fodor's Alaska '95**

✔ **Alaska. Travel Survival Kit**
Jim DuFresne 1991 (1983)

✔ **Frommer's Alaska '94–'95**

✔ **Insight Guide Alaska** 1992,

✔ **Let's Go Alaska and the Pacific North West 1995**
Includes Washington, Oregon and Western Canada.

✔ **The Smithsonian Guide to Historic America: The Pacific States, California, Oregon, Washington, Alaska, Hawaii** William Bryant Logan and Susan Ochshorn 1989

✔ **Adventure Guide to the Alaska Highway** Ed and Lynn Readicker-Henderson 1992

History

✔ **Frozen in Time. The Fate of the Franklin Expedition** Owen Beattie and John Geiger 1993 (1987)
The discovery of the corpses of three Victorian seamen led to the unravelling of the fate of the Franklin expedition.

✔ **North Pole, South Pole. Journeys to the Ends of the Earth** Bertrand Imbert 1992
A well illustrated and concise history of the various Polar expeditions.

Arctic Explorations Dr E.K. Kane 1856
A narrative of the non-scientific part of Kane's expedition to the Arctic Seas; there are some good and well observed descriptions of animal behaviour.

Safe Return Doubtful. The Heroic Age of Polar Exploration
John Maxtone-Graham 1989 (1988)
The heroic, and not so heroic, exploits and achievements of those involved in polar exploration: Sir John Franklin, William Edward Parry, George Nares, Charles Francis Hall, Fridtjof Nansen, Solomon August Andrée (the balloonist), Ernest Shackleton, Robert Peary, Scott and Amundsen.

To the Arctic. The Story of Northern Exploration from Earliest Times to the Present Jeanette Mirsky 1949 (1934)
A comprehensive history which examines Arctic exploration through the eyes of the explorers.

In Northern Mists. Arctic Exploration in Early Times Fridtjof Nansen 1911
The two volumes cover the Norse voyages and settlements and the discoveries made by the Portuguese and John Cabot.

✔ **The Arctic. A History**
Richard Vaughan 1994
A thoroughly researched and somewhat weighty history of the Arctic area from 12,000 years ago to the present day; well illustrated with maps and contemporary photographs. An extensive bibliography.

Natural History

Wildlife and Wilderness: an artist's world Keith Shackleton 1986
The artist often travelled to the Arctic and Antarctic as the naturalist on the tourist ship *Linblad Explorer*.

Photography

✔ **Alaska** *Dale Brown 1979*
In the Time–Life 'World's Wild Places' series.

✔ **Hunters of the Polar North**
Wally Herbert 1981
A photographic book with ample text in the Time–Life 'People of the Wild' series about the Eskimos.

✔ **Diary of an Arctic Year**
Stephen J. Kraseman 1991
The diary and detailed account of the seasons of the Arctic year.

The Amundsen Photographs *Edited and introduced by Roland Huntford 1987*
Amundsen, described by Roland Huntford as 'one of those driven souls who have shaped our century', had a great photographic collection which was thought to have disappeared, but was found in a box marked 'Horlicks Malted Milk' in 1986. They are records of his expeditions to the North West Passage in 1903, the South Pole in 1911 and the North East Passage in 1918.

The Living Arctic *Fritz Muller 1981*
A well illustrated book about Arctic Canada.

✔ **Northwest Passage. The Quest for an Arctic Route to the East**
Edward Struzik Photographs by Mike Beedell 1991
Maps and historical photographs as well as up-to-date material.

Travel Literature

Watkin's Last Expedition
F. Spencer Chapman 1934
Gino Watkin's second and last expedition; he disappeared from east Greenland and only his upturned kayak was found.

Letters from High Latitudes
Lord Dufferin 1989 (1903)
In 1856 Lord Dufferin commissioned the schooner *Foam* and sailed to the Arctic, visiting Reykjavik in Iceland before skirting the pack ice of the Arctic and sailing to Jan Mayen and eastwards to northern Norway.

Hell on Ice *Ranulph Fiennes 1979*
An expedition of four men and two women which started in Alert in northern arctic Canada, but which failed to reach the North Pole despite assisted air resupply. It was an exercise for the Transglobe Expedition which took place in 1979.

To the Ends of the Earth
Ranulph Fiennes 1983
The purpose of the Transglobe Expedition was to travel around the world from Greenwich back to Greenwich along the zero meridian. They set sail for Antarctica in September 1979 and finally reached the North Pole in April 1982.

Narrative of a Journey in the Shores of the Polar Sea in the Years 1819, '20, and '22 *John Franklin 1823*
An overland expedition in northwestern Canada which explored much of the coastline.

✔ **Down the Wild River North**
Constance Helmericks 1993 (1969)
In 1965 Connie Helmericks and her two teenage daughters canoed down the Peace, Slave and Mackenzie Rivers in northern Canada to the Arctic Ocean.

Across the Top of the World
Wally Herbert 1971 (1969)
The story of the British Trans-Arctic Expedition, a record-making journey from Point Barrow in Alaska across the Arctic Ocean, via the North Pole to Spitsbergen – a distance of 3,600 miles.

Lands of Silence. A History of Arctic and Antarctic Exploration *Sir Clements Markham 1921*
The author was well versed in his subject, knowing many of the explorers and having travelled widely in the Arctic.

The Voyage of the 'Fox' in the Arctic Seas: A Narrative of the Discovery of the Fate of Sir John Franklin and His Companions *Francis McClintock 1859*
An account of the last expedition which was sent by Lady Jane Franklin to try and discover the fate of her husband Sir John Franklin.

Travels in Alaska *John Muir 1979 (1915)*
Most of the book is about Muir's initial contact with Alaska in 1879; he had studied glacier markings for years before going and in Alaska was able to observe actual glaciers. He also recorded his enjoyment of nature.

Farthest North. Being the record of a voyage of exploration of the ship Fram 1893–96 and of a fifteen months' sleigh journey by Dr Nansen and Lieut. Johansen with an appendix by Otto Sverdrup captain of the Fram
Fridtjof Nansen 1897
Nansen's purpose in going to the Arctic was to investigate the hydrology of the central arctic basin by drifting in the ice near the North Pole. The expedition included a sledge

journey and a meeting with the Jackson–Harmsworth expedition. The outcome was that Nansen conclusively disproved the theory that there was an open polar sea around the North Pole.

The First Crossing of Greenland
Fridtjof Nansen 1890
A description of his expedition to cross the ice sheet and information about previous expeditions.

Journey of a Voyage for the Discovery of a North-West Passage from the Atlantic to the Pacific; Performed in the Years 1819–1820, in His Majesty's ships Hecla and Griper, under the Orders of William Edward Parry, RN, FRS ... With an Appendix, containing the Scientific and Other Observations
William Edward Parry 1821
Parry disproved Ross' theory that Lancaster Sound was an inlet by sailing round it.

The North Pole *Robert Peary* 1910
In 1909 Peary reached the North Pole with a series of four supporting dog sledging parties.

✔ **Tracks Across Alaska** *Alastair Scott* 1992 (1990)
Alastair Scott hired a dog-team and travelled 800 miles along the Arctic circle in midwinter: 'He arrived in Manley from Scotland with no dogs, no sled and no experience. As a matter of fact he's so green that he calls a sled a sledge'. (Local newspaper)

North to the Pole *Will Steger* 1987
The purpose of this American expedition was to reach the North Pole without resupply – something which had not been done since Peary's journey in 1909. They were successful, and were airlifted back to base.

✔ **The Thousand Miles with a Dog Sled** *Hudson Stuck* 1988 (1914)
A detailed and realistic account of rural Alaska; Stuck, as episcopal archdeacon of the Yukon travelled widely throughout Alaska between 1905 and 1910.

✔ **Polar Dream** *Helen Thayer* 1993
The account of the first solo journey by a woman to the North Pole. Helen Thayer aged 50, skied solo to the Pole accompanied only by a black husky named Charlie. The journey took twenty-seven gruelling days.

Mischief in Greenland *H.W. Tilman* 1964
Tilman went to southwest Greenland on two occasions to climb mountains. *Mostly Mischief* is an account of his voyages to both the Arctic and Antarctic.

ANTARCTIC

Autobiography/Biography

My Life as an Explorer *Roald Amundsen*
1927 (see 'Arctic')

Birdie Bowers of the Antarctic
G. Seaver 1947 (1938)
Bowers who was one of the four members of Scott's expedition to die at the South Pole was described by *Time and Tide* as 'A fine man, brave, honourable and very lovable and the story of his short life makes profoundly moving reading'.

Edward Wilson of the Antarctic
G. Seaver 1940 (1933)
Wilson was the doctor on both of Scott's expeditions to the Antarctic and was described, as follows, by Scott: 'Words must always fail me when I talk of Bill Wilson. I believe he really is the finest character I ever met – the closer one gets to him the more there is to admire ... I think he is the most popular member of the party, and that is saying much'.

Scott and Amundsen *Roland Huntford* 1979
A controversial book which does much to demythologize Scott's journey to the South Pole. Amundsen seems to have reached the Pole 'with no more trouble than if it had been a mountain excursion', whereas Scott used 'haphazard methods' and tragically died with four other members of his team. 'But in the course of re-telling the saga, Roland Huntford demolishes a legend. Amundsen reached the Pole on December 15 and returned safely. Scott reached it on January 17 but never came back ... In death Scott became immortal. Now his reputation and character are torn to shreds'. (*The Sunday Telegraph*)

Fiction/Poetry

✔ **The Birthday Boys** *Beryl Bainbridge* 1993 (1991)
A novel in five parts which takes place between June 1910 and March 1912, related by Petty Officer Edgar (Taff) Evans, Dr Edward (Uncle Bill) Wilson, Captain Robert Falcon (Con) Scott, Lt. Henry Robertson (Birdie) Bowers and Capt. Lawrence Edward (Titus) Oates.

✔ **The Rime of the Ancient Mariner**
Samuel Taylor Coleridge
Coleridge, who was slightly younger than Captain Cook, was well acquainted with Cook's account of his voyage to Antarctica.

When Cook reported that South Georgia was full of penguins, seals and whales, immediate carnage, which he did not live to see, took place and by 1822 it was estimated that 1,200,000 seals had been taken from South Georgia, making them almost extinct. Coleridge was aware of the precarious balance between man and nature; man's impact on the natural world prior to the eighteenth century had been minimal and his poem about the shooting of the albatross reflects this unease:
'With his cruel bow he laid full low
The harmless Albatross.'

A Victim of the Aurora *Thomas Keneally 1978 (1977)*
An old man sits on a terrace in Los Angeles and remembers his time as the artist on the New British South Polar Expedition. One of the twenty-five men on the expedition was a murderer and the challenge of finding out who, was as great as the adventure.

✔ **Moby Dick** *Herman Melville (1851)*
Melville gives excellent descriptions of whales and whaling, but he was under the misconception that whales in the waters of the Antarctic would be safe from man.

Guides

✔ **Antarctica. An Introductory Guide** *Diana Galimberti 1991*
The geography, geology and glaciology, animal life and history of discoveries.

History

Antarctica. The Last Continent *Ian Cameron 1974*
The Ancients thought of Antarctica as a Great Southern Continent filled with 'Brazil Wood, Elephants and Gold'; the first sighting of the mainland of Antarctica is attributed to the little known Russian, Thaddeus von Bellinghausen and the first landing was by John Davis, a New Englander. These facts as well as descriptions of many others who were driven to explore Antarctica are included in this well illustrated book.

✔ **North Pole, South Pole. Journeys to the Ends of the Earth** *Bertrand Imbert 1992 (see 'Arctic')*

Safe Return Doubtful. The Heroic Age of Polar Exploration *John Maxtone-Graham 1989 (1988) (see 'Arctic')*

Beyond the Frozen Sea. Visions of Antarctica *Edwin Mickleburgh 1987*
A review of the history of who went to Antarctica and what people had thought of it from the earliest times. There is a good mix between what happens in the Antarctic and what is thought about it in the rest of the world.

Natural History

Animals of the Antarctic *Robert Burton 1970*
Descriptions of penguins, birds, seals, whales and insects and how they have adapted to the freezing conditions.

Wildlife and Wilderness: an artist's world *Keith Shackleton 1986 (see 'Arctic')*

Mischief Among the Penguins *H.W. Tilman 1961*
Tilman's journey in his Bristol Channel Pilot Cutter *Mischief* to the distant Crozet and Kerguelen Islands in the Southern Indian Ocean. These remote islands are full of penguins, albatrosses and elephant seals.

Birds of the Antarctic and Sub-Antarctic *George E. Watson 1975*
An illustrated handbook which provides identification information for all the birds on land or water south of 55° latitude.

Photography

The Amundsen Photographs *Edited and introduced by Roland Huntford 1987 (see 'Arctic')*

Travel Literature

The South Pole *Roald Amundsen 1912*
The account of the Norwegian Antarctic Expedition in the *Fram* which took place from 1910–12 and which successfully reached the South Pole.

Alone *R. Byrd 1966 (1935)*
In March 1934 Byrd moved into a tiny hut at Bolling Advance Weather Base; for four and a half months he was the only person there, in temperatures which reached –83° he began to suffer from carbon monoxide poisoning from a leaking stove. The book tells of his struggle to keep alive and preserve his sanity.

✔ **The Crystal Desert. Summers in Antarctica** *David G. Campbell 1993 (1992)*
A mixture of geography, history and natural sciences and of personal meditation and philosophy: 'A non-fiction work of flawless prose,

in which the plants, rocks and glaciers of Antarctica are treated with the same particularity as the characters in a novel'. (Edna O'Brien *New York Times Book Review*)

The Worst Journey in the World. Antarctic 1910–1913   Apsley
Cherry-Garrard   1929 (1922)

A narrative of Scott's last expedition from when it left England in 1910 until its return to New Zealand in 1913. Cherry-Garrard waxes lyrical about the kinds of people who went on expeditions: 'Talk of ex-soldiers: give me ex-antarcticists, unsoured and with their ideals intact: they could sweep the world'. He writes that he would willingly serve under Scott, Amundsen, Shackleton and Wilson: Scott for a joint scientific and geographical expedition, Wilson for a Winter Journey, Amundsen for a 'dash to the Pole and nothing else' and 'if I am in the devil of a hole and want to get out of it, give me Shackleton every time'. A gripping book. [Paul Theroux]

✔ Mind Over Matter   Ranulph Fiennes
1993

Ranulph Fiennes' epic 97-day unsupported journey of the crossing of the Antarctic Continent. The two-man team had been told that their planned trip was well-nigh impossible; the book is a testimony to extraordinary endurance and courage.

To the Ends of the Earth
Ranulph Fiennes   1983 (see 'Arctic')

The Crossing of Antarctica
Sir Vivian Fuchs and Sir Edmund Hillary   1958

The account of an expedition consisting of twelve men and eight vehicles, with sledges and dog teams, which crossed more than 2,000 miles from Shackleton base to Scott base in 1957/8.

Scott's Last Expedition   L. Huxley (ed.)
1913

The journals of Scott.

Lands of Silence. A History of Arctic and Antarctic Exploration
Sir Clements Markham   1921

The author was well versed in his subject, knowing many of the explorers and having travelled there widely.

The Home of the Blizzard
Douglas Mawson   1930 (1915)

The story of the Australasian Antarctic Expedition of 1911–1914. Mawson writes that the hardships of Antarctic exploration are compensated for by ' . . . times, during the long hours of steady tramping across the trackless snow-fields, [when] one's thoughts flow in a clear and limpid stream, the mind

is unruffled and composed and the passion of a great venture springing suddenly before the imagination is sobered by the calmness of pure reason'.

The Water Beetle   Nancy Mitford   1962

An essay in the book called *A Bad Time* is about polar exploration and quotes from Apsley Cherry-Garrard's *The Worst Journey in the World*. She encourages people to read more of the 'wonderful books' which write about the expedition.

South with Scott   Admiral Lord Mountevans
1962 (1921)

Evans first started to take an interest in Antarctic exploration in 1901 when he became Second Officer in the relief ship to the Discovery expedition; the two ships *Morning* and *Terra Nova* reached the *Discovery* in January 1904. He became Second-in-Command of the British Antarctic Expedition in which Scott lost his life but did not write his account of events until 1921.

The Great White South   H.G. Ponting
1921

An account of the author's experiences with Captain Scott's South Pole expedition and of life in the Antarctic. Ponting was described by Scott as 'the most delighted of men; he declares this is the most beautiful spot he has ever seen . . . He is enraptured and uses expressions which in anyone else and alluding to any other subject might be deemed extravagant'.

The Voyage of the 'Discovery'
R.F. Scott   1948 (1905)

Scott had a chance meeting with Sir Clements Markham in Buckingham Palace Road which led him to apply to command an expedition which was going to the Antarctic in 1900. He had no previous experience of Polar exploration or travel, but proceeded to spend a year learning all he could. He quickly realized the importance of doing as much scientific work as possible on the expedition, so the ship was equipped with scientists and scientific material; the results that came back were of great value.

The Heart of the Antarctic
Ernest Shackleton   1909

The story of the British Antarctic Expedition 1907–1909

South   Sir Ernest Shackleton   1919

'One of my favourites. After Scott had been beaten to the South Pole by Amundsen, Shackleton decided to try to restore British prestige with "the first crossing of the last continent". The tales of their privations and endurance are the perfect companion when you're tucked up in front of a warm winter fire'. (Jeremy Paxman)

Crossing Antarctica *Will Steger and Jon Bowermaster 1992*
Will Steger was one of a team of six men and thirty-six huskies who took 220 days to cross the 3,700 miles of Antarctica on foot; they survived appalling conditions, windchills of −150°, and winds which raged at more than 100 miles per hour. A gruelling ordeal.

Mostly Mischief *H.W. Tilman 1966*
An account of Tilman's voyages to both the Arctic and Antarctic.

Diary of the 'Discovery' Expedition, 1901–1913 *Edward Wilson   Ann Savours (ed.) 1966*

Diary of the 'Terra Nova' Expedition 1910–1913 *Edward Wilson   H.R. King (ed.) 1972*

INDEXES

INDEX OF

Authors, Editors and Translators

INDEX OF

Titles

INDEX OF

Places

INDEX OF

Photographers and Illustrators